# Introduction

Thanks for purchasing this book and entrusting me in your journey of AWS Certification.

If you have purchased this book that means you are planning to take the AWS Certified Solutions Architect – Associate very soon in near future, kudos to your desire to learn and test your knowledge by passing the exam. It will require finding hours outside work, between family friends and sacrificing entertainment time. But in the end when you see your result that you have passed, every minute invested will be worth it, giving you dividends for years to come.

Taking certification exam is not only for proving one's knowledge, or to get a promotion, or to improve peer standing, or to get salary increase or to meet organization's mandatory requirement but it is a milestone in the journey of gaining knowledge of AWS cloud platform. When we are part of a project developing solutions for individual users or enterprises, we are only using or increasing our knowledge based on subset of AWS services being used in the project. But when we prepare for the certification, we broaden our knowledge horizon to other AWS services, use cases and solution considerations.

My intention of publishing this book is not only to help you achieve your goal of passing this certification exam but also making you a better AWS cloud platform professional in your current role and achieving more success in future roles/certifications. I have developed this book based on my experience of first failing the exam (yes I did with score of 700, pass is 720) and then passing the exam in second attempt with score of 905. I have also drawn on my experience of developing AWS solutions for my clients from startups to Fortune 100 enterprises.

I have structured this book in chapters aligned to AWS service categories, which will help you prepare for specific topic as per your study plan. The exam by itself is not easy, most of the questions will be scenario based and will test your knowledge of services, where/how they are applicable and which one/combinations will be best for a given scenario. It is very essential that you do hands on lab exercises for all the services. Every service's user guide documentation has getting started or quick start tutorial which one must do by creating an AWS account.

This book contains 1100+ questions and 2 practice exams which will help you prepare to pass the exam. The questions in every chapter have been structured with the intention to build and strengthen your fundamental AWS knowledge and develop the ability to tackle questions similar to in the exam. The answers have references to AWS service user guides, blogs, knowledge center, faqs and other url/documentation. There is easy navigation for kindle edition between Questions & Answers with Answers having embedded hyperlinks to relevant AWS documentations.

All the very best.
Avinash Thakur
*AWS Certified Solutions Architect*

# Chapter 1 Compute: Amazon EC2, Auto Scaling, AWS Lambda, AWS Elastic Beanstalk, Amazon Elastic Container Service, AWS Fargate

Q1. What are features of EC2?
    A.   Virtual computing environments, instances with Preconfigured templates known as Amazon Machine Images (AMIs)
    B.   Various configurations of CPU, memory, storage, and networking capacity for your instances, known as instance types
    C.   Provides temporary or permanent Storage volumes known as instance store volumes or Amazon EBS volumes
    D.   All of the above

Q2. Which of the following is required to launch a new EC2 instance? Choose 2.
    A.   Root or IAM Admin user access keys
    B.   EC2 instance type
    C.   Linux or Windows license
    D.   Amazon Machine Image ( AMI)

Q3. What does an Amazon Machine Image (AMI) Include? Choose 3.
    A.   Instance Type
    B.   One or more EBS snapshots, or, for instance-store-backed AMIs, a template for the root volume of the instance (for example, an operating system, an application server, and applications).
    C.   Launch permissions that control which AWS accounts can use the AMI to launch instances.
    D.   A block device mapping that specifies the volumes to attach to the instance when it's launched

Q4. What are the two root device option for AMI to launch EC2 instance?
    A.   AMIs backed by S3
    B.   AMIs backed by Amazon EC2 instance store
    C.   AMIs backed by Amazon EBS
    D.   AMIs backed by DynamoDB

Q5. Which of the following statements are true for data persistence of EC2 root device volume? Choose 2.
    A.   Data on any instance store volumes always persists only during the life of the instance.
    B.   By default, data of the EBS root volume is deleted when the instance terminates but it can be changed to persist.
    C.   Data on any EBS root volumes always persists only during the life of the instance.
    D.   By default, data of the EBS root volume is not deleted when the instance terminates but it can be changed to be deleted.

Q6. By default, the root device volume for an AMI backed by Amazon EBS is deleted when the instance terminates. How this behavior can be changed?
   A.   Set the DoNotDeleteOnTermination attribute to true
   B.   Set the DoNotDeleteOnTermination attribute to false
   C.   Set the DeleteOnTermination attribute to true
   D.   Set the DeleteOnTermination attribute to false

Q7. What are the characteristics based on which you choose the AMI? Choose 2.
   A.   Region, Operating system, Architecture (32-bit or 64-bit)
   B.   Operating system, Architecture (32-bit or 64-bit)
   C.   Launch Permissions
   D.   Launch Permissions, Storage for the Root Device- EBS/Instance

Q8. What are three different type of launch permissions for AMI?
   A.   Public: The owner grants launch permissions to all AWS accounts.
   B.   Explicit: The owner grants launch permissions to specific AWS accounts.
   C.   Implicit: The owner has implicit launch permissions for an AMI.
   D.   Private: The owner grants launch permissions to specific AWS accounts.

Q9. You can convert your Instance Store-Backed Linux AMI to an Amazon EBS-Backed Linux AMI.
   A.   True
   B.   False

Q10. You can convert an instance store-backed Windows AMI to an Amazon EBS-backed Windows AMI.
   A.   True
   B.   False

Q11. To launch EC2 instances, you are using AMIs that are backed by Amazon EBS snapshots. Amazon EC2 instances are launched from AMIs using the *RunInstances* action with encryption parameters supplied through block device mapping, either by means of the AWS Management Console or directly using the Amazon EC2 API or CLI.  In the scenario of Launch with no encryption parameters, which of the following three statements are correct?
   A.   An unencrypted snapshot is restored to an unencrypted volume, unless encryption by default is enabled, in which case all the newly created volumes will be encrypted.
   B.   An encrypted snapshot that you own is restored to a volume that is encrypted to the same CMK.
   C.   An encrypted snapshot that you do not own (i.e., the AMI is shared with you) is restored to a volume that is encrypted to original AMI owner's AWS account's default CMK.

D.  An encrypted snapshot that you do not own (i.e., the AMI is shared with you) is restored to a volume that is encrypted to your AWS account's default CMK.

Q12. To launch EC2 instances, you are using AMIs that are backed by Amazon EBS snapshots. Amazon EC2 instances are launched from AMIs using the action with encryption parameters supplied through block device mapping, either by means of the AWS Management Console or directly using the Amazon EC2 API or CLI. In the scenario of Launch with Encrypted set, but no KmsKeyId specified, which of the following three statements are correct?
A.  An unencrypted snapshot is restored to an EBS volume that is encrypted by your AWS account's default CMK.
B.  An encrypted snapshot that you own is restored to an EBS volume encrypted by the same CMK.
C.  An encrypted snapshot that you do not own (i.e., the AMI is shared with you) is restored to a volume that is encrypted by your AWS account's default CMK.
D.  An encrypted snapshot that you do not own (i.e., the AMI is shared with you) is restored to a volume that is encrypted to original AMI owner's AWS account's default CMK.
E.  An unencrypted snapshot is restored to an unencrypted volume.

Q13. To launch EC2 instances, you are using AMIs that are backed by Amazon EBS snapshots. Amazon EC2 instances are launched from AMIs using the action with encryption parameters supplied through block device mapping, either by means of the AWS Management Console or directly using the Amazon EC2 API or CLI. In the scenario of Launch with Encrypted set and also KmsKeyId specified, which of the following two statements are correct?
A.  An unencrypted snapshot is restored to an unencrypted volume.
B.  An encrypted snapshot that you do not own (i.e., the AMI is shared with you) is restored to a volume that is encrypted to original AMI owner's AWS account's default CMK.
C.  An unencrypted snapshot is restored to an EBS volume encrypted by the specified CMK.
D.  An encrypted snapshot is restored to an EBS volume encrypted not to the original CMK, but instead to the specified CMK.

Q14.Which of the following Source-Target encryption scenario is not supported when copying AMI?
A.  Unencrypted-to-unencrypted
B.  Encrypted-to-encrypted
C.  Unencrypted-to-encrypted
D.  Encrypted-to-unencrypted

Q15. You have developed a web application and plan to deploy it in your VPC in us-west region. Your VPC has three subnets mapped to three availability zones: us-west-1a, us-west-1b, us-west-1c. How many minimum web server instances should you deploy in each of three AZ so that you have at least six instances running in case one of AZ goes down within minimum cost?

    A.   Six in us-west-1a, six in us-west-1b, six in us-west-1c.

    B.   Three in us-west-1a, three in us-west-1b, three in us-west-1c.

    C.   Two in us-west-1a, two in us-west-1b, four in us-west-1c.

    D.   Four in us-west-1a, two in us-west-1b, four in us-west-1c.

Q16. What are benefits of enabling enhanced networking on your Linux instance type? Choose 3.

    A.   lower I/O performance and higher CPU utilization when compared to traditional virtualized network interfaces

    B.   higher I/O performance and lower CPU utilization when compared to traditional virtualized network interfaces

    C.   higher bandwidth, higher packet per second (PPS) performance, and consistently lower inter-instance latencies

    D.   There is no additional charge for using enhanced networking.

Q17. Which of the following is not a type of EC2 placement group?

    A.   Cluster

    B.   Spread

    C.   Partition

    D.   Enhanced

Q18. What are the two steps you will take regarding your instances if your application requirement is low network latency, high network throughput, majority of the network traffic is between the instances in the group and require highest packet-per-second network Performance? Choose 2.

    A.   Use Cluster placement groups

    B.   Use Spread Placement groups

    C.   Choose an instance type that supports enhanced networking

    D.   Choose an instance type that supports performance networking

Q19. Which placement groups can be used to deploy large distributed and replicated workloads, such as HDFS, HBase, and Cassandra, across distinct racks?

    A.   Use Cluster placement groups

    B.   Use Spread Placement groups

    C.   Use Partition Placement groups

    D.   Use Container Placement groups

Q20. Which placement groups are recommended for applications that have a small number of critical instances that should be kept separate from each other?
   A.   Use Cluster placement groups
   B.   Use Spread Placement groups
   C.   Use Partition Placement groups
   D.   Use Container Placement groups

Q21. How can you connect to your Linux EC2 instance from your local computer? Choose 3.
   A.   Local Computer is Linux, use SSH to connect to Linux EC2 instance.
   B.   Local Computer is windows, use SSH to connect to Linux EC2 instance.
   C.   Local Computer is windows, use Putty to connect to Linux EC2 instance.
   D.   Local Computer is Linux, use Putty to connect to Linux EC2 instance.

Q22. Which of the following statements are correct when you stop an EC2 instance? Choose 2.
   A.   You can only stop an instance store-backed instance and not EBS-backed instance.
   B.   You can only stop an EBS-backed instance and not an instance store-backed instance.
   C.   Any Amazon EBS volumes remain attached to the instance, and their data persists. Any data stored in the RAM of the host computer or the instance store volumes of the host computer is gone.
   D.   Any Amazon instance volumes remain attached to the instance, and their data persists. Any data stored in the RAM of the host computer or the instance store volumes of the host computer is persisted.

Q23. Which of the following statements are correct when you stop an EC2 instance? Choose 2.
   A.   The instance retains its private IPv4 addresses and any IPv6 addresses when stopped and restarted. AWS releases the public IPv4 address and assign a new one when you restart it.
   B.   The instance retains its associated Elastic IP addresses. You're charged for any Elastic IP addresses associated with a stopped instance.
   C.   The instance doesn't retains its private IPv4 addresses and any IPv6 addresses when stopped and restarted. AWS releases the public IPv4 address and assign a new one when you restart it.
   D.   The instance retains its associated Elastic IP addresses. You're not charged for any Elastic IP addresses associated with a stopped instance.

Q24. Which of the following is true about Elastic Ip Address? Choose 3.
   A.   To use an Elastic IP address, you first allocate one to your account, and then associate it with your instance or a network interface.

B. An Elastic IP address is a private IPv4 address in subnet, which is not reachable from the internet.

C. With an Elastic IP address, you can mask the failure of an instance or software by rapidly remapping the address to another instance in your account.

D. An Elastic IP address is a public IPv4 address, which is reachable from the internet.

Q25. Which of the following is true about Elastic Ip Address? Choose 4.

A. You can disassociate an Elastic IP address from a resource, and reassociate it with a different resource.

B. You are not charged if an Elastic IP address is not associated with a running instance, or if it is associated with a stopped instance or an unattached network interface.

C. A disassociated Elastic IP address remains allocated to your account until you explicitly release it.

D. Small hourly price is charged if an Elastic IP address is not associated with a running instance, or if it is associated with a stopped instance or an unattached network interface.

E. While your instance is running, you are not charged for one Elastic IP address associated with the instance, but you are charged for any additional Elastic IP addresses associated with the instance

Q26. You have developed a web application and plan to deploy it in your VPC in us-west region. Your VPC has three subnets mapped to three availability zones: us-west-1a, us-west-1b, us-west-1c. Your application requires in normal scenario nine servers but can run on a minimum 66 percent capacity. How many web server instances should you deploy in each of three AZ so that you can meet the above availability requirements in a cost effective way?

A. Six in us-west-1a, six in us-west-1b, six in us-west-1c.

B. Two in us-west-1a, two in us-west-1b, four in us-west-1c.

C. Four in us-west-1a, four in us-west-1b, four in us-west-1c.

D. Three in us-west-1a, three in us-west-1b, three in us-west-1c.

Q27. Which of the following statement are correct when you hibernate an EC2 Linux instance? Choose 4.

A. Any Amazon EBS volumes remain attached to the instance, and their data persists, the contents of the RAM are not saved.

B. Operating system performs hibernation (suspend-to-disk), which freezes all the processes, saves the contents of the RAM to the Amazon EBS root volume, and then performs a regular shutdown.

C. Any Amazon EBS volumes remain attached to the instance, and their data persists, including the saved contents of the RAM.

D. When you restart the instance, the instance boots up and the operating system reads in the contents of the RAM from the Amazon EBS root volume before unfreezing processes to resume its state.

E. The instance retains its private IPv4 addresses and any IPv6 addresses when hibernated and started. We release the public IPv4 address and assign a new one when you start it.

Q28. What is an elastic network interface? Choose 3.
A. A logical networking component in a VPC that represents a virtual network card.
B. You cannot create and configure network interfaces in your account and attach them to instances in your VPC.
C. You can create and configure network interfaces in your account and attach them to instances in your VPC.
D. A network interface can have a primary private IPv4 address attribute from the IPv4 address range of your VPC.

Q29. Which of the following is not a metrics sent by EC2 instance to cloudwatch?
A. CPUUtilization
B. DiskReadOps
C. NetworkIn
D. MemoryUtilization
E. EBSReadOps

Q30. What are the benefits of assigning multiple private ip addresses to an EC2 instance?
A. Host multiple websites on a single server by using multiple SSL certificates on a single server and associating each certificate with a specific IP address.
B. Operate network appliances, such as firewalls or load balancers that have multiple IP addresses for each network interface.
C. Redirect internal traffic to a standby instance in case your instance fails, by reassigning the secondary IP address to the standby instance.
D. All of the above

Q31. Choose two correct statements highlighting the difference between Amazon EBS-Backed AMI and Amazon Instance Store-Backed AMI?
A. Size limit for a root device: EBS-Backed AMI = 16 TiB, Instance Store-Backed AMI= 10 GB
B. Size limit for a root device: EBS-Backed AMI =10 GB, Instance Store-Backed AMI= 16 TiB
C. Modifications: EBS-Backed AMI = the instance type, kernel, RAM disk, and user data can be changed while the instance is stopped, Instance Store-Backed AMI= Instance attributes are fixed for the life of an instance.
D. Modifications: Instance Store -Backed AMI = the instance type, kernel, RAM disk, and user data can be changed while the instance is stopped, EBS-Backed AMI= Instance attributes are fixed for the life of an instance.

Q32. Which storage provides temporary block-level storage for your instance and is ideal for temporary storage of information that changes frequently, such as buffers, caches, scratch data, and other temporary content, or for data that is replicated across a fleet of instances, such as a load-balanced pool of web servers ?
   A.   S3
   B.   RDS
   C.   Instance Store
   D.   EBS

Q33. When the data in the instance store persists?
   A.   Never
   B.   The underlying disk drive fails
   C.   The instance stops
   D.   The instance terminates
   E.   The instance reboots (intentionally or unintentionally)

Q34. What do you need to connect to a new Linux EC2 instance using SSH?
   A.   Root userid and password
   B.   IAM userid and password
   C.   Digital certificate
   D.   Using the private key of the key pair linked with EC2 instance

Q35. Which of the following is not a benefit for copying an AMI across geographically diverse Regions?
   A.   Consistent global deployment: Copying an AMI from one Region to another enables you to launch consistent instances in different Regions based on the same AMI.
   B.   Scalability: You can more easily design and build global applications that meet the needs of your users, regardless of their location.
   C.   Performance: You can increase performance by distributing your application, as well as locating critical components of your application in closer proximity to your users. You can also take advantage of Region-specific features, such as instance types or other AWS services.
   D.   Cost Reduction : No charges for copying, data transfer or storage
   E.   High availability: You can design and deploy applications across AWS regions, to increase availability.

Q36. For an instance in your VPC, you have attached two security groups. One security group has a rule that allows access to TCP port 22 (SSH) from IP address 203.0.113.1 and another security group has a rule that allows access to TCP port 22 from everyone. Which of the following is correct?
   A.   Everyone has access to TCP port 22
   B.   Only IP address 203.0.113 will have access.

C. You cannot have two rules for same port for an instance.

D. No one will have access.

Q37. What are the different ways to achieve high EC2 networking bandwidth performance? Choose 3.

A. Use dedicated hosts

B. Configure your AMIs and your current-generation EC2 instances to use the Elastic Network Adapter (ENA) to get high GBPs performance

C. Put the instances in placement group

D. Enable enhanced networking on the instances

Q38. Which of the following two statements are correct regarding encryption in Amazon EBS backed AMI?

A. Snapshots of both data and root volumes can be encrypted and attached to an AMI.

B. You can launch instances and copy images with full EBS encryption support.

C. Snapshots of both data and root volumes cannot be encrypted and attached to an AMI.

D. You cannot launch instances and copy images with full EBS encryption support.

Q39. Amazon EC2 AMIs are copied using the *CopyImage* action, either through the AWS Management Console or directly using the Amazon EC2 API or CLI. The encryption parameters are *Encrypted* and *KmsKeyId*. Which of the following three statements are correct when you copy with no encryption parameters.

A. An unencrypted snapshot is copied to another unencrypted snapshot, unless encryption by default is enabled, in which case all the newly created snapshots will be encrypted.

B. An encrypted snapshot that you own is copied to a snapshot encrypted with the same key.

C. An encrypted snapshot that you do not own (that is, the AMI is shared with you) is copied to a snapshot that is encrypted to your AWS account's default CMK.

D. An encrypted snapshot that you do not own (that is, the AMI is shared with you) is copied to a snapshot that is encrypted by original owner's default CMK.

Q40. Amazon EC2 AMIs are copied using the *CopyImage* action, either through the AWS Management Console or directly using the Amazon EC2 API or CLI. The encryption parameters are *Encrypted* and *KmsKeyId*. Which of the following three statements are correct when you copy with encryption parameters *Encrypted* set, but no *KmsKeyId* specified?

A. An unencrypted snapshot is copied to a snapshot encrypted to the AWS account's default CMK.

B. An encrypted snapshot that you do not own (the AMI is shared with you) is copied to a snapshot that is encrypted by original owner's default CMK.

C. An encrypted snapshot is copied to a snapshot encrypted to the same CMK.

D.  An encrypted snapshot that you do not own (the AMI is shared with you) is copied to a volume that is encrypted to your AWS account's default CMK.

Q41. Amazon EC2 AMIs are copied using the *CopyImage* action, either through the AWS Management Console or directly using the Amazon EC2 API or CLI. The encryption parameters are *Encrypted* and *KmsKeyId*. Which of the following two statements are correct when you copy with both encryption parameters *Encrypted* and *KmsKeyId* specified?
A.  An encrypted snapshot is copied to a snapshot encrypted to the original CMK
B.  An unencrypted snapshot is copied to a snapshot encrypted to the specified CMK.
C.  An unencrypted snapshot is copied to a snapshot encrypted to the original CMK.
D.  An encrypted snapshot is copied to a snapshot encrypted not to the original CMK, but instead to the specified CMK.

Q42. Which of the following are true about instance private ip address? Choose 3.
A.  Instance private IPv4 address is not reachable over the Internet.
B.  Instance private IPv4 addresses can be used for communication between instances in the same VPC.
C.  Instance private IPv4 address is reachable over the Internet.
D.  On launch an instance receives a primary private IP address from the IPv4 address range of the subnet.

Q43. What is an instance primary private ip address? Choose 3.
A.  Each instance has a default network interface (eth0) that is assigned the primary private IPv4 address.
B.  Primary private IP addresses can be reassigned from one instance to another.
C.  You can also specify additional private IPv4 addresses, known as secondary private IPv4 addresses.
D.  Secondary private IP addresses can be reassigned from one instance to another.

Q44.What are the modifiable attributes of reserved instances? Choose 4.
A.  Change Availability Zones within the same Region
B.  Change the scope from Availability Zone to Region and vice versa
C.  Change the instance size within the same instance family
D.  Change the network platform from EC2-Classic to Amazon VPC and vice versa
E.  Change standard reserve instance to convertible reserved instance

Q45. What are general prerequisites for Connecting to your Linux instance using SSH? Choose 4.
A.  Get the public DNS name or elastic ip address of the instance.
B.  Get the default user name for the AMI that you used to launch your instance.
C.  Get a new AWS account IAM user.
D.  Enable inbound SSH traffic from your IP address to your instance.

E.   Instance private key.

Q46. Which of the following is not correct about EC2 instance's Public IPv4 Addresses and External DNS Hostnames?
   A.   An external DNS hostname is resolved to the public IP address of the instance from outside its VPC, and to the private IPv4 address of the instance from inside its VPC.
   B.   Public IP address is mapped to the primary private IP address through network address translation (NAT).
   C.   Your instance's public IP address is not released when you associate an Elastic IP address with it.
   D.   When an instance is launched into a non-default VPC, the subnet has an attribute that determines whether instances launched into that subnet receive a public IP address from the public IPv4 address pool.
   E.   Instance's public IP address is released when it is stopped or terminated. Your stopped instance receives a new public IP address when it is restarted.

Q47. You have purchased an a1.large Linux Standard Reserved Instance in us-west-1a. Which of the following ways you can modify the reservation? Choose 3.
   A.   Change it into windows instance
   B.   Change it in a1.xlarge
   C.   Change the region to us-east and AZ to us-east-1a
   D.   Change the AZ to us-west-1b
   E.   Change it into two a1.medium instances.

Q48. What are the purchasing options for EC2 instances? (Choose 4)
   A.   One Zone Instances
   B.   On-Demand Instances
   C.   Reserved Instances
   D.   Regional Instances
   E.   Spot Instances
   F.   Saving Plans

Q49. Which of the following statements are correct for reserved instances? Choose 2.
   A.   Reserved Instances are more expensive compared to On-Demand Instance pricing.
   B.   Reserved Instances provide you with a significant discount compared to On-Demand Instance pricing.
   C.   Reserved Instances are not physical instances, but rather a billing discount applied to the use of On-Demand Instances in your account.
   D.   Reserved Instances are physical instances which are allocated to your account based on region and zone you would have selected.

Q50. Your company started using AWS and initially you have T2 instances purchased at on-demand rates. After some time you purchase reserved instance that matches the attributes (instance type, region, dedicated instance, and platform) of your T2 instance. After some time you purchase reserved instance for C4 instances also. How reserved instance billing will be applied?
   A.   Reserved instance billing benefit is not applied to any of the instance.
   B.   Reserved instance billing benefit is immediately applied to C4 instance.
   C.   Reserved instance billing benefit is immediately applied to both T2 and C4 instance.
   D.   Reserved instance billing benefit is immediately applied to T2 instance.

Q51. What are the four instance attributes which determines the reserved instance pricing?
   A.   Instance Type
   B.   Scope : Regional or Zone
   C.   Tenancy : whether instance runs on shared or single-tenant hardware
   D.   Hardware memory and CPU
   E.   Operating System Platform

Q52. Which of the following three statements are correct about Standard Reserved Instance?
   A.   Instance size, can be modified during the term; however, the instance family cannot be modified.
   B.   Instance size and instance family both can be modified.
   C.   Cannot be exchange for another standard reserved instance, it can only be modified.
   D.   Can be sold in the Reserved Instance Marketplace.
   E.   Cannot be sold in the Reserved Instance Marketplace.

Q53. Which of the following two statements are correct about Convertible Reserved Instance?
   A.   Can be exchanged during the term for another Convertible Reserved Instance with new attributes including instance family, instance type, platform, scope, or tenancy.
   B.   Cannot be exchanged during the term for another Convertible Reserved Instance with new attributes including instance family, instance type, platform, scope, or tenancy.
   C.   Can be sold in the Reserved Instance Marketplace.
   D.   Cannot be sold in the Reserved Instance Marketplace.

Q54. You have the following Convertible Reserved Instances in your account:

| Reserved Instance ID | Term | Expiration date |
|---|---|---|
| aaaa1111 | 1-year | 2018-12-31 |
| bbbb2222 | 1-year | 2018-07-31 |
| cccc3333 | 3-year | 2018-06-30 |
| dddd4444 | 3-year | 2019-12-31 |

Which of the following merging and exchanging options you can do?
  A. You can merge aaaa1111 and bbbb2222 and exchange them for a 1-year Convertible Reserved Instance with expiration date 2018-12-31
  B. You can merge bbbb2222 and cccc3333 and exchange them for a 3-year Convertible Reserved Instance with expiration date 2018-07-31
  C. You can merge bbbb2222 and cccc3333 and exchange them for a 1-year Convertible Reserved Instance with expiration date 2018-07-31
  D. You can merge cccc3333 and dddd4444 and exchange them for a 3-year Convertible Reserved Instance with expiration date 2019-12-31

Q55. What is a spot instance? Choose 2.
  A. Spot instances are exactly the same as On-Demand or Reserved instances but offered at a significant discount off the On-Demand prices
  B. Spot instances are exactly the same as On-Demand or Reserved instances but offered at more cost than the On-Demand prices
  C. Spot instances can be interrupted by Amazon EC2 for capacity requirements with a 5-minute notification
  D. Spot instances can be interrupted by Amazon EC2 for capacity requirements with a 2-minute notification

Q56. What are the possible use cases and criteria for using spot instances? (Choose 2)
  A. Not suitable for sensitive workloads or databases.
  B. Stateless, non-production application, such as development and test servers, where occasional downtime is acceptable
  C. Stateful, non-production application, such as development and test servers, where occasional downtime is acceptable
  D. Stateless, production application

Q57. What are the reasons because of which spot instances can be interrupted? Choose 3.
  A. Your Spot Instances are guaranteed to run until you terminate them.
  B. Not enough unused EC2 instances to meet the demand for Spot Instances.
  C. The Spot price exceeds your maximum price.

D.  Constraints in the request such as a launch group or an Availability Zone group cannot be met.

Q58. Which of the following statements are correct about spot fleet? Choose 3.
  A.  A collection, or fleet, of Spot Instances, and optionally On-Demand Instances.
  B.  A collection, or fleet, only of Spot Instances.
  C.  The request for Spot Instances is fulfilled if there is available capacity and the maximum price you specified in the request exceeds the current Spot price.
  D.  Attempts to maintain its target capacity fleet if your Spot Instances are interrupted due to a change in the Spot price or available capacity.

Q59. Which of the following statements are correct about Standard Reserved Instance (RI) and Convertible RIs? Choose 3.
  A.  Standard RIs can only be modified. Convertible RIs can be exchanged as well as modified.
  B.  You can modify a Standard RI to change the following attributes: Availability Zone or scope, Network platform (EC2-Classic or VPC), Instance size.
  C.  You can exchange the Convertible RI for comparable RIs depending on their value, which gives you more flexibility to change the instances that your RIs will apply to later.
  D.  Standard RIs can only be modified. Convertible RIs can only be exchanged.

Q60. How zonal reserved instance are applied? Choose 2.
  A.  Reserved Instances assigned to a specific Availability Zone can provide the Reserved Instance discount to matching instance usage in every Availability Zone for the region.
  B.  Reserved Instances assigned to a specific Availability Zone provide the Reserved Instance discount to matching instance usage in that Availability Zone.
  C.  The Reserved Instance discount applies to instance usage for the specified instance type and size only.
  D.  The Reserved Instance discount applies to instance usage within the instance family, regardless of size for Amazon Linux/Unix Reserved Instances with default tenancy

Q61. How regional reserved instance are applied? Choose 2.
  A.  The Reserved Instance discount applies to instance usage in any Availability Zone in the specified Region.
  B.  Reserved Instances assigned to a region provide the Reserved Instance discount to matching instance usage in only one Availability Zone.
  C.  The Reserved Instance discount applies to instance usage for the specified instance type and size only.
  D.  The Reserved Instance discount applies to instance usage within the instance family, regardless of size for Amazon Linux/Unix Reserved Instances with default tenancy

Q62. Which are the scenarios when the instance size flexibility is not provided when applying reserved instances? Choose 3.
A. Reserved instances purchased for a region
B. Reserved instances purchased for a specific Availability Zone
C. Reserved Instances with dedicated tenancy
D. Reserved Instances for Windows, Windows with SQL Standard, Windows with SQL Server Enterprise, Windows with SQL Server Web, RHEL, and SLES

Q63. You purchased a t2.medium default tenancy Amazon Linux/Unix Reserved Instance in the US East (N. Virginia) region and you have two running t2.small instances in your account in that Region. How will the reserved instance billing benefit applied?
A. You will not get any benefit as you don't have running instance type matching to reserved instance type bought.
B. You will get benefit applied to usage of only one running t2.small.
C. You will get benefit applied to usage of both running t2.small
D. You will get benefit applied to 75% usage of both running t2.small

Q64. You purchase a t2.medium default tenancy Amazon Linux/Unix Reserved Instance in the US East (N. Virginia) and you have one running t2.large instances in your account in that Region. How will the reserved instance billing benefit applied?
A. You will not get any benefit as you don't have running instance type matching to reserved instance type bought.
B. You will get benefit applied to only 50% usage.
C. You will get 100% usage benefit
D. You will get 75% usage benefit

Q65. Which of the following statements are correct pertaining to requirements and restrictions for reserved instance modification? Choose 4.
A. You can change Availability Zones within the same Region.
B. If you change the scope from Availability Zone to Region, you lose the capacity reservation benefit.
C. If you change the scope from Region to Availability Zone, you lose Availability Zone flexibility and instance size flexibility (if applicable).
D. To change the instance size within the same instance family, the reservation must use Amazon Linux on default tenancy.
E. If you change the scope from Region to Availability Zone, you don't lose Availability Zone flexibility and instance size flexibility (if applicable).

Q66. You have a reservation for one t2.large instance. You want to modify this reservation. Which of the following statements are correct. Choose 2.
A. You can convert into one t2.small instances

B.  You can convert into two t2.medium instances
C.  You can convert into one  t2.medium instances
D.  You can convert into four t2.small instances

Q67. Which of the following are correct for Scheduled Reserved Instances? Choose 3.
   A.  Enable you to purchase capacity reservations that recur on a daily, weekly, or monthly basis, with a specified start time and duration, for a one-year term.
   B.  You are not charged if you do not use the scheduled instances.
   C.  You pay for the time that the instances are scheduled, even if you do not use them.
   D.  You can't stop or reboot Scheduled Instances, but you can terminate them manually as needed.

Q68. What is an EC2 dedicated host?
   A.  A physical server with EC2 instance capacity fully dedicated to your use.
   B.  Provides visibility of the number of sockets and physical cores.
   C.  Allows you to consistently deploy your instances to the same physical server over time.
   D.  Supports Bring Your Own License.
   E.  All of the above

Q69. What are the different type of instance tenancy attribute? Choose 3.
   A.  Default: Your instance runs on shared hardware.
   B.  Dedicated: Your instance runs on single-tenant hardware.
   C.  Shared: Your instance runs on shared hardware.
   D.  Host: Your instance runs on a Dedicated Host, which is an isolated server with configurations that you can control.

Q70. After you launch an instance, there are some limitations to changing its tenancy. Which of the following statements are correct? Choose 3.
   A.  You cannot change the tenancy of an instance from default to dedicated or host after you've launched it.
   B.  You can change the tenancy of an instance from default to dedicated or host after you've launched it.
   C.  You cannot change the tenancy of an instance from dedicated or host to default after you've launched it.
   D.  You can change the tenancy of an instance from dedicated to host, or from host to dedicated after you've launched it.

Q71. You have purchased two c4.xlarge default tenancy Linux/Unix Standard Reserved Instances in Availability Zone us-east-1a. Which of the following running instances will benefit from this?

A.  two c4.xlarge default tenancy Linux/Unix instances running in the Availability Zone us-east-1b

B.  two m4.xlarge default tenancy Linux/Unix instances running in the Availability Zone us-east-1a

C.  two c4.xlarge default tenancy Linux/Unix instances running in the Availability Zone us-east-1a

D.  four c4.large default tenancy Linux/Unix instances running in the Availability Zone us-east-1a

Q72. You are running the following On-Demand Instances in account A:
- 4 x m3.large Linux, default tenancy instances in Availability Zone us-east-1a
- 2 x m4.xlarge Amazon Linux, default tenancy instances in Availability Zone us-east-1b
- 1 x c4.xlarge Amazon Linux, default tenancy instances in Availability Zone us-east-1c

You purchase the following Reserved Instances in account A:
- 4 x m3.large Linux, default tenancy Reserved Instances in Availability Zone us-east-1a (capacity is reserved)
- 4 x m4.large Amazon Linux, default tenancy Reserved Instances in Region us-east-1
- 1 x c4.large Amazon Linux, default tenancy Reserved Instances in Region us-east-1

How the reserved instances are applied? Choose 3.

A.  reservation of the four m3.large zonal Reserved Instances is used by the four m3.large instances

B.  m4.large regional Reserved Instances billing discount applies to 100% usage of 2 x m4.xlarge Amazon Linux, default tenancy

C.  m4.large regional Reserved Instances billing discount applies to 50% usage 2 x m4.xlarge Amazon Linux, default tenancy

D.  c4.large regional Reserved Instance billing discount applies to 50% of c4.xlarge usage.

E.  c4.large regional Reserved Instance billing discount applies to 100% of c4.xlarge usage.

Q73. Which of the following three statements are correct on reserved instance modifications?

A.  You can combine a reservation for two t2.small instances into one t2.medium instance

B.  You can divide a reservation for two t2.small instances into one t2.large instance.

C.  You can divide a reservation for one t2.large instance into four t2.small instances

D.  You can combine a reservation for four t2.small instances into one t2.large instance

Q74. Which of the following is not an allocation strategy for the Spot Instances in a Spot Fleet?

A.  lowestPrice

B.  diversified
C.  capacityOptimized
D.  InstancePoolsToUseCount
E.  PerformanceOptimized

Q75. Your online gaming application gets steady traffic apart from first three days of month when you run promotion giving discounts and bonus points to gamers. During those three days the traffic triples because of new users joining and existing users playing more. Currently you have six instances on which your application runs. What is the cost effective way to plan your instances to handle this periodic traffic surge?
A.  Run 6 on demand instances then add 12 more on-demand only for first three days of the month
B.  Run 6 on demand instances then add 12 more as spot instances
C.  Use 18 reserved instances i.e. three time the normal demand all the time
D.  Run 6 reserved instance and then add 12 on demand instances for three days every month.

Q76. You have a reservation with two t2.micro instances and a reservation with one t2.small instance. Which of the following two ways you can combine them? Choose 2.
A.  Merge both reservations to a single reservation with one t2.medium instance
B.  Merge both reservations to a single reservation with two t2.small instance
C.  Merge both reservations to a single reservation with two t2.medium instance
D.  Merge both reservations to a single reservation with one t2.large instance

Q77. For a service or platform to be considered serverless, what capabilities it should provide? Choose 4.
A.  No server management – You don't have to provision or maintain any servers.
B.  Flexible scaling – You can scale your application automatically or by adjusting its capacity through toggling the units of consumption (for example, throughput, memory) rather than units of individual servers.
C.  Full control on server management – You will have the ability to install software, maintain or administer.
D.  High availability – Serverless applications have built-in availability and fault tolerance.
E.  No idle capacity – You don't have to pay for idle capacity.

Q78. Choose the services from which Lambda can read events? Choose 3.
A.  Amazon API Gateway
B.  Amazon Kinesis
C.  Amazon DynamoDB
D.  Amazon Simple Queue Service

Q79. You are a project manager for developing a web application on a tight budget with timeline of one year for end user release. You are planning to have three environments: for developers, for testers and for integration. You need four instances for each environment, minimum of two instances any time and will need them from first week itself. How can you optimize your cost for various environments instances?
A. Use 12 reserved instances covering requirement of all three environments.
B. Use 6 reserve instances and 6 spot instances
C. Use 6 reserve instances and 6 on-demand instances
D. Use 3 reserve instances and 9 spot instances

Q80. Which of the following services can be integrated with Lambda? Choose 3.
A. S3, SNS, SES, IoT events, Cloudwatch
B. ELB, Cognito, API Gateway, Cloudfront, Step Functions
C. Kinesis, DynamoDB, SQS
D. RDS, ECS, Auto Scaling

Q81. What are the different ways you can use Lambda in your application design?
A. Configure triggers to invoke a function in response to resource lifecycle events
B. Respond to incoming HTTP requests
C. Consume events from a queue
D. Run on a schedule
E. All of the above

Q82. You have an application which is using AWS services as depicted below for data ingestion, transformation and final storage in database.

Daily File Upload — Amazon S3 — AWS Lambda File Stream Create — Amazon Kinesis Data Streams — AWS Lambda Process and Transform Data — Amazon Aurora

At the end of day files are uploaded to a designated S3 bucket. Lambda mapped to S3 captures the file upload event and has the function logic to read files from s3 bucket as stream and writing the data to the kinesis stream. Second Lambda reads the Kinesis streams and has function logic to process and transform the data before saving the records in Aurora DB. While testing you are getting error and the lambda task processing the file in S3 aborts. The code works fine in your local computer dev setup with test files. What could you do to solve the issue? Choose 2.
A. Increase the timeout setting. Maximum is 15 minutes. Optimize you code execution time.
B. Increase the memory allocation. Maximum is 3 GB.

C. Check your code for concurrency issue.

D. Increase the provisioned concurrency.

Q83. Which of the following commands you can run on Linux Instance at Launch?

A. Installing web server, php, and mariadb packages.

B. Starting http service

C. Creating a simple web page to test the web server and PHP engine.

D. All of the above

Q84. Which AWS service gives you following features:

- Lets connected devices easily and securely interact with cloud applications and other devices.

- Support billions of devices and trillions of messages, and can process and route those messages to AWS endpoints and to other devices reliably and securely.

- Lets your application keep track of and communicate with all your devices, all the time, even when they aren't connected.

A. API Gateway

B. Application Load Balancer

C. IoT Core

D. Cloudfront

Q85. You have a photo upload application running in an EC2 instance. The application uses S3 to store the uploaded images. After an image is uploaded you want to create a thumbnail version of it. You know that applications that run on an EC2 instance must include AWS credentials in their AWS API requests. Which of the following is the best option?

A. Store AWS credentials directly within the EC2 instance and allow applications in that instance to use those credentials.

B. Creates role which has permissions policy that grants required access to the specified S3 bucket and attaches the role to the EC2 instance.

C. Store AWS credentials directly with the application code.

D. Create a bucket policy attached to the bucket giving required permission to the EC2 instance.

Q86. You have created an ecommerce website and leveraged Serverless architecture by using Lambda for order management, payment management, cart management and recommendation engine. You are following recommended best practices by leveraging Lambda environment variables and not storing any DEV/TEST/PRODUCTION environment configuration, third party integration or any other AWS service information in the code. As some of these environment variable information are sensitive, which of the following is the best possible encryption option for environment variables?

A. No need to do anything as first time you create or update Lambda functions that uses environment variables in a region, a default service key is created for you automatically within AWS KMS to encrypt environment variables.
B. Lambda doesn't provide a way to encrypt sensitive information.
C. Write a custom code to encrypt decrypt environment variable stores in a text file.
D. Check the "Enable helpers for encryption in transit "checkbox in AWS Lambda console and supply a custom KMS key. This masks the value you entered and results in a call to AWS KMS to encrypt the value and return it as Ciphertext.

Q87. You have a batch job which needs to run every night from 11 pm to 3 am. Which option will ensure that capacity is available for the required duration as well it is cost effective? Choose 2.
A. Use Scheduled Reserved Instances
B. Use Spot Instances
C. Use Reserved Instances
D. Use On-Demand Instances
E. On-demand Instances with Saving plans

Q88. What is the URI to view all categories of instance metadata from within a running instance?
A. http://169.254.169.254/meta-data/
B. http://169.254.169.254/latest/meta-data/
C. http://254..169.254.169/meta-data/
D. http:// 254..169.254.169/latest/meta-data/

Q89. You are a designing microservices based architecture for an online banking application on AWS. You want to leverage AWS managed services, which eliminates the architectural burden to design for scale and high availability and eliminates the operational efforts of running and monitoring the microservice's underlying infrastructure. Which of the following AWS services will meet your criteria? Choose 5
A. Amazon API Gateway
B. AWS Lambda
C. AWS Fargate
D. EC2 Auto Scaling Fleet
E. Amazon RDS
F. Amazon Aurora Serverless
G. Amazon DynamoDB

Q90. Which of the following is not a Serverless service offered by AWS? Choose 3
A. AWS Fargate
B. Amazon RDS
C. Amazon EC2

D.   Amazon DynamoDB

E.   Amazon Aurora Serverless

F.   Amazon API Gateway

G.   Amazon S3

H.   Amazon EFS

I.   Amazon EBS

J.   Amazon SNS and SQS

Q91. You have a web app that provides video transcoding services. The videos uploaded by the users are first stored in a S3 bucket where you have configured "An object created event" notification to a SQS queue. There are fleet of EC2 instances which picks up the videos from the queue and places it in another S3 bucket after transcoding the file. These consumer fleet of EC2 instance also has dynamic auto scaling policy based on custom metric 'backlog per instance'. Which type of EC2 instances you will use which will be most cost effective given that you don't have defined duration in which you have to complete the transcoding for an uploaded file?

A.   Reserved Instances

B.   On-demand Instances

C.   Saving plans Instances

D.   Spot Instances

Q92. What is the URI to instance user data from within a running instance?

A.   http://169.254.169.254/latest/meta-data/user-data

B.   http://169.254.169.254/latest/user-data

C.   http:// 254. 169. 254.169/latest/meta-data/user-data

D.   http:// 254. 169. 254.169/latest/user-data

Q93. What are differences between Dedicated Hosts and Dedicated Instances? Choose 3.

A.   Host and instance affinity: Dedicated Hosts allows you to consistently deploy your instances to the same physical server over time. Dedicated Instances don't support this feature.

B.   Bring Your Own License (BYOL): Dedicated Hosts Supports. Not supported in Dedicated Instances.

C.   Bring Your Own License (BYOL): Not supported in Dedicated Hosts. Dedicated Instances Supports.

D.   Visibility of sockets, cores, and host ID: Dedicated Hosts provides visibility of the number of sockets and physical cores. No visibility provided by Dedicated Instances.

E.   Host and instance affinity: Dedicated Hosts don't support this feature. Dedicated Instances allows you to consistently deploy your instances to the same physical server over time.

Q94. You have been tasked to migrate on-premise application hosted in Docker to AWS cloud platform. You want to simply upload your application containers without having to handle the details of capacity provisioning, load balancing, scaling, and application health monitoring. Which AWS service you will use?
    A.   CodeDeploy
    B.   ECS
    C.   Elastic Beanstalk
    D.   EC2

Q95. What are most appropriate use case for using ECS? Choose 2.
    A.   Microservice architecture based application.
    B.   Batch job workload.
    C.   GUI based desktop application.
    D.   Provide cross-platform compatibility.

Q96. To do your first PoC in AWS you deployed a small web application on an EC2 server in the public subnet of VPC. You also attached an EBS volume to the EC2 instance. After few days you stopped the EC2 instance but you were surprised to see that you are still receiving charges. What could be the reason of charges?
    A.   EC2 instances accrue charges even when they're not running.
    B.   You are being charged for using VPC.
    C.   There is billing error, you should raise a ticket to AWS support.
    D.   You are charged for EBS storage for the amount of storage provisioned to your account.

Q97. What is the underlying hypervisor used for EC2  ? Choose 2.
    A.   Xen
    B.   Nitro
    C.   Hyper-v
    D.   vSphere

Q98. How is attaching multiple network interfaces to an instance useful?
    A.   Create a management network.
    B.   Use network and security appliances in your VPC.
    C.   Create dual-homed instances with workloads/roles on distinct subnets.
    D.   Create a low-budget, high-availability solution.
    E.   All of the above

Q99. Your company is migrating existing web applications running on on-premise web servers to AWS. Your applications are using trusted IP addresses that your partners and customers have whitelisted in their firewalls.  You want to move these applications to AWS without requiring your partners and customers to change their IP address whitelists. Some applications may also have hard-coded IP address dependencies. How can you migrate such applications to AWS with minimal disruptions?

A. Submit a support request to AWS to allocation Elastic IP address which matches your existing IP address range.

B. You cannot migrate your local IP address to AWS, use the Elastic IP address allocated by AWS.

C. Leverage AWS Bring Your Own IP (BYOIP) and create Elastic IP addresses from your BYOIP address prefix and use them with AWS resources such as EC2 instances, Network Load Balancers, and NAT gateways.

D. Route internet request/response of migrated web application on AWS through on-premise VPN.

Q100. You are getting following error when trying to connect to newly launched EC2 instance using Putty.
Error: Server refused our key
Error: No supported authentication methods available
What could be the possible reasons? Choose 2.

A. Verify that you are connecting with the appropriate user name for your AMI.

B. Verify that your private key (.pem) file has been correctly converted to the format recognized by PuTTY (.ppk).

C. Verify that your IAM user policy has permission to access EC2 instance.

D. Verify that your EC2 instance security group allows SSH connection

Q101. Which of the following information are given in an Auto Scaling launch configuration?

A. ID of the Amazon Machine Image (AMI)

B. Instance Type and Key pair

C. One or more security group

D. Block device mapping

E. All of the above

Q102. What are benefits of Auto Scaling? Choose 3.

A. Better Fault tolerance

B. Better Availability

C. Better Cost management

D. Better performance

Q103. What are purchase types of instances an auto scaling group can launch?

A. On-Demand Instances only

B. Spot instance only

C. On demand instance or Spot instances or both

D. Reserved instances only

Q104. What are the different ways you can scale your EC2 auto scaling group? Choose 5.
   A.   Maintain current instance levels at all times
   B.   Manual Scaling by specifying change in the max, min and desired capacity
   C.   Scale based on demand
   D.   Account based scaling
   E.   Scale based on Schedule
   F.   Predictive Scaling

Q105. You want to define the auto scaling based on the CPU utilization of the instances. Which auto scaling policy you will use?
   A.   Maintain current instance levels at all times
   B.   Manual Scaling by specifying change in the max, min and desired capacity
   C.   Scale based on demand or dynamic Scaling
   D.   Account based scaling

Q106. . What are the key components of Amazon EC2 Auto Scaling? Choose 3.
   A.   Auto Scaling Groups
   B.   Load Balancers
   C.   Launch Templates or Launch Configurations
   D.   Scaling options

Q107. Which of the following two statements are correct about EC2 auto scaling with regard to instances in AZ and regions? Choose 2.
   A.   An Auto Scaling group can contain EC2 instances in one or more Availability Zones within the same Region.
   B.   An Auto Scaling group will have EC2 instances in one Availability Zones only.
   C.   Auto scaling groups cannot span multiple Regions.
   D.   An Auto Scaling group can contain EC2 instances in one or more Availability Zones across Regions.

Q108. You have deployed your web application EC2 instances within an auto scaling group spanning three AZs in a region and attached to an application load balancer. AWS has launched a new AMI which will be more cost effective for you. How can you ensure that your auto scaling group uses new AMI to launch new instances?
   A.    Modify the existing launch configuration to use new AMI.
   B.    Create a new launch configuration with new AMI and then update the Auto Scaling group to use the new launch configuration.
   C.    First terminate the existing instances based on old AMI then Modify the existing launch configuration to use new AMI.
   D.    First terminate the existing instances based on old AMI, create a new launch configuration with new AMI and then update the Auto Scaling group to use the new launch configuration.

Q109. How does Amazon EC2 Auto Scaling distribute instances? Choose 2.
   A.   Randomly between the Availability Zones that are enabled for Auto Scaling group
   B.   Evenly between the Availability Zones that are enabled for Auto Scaling group
   C.   Launches new instances in the Availability Zone with the fewest instances.
   D.   Launches new instances in the Availability Zone with the highest instances.

Q110. You are the solution architect for an ecommerce company. There are regular flash discounts and festivals discount offered which leads to sudden burst in orders at an unpredictable magnitude and many time more than off discount period. The architecture of the web application is shown in the diagram below. At times during the discount sales the EC2 Auto scaling is not adding instances fast enough and it is leading to performance deterioration during orders checkout and backend processing. How can you ensure none of the customer order is lost without impacting performance, scalability, and resiliency?

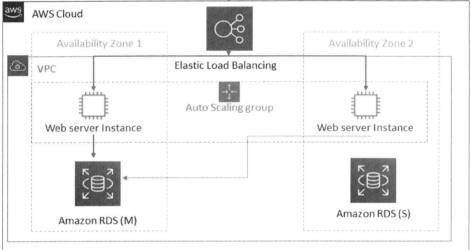

A. Increase the minimum fleet of servers saving the customers' orders.

B. Have an SQS queue for customer orders and fleet of EC2 instances in auto scale group to process the order.

C. Increase the performance and capacity of database.

D. Use lambda instead of EC2 for processing the customer order.

Q111. What are the three ways Auto Scale group can be created?

A. Using an AMI

B. Using launch template

C. Using launch configuration

D.  Using an EC2 instance

Q112. Which of the following statements are correct about auto scaling group? Choose 3.
A.  An Auto Scaling group contains a collection of Amazon EC2 instances that are treated as a logical grouping for the purposes of automatic scaling and management.
B.  An Auto Scaling group starts by launching enough instances to meet its desired capacity. It maintains this number of instances by performing periodic health checks on the instances in the group.
C.  An Auto Scaling group can launch On-Demand Instances, Spot Instances, and Reserved Instances. You can specify multiple purchase options for your Auto Scaling group only when you configure the group to use a launch template.
D.  An Auto Scaling group can launch On-Demand Instances, Spot Instances, or both. You can specify multiple purchase options for your Auto Scaling group only when you configure the group to use a launch template.

Q113.You are the solution architect for a national retail store. You have a reporting application running on EC2 instances in an auto scaling group maintaining a fixed number of instances. All the stores across the cities uploads the data every day from 1 AM-3AM for report batch processing. You notice that for last one week the performance has degraded which is affecting downstream analytical applications. What can you do to ensure that batch processing process EC2 instances are scaled at 1AM?
A.  Create a new Auto Scaling group with schedule scaling policy scheduled at 1 AM.
B.  Configure your existing Auto Scaling group to scale based on a schedule by creating a scheduled action for 1 AM.
C.  Configure your existing Auto Scaling group with Dynamic scaling policy scheduled at 1 AM.
D.  Configure your existing Auto Scaling group to scale based on a schedule by creating a scheduled action for 12.30 AM.

Q114. You are the solution architect for a national retail store. You have a sales reporting application running on EC2 spot instances in an auto scaling group. All the stores across the cities uploads the data during the day. Auto scaling group is configured with step policy to scale out using the Amazon CloudWatch CPUUtilization metric to add capacity using EC2 spot instances when the metric value exceeds 90 percent utilization for 15 minutes. You notice that number of EC2 instances have reached to 20, all running at 100 percent utilization and Auto Scaling group scaling out is failing. What could be the reason? Choose 2.
A.  New instances must be taking too much time to bootstart.
B.  Cooldown period must be high.
C.  The maximum size of your auto scaling group is 20.
D.  You have reached the maximum number of spot instance of 20 per region.

Q115. When you configure dynamic scaling, you define how to scale the capacity of your Auto Scaling group in response to changing demand. You can configure your Auto Scaling group to scale dynamically to meet this need by creating a scaling policy. Which of the following scaling policies are supported by Amazon EC2 Auto Scaling? Choose 3.
   A. Weighted Scaling
   B. Target tracking scaling
   C. Step scaling
   D. Simple scaling

Q116.You are architecting a website which will have three subdomains, for example subdomain1.site.com, subdomain2.site.com, subdomain3.site.com. Each of these subdomain's request will be served by web servers running on EC2 instances. The webserver EC2 instances can be configured in one auto scaling group or multiple auto scaling group to meet the user request volume. Your business need is that each subdomains request to be handled differently by backend EC2 instances. You are contemplating whether to set up multiple ALBs (one for each subdomain) or have only one ALB. Which of the two following options are correct?
   A. An auto scaling group can be attached to multiple ALB so you can have one ALB for each subdomain. All instances are configured under on auto scaling group.
   B. An auto scaling group can be attached to only one ALB so you cannot have one ALB for each subdomain i.e. more than one ALB mapped to one auto scaling group.
   C. You can use one ALB as it has the ability for Routing Rules (Domain and Path based) and you can have the request routed to domain specific auto scaling group.

Q117. What are the features of EC2 Auto Scaling cooldown period? Choose 3.
   A. The cooldown period helps to ensure that your Auto Scaling group doesn't launch or terminate additional instances before the previous scaling activity takes effect.
   B. After the Auto Scaling group dynamically scales in/out using a simple scaling policy, it waits for the cooldown period to complete before resuming scaling activities.
   C. The default cooldown period is 300 seconds.
   D. Cooldown period is the duration when auto scaling group don't scale out but scale in happens.

Q118. Which statements is correct when you configure the EC2 Auto Scaling group to use Elastic Load Balancing health checks?
   A. Instance is considered unhealthy if it fails either the EC2 status checks or the load balancer health checks
   B. Instance is considered unhealthy only when it fails the load balancer health checks
   C. Instance is considered unhealthy only when it fails the EC2 status checks
   D. Instance is considered unhealthy only when it fails the customized health checks

Q119. If you attach multiple load balancers to an auto scaling group. How is an instance marked as unhealthy?

A. All load balancers must report that the instance is unhealthy in order for it to consider the instance unhealthy.

B. If one load balancer reports an instance as unhealthy, the instance is marked as unhealthy and replaced by auto scaling group.

C. Majority of load balancers must report that the instance is unhealthy in order for it to consider the instance unhealthy.

D. You can designate a specific load balancers that must report that the instance is unhealthy in order for it to consider the instance unhealthy.

Q120. Which of the following statement are correct about auto scaling group? Choose 2.

A. An Auto Scaling group can contain Amazon EC2 instances from multiple Availability Zones within the same Region.

B. An Auto Scaling group can contain Amazon EC2 instances from multiple Availability Zones across Regions.

C. An Auto Scaling group can contain Amazon EC2 instances only in one Availability Zones within a Region.

D. Incoming traffic is distributed equally across all Availability Zones enabled by the load balancer attached to Auto Scaling group.

Q121. Your company has an intranet application for employees to fill up their weekly timesheet. Usage pattern analysis depicts a surge in traffic on Friday evening and Wednesday evening from 4-6 pm. Which auto scaling policy would you use to add and remove instances?

A. Schedule based auto scaling policy

B. Demand based auto scaling policy

C. Maintain current instance levels at all times

D. Manual Scaling by specifying change in the max, min and desired capacity

Q122.What is the difference between RunTask and StartTask in ECS ? Choose 2.

A. RunTask starts a new task using the specified task definition and can be placed in any container instance.

B. StartTask starts a new task from the specified task definition on the specified container instance or instances.

C. StartTask starts a new task using the specified task definition and can be placed in any container instance.

D. RunTask starts a new task from the specified task definition on the specified container instance or instances

Q123. You have deployed a fleet of EC2 instances using an auto scaling group based on target tracking dynamic scaling. Recently you notice that scaling policy is launching, terminating and relaunching many instances in an hour. This has led to increased cost as you are getting billed for every instance which is getting launched for few seconds to few minutes. What should you do so that frequency of launching and termination of instances is optimized? Choose 2.

A.   Scale out quickly but scale in slowly. Increase the duration of cooldown period.
B.   Scale out slowly and scale in quickly. Decrease the duration of cooldown period.
C.   Change the target tracking scaling metric.
D.   Analyze and change the target tracking metric target value.

Q124. You have migrated your on-premise intranet application to AWS. You deployed this as a web application in a VPC with an Application Load Balancer (ALB). Web server EC2 instances are in an auto scaling group (ASG) attached to ALB. Based on past data you know the number of instances required to serve the user requests. How can you configure the auto scaling group to maintain a fixed number of instances without compromising on fault tolerance and better availability?
A.   Set the same value for minimum, maximum, and desired capacity in ASG equal to required number of fixed instance.
B.   No need to have an ASG. Deploy the required number of instances and attach it to ALB.
C.   Set the same value for desired capacity in ASG equal to required number of fixed instance.
D.   Set the minimum value in ASG equal to required number of fixed instance.

Q125. Which of the following statement are correct regarding Manual Scaling for Amazon EC2 Auto Scaling? Choose 3.
A.   At any time, you can change the size of an existing Auto Scaling group manually.
B.   You cannot change the size of an existing Auto Scaling group manually.
C.   You can update the instances that are attached to the Auto Scaling group.
D.   You can attach EC2 Instances to your Auto Scaling Group

Q126.   You are creating proof of concept web application and want to quickly deploy and manage applications in the AWS Cloud without having to learn about the infrastructure that runs those applications. You don't want to handle the details of capacity provisioning, load balancing, scaling, and application health monitoring. Which AWS services you should leverage?
A.   EC2, ELB, Auto Scaling
B.   AWS Elastic Beanstalk
C.   Lambda, ELB, Auto Scaling
D.   EC2, S3, ELB, Auto Scaling
E.   Lambda, ELB, Auto Scaling, CloudFormation

Q127. Elastic Beanstalk supports applications developed in?
A.   Go, Java, .NET, Node.js, PHP, Python, Scala and Ruby
B.   Go, Java, .NET, Node.js, PHP, Python, React.js and Ruby
C.   Go, Java, .NET, Node.js, PHP, Python, React.js , Angular and Ruby
D.   Go, Java, .NET, Node.js, PHP, Python, Scala, Swift and Ruby

E.  Go, Java, .NET, Node.js, PHP, Python, and Ruby

Q128.You have an EC2 auto scaling group with following setting:
Auto Scaling group name = my-asg
Minimum size = 1
Maximum size = 5
Desired capacity = 2
Availability Zone = us-west-1a, Region: us-west-1 US West (N. California)

You know that AWS allows attaching instances to existing auto scaling group. What are the considerations you should check before you can attach an existing instance? Choose 3.
A.  The instance is in the running state. The AMI used to launch the instance must still exist.
B.  The instance is in AZ us-west-1a.
C.  The instance is in any AZ in us-west-1 Region.
D.  The instance is not a member of another Auto Scaling group.

Q129 You have an EC2 auto scaling group with following setting:
Auto Scaling group name = my-asg
Minimum size = 1
Maximum size = 5
Desired capacity = 3
Availability Zone = us-west-1a, Region: us-west-1 US West (N. California)

Currently there are 3 instances equal to desired capacity in running state. You want to create a separate auto scale group by detaching 2 instance, which of the following statements are applicable? Choose 3.
A.  You have the option of decrementing the desired capacity for the Auto Scaling group by the number of instances you are detaching.
B.  If you choose not to decrement the desired capacity, Amazon EC2 Auto Scaling launches new instances to replace the ones that you detach.
C.  If you choose not to decrement the desired capacity, Amazon EC2 Auto Scaling will automatically decrement the value of desired capacity as you detach instances.
D.  If you decrement the capacity but detach multiple instances from the same Availability Zone, Amazon EC2 Auto Scaling can rebalance the Availability Zones unless you suspend the AZ Rebalance process.

Q130. . You have deployed an intranet HR application on AWS Elastic Beanstalk. Initially it was rolled out to few beta user employees with single instance deployment on a t2.micro, with single instance capacity. After positive feedback it is planned to be rolled out to all the employees. What you should do so that there is no performance issues? Choose 2.

A.  No need to do anything Elastic Beanstalk will automatically handle appropriate capacity provisioning, load balancing, auto-scaling to meet performance requirements.
B.  Change the single instance type from t2.micro to t2.large.
C.  Modify the configuration to instance type as t2.large, change the root volume type to general purpose SSD with 100 GB
D.  Change the environment type from single instance to load balanced and configure auto scaling based on CPUutilization.

Q131. In which order EC2 auto scaling group implements the following rules for default termination policy when a scale-in event happens?
1.  If there are multiple unprotected instances to terminate, determine which instances are closest to the next billing hour. If there are multiple unprotected instances closest to the next billing hour, terminate one of these instances at random.
2.  Determine which Availability Zones have the most instances, and at least one instance that is not protected from scale in.
3.  Determine which instances to terminate so as to align the remaining instances to the allocation strategy for the On-Demand or Spot Instance that is terminating. This only applies to an Auto Scaling group that specifies allocation strategies.
4.  Determine whether any of the instances use the oldest launch template or configuration.

A.  1,2,3,4
B.  2, 3,4,1
C.  3,4,1,2
D.  4,3,2,1

Q132. Which scaling policy you should use if you are scaling based on a utilization metric that increases or decreases proportionally to the number of instances in an Auto Scaling group?
A.  Cloudwatch Scaling
B.  Target tracking scaling
C.  Step scaling
D.  Simple scaling

Q133. You have deployed an application that uses an Auto Scaling group and an Amazon SQS queue to send requests to a single EC2 instance. To help ensure that the application performs at optimum levels, there are two policies that control when the Auto Scaling group should scale out. One is a target tracking policy that uses a custom metric to add and remove capacity based on the number of SQS messages in the queue. The other is a step policy that uses the Amazon CloudWatch CPUUtilization metric to add capacity when the instance exceeds 90 percent utilization for a specified length of time.

What will happen when EC2 instance could trigger the CloudWatch alarm for the CPUUtilization metric at the same time that the SQS queue triggers the alarm for the custom metric resulting in scale-out and scale in criteria for both policies being met at the same time?

A. Auto Scaling group will throw an error and scale out/in will not happen.

B. Auto Scaling will execute one policy that provides the largest capacity for scale out and scale in.

C. Auto Scaling will always execute policy based on CloudWatch metric.

D. Auto Scaling will always execute policy based on SQS custom metric.

Q134. Your solution architect has configured following scaling policy in the auto scaling group for your web server instances:

- Scaling policy to keep the average aggregate CPU utilization of your Auto Scaling group at 40 percent.

- Scaling policy to keep the request count per target of your Elastic Load Balancing target group at 1000 for your Auto Scaling group.

Which type of dynamic scaling policy is this?

A. Cloudwatch Scaling

B. Target tracking scaling

C. Step scaling

D. Simple scaling

Q135. Which of the following metric will not work for target tracking policy in EC2 auto scaling group? Choose 3.

A. The number of requests received by the load balancer fronting the Auto Scaling group (that is, the Elastic Load Balancing metric RequestCount).

B. The CPU utilization of an Auto Scaling group.

C. Load balancer request latency.

D. CloudWatch SQS queue metric ApproximateNumberOfMessagesVisible.

E. A customized metric that measures the number of messages in the queue per EC2 instance.

Q136. For a proof of concept, you are planning to use Elastic Beanstalk as you can quickly deploy and manage applications in the AWS Cloud without having to learn about the infrastructure that runs the application. Which of the following is automatically handled by Elastic Beanstalk? Choose 4.

A. Data at rest and data in transit encryption

B. capacity provisioning

C. load balancing

D. scaling

E. application health monitoring

Q137. Choose the supported platforms by Elastic Beanstalk?

A. Programming languages: Go, Java, Node.js, PHP, Python, Ruby
B. Application servers :WebSphere, WebLogic, Tomcat, Passenger, Puma
C. Application servers :Tomcat, Passenger, Puma
D. Docker Containers

Q138. What elements of application can you control when using AWS Elastic Beanstalk?
   A. Select the operating system that matches your application requirements (e.g., Amazon Linux or Windows Server 2012 R2) and run other application components, such as a memory caching service, side-by-side in Amazon EC2
   B. Choose from several available database and storage options and Access log files without logging in to the application servers
   C. Enable login access to Amazon EC2 instances for immediate and direct troubleshooting and enhance application security by enabling HTTPS protocol on the load balancer
   D. Quickly improve application reliability by running in more than one Availability Zone and Adjust application server settings (e.g., JVM settings) and pass environment variables
   E. Access built-in Amazon CloudWatch monitoring and getting notifications on application health and other important events
   F. All of the above
   G. None of the above

Q139. Which of the following are correct considerations for target tracking policy in EC2 auto scaling group? Choose 2.
   A. An Auto Scaling group can have multiple scaling policies in force at the same time using same metric but different target.
   B. An Auto Scaling group can have multiple scaling policies in force at the same time, provided that each of them uses a different metric.
   C. You can disable the scale-in portion of a target tracking scaling policy.
   D. A target tracking scaling policy should have both scale-in and scale-out portion.

Q140. Which of the following adjustment types is not supported by Amazon EC2 Auto Scaling for step scaling and simple scaling?
   A. ChangeInCapacity
   B. ExactCapacity
   C. DesiredCapacity
   D. PercentChangeInCapacity

Q141. Which of the following options are true about AWS Lambda? Choose 4.
   A. AWS Lambda lets you run code without provisioning or managing servers.
   B. You pay only for the compute time you consume, there is no charge when your code is not running.

C. You can set up your code to automatically trigger from other AWS services or call it directly from any web or mobile app.

D. Stateful Processing is perfect use case for AWS Lambda

E. Stateless Processing is perfect use case for AWS Lambda

Q142. Which statements are true with regards to EC2 and Lambda? Choose 2.

A. With Amazon EC2 you are responsible for provisioning capacity, monitoring fleet health and performance, and designing for fault tolerance and scalability.

B. With Amazon EC2 you are not responsible for provisioning capacity, monitoring fleet health and performance, and designing for fault tolerance and scalability.

C. Lambda performs on your behalf, including capacity provisioning, monitoring fleet health, deploying your code, running a web service front end, and monitoring and logging your code

D. Lambda you are responsible for capacity provisioning, monitoring fleet health, deploying your code, running a web service front end, and monitoring and logging your code

Q143. What languages does AWS Lambda support? Choose 2.

A. React.js, Python, Java, Ruby

B. Angular, C#, Go and PowerShell.

C. Node.js, Python, Java, Ruby

D. C#, Go and PowerShell.

Q144. You have a web app that lets users upload images and use them online. Each image requires resizing and encoding before it can be published. The web app runs on EC2 instances in a Dynamic Auto Scaling group based on CPU utilization that is configured to handle your typical upload rates. Unhealthy instances are terminated and replaced to maintain current instance levels at all times. The app places the raw bitmap data of the images in an Amazon SQS queue for processing. There are fleet of EC2 instance acting as worker program polling the SQS queue to processes the images and then publishes the processed images where they can be viewed by users. These consumer fleet of EC2 instance also has dynamic auto scaling policy.

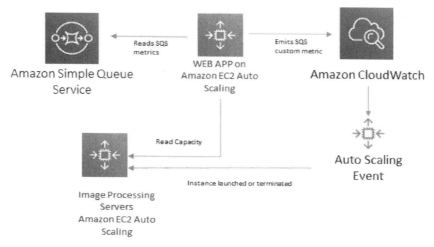

Which of the following AWS service you can use for processing the images instead of EC2 instances without compromising performance and also achieving cost optimization?

A. AWS Elastic Beanstalk
B. AWS Lambda
C. Amazon SNS
D. None of the above

Q145.You have a photo upload application and use S3 to store the uploaded images. After an image is uploaded you want to create a thumbnail version of it. Which of the following option will be most scalable and cost effective?

A. Create a Lambda function that Amazon S3 can invoke when objects are created. Then, the Lambda function can read the image object from the source bucket and create a thumbnail image target bucket.
B. Have a fleet of EC2 instances running a program which continuously reads the most latest object uploaded in S3 and converts into thumbnail.
C. S3 posts new image upload event notification as JSON to a SQS queue from which a fleet of EC2 servers will process the image.
D. S3 posts new image upload event notification as JSON to a SNS topic from which a fleet of EC2 servers will process the image.

Q146. Which of the following are suitable use cases that can be implemented with Amazon Lambda for real time data processing? Choose 3.

A. Dynamic Websites
B. Real-time File Processing
C. Real-time Stream Processing
D. Extract, Transform, Load

Q147-148 are based on following scenario.
You have web server EC2 instances in auto scaling group with dynamic step adjustment policy. You are using the CloudWatch metric ASGAverageCPUUtilization (Average CPU utilization of the Auto Scaling group) for dynamic scaling. You have an alarm with a breach threshold of 50 and a scaling adjustment type of PercentChangeInCapacity. You also have scale-out and scale-in policies with the following step adjustments:

## SCALE OUT POLICY

| Metric Lower Bound Value Increase from threshold of 50% | Metric Upper Bound Value Increase from threshold of 50% | Adjustment | Metric value In % |
|---|---|---|---|
| 0 | 10 | 0 | 50 <= *value* < 60 |
| 10 | 20 | 10 | 60 <= *value* < 70 |
| 20 | null | 30 | 70 <= *value* < +infinity |

## SCALE IN POLICY

| Metric Lower Bound Value Decrease from threshold of 50% | Metric Upper Bound Value Decrease from threshold of 50% | Adjustment | Metric value In % |
|---|---|---|---|
| -10 | 0 | 0 | 40 < *value* <= 50 |
| -20 | -10 | -10 | 30 < *value* <= 40 |
| 20 | null | 30 | - infinity< *value* <=30 |

Your group has both a current capacity and a desired capacity of 10 instances. The group maintains its current and desired capacity while the aggregated metric value is greater than 40 and less than 60.

Q147.Based on scenario given above for step scaling configuration what will happen if the metric value gets to 60 and further to 70 after sometime? Choose 2.
 A. If the metric value gets to 60, the desired capacity of the group increases by 1 instance, to 11 instances.
 B. If the metric value rises to 70, the desired capacity of the group increases by another 3 instances, to 13 instances.
 C. If the metric value rises to 70, the desired capacity of the group increases by another 3 instances, to 14 instances.

D.  If the metric value rises to 70, the desired capacity of the group increases by another 3 instances, to 15 instances.

Q148. On continuation from scenario given in Q147 above for step scaling configuration what will happen if the metric value after reaching 70 first falls to 40 and falls further to 30 after some time? Choose 2.
A.  If the metric value gets to 40, the desired capacity of the group decreases by 1 instance, to 9 instances.
B.  If the metric value gets to 40, the desired capacity of the group decreases by 1 instance, to 13 instances.
C.  If the metric value falls to 30, the desired capacity of the group decreases by another 3 instances, to 10 instances.
D.  If the metric value falls to 30, the desired capacity of the group decreases by another 3 instances, to 6 instances.

Q149. Which of the following are rules for configuring step adjustments for your policy? Choose 4.
A.  The ranges of your step adjustments can't overlap or have a gap.
B.  Only one step adjustment can have a null lower bound (negative infinity). If one step adjustment has a negative lower bound, then there must be a step adjustment with a null lower bound.
C.  Only one step adjustment can have a null upper bound (positive infinity). If one step adjustment has a positive upper bound, then there must be a step adjustment with a null upper bound.
D.  You can define a default adjustments for gaps in the range.
E.  If the metric value is above the breach threshold, the lower bound is exclusive and the upper bound is inclusive. If the metric value is below the breach threshold, the lower bound is inclusive and the upper bound is exclusive.
F.  If the metric value is above the breach threshold, the lower bound is inclusive and the upper bound is exclusive. If the metric value is below the breach threshold, the lower bound is exclusive and the upper bound is inclusive.

Q150. Amazon EC2 Auto Scaling can determine the health status of an instance using one or more of the following. Choose 3.
A.  Status checks provided by Amazon EC2
B.  Health checks provided by Elastic Load Balancing.
C.  Cloudwatch metrics.
D.  Your custom health checks.

Q151. You have created a Linux EC2 instance in the default VPC and attached key pair to it. Now you are not able to connect to EC2 instance from your windows laptop using Putty, SSH client for Windows. You have downloaded the key pair from AWS console, converted to .ppk file and configured the Putty to use it. You are using the user name 'ec2-user' and instance ip address displayed in the console. What could be the possible reason?

    A.   'ec2-user' is not the right user name for Linux EC2

    B.   To connect to your instance, security group attached to instance must have inbound rules that allow SSH access from public IP address of your computer, or a range of IP addresses in your local network.

    C.   You have to use a separate key pair to login from your laptop.

    D.   None of the above

Q152. Which of the following are correct regarding AWS lambda limits? Choose 3.

    A.   Function timeout value is 900 sec or 15 mts

    B.   Function memory allocation 128 mb to 3008 mb  in 64 MB increments

    C.   Function timeout value is 300 sec or 5 mts

    D.   Deployment package size is 50 MB (zipped, for direct upload)

Q153. How does a load balancer check the health of an EC2 instance? Choose 3.

    A.   By sending ping

    B.   Monitor Cloudwatch metric for EC2 status

    C.   Attempting connections

    D.   Sends requests

Q154. If you have configured the Auto Scaling group to use Elastic Load Balancing health checks, when it considers the instance unhealthy? Choose 2.

    A.   If it fails the EC2 status checks

    B.   If it fails the load balancer health checks.

    C.   Only when it fails the EC2 status checks.

    D.   Only when it fails the load balancer health checks.

Q155. If you attach multiple load balancers to an Auto Scaling group, which of the following statements are correct? Choose 2.

    A.   If one load balancer reports an instance as unhealthy and others report it as healthy, the Auto Scaling group treats it as healthy instance.

    B.   All load balancers must report that the instance is healthy in order for it to be considered a healthy instance by ASG.

    C.   If one load balancer reports an instance as unhealthy, the Auto Scaling group replaces the instance, even if other load balancers report it as healthy.

    D.   All load balancers must report that the instance is unhealthy in order for it to be considered an unhealthy instance by ASG.

Q156. You are developing a microservices based SaaS application for GPS tracking of trucks. This involves each trucks being fitted with a GPS device which will send real time telemetry data to the SaaS cloud application. You will also have accessibility to this application through mobile app. Which of the following is correct choice for main AWS services for the architecture?

A. AWS IoT core, Kinesis, Redshift, AWS Lambda, API Gateway, DynamoDB
B. AWS IoT core, EMR, S3, AWS Lambda, API Gateway, DynamoDB
C. AWS IoT core, RDS, S3, AWS Lambda, API Gateway, DynamoDB
D. AWS IoT core, Kinesis, S3, AWS Lambda, API Gateway, DynamoDB, RDS

Q157. You are creating a test web app based on serverless architecture. The main functionality of the app is to process the photos uploaded by the user and execute following steps:
- Extract meta data such as geolocation, time, size, format.
- create a thumbnail version
- use image recognition to tag objects in the photo

Which AWS services you will use?

A. Amazon S3, AWS Lambda, AWS Step Functions, Amazon Rekognition, Amazon DynamoDB
B. Amazon S3, EC2, AWS Step Functions, Amazon Rekognition, Amazon DynamoDB
C. Amazon RDS , EC2, AWS Step Functions, Amazon Rekognition, Amazon DynamoDB
D. Amazon RDS, AWS Lambda, AWS Step Functions, Amazon Rekognition, Amazon DynamoDB

Q158. You have a web application running in a VPC. You are leveraging different AWS services: API Gateway, ALB, Lambda, EC2 instance, RDS. EC2 instances running web server are in a public subnet and RDS is in a private subnet. Lambda is configured as target with ALB for a specific URL path. How will you ensure that this target Lambda will have access to RDS database in private subnet?

A. ALB target lambda automatically has access to all VPC subnets, private or public mapped to ALB.
B. Configure RDS as the target of lambda output.
C. Lambda cannot access private subnets.
D. Configure lambda to connect to private subnets in a virtual private cloud (VPC) in your account.

Q159. Which of the following AWS services supports Docker? Choose 2.

A. EC2
B. ECS
C. EBS
D. Elastic Beanstalk

Q160. A retail bank is planning to migrate their on-premise monolithic banking application to AWS cloud platform by re-designing into distributed microservices based architecture by decomposing the business process into smaller and independent services. They want to leverage Docker containers for this architecture. Which AWS service you can use to implement this architecture?

    A. EBS

    B. EC2

    C. ECS

    D. EKS

Q161. What is Amazon Elastic Container Service? Choose 4.

    A. Highly scalable, high performance container management service that supports Docker containers.

    B. Eliminates the need for you to install, operate, and scale your own cluster management infrastructure.

    C. With simple API calls, you can launch and stop container-enabled applications, query the complete state of your cluster, and access many familiar features like security groups, Elastic Load Balancing, EBS volumes and IAM roles.

    D. AWS Fargate is a compute engine for Amazon ECS.

    E. AWS Lambda is a compute engine for Amazon ECS.

Q162. What are two launch modes for Amazon ECS?

    A. Fargate launch type, all you have to do is package your application in containers, specify the CPU and memory requirements, define networking and IAM policies, and launch the application.

    B. Elastic Beanstalk launch type, all you have to do is package your application in containers, specify the CPU and memory requirements, define networking and IAM policies, and launch the application.

    C. EC2 launch type allows you to have server-level, more granular control over the infrastructure that runs your container applications.

    D. Lambda launch type, all you have to do is package your application in containers, specify the CPU and memory requirements, define networking and IAM policies, and launch the application.

Q163. Which statements are true about AWS Fargate? Choose 2.

    A. It is a compute engine for Amazon Elastic Beanstalk that allows you to run containers.

    B. It is a compute engine for Amazon ECS that allows you to run containers.

    C. You no longer have to provision, configure, and scale clusters of virtual machines to run containers.

    D. You have to provision, configure, and scale clusters of virtual machines to run containers.

Q164. You have written a Lambda application that returns a count of the S3 buckets that you own. You deploy it and use it in production. Your Lambda function is exposed as a REST service via an Amazon API Gateway deployment. Later on, you receive requirements that tell you that you need to change your Lambda application to count only buckets that begin with the letter "a". Before you make the change, you need to be sure that your new Lambda application works as expected. If it does have issues, you want to minimize the number of impacted users and roll back easily.

You are using SAM to define your resources for serverless application, it comes built-in with CodeDeploy where you have the option to gradually shifts customer traffic to the new version until you're satisfied that it's working as expected, or you roll back the update.

Which of the following deployment preference type you will choose if you want 10 percent of your traffic is immediately shifted to your new version and after 10 minutes, all traffic is shifted to the new version?
  A.  Canary
  B.  Linear
  C.  All-at-once
  D.  Blue-Green deployment

Q165. What are the AWS services you will use if you want to design a serverless single page web application?
  A.  API Gateway, Cloudfront, Lambda, S3, RDS MySQL
  B.  API Gateway, Cloudfront, EC2, S3, RDS MS-SQL
  C.  API Gateway, Cloudfront, ECS, S3, RDS Oracle
  D.  API Gateway, Cloudfront, Lambda, S3, DynamoDB

Q166. You have been hired as solution architect for a hospital which plans to use medical sensor devices that are wired to a patient receiving treatment at a hospital. Each sensor will be transmitting following information about the patient:
Timestamp, deviceid, patient id, patient name, patient date of birth, temperature, pulse, oxygen percent, systolic, diastolic.
The key requirements of solutions are:
• The sensor data must be ingested securely and at scale.
• It must then be de-identified to remove the patient's personal health information (PHI) so that the anonymized data can be processed in other systems downstream.
• Analyze in real-time to detect anomalies with any of the devices in the hospital and notify the appropriate device manufacturers. To achieve this enrich the ingested data with device manufacture name and model id.
• Send a SMS notification whenever an anomaly is detected.
What are the key AWS services you will use so that solution is scalable, cost efficient and can do real time ingestion and analytics of streaming data?
  A.  IoT Core, Lambda, Kinesis Firehose, EC2, Kinesis Data Streams, SNS
  B.  IoT Core, Lambda, Kinesis Firehose, Kinesis Analytics, Kinesis Data Streams, SNS
  C.  Apache Kafka, Apache Storm, Apache Zookeeper, Tableau

D. IoT Core, Lambda, Kinesis Firehose, Kinesis Analytics, EC2, Kinesis Data Streams, SNS

Q167. You are getting following error when trying to connect to newly launched EC2 instance using Putty.
Error: Host key not found, Permission denied (publickey)
Error: Authentication failed, permission denied
What could be the possible reasons? Choose 2.
   A. Verify that you are connecting with the appropriate user name for your AMI.
   B. Confirm that you are using the private key file that corresponds to the key pair that you selected when you launched the instance.
   C. Verify that your IAM user policy has permission to access EC2 instance.
   D. Verify that your EC2 instance security group allows SSH connection

Q168. Your company has a web application running on EC2 instance and using RDS MySQL database. This application is used internally by employees only during the office hours from 8AM to 6 PM. The application is idle after that. How can you save cost by stopping the instance and database during night hours?
   A. Write a custom program which runs in the background in the EC2 instance and stops both the instance and RDS at configured time.
   B. Give permission to an IAM user to manually start/stop EC2 instance and RDS database.
   C. Use the AWS Instance Scheduler to configure custom start and stop schedules for their Amazon Elastic Compute Cloud (Amazon EC2) and Amazon Relational Database Service (Amazon RDS) instances.
   D. You don't save cost as AWS charges for stopped EC2 instance and RDS database instance.

Q169. You have a critical web application running on EC2 instances in auto scaling group. The auto scaling group uses mix of on-demand instances and spot instance. How can you ensure that you get a notification whenever following events happens:
• Auto Scaling Events: Amazon EC2 Auto Scaling successfully launched an instance, Amazon EC2 Auto Scaling failed to launch an instance, Amazon EC2 Auto Scaling successfully terminated an instance.
• Spot Instance Interruption Notices
• Amazon EC2 State Change Events: shutting-down, stopped, stopping, and terminated.
   A. Using CloudWatch Events
   B. Using Cloudtrail events
   C. Using EC2 events
   D. Using VPC Flow logs

Q170. Choose 3 options from following instance meta data categories which you can get by using the following URI from an EC2 instance.
http://169.254.169.254/latest/meta-data/
  A.  route table, NACL setting, SSL certificates
  B.  ami-id, hostname, instance-id, instance-type
  C.  local-hostname, local-ipv4, vpc id, subnet id, security groups
  D.  public-hostname, public-ipv4, availability-zone

Q171. You have launched a new instance for a test environment using Amazon Linux 2, with a public DNS name that is reachable from the internet. You plan to use this server to deploy a dynamic PHP application that reads and writes information to a database. You did following procedures to install an Apache web server with PHP and MariaDB (a community-developed fork of MySQL) support on your Amazon Linux 2 instance (sometimes called a LAMP web server or LAMP stack).
  • Update the distribution software packages.
  • Installed the necessary web server, php, and mariadb packages.
  • Start httpd service and turned on via systemctl.
  • Add ec2-user to the apache group.
  • The appropriate ownership and file permissions are set for the web directory and the files contained within it.
  • A simple web page is created to test the web server and PHP engine.
How can you automate the above steps when you launch instances for QA, Integration and production environment?
  A.  Convert the tasks into a shell script and a set of cloud-init directives that executes when the instance launches using instance meta data.
  B.  Convert the tasks into a shell script and a set of cloud-init directives that executes when the instance launches using user data.
  C.  Convert the tasks into a shell script and a set of cloud-init directives that executes when the instance launches using AWS Config.
  D.  Convert the tasks into a shell script and a set of cloud-init directives that executes when the instance launches using AWS CloudFormation.

Q172. You want to launch a copy of an Amazon Elastic Cloud Compute (Amazon EC2) instance to serve clients in other geographical regions, and to create redundancy in your application. How can you create an Amazon Machine Image (AMI) of Amazon EC2 instance and then copy the AMI to another AWS Region?
  A.  Create an AMI of your EC2 instance in the current region and Copy the AMI of your EC2 instance to desired AWS Region. Apply launch permissions and then launch new instances.
  B.  Create an AMI of your EC2 instance in the current region and it can be used to launch new instance in another region.

C. You can clone current EC2 instance in the new region through Console.

D. None of the above.

Q173. Which of the following statement is not correct regarding attaching role to an EC2 instance so that your applications can securely make API requests from your instances?

A. You cannot attach multiple IAM roles to a single instance.

B. You can attach a single IAM role to multiple instances.

C. You can attach a role when you launch your instance, or attach the role to an existing instance.

D. You can attach multiple IAM roles to a single instance.

Q174. You have launched EC2 instances in an Auto Scaling Group (ASG) with an Application Load Balancer in the front to receive the requests. You know that after an instance has been marked unhealthy because of an Amazon EC2 or Elastic Load Balancing health check, it is almost immediately scheduled for replacement. What are the steps followed by ASG to replace the unhealthy instance? Choose 3.

A. If Connection Draining is enabled, the load balancer will allow existing, in-flight requests made to an instance to complete, but it will not send any new requests to the instance.

B. Amazon EC2 Auto Scaling creates a new scaling activity for terminating the unhealthy instance and then terminates it. Later, another scaling activity launches a new instance to replace the terminated instance.

C. Any Associated Elastic IP address or EBS volume will be attached to the new instance.

D. Any associated Elastic IP addresses or attached EBS volume with terminated instance are disassociated and are not automatically associated with the new instance.

Q175. You are designing a simple serverless web application which present users with an HTML based user interface and will interface on the backend with a RESTful web service to process the user request data. The application will also have user authentication functionality. Which AWS services you will use so that cost is optimized and they are managed services? Choose 4.

A. Lambda

B. S3

C. API Gateway

D. Cognito

E. EC2

Q176. What are different components of ECS using Amazon EC2?

A. Cluster, Instance, Agent

B. Task Definition, Task

C. Scheduler, Services

D.   All of the above

Q177. What are the different IAM Roles you have to create for your ECS to work properly?
Choose 5.
A.   Amazon ECS Task Execution IAM Role
B.   Amazon ECS Container Instance IAM Role
C.   Amazon ECS Instance Agent IAM Role
D.   Amazon ECS CodeDeploy IAM Role
E.   Amazon ECS CloudWatch Events IAM Role
F.   Amazon ECS Cluster IAM Role

Q178. Select the features of Elastic Fabric Adapter (EFA)? Choose 3.
A.   Brings the scalability, flexibility, and elasticity of cloud to tightly-coupled High
     Performance Computing (HPC) applications and machine learning applications.
B.   Tightly-coupled HPC applications have access to lower and more consistent latency
     and higher throughput than traditional TCP channels, enabling them to scale better.
C.   Provide all ENA devices functionalities plus a new OS bypass hardware interface
     that allows user-space applications to communicate directly with the hardware-
     provided reliable transport functionality.
D.   EFA and ENA are same.

Q179. Your web application is hosted on EC2 instances inside a VPC. You are writing a shell
scrip which will run in the instance based on following instance attributes:
VPC id, Subnet id, private ip address, public ip address, security groups, public hostname.
How will your script get this information?
A.   Using    cURL    to    get    instance    meta    data    information    from
     http://169.254.169.254/latest/user-data/
B.   Using Cloudtrail
C.   Using    cURL    to    get    instance    meta    data    information    from
     http://169.254.169.254/latest/meta-data/
D.   Using CloudWatch

Q180. An international wind turbine manufacturer is developing a product which can send its
various sensor information to cloud for real time dashboard, processing and analysis. The
manufacturer is planning to offer add-on services where
   •   Customer can see real-time dashboards in a mobile app or a web browser.
   •   Process historical information for trending and analytics.
As they roll out thousands of such smart units, the solution needs to be able to handle massive
amounts of data and scale as they grow their business without interruption. Which AWS
services you will use to design such a system?
A.   AWS IoT, Amazon EMR, Amazon DynamoDB, Amazon S3, Amazon Redshift,
     Amazon Quicksight

B. AWS IoT, Amazon Kinesis, Amazon DynamoDB, Amazon S3, Amazon Redshift, Amazon Quicksight

C. AWS IoT, Amazon Kinesis, Amazon DynamoDB, Amazon S3, Amazon Aurora, Amazon Quicksight

D. AWS IoT, Amazon Kinesis, Amazon DynamoDB, Amazon S3, Amazon RDS, Amazon Quicksight

Q181. A developer runs an application on an EC2 instance that requires access to the S3 bucket named *photos*. She doesn't want to store AWS credentials directly within the EC2 instance and allow applications in that instance to use those credentials for API request .An administrator creates the Get-pics service role and attaches the role to the EC2 instance. The role includes a permissions policy that grants read-only access to the specified S3 bucket. It also includes a trust policy that allows the EC2 instance to assume the role and retrieve the temporary credentials. Which feature will enable application that runs on the instance to use the role's temporary credentials to access the photos bucket?

A. IAM Instance Profile
B. IAM Roles
C. Systems Manager
D. STS

Q182. What are the two types of Enhanced Networking Types?

A. AMD 82599 Virtual Function (VF) interface
B. Elastic Network Adapter (ENA)
C. Intel 82599 Virtual Function (VF) interface
D. Elastic Network Interface (ENI)

Q183. Which of the following statements is incorrect as the suitable scenario for using ENI vs EN vs EFA?

A. Use ENI when you need basic networking and want to create a separate management network at low cost.
B. Use ENI when you need to accelerate High Performance Computing and machine learning application.
C. Use EN (Enhanced Networking) when you need speeds between 10GBps and 100 GBps with high throughput.
D. Use EFA when you need to accelerate High Performance Computing and machine learning application.

# Chapter 2: Networking :Amazon Virtual Private Cloud (VPC), Elastic Load Balancing, Amazon API Gateway, AWS App Mesh, AWS Direct Connect, AWS PrivateLink, AWS Global Accelerator, AWS Transit Gateway, AWS VPN

Q1. What are the characteristics of VPC security groups? Choose 3.
A. You can specify allow rules, but not deny rules.
B. You can specify separate rules for inbound and outbound traffic.
C. You can specify deny rules, but not allow rules.
D. When you create a security group, it has no inbound rules.
E. When you create a security group, it has no outbound rules.

Q2. Which of the following statements are true for security groups? Choose 3.
A. Security groups are stateful.
B. Security groups are stateless.
C. If you send a request from your instance, the response traffic for that request is allowed to flow in regardless of inbound security group rules.
D. Responses to allowed inbound traffic are allowed to flow out, regardless of outbound rules.

Q3. Which of the following statements are true for default security group? Choose 3.
A. If you don't specify a security group when you launch an instance, the instance is automatically associated with the default security group for the VPC.
B. Allows all inbound traffic from outside world.
C. Allows all inbound traffic from other instances associated with the default security group.
D. Allows all outbound traffic from the instance.
E. Denys all outbound traffic from the instance.

Q4. What are the default rules of a new security group? Choose 2.
A. Allows inbound traffic
B. Denys outbound traffic
C. Allows no inbound traffic
D. Allows all outbound traffic

Q5. You want to create a public-facing web server to host a blog. You are planning to place the Linux EC2 web server in a VPC with a subnet having an IPv4 CIDR block. You also want to access the EC2 instance form your laptop. Which of the following steps are applicable? Choose 4.
A. Create a nondefault VPC with a single public subnet and internet gateway.
B. Attach route tables to the VPC which allows traffic to flow from the subnet to the Internet gateway.
C. Create a security group for your instance that allows traffic only through specific ports to enable inbound Http, Https and access from your home network address.
D. Create a security group for your instance that allows traffic only through specific ports to enable inbound Http. Https.

E. Launch an Amazon EC2 instance into your subnet and associate an Elastic IP address with your instance.

Q6. Which of the following statements are true regarding VPC and subnets? Choose 2.

A. A VPC spans all the Availability Zones in the region.

B. Each subnet must reside entirely within one Availability Zone and cannot span zones.

C. Each subnet can span more than one availability zones.

D. A VPC needs to be mapped to availability zones in a region.

Q7, Q8, Q9 are based on figure below.

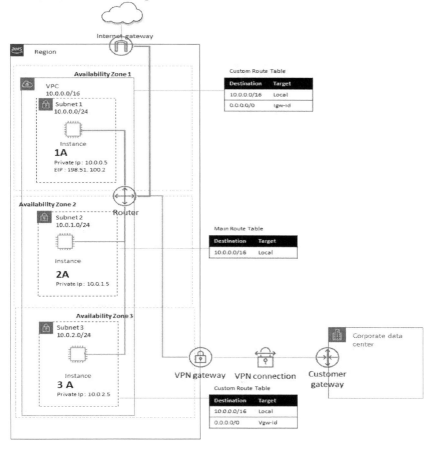

There are three subnets 1A, 2A, and 3A each with one EC2 instance. The figure above depicts the ip address of VPC, subnet and instances. The route tables attached to three subnets are also depicted on the right side of figure.

Q7. Which subnet in the figure above is a public subnet?
- A. 1A
- B. 2A
- C. 3A
- D. None of the above

Q8. Which subnet in the figure above is a private subnet?
- A. 1A
- B. 2A
- C. 3A
- D. None of the above

Q9. Which subnet in the figure above is a vpn-only subnet?
- A. 1A
- B. 2A
- C. 3A
- D. None of the above

Q10. Which of the following statements are correct regarding CIDR block range of a VPC subnet? Choose 2.
- A. The CIDR block of a subnet can be the same as the CIDR block for the VPC (for a single subnet in the VPC).
- B. The CIDR block of a subnet cannot be the same as the CIDR block for the VPC (for a single subnet in the VPC).
- C. The CIDR block of a subnet cannot be a subset of the CIDR block for the VPC (for multiple subnets).
- D. The CIDR block of a subnet can be a subset of the CIDR block for the VPC (for multiple subnets).

Q11. Which of the following statements are correct regarding IPv4 CIDR block range of a VPC subnet? Choose 2.
- A. The allowed block size is between a min: /28 netmask and max: /16 netmask.
- B. If you create more than one subnet in a VPC, the CIDR blocks of the subnets cannot overlap.
- C. If you create more than one subnet in a VPC, the CIDR blocks of the subnets can overlap.
- D. The allowed block size is between a min: /16 netmask and max: /28 netmask.

Q12. How many IP addresses in each subnet CIDR block are not available for you to use, and cannot be assigned to an instance?

A.   2
B.   3
C.   4
D.   5

Q13. Which of the following rules apply when you add IPv4 CIDR blocks to a VPC that's part of a VPC peering connection? Choose 3
A.   If the VPC peering connection is active, you can add CIDR blocks to a VPC provided they do not overlap with a CIDR block of the peer VPC.
B.   If the VPC peering connection is pending-acceptance, the owner of the requester VPC cannot add any CIDR block to the VPC, regardless of whether it overlaps with the CIDR block of the accepter VPC. Either the owner of the accepter VPC must accept the peering connection, or the owner of the requester VPC must delete the VPC peering connection request, add the CIDR block, and then request a new VPC peering connection.
C.   If the VPC peering connection is pending-acceptance, the owner of the accepter VPC can add CIDR blocks to the VPC. If a secondary CIDR block overlaps with a CIDR block of the requester VPC, the VPC peering connection request fails and cannot be accepted.
D.   If the VPC peering connection is active, you can add CIDR blocks to a VPC which overlap with a CIDR block of the peer VPC.

Q14. Which subnet security feature is extra layer of security and can be optional?
A.   Security Groups
B.   Network ACLs
C.   Routing Table
D.   Internet Gateway

Q15. You have created a VPC, Subnet, Instances as below:
•   A VPC with CIDR block 10.0.0.0/16
•   A subnet in that VPC with CIDR block 10.0.1.0/24
•   Instances running in that subnet with IP addresses 10.0.1.6 and 10.0.1.7
•   On-premises host networks using CIDR blocks 10.0.30.0/24 and 10.1.31.0/24
You have appropriately configured their security group settings so that inbound and outbound connection can be made between the VPC and your on-premise network. However when those instances in the VPC try to talk to hosts in the 10.0.30.0/24 address space in your corporate network, the traffic is dropped but they can talk to the instances in 10.1.31.0/24 address space? What could be the reason? Choose 2.
A.   You have to also configure the Network ACL for communication between VPC and your corporate address space.
B.   Your VPC address space 10.0.0.0/16 overlaps with one of your on-premise networks' prefixes 10.0.30.0/24, so the traffic to the network's prefix is dropped.

C.    Your VPC instances can talk to hosts in the 10.1.31.0/24 space because that block isn't part of 10.0.0.0/16.

D.    You have not enabled flow logs.

Q16. Which of the following statements are correct about default VPC and default subnet? Choose 3.

A.    A default subnet is a private subnet.

B.    A default subnet is a public subnet.

C.    Instances that you launch into a default subnet receive both a public IPv4 address and a private IPv4 address, and both public and private DNS hostnames.

D.    A default security group is associated with your default VPC.

Q17. By default, Amazon EC2 and Amazon VPC use which addressing protocol?

A.    IPv6

B.    TCP

C.    IPv4

D.    UDP

Q18. It is necessary to associate an IPv6 CIDR block with your VPC?

A.    True

B.    False

Q19. When you assign both IPv4 and IPv6 CIDR block to your VPC, which of the following statements are correct? Choose 2.

A.    Your VPC resources can communicate over IPv6 only.

B.    Your VPC resources can communicate over IPv4, or IPv6, or both.

C.    IPv4 and IPv6 addresses are independent of each other; you must configure routing and security in your VPC separately for IPv4 and IPv6.

D.    You must configure routing and security in your VPC only for IPv6.

Q20. What are the values you can configure within a DHCP option set for a VPC? Choose 3.

A.    Domain-name-servers and Domain-name

B.    Static Public IP address

C.    ntp-servers and netbios-name-servers

D.    netbios-node-type

Q21. How can you ensure that a network interface created in the subnet automatically receives a public IPv4 address? Choose 2

A.    Modifying the public IP addressing attribute of your VPC.

B.    Modifying the public IP addressing attribute of your AZ.

C.    Modifying the public IP addressing attribute of your subnet.

D.    Enabling or disabling the public IP addressing feature during instance launch, which overrides the subnet's public IP addressing attribute.

Q22. Which are the features provided by Amazon Virtual Private Cloud that you can use to increase and monitor the security for your virtual private cloud (VPC)? Choose 3.
   A. Security groups
   B. Network access control lists (ACLs)
   C. Flow logs
   D. Cloudwatch

Q23. Which of the following statements are true regarding security groups (SG) and network ACLs? Choose 2.
   A. SG operates at instance level and network ACLs operates at subnet level.
   B. SG supports allow rules only and network ACLs support allow and deny rules.
   C. Network ACLs operates at instance level and SG operates at subnet level.
   D. Network ACLs supports allow rules only and SG support allow and deny rules.

Q24. You have ensured that an instance interface created in the subnet automatically receives a public IPv4 address by modifying the public IP addressing attribute of your subnet and enabling the public IP addressing feature during instance launch. How can you ensure that instances launched in the VPC receive public DNS hostnames that correspond to their public IP addresses and DNS resolution through the Amazon DNS server is supported for the VPC?
   A. You don't need to do anything, DNS hostnames are automatically provided by AWS once an instance gets a public ip address.
   B. Set VPC attribute enableDnsHostnames and enableDnsSupport to true.
   C. Set only VPC attribute to *enableDnsHostnames* true for ensuring instances with public IP addresses get corresponding public DNS hostnames. This will also ensure DNS resolution.
   D. Set only VPC attribute to *enableDnsSupport* true for ensuring instances with public IP addresses get corresponding public DNS hostnames. This will also ensure DNS resolution.

Q25. You have a web server running on 5 EC2 instances in one subnet of your VPC. You add another EC2 instance to the subnet having same security group. After adding the new instance you made changes to the security group. How long will it take for the changes to take effect?
   A. Immediately only for newest one instance and after 5 minutes for existing 5 instances.
   B. Immediately for all six instances.
   C. Immediately only for existing 5 instance and after 5 minutes for new instance.
   D. After 5 minutes for all the six instances.

Q26. Which of the following statements are true regarding security groups (SG) and network ACLs? Choose 2.

A.   Network ACLs is stateful: Return traffic is automatically allowed, regardless of any rules.
B.   SG is stateful: Return traffic is automatically allowed, regardless of any rules.
C.   Network ACLs is stateless: Return traffic must be explicitly allowed by rules
D.   SG is stateless: Return traffic must be explicitly allowed by rules

Q27. How many security groups you can attach to an instance?
A.   One
B.   Three
C.   Five
D.   Two

Q28. You have instance A1 in subnet S1 and instance A2 in subnet S2 in a VPC. Both of them are attached to same custom security group called MyWebDMZ. How can you ensure that both the instance can talk to each other?
A.   Instances associated with a security group can't talk to each other unless you add rules allowing it in the security group.
B.   Instances associated with same security group can't talk to each other.
C.   Instances have to be in the same subnet to talk with each other.
D.   Instances associated with a security group can't talk to each other unless you add rules allowing it in the network ACLs.

Q29. Your VPC automatically comes with a modifiable default network ACL. Which of the following statements is true?
A.   It allows all inbound and outbound IPv4 traffic.
B.   It doesn't
C.   Allow inbound but allows all outbound traffic.
D.   It doesn't allow outbound but allows all inbound.
E.   It denies all inbound and outbound traffic until you add rules.

Q30. You can create a custom network ACL and associate it with a subnet. Which of the following statements is true?
A.   It allows all inbound and outbound IPv4 traffic.
B.   It doesn't allow inbound but allows all outbound traffic.
C.   It doesn't allow outbound but allows all inbound.
D.   It denies all inbound and outbound traffic until you add rules.

Q31. Which of the following statements are correct about network ACL mapping to subnet? Choose 2.
A.   Each subnet in your VPC must be associated with a network ACL.
B.   It is optional to associate a subnet with network ACL.

C. If you don't explicitly associate a subnet with a network ACL, the subnet is automatically associated with the default network ACL.
D. Each subnet in your VPC must be associated with a custom security group and custom network ACL.

Q32. How many network ACLs can be associated with a subnet?
A. multiple
B. Five
C. Two
D. One

Q33. How many subnets a network ACLs can be associated with?
A. multiple
B. Five
C. Two
D. One

Q34. How are the rules evaluated in a security group (SG) and network ACLs? Choose 2.
A. Network ACLs evaluate all rules before deciding whether to allow traffic.
B. SG evaluate all rules before deciding whether to allow traffic.
C. Network ACLs process rules in number order when deciding whether to allow traffic.
D. SG process rules in number order when deciding whether to allow traffic.

Q35. Your company is migrating two existing applications to AWS. Application portfolio has one internet application which will be accessed by its customers and one intranet application which will be accessed only by employees from corporate network. Your plan is to create one VPC and deploy each application instances individually in a separate subnet. You also want to ensure that whole design is fault tolerant and services should not be hampered in case one of AWS AZ goes down? How many minimum subnets should you create?
A. 2 subnets
B. 4 subnets
C. 1 subnets
D. 6 subnets

Q36. What are AWS Privatelink features? Choose 3.
A. Simplifies the security of data shared with cloud-based applications by eliminating the exposure of data to the public Internet.
B. Provides private connectivity between VPCs, AWS services, and on-premises applications, securely on the Amazon network.
C. Makes it easy to connect services across different accounts and VPCs to significantly simplify the network architecture.

D. Improves the performance of EC2 instances.
E. To use AWS PrivateLink, create an interface VPC endpoint for a service outside of your VPC. This creates an elastic network interface in your subnet with a private IP address that serves as an entry point for traffic destined to the service.

Q37. How Network ACL evaluates rules? Choose 2.
A. Rules are evaluated starting with the lowest numbered rule.
B. Rules are evaluated starting with the highest numbered rule
C. As soon as a rule matches traffic, it is applied regardless of any lower-numbered rule that may contradict it.
D. As soon as a rule matches traffic, it is applied regardless of any higher-numbered rule that may contradict it.

Q38. What feature Network ACL rules provides which ensures that if none of the rule matches the traffic is denied?
A. You have the flexibility to add a rule with highest number to specify deny unmatched traffic both for inbound and outbound.
B. Each network ACL also includes a rule whose rule number is an asterisk. This rule ensures that if a packet doesn't match any of the other numbered rules, it's denied. You can't modify or remove this rule.
C. You have the flexibility to add a rule with lowest number to specify deny unmatched traffic both for inbound and outbound.
D. If a traffic doesn't match any rule it is implicit ALLOW.

Q39. Which of the following are use cases for AWS Privatelink? Choose 3.
A. Maintain regulatory compliance. Preventing personally identifiable information (PII) from traversing the Internet helps maintain compliance with regulations such as HIPAA or PCI.
B. Advanced security features, such as security groups and network access control lists, to enable inbound and outbound filtering at the instance level and subnet level.
C. Fault tolerance by providing dual communication channel between on premise data center and AWS resources.
D. Securely access SaaS applications. With AWS PrivateLink, you can connect your VPCs to AWS services and SaaS applications in a secure and scalable manner.
E. Easily migrate services from on-premises locations to the AWS cloud. On-premises applications can connect to service endpoints in Amazon VPC over AWS Direct Connect or AWS VPN. Service endpoints will direct the traffic to AWS services over AWS PrivateLink, while keeping the network traffic within the AWS network.

Following Q40-42 are based on figure below for a network ACL setting:

| Inbound | | | | | |
|---|---|---|---|---|---|
| Rule # | Type | Protocol | Port Range | Source | Allow/Deny |
| 100 | HTTP | TCP | 80 | 0.0.0.0/0 | ALLOW |
| 110 | HTTPS | TCP | 443 | 0.0.0.0/0 | ALLOW |
| 120 | SSH | TCP | 22 | 192.0.2.0/24 | ALLOW |
| 130 | RDP | TCP | 3389 | 192.0.2.0/24 | ALLOW |
| 140 | Custom TCP | TCP | 1024-65535 | 0.0.0.0/0 | ALLOW |
| * | All traffic | All | All | 0.0.0.0/0 | DENY |

| Outbound | | | | | |
|---|---|---|---|---|---|
| Rule # | Type | Protocol | Port Range | Destination | Allow/Deny |
| 100 | HTTP | TCP | 80 | 0.0.0.0/0 | ALLOW |
| 110 | HTTPS | TCP | 443 | 0.0.0.0/0 | ALLOW |
| 120 | Custom TCP | TCP | 1024-65535 | 0.0.0.0/0 | ALLOW |
| * | All traffic | All | All | 0.0.0.0/0 | DENY |

Q40. Based on the above figure of a network ACL configured for a subnet, how the rules will be evaluated for a packet destined for the SSL port (443)?
- A. Rule 110 will be directly matched and inbound packet will be allowed.
- B. First the lower number rule 100 will be evaluated and then next 110 will be evaluated which matches.
- C. All the six rule will be evaluated at once and packet match with a rule will be done.
- D. Rules will be evaluated in descending order i.e. 140, 130, 120, 110 till the match.

Q41. Based on the above figure of a network ACL configured for a subnet, how the rules will be evaluated for a packet destined for port 139 (NetBIOS)?
- A. It doesn't match any of the rules, therefor an error 'rule not defined' will be thrown.
- B. It doesn't match any of the rules, therefor it is implicit ALLOW.
- C. It doesn't match any of the rules, and the * rule ultimately denies the packet.
- D. None of the above.

Q42. What is the significance of inbound rule 140 and outbound rule 120? Choose 2.

A. Inbound rule 140 allows inbound IPv4 traffic from the Internet for ephemeral port range to cover the different types of clients that might initiate traffic to public-facing instances in your VPC.
B. Outbound rule 120 allows outbound IPv4 responses to clients on the Internet (for example, serving web pages to people visiting the web servers in the subnet).
C. Inbound rule 140 with a wide port range is to ensure that at least one rule matches for incoming packet.
D. Outbound rule with a wide port range 120 is to ensure that at least one rule matches.

Q43. You want to troubleshoot why specific traffic is not reaching an instance and also want to diagnose overly restrictive security group rules. Which AWS service will you use?
A. AWS Cloudtrail
B. AWS Cloudwatch
C. AWS Flowlogs
D. AWS WAF

Q44. For which of the following resources you can create a flow log? Choose 3
A. VPC
B. Subnet
C. Network interface
D. Security Group

Q45. You're using flow logs to diagnose overly restrictive or permissive security group rules or network ACL rules for your VPC which has one instance to start with. You use the ping command from your home computer to your instance. Your security group's inbound rules allow ICMP traffic from your home computer IP address and the outbound rules do not allow ICMP traffic. Your network ACL permits inbound ICMP traffic from your home computer ip address but does not permit outbound ICMP traffic.
Which of the following statements are correct regarding flow log records which will get displayed? Choose 2.
A. A REJECT record for the response ping because the security group denied for outgoing ICMP.
B. There will not be any log as outgoing is denied by both security group and network ACL.
C. An ACCEPT record for the originating ping that was allowed by both the network ACL and the security group, and therefore was allowed to reach your instance.
D. A REJECT record for the response ping that the network ACL denied.

Q46. You're using flow logs to diagnose overly restrictive or permissive security group rules or network ACL rules for your VPC which has one instance to start with. You use the ping command from your home computer to your instance. Your security group's inbound rules allow ICMP traffic from your home computer IP address and the outbound rules do not allow

ICMP traffic. Your network ACL permits inbound ICMP traffic from your home computer ip address and also permit outbound ICMP traffic. Which of the following statements are correct regarding flow log records which will get displayed? Choose 2.

A. A REJECT record for the response ping because the security group denied for outgoing ICMP.
B. There will not be any log as outgoing is denied by security group.
C. An ACCEPT record for the originating ping that was allowed by both the network ACL and the security group, and therefore was allowed to reach your instance.
D. An ACCEPT record for the response ping.

Q47. You're using flow logs to diagnose overly restrictive or permissive security group rules or network ACL rules for your VPC which has one instance to start with. You use the ping command from your home computer to your instance. Your security group's inbound rules does not allow ICMP traffic from your home computer IP address and the outbound rules do not allow ICMP traffic. Your network ACL permits inbound ICMP traffic from your home computer ip address and also permit outbound ICMP traffic. Which of the following statements are correct regarding flow log records which will get displayed?

A. A REJECT record for the response ping because the security group denied for incoming ICMP.
B. A REJECT record for the response ping because the security group denied for outgoing ICMP.
C. There will not be any log as incoming and outgoing is denied by security group.
D. None of the above

Q48. What is VPC Peering? Choose 3

A. A VPC peering connection is a networking connection between two VPCs that enables you to route traffic between them using private IPv4 addresses or IPv6 addresses.
B. Instances in Master VPC can communicate with Secondary VPC as if they are within the same network.
C. Instances in either VPC can communicate with each other as if they are within the same network.
D. You can create a VPC peering connection between your own VPCs, or with a VPC in another AWS account.

Q49. Which of the following statements are correct about VPC peering? Choose 3.

A. The VPCs has to be in same region.
B. The VPCs can be in different regions.
C. Traffic always stays on the global AWS backbone, and never traverses the public internet.

D. AWS uses the existing infrastructure of a VPC to create a VPC peering connection; it is neither a gateway nor a VPN connection, and does not rely on a separate piece of physical hardware.

Q50. What are the benefits of VPC peering?
A. There is no single point of failure for communication or a bandwidth bottleneck.
B. A VPC peering connection helps you to facilitate the transfer of data or create a file sharing network.
C. Provides a simple and cost-effective way to share resources between regions or replicate data for geographic redundancy.
D. Never traverses the public internet, which reduces threats, such as common exploits, and DDoS attacks.
E. All of the above.

Q51. What are the steps involved to establish a VPC peering connection? Choose 3.
A. The owner of the requester VPC sends a request to the owner of the accepter VPC to create the VPC peering connection. The owner of the accepter VPC accepts the VPC peering connection request to activate the VPC peering connection.
B. To enable the flow of traffic between the VPCs using private IP addresses, the owner of each VPC in the VPC peering connection must manually add a route to one or more of their VPC route tables that points to the IP address range of the other VPC (the peer VPC).
C. If required, update the security group rules that are associated with your instance to ensure that traffic to and from the peer VPC is not restricted.
D. There is no need to update the security group rules that are associated with your instance to ensure that traffic to and from the peer VPC is not restricted.

Q52. Which of the following three statements are correct about VPC peering connections?
A. Transitive peering relationships is supported.
B. A VPC peering connection is a one to one relationship between two VPCs.
C. A VPC can peer with multiple VPCs in one to many relationships.
D. Transitive peering relationships are not supported.

Q53. You are doing security audit of EC2 instances. You notice that for one of the instance there are two security groups attached to it. The first allows HTTP access over port 80 from CIDR block 0.0.0.0/0. Second allows SSH access over port 22 from your company ip address range 204.0.223.0/24. What request traffic can reach your instance?
A. SSH and HTTP traffic from 0.0.0.0/0.
B. SSH and HTTP traffic from 204.0.223.0/24.
C. SSH traffic from 204.0.223.0/24 and HTTP traffic from 0.0.0.0/0.
D. No traffic can reach your instance.

Q54. You are doing security audit of EC2 instances. You notice that for one of the instance there are two security groups attached to it. The first allows HTTP access over port 80 from CIDR block 0.0.0.0/0. Second allows SSH access over port 22 from your company ip address range 204.0.223.0/24. You add another rule to allow SSH access over port 22 from address range 0.0.0.0/0 in the first security group. What request traffic can reach your instance?
   A.   SSH and HTTP traffic from 0.0.0.0/0.
   B.   SSH and HTTP traffic from 204.0.223.0/24.
   C.   SSH traffic from 204.0.223.0/24 and HTTP traffic from 0.0.0.0/0.
   D.   No traffic can reach your instance.

Q55. Which of the following statements are correct about route table? Choose 2.
   A.   Each subnet must be associated with a route table, which controls the routing for the subnet.
   B.   A subnet can only be associated with one route table at a time, but you can associate multiple subnets with the same route table.
   C.   Each subnet must be associated with multiple route table, which collectively controls the routing for the subnet.
   D.   A subnet can be associated with multiple route table at a time, but you can associate multiple subnets with the same route table.

Q56. What are the properties of a main route table? Choose 2.
   A.   You can delete the main route table.
   B.   Your VPC automatically comes with a main route table that you can modify.
   C.   You cannot delete the main route table, but you can replace the main route table with a custom table that you've created.
   D.   You have to create main route table explicitly when you create VPC.

Q57. What must you do to enable access to or from the internet for instances in a VPC subnet?
   A.   Attach an internet gateway to your VPC.
   B.   Ensure that your subnet's route table points to the internet gateway.
   C.   Ensure that instances in your subnet have a globally unique IP address (public IPv4 address, Elastic IP address, or IPv6 address).
   D.   Ensure that your network access control and security group rules allow the relevant traffic to flow to and from your instance.
   E.   All of the above

Q58. Which of the following two statements are correct about internet gateway? Choose 2.
   A.   An internet gateway is a horizontally scaled, redundant, and highly available VPC component that allows communication between instances in your VPC and the internet.

B.  An internet gateway perform network address translation (NAT) for instances that have been assigned public IPv4 addresses.

C.  An internet gateway is a horizontally scaled, redundant, and highly available VPC component that allows communication between instances in your VPC and corporate VPN.

D.  An internet gateway is a horizontally scaled, redundant, and highly available VPC component that allows communication between VPC endpoints and AWS resources.

Q59. Which VPC component allows outbound communication over IPv6 from instances in your VPC to the Internet, and prevents the Internet from initiating an IPv6 connection with your instances?

A.  Internet Gateway
B.  Egress-Only Internet Gateways
C.  NAT Gateway
D.  NAT Instance

Q60. Which VPC component enable instances in a private subnet to connect to the internet or other AWS services, but prevent the internet from initiating a connection with those instances? Choose 2.

A.  Internet Gateway
B.  Egress-Only Internet Gateways
C.  NAT Gateway
D.  NAT Instance

Q61. Which of the following two statements are correct about Egress-Only Internet Gateways?

A.  An egress-only Internet gateway is stateful.
B.  An egress-only Internet gateway is stateless.
C.  An egress-only Internet gateway forwards traffic from the instances in the subnet to the Internet or other AWS services, and then sends the response back to the instances.
D.  An egress-only Internet gateway forwards traffic from the instances in the subnet to the Internet or other AWS services, and but doesn't sends the response back to the instances.

Q62. What is a bastion host? Choose 3.

A.  A bastion host is a server whose purpose is to provide access to a private subnet from an external network, such as the Internet.
B.  Bastion hosts are instances that are in public subnet and are typically accessed using SSH or RDP.
C.  It can acts as a 'hop' or 'bridge' server, allowing you to use SSH or RDP to log in to other instances in private subnet in your VPC.

D.   Bastion host is a server to install firewall to protect your private subnet.

Q63. You have following VPCs in your AWS account
VPC A: CIDR block 172.16.0.0/16
VPC B: CIDR block 10.0.0.0/16
VPC C: CIDR block 172.16.0.0/16
Which of the following peering can be done? Choose 2.
   A.   A <-> B
   B.   A <-> C
   C.   B <-> C

Q64. You have following VPCs in your AWS account
VPC A: CIDR block 172.16.0.0/16, 172.1.0.0/16
VPC B: CIDR block 10.0.0.0/16, 10.2.0.0/16
VPC C: CIDR block 172.16.0.0/16, 172.2.0.0/16
Which of the following peering can be done?
   A.   A <-> B
   B.   A <-> C
   C.   B <-> C

Q65. You are setting up a VPC for a single tier public facing web application. You also want your cloud web application to connect with in-premise application in the corporate network. Following are the configurations you have made:
   •   A VPC with CIDR block 10.0.0.0/16
   •   A public subnet in that VPC with CIDR block 10.0.1.0/24
   •   IP address of Web server instance running in the subnet is 10.0.1.4
   •   On premise corporate network of two offices CIDR 10.0.37.0/24 and 10.1.38.0/24
Which of the following statement is correct for above configuration? Choose 2.
   A.   Traffic is dropped when the VPC web server instance tries to connect with host in 10.0.37.0/24.
   B.   Traffic is dropped when the VPC web server instance tries to connect with host in 10.1.38.0/24.
   C.   Traffic will flow between VPC instance and host instance in 10.1.38.0/24.
   D.   Traffic will flow between VPC instance and host instance in 10.0.37.0/24.

Q66. . You want to run a public-facing web application, while maintaining back-end servers that aren't publicly accessible. You will have to set up security and routing so that the web servers can communicate with the MySQL database servers. You also need to ensure that database servers can connect to the Internet for software updates but the Internet cannot establish connections to the database servers. How will you set up your VPC configuration? Choose 3.
   A.   Set up web servers in a public subnet and the database servers in a private subnet.

71

B. The DB instances in the private subnet can access the Internet by using a network address translation (NAT) gateway that resides in the public subnet.
C. Security Group attached with DB Instance should only allow read or write database requests from the web servers by configuring source as web server's security group.
D. The DB instances in the private subnet can access the Internet by using a web server EC2 instance that resides in the public subnet.

Q67. You have ensured that an instance interface created in the subnet automatically receives a public IPv4 address by modifying the public IP addressing attribute of your subnet and enabling the public IP addressing feature during instance launch. Which of the following statements are correct? Choose 3.
A. A public IP address is assigned from Amazon's pool of public IP addresses; it's not associated with your account.
B. When a public IP address is disassociated from your instance, it's released back into the pool, and is no longer available for you to use.
C. You cannot manually associate or disassociate a public IP address.
D. The assigned IP addresses are persistent.

Q68. How can you connect to a DB Instances deployed within a VPC from the Internet or from EC2 Instances outside the VPC? Choose 3.
A. It is not possible to connect to a DB instance deployed within a VPC.
B. Use a bastion host, set up in a public subnet with an EC2 instance that acts as a SSH Bastion. This public subnet must have an internet gateway and routing rules that allow traffic to be directed via the SSH host, which must then forward requests to the private IP address of your RDS DB instance.
C. Use public connectivity, create your DB Instances with the Publicly Accessible option set to yes. With Publicly Accessible active, your DB Instances within a VPC will be fully accessible outside your VPC by default.
D. Set up a VPN Gateway that extends your corporate network into your VPC, and allows access to the RDS DB instance in that VPC.

Q69. How do instances in a VPC without public IP addresses can access the internet? Choose 2.
A. Inside a VPC, they can Route their traffic through a network address translation (NAT) gateway or a NAT instance to access the internet.
B. It is not possible.
C. For Amazon VPCs with a Site-to-Site VPN connection or Direct Connect connection, instances can route their Internet traffic down the virtual private gateway to your existing datacenter.
D. Inside a VPC, they can Route their traffic through Internet Gateway to access the internet.

Q70. Which of the following statements are correct about NAT devices? Choose 3.
   A.   You can use a NAT device to enable instances in a private subnet to connect to the internet (for example, for software updates) or other AWS services, but prevent the internet from initiating connections with the instances.
   B.   A NAT device forwards traffic from the instances in the private subnet to the internet or other AWS services, and then sends the response back to the instances.
   C.   When traffic goes to the internet, the source IPv4 address is replaced with the NAT device's address and similarly, when the response traffic goes to those instances, the NAT device translates the address back to those instances' private IPv4 addresses.
   D.   NAT devices are supported for both IP4 and IPv6 traffic.

Q71. Which of the following are NAT devices offered by AWS? Choose 2.
   A.   NAT Private Gateway
   B.   NAT Internet Gateway
   C.   NAT gateway
   D.   NAT instance

Q72. Which of the following is true about difference between NAT instances and NAT gateways? Choose 3.
   A.   Type and size: NAT Gateway: Choose a suitable instance type and size, according to your predicted workload. NAT instances: Uniform offering; you don't need to decide on the type or size.
   B.   Bandwidth = NAT gateways: Can scale up to 45 Gbps. NAT instances: Depends on the bandwidth of the instance type.
   C.   Maintenance= NAT gateways: Managed by AWS.NAT instances: Managed by you.
   D.   Performance=NAT gateways: Software is optimized for handling NAT traffic. NAT instances: A generic Amazon Linux AMI that's configured to perform NAT.

Q73. You created a NAT gateway and followed the steps to configure it, but when you do a test your instances in the private subnet cannot access the internet. What could be possible reasons? Choose 4.
   A.   The NAT gateway is not ready to serve traffic.
   B.   Your route tables are not configured correctly.
   C.   You should place the instance in a public subnet.
   D.   Your security groups or network ACLs are blocking inbound or outbound traffic.
   E.   You're using an unsupported protocol.

Q74. You are using a NAT instance to enable instances in a private subnet to connect to the internet for software updates, but prevent the internet from initiating connections with the instances. The NAT instance is in the public subnet and you have ensured that security groups, network ACLs and route tables are also appropriately configured. But on testing your instance in the private subnet cannot still access the internet. What could be the possible reason?

A. Your source instance should be in public subnet to access internet.
B. Your NAT instance should also be in the private subnet.
C. You should disable source/destination check in the NAT instance.
D. All of the above

Q75. Which of the following can be used as bastion server to access private subnet instances in a VPC?
A. NAT Instance
B. NAT Gateway
C. Transit Gateway
D. Bastion Instance

Q76. You want to run a public-facing web application, while maintaining back-end servers that aren't publicly accessible. You will have to set up security and routing so that the web servers can communicate with the MySQL database servers. You also need to ensure that database servers can connect to the Internet for software updates but the Internet cannot establish connections to the database servers. How will you set up your VPC configuration?
A. Set up web servers in a public subnet and the database servers in a private subnet.
B. The DB instances in the private subnet can access the Internet by using a network address translation (NAT) instance that resides in the public subnet.
C. Security Group attached with DB Instance should only allow read or write database requests from the web servers by configuring source as web server's security group.
D. The DB instances in the private subnet can access the Internet by using a web server EC2 instance that resides in the public subnet.
E. Security Group attached with NAT Instance should allow internet access from DB server in private subnet and route response back to it.

Q77. In the following diagram Subnet 3A is a VPN-only subnet. How can instances in the subnet reach internet or AWS service? Choose 2.

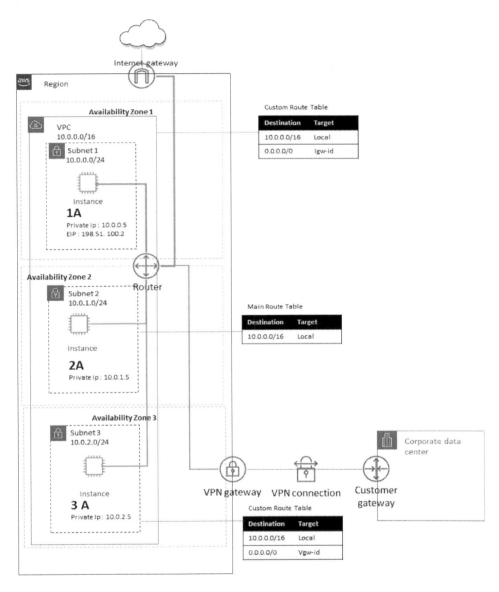

A.   Any Internet-bound traffic must first traverse the virtual private gateway to corporate network, where the traffic is then subject to firewall and corporate security policies.

B.   If the instances send any AWS-bound traffic, the requests must go over the virtual private gateway to corporate network and then egress to the Internet before reaching AWS.

C. Instances can send any AWS-bound traffic flow directly without going to corporate network.

D. Any Internet-bound traffic can flow through the internet gateway.

Q78. What you must do to enable access to or from the internet for instances in a VPC subnet? Choose 4.

A. Attach an internet gateway to your VPC.

B. Attach a Transit Gateway or VPN Gateway to your VPC.

C. Ensure that your subnet's route table points to the internet gateway.

D. Ensure that instances in your subnet have a globally unique IP address (public IPv4 address, Elastic IP address, or IPv6 address).

E. Ensure that your network access control and security group rules allow the relevant traffic to flow to and from your instance.

Q79. You have configured a VPC with public and private subnet as shown in the diagram below with:

Public subnet: web server instance, NAT instance for private subnet instances to access the internet.

Private subnet: RDS instances, fleet of EC2 instances in an auto scaling group. These instances access internet through NAT instance in the public subnet for software updates.

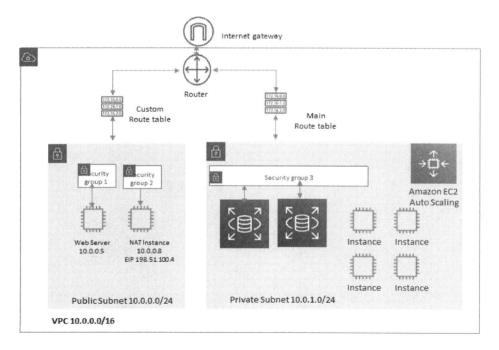

The software updates for instances in the private subnet is schedule to run every night from 11 pm – 1am. You observe recently that these updates has become very slow and some of the updates are getting time out before the maintenance window of two hours. You identify the bottleneck is NAT instance network bandwidth. What architecture changes you can do to resolve this problem?

    A.   Increase the number of NAT instances and change its instance type to one having more bandwidth.

    B.   Use NAT gateway instead of NAT instance.

    C.   Place NAT instance in the private subnet to increase network performance.

    D.   Change the maintenance window of private subnet instances so as not to overlap with one another.

Q80. Which of the following are components of a VPC? Choose 3.

    A.   S3, Lambda, EC2, RDS

    B.   IP Address Range , Subnet,

    C.   Internet Gateway, NAT Gateway, Virtual private gateway, Egress-only Internet Gateway

    D.   Direct connect, Cloudfront and Route53

    E.   Peering Connection, VPC Endpoints

Q81. Which of the following are VPC limits? Choose 2.

    A.   Default limit for number of VPC per region per account is 5

    B.   IP address range of VPC is between maximum  of /16 and minimum of /28 netmask

    C.   Default limit for number of VPC per account is 5

    D.   IP address range of VPC is between a minimum of /16 and maximum of /28 netmask

Q82. What are the features of a VPC Subnet? Choose 3.

    A.   An internal subnet is for connection only from your corporate VPN.

    B.   A subnet is a range of IP addresses in your VPC.

    C.   Public subnet is for resources that must be connected to the internet.

    D.   Private is subnet for resources that won't be connected to the internet.

Q83. You are the solution architect for a mortgage broker who has a web application running on an on-demand EC2 instance in a public subnet of VPC. The database servers are in the private subnet. This web application is for end customers to log in and check their application status. You are using security group to manage the user request reaching your instances in public and private subnet. Your IT monitoring team notice a brute force attack from an ip address outside the company network. How can you block the ip address so that request doesn't reach your web servers?

    A.   Create a rule in security group attached to web server instance to block the ip address.

B.   Create a rule in Network Access Control attached to web server instance to deny access to ip address.
C.   Move the web servers instance from public subnet to private subnet.
D.   Create a rule to block the ip address in the internet gateway.

Q84. Your Company has a VPC for the HR department, and another VPC for the finance department. The HR department requires access to all resources that are in the accounting finance, and the finance department requires access to all resources in the HR department. To enable the two departments to have full access to each other's' resources you have created VPC peer connection. What updates needs to be done in the route table? Choose 2.
A.   Add a route pointing to Finance department VPC CIDR block in the route table that's associated with HR department subnets.
B.   Add a route pointing to HR department VPC CIDR block in the route table that's associated with Finance department subnets.
C.   No need to add any entry in the Finance department subnet route tables.
D.   No need to add any entry in the HR department subnet route tables.

Q85. Which VPC component enables you to privately connect your VPC to supported AWS services and VPC endpoint services powered by PrivateLink without requiring an internet gateway, NAT device, VPN connection, or AWS Direct Connect connection? ?
A.   It is not possible
B.   Egress only Internet Gateway
C.   Transit Gateway
D.   VPC Endpoints

Q86. Which of the following are types of VPC endpoints? Choose 2.
A.   Interface endpoints
B.   Internet endpoints
C.   Gateway endpoints
D.   Service endpoints

Q87. Which of the following AWS services are supported by VPC Gateway endpoints? Choose 2.
A.   Amazon S3
B.   DynamoDB
C.   Amazon RDS
D.   Amazon EBS

Q88. You have a VPC peering connection (pcx-22223333) between VPC A and VPC B, which are in the same AWS account. VPC A CIDR block is: 172.16.0.0/16. VPC B CIDR block is: 10.0.0.0/16. Which of the following is correct configuration of route tables to enable communication from both VPCs?

A.

| Route Table | Destination | Target |
|---|---|---|
| VPC A | 172.16.0.0/16 | Local |
|  | 10.0.0.0/16 | pcx-22223333 |
| VPC B | 10.0.0.0/16 | Local |
|  | 172.16.0.0/16 | pcx-22223333 |

B.

| Route Table | Destination | Target |
|---|---|---|
| VPC A | 172.16.0.0/16 | Local |
|  | 10.0.0.0/16 | pcx-22223333 |
| VPC B | 10.0.0.0/16 | Local |
|  |  |  |

C.

| Route Table | Destination | Target |
|---|---|---|
| VPC A | 172.16.0.0/16 | Local |
|  |  |  |
| VPC B | 10.0.0.0/16 | Local |
|  | 172.16.0.0/16 | pcx-22223333 |

D.

| Route Table | Destination | Target |
|---|---|---|
| VPC A | 172.16.0.0/16 | Local |
|  |  |  |
| VPC B | 10.0.0.0/16 | Local |
|  |  |  |

Q89. You have three VPCs A, B, C. How many peer connection you need to configure so all the VPCs can access the resource of one another?

A. Two peer configuration. A-B and B-C peer configuration needs to be done. A-C transitive peering configuration will be automatically done.

B. Three peer configuration. A-B, B-C and C-A.

C. Two peer configuration. A-C and B-C peer configuration needs to be done. A-B transitive peering configuration will be automatically done.

D. None of the above.

Q90. You have 7 VPCs which you want to make a full mesh peering configuration so that every VPC can access the resources of each other? How many peering configuration you need to create.

A. 7
B. 14
C. 21
D. 28

Q91. VPC A and VPC B are peered, and VPC A has a VPN connection to a corporate network. Which of the following two statements are true.

A. You cannot use VPC A to extend the peering relationship to exist between VPC B and the corporate network.

B. Traffic from the corporate network can't directly access VPC B by using the VPN connection to VPC A.

C. You can use VPC A to extend the peering relationship to exist between VPC B and the corporate network.

D. Traffic from the corporate network can directly access VPC B by using the VPN connection to VPC A.

Q92. Which of the following services are supported by VPC Interface endpoints? Choose 3.

A. Amazon API Gateway, Elastic Load Balancing, Amazon Kinesis Data Firehose, Amazon Kinesis Data Streams

B. Amazon SNS, Amazon SQS, AWS Storage Gateway

C. Amazon S3, DynamoDB, Amazon RDS

D. AWS CloudFormation, AWS CloudTrail, AWS CodeBuild, AWS CodeCommit, AWS CodePipeline

Q93. You have a VPC peering connection between VPC A and VPC B (pcx-abababab). VPC A has an internet gateway; VPC B does not. Which of the following two statements are correct?

A. You can use VPC A to extend the peering relationship to exist between VPC B and the internet.

B. You cannot use VPC A to extend the peering relationship to exist between VPC B and the internet.

C. Traffic from the internet can't directly access VPC B by using the internet gateway connection to VPC A.

D. Traffic from the internet can directly access VPC B by using the internet gateway connection to VPC A.

Q94. You have a VPC peering connection between VPC A and VPC B (pcx-ababab). VPC A has a NAT device that provides internet access to instances in private subnets in VPC A. Which of the following two statements are correct?

A. You can use VPC A to extend the peering relationship to exist between VPC B and the internet through NAT device.

B. You cannot use VPC A to extend the peering relationship to exist between VPC B and the internet through NAT device.

C. Traffic from the internet can't directly access VPC B by using the NAT device connection to VPC A.

D. Traffic from the internet can directly access VPC B by using the NAT device connection to VPC A.

Q95. You have a VPC peering connection between VPC A and VPC B (pcx-ababab). VPC A has a VPC endpoint that connects it to Amazon S3. Which of the following two statements are correct?

A. VPC B can't directly access Amazon S3 using the VPC endpoint connection to VPC A.

B. VPC B can directly access Amazon S3 using the VPC endpoint connection to VPC A.

C. Traffic from the Amazon S3 can directly flow to VPC B by using connection to VPC A.

D. Traffic from the Amazon S3 cannot directly flow to VPC B by using connection to VPC A.

Q96. You have created a VPC with public and private subnet with instances in both the subnet. To provide internet access to instances in private subnet you are using NAT gateway. The private subnet instance daily stores and fetches data from S3 which is nearly 1 TB of size every day. This request and data is passed through the NAT gateway. You notice in your month's billing that this is one of the major cost as NAT gateway is billed both in Price per NAT gateway as $/hour as well as Price per GB data processed ($). How can you minimize the data transfer cost?

A. There is no alternate way as instance in private subnet can access internet over NAT gateway only.

B. Use VPC Gateway Endpoint which supports Amazon S3.

C. Use Amazon S3 Gateway.

D. Use Customer Gateway

Q97. You have created a peering configuration between two VPCs in your organization as shown below.

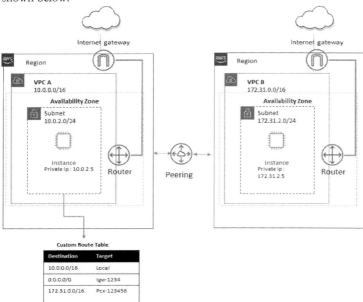

Choose 3 options which is correct for VPC A subnet routing.

A.  The traffic will not flow from VPC A to VPC B in the route table as 172.31.0.0/16 overlaps with 0.0.0.0/0 and 0.0.0.0/0 is mapped to internet gateway routing.
B.  Any traffic from the VPC A subnet that's destined for the 172.31.0.0/16 IP address range will flow through the peering connection.
C.  Any traffic destined for a target within the VPC A (10.0.0.0/16) is covered by the Local route, and therefore is routed within the VPC.
D.  Any traffic in VPC A other than *Local and Peer VPC* will flow through internet gateway.

Q98. You have created a VPC with public and private subnet with instances in both the subnet. To provide internet access to instances in private subnet you are using NAT gateway. The private subnet instance daily stores and fetches data from DynamoDB which is nearly 1 TB of size every day. This request and data is passed through the NAT gateway. You notice in our month's billing that this is one of the major cost as NAT gateway is billed both in Price per NAT gateway as $/hour as well as Price per GB data processed ($). How can you minimize the data transfer cost?

A. There is no alternate way as instance in private subnet can access internet over NAT gateway only.
B. Use Amazon DynamoDB Gateway.
C. Use Customer Gateway
D. Use VPC Gateway Endpoint which supports Amazon DynamoDB.

Q99. Your company has a VPC for the HR department, and another VPC for the finance department. The HR department requires access to all resources that are in the accounting finance, and the finance department requires access to all resources in the HR department. How can you achieve this?
A. Delete one VPC and move all the resources to another VPC.
B. Establish VPC peering connection between two VPCs.
C. Modify IAM policies in the two VPCs to enable access.
D. This is possible only when the two VPCs are in the same corporate AWS account.

Q100. Your company has multiple IT departments, each with their own VPC. Some VPCs are located within the same AWS account, and others in a different AWS account. You want to enable the IT departments to have full access to each other's' resources. How can you achieve this?
A. Delete all VPCs and move the resources to one VPC.
B. Establish VPC peering connection between VPCs.
C. Modify IAM policies in the VPCs to enable access.
D. This is possible only when the VPCs are in the same corporate AWS account.

Q101. What are components of site to site VPN? Choose 3.
A. Direct Connect
B. Virtual Private Gateway
C. AWS Transit Gateway
D. Customer Gateway

Q102. Which component of site to site VPN is on the AWS VPC side?
A. Direct Connect
B. Virtual Private Gateway
C. AWS Transit Gateway
D. Customer Gateway

Q103. Which component of site to site VPN is on the customer remote network side?
A. Direct Connect
B. Virtual Private Gateway
C. AWS Transit Gateway
D. Customer Gateway

Q104. Which component act as hub that you can use to interconnect your virtual private clouds (VPC) and on-premises networks?
    A.   Direct Connect
    B.   Virtual Private Gateway
    C.   AWS Transit Gateway
    D.   Customer Gateway

Q105. Which security protocol is supported for AWS site to site VPN connections?
    A.   PPTP
    B.   L2F
    C.   L2TP
    D.   IPSec

Q106. A Site-to-Site VPN connection offers how many VPN tunnels between a virtual private gateway or transit gateway on the AWS side and a customer gateway on the remote (customer) side ?
    A.   1
    B.   2
    C.   3
    D.   4

Q107. Your organization has adopted AWS and hosts applications that spans hundreds of VPCs. Which AWS service can minimize the operations burden of managing such a vast distributed network, Connecting and managing hundreds of VPCs via peering requiring massive route tables which is difficult to deploy, manage and can be error prone ?
    A.   AWS Direct Connect
    B.   AWS Site to Site VPN
    C.   AWS VPN Gateway
    D.   AWS Transit Gateway

Q108. You have migrated your company's in-premise application to AWS and deployed it inside a VPC. You have created security groups and network ACL as per the best practices for access over the internet (HTTP/HTTPS0 and SSH from corporate network. You want to create an alarm that alerts you if there have been 10 or more rejected attempts to connect to your instance over TCP port 22 (SSH) within a 1-hour period. How can you achieve this?
    A.   Create a filter and alarm in the CloudTrail.
    B.   Enable flow logs for your VPC and publish data directly to Cloudtrail logs, then in the CloudTrail select your VPC flow log group to create a metric filter and alarm to notify you through email.
    C.   Create a filter and alarm in the CloudWatch.

D. Enable flow logs for your VPC and publish data directly to CloudWatch logs, then in the CloudWatch select your VPC flow log group to create a metric filter and alarm to notify you through email.

Q109. You are the solution architect for a financial services company. Because of security reasons you have deployed an analytical application in a private subnet of VPC having IPv6 CIDR block. You are exploring the options to gives access to private subnet instances for downloading software updates without creating a public subnet. How will you achieve this requirement?
A. Use Egress only internet gateway
B. Use NAT Gateway
C. Use NAT Instance
D. Use Internet Gateway

Q110. When you create a custom VPC, which of the following is created for you by default? Choose 3.
A. Security Group
B. Network ACL
C. Route Table
D. Subnet

Q111.What are the benefits of having ELB? Choose 3.
A. High Availability
B. Health Checks
C. Security layer
D. High Server Performance

Q112. Choose three types of load balancers provided by AWS?
A. Application Load Balancers
B. Database Load Balancers
C. Network Load Balancers
D. Classic Load Balancers

Q113. What is the protocol supported by Application Load Balancer?
A. HTTP, HTTPS
B. TCP, UDP, TLS
C. TCP, SSL/TLS, HTTP, HTTPS
D. HTTP, HTTPS, TCP

Q114. What is the protocol supported by Network Load Balancer?
A. HTTP, HTTPS
B. TCP, UDP, TLS

C.   TCP, SSL/TLS, HTTP, HTTPS
D.   HTTP, HTTPS, TCP

Q115. What is the protocol supported by Classic Load Balancer?
A.   HTTP, HTTPS
B.   TCP, UDP, TLS
C.   TCP, SSL/TLS, HTTP, HTTPS
D.   HTTP, HTTPS, TCP

Q116. Which load balancer you should use if you need flexible application management?
A.   Application Load Balancers
B.   Database Load Balancers
C.   Network Load Balancers
D.   Classic Load Balancers

Q117. Which load balancer you should use if you have an existing application that was built within the EC2-Classic network?
A.   Application Load Balancers
B.   Network Load Balancers
C.   Classic Load Balancers
D.   Database Load Balancers

Q118. Which load balancer operates at the request level (layer 7) and can be used for HTTP/HTTPS application traffic?
A.   Network Load Balancers
B.   Classic Load Balancers
C.   Database Load Balancers
D.   Application Load Balancers

Q119. Which load balancer operates at the connection level (layer 4) and can be used for TCP and UDP traffic?
A.   Network Load Balancers
B.   Classic Load Balancers
C.   Database Load Balancers
D.   Application Load Balancers

Q120. When you enable an Availability Zone for your load balancer, Elastic Load Balancing creates a load balancer node in the Availability Zone. What is cross zone load balancing? Choose 2.
A.   When disabled, each load balancer node distributes traffic across the registered targets in all enabled Availability Zones.

B.  When enabled, each load balancer node distributes traffic across the registered targets in all enabled Availability Zones.
C.  When disabled, each load balancer node distributes traffic across the registered targets in its Availability Zone only.
D.  When enabled, each load balancer node distributes traffic across the registered targets in its Availability Zone only.

Q121. For a ELB there are two enabled Availability Zones, with 2 targets in Availability Zone A and 8 targets in Availability Zone B. Clients send requests, and Amazon Route 53 responds to each request with the IP address of one of the load balancer nodes. How the traffic will be distributed if cross zone load balancing is enabled?

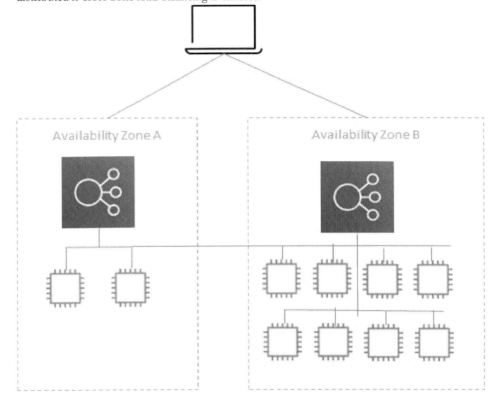

A.  Each of the 2 targets in Availability Zone A receives 50% of the traffic and each of the 8 targets in Availability Zone B receives 12.5% of the traffic.
B.  Each of the 10 targets receives 10% of the traffic.
C.  Each of the 2 targets in Availability Zone A receives 25% of the traffic and each of the 8 targets in Availability Zone B receives 6.25% of the traffic.

D.   None of the above

Q122. What are the three component of Application Load Balancer? Choose 3.
   A.   Load Balancer
   B.   Listener
   C.   Target Group
   D.   Firewall

Q123. Which of the following statements are true about internet facing load balancers? Choose 3.
   A.   The nodes of an Internet-facing load balancer have public IP addresses.
   B.   The DNS name of an Internet-facing load balancer is publicly resolvable to the public IP addresses of the nodes.
   C.   The DNS name of an Internet-facing load balancer is publicly resolvable to the private IP addresses of the nodes.
   D.   Internet-facing load balancers can route requests from clients over the Internet.

Q124. For a ELB there are two enabled Availability Zones, with 2 targets in Availability Zone A and 8 targets in Availability Zone B. Clients send requests, and Amazon Route 53 responds to each request with the IP address of one of the load balancer nodes. How the traffic will be distributed if cross zone load balancing is not enabled?

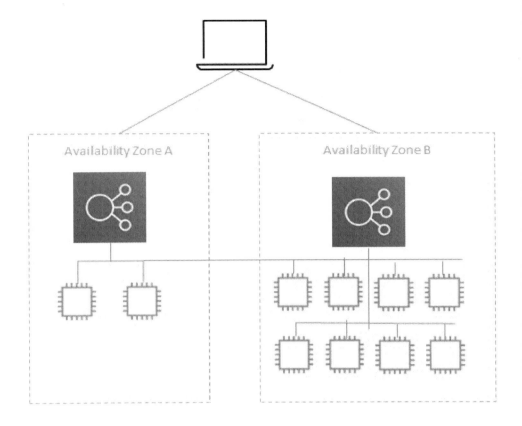

A. Each of the 2 targets in Availability Zone A receives 50% of the traffic and each of the 8 targets in Availability Zone B receives 12.5% of the traffic.

B. Each of the 10 targets receives 10% of the traffic.

C. Each of the 2 targets in Availability Zone A receives 25% of the traffic and each of the 8 targets in Availability Zone B receives 6.25% of the traffic.

D. None of the above

Q125.Which of the following statements are true about internal facing load balancers? Choose 3.

A. Internal -facing load balancers can route requests from clients over the Internet.

B. The nodes of an internal load balancer have only private IP addresses.

C. The DNS name of an internal load balancer is publicly resolvable to the private IP addresses of the nodes.

D. Internal load balancers can only route requests from clients with access to the VPC for the load balancer.

Q126. How do you decide which load balancer to select for your application?
A.  If need is to load balance HTTP requests, use Application Load Balancer.
B.  For network/transport protocols (layer4 – TCP, UDP) load balancing, and for extreme performance/low latency applications, use Network Load Balancer.
C.  If your application is built within the EC2 Classic network then you should use Classic Load Balancer.
D.  All of the above.

Q127. Which of the following statement are correct as how internet and internal load balancers route requests to target? Choose 2.
A.  Internet-facing route requests to your targets using public IP addresses and internal load balancers route requests to your targets using private IP addresses.
B.  Internet-facing and internal load balancers route requests to your targets using private IP addresses.
C.  Targets do not need public IP addresses to receive requests from an internal or an Internet-facing load balancer.
D.  Targets need public IP addresses to receive requests from an internal or an Internet-facing load balancer.

Q128. You are designing an application that will have multiple tiers, web servers that must be connected to the Internet and database servers that are only connected to the web servers, you want to design an architecture that uses both internal and Internet-facing load balancers. How load balancers will be connected with web and database tiers? Choose 2.
A.  Create an internal load balancer and register the database servers with it.
B.  Create an Internet-facing load balancer and register the web servers with it.
C.  Create an Internet-facing load balancer and register the database servers with it.
D.  The database servers receive requests from the Internet facing load balancer.

Q129. What are the benefits of migrating from a classic load balancer to application load balancer?
A.  Support for path-based routing
B.  Support for host-based routing
C.  Support for routing based on fields in the request, such as standard and custom HTTP headers and methods, query parameters, and source IP addresses.
D.  All of the above

Q130. How do you configure subnets for Application Load Balancer? Choose 2.
A.  You must specify one public subnet from at least one Availability Zones.
B.  You can specify any number of public subnet per Availability Zone.
C.  You can specify only one public subnet per Availability Zone.
D.  You must specify one public subnet from at least two Availability Zones.

Q131. What are the three target types you can select in load balancer target group?

    A.   Instance

    B.   IP

    C.   SQS Queue

    D.   Lambda Function

Q132. What will happen to targets in an availability zone if that availability zone is disabled for an application load balancer? Choose 2.

    A.   The targets in that Availability Zone will not remain registered with the load balancer.

    B.   The targets in that Availability Zone will remain registered with the load balancer.

    C.   The load balancer will not route requests to the targets.

    D.   The load balancer will keep routing requests to target as they are still part of the target group attached to load balancer.

Q133. Which of the following are correct about application load balancer listener? Choose 3.

    A.   You must add one or more listeners.

    B.   You must add one listener.

    C.   A listener is a process that checks for connection requests, using the protocol and port that you configure.

    D.   The rules that you define for a listener determine how the load balancer routes requests to the targets in one or more target groups.

Q134. What are the protocols and ports supported by application load balancer listener? Choose 2.

    A.   Protocols : HTTP, HTTPS

    B.   Ports : 1-65535

    C.   Protocols: TCP, UDP

    D.   Protocols : HTTP, HTTPS, TCP, UDP

Q135. Which of the following statements are correct about web sockets and application load balancer? Choose 2.

    A.   Application Load Balancers doesn't provide native support for WebSockets.

    B.   You cannot use WebSockets with both HTTP and HTTPS listeners.

    C.   Application Load Balancers provide native support for WebSockets.

    D.   You can use WebSockets with both HTTP and HTTPS listeners.

Q136. What does target group attached to application load balancer does?

    A.   Route requests to one or more registered targets.

    B.   Route requests to one or more registered listeners.

    C.   Route requests to one or more registered targets in a specific subnet.

    D.   Route requests to one or more registered targets in a specific availability zone.

Q137. If you choose target type IP for target group attached to application load balancer, which IP addresses you can specify from following CIDR blocks? Choose 3.
- A. Any publicly routable IP addresses.
- B. Any subnets of the VPC for the target group.
- C. 10.0.0.0/8 (RFC 1918), 100.64.0.0/10 (RFC 6598)
- D. 172.16.0.0/12 (RFC 1918), 192.168.0.0/16 (RFC 1918)

Q138. You have an application whose web server maintains state information in order to provide a continuous experience to clients. How can you ensure that your application load balancer routes the requests to the same target in a target group for all the requests from the user during a session?
- A. Have to programmatically handle at web api level to give stateful experience.
- B. Enable sticky session attribute of the target group attached to load balancer.
- C. Load balancer doesn't support stateful session management.
- D. Client should send its own generated session cookie each time with information about the target instance.

Q139. How can you ensure that the load balancer stops sending requests to instances that are deregistering or unhealthy while keeping the existing session connection open so as to complete the in-flight requests to these instances ?
- A. Programmatically keep sending requests to the same instance till session completes.
- B. Enable sticky sessions.
- C. Enable connection draining.
- D. All of the above.

Q140. How an application load balancer checks the status of registered targets?
- A. Through health checks
- B. Through connection draining checks
- C. Through Session checks
- D. Targets ping their status to load balancer

Q141. Which of the following statements are correct about an application load balancer health checks? Choose 3.
- A. Each load balancer node routes requests only to the healthy targets in the enabled Availability Zones for the load balancer.
- B. After your target is registered, it must pass at least two consecutive health check to be considered healthy.
- C. After your target is registered, it must pass one health check to be considered healthy.
- D. Health checks do not support WebSockets.

Q142. Which of the following are correct about application load balancer listener rule? Choose 3.
   A.   Each listener has a default rule, and you can optionally define additional rules.
   B.   Each rule consists of a priority, one or more actions, and one or more conditions.
   C.   Rules are evaluated in priority order, from the lowest value to the highest value. The default rule is evaluated last.
   D.   Rules are evaluated in priority order, from the lowest value to the highest value. The default rule is evaluated first.

Q143. Which of the following reasons are valid reasons to use application load balancers?
   A.   To have the ability to manage load between micro services and general requests.
   B.   To have better availability and fault tolerance of your application instances.
   C.   To balance load across application which are in containers
   D.   All of the above

Q144. You have configured an application load balancer in front of four instances running your web server. These four instances are distributed two each in two separate availability zone (AZ-A, AZ-B) enabled for the load balancer. As the load increases you have added two more instance in a new availability zone (AZ-C) to the target group. However you notice that the new target instance is taking longer than expected to enter the InService state and it might be failing health checks. What are the possible reasons you will check?
   A.   Security group of the instance may not be allowing traffic from load balancer.
   B.   Network access control list (ACL) of the new instance's subnet may not be allowing traffic.
   C.   Availability zone AZ-C may not be enabled for the load balancer.
   D.   The health check ping path may not be existing in the instance.
   E.   All of the above.

Q145. What are the possible reasons you will check if clients cannot connect to an Internet-facing application load balancer? Choose 3.
   A.   Load balancer is attached to a public subnet.
   B.   Load balancer is attached to a private subnet.
   C.   The security group for the load balancer must allow inbound traffic from the clients and outbound traffic to the clients on the listener ports.
   D.   Network ACLs for the load balancer subnets must allow inbound traffic from the clients and outbound traffic to the clients on the listener ports.

Q146. Which of the following two statement are correct for application load balancer health checks?
   A.   If there is at least one healthy target in a target group, the load balancer routes requests only to the healthy targets.
   B.   Load balancer will never send request to unhealthy targets.

C.   If a target group contains only unhealthy targets, the load balancer routes requests to the unhealthy targets.

D.   Load balancer will always send request to targets in a target group irrespective of health status.

Q147. Which load balancer you should use if you need extreme performance and static IP is needed for your application?
A.   Application Load Balancers
B.   Classic Load Balancers
C.   Database Load Balancers
D.   Network Load Balancers

Q148. What are the benefits of migrating from a classic load balancer to network load balancer?
A.   Ability to handle volatile workloads and scale to millions of requests per second.
B.   Support for static IP addresses for the load balancer. You can also assign one Elastic IP address per subnet enabled for the load balancer.
C.   Support for routing requests to multiple applications on a single EC2 instance.
D.   Support for containerized applications.
E.   All of the above.

Q149. What are the protocols and ports supported by network load balancer? Choose 2.
A.   Protocols: TCP, TLS, UDP, TCP_UDP
B.   Ports: 1-65535
C.   Protocols: HTTP, HTTPS
D.   Protocols: HTTP, HTTPS, TCP, UDP

Q150. What are the possible target types for network load balancer target groups? Choose 2.
A.   Instance
B.   IP Address
C.   Lambda function
D.   SQS Queue

Q151. You are using instance id as the target types for network load balancer target groups. What should you do so that the source IP addresses of the clients are preserved and provided to your applications?
A.   Enable Proxy Protocol and get the client IP addresses from the Proxy Protocol header.
B.   You don't need to do anything the source IP addresses of the clients are preserved and provided to your applications.
C.   Enable sticky sessions in the load balancer.
D.   Send the ip address through client cookie.

Q152. You are using instance ip address as the target types for network load balancer target groups. What should you do so that the source IP addresses of the clients are preserved and provided to your applications?

A. Enable Proxy Protocol and get the client IP addresses from the Proxy Protocol header.

B. You don't need to do anything the source IP addresses of the clients are preserved and provided to your applications.

C. Enable sticky sessions in the load balancer.

D. Send the ip address through client cookie.

Q153. You are the solution architect for a SaaS application in which you provide different domain to each tenant. How will you configure multiple certificates for different domains using Elastic Load Balancing (ELB) so that multi-tenant SaaS applications can run behind the same load balancer? Choose 2.

A. Use a Subject Alternative Name (SAN) certificate to validate multiple domains behind the load balancer, including wildcard domains, with AWS Certificate Manager (ACM).

B. Use an Application Load Balancer (ALB), which supports multiple SSL certificates and smart certificate selection using Server Name Indication (SNI).

C. It is not possible.

D. Use a Classic Load Balancer, which supports multiple SSL certificates and smart certificate selection using Server Name Indication (SNI).

Q154 If you are using an internet facing ELB (Elastic Load Balancer), what are the security group configuration you need to do so that ELB can communicate with instances running a web server? Choose 3.

A. ELB Security Group Inbound Setting: Protocol = TCP, Port for 80(HTTP) and 443(HTTPS), Source IP =0.0.0.0/0 (all IPv4 addresses)

B. ELB Security Group Outbound Setting: Protocol = TCP, Port for 80(HTTP) and 443(HTTPS), Destination IP = The ID of the instance security group

C. Instance Security Group Inbound Setting: Protocol = TCP, Port for 80(HTTP) and 443(HTTPS), Source IP = The ID of the ELB security group

D. Instance Security Group Outbound Setting: Protocol = TCP, Port for 80(HTTP) and 443(HTTPS), Destination IP = The ID of the ELB security group

Q155. If you are using an internal ELB (Elastic Load Balancer), what are the security group configuration you need to do so that ELB can communicate with instances running a web server? Choose 3.

A. ELB Security Group Inbound Setting: Protocol = TCP, Port for 80(HTTP) and 443(HTTPS), Source IP =0.0.0.0/0 (all IPv4 addresses)

B. ELB Security Group Inbound Setting: Protocol = TCP, Port for 80(HTTP) and 443(HTTPS), Source IP = the IPv4 CIDR block of the VPC
C. ELB Security Group Outbound Setting: Protocol = TCP, Port for 80(HTTP) and 443(HTTPS), Destination IP = The ID of the instance security group
D. Instance Security Group Inbound Setting: Protocol = TCP, Port for 80(HTTP) and 443(HTTPS), Source IP = The ID of the ELB security group
E. Instance Security Group Outbound Setting: Protocol = TCP, Port for 80(HTTP) and 443(HTTPS), Destination IP = The ID of the ELB security group

Q156. . Which load balancer you will use for network/transport protocols (layer4 – TCP, UDP) load balancing, and for extreme performance/low latency applications?
A. Application load balancer
B. Network load balancer
C. Classic load balancer
D. None of the above

Q157. Which of the following is not an action type for listener rules?
A. authenticate-cognito
B. authenticate-oidc
C. SSL
D. fixed-response
E. forward
F. redirect

Q158. Which of the following is not a rule condition type for listener rules?
A. host-header
B. http-request-method
C. http-header
D. geo-location
E. path-pattern
F. query-string
G. source-ip

Q159. You have configured an application load balancer listening on port 80 and mapped it to a target group of EC2 instances also listening on port 80. When a client request reaches load balancer with correct protocol and port, how many connection load balancer maintains between client and target EC2 instance?
A. 1
B. 2
C. 3
D. 4

Q160 You want to perform maintenance activities on your EC2 instances such as deploying software upgrades or replacing back-end instances .What configuration should you do to your ELB and auto scale group so that your users experience is not impacted during maintenance activities?

A. Shut down all the instances for a period of time when you are doing upgrade or replacing instances.

B. Enable Connection draining on ELBs.

C. Wait for the instance to have zero user connection and then stop the instance for maintenance.

D. Abruptly stop the instance even when they have user connection as they can reconnect to another healthy instance on next try.

Q161. You have deployed your web application within an auto scaling group spanning three AZs in a region and attached to an application load balancer. You observe that instances in two AZs are receiving traffic but instances in third AZ is not receiving traffic? You verify that security group and network ACL setting for ALB and instances are as per guideline what could be the possible reason?

A. ALB works with only two AZs

B. Auto scaling works with only two AZs

C. Third AZ is not added to the ALB

D. None of the above

Q162. What are the recommended security group rules for internet facing application load balancer? Choose 3.

A. Inbound : Source=0.0.0.0/0, Port Range = *listener port*

B. No need to configure outbound rule

C. Outbound : Destination=instance security group, Port Range=instance listener port

D. Outbound : Destination=instance security group, Port Range= health check port

Q163. What are the recommended security group rules for internal facing application load balancer? Choose 3.

A. Inbound : Source= VPC CIDR, Port Range = listener port

B. No need to configure outbound rule

C. Outbound : Destination=instance security group, Port Range=instance listener port

D. Outbound : Destination=instance security group, Port Range= health check port

Q164. Which service you can use with your Application Load Balancer to allow or block requests based on the rules in a web access control list (web ACL)?

A. Amazon Inspector

B. Amazon Guard Duty

C. Amazon Cognito

D. AWS WAF

Q165. Which of the following load balancer supports TLS termination?
 A. Application load balancer
 B. Network load balancer
 C. Classic load balancer
 D. None of the above

Q166. Which of the following load balancer supports SSL termination? Choose 2.
 A. Application load balancer
 B. Network load balancer
 C. Classic load balancer
 D. None of the above

Q167. You have an ecommerce web application deployed in a VPC behind an application load balancer (ALB) and has EC2 instances in an auto scaling group in two availability zones. Both the availability zones are mapped to the load balancer. Security group and network ACLs are configured appropriately and instances in both the AZs are receiving traffic from ALB. You are also leveraging Route53 and Cloudfront in your architecture. How can you ensure that instances in both the AZ receive equal amount of traffic. ?
 A. Configure Route53 simple routing policy to distribute traffic evenly across all instances.
 B. Configure Route53 weighted routing policy to distribute traffic evenly across all instances.
 C. No need to do anything Route53 will distribute traffic evenly across all instances.
 D. Enable cross zone load balancing in the ALB configuration.

Q168. Your company is in the transition phase of an application migration to AWS and want to use AWS to augment on-premises resources with EC2 instances. How can you configure Application Load Balancer to distribute application traffic across both your AWS and on-premises resources? Choose 3.
 A. It is not possible to use Application Load Balancer for on premise instances as target.
 B. Provision Direct Connect or VPN between on premise and AWS VPC. Use IP addresses based target groups in ALB.
 C. Register all the resources (AWS and on-premises) to the same target group and associate the target group with a load balancer.
 D. You can use DNS based weighted load balancing across AWS and on-premises resources using two load balancers i.e. one load balancer for AWS and other for on-premises resources.

Q169 which of the following CloudWatch metrics are available for application load balancer?
 A. The total number of concurrent TCP connections active from clients to the load balancer and from the load balancer to targets.

B. The total number of bytes processed by the load balancer over IPv4 and IPv6.

C. The number of targets that are considered healthy and unhealthy.

D. All of the above.

Q170. To analyze traffic patterns and troubleshoot issues, you want to capture detailed information about requests sent to your load balancer such as the time the request was received, the client's IP address, latencies, request paths, and server responses. Which AWS service or feature you will use?

A. Cloudwatch

B. Access logs

C. Request Tracing

D. Cloudtrail logs

Q171. Which service you will use to capture detailed information about the traffic going to and from your Network Load Balancer?

A. Access logs

B. VPC Flow Logs

C. CloudTrail logs

D. CloudWatch metrics

Q172. Which service you will use to capture detailed information about the TLS requests sent to your Network Load Balancer?

A. Access logs

B. VPC Flow Logs

C. CloudTrail logs

D. CloudWatch metrics

Q173. How can you get a history of Application Load Balancing API calls made on your account for security analysis and operational troubleshooting purposes?

A. Access logs

B. VPC Flow Logs

C. CloudTrail

D. CloudWatch

Q174.Using which AWS service you can establish private connectivity between AWS and your datacenter, office, or colocation environment, which in many cases can reduce your network costs, increase bandwidth throughput, and provide a more consistent network experience than Internet-based connections?

A. AWS Transit Gateway

B. AWS VPN

C. AWS Direct Connect

D. AWS Storage Gateway

Q175.Which of the following statements are correct about AWS Direct Connect? Choose 3.
- A. It is a network service that provides an alternative to using the Internet to connect customer's on premise sites to AWS.
- B. Enable access to your remote network from your VPC by creating an AWS Site-to-Site VPN (Site-to-Site VPN) connection
- C. Data that would have previously been transported over the Internet can now be delivered through a private network connection between AWS and your datacenter or corporate network.
- D. It can reduce costs, increase bandwidth, and provide a more consistent network experience than Internet-based connections.

Q176.In AWS what are the approaches in which you can leverage cost effective resources? Choose 4.
- A. Appropriate provisioning and right sizing
- B. Using appropriate purchasing options to meet use case
- C. Using EC2 and VPC for deploying workloads
- D. Geographic location selection
- E. Using managed services and optimizing data transfer

Q177. Which of the following two services supports and helps in optimizing data transfer? Choose 2.
- A. AWS RDS
- B. AWS VPN
- C. AWS Direct Connect
- D. Amazon CloudFront content delivery network (CDN)

Q178 A building construction company's architects use CAD software installed in their workstation to design architecture blueprints. These blueprint files are very large. The company started using S3 and AWS Storage gateway for file storage and back up. After a while as number of users increased after rolling it out across different global office locations, it was found that transferring/fetching large data files speed was slow. What should they do to decrease the amount of time required to transfer data in a cost effective way?
- A. Increase the bandwidth with your Internet service provider.
- B. Create VPN connection with AWS resources.
- C. Use AWS Direct Connect to connect with AWS resources.
- D. Use AWS Transit Gateway to connect with AWS resources.

Q179. Choose 3 use cases for which AWS Direct Connect is suitable?
- A. Applications that use real-time data feeds from on-premise.
- B. Hybrid environments that satisfy regulatory requirements requiring the use of private connectivity.

C. Transferring large data sets over the Internet from on-premise data centers.

D. Applications that can work solely on cloud and doesn't need integration with on-premise.

Q180. Which AWS service gives you the ability to build a hub-and-spoke network topology and flexibility to your Amazon Virtual Private Clouds (VPCs) and on-premises networks to a single gateway?
A. AWS DirectConnect
B. AWS Privatelink
C. AWS VPN
D. AWS Transit Gateway

Q181. You have created a VPC subnet with CIDR block 10.0.0.0/28. How many instances you can have in this subnet?
A. 11
B. 12
C. 14
D. 16

Q182. You are configuring a subnet for your VPC where you want to deploy 16 EC2 instances. Which of the following CIDR block will be correct?
A. 10.0.0.0/28
B. 10.0.0.0/27
C. 10.0.0.0/29
D. 10.0.0.0/30

Q183. Which of the following two services you can leverage to build a hybrid cloud architecture connecting your on premise application to cloud applications?
A. AWS Direct Connect
B. AWS VPN
C. AWS Transit Gateway
D. AWS Privatelink

Q184. You are the solution architect for a financial services company who is migrating their in-house application to AWS. Because of the sensitive financial data and security requirement you are planning to house the application instances in private subnet that are not publicly reachable. How can you connect a public-facing load balancer to instances that have private IP addresses?
A. Associate your internet-facing load balancer with private subnet of your instances.
B. It is not possible to connect internet-facing load balancer with private subnet of your instances.

C. Create a public subnet with NAT gateway. Map the public subnet to load balancer and NAT gateway to private instances.

D. Create public subnets in the same Availability Zones as the private subnets that are used by your private instances. Then associate these public subnets to the internet-facing load balancer.

Q185. You are the solution architect for a financial services company who is migrating their in-house application to AWS. Because of the sensitive financial data and security requirement you are planning to house the application instances in private subnet that are not publicly reachable. Your architecture consists of

- A public-facing load balancer to distribute the load across the instances in the private subnets.
- Two tier: Application and Database tiers. Application tier consists of EC2 instances in auto scaling group. Database tier using RDS in a Multi-AZ deployment.
- Application and Database tiers should be in separate private subnets.
- Application which should be highly available and scalable.

How many minimum subnets you will need to create?

A. Total 4. Across Two AZs, each with two private subnets.
B. Total 6. Across Two AZs, each having one public subnet and two private subnets.
C. Total 6. One AZ, having two public subnet and four private subnets.
D. Total 5. One AZ, having one public subnet and four private subnets.

Q186. You have created a VPC with CIDR block 10.0.0.0/24, which of the following two statements are correct? Choose 3.

A. It supports 256 IP addresses.
B. You can break this CIDR block into two subnets, each supporting 128 IP addresses. One subnet uses CIDR block 10.0.0.0/25 (for addresses 10.0.0.0 - 10.0.0.127) and the other uses CIDR block 10.0.0.128/25 (for addresses 10.0.0.128 - 10.0.0.255).
C. The first four IP addresses and the last IP address in each subnet CIDR block are not available for you to use, and cannot be assigned to an instance.
D. The first IP addresses and the last four IP address in each subnet CIDR block are not available for you to use, and cannot be assigned to an instance.

Q187. You have two public subnet in your VPC having one instance each. The security group of both the instance has 'Local' with VPC CIDR as default rule so that they can communicate with each other. You are using default Network ACL. However when you try to ping from one instance to another you are getting timeout. What could be the possible reason?

A. You need to add rule in their security group to allow RDP traffic as ping command is a type of RDP traffic.
B. You need to add rule in their security group to allow SSH traffic as ping command is a type of SSH traffic.

C. You need to add rule in their security group to allow ICMP traffic as ping command is a type of ICMP traffic.

D. The instances may not have public IP address.

Q188. You have created an online event ticket platform in which users can buy tickets for county and state fairs. The platform supports user request originating from multiple channels of desktop web, mobile web and native mobile app in iOS/Android. You have designed and deployed your instances in such a way that there are different instances to serve the request based on source channel. The request URL when user starts to buy a ticket are:

Web: www.statefair.com/web/buytickets
Mobile Web: www.statefair.com/mobileweb/buytickets
Native mobile app: www.statefair.com/mobileapp/buytickets

Your architecture has one application load balancer to serve the requests originating from different channels. How can you configure the load balancer so that request are served by their respective instances?

A. Replace your application load balancer with network load balancer and configure path based routing in your application load balancer to route request to different target group of instances.

B. Replace your application load balancer with network load balancer and configure host based routing in your application load balancer to route request to different target group of instances.

C. Configure path based routing in your application load balancer to route request to different target group of instances.

D. Configure host based routing in your application load balancer to route request to different target group of instances.

Q189. You have created an online event ticket platform in which users can buy tickets for county and state fairs. The platform supports user request originating from multiple channels of desktop web, mobile web and native mobile app in iOS/Android. You have designed and deployed your instances in such a way that there are different instances to serve the request based on source channel. The request URL when user starts to buy a ticket are:

Web: web.statefair.com/buytickets
Mobile Web: webmobile.statefair.com/buytickets
Native mobile app: mobile.statefair.com/buytickets

Your architecture has one application load balancer to serve the requests originating from different channels. How can you configure the load balancer so that request are served by their respective instances?

A.   Replace your application load balancer with network load balancer and configure path based routing in your application load balancer to route request to different target group of instances.
B.   Replace your application load balancer with network load balancer and configure host based routing in your application load balancer to route request to different target group of instances.
C.   Configure path based routing in your application load balancer to route request to different target group of instances.
D.   Configure host based routing in your application load balancer to route request to different target group of instances.

Q190. You have designed your web application to use a microservices architecture to structure your application as services that you can develop and deploy independently. You want to install one or more of these services on each EC2 instance, with each service accepting connections on a different port. How can you use a load balancer with this design? Choose 2.
A.   Use a single Application Load Balancer to route requests to all the services for your application.
B.   Use a single Classic Load Balancer to route requests to all the services for your application.
C.   Register an EC2 instance with a target group, you can register it multiple times; for each service, register the instance using the port for the service.
D.   You have to deploy each microservice in a separate instance as you can attach an instance only once to a target group.

Q191. Your Amazon ECS service can optionally be configured to use Elastic Load Balancing to distribute traffic evenly across the tasks in your service.
A.   TRUE
B.   FALSE

Q192. Which type of AWS cloud infrastructure deployment places compute, storage, database, and other select services closer to large population, industry, and IT centers, enabling you to deliver applications that require single-digit millisecond latency to end-users?
A.   Availability Zone
B.   Local Zone
C.   Outpost
D.   Region

Q193. You have an ecommerce application which has its web servers and databases in private subnet of a VPC. There are three stacks of web tier and data tier deployed in private subnet in three different AZ for fault tolerance and availability. Application load balancer receives the user request and balances the load across three stacks of web-data servers. The web tier instances in these three private subnet have to access a third party payment gateway over the internet for customer credit card processing. Which option will be highly available?

A. Provision a NAT gateway in a public subnet of each AZ and configure the routing to ensure that web server uses the NAT gateway in their respective AZ.

B. Provision a NAT gateway in in a public subnet of one AZ and configure the routing to ensure that web server in all three AZ uses the NAT gateway.

C. Provision a NAT gateway in a private subnet of each AZ and configure the routing to ensure that web server uses the NAT gateway in their respective AZ.

D. Provision a NAT gateway in in a private subnet of one AZ and configure the routing to ensure that web server in all three AZ uses the NAT gateway.

Q194. Which of the following virtual interfaces you don't need to create to begin using your AWS Direct Connect connection?

A. Private virtual interface

B. Public virtual interface

C. Transit virtual interface

D. VPC virtual interface

Q195. Using AWS Direct Connect, you want to establish private connectivity between AWS and your datacenter to reduce your network costs, increase bandwidth throughput, and provide a more consistent network experience than Internet-based connections. Your virtual interface is up and you've established a BGP peering session. If you cannot route traffic over the virtual interface, what steps you will take to diagnose the issue? Choose 3.

A. For a private virtual interface, ensure that your VPC route tables have prefixes pointing to the virtual customer gateway to which your private virtual interface is connected.

B. Ensure that you are advertising a route for your on-premises network prefix over the BGP session.

C. For a private virtual interface, ensure that your VPC security groups and network ACLs allow inbound and outbound traffic for your on-premises network prefix.

D. For a private virtual interface, ensure that your VPC route tables have prefixes pointing to the virtual private gateway to which your private virtual interface is connected.

Q196. What are the different options in AWS to connect your on-premise corporate data center to your VPC in the cloud?

A. AWS PrivateLink

B. AWS Direct Connect

C. AWS Managed VPN

D. AWS Transit Gateway or Transit VPC

Q197. How can you capture client IP addresses in ELB access logs? Choose 3.

A.  For Application Load Balancers and Classic Load Balancers with HTTP/HTTPS listeners, you must use X-Forwarded-For headers
B.  For Application Load Balancers with TCP/SSL listeners, you must enable Proxy Protocol support on the Classic Load Balancer and the target application.
C.  For Classic Load Balancers with TCP/SSL listeners, you must enable Proxy Protocol support on the Classic Load Balancer and the target application.
D.  For Network Load Balancers, you can register your targets by instance ID to capture client IP addresses without additional web server configuration.

Q198. Your multinational company has IT departments in different regional headquarters around the globe. Each regional IT department has created VPCs in AWS region overlapping or near to their geographic location. What AWS networking capabilities you can leverage which will:

• Provide VPCs full access to each other's resources or to provide a set of VPCs partial access to resources in a central VPC.

• Be simple and cost-effective way to share resources between regions or replicate data for geographic redundancy.

• Communicate privately and securely with one another for sharing data or applications.

• Stay on the AWS global network backbone and never traverses the public internet, thereby reducing threat vectors, such as common exploits and DDoS attacks.
A.  Using VPC endpoints
B.  It is not possible to Peer VPCs across regions.
C.  Using Corporate Network Backbone
D.  Using Inter-region VPC Peering

Q199. Which of the following statement is correct about AWS Region? Choose 2.
A.  It is a physical location around the world which has cluster of data centers.
B.  Each region maps to one data center at a geographic location.
C.  Each AWS Region is an extension of an AWS Local Zone where you can run your latency sensitive applications using AWS services.
D.  Each AWS Region consists of multiple, isolated, and physically separate AZ's within a geographic area.

Q200. Which of the following statement is not correct about AWS Local Zones?
A.  AWS Local Zones place compute, storage, database, and other select AWS services closer to end-users.
B.  With AWS Local Zones, you can easily run highly-demanding applications that require single-digit millisecond latencies.
C.  Each AWS Local Zone location is an extension of an AWS Region where you can run your latency sensitive applications using AWS services
D.  Each Local Zone maps to an AZ in a region.

Q201. Which of the following statement is not correct about AZ? Choose 2.

    A.   An Availability Zone (AZ) is one discrete data centers with redundant power, networking, and connectivity in an AWS Region.

    B.   All AZ's in an AWS Region are interconnected with high-bandwidth, low-latency networking, over fully redundant, dedicated metro fiber providing high-throughput, low-latency networking between AZ's.

    C.   Traffic between AZ's is not encrypted.

    D.   AZ's give customers the ability to operate production applications and databases that are more highly available, fault tolerant, and scalable than would be possible from a single data center.

Q202. You have web server running on two EC2 instances behind an Application Load Balancer. How can you improve the fault tolerance of application using Auto Scaling? Choose 3.

    A.   After you create the Auto Scaling group, attach your existing load balancer to it.

    B.   Your Auto Scaling group region and Availability Zones not necessarily has to be same as the load balancer.

    C.   You have to create a new load balancer to attach to the Auto Scaling group.

    D.   Create your Auto Scaling group in the same region and Availability Zone as your load balancer.

    E.   Create an Auto Scaling group that launches copies of instances you've already configured, or create a launch configuration that uses an Amazon Machine Image (AMI) instead.

Q203. Which AWS service you will use to direct your users to application based on their geographic location, application health, and weights that you can configure. You also want to use static IP addresses that are globally unique for your application so that there is no need to update clients as your application scales. Your application has Application Load Balancers.

    A.   CloudFront

    B.   Route53

    C.   Application Load Balancer

    D.   Global Accelerator

Q204. Which of the following are components of AWS Global Accelerator? Choose 3.

    A.   Load Balancer, DNS Hosted Zone

    B.   Static IP addresses, Accelerator

    C.   DNS name, Listener

    D.   Endpoint group, Endpoint

Q205. What are the use cases for using AWS Global Accelerator? Choose 2.

    A.   For applications, such as gaming, media, mobile applications, and financial applications, which need very low latency for a great user experience.

B. Useful for IoT, retail, media, automotive and healthcare use cases in which client applications cannot be updated frequently.
C. Speed up the delivery of your static content (e.g., images, style sheets, JavaScript, etc.) to viewers across the globe.
D. Private connectivity between VPCs, AWS services, and on-premises applications, securely on the Amazon network.

Q206. How is AWS Global Accelerator different from Amazon CloudFront? Choose 2.
A. Global Accelerator improves performance for both cacheable content (such as images and videos) and dynamic content (such as API acceleration and dynamic site delivery).
B. CloudFront improves performance for both cacheable content (such as images and videos) and dynamic content (such as API acceleration and dynamic site delivery).
C. Global Accelerator improves performance for a wide range of applications over TCP or UDP by proxying packets at the edge to applications running in one or more AWS Regions.
D. CloudFront improves performance for a wide range of applications over TCP or UDP by proxying packets at the edge to applications running in one or more AWS Regions.

Q207. What are two ways that you can customize how AWS Global Accelerator sends traffic to your endpoints?
A. Change the traffic dial to limit the traffic for one or more endpoint groups.
B. Change the traffic dial to limit the traffic for endpoints in a group.
C. Specify weights to change the proportion of traffic to the endpoint group.
D. Specify weights to change the proportion of traffic to the endpoints in a group.

Q208. You have two endpoint groups for your AWS Global Accelerator, one for the us-west-2 Region and one for the us-east-1 Region. You've set the traffic dials to 50% for each endpoint group. Now if 100 requests coming to your accelerator, with 50 from the East Coast of the United States and 50 from the West Coast which of the following two statements are correct as how the traffic will be directed?
A. First 25 requests are directed to the endpoint group in us-west-2 and 25 are directed to the endpoint group in us-east-1.
B. The next 25 requests from the East Coast are served by us-west-2, and the next 25 requests from the West Coast are served by us-east-1.
C. First 50 request are served by us-west-2 and next 50 requests are served by us-east-1.
D. First 50 request are served by us-east-1 and next 50 requests are served by us-west-2.

Q209. What are the options for preserving and accessing the client IP address for AWS Global Accelerator for different endpoints? Choose 3.

A. Global Accelerator does not support client IP address preservation when you use an internal Application Load Balancer or an EC2 instance.

B. When you use an internet-facing Application Load Balancer as an endpoint with Global Accelerator, you can choose to preserve the source IP address of the original client for packets that arrive at the load balancer by enabling client IP address preservation.

C. When you use an internal Application Load Balancer or an EC2 instance with Global Accelerator, the endpoint always has client IP address preservation enabled.

D. Global Accelerator does not support client IP address preservation for Network Load Balancer and Elastic IP address endpoints.

# Chapter 3 Storage: Amazon Simple Storage Services (S3), EBS, EFS, Storage Gateway, Snowball, FsX, DataSync

Q1. What are some of the key characteristics of Amazon S3? Choose 3.
   A.  Data is stored as objects within resources called "buckets"
   B.  With S3 Versioning, you can easily preserve, retrieve, and restore every version of an object stored in Amazon S3
   C.  With S3 Cross-Region Replication (CRR), you can replicate objects (and their respective metadata and object tags) into other AWS Regions
   D.  S3 can be attached to an EC2 instance to provide block storage

Q2. What are storage classes provided by S3? Choose 3.
   A.   Standard, Intelligent-Tiering, Standard-Infrequent Access `
   B.  One Zone-Infrequent Access (One Zone-IA), Glacier (S3 Glacier)
   C.  Glacier Deep Archive
   D.  Elastic File System and Elastic Block Storage
   E.  Storage Gateway

Q3. Which of the following are use cases for using Amazon Simple Storage Service (Amazon S3)? Choose 4.
   A.  File System - mounted to EC2 instance
   B.  For Backup and Storage
   C.  To Provide application hosting services that deploy, install, and manage web applications
   D.  To build a redundant, scalable, and highly available infrastructure that hosts video, photo, or music uploads and downloads.
   E.  To host software applications that customers can download

Q4. A construction engineering company wants to leverage cloud storage to store their large architecture blueprints files which are saved as pdfs in network shared folder through a collaboration application between project team members. The blueprint files for the active projects should be accessible fast while files pertaining to completed projects are not accessed frequently. What is the best cloud storage solution for them which will work with existing application?
   A.  Store latest project files in s3-Standard and store files more than one month old S3-IA. Create a life cycle policy to move files accordingly.
   B.  Install an AWS Storage volume gateway in cached mode.
   C.  Install an AWS Storage volume gateway in stored mode.
   D.  Install AWS Storage File Gateway.

Q5. Which of the following statements are correct for Amazon S3 Data consistency model?
   A.  A process writes a new object to Amazon S3 and immediately lists keys within its bucket. Until the change is fully propagated, the object might not appear in the list.
   B.  A process replaces an existing object and immediately attempts to read it. Until the change is fully propagated, Amazon S3 might return the prior data.

C. A process deletes an existing object and immediately attempts to read it. Until the deletion is fully propagated, Amazon S3 might return the deleted data.

D. A process deletes an existing object and immediately lists keys within its bucket. Until the deletion is fully propagated, Amazon S3 might list the deleted object.

E. All of the above

Q6. Jason creates a S3 bucket 'mywestwebsite' in 'us-west-1' region. Which of these are correct url to access this bucket? Choose 3.
   A. https://amazonaws. s3.us-west-1.com/mywestwebsite
   B. https://s3.us-west-1.amazonaws.com/mywestwebsite
   C. https://s3.amazonaws.com/mywestwebsite
   D. https://mywestwebsite.s3.amazonaws.com
   E. https://mywestwebsite.s3.us-west-1.amazonaws.com

Q7. Jason creates a S3 bucket 'myeastwebsite' in 'us-east-1' region. Which of these are correct url to access this bucket? Choose 4.
   A. https://amazonaws.s3.us-east-1.com/myeastwebsite
   B. https://s3.us-east-1.amazonaws.com/myeastwebsite
   C. https://s3.amazonaws.com/myeastwebsite
   D. https://myeastwebsite.s3.amazonaws.com
   E. https://myeastwebsite.s3.us-east-1.amazonaws.com

Q8. Based on the following Amazon S3 URL of an object, which of the following statement are correct? Choose 2.
https://mywestwebsite.s3.amazonaws.com/photos/whale.jpg
   A. "whale.jpg" is stored in the folder "photos" inside the bucket "mywestwebsite".
   B. The key of the object will be "photos/whale.jpg"
   C. The key of the object will be "whale.jpg"
   D. The object "whale.jpg" is stored in the main bucket folder "mywestwebsite"

Q9. John Smith has an object saved in S3 with attribute value "color=violet". He updates the object with attribute value to "color=red". He GET the object after 2 seconds and reads the attribute value of color. What will be the value?
   A. The value will be " violet"
   B. The value will be "red"
   C. The value can be either " violet" or "red"
   D. He will get 404 object not found error.

Q10. Agrim uses S3 to store all his personal photos. He has a bucket name "personalgallery" in us-east-1 region. After he came back from a vacation in Alaska, he uploads all camera snaps in his laptop desktop folder "alaskaphotos". The photos have file name photo1.jpg, photo2.jpg etc. He logs into his AWS account and opens the S3 console. He then drags the desktop folder "alaskaphotos" inside the "personalgallery" bucket to upload files. Which of the following is correct? Choose 2.

A. All the snap files photo1.jpg, photo2.jpg etc. will be visible in the S3 console inside the main bucket folder "personalgallery"

B. All the snap files photo1.jpg, photo2.jpg etc. will be visible in the S3 console inside another folder "alaskaphotos" under the main bucket folder "personalgallery"

C. The key name of the photos files will be "photo1.jpg" "photo2.jpg" etc.

D. The key name of the photos files will be "/alaskaphotos/photo1.jpg" "/alaskaphotos/photo2.jpg" etc.

Q11. John hosts his personal blog website as static website on S3. The bucket name he uses to store his website files is 'west-bucket' in 'us-west-2' region. The photos are uploaded under the main bucket folder using the S3 console. What is the url of john's static website?

A. http:// s3-us-west-2.amazonaws.com/ west-bucket

B. http://west-bucket.s3-us-west-2.amazonaws.com/

C. http://west-bucket.s3-website-us-west-2.amazonaws.com/

D. http:// s3-website-us-west-2.amazonaws.com/west-bucket

Q12. James hosts his personal blog website as static website on S3. The bucket name he uses to store his website files is 'eu-bucket' in 'eu-central-1' region. The photos are uploaded under the main bucket folder using the S3 console. What will be url of James' static website?

A. http:// s3- eu-central-1.amazonaws.com/eu-bucket

B. http://eu-bucket.s3-website. eu-central-1.amazonaws.com/

C. http://eu-bucket.s3-website-eu-central-1.amazonaws.com/

D. http:// s3-website- eu-central-1amazonaws.com/eu-bucket

Q13. You are an architect who has been tasked to build a static website using S3. What are the essential prerequisite steps? Choose 2.

A. Register a custom domain name in Route 53.

B. Configure the bucket's property for static website hosting with an index, error file and redirection rule.

C. Enable HTTP on the bucket.

D. Ensure that bucket and its objects must have public read access.

Q14. Which S3 storage class is not designed to be resilient to simultaneous complete data loss in a single Availability Zone and partial loss in another Availability Zone?

A. STANDARD_IA

B. ONEZONE_IA

C. INTELLIGENT_TIERING

D. DEEP_ARCHIVE

Q15. Which S3 storage class are designed for long-lived and infrequently accessed data? Choose 2.

A.   STANDARD_IA
B.   ONEZONE_IA
C.   GLACIER
D.   DEEP_ARCHIVE

Q16. The GLACIER and DEEP_ARCHIVE storage classes offer the same durability and resiliency as the STANDARD storage class.
A.   True
B.   False

Q17. What are the benefits of AWS Storage Gateway? Choose 3.
A.   Hybrid storage service that enables your on-premises applications to seamlessly use AWS cloud storage.
B.   You can use the service for backup and archiving, disaster recovery, cloud data processing, storage tiering, and migration.
C.   In premise solution for enhancing your company data center storage capability without connecting to AWS cloud storage.
D.   Your applications connect to the service through a virtual machine or hardware gateway appliance using standard storage protocols, such as NFS, SMB and iSCSI.

Q18. What are the three storage interfaces supported by AWS Storage Gateway?
A.   File Gateway
B.   Volume Gateway
C.   Tape Gateway
D.   Network Gateway

Q19. What is the minimum file size that can be store in S3?
A.   1 Byte
B.   0 Byte
C.   1 KB
D.   1 MB

Q20. What is the largest object size that can be uploaded to S3 in a single PUT?
A.   5GB
B.   5TB
C.   5MB
D.   5KB

Q21. What is the maximum file size that can be stored on S3?
A.   5GB
B.   5TB
C.   5MB
D.   5KB

Q22. A law firm has an internal tablet/mobile application used by employees to download large word documents in their devices for offline review. These document's size are in the range of 10-20 MB. The employees save the document in local device storage, edit it in offline mode and then use the feature in app to upload file to cloud storage. Most of the time users are expected to be in area of high mobile bandwidth of LTE or WIFI but some time they may be in area using a slow speed network (EDGE) or 3G with lots of fluctuations. The files are stored in AWS S3 buckets. What approach should the architect recommend for file upload in application?

A. Use Single PUT operation to upload the files to S3
B. Use Multipart upload to upload the files to S3
C. Use Amazon S3 Transfer Acceleration to upload the files
D. Use Single POST operation to upload the files to S3

Q23. What are the recommended scenarios to use multipart uploading to S3? Choose 2.

A. If you're uploading any size objects over a stable high-bandwidth network, use multipart uploading to maximize the use of your available bandwidth by uploading object parts in parallel for multi-threaded performance.
B. If you're uploading large objects over a stable high-bandwidth network, use multipart uploading to maximize the use of your available bandwidth by uploading object parts in parallel for multi-threaded performance.
C. If you're uploading over a stable high-bandwidth network, use multipart uploading to increase resiliency to network errors by avoiding upload restarts.
D. If you're uploading over a spotty network, use multipart uploading to increase resiliency to network errors by avoiding upload restarts.

Q24. What is S3 transfer acceleration? Choose 2.

A. Enables fast, easy, and secure transfers of files over long distances between your client and your Amazon S3 bucket.
B. Enables fast, easy, and secure transfers of files over short distances between your client and your Amazon S3 bucket.
C. Leverages Amazon CloudFront's globally distributed AWS Edge Locations.
D. Leverages Amazon CloudFront's regionally distributed AWS Edge Locations.

Q25. You have designed an intranet web application for your employees to upload files to S3 buckets for archive. One of employee is trying to upload a 6 GB file to S3 but keep getting the following AWS error message "Your proposed upload exceeds the maximum allowed object size.". What can be the possible reason?

A. Your intranet firewall is not allowing upload of that object size.
B. Your browser is not allowing upload of that object size.
C. Maximum size of object that can be uploaded to S3 in single PUT operation is 5 GB.
D. The S3 bucket cannot store object of that size.

Q26. In general, at what object size AWS recommends using multipart uploads instead of uploading the object in a single operation?
- A.   5 MB
- B.   50 MB
- C.   100 MB
- D.   5 GB

Q27. What are the reasons to use S3 Transfer acceleration? Choose 2.
- A.   Applications that upload to a centralized bucket from all over the world.
- B.   Transfer gigabytes to terabytes of data on a regular basis across continents.
- C.   To improve application performance
- D.   To improve snapshot copy of EC2 EBS volume.

Q28. Amazon EBS provide which type of storage?
- A.   Block based Storage
- B.   Object based Storage
- C.   Magnetic Storage
- D.   File Storage

Q29. Your company is planning to store their important documents in S3 storage. The compliance unit wants to be intimated when documents are created or deleted along with the user name. You know that S3 has the feature of event notification for object events like s3: ObjectCreated:*, s3: ObjectRemoved:*. What are the destination where S3 can publish events? Choose3.
- A.   Amazon SES
- B.   Amazon Simple Notification Service (Amazon SNS) topic
- C.   Amazon Simple Queue Service (Amazon SQS) queue
- D.   AWS Lambda

Q30.   You want to host your own cloud blog website with custom domain as "www. Mycloudblog.com" as static website using S3. What are the essential prerequisite steps? Choose 4.
- A.   Register the custom domain name in Route 53. Create the alias records that you add to the hosted zone for your domain name.
- B.   Configure the bucket's property for static website hosting with an index, error file and redirection rule.
- C.   The bucket names must match the names of the website that you are hosting.
- D.   Enable HTTP on the bucket
- E.   Ensure that bucket and its objects must have public read access

Q31. What are the benefit of using versioning in S3? Choose 2.

A. To restrict access to bucket.
B. To preserve, retrieve, and restore every version of every object stored in your Amazon S3 bucket.
C. To encrypt objects stored in the bucket.
D. To recover from both unintended user actions and application failures.

Q32. What is the version id of the stored objects before the version is enabled on the bucket?
A. 111111
B. 222222
C. 999999
D. Null

Q33. How does versioning-enabled buckets enable you to recover objects from accidental deletion or overwrite? Choose 2.
A. If you delete or overwrite an object AWS keeps a copy in the archive folder.
B. If you delete an object, instead of removing it permanently, Amazon S3 inserts a delete marker, which becomes the current object version.
C. If you overwrite an object, it results in a new object version in the bucket.
D. If you delete or overwrite an object AWS emails you a copy of the previous version.

Q34. Choose the statements that are true? Choose 3.
A. Buckets can be in one of three states: unversioned (the default), versioning-enabled, or versioning-suspended.
B. Buckets can be in one of two states: unversioned (the default) or versioning-enabled.
C. Once you version-enable a bucket, it can never return to an unversioned state.
D. Once you version-enable a bucket, it can return to an unversioned state.
E. Once you version-enable a bucket, you can only suspend versioning on that bucket.

Q35. Your company stores customer contract documents in S3. One of the Account Manager deleted the signed contracts of his accounts. As a result of this you have been asked to configure S3 storage in such a way that files can be protected against inadvertent or intentional deletion. How will you configure the S3? Choose 2.
A. Enable Versioning on the bucket.
B. Write a lambda program which copies the file in another backup bucket.
C. Enable MFA delete on the bucket.
D. Use lifecycle policy which copies the data after POST/UPDATE into another bucket.
E. Use cross region replication which copies the data after POST/UPDATE into another bucket.

Q36. What is S3 cross region replication?

A. Enables automatic, synchronous copying of objects across buckets in same AWS Regions

B. Enables automatic, synchronous copying of objects across buckets in different AWS Regions

C. Enables automatic, asynchronous copying of objects across buckets in different AWS Regions

D. Enables automatic, asynchronous copying of objects across buckets in same AWS Regions

Q37. What are the reasons to enable cross region replication on your S3 buckets?
  A. Comply with compliance requirements
  B. Minimize latency
  C. Increase operational efficiency
  D. Maintain object copies under different ownership
  E. All of the above

Q38. What are pre-requisite to enable Cross Region Replication? Choose 4.
  A. The source and destination bucket owner must have their respective source and destination AWS Regions enabled for their account.
  B. Both source and destination buckets must be in different region having their versioning enabled.
  C. Amazon S3 must have permissions to replicate objects from the source bucket to the destination bucket.
  D. If the owner of the source bucket doesn't own the object in the bucket, the object owner must grant the bucket owner READ and READ_ACP permissions with the object access control list (ACL).
  E. Both source and destination buckets must be in same region having their versioning enabled
  F. Amazon S3 needs to have only one permission to read objects in the source bucket.

Q39. What is S3 Object expiration?
  A. When an object reaches the end of its lifetime, Amazon S3 queues it for removal and removes it synchronously
  B. When an object reaches the end of its lifetime, Amazon S3 queues it for removal and removes it asynchronously
  C. When an object reaches the end of its lifetime, Amazon S3 queues it for removal and moves it to DEEP_ARCHIVE
  D. When an object reaches the end of its lifetime, Amazon S3 queues it for removal and moves it to GLACIER

Q40. What isn't replicated by default when you enable Cross Region Replication on your S3 bucket? Choose 3.

A.  Objects with file type .doc, .pdf, png
B.  Objects that existed before you added the replication configuration to the bucket.
C.  Objects in the source bucket that the bucket owner doesn't have permissions for.
D.  Objects created with server-side encryption using customer-provided (SSE-C) encryption keys.
E.  Objects encrypted using Amazon S3 managed keys (SSE-S3)

Q41. Suppose that you are a solution architect of a global company having regional headquarters in US-East, Ireland and Sydney. You have configured cross-region replication where bucket 'myuseastbucket' in 'us-east-1' US East (N. Virginia) region is the source and bucket 'myeuwestbucket' in 'eu-west-1' EU (Ireland) is the destination. Now you added another cross-region replication configuration where bucket 'myeuwestbucket' is the source and bucket 'mysoutheastbucket' in Asia Pacific (Sydney) 'ap-southeast-2' is the destination.
You notice that file created in 'myuseastbucket' is getting replicated in 'myeuwestbucket' but not in 'mysoutheastbucket' ? What is the possible reason?
A.  You have not configured cross region replication for 'myuseastbucket'   to mysoutheastbucket'
B.  Daisy Chain replication is not supported by S3.
C.  You have not called S3 support and get cross region replication to more than two destination.
D.  You have not given S3 permission to replicated objects to 'mysoutheastbucket'

Q42. What are the actions that can be configured in the S3 object lifecycle? Choose 2.
A.  Define when objects transition to another storage class.
B.  Define when objects expire.
C.  Define when object versioning is to be started.
D.  Define when object cross region replication is to be started.

Q43. Which statements on Amazon S3 pricing are true? Choose 3.
A.  If you create a lifecycle expiration rule that causes objects that have been in INTELLIGENT_TIERING, STANDARD_IA, or ONEZONE_IA storage for less than 30 days to expire, you are charged for 30 days
B.  You are always only charged for number of days objects are in the INTELLIGENT_TIERING, STANDARD_IA, or ONEZONE
C.  If you create a lifecycle expiration rule that causes objects that have been in GLACIER storage for less than 90 days to expire, you are charged for 90 days.
D.  If you create a lifecycle expiration rule that causes objects that have been in DEEP_ARCHIVE storage for less than 180 days to expire, you are charged for 180 days.

Q44. Which of the following lifecycle transitions between storage classes are supported? Choose 2.

A. You can only transition from STANDARD to STANDARD_IA or ONEZONE_IA

B. You can transition from the STANDARD storage class to any other storage class.

C. You can only transition from STANDARD to the GLACIER or DEEP_ARCHIVE storage classes.

D. You can transition from any storage class to the GLACIER or DEEP_ARCHIVE storage classes.

Q45. Which lifecycle transitions between storage classes are supported? Choose 3.

A. You can transition from the STANDARD_IA storage class to the INTELLIGENT_TIERING or ONEZONE_IA storage classes.

B. You can transition from any storage class to the STANDARD storage class.

C. You can transition from the INTELLIGENT_TIERING storage class to the ONEZONE_IA storage class.

D. You can transition from the DEEP_ARCHIVE storage class to any other storage class.

E. You can transition from the GLACIER storage class to the DEEP_ARCHIVE storage class.

Q46. Which lifecycle transitions between storage classes are not supported? Choose 4.

A. Transition from any storage class to the STANDARD storage class.

B. Transition from the STANDARD storage class to any other storage class.

C. Transition from the INTELLIGENT_TIERING storage class to the STANDARD_IA storage class.

D. Transition from the ONEZONE_IA storage class to the STANDARD_IA or INTELLIGENT_TIERING storage classes.

E. Transition from the DEEP_ARCHIVE storage class to any other storage class.

Q47. A manufacturing company has been using in-premise servers for storage. They have nearly used their installed storage capacity but don't want to spend on adding new storage capacity to in-premise. They want to leverage AWS but don't want to migrate their whole current in-premise data to cloud. Which AWS service can they use to achieve their requirement?

A. Amazon S3
B. Amazon EBS
C. Amazon Storage Gateway
D. Amazon RDS

Q48. Which option of AWS Storage Gateway provides cloud-backed storage volumes that you can mount as Internet Small Computer System Interface (iSCSI) devices from your on-premises application servers?

A. File Gateway

B.   Volume Gateway
C.   Tape Gateway
D.   iSCSI Gateway

Q49. You are creating a bucket with name 'mybucket' but you get an error message that 'bucket name already exist'. You don't have a bucket with same name nor you created a bucket with similar name earlier, what is the reason you are getting this error?
  A.   S3 doesn't allow you to create a bucket with name 'mybucket', it is reserved.
  B.   You cannot have substring 'bucket' in you bucket name.
  C.   Bucket names must be unique across all existing bucket names in Amazon S3.
  D.   'mybucket' is not a DNS-compliant bucket name

Q50. Which option of AWS Storage Gateway provides you feature to store and retrieve objects in Amazon S3 using industry-standard file protocols such as Network File System (NFS) and Server Message Block (SMB)?
  A.   File Gateway
  B.   Volume Gateway
  C.   Tape Gateway
  D.   iSCSI Gateway

Q51. Which of the following statements are correct about Volume Gateway? Choose 2.
  A.   Cached volumes store your data in Amazon S3 and retains a copy of frequently accessed data subsets locally.
  B.   Stored volumes provides low-latency access to your entire dataset by storing all your data locally.
  C.   Stored volumes store your data in Amazon S3 and retains a copy of frequently accessed data subsets locally.
  D.   Cached volumes provides low-latency access to your entire dataset by storing all your data locally.

Q52. What are the advantages provided by multipart upload? Choose 4.
  A.   Ability to upload parts in parallel to improve throughput.
  B.   Ability to begin an upload before knowing the object size.
  C.   Ability to pause and resume the upload.
  D.   Quick recovery from network issues.
  E.   Ability to upload 10 MB to 5 GB, last part can be < 10 MB.

Q53. What are the hosting options for AWS Storage Gateway? Choose 3.
  A.   On-premises as a VM appliance
  B.   Hardware appliance
  C.   In AWS Elastic Beanstalk
  D.   In AWS as an Amazon EC2 instance

Q54. Which of the following options are correct for File Storage Gateway? Choose 3.

A.  File gateway presents a file-based interface to Amazon S3, which appears as a network file share. It enables you to store and retrieve Amazon S3 objects through standard file storage protocols.

B.  With file gateway, your configured S3 buckets will be available as Network File System (NFS) mount points or Server Message Block (SMB) file shares to your existing file-based applications or devices.

C.  With file gateway, your configured S3 buckets will be available as iSCSI shares to your existing file-based applications or devices.

D.  The gateway translates these file operations into object requests on your S3 buckets. Your most recently used data is cached on the gateway for low-latency access, and data transfer between your data center and AWS is fully managed and optimized by the gateway.

Q55. Which S3 storage class is suitable for performance-sensitive use cases (those that require millisecond access time) and frequently accessed data?

A.  INTELLIGENT_TIERING
B.  STANDARD
C.  STANDARD-IA
D.  ONEZONE_IA

Q56. Your company is adopting AWS and want to minimize on-premises storage footprint, but need to retain on-premises access to storage for their existing apps. You would like to leverage AWS services as a way to replace on-premises storage with cloud-backed storage, which allows existing applications to operate without changes, while still getting the benefits of storing and processing this data in AWS. Which AWS service will be appropriate?

A.  Amazon S3
B.  Amazon RDS
C.  Amazon EBS
D.  Amazon Storage Gateway

Q57. Which of the following are applicable use cases for AWS Storage Gateway? Choose 3.

A.  Increase performance and reduce latency of on premise storage.

B.  Moving on-premises backups to AWS.

C.  Replace on-premises storage with cloud-backed storage, while allowing their existing applications to operate without changes, while still getting the benefits of storing and processing this data in AWS.

D.  Run apps in AWS and make the results available from multiple on-premises locations such as data centers or branch and remote offices. Also, customers that have moved their on-prem archives to AWS often want to make this data available for access from existing on-premises applications.

Q58. Which of the following server side encryption methods are supported in S3?
   A.   Server-Side Encryption with Amazon S3-Managed Keys (SSE-S3)
   B.   Server-Side Encryption with AWS KMS-Managed Keys (SSE-KMS)
   C.   Server-Side Encryption with Customer-Provided Keys (SSE-C)
   D.   All of the above

Q59. What is a Tape Gateway? Choose 3.
   A.   Cloud based Virtual Tape Library.
   B.   Cloud based File and Object Library.
   C.   Provides virtual tape library (VTL) interface for existing tape-based backup infrastructure to store data on virtual tape cartridges that you create on your tape gateway.
   D.   After you deploy and activate a tape gateway, you mount the virtual tape drives and media changer on your on-premises application servers as iSCSI devices.
   E.   After you deploy and activate a tape gateway, you mount the virtual tape drives and media changer on your on-premises application servers as File share.

Q60. Which of the following two statements are correct for appropriate use for STANDARD_IA and ONEZONE_IA?
   A.   ONEZONE_IA —Use for your primary or only copy of data that can't be recreated.
   B.   STANDARD_IA—Use for your primary or only copy of data that can't be recreated.
   C.   ONEZONE_IA—Use if you can recreate the data if the Availability Zone fails, and for object replicas when setting cross-region replication (CRR).
   D.   STANDARD_IA —Use if you can recreate the data if the Availability Zone fails, and for object replicas when setting cross-region replication (CRR).

Q61. If you encrypt a bucket on S3, what type of encryption does AWS use?
   A.   1028-bit Advanced Encryption Standard (AES-1028)
   B.   256-bit Advanced Encryption Standard (AES-256)
   C.   128-bit Advanced Encryption Standard (AES-128)
   D.   192-bit Advanced Encryption Standard (AES-192)

Q62. Your company is exploring AWS Storage Gateway for extending their on-premise storage. One of the key criteria is to have AWS as the primary storage but still there should be fast and low latency access to frequently accessed data. Which Storage Gateway option will meet this criteria? Choose 2.
   A.   Tape Gateway
   B.   File Gateway
   C.   Volume Stored Gateway
   D.   Volume Cached Gateway

Q63. How can you protect data in transit to S3?
   A.   Using an AWS KMS–Managed Customer Master Key (CMK)
   B.   Using a Client-Side Master Key
   C.   Using SSL between client and S3
   D.   All of the above

Q64. You have an object saved in S3 with attribute "color=yellow". There are two applications 'Client1' and 'Client 2' which update the value of attribute to 'Red' and 'Ruby' one after another as shown in the figure below. Client 1 does a read operation 'R1' after the write W2 from client 2 and Client 2 does a read operation after the R1 as shown in the timeline in the figure below. What will be value of color for R1 read? Choose 3.

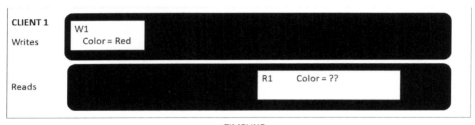

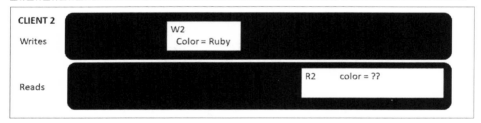

   A.   For R1 the value of Color = Red
   B.   For R1 the value of Color = Ruby
   C.   For R1 the value of Color = Yellow
   D.   For R1 the value of Color = Null

Q65. How can you protect data at rest in S3? Choose 2.
   A.   Using server side encryption
   B.   Using client side encryption
   C.   Using SSL between client and S3

Q66. What is Amazon S3 Block Public Access feature? Choose 3.

A. With S3 Block Public Access, account administrators and bucket owners can easily set up centralized controls to limit public access to their Amazon S3 resources that are enforced regardless of how the resources are created.

B. You can enable block public access settings only for access points, buckets, and AWS accounts.

C. Amazon S3 evaluates whether an operation is prohibited by a block public access setting, it rejects any request that violates setting.

D. You can enable block public access settings only for objects, buckets, and AWS accounts.

Q67.You have a S3 bucket named Photos with versioning enabled. You do following steps:
1. PUT a new object photo.gif which gets version ID = 111111
2. PUT a new version of photo.gif.
3. DELETE photo.gif
Which of the following two statements are correct?

A. After Step2, Amazon S3 generates a new version ID (121212), and adds the newer version to the bucket retaining the older version with ID=111111.There is two versions of photo.gif.

B. After Step2, Amazon S3 overwrites the older version with ID=111111 and grants it new ID. There is only one version of photo.gif.

C. After Step 3, when you DELETE an object, all versions remain in the bucket and Amazon S3 inserts a delete marker.

D. After Step 3, when you DELETE an object, all versions are deleted from the bucket.

Q68. As a solution architect you want to ensure that Amazon Simple Storage Service (Amazon S3) buckets and objects are secure. The resources that needs to be private must be private. What are the ways to limit permission to Amazon S3 resources? Choose 4.

A. Writing AWS Identity and Access Management (IAM) user policies that specify the users that can access specific buckets and objects.

B. Writing bucket policies that define access to specific buckets and objects.

C. Using Client side encryption

D. Using Amazon S3 Block Public Access as a centralized way to limit public access.

E. Using server side encryption

F. Setting access control lists (ACLs) on your buckets and objects.

Q69. When should you use an ACL-based Access Policy (Bucket and Object ACLs)? Choose 4.

A. When an object ACL is the only way to manage access to objects not owned by the bucket owner.

B. When permissions vary by object and you need to manage permissions at the object level.

C. When you want to define permission at object level.

D. To grant write permission to the Amazon S3 Log Delivery group to write access log objects to your bucket.

E. When the AWS account that owns the object also owns the bucket and you need to manage object permissions.

Q70. You have a S3 bucket named Photos with versioning enabled. You do following steps:
1. PUT a new object photo.gif which gets version ID = 111111
2. PUT a new version of photo.gif get version ID=222222
3. DELETE photo.gif. Delete marker with version ID = 456789
4. GET object

Which of the following two statements are correct?
   A. GET object will return object with version ID = 111111
   B. GET object will return object with version ID = 222222
   C. GET Object returns a 404 not found error.
   D. GET object will return delete marker object with version ID = 456789

Q71. By default all S3 buckets are public and can be accessed only by users that are explicitly granted access.
   A. True
   B. False

Q72. You have a S3 bucket named Photos with versioning enabled. You do following steps:
1. PUT a new object photo.gif which gets version ID = 111111
2. PUT a new version of photo.gif get version ID=222222
3. DELETE photo.gif. Delete marker with version ID = 456789

Which of the following two statements are correct?
   A. You can GET a specific object version.
   B. You can permanently delete a specific object by specifying the version you want to delete.
   C. You can permanently delete only latest version of object. version ID=222222
   D. You can GET only latest version of object. version ID=222222

Q73. In which of the following use case you will not use S3 lifecycle configurations?
   A. If you upload periodic logs to a bucket, your application might need them for a week or a month. After that, you might want to delete them.
   B. Some documents are frequently accessed for a limited period of time. After that, they are infrequently accessed. At some point, you might not need real-time access to them, but your organization or regulations might require you to archive them for a specific period. After that, you can delete them.
   C. Daily upload of data from regional offices to a central bucket for ETL processing.

D.  You might upload some types of data to Amazon S3 primarily for archival purposes, long-term database backups, and data that must be retained for regulatory compliance.

Q74. When should you choose IAM policies for S3 permissions? Choose 3.
A.  You prefer to keep access control policies in the IAM environment not only for S3 but for other AWS resources
B.  If you're more interested in "What can this user do in AWS?"
C.  If you're more interested in "Who can access this S3 bucket?"
D.  You have numerous S3 buckets each with different permissions requirements.

Q75. In order to determine whether the requester has permission to perform the specific operation, put in order following steps which Amazon S3 does when it receives a request?

1.  Converts all the relevant access policies (user policy, bucket policy, ACLs) at run time into a set of policies for evaluation.
2.  Object context – If the request is for an object, Amazon S3 evaluates the subset of policies owned by the object owner.
3.  User context – Amazon S3 evaluates a subset of policies owned by the parent account.
4.  Bucket context – In the bucket context, Amazon S3 evaluates policies owned by the AWS account that owns the bucket.
A.  1,2,3,4
B.  2,3,4,1
C.  3,4,1,2
D.  1,3,4,2

Q76. How S3 evaluates request for a bucket operation requested by an IAM Principal whose parent AWS account is also the bucket owner?
Principal: Jill
Jill's Parent Account: 1111-1111-1111
A.  In the user context Amazon S3 evaluates all policies that belongs to the parent AWS account to determine if Principal has permission to perform the operation.
B.  Amazon S3 evaluates the user context by reviewing the policies authored by the account to verify that Principal has the necessary permissions, then it evaluates the bucket context, to verify that bucket owner has granted Jill (or her parent AWS account) permission to perform the requested operation.
C.  Amazon S3 evaluates the user context by reviewing the policies authored by the account to verify that Principal has the necessary permissions, then it evaluates the bucket context, to verify that bucket owner has granted Jill (or her parent AWS account) permission to perform the requested operation and last object context

evaluates the object ACL to determine if Jill has permission to access the objects in the bucket.

D.  Amazon S3 evaluates the bucket context, to verify that bucket owner has granted Jill (or her parent AWS account) permission to perform the requested operation and in object context evaluates the object ACL to determine if Jill has permission to access the objects in the bucket.

Q77. When should you choose Bucket policy for S3 permissions? Choose 4.
A.  If you're more interested in "What can this user do in AWS?"
B.  If you're more interested in "Who can access this S3 bucket?"
C.  You want a simple way to grant cross-account access to your S3 environment, without using IAM roles.
D.  Your IAM policies are reaching the size limit (up to 2 kb for users, 5 kb for groups, and 10 kb for roles). S3 supports bucket policies of up 20 kb.
E.  You prefer to keep access control policies in the S3 environment.

Q78 How S3 evaluates request for a bucket operation requested by an IAM Principal whose parent AWS account is not the bucket owner?
Principal: Jill
Jill's Parent Account: 1111-1111-1111
Bucket Owner: 2222-2222-2222

A.  In the user context Amazon S3 evaluates all policies that belong to the parent AWS account to determine if Principal has permission to perform the operation.
B.  Amazon S3 evaluates the user context by reviewing the policies authored by the account to verify that Principal has the necessary permissions, then it evaluates the bucket context, to verify that bucket owner has granted Jill (or her parent AWS account) permission to perform the requested operation.
C.  Amazon S3 evaluates the user context by reviewing the policies authored by the account to verify that Principal has the necessary permissions, then it evaluates the bucket context, to verify that bucket owner has granted Jill (or her parent AWS account) permission to perform the requested operation and last object context evaluates the object ACL to determine if Jill has permission to access the objects in the bucket.
D.  Amazon S3 evaluates the bucket context, to verify that bucket owner has granted Jill (or her parent AWS account) permission to perform the requested operation and in object context evaluates the object ACL to determine if Jill has permission to access the objects in the bucket.

Q79. Which of the following statements are correct about S3 ACLs? Choose 4.
A.  Resource-based access policy options that you can use to manage access to your buckets and objects.

B. You can grant permissions only to other AWS accounts; you cannot grant permissions to users in your account.

C. A grantee can be an AWS account or IAM user.

D. You cannot grant conditional permissions, nor can you explicitly deny permissions.

E. A grantee can be an AWS account or one of the predefined Amazon S3 groups.

Q80. A building architecture company stores all its project architecture documents in S3. As an added security measure they want to allow access to S3 only from their corporate network ip addresses. How this can be achieved?

A. Create bucket policies with Action=Allow and the condition block element *IpAddress* having values for the corporate domain ip address.

B. Create IAM policy with Action=Deny the condition block element if *NotIpAddress* having values for the corporate domain ip address.

C. Create IAM policy with Action=Allow the condition block element if *IpAddress* having values for the corporate domain ip address.

D. All of the above

Q81. A pharmaceutical company has an on-premise analytics application which has 100 GB of data. They don't want to invest in extending the on-premise storage but want to leverage the AWS cloud storage without making considerable changes to the analytics application. They also want to have low latency access to data of last one month which is more frequently used and should be stored in-premise. Which storage option will you use?

A. Amazon RDS

B. Amazon Volume Storage Gateway Cached

C. Amazon EBS

D. Amazon S3

E. Amazon Volume Storage Gateway Stored

Q82. You are using S3 bucket for data backup of on-premise data. You have created a lifecycle policy to Transition the data from Standard storage class to Standard IA 3 days after data is created in S3 bucket. If you have uploaded a file to backup S3 folder on 1/15/2020 10.30 AM UTC when will S3 transition it to Standard IA storage class?

A. 1/18/2020 10.30 AM UTC

B. 1/18/2020 10.30 PM UTC

C. 1/19/2020 00:00 UTC

D. 1/18/2020 00:00 UTC

Q83. You are a solution architect having your own website on wildlife videography. You have uploaded videos from your recent visit to Brazil's amazon forest on the website. In the backend you store these videos in a S3 folder which is not publically accessible. You want to ensure that these videos can be downloaded only by registered users of your website. How can you do this?

A.  Make the S3 folder publically accessible
B.  Attach a bucket policy to the folder so that it is accessible by the registered users
C.  Generate a pre-signed URL to grant time-limited permission to download the video file
D.  Create IAM users for the users registered in the website and give access to S3 bucket

Q84. Your company has decided to start their journey to cloud by moving secondary workloads, such as backups and archives. They want to migrate back up on-premises data currently being stored on physical tapes without changing their current backup workflows or backup applications. As a cloud migration consultant what is the strategy you will adopt?
A.  Use AWS Tape Gateway.
B.  Use a third party software to convert data in tape to a block storage for storing in in premise EFS.
C.  Use a third party software to convert data in tape to an object storage for uploading to S3.
D.  Use AWS File Gateway.
E.  Use AWS Volume Cached Gateway

Q85. You are the solution architect for a pharmaceutical company which has been using a client application to manage their on-premise data backup and archival. The application uses iSCSI protocol to transfer data between application and on-premise storage. The on-premise storage currently store TBs of data and is reaching near capacity. The company doesn't want to invest in expanding the on-premise storage capacity. Which AWS service company should leverage so that there is minimum or no change to existing backup & archiving application as well as low latency is provided for frequently used data?
A.  Use AWS Tape Gateway.
B.  Use AWS Volume Storage Gateway.
C.  Use AWS File Gateway.
D.  Use AWS Volume Cached Gateway

Q86. Which S3 storage class is designed to optimize storage costs by automatically moving data to the most cost-effective storage access tier, without performance impact or operational overhead?
A.  INTELLIGENT_TIERING
B.  STANDARD
C.  STANDARD-IA
D.  ONEZONE_IA

Q87. You are the solution architect for pharmaceutical company which has been using a client application to manage their in-premise data backup and archival. The application uses iSCSI protocol to transfer data between application and in-premise storage. The on-premise storage currently store TBs of data and is reaching near capacity. The company doesn't want to invest

in expanding the on-premise storage capacity. Which AWS service should company leverage so that there is minimum or no change to existing backup & archiving application as well low latency is provided for all data using cloud as secondary storage?
   A.  Use AWS Tape Gateway.
   B.  Use AWS Volume Stored Gateway.
   C.  Use AWS File Gateway.
   D.  Use AWS Volume Cached Gateway

Q88. Suppose that for a S3 bucket you have created a lifecycle rule and specified a date-based Expiration action to delete all objects. Select three correct statements from following.
   A.  On the specified date, S3 expires all the qualified objects in the bucket.
   B.  S3 will expire subsequent new objects created in the bucket.
   C.  S3 continues to apply the date-based action even after the date has passed, as long as the rule status is Enabled.
   D.  S3 will apply the date based rule only for that day on the existing and new objects created till 11:59:59 PM.

Q89. Which S3 storage class are designed for low cost data archiving? Choose 2.
   A.  STANDARD_IA
   B.  ONEZONE_IA
   C.  GLACIER
   D.  DEEP_ARCHIVE

Q90. You have created a static blog website using S3. The name of the bucket is 'mycloudblogs.com' created in us-west-2 region. The website is available at the following Amazon S3 website endpoint:
http://mycloudblogs.com.s3-website-us-west-2.amazonaws.com/

Your website also has JavaScript on the webpages that are stored in this bucket to be able to make authenticated GET and PUT requests against the same bucket by using the Amazon S3 API endpoint for the bucket:
mycloudblogs.com.s3-us-west-2.amazonaws.com

You have also created the alias record for mycloudblogs.com in Route 53 so that your user can access the website by using the url http://mycloudblogs.com.

When you tested the website by invoking the website endpoint url on your browser you are getting following error:
'No 'Access-Control-Allow-Origin' header is present on the requested resource'.

What could be the reason?

A. You need to pass a unique header value from browser to Amazon S3 for every request.

B. You need to pass a unique header value from Amazon S3 to browser for every request.

C. Need to configure your CORS Settings for your bucket on amazon S3 console.

D. Need to configure your CORS Settings for your bucket in Route 53 record.

Q91. You are the solution architect for financial services company who has been using a client application to manage their on-premise data backup and archival. The application uses NFS or SMB protocol to transfer data between application and on-premise storage. The on-premise storage currently store TBs of data and is reaching near capacity. The company doesn't want to invest in expanding the in-premise storage capacity. Which AWS service company should leverage so that there is minimum or no change to existing backup & archiving application as well low latency is provided for frequently used data?

A. Use AWS Tape Gateway.

B. Use Volume Storage Gateway.

C. Use AWS File Gateway.

D. Use AWS Volume Cached Gateway

Q92. A company wants to use S3 to store the paid invoices by its customers. These paid invoices are accessed by various departments from finance, sales, and department heads and customer representatives for 30 days. The invoices that are paid more than 30 days before are infrequently accessed only by accounting department for auditing purpose. After the financial year these invoices are rarely accessed by any one and even if accessed, fast retrieval is not a consideration. How the solution architect of the company should plan on using different storage tiers in most cost effective way?

A. Use STANDARD tier for storing paid invoice for first 30 days. Configure lifecycle rule to move the invoice to ONEZONE_IA after 30 days and to GLACIER after the financial year is over.

B. Use STANDARD tier for storing paid invoice for first 30 days. Configure lifecycle rule to move the invoice to STANDARD _IA after 30 days and to GLACIER after the financial year is over.

C. Use STANDARD tier for storing paid invoice for first 30 days. Configure lifecycle rule to move the invoice to STANDARD _IA after 30 days and to DEEP_ARCHIVE after the financial year is over.

D. Use STANDARD tier for storing paid invoice for first 30 days. Configure lifecycle rule to move the invoice to STANDARD _IA after 30 days and to DEEP_ARCHIVE after the financial year is over.

Q93. Which of the following two statements are correct about data archiving storage classes in S3? Choose 2.

A.  GLACIER—used for archives where portions of the data might need to be retrieved in minutes.
B.  DEEP_ARCHIVE —used for archives where portions of the data might need to be retrieved in minutes.
C.  GLACIER —Use for archiving data that rarely needs to be accessed.
D.  DEEP_ARCHIVE—Use for archiving data that rarely needs to be accessed.

Q94. Which of the following two statements are correct about data archiving storage classes in S3? Choose 2.
A.  Objects that are stored in the GLACIER or DEEP_ARCHIVE storage classes are available in real time.
B.  You must first initiate a restore request and then a temporary copy of the object is available immediately for the duration that you specify in the request.
C.  Objects that are stored in the GLACIER or DEEP_ARCHIVE storage classes are not available in real time.
D.  You must first initiate a restore request and then wait until a temporary copy of the object is available for the duration that you specify in the request.

Q95. Which of the following statement are true for S3 lifecycle management configuration? Choose 2.
A.  The configuration rules does not apply to existing objects.
B.  The configuration rules applies to existing objects.
C.  The configuration rules applies to objects that you add later.
D.  The configuration rules applies only to existing objects and not to objects that you add later.

Q96.Choose two correct statements for S3 multipart upload?
A.  Part Size can be from 5 MB to 5 GB
B.  Part Size can be from 50 MB to 5 GB
C.  Last part can be < 5 MB
D.  Last part can be < 5 KB

Q97. You have a version enabled bucket with two version of an object as shown in the figure below:

What will happened when you invoke the delete API specifying only the object's key, and not the version ID?

A.  S3 will return an error.
B.  S3 deletes all the versions in the bucket.
C.  S3 creates a delete marker and returns its version ID in the response.
D.  S3 will delete the current object ID =222222

Q98. You are solution architect for a Stock Trading web application provider company. Financial regulation mandates them to keep the trading data for five years. From analysis of past internal and customer access behavior you are certain that data more than two year old is unlikely to be accessed, data less than two year old but more than six months old is infrequently accessed. Any data less than six months old will need to have faster access. Currently 150 TB data are stored in in-premise data storage which company is planning to move to AWS cloud storage to save cost. Which is the most cost effective option?
A.  Store the data on Amazon S3 with lifecycle policy that change the storage class from Standard to Standard-IA in six months, from Standard-IA to Glacier in 1.5 years and expiration in 3.5 years.
B.  Store the data on Amazon S3 with lifecycle policy that change the storage class from Standard to Standard-IA in six months, from Standard-IA to Glacier in two year and expiration in five years.
C.  Store all the data in Redshift data warehouse.
D.  Store all the data in EBS general purpose volume attached to EC2 cheapest instance.

Q99. You have a bucket with following object versions after you have placed a delete marker.

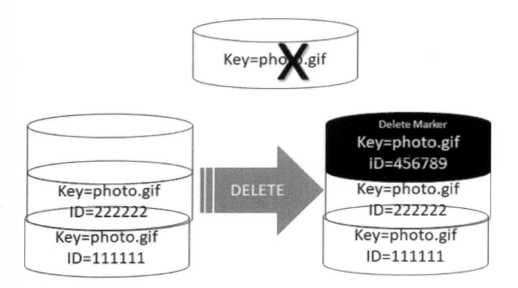

Choose two correct statements from below when you invoke the delete API specifying both the key and object ID.
  A.  Delete API invoked with Key=photo.gif and ID=111111, will return an error.
  B.  Delete API invoked with Key=photo.gif and ID=456789, will return an error.
  C.  Delete API invoked with Key=photo.gif and ID=111111, will delete that version.
  D.  Delete API invoked with Key=photo.gif and ID=456789, will delete the delete marker. This makes the object reappear in your bucket.

Q100. You're a developer at a large retailer, you need to extract and analyze the weekly sales data from a single store, but the data for all 200 stores is saved in a new GZIP-ed CSV every day. Which Amazon S3 feature you will leverage to filter this data to single store thus reducing the amount of data that Amazon S3 transfers, and also reducing the cost and latency to retrieve this data?
  A.  S3 SQL
  B.  S3 Select
  C.  S3 Download
  D.  S3 Filter

Q101. A solution architect is not sure whether to store the data associated with Amazon EC2 instance in an instance store or in an attached Amazon Elastic Block Store (Amazon EBS) volume. What should be the criteria for choosing storage type? Choose 2.

  A.  The Amazon Elastic Block Store (Amazon EBS) volumes is ideal for temporary storage
  B.  The instance store is ideal for temporary storage
  C.  For data to retain longer, or encrypt the data, use Amazon Elastic Block Store (Amazon EBS) volumes
  D.  For data to retain longer, or encrypt the data, use instance store

Q102. How are two different EBS volume types optimized for? Choose 2.
  A.  SSD-backed volumes optimized for transactional workloads involving frequent read/write operations with small I/O size, where the dominant performance attribute is IOPS
  B.  HDD-backed volumes optimized for transactional workloads involving frequent read/write operations with small I/O size, where the dominant performance attribute is IOPS
  C.  SSD-backed volumes optimized for large streaming workloads where throughput (measured in MiB/s) is a better performance measure than IOPS
  D.  HDD-backed volumes optimized for large streaming workloads where throughput (measured in MiB/s) is a better performance measure than IOPS

Q103. What is the main characteristics of two SSD based EBS volume? Choose 2.

A.  General purpose SSD volume balances price and performance for a wide variety of workloads
B.  Provisioned IOPS SSD is highest-performance SSD volume for mission-critical low-latency or high-throughput workloads
C.  Provisioned IOPS SSD volume balances price and performance for a wide variety of workloads
D.  General purpose is highest-performance SSD volume for mission-critical low-latency or high-throughput workloads

Q104. Which of the following statements are true about Amazon EBS? Choose 4.
A.  Provides block level storage volumes for use with EC2 instances.
B.  You can mount multiple volumes on the same instance, and each volume can also be attached to more than one instance at a time.
C.  You can mount multiple volumes on the same instance, but each volume can be attached to only one instance at a time.
D.  You can create a file system on top of these volumes, or use them in any way you would use a block device (like a hard drive).
E.  EBS volumes that are attached to an EC2 instance are exposed as storage volumes that persist independently from the life of the instance.

Q105. Which Amazon EBS volume type you will use for critical business applications that require sustained IOPS performance, low latency or high-throughput workloads?
A.  General Purpose SSD (gp2)
B.  Provisioned IOPS SSD (io1)
C.  Throughput Optimized HDD (st1)
D.  Cold HDD (sc1)

Q106. Which Amazon EBS volume type you will use for large database workloads, such as: MongoDB, Cassandra, Microsoft SQL Server, MySQL, PostgreSQL, Oracle?
A.  General Purpose SSD (gp2)
B.  Provisioned IOPS SSD (io1)
C.  Throughput Optimized HDD (st1)
D.  Cold HDD (sc1)

Q107. Which Amazon EBS volume type you will use for
• Streaming workloads requiring consistent, fast throughput at a low price
• Big data or Data warehouses
• Log processing
A.  General Purpose SSD (gp2)
B.  Provisioned IOPS SSD (io1)
C.  Throughput Optimized HDD (st1)
D.  Cold HDD (sc1)

Q108. You have a corporate intranet web application that required 500GB of block storage at 1000 IOPS throughout the day apart from 40 minutes at night when you run a schedule batch process to generate reports during which you require 3000 IOPS. Which Amazon EBS volume will be cost effective?
- A. General Purpose SSD (gp2)
- B. Provisioned IOPS SSD (io1)
- C. Throughput Optimized HDD (st1)
- D. Cold HDD (sc1)

Q109. You want to create a test environment which will be replica of production environment. To achieve this replication you are planning to use the production environment EC2 instance EBS snapshot to create the new test environment volume. Which of the following statements are correct? Choose 2.
- A. New volumes created from existing EBS snapshots load lazily in the background.
- B. New volumes created from existing EBS snapshots doesn't load lazily in the background.
- C. After test environment EBS volume is created from production EBS snapshot, there is no need to wait for all of the data to transfer from Amazon S3 to test EBS volume before your attached test EC2 instance can start accessing the volume and all its data.
- D. After test environment EBS volume is created from production EBS snapshot, you have to wait for all of the data to transfer from Amazon S3 to test EBS volume before your attached test EC2 instance can start accessing the volume and all its data.

Q110. Which of the following are best practices for getting optimal performance from your EBS volumes? Choose 3.
- A. Use EBS-Optimized Instances
- B. Use Compute intensive Instance
- C. Be Aware of the Performance Penalty When Initializing Volumes from Snapshots
- D. Use RAID 0 to Maximize Utilization of Instance Resources

Q111. Which EBS RAID configuration you will use when fault tolerance is more important than I/O performance?
- A. RAID 0
- B. RAID 1
- C. RAID 5
- D. RAID 6

Q112. Which EBS RAID configuration you will use when I/O performance is more important than fault tolerance; for example, as in a heavily used database (where data replication is already set up separately)?
- A. RAID 0

B.  RAID 1
C.  RAID 5
D.  RAID 6

Q113. You are evaluating RAID 0 and RAID 1 options for EBS volumes with two 500 GiB Amazon EBS io1 volumes with 4,000 provisioned IOPS and 500 MiB/s of throughput each. Which of the following two statements are correct?
A.  You can create a 1000 GiB RAID 1 array with an available bandwidth of 8,000 IOPS and 1,000 MiB/s of throughput.
B.  You can create a 500 GiB RAID 0 array with an available bandwidth of 4,000 IOPS and 500 MiB/s of throughput
C.  You can create a 1000 GiB RAID 0 array with an available bandwidth of 8,000 IOPS and 1,000 MiB/s of throughput.
D.  You can create a 500 GiB RAID 1 array with an available bandwidth of 4,000 IOPS and 500 MiB/s of throughput.

Q114. Which two statements are correct given volume configuration, how I/O characteristics drive the performance behavior for your EBS volumes?
A.  General Purpose SSD (gp2) and Provisioned IOPS SSD (io1)—deliver consistent performance whether an I/O operation is large or sequential.
B.  General Purpose SSD (gp2) and Provisioned IOPS SSD (io1)—deliver consistent performance whether an I/O operation is random or sequential.
C.  HDD-backed volumes—Throughput Optimized HDD (st1) and Cold HDD (sc1)— deliver optimal performance only when I/O operations are large and sequential.
D.  HDD-backed volumes—Throughput Optimized HDD (st1) and Cold HDD (sc1)— deliver optimal performance only when I/O operations are random and sequential.

Q115. You have recently launched a web application. Backend database is on a high end compute EC2 instance with 500 GB Provisioned IOPS SSD (io1) EBS drive. On analyzing the CloudWatch metrics for EBS you notice that write operation needs performance improvement. Which of the following is the best way to improve write performance of EBS database? Choose 2.
A.  Have two 500 GiB Amazon EBS io1 volumes in RAID 1 configuration.
B.  Use EC2 instance with enhanced networking and put in placement group.
C.  Have two 500 GiB Amazon EBS io1 volumes in RAID 0 configuration.
D.  Use EBS optimized EC2 instance.

Q116. Which RAID configuration are recommended for Amazon EBS volumes? Choose 2.
A.  RAID 0
B.  RAID 1
C.  RAID 5
D.  RAID 6

Q117. How can you create a new empty EBS volume with encryption? Choose 2.
A. By enabling encryption by default, the volume will be automatically encrypted.
B. Amazon EBS doesn't support encryption of new empty EBS volume other than default key encryption.
C. Amazon EBS supports encryption of EBS snapshots only and not of new volume.
D. By enabling encryption for the specific volume creation operation, you can specify the CMK to be used to encrypt the volume.

Q118. Which of the following statements are correct about Amazon EBS snapshots encryption? Choose 3.
A. Snapshots of encrypted volumes are automatically encrypted.
B. Volumes that you create from encrypted snapshots are automatically encrypted.
C. Snapshots of encrypted volumes are not automatically encrypted.
D. Volumes that you create from encrypted snapshots are not automatically encrypted.
E. Volumes that you create from an unencrypted snapshot that you own or have access to can be encrypted on-the-fly.
F. Volumes that you create from an unencrypted snapshot that you own or have access to cannot be encrypted on-the-fly.

Q119. Which of the following statements are correct about Amazon EBS encryption? Choose 2.
A. When you copy an unencrypted snapshot that you own, you cannot encrypt it during the copy process.
B. When you copy an encrypted snapshot that you own or have access to, you cannot reencrypt it with a different key during the copy process.
C. When you copy an unencrypted snapshot that you own, you can encrypt it during the copy process.
D. When you copy an encrypted snapshot that you own or have access to, you can reencrypt it with a different key during the copy process.

Q120. When you create an encrypted EBS volume and attach it to a supported instance type, which types of data are encrypted?
A. Data at rest inside the volume
B. All data moving between the volume and the instance
C. All snapshots created from the volume
D. All volumes created from those snapshots
E. All of the above

Q121. Your company is using EBS for various workloads hosted in AWS. As per new company policies and regulatory requirements for audit and backups you have been instructed to automate creation, retention, and deletion of Amazon Elastic Block Storage (Amazon EBS) snapshots used for backing up Amazon EBS volumes wherever possible. How can you do that?

A.  Use Amazon Data Lifecycle Manager (DLM) to create lifecycle policies to automate EBS snapshot management.

B.  Use AWS Glue to create lifecycle policies to automate EBS snapshot management.

C.  Use AWS Data pipeline to create lifecycle policies to automate EBS snapshot management.

D.  Create a scheduled job which runs twice a day across the workloads system.

Q122. With changes in security compliance in your organization all the data-in-rest has to be encrypted. To comply with this policy you have to encrypt all the unencrypted EBS volumes attached to EC2 instances running in your corporate applications. How will you convert an unencrypted EBS to encrypted? Choose 2.

A.  An unencrypted EBS volume cannot be converted to encrypt in any way.

B.  Create an EBS snapshot of the volume you want to encrypt. Copy the EBS snapshot, encrypting the copy in the process.

C.  Create a new EBS volume from your new encrypted EBS snapshot. The new EBS volume will be encrypted. Detach the original EBS volume and attach your new encrypted EBS volume, making sure to match the device name.

D.  Create a new, empty EBS volume by enabling encryption by default, the volume is automatically encrypted. Detach the original EBS volume and attach your new encrypted EBS volume, making sure to match the device name.

Q123. You have used Amazon Data Lifecycle Manager to automate the creation of snapshots of an EBS volume every day at 11 PM, when the EC2 instance to which it is attached is least used. Which of the following is correct for the scenario when EBS snapshot creation is under progress? Choose 2.

A.  An in-progress snapshot is not affected by ongoing reads and writes to the volume.

B.  You cannot use the EBS while the snapshot is in progress.

C.  EBS volume can be used in read only mode while snapshot is in progress.

D.  Snapshots only capture data that has been written to your Amazon EBS volume at the time the snapshot command is issued.

Q124. With changes in security compliance in your organization all the data-in-rest and data in transit has to be encrypted. You are releasing a web application to production live which has backend relation database on an EC2 instance with an EBS volume. How can you ensure that data encryption compliance needs are met in most efficient way? Choose 3.

A.  Modify the web application business layer program to encrypt/decrypt the data in transit and data at rest.

B.  Use AWS IAM to encrypt/decrypt the data in transit and data at rest.

C.  Configure your AWS account to enforce the encryption of the new EBS volumes and snapshot copies that you create.

D. When you create a new, empty EBS volume, you can encrypt it by enabling encryption for the specific volume creation operation.

E. Use HTTPS/TLS protocol for communication between user and webserver to encrypt data in transit.

Q125. You are migrating to AWS, an on-premise legacy application which stores state in files on disk. The current storage size is 2 PB. For application layer you will be using a fleet of EC2 instances in an auto scale group which will access these files concurrently. You are evaluating different storage options in AWS based on following criteria:

- Should be able to scale on demand to petabytes without disrupting applications, growing and shrinking automatically as you add and remove files, eliminating the need to provision and manage capacity to accommodate growth.

- Ability to enable lifecycle management on your file system, files not accessed according to the lifecycle policy should be automatically and transparently moved into lower cost storage class

- Parallel shared access to multiple Amazon EC2 instances, enabling your applications to achieve high levels of aggregate throughput and IOPS with consistent low latencies.

Which storage options you should choose?

A. S3

B. EFS

C. EBS

D. RDS

Q126. What is the main characteristics of two HDD based EBS volume? (Choose 2)

A. Throughput Optimized HDD is Low-cost HDD volume designed for frequently accessed, throughput-intensive workloads

B. Cold HDD is Lowest cost HDD volume designed for less frequently accessed workloads

C. Throughput Optimized is Lowest cost HDD volume designed for less frequently accessed workloads

D. Cold HDD is Low-cost HDD volume designed for frequently accessed, throughput-intensive workloads

Q127. You have attached an EBS volume to an EC2 instance in us-west-1a AZ. Is an EBS volume fault tolerant to full AZ failure?

A. Yes EBS volume is automatically replicated to three AZs in the region it is created.

B. Yes if Multi-AZ is enabled for the EBS volume.

C. No, EBS volume is automatically replicated within one zone only in which it is created.

D. Yes if the EC2 instance auto scale to multi AZs.

Q128. Which Amazon EBS volume type you will use that balances price and performance for a wide variety of workloads?
  A.   General Purpose SSD (gp2)
  B.   Provisioned IOPS SSD (io1)
  C.   Throughput Optimized HDD (st1)
  D.   Cold HDD (sc1)

Q129. You run an online photo editing website for two type of members: free members and fee paying premium members. The set of editing requests and photos is placed asynchronously in a SQS queue which is then processed by worker EC2 instances in an auto scaling group. The architecture has two SQS queues, one for premium members and one for free members editing task. You have on-demand EC2 instances in an auto scale group to process the messages in the premium members queue and spot instances for processing the message from free member queue. You want to use S3 for storing the photo image files. Which of the following will be most cost optimized way of leveraging S3 without compromising best performance service to premium members and free members?
  A.   Use S3-Standard-IA for premium members and S3-One Zone-IA for free members.
  B.   Use S3-Standard for free members and S3-One Zone-IA for premium members.
  C.   Use S3-Standard for premium members and S3-Glacier for free members.
  D.   Use S3-Standard for premium members and S3-One Zone-IA for free members.

Q130. Which Amazon EBS volume type is a low-cost HDD volume designed for frequently accessed, throughput-intensive workloads?
  A.   General Purpose SSD (gp2)
  B.   Provisioned IOPS SSD (io1)
  C.   Throughput Optimized HDD (st1)
  D.   Cold HDD (sc1)

Q131. Amazon S3 offers eventual consistency for overwrite PUTS and DELETES in all Regions. Which of the following operation can result in stale old data? Choose 3.
  A.   GET after a DELETE
  B.   LIST after a DELETE
  C.   GET after PUT to an existing object
  D.   GET after PUT of new object

Q132. Which Amazon EBS volume type is lowest cost HDD volume designed for less frequently accessed workloads?
  A.   General Purpose SSD (gp2)
  B.   Provisioned IOPS SSD (io1)
  C.   Throughput Optimized HDD (st1)
  D.   Cold HDD (sc1)

Q133. You are the solution architect for a law firm which is using S3 to store numerous documents related to cases handled by their lawyers. Recently one of the employee inadvertely deleted few important documents stored in bucket. Luckily another employee had the local copy in his computer and you were able to restore the document in the bucket. You have been asked to do configuration changes in S3 so that such unintentional mistakes can be avoided and even if it happens there should be easier way to recover form it ?Choose 3.

    A.   Set S3 object lock
    B.   Enable S3 cross region replication
    C.   Enable bucket versioning
    D.   Enable MFA delete on a bucket

Q134. You want to automate the creation, retention, and deletion of snapshots taken to back up your Amazon EBS volumes. How can you achieve this?

    A.   Write a java or .net program which will run at a scheduled time.
    B.   Use Cloudtrail , CloudWatch and CloudFormation
    C.   User EBS Automate
    D.   Use Amazon Data Lifecycle Manager (Amazon DLM)

Q135. Which S3 feature evaluates your bucket access policies and enables you to discover and swiftly remediate buckets with potentially unintended access?

    A.   Access Analyzer for S3
    B.   Policy Analyzer for S3
    C.   Bucket Analyzer for S3
    D.   Amazon Inspector

Q136. What are available retrieval options when restoring an archived object from S3? Choose 3.

    A.   Expedited
    B.   Standard
    C.   Urgent
    D.   Bulk
    E.   Immediate

Q137. You want to host your static website on Amazon S3. You registered a domain example.com in Route 53, and you want requests for http://www.example.com and http://example.com to be served from your Amazon S3 content. Which of the following steps you will do to achieve this? Choose 3.

    A.   Create only one bucket example.com to host your content. Upload your index document and optional website content to your bucket.
    B.   Create two buckets. You will host your content out of the root domain bucket (example.com), and you will create a redirect request for the subdomain bucket

(www.example.com). Upload your index document and optional website content to your root domain bucket.

    C.   Make example.com bucket publically readable. Disable block public access for the bucket and write a bucket policy that allows public read access.

    D.   Create the alias records in the hosted zone for your domain maps example.com and www.example.com. The alias records use the Amazon S3 website endpoints.

Q138. You are the solution architect for a financial services company who needs to store a set of trading records for 7 years to meet regulatory compliance requirements. The records should be immutable during this period. You also never want any user, including the root user in your AWS account, to be able to delete the objects during the retention period. What features of S3 you should use to achieve this requirements?

    A.   Use Object Locking with retention period of 7 years in compliance mode.

    B.   Use Object Locking with retention period of 7 years in governance mode.

    C.   Use Object Locking with legal period of 7 years in compliance mode.

    D.   Use Object Locking with legal period of 7 years in governance mode.

Q139. For which events Amazon S3 can publish notifications? Choose 5.

    A.   New object created events

    B.   Object removal events

    C.   New bucket created events

    D.   Bucket removal events

    E.   Restore object events

    F.   Reduced Redundancy Storage (RRS) object lost events

    G.   Replication events

Q140. What are different typed of object replication available in S3? Choose 2.

    A.   Cross-Region replication (CRR)

    B.   Subnet-to-Subnet replication (SSR)

    C.   Account-to-Account replication (AAR)

    D.   Same-Region replication (SRR)

Q141. Why should you use S3 Replication? Choose 4.

    A.   Replicate objects while retaining metadata

    B.   Replicate objects into different storage classes

    C.   Replicate objects across VPCs

    D.   Maintain object copies under different ownership

    E.   Replicate objects within 15 minutes

Q142. Which of the following is not a use case for S3 Same Region Replication (SRR)?

    A.   Aggregate logs into a single bucket

    B.   Production and test accounts that uses same data

C. Store multiple copies of your data in separate AWS accounts within a certain Region to abide by data sovereignty rules.

D. Reduce latency of global users.

Q143. Replication enables automatic, asynchronous copying of objects across Amazon S3 buckets. What is replicated by default in S3? Choose 3.
A. Objects that existed before you added the replication configuration to the bucket.
B. Objects created after you add a replication configuration.
C. Unencrypted objects and Objects encrypted at rest under Amazon S3 managed keys (SSE-S3) or customer master keys (CMKs) stored in AWS Key Management Service (SSE-KMS).
D. Only objects in the source bucket for which the bucket owner has permissions to read objects and access control lists (ACLs).
E. Objects created with server-side encryption using customer-provided (SSE-C) encryption keys.

Q144. Suppose that you configure replication where bucket A is the source and bucket B is the destination. Now suppose that you add another replication configuration where bucket B is the source and bucket C is the destination. Which of the following is correct?
A. After you configure B as the source bucket, object replication from A to B will stop.
B. You cannot configure an existing 'destination' bucket as 'source' bucket.
C. Objects in bucket B that are replicas of objects in bucket A are replicated to bucket C.
D. Objects in bucket B that are replicas of objects in bucket A are not replicated to bucket C.

Q145. Suppose that you configure replication where bucket A is the source and bucket B is the destination. Which of the following statement is correct when in bucket A you specify an object version ID in a DELETE request?
A. Amazon S3 adds a delete marker in bucket A. It does replicate the delete marker in the destination bucket B.
B. Amazon S3 deletes that object version in the bucket A. But it doesn't replicate the deletion in the destination bucket B.
C. Amazon S3 deletes that object version in the bucket A and replicates the deletion in the destination bucket B.
D. Amazon S3 adds a delete marker in bucket A. But it doesn't replicate the delete marker in the destination bucket B.

Q146. Which Amazon service has following features:
- Fully managed elastic NFS file system for use with AWS Cloud services and on-premises resources

- Built to scale on demand to petabytes without disrupting applications, growing and shrinking automatically as you add and remove files, eliminating the need to provision and manage capacity to accommodate growth.
- Designed to provide massively parallel shared access to thousands of Amazon EC2 instances, enabling your applications to achieve high levels of aggregate throughput and IOPS with consistent low latencies.

A. Amazon S3
B. Amazon RDS
C. Amazon EFS
D. Amazon EBS

Q147. Your company is planning to use WordPress hosted on AWS for corporate website. You are planning to run your WordPress site using an auto scaling group of Amazon EC2 instances and database layer on Amazon RDS Aurora. Which Amazon service you should use to store shared, unstructured WordPress data like php files, config themes, plugin etc. This storage service should be accessible by multiple WordPress EC2 instances.

A. Amazon S3
B. Amazon RDS
C. Amazon EFS
D. Amazon EBS

Q148. You can mount your Amazon EFS file systems on your on-premises servers, and move file data to and from Amazon EFS using standard Linux tools and scripts or AWS DataSync. Which use cases can you do by enabling access to EFS file systems from on-premises servers with ability to move file data to and from Amazon EFS file?

A. You can migrate data from on-premises datacenters to permanently reside in Amazon EFS file systems.
B. You can support cloud bursting workloads to offload your application processing to the cloud. You can move data from your on-premises servers into your EFS file systems, analyze it on a cluster of EC2 instances in your Amazon VPC, and store the results permanently in your EFS file systems or move the results back to your on-premises servers.
C. You can periodically copy your on-premises file data to EFS to support backup and disaster recovery scenarios.
D. All of the above

Q149. You are the solution architect for a media company which is planning to migrate on-premise applications to AWS. You are analyzing the workflows like video editing, studio production, broadcast processing, sound design, and rendering which uses an existing shared storage to process large files. Which Amazon service you will use that provides a:

- strong data consistency model with high throughput
- scale on demand to petabytes without disrupting applications

- growing and shrinking automatically as you add and remove files
- shared file access which can cut the time it takes to perform these jobs
- ability to consolidate multiple local file repositories into a single location accessible by application deployed on multiple EC2 instances
  A.  Amazon EFS
  B.  Amazon EBS
  C.  Amazon S3
  D.  Amazon RDS

Q150. Which AWS service provides detailed records for the requests that are made to a bucket in form of  requester, bucket name, request time, request action, response status, and an error code, if relevant.?
  A.  Cloud trail
  B.  VPC Flow Logs
  C.  Cloudwatch
  D.  Server Access Logging

Q151. You have created a bucket to store photos which you took during your wildlife safari in Africa. By default, Block Public Access settings is set to True on this bucket. Some of the photos captures the natural landscape beauty which you want to make it publicly readable. Other photos you don't want to make publicly readable as they are personal. You have tagged the photos which you want to make publicly readable. How can you change the permissions to do that? Choose 3.
  A.  Create an IAM role and attach it to the bucket.
  B.  Remove Block Public Access settings on the bucket.
  C.  Use a bucket policy that grants public read access to a specific object tag.
  D.  Update the object's access control list (ACL) for photo objects which you want to make accessible.

Q152. Your company is planning to migrate their on-premise archive storage of 5 TB to AWS. You have a 1000 Mbs connection that you can solely dedicate to transferring your data to S3.What will be most economical choice to transfer data to S3?
  A.  Snowball
  B.  Snowball Edge
  C.  Internet
  D.  None of the above

Q153. What are the different storage models available for Snowball and Snowball Edge? Choose 2.
  A.  Snowball : 80 TB and 50 TB models
  B.  Snowball edge: 80 TB and 50 TB models
  C.  Snowball: 100 TB

D.   Snowball edge : 100 TB

Q154. You have 80 TB of on premise data which you want to upload to S3. You have a 100 Mbs connection that you can solely dedicate to transferring your data. Which of the following is best cost optimized way to import data to S3 as soon as possible?
A.   Use one Snowball 80 TB device
B.   Use two Snowball 50 TB device
C.   Use one Snowball Edge 100 TB storage optimized device
D.   Through 100mbs internet connection

Q155.You are using Amazon File Storage Gateway with your intranet client application. You know that files are stored as objects in your S3 buckets and you can configure the initial storage class for objects that file gateway creates. There is a one-to-one relationship between files and objects, and you can configure the initial storage class for objects that file gateway creates.
You have created a file gateway with hostname *file.amazon.com* and have mapped it with S3 bucket *my-bucket*. The mount point exposed by File Gateway is *file.amazon.com:/export/my-bucket*. You have mounted this locally on */mnt/my-bucket* and created a file named *file.html* in a directory */mnt/my-bucket/dir*. How this file be stored in the S3 bucket?
A.   This file will be stored as a file in the S3 bucket *my-bucket* with a key of *dir/file.html*.
B.   This file will be stored as an object in the S3 bucket *my-bucket* with a key of *dir/file.html*.
C.   This file will be stored as a file in the S3 bucket *my-bucket* with a key of *file.html*.
D.   This file will be stored as an object in the S3 bucket *my-bucket* with a key of *file.html*.

Q156. What you must do to enable S3 server access logging? Choose 2.
A.   Grant the Amazon S3 Log Delivery group write permission on the source bucket for which you want Amazon S3 to deliver access logs.
B.   Turn on the log delivery by adding logging configuration on the source bucket for which you want Amazon S3 to deliver access logs.
C.   Grant the Amazon S3 Log Delivery group write permission on the target bucket where you want the access logs saved.
D.   Turn on the log delivery by adding logging configuration on the target bucket where you want the access logs saved.

Q157. How are Amazon S3 and Amazon S3 Glacier designed to achieve 99.999999999% durability? Choose 2.
A.   Amazon S3 Standard, S3 Standard-IA, and S3 Glacier storage classes redundantly store your objects on multiple devices across a minimum of three Availability Zones (AZs)
B.   S3 One Zone-IA storage class stores data redundantly across multiple devices within a single AZ.

C. Amazon S3 Standard, S3 Standard-IA, and S3 Glacier storage classes redundantly store your objects on multiple devices across a minimum of two Availability Zones (AZs)

D. Amazon S3 Standard, S3 Standard-IA, and S3 Glacier storage classes redundantly store your objects on multiple devices across a minimum of six Availability Zones (AZs)

Q158. You are the solution architect for a company that provides online stock trading website. To comply with financial regulation you have to store the trading data for five years. You are evaluating different S3 storage options for archive storage. Your evaluation criteria are:
-   Optimized cost
-   Retrieval time in 1-5 minutes
-   Reliable and predictable access to a subset of your data in minutes.
    Which of the following statement is correct? Choose 2.
A. Store the data in Deep Archive and use Expedited retrieval option
B. Purchase provisioned retrieval capacity if your workload requires highly reliable and predictable access to a subset of your data in minutes
C. Store the data in Glacier and use Standard retrieval option
D. Store the data in Glacier and use Expedited retrieval option

Q159. IOPS are a unit of measure representing input/output operations per second measured in KiB. What is the maximum amount of data that an Amazon EBS volume type counts as a single I/O? Choose 2.
A. I/O size is capped at 256 KiB for HDD volumes
B. I/O size is capped at 1,024 KiB for HDD volumes
C. I/O size is capped at 256 KiB for SSD volumes
D. I/O size is capped at 1,024 KiB for SSD volumes

Q160. For an Amazon EBS SSD volumes, a single 1,024 KiB I/O operation will be counted as how many operation/s?
A. 1 operation
B. 16 operations
C. 32 operations
D. 4 operations

Q161. You are using a General Purpose SSD (gp2) EBS volume of size 1000 GiB You know that with this volume size you will have burst credits available to an IOPS limit of 3,000 and a volume throughput limit of 250 MiB/s. Which of the following will be appropriate I/O size?
A. 256 KiB
B. 1024 KiB
C. 16KiB
D. 128KiB

Q162. You are using a Provisioned IOPS SSD (io1) EBS Volume of size 100 GiB. What is the maximum IOPS you can provision for this volume?
  A.  100
  B.  300
  C.  3000
  D.  5000

Q163. Which of the following is correct for credits and burst performance feature of Throughput Optimized HDD (st1) EBS Volumes? Choose 2.
  A.  St1 provides Throughput Credits and Burst Performance.
  B.  For a 1-TiB st1 volume, burst throughput is limited to 250 MiB/s, the bucket fills with throughput credits at 40 MiB/s, and it can hold up to 1 TiB-worth of credits.
  C.  St1 provides I/O Credits and Burst Performance.
  D.  For a 1-TiB st1 volume, burst I/O is limited to 3000, the credit bucket is not applicable.

Q164. For greater I/O performance you are using RAID 0 configuration for EBS volumes attached to your EC2 instances with two 500 GiB Amazon EBS io1 volumes with 4,000 provisioned IOPS each. Your company's backup and disaster recovery strategy mandates taking regular snapshots of EBS volumes. Which of the following statements is correct for creating snapshots of Amazon Elastic Block Store (Amazon EBS) volumes that are configured in a RAID array?
  A.  You cannot create snapshots for Amazon EBS volumes that are configured in a RAID array.
  B.  To create snapshots for Amazon EBS volumes that are configured in a RAID array, use the multi-volume snapshot feature of your instance.
  C.  Follow a mutli-step process: pause I/O or stop the instance to temporarily disable write access, create snapshots for each of your volumes, and then resume I/O.
  D.  You can create snapshots for each of your volumes individually, AWS will ensure that they are in sync with relative to each other.

Q165. You are a solution architect for a global steel manufacturing company having plants across the globe. Recently an analytical and reporting application was launched in us-west region which involves each manufacturing plant uploading their weekly production data across the globe to a S3 bucket in us-west-1 region. The size of weekly production data file ranges from gigabytes to petabytes. After the first week of release feedback came from plants in countries other than US that they are experiencing slow upload times. How can you make the process of uploading the files to S3 faster?
  A.  Use S3 multipart upload.
  B.  Change you design to first upload the data in region closest to the plan , then replicate it to us-west-1 central bucket using cross-region replication.

C. Use S3 Transfer Acceleration.

D. Use Amazon Cloudfront.

Q166. You are evaluating which type of EBS volume to use for large, sequential cold-data workloads. This volume type should be optimized for workloads involving large, sequential I/O. Which is the appropriate choice if you require infrequent access to your data and are looking to save costs?

A. Cold HDD (sc1) Volumes

B. Throughput Optimized HDD (st1) Volumes

C. Provisioned IOPS SSD (io1)

D. General Purpose SSD (gp2)

Q167. You are evaluating which type of EBS volume to use for large, sequential workloads. This volume type should be optimized for workloads involving large, sequential I/O. Which is the appropriate choice if you require frequent access to your data and are looking to save costs?

A. Cold HDD (sc1) Volumes

B. Throughput Optimized HDD (st1) Volumes

C. Provisioned IOPS SSD (io1)

D. General Purpose SSD (gp2

Q168. You have are designing a web application on AWS and contemplating which type of EBS volume to use for your OLTP database.The volume should be optimized for transactional workloads involving frequent read/write operations with small I/O size, where the dominant performance attribute is IOPS. Your analysis shows that the volume should support Max IOPS of nearly 50,000. Which EBS volume will meet the design criteria?

A. Cold HDD (sc1) Volumes

B. Throughput Optimized HDD (st1) Volumes

C. Provisioned IOPS SSD (io1)

D. General Purpose SSD (gp2

Q169. You are designing an internal application in which you are using S3 to store documents to be uploaded by the employees. You don't want to create separate IAM user for each employee to manage access. How can you ensure that employees have only 'upload' access to the bucket?

A. You will have to create IAM user for each employee and attach only 'upload' permission for the user to that bucket.

B. Create a persigned url to upload an object to the bucket and share it with employees.

C. Make the bucket public and as soon as employees have uploaded the document change it to be private.

D. You will have to create IAM role for each employee and attach only 'upload' permission for the user to that bucket.

Q170. Which of the following statement is not correct about S3 storage classes? Choose 2.
   A.   Standard – Designed for frequently accessed data.
   B.   Standard-IA – Designed for long-lived, infrequently accessed data.
   C.   One Zone-IA – Designed for long-lived, infrequently accessed, non-critical data.
   D.   Glacier – Designed for long-lived, infrequent accessed, archived critical data.
   E.   Standard – Designed for long-lived, infrequently accessed data.
   F.   Glacier Deep Archive - Lowest cost storage class designed for long-term retention of data that will be retained for 7-10 years and Retrieval time within 12 hours
   G.   One Zone-IA – Designed for long-lived, infrequently accessed, critical data.

Q171. Your company is planning to use S3 for storing daily transaction records. You know that transaction records will be accessed very infrequently after one year. You want to move the transaction record files to lower cost infrequent access storage if it has not been accessed for 30 days. But you cannot configure the lifecycle from the day of the creation to one year as there is no defined access patterns and it is unpredictable. What should you do to optimize your cost?
   A.   Use Intelligent-Tiering storage class for your transaction record objects.
   B.   Use Standard storage class for your transaction record objects and create a lifecycle policy to movie it to Standard-IA after 30 days.
   C.   Use Standard storage class for your transaction record objects and write a custom program which moves objects to Standard-IA if not accessed in last 30 days.
   D.   Use Standard storage class for your transaction record objects and create a lifecycle policy to movie it to OneZone-IA after 30 days.

Q172. Which of the following is not a feature of S3 Glacier storage class?
   A.   Data is stored in Amazon S3 Glacier in "archives."
   B.   A single archive can be as large as 40 terabytes. You can store an unlimited number of archives and an unlimited amount of data in Amazon S3 Glacier.
   C.   Data stored in Amazon S3 Glacier is mutable, meaning that after an archive is created it can be updated.
   D.   Amazon S3 Glacier uses "vaults" as containers to store archives. You can also set access policies for each vault to grant or deny specific activities to users.
   E.   You can specify controls such as "Write Once Read Many" (WORM) in a Vault Lock policy and lock the policy from future edits.
   F.   Data stored in Amazon S3 Glacier is immutable, meaning that after an archive is created it cannot be updated.

Q173. Your company employees' uses Linux based desktop. The company has a local network folder having more than 10 TB of word and excel files. Any newly created file is infrequently accessed after 30 days. As the company has adopted AWS as part of their IT strategy. Which

AWS services should they use so that files are accessible from on premise and also leverage low cost storage for infrequently access data?

A. Use File Gateway after migrating files to Amazon S3, File gateway supports Amazon S3 Standard, S3 Standard - Infrequent Access (S3 Standard - IA) and S3 One Zone – IA, access files using Network File System (NFS)

B. Use EFS which supports the Network File System. Migrate documents to EFS. Amazon EFS offers two storage classes, Standard and Infrequent Access. Create and Mount a File System On-Premises with AWS Direct Connect and VPN

C. Migrate documents to S3 and make use of Standard and Infrequent Access storage class.

D. Use Volume Gateway after migrating files to Amazon S3, Volume gateway supports Amazon S3 Standard, S3 Standard - Infrequent Access (S3 Standard - IA) and S3 One Zone – IA, access files using Network File System (NFS)

Q174. What is the smallest file size that can be stored in S3?
A. 0 bytes
B. 1 bytes
C. 1 KB
D. 100 KB

Q175. What HTTP response code you will receive after successful upload of an object to S3 bucket?
A. HTTP 100
B. HTTP 200
C. HTTP 300
D. HTTP 400

Q176. For which operation S3 offers eventual consistency model? Choose 2.
A. Overwrite PUTs of existing object
B. PUTs of new object
C. GET
D. DELETEs

Q177. For which operation S3 offers read after write consistency model?
A. Overwrite PUTs of existing object
B. PUTs of new object
C. GET
D. DELETEs

Q178. To add another layer of security you have enabled MFA (multi-factor authentication) Delete for a bucket. Which operation will require additional authentication? Choose 2.
A. To Create a new object

B.  To Update object ACL
C.  To Change the versioning state of your bucket
D.  To Permanently delete an object version

Q179. Which of the following can be used to store files? Choose 3.
A.  S3
B.  EBS
C.  EMR
D.  EFS
E.  RDS MySQL

Q180. How can you securely upload/download your data to Amazon S3?
A.  SSL endpoints using the HTTP protocol
B.  SSL endpoints using the HTTPS protocol
C.  VPC  endpoints using the HTTP protocol
D.  VPC endpoints using the HTTPS protocol

Q181. How can you troubleshoot slow downloads from or uploads to Amazon Simple Storage Service (Amazon S3)? When you download from or upload to Amazon S3 from a specific network or machine, your requests might get higher latency. How can you diagnose the high latency? Choose 3.
A.  Test the impact of geographical distance between the client and the S3 bucket.
B.  There might be latency introduced in your application or how your host that's making the requests is handling the requests sent and responses received.
C.  Check the storage class for the object.
D.  Supported request rate per prefix may be exceeded.

Q182. Your company is adopting AWS cloud platform for all new application development as well as migrating current on-premise application. One of the strategy is to leverage S3 for storage. What are the performance design patterns you should follow? Choose 4.
A.  Using Caching for Frequently Accessed Content with Amazon CloudFront, Amazon ElastiCache, or Amazon S3 Transfer Acceleration
B.  Using Caching for Frequently Accessed Content with Amazon CloudFront, Amazon ElastiCache, or AWS Elemental MediaStore
C.  Timeouts and Retries for Latency-Sensitive Applications
D.  Horizontal Scaling and Request Parallelization for High Throughput
E.  Using Amazon S3 Transfer Acceleration to Accelerate Geographically Disparate Data Transfers
F.  Using Amazon CloudFront to Accelerate Geographically Disparate Data Transfers

Q183. Which of the following is not a performance guideline for S3?

A.  Combine Amazon S3 (Storage) and Amazon EC2 (Compute) in the Same AWS Region
B.  Use Amazon S3 Transfer Acceleration to Minimize Latency Caused by Distance
C.  Randomizing prefix naming with hashed characters to optimize performance for frequent data retrievals
D.  Using the Range HTTP header in a GET Object request, fetch a byte-range from an object, transferring only the specified portion.

Q 184. Which of the following is not a way to improve the transfer speeds for copying data between S3 bucket and EC2 instance? Choose 2.
A.  Use enhanced networking on the EC2 instance.
B.  Use parallel workloads for the data transfer.
C.  EC2 and S3 bucket should be in different region.
D.  Use an Amazon Virtual Private Cloud (Amazon VPC) endpoint for Amazon S3.
E.  Use S3 Transfer Acceleration between geographically distant AWS Regions.
F.  Use EC2 in cluster placement group.
G.  Upgrade your EC2 instance type.
H.  Use chunked transfers.

Q185. What are the features of S3 Batch operations? Choose 3.
A.  To perform large-scale batch operations on Amazon S3 objects and can execute a single operation on lists of Amazon S3 objects that you specify.
B.  Can be used to copy objects and set object tags or access control lists (ACLs).
C.  You can also initiate object restores from Amazon S3 Glacier or invoke an AWS Lambda function to perform custom actions using your objects.
D.  To perform ETL jobs on data stored in S3.

Q186. You can't access a certain prefix or object that's in your Amazon Simple Storage Service (Amazon S3) bucket but can access the rest of the data in the bucket. What should you verify as the reason? Choose 4.
A.  Security Group and NACL setting
B.  Ownership of the prefix or object
C.  Restrictions in the bucket policy
D.  Restrictions in your AWS Identity and Access Management (IAM) user policy
E.  Permissions to object encrypted by AWS Key Management Service (AWS KMS)

Q187. You want to enable default encryption using AWS Key Management Service (AWS KMS) on your Amazon Simple Storage Service (Amazon S3) bucket. You already have objects stored in the bucket. If you enable default encryption, what happens to the encryption of existing objects? Choose 2.
A.  Enabling default encryption doesn't change the encryption of objects that are already in the bucket, the encryption that you set applies only to future uploads.

B.   Enabling default encryption will change the encryption of existing objects as well as future uploads.

C.   Any objects already encrypted using Amazon S3-managed keys (SSE-S3) they are re-encrypted with KMS.

D.   Any unencrypted objects already in the bucket remain unencrypted or any objects already encrypted using Amazon S3-managed keys (SSE-S3) remain encrypted with SSE-S3.

Q188. What are the key differences between the Amazon REST API endpoint and the website endpoint? Choose 3.

A.   REST API Endpoint Supports both public and private content, Website Endpoint Supports only publicly readable content.

B.   REST API Endpoint Supports only publicly readable content, Website Endpoint Supports both public and private content.

C.   REST API Endpoint Supports SSL connections. Website Endpoint Does not support SSL connections.

D.   REST API Endpoint does not Support SSL connections. Website Endpoint support SSL connections

E.   REST API Endpoint Supports all bucket and object operations, Website Endpoint Supports only GET and HEAD requests on objects.

Q189. What are differences between EFS and EBS? Choose 3.

A.   EFS: Data is stored redundantly across multiple AZs. EBS: Data is stored redundantly in a single AZ.

B.   EBS: Data is stored redundantly across multiple AZs. EFS: Data is stored redundantly in a single AZ.

C.   EBS: Up to thousands of Amazon EC2 instances, from multiple AZs, can connect concurrently to an EBS volume. EFS: A single Amazon EC2 instance in a single AZ can connect to a file system.

D.   EFS Use cases: Big data and analytics, media processing workflows, content management, web serving, and home directories. EBS use cases: Boot volumes, transactional and NoSQL databases, data warehousing, and ETL.

E.   EFS: Up to thousands of Amazon EC2 instances, from multiple AZs, can connect concurrently to a file system. EBS: A single Amazon EC2 instance in a single AZ can connect to an EBS volume.

Q190. Which EFS performance mode you will choose for latency-sensitive use cases, like web serving environments, content management systems, home directories, and general file serving?

A.   Default Performance Mode

B.   Max IOPS performance Mode

C.   General Purpose Performance Mode

D.   Max I/O Performance Mode

Q191. Which EFS performance mode you will choose highly parallelized applications and workloads, such as big data analysis, media processing, and genomics analysis?
A.   Default Performance Mode
B.   Max IOPS performance Mode
C.   General Purpose Performance Mode
D.   Max I/O Performance Mode

Q192. What are the two throughput modes to choose for your EFS?
A.   IOPS Mode
B.   Bursting Mode
C.   Provisioned Mode
D.   I/O Mode

Q193. Which of the following statements are true? Choose 2.
A.   You can't use Amazon EFS with Microsoft Windows–based Amazon EC2 instances.
B.   You can't use Amazon EFS with Linux–based Amazon EC2 instances.
C.   You can use Amazon EFS with Microsoft Windows–based Amazon EC2 instances.
D.   You can use Amazon EFS with Linux–based Amazon EC2 instances.

Q194. You are migrating your on premise Windows-based custom build .Net applications to AWS cloud platform using Lift-and-Shift strategy. These applications require shared file storage provided by Windows-based file systems (NTFS) and that uses the SMB protocol. Which AWS services you will use? Choose 2.
A.   Lambda
B.   EFS
C.   EBS
D.   EC2
E.   FSx for Windows File Server

Q195. Which of the following are correct statements as when should you use Amazon FSx Windows File Servers vs. Amazon EFS vs. Amazon FSx for Lustre? Choose 3.
A.   For Windows-based applications, Amazon FSx provides fully managed Windows file servers with features and performance optimized for "lift-and-shift" business-critical application workloads including home directories (user shares), media workflows, and ERP applications via SMB protocol.
B.   If you have Linux-based applications, Amazon EFS is a cloud-native fully managed file system that provides simple, scalable, elastic file storage accessible from Linux instances via the NFS protocol.
C.   For compute-intensive and fast processing workloads, like high performance computing (HPC), machine learning, EDA, and media processing, Amazon FSx for

Lustre, provides a file system that's optimized for performance, with input and output stored on Amazon S3.

D. If you have Windows-based applications, Amazon EFS is a cloud-native fully managed file system that provides simple, scalable, elastic file storage accessible from EC2 windows instances via the NFS protocol

Q196: What instance types and OS versions can connect to FSx on windows server? Choose 3.
A. IBM I, MacOS, OS 400
B. Amazon EC2, VMware Cloud on AWS,
C. Amazon WorkSpaces, and Amazon AppStream 2.0 instances
D. Windows Server 2008 and Windows 7, and current versions of Linux

Q197. You are designing a business critical custom .Net application running on Windows server EC2 instance which access a files system created by Amazon FSx for windows server. You are provisioning EC2 instances in an auto-scale group across Multi AZs for availability and fault tolerance. How can you ensure high availability and durability of FSx file systems? Choose 3.
A. Amazon FSx automatically replicates your data within an Availability Zone (AZ) to protect it from component failure, continuously monitors for hardware failures, and automatically replaces infrastructure components in the event of a failure.
B. Create a Read Replica file system, which provides performance and redundancy across multiple AZs.
C. Create a Multi-AZ file system, which provides redundancy across multiple AZs.
D. Amazon FSx also takes highly durable backups (stored in S3) of your file system daily using Windows's Volume Shadow Copy Service, and allows you to take additional backups at any point.

Q198. Which of the following is not a feature of FSx for windows server Multi-AZ files systems?
A. Automatically replicates your data within an Availability Zone (AZ) to protect it from component failure, continuously monitors for hardware failures, and automatically replaces infrastructure components in the event of a failure.
B. Automatically provisions and maintains a standby file server in a different Availability Zone.
C. Any changes written to disk in your file system are synchronously replicated across AZs to the standby.
D. In the event of planned file system maintenance or unplanned service disruption, Amazon FSx automatically fails over to the secondary file server
E. Any changes written to disk in your file system are asynchronously replicated across AZs to the standby.

Q199. What events would cause a Multi-AZ Amazon FSx file system to initiate a failover to the standby file server? Choose 3.
A. File Server EC2 instance client goes down.
B. An Availability Zone outage occurs.
C. The preferred file server becomes unavailable.
D. The preferred file server undergoes planned maintenance.

Q200. You have connected windows client and Linux client to a Multi-AZ Amazon FSx file system. What will happen if the preferred file server becomes unavailable? Choose 3.
A. For windows client there will be automatic failover without manual intervention from the preferred file server to the standby file server.
B. Linux clients do not support automatic DNS-based failover. Therefore, they don't automatically connect to the standby file server during a failover.
C. For Linux client there will be automatic failover without manual intervention from the preferred file server to the standby file server.
D. For windows client after the resources in the preferred subnet are available, Amazon FSx automatically fails back to the preferred file server in the preferred subnet.

Q201. What are the two options for using your Amazon FSx for Windows File Server file system with Active Directory?
A. Using Amazon FSx with AWS AD Connector
B. Using Amazon FSx with AWS Directory Service for Microsoft Active Directory
C. Using Amazon FSx with Your Self-Managed Microsoft Active Directory.
D. Using Amazon FSx with AWS Simple AD

Q202. How can you optimize total cost of ownership of FSx for windows server?
A. Turning on data deduplication
B. Turning on data compression
C. Turning on data intelligent tie
D. Turing on FSx Analysis

Q203. How much data can you store in one file system of Amazon FSx for Windows File Server?
A. 10 TB
B. 16 TB
C. 32 TB
D. 64 TB

Q204. In your company multiple departments have created their own file share using Amazon FSx for window server. There are separate file shares for marketing, finance, sales, supply chain and HR. How can you unify access to your file shares across multiple file systems and also improve performance?

A. Delete and merge all separate file systems in single file system.
B. Use DFS Namespaces to group file shares on multiple file systems into one common folder structure (a namespace)
C. Use Multi-AZ deployment in all the file systems.
D. Use Read Replicas in all the files systems.

Q205. What are the benefits of using AWS DataSync? Choose 2.
A. Your data can be used on-premises and stored durably in AWS Cloud storage services, including Amazon S3, Amazon S3 Glacier, Amazon S3 Glacier Deep Archive, and Amazon EBS.
B. Easy for you to move data over the network between on-premises storage and AWS.
C. Transfer data rapidly over the network into AWS, up to 10 times faster than is common with open-source tooling.
D. A single device can transport multiple terabytes of data and multiple devices can be used in parallel to transfer petabytes of data into or out of an Amazon S3 bucket

Q206. What are the main use cases for AWS DataSync? Choose 3.
A. Data migration – Move active datasets rapidly over the network into Amazon S3, Amazon EFS, or Amazon FSx for Windows File Server.
B. Data movement for timely in-cloud processing – Move data into or out of AWS for processing when working with systems that generate data on-premises.
C. Data archiving – Move cold data from expensive on-premises storage systems directly to durable and secure long-term storage such as Amazon S3 Glacier or S3 Glacier Deep Archive.
D. Hybrid cloud workloads: manage hybrid file and object workloads that run across both your organization and the AWS Cloud.

Q207. You are planning a strategy to migrate over 600 terabytes (TB) of data from on-premises storage system to Amazon S3 and Amazon EFS. You don't want to use other AWS offline data transfer services. You need to move data from their on-premises storage to AWS via Direct Connect or VPN, without traversing the public internet, to further increase the security of the copied data. Which AWS service you will use?
A. AWS Snowball
B. AWS Snowball Edge
C. AWS Snowmobile
D. AWS DataSync
E. AWS AppSync

Q208. You are planning to use AWS DataSync to migrate on-premise data to S3 storage in cloud. How can you ensure data transferred between your AWS DataSync agent deployed on-premises or in-cloud, doesn't traverse the public internet? Choose 2.

A. Utilize public service endpoints in their respective AWS Regions (such as datasync.us-east-1.amazonaws.com)
B. Use VPC Internet Gateway
C. Use VPC Endpoints
D. From on-premise have Direct Connect or VPN to your VPC

Q209.When do you use AWS DataSync and when do you use AWS Snowball Edge? Choose 2.
A. AWS DataSync is ideal for online data transfers.
B. AWS Snowball Edge is suitable for offline data transfers
C. AWS Snowball Edge is ideal for online data transfers.
D. AWS DataSync is suitable for offline data transfers

Q210. In which of the following scenario you should not use DataSync?
A. If you want to transfer data from existing storage systems (e.g. Network Attached Storage), If you want to transfer data from instruments that cannot be changed (e.g. DNA sequencers, video cameras)
B. If your applications are already integrated with the Amazon S3 API, and you want higher throughput for transferring large files to S3.
C. If you want to automate moving data to multiple destinations with built-in retry and network resiliency mechanisms, data integrity verification

Q211. For an Amazon EBS HDD volumes, a single 1,024 KiB I/O operation will be counted as how many operation/s?
A. 1 operation
B. 16 operations
C. 32 operations
D. 4 operations

Q212. What are the features of Amazon FSx for Lustre? Choose 3
A. Integrates with Amazon RDS, making it easy to process data sets with the Lustre file system.
B. As a fully managed service, Amazon FSx for Lustre enables you to launch and run the world's most popular high-performance file system. Lustre file systems for any workload where storage speed matters.
C. Integrates with Amazon S3, making it easy to process data sets with the Lustre file system.
D. It is POSIX-compliant, so you can use your current Linux-based applications without having to make any changes.
E. It is POSIX-compliant, so you can use your current Windows-based applications without having to make any changes.

Q213. What are the suitable use cases for using Amazon FSx for Lustre? Choose 5.

A. Media processing and transcoding
B. Machine learning
C. Click stream analysis
D. ETL Jobs
E. High performance computing
F. Autonomous Vehicles
G. Electronic Design Automation (EDA)

Q214. When should you use EFS vs FSx for Windows vs FSx for Lustre? Choose 3.

A. Use EFS, for Windows Applications and Windows instances when you need simple, scalable, fully managed elastic NFS file.

B. Use FSx for Windows File Server, for Linux based application when you need centralized storage having native support for POSIX file system features and support for network access through industry-standard Server Message Block (SMB) protocol.

C. Use EFS, for Linux Applications and Linux instances when you need simple, scalable, fully managed elastic NFS file.

D. Use FSx for Windows File Server, for Windows based application when you need centralized storage having native support for Windows file system features and support for network access through industry-standard Server Message Block (SMB) protocol.

E. Use FSx for Lustre, when you need to launch and run the popular, high-performance Lustre file system for workloads where speed matters, such as machine learning, high performance computing (HPC), video processing, and financial modeling.

# Chapter 4: Databases: Amazon RDS, Amazon Aurora, Amazon DynamoDB, Amazon ElastiCache, Amazon DocumentDB

Q1. How can you increase the high availability of Amazon RDS?
  A.   Create periodic snapshot of main DB Instance in another AZ
  B.   Use RDS Multi-AZ deployment
  C.   Use RDS Read Replicas
  D.   Create two similar DB instances in separate AZ and do periodic synchronization

Q2. How Amazon RDS provides high availability? Choose 2.
  A.   Amazon RDS provides high availability through Multi-AZ deployment
  B.   Amazon RDS provides high availability through Read Replicas
  C.   In a Multi-AZ deployment automatically provisions and maintains a synchronous standby replica in a different Availability Zone.
  D.   In a Multi-AZ deployment automatically provisions and maintains an asynchronous standby read replica in a different Availability Zone.

Q3. Which database engines are supported by Amazon RDS?
  A.   MySQL, MariaDB, PostgreSQL, Oracle, Microsoft SQL Server
  B.   MySQL, MariaDB, PostgreSQL, Oracle, Microsoft SQL Server, Amazon Aurora
  C.   MySQL, PostgreSQL, Oracle, Microsoft SQL Server, Amazon Aurora
  D.   MySQL, MariaDB, Oracle, Microsoft SQL Server, Amazon Aurora

Q4. Which AWS database service will you choose for Online Transaction Processing (OLTP)?
  A.   Amazon RDS
  B.   Amazon Redshift
  C.   Amazon Glacier
  D.   Amazon DynamoDB

Q5.What are three types of instance classes supported by Amazon RDS?
  A.   Standard
  B.   Memory Optimized
  C.   Burstable Performance
  D.   Performance Optimized

Q6. Which automated monitoring tools you can use to watch Amazon RDS and report when something is wrong? Choose 4.
  A.   Amazon RDS Events
  B.   Database log files
  C.   Amazon Inspector
  D.   Amazon RDS Enhanced Monitoring
  E.   Amazon CloudWatch

Q7. What does Amazon RDS manages on user's behalf? Choose 2.
  A.   Provisioning the infrastructure capacity requested to installing the database software.

B.  Once database is up and running, Amazon RDS automates common administrative tasks such as performing backups and patching the software that powers your database

C.  Managing the database settings that are specific to your application.

D.  Automatic performance tuning to optimize your database for your application's workflow.

Q8. What are the steps taken by RDS when you modify DB instance in a Single-AZ deployment to be a Multi-AZ deployment (for engines other than SQL Server or Amazon Aurora)? Choose 2.

A.  Step 1. Amazon RDS takes a snapshot of the primary DB instance from your deployment and then restores the snapshot into another Availability Zone.

B.  Step 1. Amazon RDS creates a fresh DB instance with similar configuration as primary DB instance and then copies data from primary to secondary.

C.  Step2. Amazon RDS then sets up asynchronous replication between your primary DB instance and the new instance.

D.  Step2. Amazon RDS then sets up synchronous replication between your primary DB instance and the new instance.

Q9. What are the possible scenarios in case of RDS Multi-AZ deployment when primary DB instance switches over automatically to the standby replica? Choose 3.

A.  An Availability Zone outage or when the primary DB instance fails.

B.  The DB instance's server type is changed or the operating system of the DB instance is undergoing software patching.

C.  A manual failover of the DB instance was initiated using Reboot with failover or when an Availability Zone outage or when the primary DB instance fails.

D.  When server performance is deteriorating.

Q10. You are an IT administrator of a company which has a SaaS product developed using AWS platform. You have enabled multi-AZ deployment for the product RDS database. Few days after the release you get an alert from DB event notification on your mobile phone that your primary Amazon RDS instance has failed. What should you do ensure that your production environment is available to users by ensuring a fast seamless failover to secondary instance?

A.  Update the DB connection string used by application server to secondary database instance.

B.  Create a new primary instance by making a copy from the secondary instance.

C.  No need to do anything, Amazon RDS handles failovers automatically so you can resume database operations as quickly as possible without administrative intervention.

D.  Update the DNS record of the DB instance to point to the standby DB instance.

Q11. Which database engines supported by Amazon RDS have multi-AZ?
- A.   MySQL, MariaDB, PostgreSQL, Oracle, Microsoft SQL Server
- B.   MySQL, MariaDB, PostgreSQL, Oracle, Microsoft SQL Server, Amazon Aurora
- C.   MySQL, PostgreSQL, Oracle, Microsoft SQL Server, Amazon Aurora
- D.   MySQL, MariaDB, Oracle, Microsoft SQL Server, Amazon Aurora

Q12. You are an IT administrator of a company which has a SaaS product developed using AWS platform. You have enabled multi-AZ deployment for the product RDS database. You know that AWS automatically failovers to secondary instance when primary instance fails. Before going to production you want to simulate and test this failover. What is the simplest way to test?
- A.   You have to wait for the new software patch to download for the DB instance.
- B.   Initiate the snapshot creation of primary instance which will make AWS switch to secondary.
- C.   Reboot the primary instance.
- D.   Delete the primary instance.

Q13. What are the features provided by Amazon RDS Multi-AZ deployments? Choose 2.
- A.   Enhanced availability
- B.   Enhanced Durability
- C.   Enhanced performance
- D.   Network latency reduction

Q14.  What is the differences between Single-AZ and Multi-AZ deployment during backup activity? Choose 3.
- A.   In Single-AZ deployments, I/O activity is suspended on your primary during backup.
- B.   In Multi-AZ deployments, I/O activity is not suspended on your primary during backup, because the backup is taken from the standby.
- C.   In Multi-AZ deployments, I/O activity is suspended on your primary during backup.
- D.   There will be elevated latencies for a few minutes during backups for Multi-AZ deployments.

Q15. How is instance failure handled in Amazon Aurora deployment? Choose 2.
- A.   Amazon Aurora uses RDS Multi-AZ technology to automate failover to one of up to 15 Amazon Aurora Replicas created in any of three Availability Zones.
- B.   Amazon Aurora Multi-AZ deployment feature has to be enabled specifically to automate failover to one of up to 15 Amazon Aurora Replicas created in any of three Availability Zones.
- C.   If no Amazon Aurora Replicas have been provisioned, in the case of a failure, you have to manually create a new Amazon Aurora DB instance.

D. If no Amazon Aurora Replicas have been provisioned, in the case of a failure, Amazon RDS will attempt to create a new Amazon Aurora DB instance for you automatically.

Q16. How Amazon Aurora MySQL provides Fault-Tolerant and Self-Healing Storage? Choose 3.

A. Each 10GB chunk of your database volume is replicated six ways, across three Availability Zones.

B. Transparently handles the loss of up to two copies of data without affecting database write availability and up to three copies without affecting read availability.

C. Data blocks and disks are continuously scanned for errors and replaced automatically.

D. Each 10GB chunk of your database volume is replicated three ways, across three Availability Zones.

Q17. You are designing an application whose storage needs is very hard to predict. You don't want to continuously monitor and increase the storage size of your RDBMS database. You want to use MySQL DB. Cost, availability and reliability is also your consideration. Which Amazon service you will use? Choose 2.

A. MySQL installed on EC2

B. RDS with MySQL

C. Aurora with MySQL

D. Serverless Aurora

Q18. What is the maximum retention value you can set in RDS?

A. 15 days

B. 35 days

C. 25 days

D. 45 days

Q19. How many copies of your data Aurora stores?

A. 3

B. 4

C. 5

D. 6

Q20. What is Aurora Global Database? Choose 2

A. Aurora global database consists of one primary AWS Region where your data is mastered, and one read-only, secondary AWS Region

B. Aurora global database consists of one primary AWS AZ where your data is mastered, and one read-only, secondary AZ

C. Only the primary cluster performs write operations.

D.   Secondary performs both read and write.

Q21. What is the default backup retention period if you create the RDS DB instance using the console?
   A.   1 day
   B.   7 days
   C.   35 days
   D.   0 day

Q22. What is the default backup retention period if you create the RDS DB instance using Amazon RDS API or the AWS CLI.?
   A.   1 day
   B.   7 days
   C.   35 days
   D.   0 day

Q23. You can set up the RDS backup retention period to between 0 and 35 days. What is the effect of setting the value to 0?
   A.   Retention period is set to 1 hour
   B.   Retention period is set to default value of seven days
   C.   Disables automated backups
   D.   Retention period is set to default value of one day

Q24. Which of the following statements are correct about RDS backups? Choose 3.
   A.   Amazon RDS creates and saves automated backups of your DB instance.
   B.   Amazon RDS creates a storage volume snapshot of your DB instance, backing up the entire DB instance and not just individual databases.
   C.   Amazon RDS creates a storage volume snapshot of your DB instance, backing up only individual databases chosen by you.
   D.   You can also back up your DB instance manually, by manually creating a DB snapshot.

Q25. You have used Multi-AZ deployment for Amazon RDS instances for your web application to achieve enhanced database availability and durability. You know that Amazon RDS maintains an up-to-date standby instance which is synchronously updated. What happens during Multi-AZ failover? Choose 2.
   A.   Failover is automatically handled by Amazon RDS so that you can resume database operations as quickly as possible without administrative intervention.
   B.   Amazon RDS simply flips the canonical name record (CNAME) for your DB instance to point at the standby, which is in turn promoted to become the new primary.

C. Amazon RDS simply flips the canonical name record (CNAME) for your DB instance to point at alternate 'failover' record which needs to be created by you in the Route 53 hosted zone .

D. Amazon RDS simply flips the A Record type for your DB instance to point at the standby, which is in turn promoted to become the new primary.

E. Amazon RDS simply flips the A Record type for your DB instance to point at alternate 'failover' record which needs to be created by you in the Route 53 hosted zone.

Q26. Which of the following statements is correct about RDS backups?
A. Amazon RDS creates automated backups of your DB instance during the backup window of your DB instance.
B. Amazon RDS saves the automated backups of your DB instance according to the backup retention period that you specify.
C. You can recover your database to any point in time during the backup retention period.
D. All of the above

Q27. RDS Automated backups occur daily during the preferred backup window. While creating the RDS DB instance you didn't specified the preferred backup window. What will happen?
A. RDS will not take automated backups.
B. RDS assigns a default 30-minute backup window.
C. RDS will not allow to take manual backups.
D. RDS will not create the DB instance.

Q28. RDS gives you the flexibility of automated backup as well as manual backup by taking snapshots. Which of the following three statements are correct? Choose 3.
A. The first snapshot of a DB instance contains the data for the full DB instance.
B. Subsequent snapshots of the same DB instance are incremental, which means that only the data that has changed after your most recent snapshot is saved.
C. Subsequent snapshots of the same DB instance also contains the data of the full DB instance.
D. You can copy both automatic and manual DB snapshots, and share manual DB snapshots.

Q29. You are sun setting an application. As part of the process you are going to delete the RDS DB instance but you want to retain the automated backups. What step can you take?
A. If you delete a RDS DB Instance there is no option to retain the automated backups.
B. You have to manually create copies of automated backups.
C. You can take snapshot of DB Instance before deleting it.
D. Choose Retain automated backups when you delete a DB instance.

Q30. What is DB parameter group and DB option group? Choose 2.
- A.   A DB option group acts as a container for engine configuration values that are applied to one or more DB instances.
- B.   A DB parameter group acts as a container for engine feature which is empty by default.
- C.   A DB parameter group acts as a container for engine configuration values that are applied to one or more DB instances.
- D.   A DB option group acts as a container for engine feature which is empty.

Q31. What is Recovery Time Objective (RTO)?
- A.   The time it takes after a disruption to restore a database to its service level, as defined by the operational level agreement (OLA).
- B.   The acceptable amount of performance loss measured in time.
- C.   The time it takes after a disruption to restore a business process to its service level, as defined by the operational level agreement (OLA).
- D.   The acceptable amount of data loss measured in time.

Q32. What is Recovery Point Objective (RPO)?
- A.   The time it takes after a disruption to restore a database to its service level, as defined by the operational level agreement (OLA).
- B.   The acceptable amount of performance loss measured in time.
- C.   The time it takes after a disruption to restore a business process to its service level, as defined by the operational level agreement (OLA).
- D.   The acceptable amount of data loss measured in time.

Q33.Which Amazon RDS storage types will you choose for High-performance OLTP workloads and Database workloads with moderate I/O requirements? Choose 2.
- A.   High-performance OLTP workloads: Amazon RDS Provisioned IOPS (SSD) Storage
- B.   Database workloads with moderate I/O requirements: Amazon RDS General Purpose (SSD) Storage
- C.   High-performance OLTP workloads: Amazon RDS General Purpose (SSD) Storage
- D.   Database workloads with moderate I/O requirements: Amazon RDS Provisioned IOPS (SSD) Storage

Q34. Where are RDS automated backups and DB snapshots stored?
- A.   EBS
- B.   DynamoDB
- C.   S3
- D.   DocumentDB

Q35. What DB instances for Amazon RDS for MySQL, MariaDB, PostgreSQL, Oracle, and Microsoft SQL Server use for database and log storage?
 A. S3
 B. EBS
 C. EFS
 D. Redshift

Q36. If a disaster occurs at 12:00 PM (noon) and the RTO is eight hours, by what time the DR process should restore the business process to the acceptable service level?
 A. 8 PM
 B. 4 AM
 C. 4 PM
 D. 8AM

Q37. If a disaster occurs at 12:00 PM (noon) and the RPO is one hour, by how much time system should recover data?
 A. 11 PM
 B. 11 AM
 C. 1 PM
 D. 1 AM

Q38. DB instances for Amazon RDS use following for database and log storage.
 A. Elastic Block Store (Amazon EBS) volumes
 B. Amazon S3
 C. Amazon Aurora
 D. MySQL, MariaDB, PostgreSQL, Oracle, and Microsoft SQL Server

Q39. What are the three storage types provided by RDS?
 A. Throughput Optimized
 B. General Purpose SSD
 C. Provisioned IOPS
 D. Magnetic

Q40. Which storage types provided by RDS will you use for production application that requires fast and consistent I/O performance?
 A. Throughput Optimized
 B. General Purpose SSD
 C. Provisioned IOPS
 D. Magnetic

Q41. What are the characteristics of RDS Provisioned IOPS SSD Storage type? Choose 3.
 A. Delivers predictable performance, and consistently low latency.

  B. Optimized for online transaction processing (OLTP) workloads that have consistent performance requirements.

  C. When you create a DB instance, you specify an IOPS rate and the size of the volume.

  D. Designed for throughput-intensive workloads.

Q42. What are the factors that can affect RDS storage performance?

  A. System activities: Multi-AZ standby creation, Read replica creation, changing storage types

  B. Database or application design resulting in concurrency issues, locking, or other forms of database contention.

  C. Instance type not with enough bandwidth to support your storage type.

  D. All of the above

Q43. Which amazon RDS database engine supports read replica?

  A. MySQL, MariaDB, PostgreSQL, Oracle, Microsoft SQL Server

  B. MySQL, MariaDB, PostgreSQL, Oracle,  Amazon Aurora

  C. MySQL,  PostgreSQL, Oracle, Microsoft SQL Server, Amazon Aurora

  D. MySQL, MariaDB, Oracle, Microsoft SQL Server, Amazon Aurora

Q44. Which of the following scenarios are apt for deploying one or more Read Replicas for a given source DB instance? Choose 2.

  A. Scaling beyond the compute or I/O capacity of a single DB instance for read-heavy database workloads.

  B. Serving read traffic while the source DB instance is unavailable.

  C. Improving performance of a single DB instance for update heavy database workloads.

  D. Serving update traffic while the source DB instance is unavailable.

Q45. Which of the following scenarios are apt for deploying one or more Read Replicas for a given source DB instance? Choose 2.

  A. Business reporting or data warehousing scenarios where you might want business reporting queries to run against a Read Replica, rather than your primary, production DB instance.

  B. For storing user session data.

  C. Implementing disaster recovery.

  D. All of the above.

Q46. Which of the following statements are true regarding Amazon RDS Read Replica? Choose 2.

  A. Amazon RDS takes a snapshot of the source instance and creates a read-only instance from the snapshot.

B.   Amazon RDS uses the synchronous replication method for the DB engine to update the Read Replica whenever there is a change to the source DB instance.

C.   You have to create manually a separate copy of the main primary DB instance and mark it as Read Replica.

D.   Amazon RDS uses the asynchronous replication method for the DB engine to update the Read Replica whenever there is a change to the source DB instance.

Q47. Which of the following statements are true regarding Amazon RDS Read Replica? Choose 2.

A.   The Read Replica operates as a DB instance that allows update-only connections.

B.   Amazon RDS replicates only those databases chosen by the user in the source DB instance.

C.   The Read Replica operates as a DB instance that allows read-only connections.

D.   Amazon RDS replicates all databases in the source DB instance.

Q48. Which of the following statements are false regarding Amazon RDS Read Replica? Choose 2.

A.   Amazon RDS doesn't support circular replication.

B.   Amazon RDS supports circular replication.

C.   Read Replica can resides in a different AWS Region than its source DB instance.

D.   Read Replica cannot resides in a different AWS Region than its source DB instance.

Q49. Which Amazon RDS database engine is fully compatible with MySQL and PostgreSQL?

A.   Amazon RDS for MySQL

B.   Amazon RDS for PostgreSQL

C.   Amazon RDS Aurora

D.   Amazon RDS for Oracle

Q50. What are the characteristics of Amazon Aurora DB Cluster? Choose 3.

A.   Two types of DB instances make up an Aurora DB cluster: Primary DB instance & Aurora Replica

B.   For primary DB instance failover you need to have a separate instance apart from Replica.

C.   Primary DB instance supports read and write operations, and performs all of the data modifications to the cluster volume. Each Aurora DB cluster has one primary DB instance.

D.   Aurora Replica connects to the same storage volume as the primary DB instance and supports only read operations. Each Aurora DB cluster can have up to 15 Aurora Replicas in addition to the primary DB instance.

Q51. What are different endpoints available in RDS Aurora? Choose 3.

A.   Cluster endpoint

B.    Reader endpoint
C.    Write endpoint
D.    Custom endpoint

Q52. Select statements which are correct for RDS Aurora storage? Choose 3.
    A.    Aurora cluster volumes automatically grow as the amount of data in your database increases.
    B.    An Aurora cluster volume can grow to a maximum size of 64 tebibytes (TiB).
    C.    An Aurora cluster volume can grow to a maximum size of 64 terabytes (TB).
    D.    Aurora data is stored in the cluster volume consisting of copies of the data across multiple Availability Zones in a single AWS Region.

Q53. You are the architect of a payment gateway provider and anticipating a fivefold increase in traffic in the upcoming shopping season. You are using RDS with MySQL as database engine. During load testing you notice a decrease in query performance with increase in traffic. Which of the following options you could do immediately to increase database performance?
    A.    Instead of MySQL use Oracle or SQL Server.
    B.    Instead of MySQL use DynamoDB.
    C.    Use Multi-AZ deployment option to increase read and write performance.
    D.    Use Read Replicas and redirect read queries to those replicas.

Q54. How many read replicas you can create for RDS MySQL?
    A.    5
    B.    10
    C.    15
    D.    20

Q55. How many read replicas you can create for RDS Aurora?
    A.    5
    B.    10
    C.    15
    D.    20

Q56. What is the main benefit of Read Replica?
    A.    Improving performance
    B.    Improving Security
    C.    Improving Availability
    D.    Improving Durability

Q57. How does read replica provide increase availability? Choose 2.
    A.    You can make a snapshot from a read replica and promote if the source DB instance fails.

B. You can promote a read replica if the source DB instance fails.

C. You can set up a read replica with its own standby instance in different AZ.

D. Read replica automatically enables Multi-AZ deployment.

Q58. Which RDS features you can combine to architect your application database for high availability and read scalability? Choose 2.

A. Configure source database as Multi-AZ for high availability

B. Create Read Replica for read scalability

C. Create Read Replica for high availability

D. Configure Multi-AZ for read scalability

Q59. With RDS for MySQL, MariaDB, PostgreSQL, and Oracle how you can use the read replica as a DR target?

A. Read Replicas are enabled as DR target by default.

B. Set the read replica as Multi-AZ, allowing you to use the read replica as a DR target.

C. Set the read replica as Single-AZ, allowing you to use the read replica as a DR target.

D. None of the above.

Q60. Amazon RDS read replicas complement Multi-AZ deployments. While both features maintain a second copy of your data, choose two differences from the following list.

A. In Read Replicas only database engine on primary instance is active while in Multi-AZ all replicas are accessible and can be used for read scaling.

B. Multi-AZ Deployments have synchronous replication and is highly durable while Read Replicas have Asynchronous replication and is highly scalable.

C. In Multi-AZ only database engine on primary instance is active while in Read Replicas all read replicas are accessible and can be used for read scaling.

D. Read Replicas have synchronous replication and is highly durable while Multi-AZ have Asynchronous replication and is highly scalable.

Q61. Amazon RDS read replicas complement Multi-AZ deployments. While both features maintain a second copy of your data, choose two differences from the following list.

A. In Multi-AZ Automated backups are taken from standby while in Read Replicas no backups configured by default.

B. In Read Replicas Automated backups are taken from standby while In Multi-AZ no backups configured by default.

C. Read Replicas always span two Availability Zones within a single Region while Multi-AZ can be within an Availability Zone, Cross-AZ, or Cross-Region.

D. Multi-AZ always span two Availability Zones within a single Region while Read Replicas can be within an Availability Zone, Cross-AZ, or Cross-Region.

Q62. Which of the following statements are correct for RDS Multi-AZ and Read Replica? Choose 2.

A.  In Multi-AZ automatic failover to standby when a problem is detected.
B.  In Read Replica automatic failover to standby when a problem is detected.
C.  In Multi-AZ, instance can be manually promoted to a standalone database instance.
D.  In Read Replica, instance can be manually promoted to a standalone database instance.

Q63. In RDS when you deploy in single AZ, what is the effect on I/O operation when a database snapshot or backup is being taken?
A.  I/O may be briefly suspended while the backup process initializes (typically under a few seconds) and you may experience a brief period of elevated latency.
B.  No effect on I/O
C.  There is no I/O suspension, since the backup is taken from the standby.
D.  None of the above

Q64. Your company has SaaS product which provides different kind of reports to various subscribed customers. The reports ranges from adhoc, daily and monthly on various metrics. This is resulting in very high read traffic to underlying Amazon RDS MySQL instance. What can you do to improve the performance without affecting the user experience?
A.  Ensure that underlying RDS MySQL instance is Multi-AZ enabled.
B.  Create a read replica for underlying RDS MySQL.
C.  Change the RDS instance from MySQL to PostgreSQL.
D.  Analyze and improve the performance of read queries.

Q65. You are sunsetting an application along with its backend RDS. You had enabled automated backups for RDS instance during the life of application. What step you should take before deleting the instance so that in future you can re-create the RDS instance again?
A.  No need to do anything, automated backup are retained even after deleting the DB instance.
B.  Create a final user created DB snapshot upon deletion.
C.  No need to do anything, RDS automatically creates a final DB snapshot when deleting the DB instance is initiated.
D.  There is no way to recreate a RDS instance after it is deleted.

Q66. Your company is launching a new SaaS application for mortgage industry. Which of the following are two options for session management in AWS?
A.  Sticky Sessions with Local Session Caching including a client-side cookies or via configurable duration parameters that can be set at the load balancer which routes requests to the web servers.
B.  Distributed Session Management using ElastiCache, Redshift, RDS
C.  Distributed Session Management using ElastiCache, DynamoDB, RDS
D.  Distributed Session Management using ElastiCache, S3, RDS

Q67. What is a DB subnet group?
   A.   A collection of subnets that you may want to designate for your RDS DB Instances in a VPC.
   B.   When creating a DB Instance in VPC, you will need to select a DB Subnet Group.
   C.   When creating a DB Instance in VPC, you don't need to select a DB Subnet Group.
   D.   Each DB Subnet Group should have at least one subnet for every Availability Zone in a given Region.

Q68. Which of the following statements are true regarding Multi-AZ and Read Replicas? Choose 2.
   A.   You cannot create a read replica with a Multi-AZ DB instance deployment as its source.
   B.   You can create a read replica with a Multi-AZ DB instance deployment as its source.
   C.   You can configure read replicas themselves as Multi-AZ
   D.   You cannot configure read replicas themselves as Multi-AZ

Q69. If read replica(s) uses a Multi-AZ DB instance deployment as a source, what happens if Multi-AZ failover occurs?
   A.   You cannot create a read replica with a Multi-AZ DB instance deployment as its source.
   B.   Any associated and available read replicas will automatically resume replication once failover has completed.
   C.   You have to manually map the read replicas to newly promoted primary to resume replication.
   D.   You have to delete the old read replicas and new read replicas will be created by RDS after a new primary is promoted.

Q70. What are DB Parameter groups? Choose 2.
   A.   A database parameter group (DB Parameter Group) acts as a "container" for engine configuration values that can be applied to one or more DB Instances.
   B.   You cannot create a new DB parameter group with custom configuration engine values.
   C.   RDS provides a default parameter group optimized for DB instance.
   D.   It is mandatory to specify a DB parameter group when creating a DB instance.

Q71. What are the metrics provided by Amazon RDS that you can use to determine how your DB instance is performing? Choose 4
   A.   IOPS
   B.   Latency
   C.   Network Bandwidth
   D.   Throughput
   E.   Queue Depth

Q72. Which of the following factor will not have negative affect on DB Instance storage performance?
A. Multi-AZ standby creation.
B. Read replica creation.
C. Changing storage types.
D. EBS-optimized instances and instances with 10-gigabit network connectivity.

Q73. You have web application architecture with web servers running on EC2 instances in auto scaling group and using RDS MySQL database. Due to sensitive nature of application you have to encrypt the in-transit data between web server and RDS database. How can you do it?
A. Download Amazon RDS root CA certificate to your web server and use Secure Socket Layer (SSL) or Transport Layer Security (TLS) from your application to encrypt a connection to DB instance.
B. All the connection between EC2 instances and RDS databases are by default encrypted.
C. Force all connections to your DB instance to use SSL by setting the rds.force_ssl parameter to 1 (on)
D. Add the SSL option to the option group associated with the DB instance.

Q74 Because of a new regulatory compliance requirement you have to encrypt all your encrypted existing application RDS DB instances. You know that in AWS RDS DB instance you can only enable encryption for an Amazon RDS DB instance when you create it, not after the DB instance is created. What steps you should take to meet the compliance requirements? Choose 2.
A. Step1: You create a new DB instance with encryption enabled
B. Step 2: Copy data from the old DB instance to new encrypted DB instance
C. Step1: You can create a snapshot of your DB instance, and then create an encrypted copy of that snapshot.
D. Step2: You can then restore a DB instance from the encrypted snapshot, and thus you have an encrypted copy of your original DB instance.

Q75. What is the encryption algorithm used in Amazon RDS to encrypt DB instances data on the server that hosts your Amazon RDS DB instances?
A. AES-128
B. AES-256
C. DES-256
D. DES-128

Q76. Which of the following statements are correct regarding enabling Amazon RDS Encryption for a DB Instance? Choose 3.
A. When you create an encrypted DB instance, you can also supply the AWS KMS key identifier for your encryption key.

B. If you don't specify an AWS KMS key identifier, then Amazon RDS uses your default encryption key for your new DB instance.

C. Once you have created an encrypted DB instance, you can change the type of encryption key used by that DB instance.

D. Once you have created an encrypted DB instance, you can't change the type of encryption key used by that DB instance.

Q77. Which three types of security groups are used with DB Instance?
A. DB security group
B. VPC security group
C. EC2 security group
D. RDS Security group

Q78. Three types of security groups are used with Amazon RDS: DB security groups, VPC security groups, and Amazon EC2 security groups. Choose three correct statement pertaining to DB security groups (SG) and VPC security groups.

A. DB SG controls access to DB instances outside a VPC while VPC SG controls access to DB instances in VPC.

B. In both DB SG and VPC SG when you add a rule to a group, you need to specify the protocol as TCP. In addition, specify the same port number that you used to create the DB instances (or options) that you plan to add as members to the group.

C. In DB SG when you add a rule to a group, you don't need to specify port number or protocol. In VPC SG when you add a rule to a group, you need to specify the protocol as TCP. In addition, specify the same port number that you used to create the DB instances (or options) that you plan to add as members to the group.

D. DB SG allow access from EC2 security groups in your AWS account or other accounts. VPC SG allow access from other VPC security groups in your VPC only.

Q79. What are the impacts of disabling automated backups in Amazon RDS? Choose 2.
A. Once you disable and you cannot re-enable automated backups
B. It disables point-in-time recovery
C. Deletes all existing automated backups for the instance
D. Existing automated backups for the instance are retained

Q80. You are the DB administrator for your company. You are responsible for running the database update scripts for a recent patch release that needs to be done over the weekend. You are using Amazon RDS MySQL which was created through console with default settings. The plan is to do patch update over the weekend when there is no user activity and in case there is any issue all changes should be rolled back. What feature of RDS can you use to roll back the changes?

A. You have to manually delete new scripts to come back to original state.

B. RDS MySQL has the feature 'Restore to point in time' to restore a DB instance to a specific point in time.

C. To manage risk first do the patch release in a DB copy without impacting original DB.

D. Enable Read Replica before making changes, to roll back delete the main DB.

Q81. How can you encrypt your Amazon RDS DB instances and snapshots at rest? Choose 2.
A. No configuration required as Amazon RDS always encrypts the data at rest.
B. You can encrypt data in RDS DB instance but cannot encrypt snapshots.
C. Enabling the encryption option for your Amazon RDS DB instances while creation.
D. While database creation supply the AWS KMS key identifier for your encryption key otherwise Amazon RDS uses your default encryption key for your new DB instance.

Q82. You are using RDS MySQL database for your web application. To achieve fault tolerance and read performance, you have also enabled Multi-AZ deployment and Read Replicas. You want to monitor different metrics ( CPU Utilization, Free Memory, Active Memory, Device Write I//Os etc) in real time for the operating system (OS) that your DB instance runs on for the primary DB instance and its Multi-AZ standby replica as well. Which of the following is the appropriate AWS feature you will use?
A. Enable RDS Enhanced Monitoring
B. Use Amazon CloudWatch to monitor
C. Create custom program which collect data for any metric.
D. Use Amazon Cloudtrail logs to extract data for any metric.

Q83. Which of the following is not correct about RDS reserved instances?
A. Reserved Instance prices cover instance costs only. Storage and I/O are still billed separately.
B. The RI discounted rate will apply to usage of Single-AZ configurations only for the same database engine and instance family. It will not be applicable for Multi-AZ configuration.
C. Reserved Instances are available in all the AWS regions and for all supported DB Engines.
D. Reserved Instances for the MySQL, MariaDB, PostgreSQL, and Amazon Aurora database engines as well as the "Bring your own license" (BYOL) edition of the Oracle database engine offer instance size flexibility.

Q84. Which of the following Data transfer scenario is not free for RDS MySQL? Choose 2.
A. Data transferred between Amazon RDS and Amazon EC2 Instances in the same Availability Zone
B. Data transferred between Availability Zones for replication of Multi-AZ deployments
C. Data transferred to copy the DB snapshot data across regions.

D.  Data transferred between an Amazon EC2 instance and Amazon RDS DB Instance in different Availability Zones of the same Region

Q85. You have a blog site that is only used for a few minutes several times per day. You want to design the application on Serverless architecture so that you consume resources on usage basis. You also don't want to compromise on scalability and performance. Which AWS services you will use? Choose 2
A.  Lambda
B.  Aurora Serverless
C.  S3
D.  RDS MySQL

Q86. Which use cases are apt for using Aurora Serverless? Choose 3.
A.  Predictable workloads
B.  Infrequently used applications
C.  New applications where you are unsure of capacity requirements.
D.  Variable and unpredictable workloads

Q87. Your company does a quarterly customer survey and uses an Amazon Elastic Compute Cloud (Amazon EC2) instance to host the customer survey website and a DB instance that is used to store the survey results. How can you save the cost in most optimized way?
A.  Take a DB snapshot of the DB instance after the survey is completed, delete the DB instance, and then restore the DB instance along with web application on EC2 when you need to conduct the survey again.
B.  AWS will not charge for EC2 and DB instance between the quarters when application is not being used.
C.  Buy reserve capacity for EC2 and DB instance.
D.  After the quarterly survey, when the application is not being used till next survey, change the instance class and storage of both EC2 and DB to lowest possible

Q88. Which storage type should you use for most RDS database workloads if your key criteria is cost optimization?
A.  Magnetic Storage
B.  Provisioned IOPS Storage
C.  General Purpose SSD Storage
D.  Throughput Optimized Storage

Q89. You are a DB Architect who is designing AWS RDS MySQL configuration for an intranet application. You don't need high I/O performance for most of the time apart from daily nightly batch data load. You have been given the mandate to design a cost optimized solution. Which RDS database storage type will you choose?
A.  Magnetic Storage

181

B.   Provisioned IOPS Storage
C.   Throughput Optimized Storage
D.   General Purpose SSD Storage

Q90. How is reserved instances applicable for RDS Multi-AZ and Read Replicas? Choose 2.
A.   Reserved instances are not available for RDS Multi-AZ
B.   Reserved instances are not available for RDS Read Replicas
C.   Reserved instances are available for RDS Multi-AZ
D.   Reserved instances are available for RDS Read Replicas

Q91. You are the DB administrator for your company. You are responsible for running the database update scripts for a recent patch release that needs to be done over the weekend. You are using Amazon Aurora MySQL which was created through console with default settings. The plan is to do patch update over the weekend when there is no user activity and in case there is any issue all changes should be rolled back. What feature of RDS can you use to roll back the changes? Choose 2.
A.   You have to manually delete new scripts to come back to original state.
B.   RDS Aurora MySQL has the feature 'Restore to point in time' to restore a DB cluster to a specific point in time.
C.   To manage risk first do the patch release in a DB copy without impacting original DB.
D.   RDS Aurora MySQL has the feature to backtrack a DB Cluster to specific point in time, without restoring data from backup.

Q92. What are the different automated monitoring tool options for Amazon RDS? Choose 3.
A.   Amazon RDS Enhanced Monitoring
B.   Amazon CloudWatch
C.   Amazon RDS Events and Database log files
D.   Amazon Flow logs

Q93. What are the features of performance insights? Choose 3.
A.   Monitors your Amazon RDS DB instance load so that you can analyze and troubleshoot your database performance.
B.   The central metric for Performance Insights is DB Load, which represents the average number of active sessions for the DB engine.
C.   The central metric for Performance Insights is DB Session, which represents the average number of active sessions for the DB engine.
D.   You can visualize the database load and filter the load by waits, SQL statements, hosts, or users.

Q94. If you have trouble connecting to your RDS DB instance in a public subnet of a VPC from your home computer, what are the checks you will do? Choose 6

A. Publicly Accessible property of the instance should be set to No.
B. Publicly Accessible property of the instance should be set to Yes.
C. The RDS DB instance is in a state other than available, so it can't accept connections.
D. The source you use to connect to the instance is missing from the sources authorized to access the RDS DB instance in your security group, network ACLs, or local firewalls.
E. The incorrect DNS name or endpoint was used to connect to the DB instance.
F. The Multi-AZ instance failed over, and the secondary instance uses a subnet or route table that doesn't allow inbound connections.
G. The user authentication is incorrect.

Q95. You are solution architect for a sports media company that hosts its websites on AWS. Most of the users visits the website for reading latest news, videos and articles on different sports available on the website, only minority of users write reviews or comments. Website server runs on Amazon EC2 auto scale enabled instances along with single EC2 instance for MySQL. With increase in the popularity of the website you have been tasked to make it more resilient and improve the performance. How can you do that? Choose 2.
A. Migrate MySQL to Amazon RDS with Multi-AZ for performance.
B. Migrate MySQL to Amazon RDS with Multi-AZ for resiliency.
C. Enable Read Replicas on Amazon RDS and distribute read traffic for performance improvement.
D. Enable Read Replicas on Amazon RDS and distribute read traffic for resiliency.

Q96. Which of the following AWS service provide caching services to improve performance? Choose 4
A. Amazon EBS
B. Amazon ElastiCache
C. Amazon DynamoDB Accelerator (DAX)
D. Amazon CloudFront
E. AWS Greengrass
F. Route 53

Q97. Which of the following services provide high availability by being inherently Multi-AZ and you don't have to enable or configure it explicitly? Choose 3
A. RDS
B. DynamoDB
C. S3
D. EC2
E. SQS
F. ELB

Q98. Which of the following AWS services does not provide cost savings through reservation model?
- A. EC2
- B. EBS
- C. RDS
- D. ElastiCache
- E. Redshift
- F. DynamoDB
- G. S3

Q99. How DynamoDB provides high durability and availability?
- A. You can take DynamoDB snapshots and store it in S3.
- B. You can enable Multi-AZ deployment of DynamoDB.
- C. You can enable Read Replica of DynamoDB in different AZ.
- D. Data is automatically replicated across multiple Availability Zones in an AWS Region.

Q100. For a website which AWS database service you will choose that has no servers to provision, patch, or manage and no software to install, maintain, or operate, it automatically scales tables up and down to adjust for capacity and maintain performance, with built-in security, backup and restore, and in-memory caching for internet-scale applications ?
- A. ElastiCache
- B. RDS
- C. DynamoDB
- D. Redshift

Q101. Which AWS database service will you choose for non-relational database?
- A. Amazon RDS
- B. Amazon Redshift
- C. Amazon Glacier
- D. Amazon DynamoDB

Q102. Which of the following statements are correct for DynamoDB? Choose 3
- A. DynamoDB is a NoSQL database that supports key-value and document data models.
- B. DynamoDB global tables replicate your data automatically across your choice of AWS Regions and automatically scale capacity to accommodate your workloads.
- C. With DynamoDB, there are no servers to provision, patch, or manage, and no software to install, maintain, or operate.
- D. DynamoDB is a RDBMS database that supports key-value and document data models.

Q103. Which data types are allowed for DynamoDB primary key attributes? Choose 3.

A.  JSON
B.  String
C.  Number
D.  Binary

Q104. Which of the following statements are true about DynamoDB? Choose 3.
A.  DynamoDB automatically spreads the data and traffic for your tables over a sufficient number of servers to handle your throughput and storage requirements, while maintaining consistent and fast performance.
B.  All of your data is stored on solid state disks (SSDs) and automatically replicated across multiple Availability Zones in an AWS region, providing built-in high availability and data durability.
C.  Amazon DynamoDB does not provide on-demand backup capability.
D.  Amazon DynamoDB provides on-demand backup capability.

Q105. What are the two types of read consistency supported by DynamoDB?
A.  Read After Write
B.  Eventually Consistent Reads
C.  Strongly Consistent Reads
D.  Lazy Read

Q106. What are the two type of read/write capacity mode in DynamoDB?
A.  Reserved
B.  On-Demand
C.  Provisioned
D.  Spot

Q107. For which of the following scenarios will DynamoDB on-demand read/write capacity mode is appropriate. Choose 3.
A.  Able to forecast capacity requirements to control costs.
B.  Creating new tables with unknown workloads.
C.  Unpredictable application traffic.
D.  Prefer the ease of paying for only what you use.

Q108. For which of the following scenarios will DynamoDB provisioned read/write capacity mode is appropriate. Choose 3.
A.  Ability to forecast capacity requirements to control costs.
B.  Predictable application traffic.
C.  Unpredictable application traffic.
D.  Applications whose traffic is consistent or ramps gradually.

Q109. DocumentDB provides compatibility to workloads from which of the following database?

A. MongoDB
B. MySQL
C. PostgreSQL
D. Redis

Q110. Which of the following statements are correct for read capacity of a DynamoDB provisioned table? Choose 2.
    A. A read capacity unit represents one strongly consistent read per second, or two eventually consistent reads per second, for an item up to 4 KB in size.
    B. A read capacity unit represents one strongly consistent read per second, or two eventually consistent reads per second, for an item up to 8 KB in size.
    C. Transactional read requests require two read capacity units to perform one read per second for items up to 4 KB.
    D. Transactional read requests require two read capacity units to perform one read per second for items up to 8 KB.

Q111. Which of the following statements are correct for read capacity of a DynamoDB provisioned table? Choose 3.
    A. If you perform a read operation on an item that does not exist, DynamoDB still consumes provisioned read throughput.
    B. If you perform a read operation on an item that does not exist, DynamoDB does not consumes provisioned read throughput.
    C. One read capacity unit represents one strongly consistent read per second, or two eventually consistent reads per second, for an item up to 4 KB in size.
    D. Transactional read requests require two read capacity units to perform one read per second for items up to 4 KB.

Q112. Which of the following statements are correct for write capacity of a DynamoDB provisioned table? Choose 2.
    A. One write capacity unit represents one write per second for an item up to 2 KB in size.
    B. Transactional write requests require 1 write capacity units to perform one write per second for items up to 2 KB.
    C. One write capacity unit represents one write per second for an item up to 1 KB in size.
    D. Transactional write requests require 2 write capacity units to perform one write per second for items up to 1 KB.

Q113.Which database will you use for storing non-relational data?
    A. Amazon RDS
    B. Amazon DynamoDB
    C. Amazon Redshift

D.   Amazon S3

Q114. Suppose that you created a DynamoDB provisioned table with 6 read capacity units. With these settings, choose three options which your application could do.
   A.   Perform strongly consistent reads of up to 24 KB per second
   B.   Perform eventually consistent reads of up to 24 KB per second
   C.   Perform eventually consistent reads of up to 48 KB per second
   D.   Perform transactional read requests of up to 12 KB per second.

Q115. Suppose that you created a DynamoDB provisioned table with 6 write capacity units. With these settings, choose two options which your application could do.
   A.   Write up to 6 KB per second.
   B.   Perform transactional write requests of up to 6 KB per second.
   C.   Write up to 3 KB per second.
   D.   Perform transactional write requests of up to 3 KB per second.

Q116. What is the default consistency model in DynamoDB?
   A.   Eventually consistent reads
   B.   Strongly consistent reads
   C.   Eventually consistent write
   D.   Strongly consistent write

Q117. You are designing a B2B ecommerce application that will have hundreds of concurrent users. Which database will you use to store the user session data?
   A.   Amazon RDS
   B.   Amazon Redshift
   C.   Amazon DynamoDB
   D.   Amazon S3

Q118. What are the two different primary keys supported in a DynamoDB table? Choose 2.
   A.   Partition key
   B.   Global secondary key
   C.   Local secondary key
   D.   Partition key and sort key

Q119. Which two secondary indexes you can create on a DynamoDB table? Choose 2.
   A.   Global secondary index – An index with a partition key and sort key that can be different from those on the table.
   B.   Local secondary index – An index that has the same partition key as the table, but a different sort key.
   C.   Global secondary index – An index with a partition key and sort key that can be same as those on the table.

D.  Local secondary index – An index that has the same partition key as the table, but two different sort key.

Q120.  You are architecting an IoT application to store time series information from water pump installed at different manufacturing plants across the country.  Each water pump will have its own device id and will be sending different machine parameter values every 5 minutes. Which database will be best to be used for storing this information?
A.  Amazon RDS
B.  Amazon Redshift
C.  Amazon DynamoDB
D.  Amazon S3

Q121. Choose three best practices for NoSQL design in DynamoDB database?
A.  You should start designing your schema only after you have understood business problems and the application use cases.
B.  You design for flexibility without worrying about implementation details or performance.
C.  You should maintain as few tables as possible in a DynamoDB application.
D.  You design your schema specifically to make the most common and important queries as fast and as inexpensive as possible.

Q122 You have a company social network application where employees in the company can exchange messages, have discussion, create profile pages and post photos. DynamoDB is the core database service used in the architecture to store the data. Database workloads is expected to be cyclical in nature or difficult to predict in advance as it is rolled out across global employee base. You don't want to manually intervene to scale database resources up or down in response to varying usage levels or sudden burst in activity. Your application is running on EC2. Which of the following two options you should do to ensure that performance of DynamoDB is at optimum level?
A.  Manage Throughput Capacity Automatically with DynamoDB Auto Scaling
B.  Use DAX which is in-memory cache for DynamoDB
C.  Use Internal Application Load Balancer with DynamoDB
D.  Use EC2 auto scaling for DynamoDB.

Q123.What factors you will consider for choosing initial throughput settings on DynamoDB provisioned tables? Choose 3.
A.  Item sizes
B.  Expected read and write request rates
C.  Read consistency requirement
D.  Write consistency requirement

Q124. You have an intranet project collaboration chat messaging application where employees in the company can exchange messages with each other. You are storing all the messages in DynamoDB table having attributes: employeeid, message, and timestamp. Which attributes should you choose for partition key and sort key?

A. Timestamp, Employeeid
B. Employeeid, Timestamp
C. Message, Employeename
D. Employeeid, message

Q125. Which DynamoDB feature captures data modification events in DynamoDB tables?

A. DynamoDB Events
B. DynamoDB Streams
C. DynamoDB DAX
D. DynamoDB Triggers

Q126. Which of the following is not a use case for using DynamoDB Streams?

A. An application in one AWS Region modifies the data in a DynamoDB table. A second application in another Region reads these data modifications and writes the data to another table, creating a replica that stays in sync with the original table.

B. A popular mobile app modifies data in a DynamoDB table, at the rate of thousands of updates per second. Another application captures and stores data about these updates, providing near-real-time usage metrics for the mobile app.

C. A global multi-player game has a multi-master topology, storing data in multiple AWS Regions. Each master stays in sync by consuming and replaying the changes that occur in the remote Regions.

D. Tracking the session time inactivity for a website user and logging out it after pre-defined duration expiry.

E. An application automatically sends notifications to the mobile devices of all friends in a group as soon as one friend uploads a new picture.

F. A new customer adds data to a DynamoDB table. This event invokes another application that sends a welcome email to the new customer.

Q127. You are determining the initial throughput settings for a DynamoDB provisioned table which has following Read Requirements:
• You want to read 80 items per second from a table.
• The items are 3 KB in size, and you want strongly consistent reads.
Which of the following two statements are correct for this scenario?

A. Each read will require half provisioned read capacity unit.
B. You have to set the table's provisioned read throughput to 40 read capacity units.
C. Each read will require one provisioned read capacity unit.
D. You have to set the table's provisioned read throughput to 80 read capacity units.

Q128. Which of the following statements are true regarding DynamoDB secondary indexes? Choose 2.
- A. A global secondary index is considered "global" because queries on the index can span all of the data in the base table, across all partitions.
- B. A global secondary index is considered "global" because queries on the index cannot span all of the data in the base table, across all partitions.
- C. A local secondary index is "local" in the sense that every partition of a local secondary index is scoped to a base table partition that has the same partition key value.
- D. A local secondary index is "local" in the sense that every partition of a local secondary index is scoped to a base table partition that has the different partition key value.

Q129. Which of the following statements are true regarding DynamoDB secondary indexes? Choose 4.
- A. Queries on global secondary indexes support eventual consistency only.
- B. Every local secondary index has its own provisioned throughput settings for read and write activity.
- C. When you query a local secondary index, you can choose either eventual consistency or strong consistency.
- D. Every global secondary index has its own provisioned throughput settings for read and write activity.
- E. Queries or scans on a local secondary index consume read capacity units from the base table.

Q130. You are determining the initial throughput settings for a DynamoDB provisioned table which has following requirements:
Write Requirements:
- You want to write 100 items per second to your table, and that the items are 512 bytes in size.

Which of the following two statements are correct for this scenario?
- A. Each write will require half provisioned write capacity unit.
- B. You have to set the table's provisioned throughput to 50 write capacity units.
- C. Each write will require one provisioned write capacity unit.
- D. You have to set the table's provisioned write throughput to 100 write capacity units.

Q131. What is DynamoDB Accelerator (DAX)? Choose 3.
- A. DAX is a DynamoDB-compatible caching service that enables you to benefit from fast in-memory performance.
- B. DAX is a DynamoDB-compatible auto scaling service that enables you to benefit from fast in-memory performance.

C.   DAX is suitable for use case where you have applications that are read-intensive, but are also cost-sensitive.

D.   DAX is suitable for use case where you have applications that require repeated reads against a large set of data.

Q132. You are the solution architect for an online gaming portal where users will have an account and can play any games available on the portal. You are saving the user games data in DynamoDB table named GameScores that tracks users and scores. Each item in GameScores is identified by a partition key (UserId) and a sort key (GameTitle). The following diagram shows how the items in the table is organized.

| UserId | GameTitle | TopScore | TopScoreDateTime | Win | Lose |
|--------|-----------|----------|------------------|-----|------|
| 101 | Battleships | 6000 | 2019-12-12:15:24:03 | 12 | 112 |
| 101 | FighterPlane | 1000 | 2019-01-01:08:14:35 | 21 | 32 |
| 101 | StarGate | 100 | 2019-11-12:22:24:23 | 8 | 19 |
| 102 | Aliens | 200 | 2019-04-18:08:26:21 | 22 | 122 |
| 102 | Battleships | 0 | 2019-07-05:18:06:12 | 0 | 6 |
| 103 | Battleships | 10 | 2019-09-09:11:55:01 | 11 | 28 |
| 103 | FighterPlane | 2000 | 2019-10-25:12:32:23 | 4 | 23 |
| 103 | Forumla1 | 1000 | 2019-12-30:16:26:07 | 11 | 42 |
| 103 | StarGate | 50 | 2019-02-28:28:06:02 | 8 | 91 |

Which of the following statements are correct about the design? Choose 2.

A.   A query that specified the key attributes (UserId and GameTitle) would be very efficient for a leaderboard application to display top scores for each game for a given userid.

B.   A query that specified the key attributes (UserId and GameTitle) would be very inefficient for a leaderboard application to display top scores for each game for a given userid.

C.   If the application needed to retrieve data from GameScores based on GameTitle only, it would need to use a Scan operation.

D.   If the application needed to retrieve data from GameScores based on GameTitle only, it would need to use a Query operation.

Q133. Based on the table design in previous question 131. As part of the new features your product manager wants to display following leaderboards:
- top score ever recorded for every game
- a user's highest score for every game

What changes if required will you do in the DynamoDB table design?

A. No change required, the table design will work efficiently for retrieving required data.

B. Create a global secondary index with attributes, partition key of *GameTitle* and a sort key of *TopScore*.

C. Create a global secondary index with attributes, partition key of *GameTitle* and a sort key of *UserID*.

D. Create a global secondary index with attributes, partition key of *UserID* and a sort key of *GameTitle*.

Q134. You are the chief architect of an online gaming company which has a very popular car racing game and uses DynamoDB as database for the gaming application. Your company is going to launch a new version of the game which will be available for only North American users for subscription. You are expecting a major spike in the usage only during day time in North American regions and then the load will decrease during night. This day night spike and down is expected at least for a month. What you should you do for the Dynamo DB database layer to meet this scenario in cost effective way?

A. Create new instances of DynamoDB and other application layer which caters only to North American user for one month.

B. Increase the provisioned capacity of DynamoDB tables during day time and decrease it during night

C. Use DynamoDB auto scaling to dynamically adjust provisioned throughput capacity on your behalf, in response to actual traffic patterns.

D. Create more secondary indexes for every table to optimize the query performance

Q135. Which of the following statements are true about DynamoDB Streams? Choose 3.

A. When a new item is added to the table, the stream captures an image of the entire item, including all of its attributes.

B. When an item is updated in the table, the stream captures the "before" and "after" image of any attributes that were modified in the item.

C. When an item is updated in the table, the stream captures only the "after" image of any attributes that were modified in the item.

D. When an item is deleted from the table, the stream captures an image of the entire item before it was deleted.

Q136. Which of the following use cases are ideal for using DynamoDB DAX? Choose 4.

A. Applications that require the fastest possible response time for reads.

B. Applications that read a small number of items more frequently than others.

C. Applications that are write-intensive, or that do not perform much read activity.

D. Applications that are read-intensive, but are also cost-sensitive.

E. Applications that require repeated reads against a large set of data.

Q137. Which of the following is correct about attribute projection in DynamoDB Global Secondary Index? Choose 2.
    A. The partition key and sort key of the table are always projected into the index.
    B. You can project other attributes apart from partition and sort key.
    C. Only the partition key of the table is projected into the index.
    D. Only the sort key of the table is projected into the index.
    E. You can project maximum of three attributes apart from partition and sort key.

Q138. . Which engines are supported by Amazon ElastiCache?
    A. Memcached only
    B. Redis Only
    C. Memcached and Redis
    D. Varnish
    E. Varnish, Memcached and Redis

Q139. You are using DynamoDB table to track the session history of your application users. You want to delete an entry from the table two hours after it was created. How can you achieve this in an efficient way?
    A. Enable Time to Live on the session data table.
    B. Write a program which continuously reads the table entries and deletes records which are expired.
    C. Write a program which runs every two hours, reads the table entries and deletes records which are expired.
    D. Write a stored procedure which deletes records which are more than two hours old.

Q140. Which of the following use cases are not ideal for using DynamoDB DAX? Choose 4.
    A. Applications that require strongly consistent reads.
    B. Applications that do not require microsecond response times for reads, or that do not need to offload repeated read activity from underlying tables.
    C. Applications that are write-intensive, or that do not perform much read activity.
    D. Applications that are already using a different caching solution with DynamoDB, and are using their own client-side logic for working with that caching solution.
    E. Application that require eventually consistent reads.

Q141 Which AWS service can be used for application where the requirement is to have an in-memory database to have real time access to data and the latency should be at microsecond?
    A. Amazon ElastiCache
    B. Amazon Neptune
    C. Amazon DynamoDB
    D. Amazon DocumentDB

Q142. What are differences between Memcached and Redis engines? Choose 3.

A.  Memcached supports transactions which let you execute a group of commands as an isolated and atomic operation. Redis does not.
B.  Memcached is multithreaded and Redis is not.
C.  Redis supports snapshots and replications. Memcached does not.
D.  Redis has geospatial support, Memcached does not.

Q143. You are developing an online car racing gaming website. One of the feature you will be having is a leaderboard displaying top 10 scores. Which caching service you will use to develop this feature?
A.  Amazon ElastiCache for Redis
B.  Amazon ElastiCache for Memcached
C.  Amazon DynamoDB
D.  Amazon S3

Q144. When should you consider caching your data? Choose 3.
A.  It is slow or expensive to acquire when compared to cache retrieval.
B.  It is accessed with sufficient frequency.
C.  It is dynamic, or if rapidly changing, it should be real time value.
D.  It is relatively static, or if rapidly changing, staleness is not a significant issue.

Q145. What are the different strategies for caching data? Choose 3.
A.  Lazy loading strategy that loads data into the cache only when necessary.
B.  Write through strategy adds data or updates data in the cache whenever data is written to the database.
C.  Periodic time based refreshing of whole data in the cache.
D.  Adding a time to live (TTL) value to each write.

Q146. When should you choose Memcached? Choose 3.
A.  You need the simplest model possible.
B.  You need complex data types, such as strings, hashes, lists, sets, sorted sets, and bitmaps.
C.  You need to run large nodes with multiple cores or threads.
D.  You need the ability to scale out and in, adding and removing nodes as demand on your system increases and decreases. You need to cache objects, such as a database.

Q147. For an AWS discussion forum portal you have designed following DynamoDB 'Thread' table with Forumname as the partition key and Subject as the sort key.

| ForumName | Subject | LastPostDateTime | Replies |
| --- | --- | --- | --- |
| S3 | aaa | 2019-12-12:15:24:03 | 12 |
| S3 | bbb | 2019-01-01:08:14:35 | 23 |
| S3 | ccc | 2019-11-12:22:24:23 | 7 |
| S3 | ddd | 2019-04-18:08:26:21 | 1 |
| EC2 | yyy | 2019-07-05:18:06:12 | 6 |
| EC2 | zzz | 2019-09-09:11:55:01 | 8 |
| RDS | rrr | 2019-10-25:12:32:23 | 3 |
| RDS | sss | 2019-12-30:16:26:07 | 4 |
| RDS | ttt | 2019-02-28:28:06:02 | 9 |

Suppose that an application needs to find all of the threads that have been posted within the last three months and display 'ForumName' 'Subject'. What change in the design you should do?

A. No change required in the current table design.

B. Create a local secondary index having partition key with *Subject*, but with sort key as *LastPostDateTime*.

C. Create a local secondary index having partition key with *LastPostDateTime*, but with sort key as *Subject*.

D. Create a local secondary index having partition key same as that of the *Thread* table, but with sort key as *LastPostDateTime*.

Q148. Which of the following DynamoDB table partition key schemes will result in better provisioned throughput efficiency? Choose 2.

A. User ID, where the application has many users.

B. Status code, where there are only a few possible status codes.

C. Item creation date, rounded to the nearest time period (for example, day, hour, or minute).

D. Device ID, where each device accesses data at relatively similar intervals.

E. Device ID, where even if there are many devices being tracked, one is by far more popular than all the others.

Q149 You have a web application using RDS MySQL database with read replica enabled. To further boost the application performance you are planning to add an in-memory caching layer to your relational database. You will implement a cache-aside strategy using Amazon

ElastiCache for Redis on top of MySQL database. How Amazon ElastiCache improves database performance?

A.  By serving high-volume application read traffic.

B.  By caching the database query results.

C.  By delivering up to a 10x performance improvement – from milliseconds to microseconds – even at millions of requests per second.

D.  By securely delivering data, videos, applications, and APIs to customers globally with low latency, high transfer speed.

Q150. You are using DynamoDB to host a discussion forum website on AWS topics (S3, VPC, ELB….). Users can subscribe to notification whenever there is a new discussion thread or post on topics they have chosen. For example user Smith has chosen to be notified for (RDS, EC2, ECS). How can you achieve this?

A.  Use Lambda with DynamoDB stream to capture the new post or topic record insertion in the table, function will have logic to query the list of users subscribed to that discussion topic then it will send notification to subscribed users through SNS.

B.  Use Cloudwatch with DynamoDB stream to capture the new post or topic record insertion in the table, trigger a Lambda to query the list of users subscribed to that discussion topic then it will send notification to subscribed users through SNS.

C.  Use Cloudtrail with DynamoDB stream to capture the new post or topic record insertion in the table, trigger a Lambda to query the list of users subscribed to that discussion topic then it will send notification to subscribed users through SNS.

D.  Use a scheduled job running in an EC2 server to continuously read the DynamoDB table and send the notification to subscribed users through SNS.

Q151. When should you choose Redis for caching strategy? Choose 3.

A.  You need complex data types, such as strings, hashes, lists, sets, sorted sets, and bitmaps.

B.  You need to sort or rank in-memory datasets. You need persistence of your key store.

C.  You need to replicate your data from the primary to one or more read replicas for read intensive applications.

D.  You need to store object data types only.

Q152. When should you choose Redis for caching strategy? Choose 3.

A.  You don't need automatic failover if your primary node fails.

B.  You need automatic failover if your primary node fails.

C.  You need publish and subscribe (pub/sub) capabilities—to inform clients about events on the server.

D.  You need backup and restore capabilities. You need to support multiple databases.

Q153. What are the features of ElastiCache for Redis to enhance reliability? Choose 4.

A. Automatic detection and recovery from cache node failures.
B. Multi-AZ with automatic failover of a failed primary cluster to a read replica in Redis clusters that support replication.
C. Multi-AZ with automatic failover of a failed primary cluster to a standby instance in Redis clusters that support replication.
D. Redis (cluster mode enabled) supports partitioning your data across up to 90 shards.
E. Starting with Redis version 3.2.6, all subsequent supported versions support in-transit and at-rest encryption with authentication so you can build HIPAA-compliant applications

Q154. What are the components of an ElastiCache for Redis? Choose 3.
A. Node
B. Shards
C. Cluster
D. Threads

Q155. How many shards a Redis cluster has in cluster mode disabled?
A. 1 shard
B. 1-30 shards
C. 1-60 shards
D. 1-90 shards

Q156. How many shards a Redis cluster can have in cluster mode enabled?
A. 1 shard
B. 1-30 shards
C. 1-60 shards
D. 1-90 shards

Q157. You are designing an online gaming portal where uses can register to play variety of games. You are planning to use DynamoDB database to store the user's scores. The pattern of the workload will be unpredictable. What are the best practices you should follow so that read or write operations on Amazon DynamoDB table are not throttled and cost is also optimized? Choose 2.
A. Distribute read and write operations as evenly as possible across your table.
B. Enable Adaptive capacity to run imbalanced workloads indefinitely.
C. Use DynamoDB Auto Scaling with reserved capacity.
D. Use On-demand capacity mode.

Q158. You are designing an online gaming application for users across the world. As the game comprise of augmented reality, high performance and very low latency is one of the important criteria for providing best gaming experience. Because of this reason you want to design a multiregional architecture using DynamoDB as the database. Which of the following will you use in the application to meet these design criteria? Choose 2.

A.   Use Cloudfront with DynamoDB as origin
B.   Enable DynamoDB Accelerator (DAX) and DynamoDB auto scaling
C.   Use DynamoDB Global Tables
D.   Enable DynamoDB Adaptive Capacity

Q159. If you are launching a RDS instance inside a VPC group, which of the following will not be applicable? Choose 2.
A.   Your VPC must have at least two subnets. These subnets must be in two different Availability Zones in the AWS Region where you want to deploy your DB instance.
B.   If you want your DB instance in the VPC to be publicly accessible, you must enable the VPC attributes DNS hostnames and DNS resolution.
C.   You create a DB subnet group by specifying the subnets you created. Amazon RDS uses that DB subnet group and your preferred Availability Zone to choose a subnet and an IP address within that subnet to assign to your DB instance.
D.   Your VPC must have at least three subnets. These subnets must be in three different Availability Zones in the AWS Region where you want to deploy your DB instance.
E.   If you want your DB instance in the VPC to be publicly accessible, you must enable the RDS attributes DNS hostnames and DNS resolution.

Q160.  What is a Redis Shards? Choose 3.
A.   A shard (API/CLI: node group) is a collection of one to six Redis nodes.
B.   A Redis (cluster mode enabled) cluster will never have more than one shard.
C.   Redis (cluster mode enabled) clusters can have from 1 to 90 shards.
D.   A Redis (cluster mode disabled) cluster will never have more than one shard.

Q161. What are the two ways in which Redis implements replication? Choose 2.
A.   With a single shard that contains all of the cluster's data in each node—Redis cluster mode disabled
B.   With data partitioned across up to 90 shards—Redis cluster mode enabled
C.   With a single shard that contains all of the cluster's data in each node—Redis cluster mode enabled
D.   With data partitioned across up to 90 shards—Redis cluster mode disabled

Q162. What is the range option of Redis cluster possible? Choose 2.
A.   90 replicas and 0 shards
B.   90 shards and 0 replicas
C.   15 shards and 5 replicas
D.   5 shards and 0 replicas

Q163.  You were doing a PoC for a web application using a simple three tier architecture as shown below.

Users

Amazon Route 53

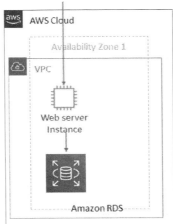

Now you want to leverage other AWS services and features to change this architecture for production environment for global user base. The key architecture criteria are:
- It should be resilient.
- It should be elastic to grow for handling the increased load.
- Reduce latency for global user base and high performance.
- Though application is stateless, it should be able to track user session.
- Storage for static assets and backups.

What services you will use to meet above criteria?

A. Application Load Balancer, RDS Multi-AZ & Read Replica, Web EC2 Instance Auto Scale Multi AZ, ElastiCache, Cloudfront, S3

B. Application Load Balancer, RDS , Web EC2 Instance Auto Scale Multi AZ, DynamoDB, ElastiCache, Cloudfront, S3

C. Application Load Balancer, RDS Multi-AZ & Read Replica, Web EC2 Instance Auto Scale Multi AZ, S3

D. Application Load Balancer, RDS, Web EC2 Instance Auto Scale Multi AZ, DynamoDB, ElastiCache, Cloudfront, S3

Q164. You are designing an ecommerce application where you want to capture 'like' or 'dislike' for a product by the user and keep updating the count. You also want to maintain a list of

everyone who has liked or disliked a product. Which AWS service will be most apt to implement this functionality where performance and low latency is also a consideration?
A.   ElastiCache for Memcache
B.   ElastiCache for Redis
C.   RDS
D.   DynamoDB

Q165. How is replication implemented in ElastiCache for Redis? Choose 2.
A.   With a single shard that contains all of the cluster's data in each node—Redis cluster mode enabled
B.   With data partitioned across up to 90 shards—Redis cluster mode disabled
C.   With a single shard that contains all of the cluster's data in each node—Redis cluster mode disabled
D.   With data partitioned across up to 90 shards—Redis cluster mode enabled

Q166. Which of the following statements are correct about ElastiCache Redis cluster mode disabled? Choose 4.
A.   It has a single shard, inside of which is a collection of Redis nodes; one primary read/write node and up to five secondary, read-only replica nodes.
B.   Each read replica maintains a copy of the data from the cluster's primary node. Asynchronous replication mechanisms are used to keep the read replicas synchronized with the primary.
C.   Applications can read from any node in the cluster. Applications can write only to the primary node.
D.   Read replicas improve read throughput and guard against data loss in cases of a node failure.
E.   Each read replica maintains a part of the data from the cluster's primary node. Synchronous replication mechanisms are used to keep the read replicas synchronized with the primary.

Q167. Which of the following statements are correct about ElastiCache Redis cluster mode enabled?
A.   Cluster is comprised of from 1 to 90 shards (API/CLI: node groups). Each shard has a primary node and up to five read-only replica nodes.
B.   The configuration can range from 90 shards and 0 replicas to 15 shards and 5 replicas, which is the maximum number or replicas allowed.
C.   Data is partitioned across the shards.
D.   Each shard contains full copy of the data, data is not partitioned across the shards.
E.   Each read replica in a shard maintains a copy of the data from the shard's primary. Asynchronous replication mechanisms are used to keep the read replicas synchronized with the primary.

Q168. When choosing between Redis (cluster mode disabled) or Redis (cluster mode enabled), which of the following factors you will consider? Choose 3.
A. Availability and Resiliency
B. Scaling v. partitioning
C. Node size v. number of nodes
D. Reads v. writes

Q169. You are designing a gaming application for training your company employees and decided to use ElastiCache for Redis. Based on your analysis you estimate that data size will not be huge, the functionality requires more read than write and there will be need to scale your read capacity as the application is rolled out across different offices resulting in increase in number of users. Between Redis (cluster mode disabled) and Redis (cluster mode enabled) which will you choose?
A. Redis (cluster mode disabled)
B. Redis (cluster mode enabled)

Q170. You are designing an online gaming application and decided to use ElastiCache for Redis. Based on your analysis you estimate that data size will be huge, the functionality requires more write than read and there will be need to scale your capacity as the application number of users increases. Between Redis (cluster mode disabled) or Redis (cluster mode enabled) which will you choose?
A. Redis (cluster mode disabled)
B. Redis (cluster mode enabled)

Q171. Which of the following are NoSQL database services offered by AWS? Choose 2.
A. Amazon RDS
B. Amazon DynamoDB
C. Amazon DocumentDB
D. Amazon Aurora

Q172. ElastiCache for Memcached clusters are comprised of how many nodes?
A. 1-20 nodes
B. 1-10 nodes
C. 1-100 nodes
D. 1-90 nodes

Q173. What is Auto Discovery supported by AWS ElastiCache in clusters running the Memcached engine? Choose 2.
A. The ability for client programs to automatically identify primary node in the cluster.
B. Your application does not need to manually connect to individual cache nodes; instead, your application connects to one primary Memcached node.

C. The ability for client programs to automatically identify all of the nodes in a cache cluster, and to initiate and maintain connections to all of these nodes.

D. Your application does not need to manually connect to individual cache nodes; instead, your application connects to one Memcached node and retrieves the list of nodes.

Q174. You have an application server in Amazon EC2 which is using Memcached currently. What you should do to migrate to Amazon ElastiCache? Choose 2.

A. Update application's Memcached config file to include the endpoints of the servers (nodes).

B. Recompile and re-linking application as the libraries currently used will not continue to work.

C. Switch to using Amazon ElastiCache without recompiling or re-linking your applications - the libraries currently being used will continue to work.

D. You can migrate your application after making code changes as Amazon ElastiCache is not protocol-compliant with Memcached.

Q175. You are using Amazon ElastiCache for Memcache to cache queries of your web application RDS MySQL. You have just released the web application to beta users with minimum number of nodes in the ElastiCache cluster. As the number of users will increase you will need to increase the number of cluster nodes. What you should do minimize the changes in your caching when scale out is done?

A. On adding new nodes, update the list of cache node endpoints manually in the configuration file and re-initialize the application by restarting it.

B. Auto Discovery capable client must be used to connect to Amazon ElastiCache Cluster.

C. Auto Discovery capable server must be used to connect to Amazon ElastiCache Cluster.

D. None of the above

Q176. Which of the following is not a type of NoSQL database in AWS?

A. Key value: DynamoDB
B. Document: DocumentDB
C. Relational: RDS
D. Graph: Neptune
E. In-memory: ElastiCache
F. Search: Elasticsearch

Q177. You are the chief cloud architect for a multinational company having offices all across the world. You are designing a web application which will be hosted on AWS and used by global user base of employees. Which AWS database service you will you use that provides a

fully managed, multiregion, and multimaster database so that you can deliver low-latency data access to your users no matter where they are located on the globe ?
   A.   RDS instance in different AWS regions with Multi-AZ deployment
   B.   DynamoDB with Global Tables
   C.   S3 with cross region replication
   D.   Database deployed in EC2 instances with EBS volumes

Q178. What are the steps involved in adding encryption to a previously unencrypted database instance?
   A.   Create a snapshot of the unencrypted database instance.
   B.   Copy the snapshot to a new, encrypted snapshot. Enable encryption and specify the desired KMS key as you do so.
   C.   Create a new database instance with encryption enabled.
   D.   Copy the data from existing to new database.
   E.   Restore the encrypted snapshot to a new database instance

Q179. How can you implement disaster recovery or fault tolerance for my Amazon ElastiCache Redis cluster?
   A.   Multi-AZ with Automatic Failover
   B.   Daily automatic backups
   C.   Manual backups using Redis append-only file (AOF)
   D.   All of the above

Q180. An ElastiCache Redis replication group is comprised of a single primary node which your application can both read from and write to, and from 1 to 5 read-only replica nodes. Whenever data is written to the primary node it is also asynchronously updated on the read replica nodes. What happens when a read replica fails?
   A.   ElastiCache detects the failed read replica.
   B.   ElastiCache takes the failed node off line.
   C.   ElastiCache launches and provisions a replacement node in the same AZ.
   D.   ElastiCache launches and provisions a replacement node in the same or different AZ.
   E.   The new node synchronizes with the one of most updated Read Replica.
   F.   The new node synchronizes with the Primary node.

Q181. In case of ElastiCache Redis choose the two correct statements applicable for a Primary node failure when Multi-AZ with Auto Failover is enabled and when it is disabled?
   A.   Enabled: ElastiCache promotes the read replica node with the least replication lag to primary node, the other replicas sync with the new primary node and new replica is created in failed primary's AZ.
   B.   Disabled: ElastiCache promotes the read replica node with the least replication lag to primary node, the other replicas sync with the new primary node and new replica is created in failed primary's AZ.

C.  Enabled: ElastiCache creates and provisions a new Primary node to replace the failed Primary and syncs the new Primary with one of the existing replicas.
D.  Disabled: ElastiCache creates and provisions a new Primary node to replace the failed Primary and syncs the new Primary with one of the existing replicas.

Q182. What are the use cases for using Amazon DocumentDB? Choose 2.
A.  Content management applications such as blogs and video platforms.
B.  For storing catalog information such as in an e-commerce application.
C.  Real-time bidding applications such as buying and selling of online ad impressions.
D.  Gaming leaderboard shows a gamer's position relative to other players of a similar rank.

Q183. Which of the following are features of Amazon DocumentDB? Choose 5.
A.  Compatible with MongoDB 3.6 drivers and tools.
B.  Compatible with DynamoDB 3.6 drivers and tools.
C.  Automatically grows the size of your storage volume as your database storage needs grow. Your storage volume grows in increments of 10 GB, up to a maximum of 64 TB.
D.  You can increase read throughput to support high-volume application requests by creating up to 15 replica instances.
E.  You can increase write throughput to support high-volume application requests by creating up to 15 replica instances.
F.  Automates failover to one of up to 15 Amazon DocumentDB replicas you have created in any of three Availability Zones. If no Amazon DocumentDB replicas have been provisioned, in the case of a failure, Amazon DocumentDB will attempt to create a new instance for you automatically.
G.  Each 10GB portion of your storage volume is replicated six ways, across three Availability Zones.

Q184. Which of the following are components of DocumentDB cluster? Choose 2.
A.  Cluster volume
B.  Writer Volume
C.  Reader Volume
D.  Instances

Q185. How is failover handled in DocumentDB? Choose 2.
A.  If you do not have an Amazon DocumentDB replica, you will need to create a new one manually in the same or a different Availability Zone, then flip the canonical name record (CNAME) for your cluster endpoint to new instance.
B.  If you have an Amazon DocumentDB replica, in the same or a different Availability Zone, when failing over, Amazon DocumentDB flips the canonical name record

(CNAME) for your cluster endpoint to a healthy replica, which is in turn is promoted to become the new primary.

C.  If you do not have an Amazon DocumentDB Replica (i.e. single instance), Amazon DocumentDB will first attempt to create a new instance in the same Availability Zone as the original instance. If unable to do so, Amazon DocumentDB will attempt to create a new instance in a different Availability Zone.

D.  If you have an Amazon DocumentDB Replica, Amazon DocumentDB will first attempt to create a new instance in the same Availability Zone as the original instance. If unable to do so, Amazon DocumentDB will attempt to create a new instance in a different Availability Zone.

# Chapter 5 Analytics: Amazon Athena, Amazon EMR, Amazon Kinesis, Amazon Redshift, AWS Glue, AWS Data Pipeline, Amazon QuickSight, AWS Lake Formation, Elasticsearch

Q1. Which AWS service you will use for real time analytics of streaming data such as IoT telemetry data, application logs, and website clickstreams. ?
    A.   Amazon Athena
    B.   Amazon Kinesis
    C.   Amazon Elasticsearch Service
    D.   Amazon QuickSight

Q2. Which of the following are Kinesis services? Choose 4.
    A.   Kinesis Video Streams
    B.   Kinesis Data Streams
    C.   Kinesis Data Firehose
    D.   Kinesis QuickSight
    E.   Kinesis Data Analytics

Q3. You want to collect log and event data from sources such as servers, desktops, and mobile devices and then have a custom application continuously process the data, generate metrics, power live dashboards, and emit aggregated data into stores such as Amazon S3. Which is the main AWS service you will use?
    A.   Kinesis Data Streams
    B.   Kinesis Data Firehose
    C.   Kinesis Video Streams
    D.   Kinesis Data Analytics

Q4. Which of the following are ideal use case for Kinesis Data Streams? Choose 3.
    A.   Real time data analytics
    B.   Long term data storage and analytics
    C.   Log and data feed intake and processing
    D.   Real time metrics and reporting
    E.   ETL Batch jobs

Q5. What are features of AWS Redshift? Choose 3.
    A.   Fully managed data warehouse service.
    B.   Allows you to run complex analytic queries against petabytes of structured data using sophisticated query optimization, columnar storage on high-performance storage, and massively parallel query execution.
    C.   Also includes Amazon Athena, allowing you to directly run SQL queries against exabytes of unstructured data in Amazon S3 data lakes
    D.   Also includes Amazon Redshift Spectrum, allowing you to directly run SQL queries against exabytes of unstructured data in Amazon S3 data lakes
    E.   Fully managed data lake service.

Q6. You are working as a solution architect for a financial services company which is planning to create a new data warehouse solution leveraging AWS Redshift. The raw data will be fist exported to S3 and EMR cluster and then copied into Redshift. The query results will be exported to another S3 data lake. How can you ensure that all data exchange (COPY, UNLOAD) between Redshift and other AWS resources should not traverse through internet and also to leverage the VPC security and monitoring features?

A. Use AWS Glue to copy and upload data to Redshift cluster

B. Use AWS Data pipeline to copy and upload data to Redshift cluster

C. Enable enhanced VPC routing on your Redshift cluster

D. Enable VPC flow logs on your Redshift cluster

Q7. Which AWS service you will use for business analytics dashboards and visualizations?

A. Amazon Athena

B. Amazon EMR

C. Amazon Elasticsearch Service

D. Amazon QuickSight

Q8. You are the solution architect for a national retail chain having stores in major cities. Each store use an on premise application for sales transaction. At the end of the day at 11 pm data from each store should be uploaded to Amazon storage which will be in excess of 30TB of data, the data then should be processed in Hadoop and results stored in data warehouse. What combination of AWS services you will use?

A. Amazon Data Pipeline, Amazon S3, Amazon EMR, Amazon DynamoDB

B. Amazon Data Pipeline, Amazon Elastic Block Storage, Amazon S3, Amazon EMR, Amazon Redshift

C. Amazon Data Pipeline, Amazon S3, Amazon EMR, Amazon Redshift

D. Amazon Data Pipeline, Amazon Kinesis, Amazon S3, Amazon EMR, Amazon Redshift, Amazon EC2

Q9. Which AWS Analytics services gives you the ability to process nearly unlimited streams of data?

A. Amazon Kinesis Streams

B. Amazon Kinesis Firehose

C. Amazon EMR

D. Amazon Redshift

Q10. Which of the following are scenarios where Amazon Quicksight cannot be used?

A. Highly formatted canned Reports

B. Quick interactive ad-hoc exploration and optimized visualization of data. Create and share dashboards and KPI's to provide insight into your data

C. Analyze and visualize data in various AWS resources, e.g., Amazon RDS databases, Amazon Redshift, Amazon Athena, and Amazon S3.

D. Analyze and visualize data from on premise databases like SQL Server, Oracle, PostgreSQL, and MySQL

E.   Analyze and visualize data in data sources that can be connected to using JDBC/ODBC connection.

Q11. Which of the following AWS services you can leverage to analyze logs for customer facing applications and websites? Choose 2.
A.   Amazon S3
B.   Amazon Elasticsearch
C.   Amazon Athena
D.   Amazon Cloudwatch

Q12. Which AWS service you will use for data warehouse and analytics requirements?
A.   DynamoDB
B.   Aurora
C.   Redshift
D.   S3

Q13. Which AWS database service will you choose for Online Analytical Processing (OLAP)?
A.   Amazon RDS
B.   Amazon Redshift
C.   Amazon Glacier
D.   Amazon DynamoDB

Q14. . Which AWS service reduces the complexity and upfront costs of setting up Hadoop by providing you with fully managed on-demand Hadoop framework?
A.   Amazon Redshift
B.   Amazon Kinesis
C.   Amazon EMR
D.   Amazon Hadoop

Q15. Which of the following use cases is not well suited for Amazon EMR?
A.   Log processing and analytics
B.   Large extract, transform, and load (ETL) data movement
C.   Ad targeting and click stream analytics
D.   Genomics, Predictive analytics, Ad hoc data mining and analytics
E.   Small Data Set and ACID transaction requirements
F.   Risk modeling and threat analytics

Q16. You want to do click stream analysis of website to detect user behavior by analyzing the sequence of clicks a user makes, the amount of time the user spends, where they usually begin the navigation, and how it ends. By tracking this user behavior in real time, you want to update recommendations, perform advanced A/B testing, push notifications based on session length, and much more. Which AWS services you will use to ingest the captured clickstream data and analyze the sessions?

A. Data ingestion: Kinesis Data Streams, Data sessionization Analytics : Kinesis Data Analytics

B. Data ingestion: Kinesis Firehose , Data sessionization Analytics : Kinesis Data Analytics

C. Data ingestion: Kinesis Data Streams, Data sessionization Analytics : AWS Glue

D. Data ingestion: Kinesis Data Streams, Data sessionization Analytics : AWS EMR

Q17. Which kinesis service is integrated with Amazon S3, Amazon Redshift, and Amazon Elasticsearch Service?

A. Kinesis Data Streams
B. Kinesis Data Firehose
C. Kinesis Quicksight
D. Kinesis Data Analytics

Q18. Your company has recently migrated on-premise application to AWS and deploying them in VPCs. As part of the proactive monitoring and audit purpose they want to continuously analyze the Cloudtrail event logs to collect different operational metrics in real time. For example:

- Total calls by IP, service, API call, IAM user
- Amazon EC2 API failures (or any other service)
- Anomalous behavior of Amazon EC2 API (or any other service)
- Top 10 API calls across all services

Which AWS services you will use?

A. S3, Kinesis Data Analytics, Lambda, DynamoDB
B. EC2, S3, Kinesis Data Analytics, DynamoDB
C. EC2, S3, Kinesis Data Analytics, Lambda, DynamoDB
D. Kinesis Data Firehose, S3, Kinesis Data Analytics, Lambda, DynamoDB

Q19. Which of the following are features of EMR HDFS File System? Choose 4.

A. It is a distributed, scalable, and portable file system for Hadoop. HDFS is an implementation of the Hadoop FileSystem API, which models POSIX file system behavior.

B. It allows clusters to store data in Amazon S3.

C. Instance store and/or EBS volume storage is used for HDFS data.

D. Amazon EBS volumes attached to EMR clusters are ephemeral: the volumes are deleted upon cluster and instance termination.

E. HDFS is common choice for persistent clusters.

F. HDFS is common choice for transient clusters.

Scenario for Q20-Q21. ABC Tolls, operates toll highways throughout the country. Customers that register with ABC Tolls receive a transceiver for their automobile. When the customer drives through the tolling area, a sensor receives information from the transceiver and records details of the transaction to a relational database. Their current solution stores records in a file system as part of their batch process.

ABC Tolls has a traditional batch architecture. Each day, a scheduled extract-transform-load (ETL) process is executed that processes the daily transactions and transforms them so they can be loaded into their Amazon Redshift data warehouse.

Then next day, the ABC Tolls business analysts review the data using a reporting tool. In addition, once a month (at the end of the billing cycle) another process aggregates all the transactions for each of the ABC Tolls customers to calculate their monthly payment.
ABC Tolls would like to make some modifications to its system. Q20-Q21 are each specific to one requirement.

Q20. The first requirement comes from its business analyst team. They have asked for the ability to run reports from their data warehouse with data that is no older than 30 minutes. The ABC Tolls engineering team determines that their current architecture needs some modifications to support these requirements. They have decided to build a streaming data ingestion and analytics system to support this requirement. Which of the following statement is correct to meet this requirement? Choose 2.
    A.   Create a Kinesis Firehose delivery stream and configure it so that it would copy data to their Amazon Redshift table every 15 minutes.
    B.   Use the Amazon Kinesis Agent on servers to forward their data to Kinesis Firehose.
    C.   Create a Kinesis data stream and configure it so that it would copy data to their Amazon Redshift table every 15 minutes.
    D.   Use the Amazon Kinesis Agent on servers to forward their data to Kinesis data stream.

Q21. ABC Tolls is also developing a new mobile application for its customers. While developing the application, they decided to create some new features. One feature will give customers the ability to set a spending threshold for their account. If a customer's cumulative toll bill surpasses this threshold, ABC Tolls wants to send an in-application message to the customer to notify them that the threshold has been breached within 10 minutes of the breach occurring. Which AWS services they will use to achieve this feature such that solution is scalable and cost effective?
    A.   Kinesis Analytics, Kinesis Streams, EC2, SNS, DynamoDB
    B.   Kinesis Analytics, Kinesis Streams, Lambda, SQS, DynamoDB
    C.   Kinesis Analytics, Kinesis Streams, EC2, SQS, DynamoDB
    D.   Kinesis Analytics, Kinesis Streams, Lambda, SNS, DynamoDB

Q22. You want to leverage Amazon Web Services to build an end-to-end log analytics solution that collects, ingests, processes, and loads both batch data and streaming data, and makes the processed data available to your users in analytics systems they are already using and in near real-time. The solution should be highly reliable, cost-effective, scales automatically to varying data volumes, and requires almost no IT administration. This solution should be extensible to use cases like analyze log data from websites, mobile devices, servers, sensors, and more for a wide variety of applications such as digital marketing, application monitoring, fraud detection, ad tech, gaming, and IoT. Which services you will use to build this log analytics solution?

    A.   Kinesis Firehose, Kinesis Analytics, S3, Elasticsearch, Kibana

    B.   Kinesis Firehose, Kinesis Analytics, RDS Aurora, Elasticsearch, Kibana

    C.   Kinesis Firehose, Kinesis Analytics, DynamoDB, Elasticsearch, Kibana

    D.   EC2, Lambda, S3, Elasticsearch, Kibana

Q23. You want to leverage AWS native components to do Clickstream analytics by collecting, analyzing, and reporting aggregate data about which webpages someone visits and in what order in your website. The clickstream analytics solution should provide these capabilities:

- Streaming data ingestion, which can process millions of website clicks (clickstream data) a day from global websites.

- Near real-time visualizations and recommendations, with web usage metrics that include events per hour, visitor count, web/HTTP user agents (e.g., a web browser), abnormal events, aggregate event count, referrers, and recent events. You want to build a recommendation engine on a data warehouse.

- Analysis and visualizations of your clickstream data both real time and analytical.

Which AWS native services you will use to build this solution?

    A.   Amazon IoT core, Amazon Elasticsearch Amazon S3, Amazon RDS, Amazon Redshift, Amazon Quicksight, Amazon Athena

    B.   Amazon Kinesis Data Firehose, Amazon Elasticsearch Amazon S3, Amazon Redshift, Amazon Quicksight, Amazon Athena

    C.   Amazon IoT core, Amazon Elasticsearch Amazon S3, Amazon DynamoDB, Amazon Redshift, Amazon Quicksight, Amazon Athena

    D.   Amazon EC2, Amazon Elasticsearch Amazon S3, Amazon Redshift, Amazon Quicksight, Amazon Athena

Q24. Which of the following are features for EMR EMRFS File System? Choose 3.

    A.   EMRFS is common choice for persistent clusters.

    B.   EMRFS is common choice for transient clusters.

    C.   Is an implementation of the Hadoop file system used for reading and writing regular files from Amazon EMR directly to Amazon S3.

    D.   Provides the convenience of storing persistent data in Amazon S3 for use with Hadoop while also providing features like Amazon S3 server-side encryption, read-after-write consistency, and list consistency.

Q25. Which AWS services is fully managed ETL (extract, transform, and load) service that is serverless, makes it simple and cost-effective to categorize your data, clean it, enrich it, and move it reliably between various data stores?
  A.  AWS EMR
  B.  AWS Datapipeline
  C.  AWS Glue
  D.  AWS Data Migration Service

Q26.Which of the following is not a use case for using AWS Glue?
  A.  To build a data warehouse to organize, cleanse, validate, and format data.
  B.  Run serverless queries against your Amazon S3 data lake.
  C.  Create event-driven ETL pipelines with AWS Glue.
  D.  Create business intelligence dashboard on top of data warehouse.

Q27. You are using Kinesis data stream and kinesis data analytics for ingestion and real time clickstream analytics of new launched website. The solution was working fine when there were limited users, but as the popularity of website increased you are observing performance issues and exceptions in the logs. What you should do to improve the performance?
  A.  Increase the number of shards in the kinesis stream.
  B.  Decrease the number of shards in the kinesis stream.
  C.  Replace the kinesis data stream by kinesis data firehose.
  D.  Replace the kinesis data stream by lambda.

Q28. You are building an ETL solution for daily sales report analysis. All the regional headquarter in the country upload their sales data between 7pm-11pm to a S3 bucket. Upon upload each file should be transformed and loaded into a data warehouse. What services you will use to design this solution in a most cost effective way? Choose 2.
  A.  Configure S3 event notification to trigger a lambda function which will kick start ETL job whenever a file is uploaded.
  B.  Use AWS Glue for ETL and Redshift for Data warehouse
  C.  Use AWS Data Pipeline for ETL and Redshift for Data warehouse
  D.  Use AWS Glue for ETL and Amazon EMR for Data warehouse

Q29. You are launching an Amazon Redshift a cluster in a virtual private cloud (VPC). What information you need to provide apart from VPC id?
  A.  Redshift Subnet Group
  B.  DW Subnet Group
  C.  Cluster Subnet Group
  D.  DB Subnet Group

Q30. What are differences between AWS Glue vs. AWS Data Pipeline? Choose 3.

A.   AWS Glue provides a managed ETL service that runs on a serverless Apache Spark environment. AWS Data Pipeline provides a managed orchestration service that gives you greater flexibility in terms of the execution environment, access and control over the compute resources that run your code, as well as the code itself that does data processing.

B.   AWS Data Pipeline, you don't have to worry about configuring and managing the underlying compute resources. AWS Glue launches compute resources in your account allowing you direct access to the Amazon EC2 instances or Amazon EMR clusters.

C.   AWS Glue, you don't have to worry about configuring and managing the underlying compute resources. AWS Data Pipeline launches compute resources in your account allowing you direct access to the Amazon EC2 instances or Amazon EMR clusters.

D.   AWS Glue ETL jobs are Scala or Python based. AWS Data Pipeline, you can setup heterogeneous set of jobs that run on a variety of engines like Hive, Pig, etc.

E.   AWS Data Pipeline provides a managed ETL service that runs on a serverless Apache Spark environment. AWS Glue provides a managed orchestration service that gives you greater flexibility in terms of the execution environment, access and control over the compute resources that run your code, as well as the code itself that does data processing.

Q31. Which of the following are components of AWS Data Pipeline? Choose 3.
   A.   Pipeline definition
   B.   Pipeline
   C.   Data Catalog
   D.   Task Runner

Q32. Which of the following are not components of AWS Glue? Choose 2.
   A.   AWS Glue Data Node
   B.   AWS Glue Console
   C.   AWS Glue Data Catalog
   D.   AWS Glue Job Scheduler
   E.   AWS Glue Crawlers and Classifiers
   F.   AWS Glue ETL Operations
   G.   AWS Glue Jobs System

Q33. Which of the following are features of Amazon Athena? Choose 3.
   A.   Is an interactive query service that makes it easy to analyze data in Amazon S3 using standard SQL.
   B.   Query jobs are executed on a clusters of EC2 instances.
   C.   Is serverless, so there is no infrastructure to setup or manage, and you can start analyzing data immediately.

    D.   Uses Presto with full standard SQL support and works with a variety of standard data formats, including CSV, JSON, ORC, Apache Parquet and Avro.

    E.   Is an interactive query service that makes it easy to analyze data in Amazon RDS using standard SQL

Q34. Which of the following data sources is not supported by Amazon QuickSight?
   A.   Amazon RDS, Amazon Aurora, Amazon Redshift
   B.   Amazon Athena and Amazon S3
   C.   Excel spreadsheets or flat files (CSV, TSV, CLF, and ELF)
   D.   EBS and EFS
   E.   Connect to on-premises databases like SQL Server, MySQL and PostgreSQL
   F.   Import data from SaaS applications like Salesforce

# Chapter 6 Content Delivery: Amazon Route 53, Amazon CloudFront

Q1. What are the three functions provided by Amazon Route 53? Choose 3.
   A.   Domain registration
   B.   Digital Certificates
   C.   DNS routing
   D.   Health checking

Q2. Which of the following AWS resource you can route traffic to using Route 53? Choose 3.
   A.   Amazon API Gateway, Amazon CloudFront, Amazon EC2
   B.   AWS Elastic Beanstalk, Elastic Load Balancing, Amazon RDS
   C.   AWS Step Functions , AWS CloudFormation , AWS OpsWorks
   D.   Amazon S3, Amazon Virtual Private Cloud (Amazon VPC), Amazon WorkMail

Q3. What are the different types of hosted zone that can be created in Amazon Route 53?
   1.   Public hosted zone
   2.   VPC hosted zone
   3.   Private hosted zone
      A.   1 and 2
      B.   2 and 3
      C.   1,2,3
      D.   1 and 3

Q4. Which of the following statements are correct about Route 53 hosted zone? Choose 4.
   A.   A hosted zone is a container for records, and records contain information about how you want to route traffic for a specific domain.
   B.   A hosted zone and the corresponding domain have the same name.
   C.   A hosted zone and the corresponding domain name can be different.
   D.   Public hosted zones contain records that specify how you want to route traffic on the internet.
   E.   Private hosted zones contain records that specify how you want to route traffic in an Amazon VPC.

Q5. Which of the following records can be in the hosted zone *example.com*? Choose 3.
   A.   www.example.com
   B.   www.example.us
   C.   accounting.tokyo.example.com
   D.   ichiro@example.com

Q6. You have registered the DNS name *example.com*, for which of the following you cannot create a CNAME record type in the hosted zone?
   A.   example.com
   B.   www.example.com
   C.   newproduct.example.com

D.  mail.example.com

Q7. Which DNS record type is used to route traffic to an IPv4 address?
A.  An A record
B.  An AAAA record
C.  A CNAME record
D.  A PTR record

Q8. Which DNS record type is used to route traffic to an IPv6 address?
A.  An A record
B.  An AAAA record
C.  A CNAME record
D.  A PTR record

Q9. Which DNS record type is used to resolve a domain name to another domain name?
A.  A NS record
B.  A SOA record
C.  A CNAME record
D.  A PTR record

Q10. Which DNS record type is used to resolve an ip address to another domain name?
A.  A NS record
B.  A SOA record
C.  An Alias record
D.  A PTR record

Q11. Which DNS record type is used to define the mail server used for a domain and ensure the email messages are routed correctly?
A.  An A record
B.  A MX  record
C.  An Alias record
D.  A PTR record

Q12. Which DNS record type is used by mail server to combat spam and tells a receiving mail server what IP addresses are authorized to send an email from a particular domain?
A.  An SPF record
B.  A MX  record
C.  A Text record
D.  A PTR record

Q13. Which DNS record type is used to store text information?
A.  An SPF record

B.   A MX  record
C.   A Text record
D.   A PTR record

Q14. Which of the following statements are correct for Route 53 Alias record type? Choose 2.
A.   An alias record can only redirect DNS queries to selected AWS resources.
B.   An alias record can redirect DNS queries to any DNS record.
C.   In most configurations, you can create an alias record that has the same name as the hosted zone (the zone apex).
D.   You can't create an alias record that has the same name as the hosted zone (the zone apex).

Q15. For which of the following you can create route 53 alias record? Choose 3.
A.   Amazon API Gateway custom regional API or edge-optimized API, Amazon VPC interface endpoint,  CloudFront distribution, Elastic Beanstalk environment
B.   ELB load balancer, AWS Global Accelerator, Amazon S3 bucket
C.   Another Route 53 record in the same hosted zone
D.   AWS OpsWorks, Aws CodePipeline, AWS CloudFormation

Q16. You are using Amazon Route 53 for domain registration and DNS service for your web application which you will be deploying on EC2 instances behind an ELB. The domain name of your web application is mywebapp.com which you have registered in the Route 53. You know that you can create an alias record with 'A' record type for both zone apex mywebapp.com and sub-domain www.mywebapp.com pointing to ELB load balancer DNS url lb1-1234.us-west-2.elb.amazonaws.com. If the IP address of the load balancer changes what you need to do?
A.   Instead of A record type create a CNAME record type.
B.   Instead of A record type create a PTR record type.
C.   You don't need to do anything, Route 53 automatically starts to respond to DNS queries using the new IP address.
D.   You can't create an alias for ELB which doesn't have static ip address.

Q17. In your route 53 hosted zone, you have created two record sets associated with one DNS name—one with weight 3 and one with weight 1. Which of the following is true.
A.   30% of the time Route 53 will return the record set with weight 1 and 10% of the time Route 53 will return the record set with weight 3
B.    30% of the time Route 53 will return the record set with weight 3 and 10% of the time Route 53 will return the record set with weight 1
C.   75% of the time Route 53 will return the record set with weight 1 and 25% of the time Route 53 will return the record set with weight 3
D.    75% of the time Route 53 will return the record set with weight 3 and 25% of the time Route 53 will return the record set with weight 1

Q18. You are the solution architect for a global financial services company providing banking and stock market trading to its customers. Because of compliance and regulatory reasons the application must be hosted in respective country of the users. For example a U.S citizen request must be routed to application hosted in US-East region and for a European Union user it must be routed to application hosted in EU-Central region. Which routing policy you will configure in the Route 53 to achieve this requirement?

    A.   Geolocation Routing

    B.   Geoproximity Routing

    C.   User Location Routing

    D.   User Profile Routing

Q19. You host a global sports news website across multiple regions in the world. The primary criteria for you while configuring the Route 53 routing policy is to ensure that users will get fastest performance. Which routing policy you will use?

    A.   Geolocation routing

    B.   Geoproximity routing

    C.   Latency based routing

    D.   Performance based routing

Q20. You are planning to roll out two new version of your SaaS web application for your users but you don't want to make it accessible to all the users. Your company's plan is to have three versions of application two new and one existing running simultaneously with 20% of traffic going to new version I, 30% of traffic going to version II and 50% of traffic going to existing version. Which routing policy will you configure in Route 53?

    A.   Version routing

    B.   % Allocation routing

    C.   Simple routing

    D.   Weighted routing

Q21. Which of the following best describes the difference between Geolocation routing and Geoproximity routing? Choose 2.

    A.   Geoproximity routing lets Amazon Route 53 route traffic to your resources based on the geographic location of your users and your resources. Geolocation routing lets you choose the resources that serve your traffic based on the geographic location of your users, meaning the location that DNS queries originate from.

    B.   In Geoproximity routing you can specify geographic locations by continent, by country, or by state in the United States to map user location to resources. You create Geolocation rules for your resources and specify the AWS Region that you created the resource in or the latitude and longitude of the resource.

    C.   Geolocation routing lets Amazon Route 53 route traffic to your resources based on the geographic location of your users and your resources. Geoproximity routing lets you choose the resources that serve your traffic based on the geographic location of your users, meaning the location that DNS queries originate from.

D. In Geolocation routing you can specify geographic locations by continent, by country, or by state in the United States to map user location to resources. You create Geoproximity rules for your resources and specify the AWS Region that you created the resource in or the latitude and longitude of the resource.

Q22. Your disaster recovery plan for a web application is to have a production environment behind one domain and a standby environment behind another domain. Which Route 53 routing policy should you configure in the hosted zone so that if the production environment is down, requests are automatically served from the standby server?

A. Health Check Routing
B. Failover Routing
C. Latency Routing
D. Weighted Routing

Q23. Which routing policy you will use when you want Route 53 to respond to DNS queries with up to eight healthy records selected at random?

A. Latency Routing
B. Weighted Routing
C. Multivalue answer Routing
D. Failover Routing

Q24. To comply with DNS standards, Route 53 responses sent over UDP are limited to 512 bytes in size. Responses exceeding 512 bytes are truncated and the resolver must re-issue the request in which protocol?

A. HTTPS
B. TCP
C. MQTT
D. HTTP

Q25. You have developed your own blog website 'www.mycloudblogs.com' in which you write about AWS, Cloud and Digital topics. It also has other features of discussion forums and ability for the user to take mock tests. You have deployed it in a VPC, web server on EC2 instances with Auto Scaling group and an Application Load Balancer (ALB) in the front. The domain name 'www.mycloudblogs.com' will be pointing to the ALB. You are also using Route 53 to manage DNS Which record types will you create in Route 53 assuming you have configured your VPC and ALB to route only IPv4 traffic?

A. 'AAAA' Alias record with Alias Target as the ALB
B. 'A' Alias record with Alias Target as the ALB
C. 'A' Non Alias record with Alias Target as the ALB
D. 'AAAA' Non Alias record with Alias Target as the ALB

E.   CNAME record with Alias Target as the ALB

Q26. You have a fleet of identical five web servers to serve your user requests. You are using Route 53 to serve traffic. Which routing policy you will use so that traffic is served from any of the five servers randomly?
A.   Latency Routing
B.   Weighted Routing
C.   Failover Routing
D.   Multivalue answer Routing

Q27. Which of the following statements are correct about Route 53 Traffic flow? Choose 3.
A.   Route 53 traffic flow provides a visual editor that helps you create complex trees in a fraction of the time with a fraction of the effort or to quickly find resources that you need to update and apply the updates to one or more DNS names.
B.   A traffic policy includes information about the routing configuration that you want to create: the routing policies that you want to use and the resources that you want to route DNS traffic to, such as the IP address of each EC2 instance and the domain name of each ELB load balancer.
C.   A policy record includes information about the routing configuration that you want to create, the routing policies that you want to use and the resources that you want to route DNS traffic to, such as the IP address of each EC2 instance and the domain name of each ELB load balancer.
D.   A traffic policy is where you specify the hosted zone in which you want to create the configuration that you defined in your policy record and to specify the DNS name that you want to associate the configuration with.
E.   A policy record is where you specify the hosted zone in which you want to create the configuration that you defined in your traffic policy and to specify the DNS name that you want to associate the configuration with.

Q28.  How does the geoproximity bias value of an endpoint affect DNS traffic routing to other endpoints? Choose 2.
A.   Changing the geoproximity bias value on an endpoint can expands the area from which Route 53 routes traffic to a resource.
B.   Changing the geoproximity bias value on an endpoint doesn't have any effect on the area from which Route 53 routes traffic to a resource.
C.   Changing the geoproximity bias value on an endpoint can shrinks the area from which Route 53 routes traffic to a resource.
D.   Changing the geoproximity bias value on an endpoint improves the latency of traffic to a resource.

Q29. What is difference between Availability Zone and Edge Location? Choose 2.

A.   Availability Zones is a data center site around the world that CloudFront uses to cache copies of your content for faster delivery to users at any location.

B.   Edge location consist of one or more discrete data centers, each with redundant power, networking, and connectivity, housed in separate facilities.

C.   Edge location is a data center site around the world that CloudFront uses to cache copies of your content for faster delivery to users at any location.

D.   Availability Zones consist of one or more discrete data centers, each with redundant power, networking, and connectivity, housed in separate facilities.

Q30. What is the main advantage of using Amazon CloudFront? Choose 2.

A.   Speeds up distribution of your static and dynamic web content, such as .html, .css, .js, and image files, to your users.

B.   An extremely reliable and cost effective way to route end users to Internet applications by translating names like www.example.com into the numeric IP addresses like 192.0.2.1 that computers use to connect to each other.

C.   When a user requests content that you're serving with CloudFront, the user is routed to the edge location that provides the lowest latency (time delay), so that content is delivered with the best possible performance.

D.   An object storage service that offers industry-leading scalability, data availability, security, and performance.

Q31. Which of the following are use cases for Cloudfront? Choose 3.

A.   Storage for Static Website Content.

B.   Accelerate Static Website Content Delivery.

C.   Serve On-Demand or Live Streaming Video.

D.   Serve private content from your own custom origin, as an option to using signed URLs or signed cookies.

Q32 You want to store files in an Amazon Simple Storage Service (Amazon S3) bucket and then serve them using Amazon CloudFront. What are the steps involved in it?  Choose 2.

A.   Grant public read permissions to the S3 bucket storing files.

B.   Retain the default private setting of bucket.

C.   Create a Cloudfront distribution for Origin Domain Name by choosing the Amazon S3 bucket which has files.

D.   Create a Cloudfront distribution for Origin Domain Name by choosing the file objects in Amazon S3 bucket.

Q33. Which of the following distributions you can configure in the Cloud front to be served over HTTP or HTTPS? Choose 3.

A.   Static and dynamic download content, for example, .html, .css, .js, and image files.

B.   Video on demand in different formats, such as Apple HTTP Live Streaming (HLS) and Microsoft Smooth Streaming.

C.  Adobe Flash multimedia content.
D.  A live event, such as a meeting, conference, or concert, in real time.

Q34. When you want to use CloudFront to distribute your content, which of the following configurations you need to do to in Cloudfront for creating a distribution? Choose 4.
    A.  Your content origin that is, the Amazon S3 bucket, MediaPackage channel, or HTTP server from which CloudFront gets the files to distribute.
    B.  Access whether you want the files to be available to everyone or restrict access to some users. Security whether you want CloudFront to require users to use HTTPS to access your content.
    C.  DNS service alternate CNAME domain name registration.
    D.  Cookie or query-string forwarding whether you want CloudFront to forward cookies or query strings to your origin. Geo-restrictions whether you want CloudFront to prevent users in selected countries from accessing your content.
    E.  Access logs whether you want CloudFront to create access logs that show viewer activity.

Q35. Which of the following can be configured as origin servers for Amazon Cloudfront? Choose 4.
    A.  Amazon S3 Bucket
    B.  HTTP server on an Amazon Elastic Compute Cloud (Amazon EC2) instance
    C.  On-premise HTTP server
    D.  Amazon Lambda
    E.  Amazon Route 53 Hosted zone
    F.  MediaStore container or a MediaPackage channel

Q36. Which of the following are good uses cases for using Amazon Cloudfront? Choose 3.
    A.  A sports web site which streams live games and also on demand videos of old events to global users.
    B.  A corporate website that serves training videos to employees located in one office.
    C.  A corporate website that serves training videos to employees located in offices across globe.
    D.  A corporate website that serves training videos to employees located in offices across globe but accessible only through corporate VPN.
    E.  A popular pc games download site for global subscriber users.

Q37. You are solution architect for a new global tennis sports news web site. Web site will be hosted on a fleet of EC2 instances. Which AWS services you can use to ensure that when load on website increases, users will not experience slow response? Choose 3.
    A.  Amazon ElastiCache as in memory data store for web caching.
    B.  AWS Auto Scaling for web site resources.

C.  CloudFormation to deploy the application in AWS region with maximum online users.
D.  AWS CloudFront with website as the custom origin.

Q38. You are the solution architect of a soccer sports news website covering different soccer leagues in Europe. You have the application hosted in EU-Central-1 region. Recently you have started promoting the website in USA and also started covering soccer leagues in USA. This has led to increase in users hitting the website from North American Region, however the users have been complaining about latency issues in the website browsing experience. As a solution architect you are analyzing the different components of website architecture (as shown in diagram below) to improve the performance.

-   Web servers are running in EC2 instance in an auto scale group. EC2 instances are high compute optimized instances. Auto scale group scales out whenever CPU utilization reaches 75%.
-   RDS instance is already optimized for performance with high configuration and read replica enabled.
-   S3 is being used for storing the static content and media files.

What else you can do to improve performance? Choose 3.

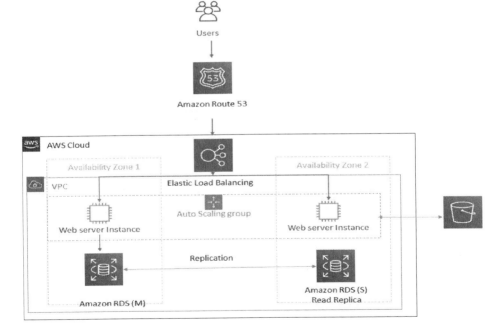

A.  Use Amazon Cloudfront with S3 and EC2 as origin servers.

B.  Have another production site running in US-East region and configure latency based routing in Route 53.

C.  Replace web server on EC2 instance with Elastic Beanstalk service.

D.  Configure Auto scale group to scales out whenever CPU utilization reaches 60%.

E.  Implement a cache-aside strategy using Amazon ElastiCache for Redis on top of RDS database.

Q39. What are the different types of health check you can create in Route 53? Choose 3.

A.  Health checks that monitor an endpoint

B.  Health checks that monitor other health checks (calculated health checks)

C.  Health checks that monitor CloudWatch alarms

D.  Health check that monitor ELB

Q40. How Route 53 determines the status of health checks that monitors an endpoint? Choose 3.

A.  Response time of the request sent by the health checker to the endpoint.

B.  Whether the endpoint responds to a number of consecutive health checks that you specify (the failure threshold).

C.  The number of child health checks that must be healthy for the status of the parent health check to be considered healthy.

D.  If more than 18% of health checkers report that an endpoint is healthy, Route 53 considers it healthy.

Q41. Which of the following is not a valid origin domain name configured in Cloudfront?

A.  Amazon S3 bucket – aws-s3-bucket1.s3.us-west-2.amazonaws.com

B.  Amazon S3 bucket configured as a website – https://bucket-name.s3-website.us-west-2.amazonaws.com

C.  MediaStore container – mymediastore.data.mediastore.us-west-1.amazonaws.com

D.  MediaPackage endpoint – mymediapackage.mediapackage.us-west-1.amazon.com

E.  Amazon EC2 instance – ec2-203-0-113-25.compute-1.amazonaws.com

F.  RDS endpoint value    -    mycluster.cluster-123456789012.us-east-1.rds.amazonaws.com:3306

G.  Elastic Load Balancing load balancer – my-load-balancer-1234567890.us-west-2.elb.amazonaws.com

H.  Your own web server – https://example.com

Q42. Till recently you were using S3 to store and share objects directly to your users. Now you are planning to configure Cloudfront to get your objects from S3 and then distribute them to your users? Which of the following two statements are correct?

A.  Using CloudFront can be more cost effective if your users access objects frequently because, at higher usage, the price for CloudFront data transfer is lower than the price for Amazon S3 data transfer.

B. Using CloudFront can be more costly if your users access objects frequently because, at higher usage, the price for CloudFront data transfer is higher than the price for Amazon S3 data transfer.

C. Downloads will be slower with CloudFront than with Amazon S3 alone because your objects are stored at edge location far from Amazon S3 origin server.

D. Downloads are faster with CloudFront than with Amazon S3 alone because your objects are stored closer to your users.

Q43. You have a website www.example.com which has its static images stored in S3. The domain name of distribution you have created in the CloudFront for S3 as origin is: d111111abcdef8.cloudfront.net. You don't want to use CloudFront domain name for your files. For example the URL for a file called /images/image.jpg will be:

http://d111111abcdef8.cloudfront.net/images/image.jpg

Your solution architect told you that you can use your own domain name, www.example.com, instead of the cloudfront.net domain name by adding 'www.example.com 'as an alternate domain name to your distribution setting. Which of the following steps are required to use alternate domain name? Choose 4.

A. 'www.example.com 'should be registered domain name with Route 53 or another domain provider.

B. Add a certificate from an authorized certificate authority (CA) to CloudFront that covers the 'www.example.com 'domain name to validate that you are authorized to use the domain.

C. Update the 'Alternate Domain Name (CNAME) 'distribution settings field with 'www.example.com'.

D. There is no need to configure the DNS service for the domain to route traffic for the domain 'www.example.com', to the CloudFront domain name for your distribution 'd111111abcdef8.cloudfront.net'.

E. Configure the DNS service for the domain to route traffic for the domain 'www.example.com', to the CloudFront domain name for your distribution 'd111111abcdef8.cloudfront.net'.

Q44. You recently launched your website to your global users. After few hours you got to know that some of the static images you are distributing through Cloudfront needs to be changed as they are of older version. You know that default expiration of content served from Cloudfront edge server is 24 hours. What should you do so that new version of images are immediately reflected in user requests? Choose 2.

A. Invalidate the file from edge caches.

B. Validate the file from edge caches.

C. Replace the files in the origin servers with new files having same name.

D. Use file versioning to serve a different version of the file that has a different name.

Q45. What are the different options in CloudFront for configuring secure access and limiting access to content? Choose 6.
  A. Configuring HTTPS connections
  B. Using AWS WAF to control access to your content
  C. Setting up field-level encryption for specific content fields
  D. Prevent users in specific geographic locations from accessing content distributed through a web distribution
  E. Using AWS Shield to control access to you content.
  F. Option of limiting access to private content by requiring that users access that content by using CloudFront signed URLs or signed cookies.
  G. Restricting Access to Amazon S3 Content by Using an Origin Access Identity

Q46. How can you restrict access to content like documents, business data, media streams, or content that is intended for selected users when you are securely serving these private content through CloudFront? Choose 2.
  A. Require that your users access your private content by using special CloudFront signed URLs or signed cookies.
  B. Require that content is always encrypted.
  C. Require that your users access your content by using CloudFront URLs, not URLs that access content directly on the origin server (for example, Amazon S3 or a private HTTP server).
  D. Require that it is always through HTTPS.

Q47. You are the solution architect for a gaming company which has a website from which user can download PC games after online payment. The game executable files are stored in Amazon S3 buckets and distribution is configured in CloudFront. How can you ensure that your users can access your files using only CloudFront URL and not through Amazon S3 URLs? Choose 2.
  A. Require that your users access your private files by using special CloudFront signed URLs.
  B. Require that your users access your private files by using signed cookies.
  C. Create an origin access identity, which is a special CloudFront user, and associate the origin access identity with your distribution
  D. Change the permissions either on your Amazon S3 bucket or on the files in your bucket so that only the origin access identity has read permission (or read and download permission).

Q48. You need to prevent users in specific countries from accessing your content stored in S3 and distributed through CloudFront. How can you achieve this?
  A. Use the S3 geo restriction feature.
  B. Use the CloudFront geo restriction feature.
  C. Use the CloudFront ip restriction feature.

D.  You cannot restrict the access based on countries.

Q49. What is Lambda@Edge?
- A.  Feature of Amazon Route 53 that lets you run code closer to users of your application, which improves performance and reduces latency.
- B.  Feature of Amazon IoT that lets you run code closer to users of your application, which improves performance and reduces latency.
- C.  Feature of Amazon ELB that lets you run code closer to users of your application, which improves performance and reduces latency.
- D.  Feature of Amazon CloudFront that lets you run code closer to users of your application, which improves performance and reduces latency.

Q50. Which combination of following three options you will use to deliver on-demand corporate videos to your users using AWS Cloudfront?
1.  Upload your original corporate training video content to an Amazon S3 bucket.
2.  Use MediaConvert to convert your video into the formats required by the players your viewers will be using. MediaConvert outputs the transcoded video to an S3 bucket.
3.  Deliver the converted content from MediaConvert by using a CloudFront distribution, so viewers can watch it on any device, whenever they like.
- A.  1 only
- B.  2,3 only
- C.  1,2,3
- D.  None of the above

Q51. What are the two ways you can use AWS Media Services with CloudFront to deliver live content to a global audience?
- A.  Use AWS Elemental MediaPackage to convert your video content from a single format to multiple formats, and then package the content for different device types.
- B.  Use AWS Elemental MediaStore to convert your video content from a single format to multiple formats, and then package the content for different device types.
- C.  If your encoder already outputs content in the formats required by all of the devices that your viewers use, you can serve the content by using a highly-scalable origin like an AWS Elemental MediaPackage container.
- D.  If your encoder already outputs content in the formats required by all of the devices that your viewers use, you can serve the content by using a highly-scalable origin like an AWS Elemental MediaStore container.

Q52. You can associate a CloudFront distribution with a Lambda@Edge function so that CloudFront intercepts requests and responses at CloudFront edge locations. What are the CloudFront events for which you can execute Lambda Functions?
- a)  When CloudFront receives a request from a viewer (viewer request)

b) Before CloudFront forwards a request to the origin (origin request)
c) When CloudFront receives a response from the origin (origin response)
d) Before CloudFront returns the response to the viewer (viewer response)
A. 1 and 4
B. 2 and 3
C. 1,2,3,4
D. 1 and 3
E. 3 and 4

Q53. What are the use cases suitable for using Lambda@Edge processing? Choose 5
A. Inspect cookies and rewrite URLs so that users see different versions of a site for A/B testing.
B. Return different objects to viewers based on the device they're using by checking the User-Agent header, which includes information about the devices.
C. Content Cache expiration check
D. Generate HTTP responses when CloudFront viewer request or origin request events occur.
E. Inspect headers or authorization tokens, and insert a header to control access to your content before CloudFront forwards the request to your origin.
F. Make network calls to external resources to confirm user credentials, or fetch additional content to customize a response.

Q54. You are planning to deploy a soccer news website for global users. To mitigate the latency for users specific to region the plan is to have a replica deployment in different regions: US-East, EU-Central and Asia Pacific. Which of the following services in architecture given below doesn't need to be specific for every region and is global? Choose 3.
A. Identity and Access Management (IAM) Roles and Users
B. EC2 Instances
C. ElastiCache for Redis
D. Route 53
E. Cloudfront
F. Elastic Load Balancer
G. S3
H. RDS
I. VPC

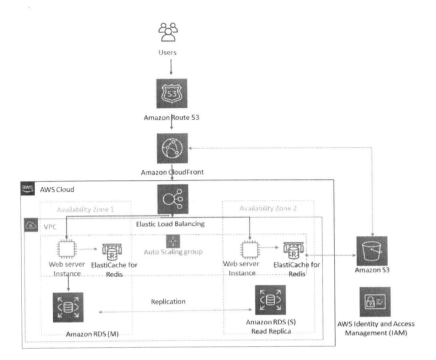

Q55. You recently launched your website to your global users. After few hours you got to know that some of the static images you are distributing through Cloudfront needs to be changed as they are of older version. Default expiration of content served from Cloudfront edge server is 24 hours. You replaced the files in the origin servers with new files having same name, still the new user request are viewing the old wrong files? What could be the reason?

A. New file with same name as the older version will be served only after expiration.

B. You cannot replace a file with same name.

C. You can only replace a file using version management.

D. After replacing the new file with same name you have to invalidate the file from the edge servers.

Q56. How Route 53 determines the status of health checks that monitor other health checks? Choose 2.

A. Route 53 adds up the number of parent health checks that are considered to be healthy.

B. Route 53 adds up the number of child health checks that are considered to be healthy.

C. Route 53 compares that number with the number of child health checks that must be healthy for the status of the parent health check to be considered healthy.

D. Route 53 compares that number with the number of parent health checks that must be healthy for the status of the child health check to be considered healthy.

Q57. How Route 53 Determines the Status of Health Checks that monitor CloudWatch alarms? Choose 2.

A. If the Cloudwatch data stream indicates that the state of the alarm is OK, the health check is considered healthy.

B. If the Cloudwatch data stream indicates that the state is Alarm, the health check is considered unhealthy.

C. If the Cloudwatch data stream indicates that the state of the alarm is OK, the health check is considered unhealthy.

D. If the Cloudwatch data stream indicates that the state is Alarm, the health check is considered healthy.

Q58. You have done Route 53 routing policy and health check configuration for domain name as shown below:

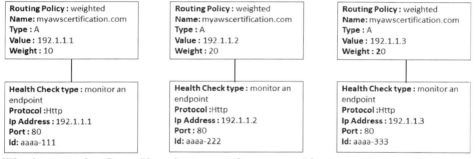

What happens when Route 53 receives a query for myawscertification.com? Choose 3.

A. Route 53 determines the current health of the all records by checking the status of the health check for that record and then selects one healthy record based on routing policy.

B. Route 53 chooses a record based on the routing policy and determines the current health of the selected record by checking the status of the health check for that record.

C. If the selected record is unhealthy, Route 53 chooses a different record. This time, the unhealthy record isn't considered.

D. When Route 53 finds a healthy record, it responds to the query with the applicable value, such as the IP address in an A record.

Q59. The following diagram shows a group of weighted records in which the third record is unhealthy. How will Route 53 select the first record based on routing policy?

| Routing Policy : weighted | Routing Policy : weighted | Routing Policy : weighted |
|---|---|---|
| Name: myawscertification.com | Name: myawscertification.com | Name: myawscertification.com |
| Type : A | Type : A | Type : A |
| Value : 192.1.1.1 | Value : 192.1.1.2 | Val **Unhealthy** |
| Weight : 10 | Weight : 20 | Weight : 20 |

| Health Check type : monitor an | Health Check type : monitor an | Health Check type : monitor an |
|---|---|---|
| endpoint | endpoint | endpoint |
| Protocol :Http | Protocol :Http | Protocol :Http |
| Ip Address : 192.1.1.1 | Ip Address : 192.1.1.2 | Ip Address : 1 **Failed** |
| Port : 80 | Port : 80 | Port : 80 |
| Id: aaaa-111 | Id: aaaa-222 | Id: aaaa-333 |

A. About 20% of the time
B. About 33% of the time
C. About 50% of the time
D. About 100% of the time

Q60. You are the solution architect for a gaming company which has a website from which user can download PC games after online payment. The game executable files are stored in web server running in an EC2 instance configured as custom origin distribution in CloudFront. How can you ensure that your users can access your files using only CloudFront URL? Choose 2.

A. Require that your users access your private files by using special CloudFront signed URLs or signed cookies.
B. Configure CloudFront to forward custom headers to your origin.
C. Create an origin access identity, which is a special CloudFront user, and associate the origin access identity with your distribution.
D. Configure Viewer Protocol Policy and Origin Protocol Policy to ensure that your custom headers are encrypted between the viewer and your origin.

Q61. Which of the following criteria Route 53 uses when choosing a healthy record for a domain query? Choose 2.

A. Records without a health check are always healthy
B. If no record is healthy, all records are unhealthy
C. Records without a health check are always unhealthy
D. If no record is healthy, all records are healthy

Q62. You have associated multiple records with a single domain name (example.com) and configured weighted routing policy in Route 53 host zone. You also added health checks to all the records in the group of weighted records, but you gave nonzero weights to some records and zero weights to others. How will Route53 health work in this scenario? Choose2.

A. Route 53 initially considers only the zero weighted records.

B. Route 53 considers the zero-weighted records on par with non-zero weighted records.

C. Route 53 initially considers only the nonzero weighted records, if any.

D. If all the records that have a weight greater than 0 are unhealthy, then Route 53 considers the zero-weighted records.

Q63. You are the solution architect for a global soccer news website. As soccer fans from all over the world be accessing this website you have deployed the web servers in each of AWS regions across the continents: US-East-1, US-West-1, EU-Central-1, sa-east-1, ap-south-1, eu-central-1 and me-south-1. You are planning to use Route 53 health checking and routing policy to configure in such a way so that all of your resources are available the majority of the time. Which of the following is the correct way to configure this scenario?

A. Configure active-active failover with weighted routing policy.

B. Configure active-active failover with failover routing policy.

C. Configure active-passive failover with weighted routing policy.

D. Configure active-passive failover with failover routing policy.

Q64. How can you allow access to an Amazon S3 bucket only from a CloudFront distribution? Choose 2.

A. Make the S3 bucket private.

B. No need to do anything, when you configure S3 as origin for CloudFront automatically AWS restrict another access.

C. Add an origin access identity (OAI) to your distribution

D. Ensure in your bucket policy and Amazon S3 access control list (ACL) that Only the OAI can access your bucket.

Q65. You are using Cloudfront with S3 bucket as origin for your application. You want to improve the availability of content delivered to your end users by having an active-passive failover. How can you achieve this? Choose 2.

A. Enable Origin Failover for your Amazon CloudFront distributions.

B. Create an origin group having two Amazon S3 buckets that serve as your origin that you independently upload your content to, setting one as the primary.

C. Have a second S3 bucket which is kept in sync with the first one. Change the Cloudfront origin to second in case of failover.

D. Failover cannot be configured at Cloudfront distribution level.

Q66. For which reasons CloudFront will return an HTTP 504 status code (Gateway Timeout)? Choose 3.

A. Traffic is blocked to the origin by a firewall or security group.

B. Origin isn't accessible on the internet.

C. SSL/TLS negotiation failure between CloudFront and a custom origin server.

D. Application delays and server timeouts.

Q67. Which of the following is not a reason for CloudFront HTTP 502 Status Code (Bad Gateway) indicating that CloudFront wasn't able to serve the requested object because it couldn't connect to the origin server? Choose 2.
- A. SSL/TLS negotiation failure between CloudFront and a custom origin server
- B. Origin is not responding with supported ciphers/protocols
- C. CloudFront caused the error due to limited resources at the edge location
- D. SSL/TLS certificate on the origin is expired, invalid, self-signed, or the certificate chain is in the wrong order
- E. Origin server does not have enough capacity to support the request rate
- F. Origin is not responding on specified ports in origin settings
- G. CloudFront was not able to resolve your origin domain due to DNS issues
- H. Lambda Function Associated with Your Distribution Includes Execution Errors

Q68. Your CloudFront distribution's origin is an Amazon S3 bucket. The S3 bucket is created in 'us-east-1' region. You deleted the S3 bucket, then later you created a new bucket with the same bucket name in 'us-west-2' region. How the CloudFront distribution will work after this change?
- A. CloudFront will work as it is with no change in request response.
- B. CloudFront will throw HTTP 400 Status Code (Bad Request) error.
- C. CloudFront will throw HTTP 504 Status Code (Gateway Timeout) error.
- D. CloudFront will throw HTTP 502 Status Code (Bad Gateway) error.

Q69. You have set up CloudFront for web distribution object caching setting Minimum TTL = 0 Seconds. Which of the following is not correct?
- A. If you set the Maximum TTL to 5 minutes (300 seconds) and the Cache-Control max-age header to 1 hour (3600 seconds), then CloudFront caches the object for 5 minutes instead of 1 hour.
- B. If you set the Maximum TTL to 5 minutes (300 seconds) and the Expires header to 1 month, then CloudFront caches the object for 5 minutes instead of 1 month.
- C. If you set the Default, Minimum, and Maximum TTL to 0 seconds, then CloudFront always verifies that it has the most recent content from the origin.
- D. If you set the Maximum TTL to 5 minutes (300 seconds) and the Cache-Control max-age header to 1 hour (3600 seconds), then CloudFront caches the object for 1 hour.

Q70. You have set up CloudFront for web distribution object caching setting Minimum TTL > 0 Seconds and the origin adds a Cache-Control max-age directive to objects. Which of the following is not correct on CloudFront caching?
- A. Minimum TTL < max-age < maximum TTL: CloudFront caches objects for the value of the Cache-Control max-age directive.

B. Max-age < minimum TTL: CloudFront caches objects for the value of the CloudFront minimum TTL.

C. Max-age > maximum TTL: CloudFront caches objects for the value of the CloudFront max-age.

D. Max-age > maximum TTL: CloudFront caches objects for the value of the CloudFront maximum TTL.

Q71. You have set up CloudFront for web distribution object caching setting Minimum TTL > 0 Seconds and the origin adds an Expires header to objects. Which of the following is not correct on CloudFront caching?

A. Minimum TTL < Expires < maximum TTL: CloudFront caches objects until the date and time in the Expires header.

B. Expires < minimum TTL: CloudFront caches objects for the value of the CloudFront minimum TTL.

C. Minimum TTL < Expires < maximum TTL: CloudFront caches objects until maximum TTL.

D. Expires > maximum TTL: CloudFront caches objects for the value of the CloudFront maximum TTL.

Q72. Your website is available in five languages. The directory structure and file names for all five versions of the website are identical. As a user views your website, requests that are forwarded to CloudFront include a language query string parameter based on the language that the user choses.

http://d111111abcdef8.cloudfront.net/main.html?language=de
http://d111111abcdef8.cloudfront.net/main.html?language=en
http://d111111abcdef8.cloudfront.net/main.html?language=es
http://d111111abcdef8.cloudfront.net/main.html?language=fr
http://d111111abcdef8.cloudfront.net/main.html?language=jp

You want your origin server to returns different versions of your objects for all query string parameters. How should you configure the Cloudfront distribution?

A. Configure CloudFront to forward query strings to the origin and to cache based on the language parameter.

B. Configure CloudFront to forward OAI to the origin and to cache based on the language parameter.

C. Configure CloudFront to forward cookies to the origin and to cache based on the language parameter.

D. Configure CloudFront to forward headers to the origin and to cache based on the language parameter.

Q73. What is the default duration for which a file is cached before expiring in CloudFront?

A. 12 hours

B. 24 hours

C.  8 hours

D.  4 hours

Q74. You are using Amazon CloudFront to serve objects stored in Amazon Simple Storage Service (Amazon S3). You have updated objects in S3, but CloudFront distribution is still serving the previous versions of those files. Why isn't Amazon S3 content updating on CloudFront? How can you fix this so that updated objects are served immediately? Choose 2.

A.  Invalidate the S3 objects.

B.  Use object versioning.

C.  Delete and create new S3 object.

D.  Wait for the default TTL

# Chapter 7 Application Integration: Amazon SQS, Amazon SNS, Amazon MQ, Amazon SWF, AWS Step Functions, AWS AppSync

Q1. How is SQS different from SNS? Choose 2.
- A. SNS is a distributed publish-subscribe system. Messages are pushed to subscribers as and when they are sent by publishers to SNS.
- B. SQS is distributed queuing system. Messages are NOT pushed to receivers. Receivers have to poll or pull messages from SQS.
- C. SNS is a distributed publish-subscribe system. Messages are polled by subscribers as and when they are sent by publishers to SNS.
- D. SQS is distributed queuing system. Messages are pushed to receivers.

Q2. You have on-premise distributed applications connected through message broker supporting JMS APIs and AMQP/ MQTT Protocols. You are planning to migrate the whole application portfolio to AWS and re-develop using native AWS services. Which AWS service should you use to replace the message broker architecture layer?
- A. Amazon Message Broker
- B. Amazon SQS
- C. Amazon SWF
- D. Amazon MQ

Q3. Which of the following statements are correct about SQS Standard Queues? Choose 2.
- A. Makes a best effort to preserve the order of messages, but more than one copy of a message might be delivered out of order.
- B. The order in which messages are sent and received is strictly preserved and a message is delivered once and remains available until a consumer processes and deletes it.
- C. Duplicates aren't introduced into the queue.
- D. Ensures At-Least-Once Delivery but may result in duplicate messages on rare occasions.

Q4. How does Amazon SQS provide message ordering?
- A. SQS doesn't provide message ordering
- B. Through FIFO: First In First Out queues
- C. Through Standard Queues
- D. Through LIFO: Last In First Out queues
- E. Through LILO: Last In Last Out queues

Q5. Which AWS service you will use if you have to build, run, and scale background jobs that have parallel or sequential steps?
- A. Amazon Lambda
- B. Amazon Simple Workflow Service (SWF)
- C. Amazon Simple Queue Service ( SQS)
- D. Amazon Simple Notification Service ( SNS)

Q6. What is visibility timeout in SQS?

A.   A period of time during which Amazon SQS makes the message available to other consumers to receive and process the message.

B.   A period of time during which Amazon SQS prevents other consumers from receiving and processing the message.

C.   A period of time for which delivery of new message is postponed.

D.   A period of time during which a message is processed by the consumer.

Q7. What is delay queue in SQS?

A.   A period of time during which Amazon SQS makes the message available to other consumers to receive and process the message.

B.   A period of time during which Amazon SQS prevents other consumers from receiving and processing the message.

C.   A period of time for which delivery of new message is postponed.

D.   A period of time during which a message is processed by the consumer.

Q8. Which architecture design consideration will make you choose SQS standard queue over FIFO queue?

A.   At-Least-Once Delivery, Unlimited Throughput, Best-Effort Ordering

B.   High Throughput, Exactly-Once Processing, First-In-First-Out Delivery

C.   Best-Effort Ordering, First-In-First-Out Delivery, Exactly-Once Processing

D.   At-Least-Once Delivery, Unlimited Throughput, Exactly-Once Processing,

Q9. The minimum and maximum SQS delay queue settings are?

A.   0 secs, 15 mts

B.   15mts, 30 mts

C.   5mts, 15 mts

D.   10 sec, 15mts

Q10. By default for how many days messages are retained in SQS queue?

A.   1 minute

B.   2 days

C.   4 days

D.   14 days

Q11. You are using Amazon SQS in your ecommerce application to send order confirmation email asynchronously. You have created a program which polls the SQS queue frequently for new order message and then sends the email after fetching new order message from the queue. You observe that at times the program is getting empty response to the *ReceiveMessage* request. What should you do to eliminate empty responses to reduce cost?

A.   Create a delay queue.

B.   Increase the duration of visibility timeout value to higher number.

C.  Make wait time for the ReceiveMessage API action is greater than 0 to effect long polling.

D.  Make wait time for the ReceiveMessage API action is greater than 0 to effect short polling.

Q12.  In Amazon SQS what is the difference between delay queue and visibility time out?

A.  There is no difference, both of them are same as they make messages unavailable to consumers for a specific period of time.

B.  Delay queues makes a message hidden when it is first added to queue, whereas for visibility timeouts a message is hidden only after it is consumed from the queue.

C.  Delay queues makes a message hidden after it is consumed from the queue, whereas for visibility timeouts a message is hidden when it is first added to queue.

D.  There is no difference, both of them are same as they make messages available to consumers for a specific period of time.

Q13.  Which architecture design consideration will make you choose FIFO queue over SQS standard queue?

A.  At-Least-Once Delivery, Unlimited Throughput, Best-Effort Ordering

B.  High Throughput, Exactly-Once Processing, First-In-First-Out Delivery

C.  Best-Effort Ordering, First-In-First-Out Delivery, Exactly-Once Processing

D.  At-Least-Once Delivery, Unlimited Throughput, Exactly-Once Processing,

Q14.  Which of the following is correct about message delivery to SQS Standard queue? Choose 2.

A.  Messages are delivered at least once.

B.  Messages are delivered only once.

C.  Messages are delivered in FIFO.

D.  Attempts to preserve the order of messages.

Q15.  What is the minimum and maximum retention time for which messages can be retained in SQS queue? Choose 2.

A.  1 minute

B.  2 days

C.  4 days

D.  14 days

Q16.  What is default visibility timeout period for a message in SQS?

A.  1 minute

B.  0 seconds

C.  30 seconds

D.  2 minute

Q17. What is minimum and maximum visibility timeout period for a message in SQS? Choose 2.

    A.   12 hours

    B.   14 days

    C.   30 seconds

    D.   0 seconds

Q18. What are the different methods using which message can be delivered to a subscriber to a SNS topic? Choose 2.

    A.   AWS lambda, AWS SQS, HTTP/s

    B.   Email, SMS

    C.   AWS lambda, AWS SQS, HTTP/s, S3

    D.   Email, SMS, DynamoDB

Q19. What is a 'fan out 'scenario?

    A.   A publisher sends same message to multiple SNS topics or SQS queues

    B.   Amazon SNS message is sent to a topic and then replicated and pushed to multiple Amazon SQS queues, HTTP endpoints, or email addresses.

    C.   Message is sent to a SQS queue and then replicated and pushed to multiple Amazon SNS topics.

    D.   Message is sent to a SQS queue and then replicated and pushed to multiple Amazon SQS queues.

Q20. You are the solution architect of a financial services company. You are planning to use Amazon SQS while designing a distributed trading application. Key functional requirements pertaining to message queue are: processing of the messages in a sequential order, message should be processed only once and there should not be duplicate messages in the queue. How will you ensure the above requirements? Choose 3 options.

    A.   Use SQS Standard Queues.

    B.   Use SQS FIFO queues.

    C.   Use SWF FIFO.

    D.   Enable content-based deduplication.

    E.   Explicitly provide the message deduplication ID (or view the sequence number) for the message.

Q21. You are designing a stock trading application. Your design includes using SQS for receiving trade confirmation messages from third party systems. You want to have the ability to isolate messages that can't be processed correctly to determine why their processing didn't succeed. How can you achieve this?

    A.   Map the Standard or FIFO Queue to S3 to store the exception messages.

    B.   Create a logic in message processing program to store the exception messages in DynamoDB.

    C.   Create an Amazon SQS Dead Letter Queue

D.   Create an Amazon SQS Exception Queue

Q22. You want to offer an online photo processing services for consumers. Users can upload the photo to the website and specify different operations like redeye reduction, cropping, thumb nail creation, photo filter, contract, brightening etc. Users can submit from few to hundreds of photos at a time. Which AWS services you will use to build a scalable and reliable web application?
   A.   Webserver- EC2, Web Database – RDS, Photo Asynchronous processing – SQS-Lambda, Photo Storage- RDS
   B.   Webserver- EC2, Web Database – RDS, Photo Asynchronous processing – SWF-Lambda, Photo Storage- S3
   C.   Webserver- EC2, Web Database – RDS, Photo Asynchronous processing – SNS-Lambda, Photo Storage- S3
   D.   Webserver- EC2, Web Database – RDS, Photo Asynchronous processing – SQS-Lambda, Photo Storage- S3

Q23. You are using SQS FIFO queue in your web application for asynchronous processing of messages. While doing unit testing you notice that producer is sending the message to queue successfully but downstream functional steps to be executed on message processing is not getting executing completely and there is an exception in the logs. After doing debugging you notice that at first, consumer program is picking up each unique message and then that message again reappears in the queue after the visibility time set of 5 minutes. Then that reappeared message is again picked up by the consumer program and reappears again. What could be the reason?
   A.   Visibility time of 5 mts is less than the time required by consumer program to process the message.
   B.   Message processing is failing because of which message reappears in the queue as consumer program is not deleting it from queue.
   C.   Message processing is successful but consumer program is not deleting the message from the queue.
   D.   Producer is sending duplicate messages into the queue.

Q24. What does SWF stands for?
   A.   Synchronous Workflow
   B.   Simple Workflow
   C.   Simple Work Foundation
   D.   Synchronous Work Foundation

Q25. What are benefits of SQS message Queues? Choose 4
   A.   Better performance
   B.   Increased Reliability and Resiliency
   C.   Cost Optimization

D.   User Security
E.   Granular Scalability
F.   Simplified Decoupling

Q26. A manufacturing company is developing an application running on EC2 which processes messages uploaded on a SQS queue from their plants all over the country. During the beta testing phase you have scheduled the application to run only over the weekend with default settings of SQS queue. After running the beta testing for two weekends when you are doing the analysis of the results you notice that not all messages were processed by the application. What could be the possible reason?
A.   The default visibility time of 30 sec is less than time taken to process the messages.
B.   The SQS application default setting of short polling.
C.   By default messages in SQS are retained for only 4 days.
D.   The default (minimum) delay for a message is 0 seconds.

Q27. You are solution architect for a startup designing a SaaS Mortgage Application. There are multiple business process which you want to design as discrete distributed application interacting with each other. What are the different AWS services you can use to coordinate task across distributed application components? Choose 2.
A.   Amazon SQS
B.   Amazon SWF
C.   Amazon Step Functions
D.   Amazon MQ

Q28. You are using SQS FIFO queue in your web application for asynchronous processing of messages. While doing unit testing you notice that producer is sending the message to queue successfully, downstream functional steps to be executed on message processing is also getting executed successfully. After doing debugging you notice that consumer program is picking up each unique message and then that message reappears in the queue after the visibility time set of 5 minutes. Then that message is again picked up by the consumer program. What could be the reason?
A.   Visibility time of 5 mts is less than the time required by consumer program to process the message.
B.   Message processing is failing because of which message reappears in the queue as consumer program is not deleting it from queue.
C.   Message processing is successful but consumer program is not deleting the message from the queue.
D.   Producer is sending duplicate messages into the queue.

Q29. You are an architect for an ecommerce application. You are using SQS standard queue to receive order message and each order message is processed by a consumer lambda program which send email confirmation to the user. Lately you have been observing few instances of duplicate confirmation email messages being sent to the customers. You cannot compromise on the throughput of the queue. What changes you can make in the architecture to solve this duplicate message processing?

A. Decrease the visibility timeout period of the queue.
B. Convert standard queue to FIFO queue which has features to remove duplicate messages in the queue.
C. Have unique identifier in the message attribute and consumer lambda program use DynamoDB to keep track of them in establishing which message process are in progress, and which are complete. Check against before processing each message to check if the message is already processed or not.
D. Use delay queue.

Q30-Q31 are based on following scenario

You have a web app that lets users upload images and use them online. Each image requires resizing and encoding before it can be published. The web app runs on EC2 instances in a Dynamic Auto Scaling group based on CPU utilization that is configured to handle your typical upload rates. Unhealthy instances are terminated and replaced to maintain current instance levels at all times. The app places the raw bitmap data of the images in an Amazon SQS queue for processing. There are fleet of EC2 instance acting as worker program polling the SQS queue to processes the images and then publishes the processed images where they can be viewed by users. These consumer fleet of EC2 instance also has dynamic auto scaling policy.

Q30 what is the benefit of using SQS in this architecture design? Choose 3.

A. Better performance by giving option of horizontal scaling of processing EC2 instances
B. Simplified Decoupling and asynchronous processing.
C. Increased Reliability
D. Simplified Decoupling and synchronous processing.

Q31. The consumer EC2 instances are scaled up and down based on auto scale policy for the purposes of processing messages from an SQS queue. How will you configure the auto dynamic scaling policy? Choose 2.

A. A custom metric, *number of messages in the queue*, to send to Amazon CloudWatch that measures the number of messages in the queue per EC2 instance in the Auto Scaling group.
B. A target tracking policy that configures your Auto Scaling group to scale based on the custom metric and a set target value, *number of messages in the queue per instance*. CloudWatch alarms invoke the scaling policy.
C. A custom metric, *backlog per instance*, to send to Amazon CloudWatch that measures the number of messages in the queue per EC2 instance in the Auto Scaling group.

D.  A target tracking policy that configures your Auto Scaling group to scale based on the custom metric and a set target value, *acceptable backlog per instance*. CloudWatch alarms invoke the scaling policy.

Q32. Which are the two service provided by AWS for workflow implementation?
    A.  Simple Workflow Service (SWF)
    B.  Step Functions
    C.  API Gateway
    D.  SQS

Q33. You are learning AWS by watching tutorial videos which are in English. To test your learning you want to create a PoC application which will take a video file as an input and generate subtitles in Spanish. The system will receive a video input, extract the audio track, transcribe it, and generate different subtitle files for your video. Your initial core design is to use:

- Amazon Elastic Transcoder to extract the audio from the video
- Amazon Transcribe to convert the audio to text
- Amazon Translate to achieve fast, high-quality language translation

You will also include a workflow management component which will coordinate components and steps through the functions of your application. What are other services you will use to design a cost optimized PoC application?
    A.  S3, Lambda, Cognito, DynamoDB
    B.  S3, Lambda, Step functions, Cognito, DynamoDB
    C.  S3, EC2, Step functions, Cognito, DynamoDB
    D.  S3, ECS, Step functions, Cognito, DynamoDB

Q34. Which of the following are type of actor in SWF? Choose 3.
    A.  Workflow starters
    B.  Deciders
    C.  Task worker
    D.  Activity workers

Q35. While designing a web application to process customer order you have followed best practices as depicted in the diagram below. Your design includes implementing load balancing, dynamic scaling across multiple Availability Zones and persisting orders in a Multi-AZ Amazon RDS database instance. The application receives and persisting the order data, as well as scales with increases in traffic for popular items.

One potential point of vulnerability in the order processing workflow is in saving the order in the database. The business expects that every order should be persisted into the database. However, any potential deadlock, race condition, or network issue could cause the persistence of the order to fail. Then, the order is lost with no recourse to restore the order.

What change you can make in your architecture to address this issue?

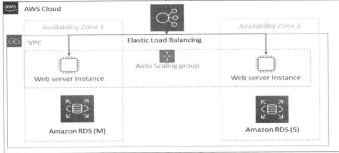

A. Change the family of web server EC2 instance to higher family with more CPU, memory and use Provisioned IOPS SSD backed EBS volumes.

B. Change the RDS storage to use Provisioned IOPS SSD. Provision a high IOPS and storage for database.

C. Use SQS queue to isolates the processing logic into its own component and runs it in a separate process from the web application.

D. All of the above.

Q36. Which AWS service is appropriate for creating, publishing, maintaining, monitoring, and securing REST and WebSocket APIs at any scale?

A. AWS ELB

B. Amazon API Gateway

C. AWS AppSync

D. Amazon Cognito

Q37. You are a solution architect for a mortgage processing SaaS application. You were having a design discussion with business analyst to break down the mortgage process from loan application to disbursal of money in multiple workflows. You made a list of multiple workflows which needs to interact with each other. How should you design these workflows in Amazon SWF?

A.  Collapse all multiple workflows into a single workflow and place it in a single domain, as workflows cannot interact across domains.
B.  Place each workflow in its own individual separate domain and design the workflows to interact across the domains.
C.  You cannot use SWF as workflow cannot interact with each other in SWF.
D.  Place the workflows which needs to interact with each other in a same domain, as workflows cannot interact across domains.

Q38. What are the different types of Amazon SWF tasks? Choose 3.
  A.  Notification task
  B.  Activity task
  C.  Lambda task
  D.  Decision task

Q39. Amazon SWF provides you with the feature of Signals that enables you to inject information into a running workflow execution. This helps in scenarios where you might want to add information to a running workflow execution to let it know that something has changed or to inform it of an external event. Which of the following is not an appropriate use case for using this feature?
  A.  For cases in which workflow has to be cancelled. (e.g., the order was cancelled by the customer).
  B.  Pausing workflow executions from progressing until a signal is received (e.g., waiting for an inventory shipment).
  C.  Providing information to a workflow execution that might affect the logic of how deciders make decisions. This is useful for workflows affected by external events (e.g., trying to finish the sale of a stock after the market closes).
  D.  Updating a workflow execution when you anticipate that changes might occur (e.g., changing order quantities after an order is placed and before it ships).

Q40. Which AWS service enables developers to manage and synchronize mobile app data in real time across devices and users, but still allows the data to be accessed and altered when the mobile device is in an offline state?
  A.  Amazon API Gateway
  B.  Amazon Cognito
  C.  AWS DataSync
  D.  AWS AppSync

Q41. You run an online photo editing website for two type of members: free members and fee paying premium members. The set of editing requests and photos is placed asynchronously in a SQS queue which is then processed by EC2 instances in an auto scaling group. How can you modify the architecture to ensure that your premium members editing upload get higher request than free member photo uploads?

A. Set the *message timer* attribute for free member's message so that those category messages are delayed for processing.

B. Create two queues, one for premium members and one for free members editing task. EC2 processing program should poll premium member's queue first and only if message request is empty then it should poll the free member's queue.

C. Set the priority in a message attribute and EC2 program will process the message accordingly.

D. Create a separate delay queue for free member's messages.

Q42. What are difference between Standard and Express workflows in AWS Step Functions? Choose 2.

A. Standard Workflows are ideal for long-running, durable, and auditable workflows. Express Workflows are ideal for high-volume, event-processing workloads.

B. Standard Workflows employ an at-most-once model. Express Workflows employ an at-least-once model

C. Express Workflows are ideal for long-running, durable, and auditable workflows. Standard Workflows are ideal for high-volume, event-processing workloads.

D. Express Workflows employ an at-most-once model. Standard Workflows employ an at-least-once model

Q43. What are different states you can define in an AWS Step Function? Choose 3.

A. Cancel, Retry

B. Task, Choice, Pass

C. Fail/Succeed, Wait

D. Parallel, Map

Q44. Which structured language is used to define your AWS Step function state machine?

A. Amazon Step Function Language

B. Amazon States Language

C. Amazon Step Function Policy

D. Amazon Step Function Access Control Language

Q45. Which of the following is not a use case for AWS Step functions?

A. Data processing: consolidate data from multiple databases into unified reports, refine and reduce large data sets into useful formats, or coordinate multi-step analytics and machine learning workflows

B. Container orchestration service : run, scale, and secure Docker container applications

C. DevOps and IT automation: build tools for continuous integration and continuous deployment, or create event-driven applications that automatically respond to changes in infrastructure

D. E-commerce: automate mission-critical business processes, such as order fulfillment and inventory tracking

E. Web applications: implement robust user registration processes and sign-on authentication

Q46.You are designing an online mortgage loan application based on Serverless microservices based architecture. The business logic for different application processing steps will be microservices developed using AWS Lambda. The data tier will comprise of S3 and DynamoDB. Users will also access this application using native mobile application running on their smartphones and will be authenticated using Amazon Cognito. Which AWS service you will use to expose the microservices as well as defined RESTful APIs and the service should scale with traffic?

A. Cognito
B. Network Load Balancer
C. API Gateway
D. Application Load Balancer

Q47. You run an online photo editing website for two type of members: free members and fee paying premium members. The set of editing requests and photos is placed asynchronously in a SQS queue which is then process by worked EC2 instances in an auto scaling group. The architecture has two SQS queues, one for premium members and one for free members editing task. You have on-demand EC2 instances in an auto scale group to process the messages in the premium members queue and spot instances for processing the message from free member queue. At times spot instances are terminated by AWS. What will happen to messages which are in-process by those terminated instances?

A. The message will be deleted by SQS.
B. The message will be deleted by the terminated instance and will not appear in the queue.
C. The message will be visible immediately in the queue and picked up for processing by other live spot instance.
D. The message will be visible in the queue after the visibility time is over and picked up for processing by other live spot instance.

Q48. Which type of Step function workflow you will use for use cases like streaming data processing, IoT data ingestion, mobile backend, and other high-throughput use-cases?

A. Standard workflow
B. Express workflow
C. Streaming workflow
D. Serverless workflow

Q49. Which type of Step function workflow you will use for orchestrating non-idempotent actions, such as starting an Amazon EMR cluster or processing payments. ?

A. Standard workflow
B. Express workflow

C. Streaming workflow

D. Serverless workflow

Q50. What are difference between Amazon SWF vs. AWS Step Functions? Choose 2.

A. AWS SWF provides a more productive and agile approach to coordinating application components using visual workflows with writing state machines in declarative JSON.

B. Amazon Step Functions gives you complete control over your orchestration logic, but increases the complexity of developing applications. You may write decider programs in the programming language of your choice, or you may use the Flow framework.

C. Amazon SWF gives you complete control over your orchestration logic, but increases the complexity of developing applications. You may write decider programs in the programming language of your choice, or you may use the Flow framework.

D. AWS Step Functions provides a more productive and agile approach to coordinating application components using visual workflows with writing state machines in declarative JSON.

Q51. Which of the following is not a correct scenario for using SNS? Choose 2.

A. Use Amazon SNS to push targeted news headlines to subscribers by email or SMS.

B. An application that sends a message to an Amazon SQS queue whenever an order is placed for a product. Then, the Amazon SNS topics that are subscribed to that queue would receive identical notifications for the new order.

C. Use Amazon SNS for sending notifications to an app, indicating that an update is available. The notification message can include a link to download and install the update.

D. Use Amazon SNS for authenticating mobile app users with Cognito.

E. An application that sends an Amazon SNS message to a topic whenever an order is placed for a product. Then, the Amazon SQS queues that are subscribed to that topic would receive identical notifications for the new order.

Q52. How can you improve the latency of requests to your API Gateway and also reduce the number of calls made to your API endpoint?

A. Use ElastiCache with API Gateway

B. Enable API caching in the API Gateway setting

C. Use CloudFront with API Gateway

D. Configuring API-level and Stage-Level Throttling in a Usage Plan

Q53. Which of the following are features of Amazon SNS? Choose 4.

A. Provides developers with a highly scalable, flexible, and cost-effective capability to publish messages from an application and immediately deliver them to subscribers or other applications

B. Follows the "publish-subscribe" (pub-sub) messaging paradigm, with notifications being delivered to clients using a "poll" mechanism that eliminates the need to periodically "push" new information and updates.

C. Follows the "publish-subscribe" (pub-sub) messaging paradigm, with notifications being delivered to clients using a "push" mechanism that eliminates the need to periodically check or "poll" for new information and updates.

D. A subscriber sends messages to topics that they have created or to topics they have permission to publish to.

E. A publisher sends messages to topics that they have created or to topics they have permission to publish to.

F. Subscribers receive all messages published to the topics to which they subscribe, and all subscribers to a topic receive the same messages.

Q54. You are the solution architect for an ecommerce company. There are regular flash discounts and festivals discount offered which leads to sudden burst in orders at an unpredictable magnitude and many time more than off discount period. How can you ensure none of the customer order is lost without impacting performance, scalability, and resiliency?

A. Increase the minimum fleet of servers saving the customers' orders.

B. Have an SQS queue for customer orders and fleet of EC2 instances in auto scale group to process the order.

C. Increase the performance and capacity of database.

D. Use lambda instead of EC2 for processing the customer order.

Q55. How is Amazon SNS different from Amazon SQS? Choose 2.

A. Amazon SNS allows applications to send time-critical messages to multiple subscribers through a "push" mechanism, eliminating the need to periodically check or "poll" for updates.

B. Amazon SQS allows applications to send time-critical messages to multiple subscribers through a "push" mechanism, eliminating the need to periodically check or "poll" for updates.

C. Amazon SQS is a message queue service used by distributed applications to exchange messages through a polling model, and can be used to decouple sending and receiving components.

D. Amazon SNS is a message queue service used by distributed applications to exchange messages through a polling model, and can be used to decouple sending and receiving components.

Q56. Which of the following Apps will not be suitable to use AWS AppSync?

A. Gaming apps with real-time scoreboards, News feeds and financial data

B. Customer service dashboards, Social Media with content feeds and search/discovery/messaging

C. Shared wallet, travel or itinerary tracking with offline usage

D. Business Intelligence interactive dashboard with drill down capability

E.   Dating apps with likes, messaging and geo/proximity awareness
F.   Field service apps that need to allow for querying and CRUD operations, even when disconnected
G.   Chat apps, including presence indicators and conversation history

Q57. Which AWS Service is a fully managed serverless GraphQL service for real-time data queries, synchronization, communications and offline programming features?
A.   Amazon Athena
B.   AWS Amplify
C.   AWS DataSync
D.   AWS AppSync

Q58. Which of the following are not features of AppSync? Choose 2.
A.   Uses GraphQL, a data language that enables client apps to fetch, change and subscribe to data from servers.
B.   Best for creating RESTful APIs using either HTTP APIs (Preview) or REST APIs.
C.   Let's you specify which portions of your data should be available in a real-time manner using GraphQL Subscriptions.
D.   Provides a queryable on-device DataStore for web, mobile and IoT developers with a local-first and familiar programming model to interact with data seamlessly whether you're online or offline.
E.   Makes it easy for developers to publish, maintain, monitor, secure, and operate APIs at any scale.
F.   Gives client applications the ability to specify data requirements with GraphQL so that only the needed data is fetched, allowing for both server and client filtering.
G.   Server-side data caching capabilities reduce the need to directly access data sources by making data available in high speed in-memory managed caches, delivering data at low latency.

Q59. Your company is planning to migrate portfolio of distributed applications to AWS. Currently ActiveMQ is the message broker used between in-premise applications. Which AWS service you should use to replace the message broker component of the architecture?
A.   Amazon SQS
B.   Amazon SNS
C.   Amazon MQ
D.   Amazon ActiveMQ

# Chapter 8 Security Identity and Compliance: AWS Identity and Access Management, AWS Artifact, AWS Certificate Manager, AWS CloudHSM, Amazon Cognito, AWS Directory Service, AWS Firewall Manager, Amazon GuardDuty, Amazon Inspector, AWS Key Management Service, Amazon Macie, AWS Security Hub, AWS Shield, AWS Single Sign-On, AWS WAF

Q1. What protection Aws Shield provide?

A. Block common attack patterns, such as SQL injection or cross-site scripting
B. Protection against Distributed Denial of Service (DDoS) attacks
C. Protection against In-Transit data spoofing
D. Protection against EC2 hacking
E. Protection against encryption key loss

Q2. What is difference between AWS Shield Standard and AWS Shield Advanced? Choose 2.

A. AWS Shield Standard provides protection for all AWS customers against common and most frequently occurring infrastructure (layer 3 and 4) attacks like SYN/UDP floods, reflection attacks.

B. AWS Shield Advanced provides protection for all AWS customers against common and most frequently occurring infrastructure (layer 3 and 4) attacks like SYN/UDP floods, reflection attacks.

C. AWS Shield Standard provides enhanced protections for your applications running on protected Amazon EC2, Elastic Load Balancing (ELB), Amazon CloudFront, AWS Global Accelerator, and Route 53 resources against more sophisticated and larger attacks.

D. AWS Shield Advanced provides enhanced protections for your applications running on protected Amazon EC2, Elastic Load Balancing (ELB), Amazon CloudFront, AWS Global Accelerator, and Route 53 resources against more sophisticated and larger attacks.

Q3. Which AWS service lets you monitor the HTTP and HTTPS requests that are forwarded to an Amazon API Gateway, Amazon CloudFront or an Application Load Balancer and gives you control over which traffic to allow or block to your web applications by defining customizable web security rules?

A. AWS Shield
B. AWS Cloudtrail
C. AWS Cloudwatch
D. AWS WAF

Q4. What are the different conditions you can define in AWS WAF to watch for in web requests? Choose 4.

A. Cross-site scripting: Scripts that are likely to be malicious. Attackers embed scripts that can exploit vulnerabilities in web applications.

B. IP addresses or address ranges, country or geographical location that requests originate from.

C. Length of specified parts of the request, such as the query string. Strings that appear in the request.

D. User credentials authentication.

E. SQL injection: SQL code that is likely to be malicious. Attackers try to extract data from your database by embedding malicious SQL code in a web request.

Q5. Which Amazon service offers threat detection that enables you to continuously monitor and protect your AWS accounts and workloads by continuously analyzing streams of meta-data generated from your account and network activity found in AWS CloudTrail Events, Amazon VPC Flow Logs, and DNS Logs?
   A. AWS WAF
   B. AWS Shield
   C. Amazon GuardDuty
   D. Amazon Macie

Q6. What is Rate-based Rule in AWS WAF? Choose 2.
   A. Allows you to specify the number of web requests that are allowed by a client IP in a trailing, continuously updated, 15 minute period.
   B. Allows you to specify the number of web requests that are allowed by a client IP in a trailing, continuously updated, 5 minute period.
   C. If an IP address breaches the configured limit, new requests will be blocked until the request rate falls below the configured threshold.
   D. If an IP address breaches the configured limit, new requests will be blocked for 5 minutes.

Q7. What is AWS security shared responsibility model? Choose 3.
   A. Security of the cloud – AWS is responsible for protecting the infrastructure that runs AWS services in the AWS Cloud. This infrastructure is composed of the hardware, software, networking, and facilities that run AWS Cloud services.
   B. AWS compliance programs doesn't includes testing by third party auditors who verify the effectiveness of security.
   C. Security in the cloud – Your responsibility is determined by the AWS service that you use. This determines the amount of configuration work the customer must perform as part of their security responsibilities.
   D. Security in the cloud -You are also responsible for other factors including the sensitivity of your data, your organization's requirements, and applicable laws and regulations.

Q8. What are the different types of policy types available in AWS? Choose 6.
   A. Identity-based policies
   B. Certificate based policies
   C. Resource-based policies
   D. Permissions boundaries
   E. User Policies
   F. Organizations SCPs
   G. Access control lists (ACLs)
   H. Session policies

Q9. Based on recent pattern of brute attack on your web site, you have analyzed that the requests come from 192.0.2.44 and they contain the value BadBot in the User-Agent header. You just don't want to block the ip-address but want to block it only when there is more than 1000 requests from the ip in a duration of 5 minutes. How can you set up this rule?

    A.   Create a rate based rule in AWS Shield

    B.   Create a rate based rule in AWS Firewall Manager

    C.   Create a rate based rule in AWS WAF

    D.   Create a rate based rule in EC2

Q10. How can you use WAF Rate-based rule to limit access to certain parts of your web login page? Choose from following rate-based rule configuration:

String match Condition settings:

1. The "Part of the request to filter" on is *URI*.

2. The "Match Type" is *Starts with*.

3. A "Value to match" is *login*

Rate limit setting:

4. A Rate limit of 1000.

IP match Condition settings:

5. Specify the IPv4 address 192.0.2.44/32.

    A.   1,2,3,4

    B.   13,4,5

    C.   3,4,5

    D.   2,3,4,5

Q11. Which AWS service simplifies your AWS WAF, AWS Shield Advanced, and Amazon VPC security group's administration and maintenance tasks across multiple accounts and resources?

    A.   AWS System Manager

    B.   AWS Trusted Advisor

    C.   AWS Firewall Manager

    D.   AWS Security

Q12. Which AWS Directory Service is a Microsoft Active Directory compatible directory that is powered by Samba 4 and hosted on the AWS cloud?

    A.   AWS Managed Microsoft AD

    B.   AD Connector

    C.   Amazon Cloud Directory

    D.   Simple AD

Q13. Which AWS Directory Service provides an easy way to connect compatible AWS applications to your existing on-premises Microsoft Active Directory?

A.   AWS Managed Microsoft AD
B.   AD Connector
C.   Amazon Cloud Directory
D.   Amazon Cognito

Q14. Which AWS Directory Service is best choice if you have more than 5,000 users and need a trust relationship set up between an AWS hosted directory and your on-premises directories?
A.   AWS Managed Microsoft AD
B.   AD Connector
C.   Amazon Cloud Directory
D.   Simple AD

Q15. Your company has around 3000 users and want to use Microsoft Active Directory compatible features to manage their EC2 instances running Windows and other AWS applications such as Amazon workspaces, Amazon Workdocs or Amazon WorkMail. You don't want to set a trust relationship with on-premise AD. Which AWS service will you use?
A.   AWS Managed Microsoft AD
B.   AD Connector
C.   Amazon Cloud Directory
D.   Simple AD

Q16.   How is web identity federation i.e. providing access to externally authenticated users supported in AWS? Choose 3.
A.   Using Amazon Cognito as an identity broker which does much of the federation work.
B.   If you are creating a mobile app or web-based app it blocks users who have Login with Amazon, Facebook, Google, or any OpenID Connect (OIDC) compatible identity provider.
C.   You can create a mobile app or web-based app that can let users identify themselves through an Internet identity provider like Login with Amazon, Facebook, Google, or any OpenID Connect (OIDC) compatible identity provider, the app can use federation to access AWS.
D.   Using Web Identity Federation API Operations for Mobile Apps.

Q17.   What are IAM Identity-based and Resource-based Policies? Choose 2.
A.   Identity-based policies are permissions policies that you attach to an IAM identity, such as an IAM user, group, or role.
B.   Resource-based policies are permissions policies that you attach to a resource such as an Amazon S3 bucket or an IAM role trust policy.
C.   Identity-based policies are permissions policies that you attach to an IAM identity, such an Amazon S3 bucket or an IAM role trust policy.

D. Resource-based policies are permissions policies that you attach to a resource such as an IAM user, group, or role.

Q18. How many types of IAM Identity Managed policies are there? Choose 2.
A. Inline policies
B. AWS managed policies
C. Resource-based policies
D. Customer managed policies

Q19. What is a principal in AWS IAM terms? Choose 2.
A. A person that uses the AWS account root user, an IAM user, or an IAM role to sign in and make requests to AWS.
B. An application that uses the AWS account root user, an IAM user, or an IAM role to sign in and make requests to AWS.
C. An encryption API that uses the AWS account root user, an IAM user, or an IAM role to sign in and make requests to AWS.
D. A replication service that uses the AWS account root user, an IAM user, or an IAM role to sign in and make requests to AWS.

Q20. Choose IAM best practices which should be followed? Choose 4.
A. Use Roles for Applications That Run on Amazon EC2 Instances
B. Share user credentials to delegate permissions
C. Use Roles to Delegate Permissions
D. Enable MFA for Privileged Users
E. Do Not Share Access Keys
F. Store access keys in your application configuration file

Q21. What are the scenarios when you should create an IAM 'user' instead of a 'role'? Choose 3.
A. You're creating an application that runs on an Amazon Elastic Compute Cloud (Amazon EC2) instance and that application makes requests to other AWS resources.
B. You created an AWS account and you're the only person who works in your account.
C. Other people in your group need to work in your AWS account, and your group is using no other identity mechanism.
D. You want to use the command-line interface (CLI) to work with AWS.
E. Users in your company are authenticated in your corporate network and want to be able to use AWS without having to sign in again.

Q22. An IAM user with administrator permissions is not the same thing as the AWS account root user.
A. True
B. False

Q23. What are the different ways to access AWS depending on user credentials? Choose 4.
   A.  Access Keys
   B.  Console password
   C.  SSH keys for use with CodeCommit
   D.  Server Certificate
   E.  Telnet Putty

Q24. Which statements are true about IAM users? Choose 4.
   A.  By default, a brand new IAM user has no permissions to do anything.
   B.  You could use an ARN to specify the user as a Principal in an IAM policy. Arn: aws: iam: account-ID-without-hyphens: user/James.
   C.  By default, a brand new IAM user has administrator permissions to do anything.
   D.  Each IAM user can be associated with more than one AWS account.
   E.  An IAM user can represent a person or an application that uses its credentials to make AWS requests.
   F.  Each IAM user is associated with one and only one AWS account.

Q25. What signature versions are supported by AWS? Choose 2.
   A.  Signature Version 1
   B.  Signature Version 2
   C.  Signature Version 3
   D.  Signature Version 4
   E.  Signature Version 5

Q26. Choose ways you can change the permissions for an IAM user in your AWS account?
   A.  By changing its group memberships
   B.  By copying permissions from an existing user
   C.  By attaching policies directly to a user
   D.  By setting a permissions boundary
   E.  All of the above

Q27. Which statements are true for IAM groups? Choose 3.
   A.  A group can contain many users, and a user can belong to multiple groups.
   B.  Groups can't be nested; they can contain only users, not other groups.
   C.  Groups can be nested; they can contain only users, not other groups.
   D.  There's no default group that automatically includes all users in the AWS account. If you want to have a group like that, you need to create it and assign each new user to it.
   E.  Groups can't be nested; they can contain only roles, not other groups.
   F.  A group can contain many roles, and a role can belong to multiple groups.

Q28. A group is not truly an "identity" in IAM because it cannot be identified as a Principal in a permission policy. It is simply a way to attach policies to multiple users at one time.
- A. True
- B. False

Q29. An IAM role is not an IAM identity that you can create in your account that has specific permissions.
- A. True
- B. False

Q30. Roles can be used by the following.
- A. An IAM user in the same AWS account as the role.
- B. An IAM user in a different AWS account than the role.
- C. A web service offered by AWS such as Amazon Elastic Compute Cloud (Amazon EC2).
- D. An external user authenticated by an external identity provider (IdP) service that is compatible with SAML 2.0 or OpenID Connect, or a custom-built identity broker.
- E. All of the above.

Q31. Delegation of a role involves setting up a trust between the account that owns the resource (the trusting account), and the account that contains the users that need to access the resource (the trusted account). The trusted and trusting accounts can be any of the following. Choose 3:
- A. The same account.
- B. It can never be in two accounts owned by different organization.
- C. Separate accounts that are both under your organization's control.
- D. Two accounts owned by different organizations.

Q32. Assuming that for a live web application you are maintaining two AWS accounts to isolate development and production environment. Development account users are assigned to two IAM groups of *Testers* and *Developers*. Some of the users in development account belonging to *Developer* user group will require access to production environment. What steps you will take to leverage IAM Roles so that some of the users in the *Developer* group in development account environment will have cross account access to production account environment? Choose 3.
- A. In the production account use IAM to create a role in that account and defines a trust policy that specifies the development account as a Principal. Also defines a permissions policy for the role that specifies which role users have read and write permissions to AWS resources.
- B. Share the account number and name of the role (for AWS console users) or the Amazon Resource Name (ARN) (for AWS CLI or AWS API access) to Development environment users for whom you want to give access.

C. Create separate identities and passwords in each environment for users who work in both accounts.

D. In the development account grant specific required members of the Developers group permission to switch to the role. This is done by granting the Developers group permission to call the AWS Security Token Service (AWS STS) AssumeRole API for the role created in production account.

Q33. You have VPC where you have web server instances in public subnet and database servers in the private subnet. There is an Application Load Balancer in the front listening at port 80 mapped to web server instances in public subnet. You are also leveraging Cloudfront for low latency and high transfer speeds for your end user. How can you minimize the impact of a DDoS attack or brute force attack from one ip address on your application? You want to ensure that attack requests should not reach your web server instances? Choose 2.

A. On discovering attack update the web server instance security group to block access to ip address/es.

B. Use AWS Shield together with AWS WAF rules to create a comprehensive DDoS attack mitigation strategy.

C. Have your web server instances in private subnet.

D. Add CloudFront IP addresses to your security groups to ensure ELB only responds to requests that are served by CloudFront (and therefore inspected by AWS WAF).

Q34. What are the features of IAM user access keys? Choose 3.

A. Access keys are long-term credentials for an IAM user or the AWS account root user.

B. You can use access keys to sign programmatic requests to the AWS CLI or AWS API (directly or using the AWS SDK).

C. You must use either the access key ID or secret access key to authenticate your requests.

D. Access keys consist of two parts: an access key ID and a secret access.

Q35. Your company first project in AWS cloud is an internal web application to be used by employees only. You want to provide single sign on where employee can use their existing corporate sign on identities. You don't want to a have separate user management module in the new application which will require your employees to have a separate authentication userid/password. Essentially this will enable your employees to have single sign on to new web application using existing corporate identities. You found that AWS supports this by way of user federation for authenticating using existing corporate identities. Which of the following consideration have to be kept in mind to use this user federation feature? Choose 3.

A. Existing corporate Identity Provider should be compatible with Security Assertion Markup Language 2.0 (SAML 2.0) to provide single-sign on (SSO) access.

B. If your corporate Identity Provider is Microsoft Active Directory Federation Service (AD FS), you cannot configure SSO.

C. If your corporate Identity Provider is Microsoft Active Directory Federation Service (AD FS), you can configure SSO.

D. If your corporate directory is not compatible with SAML 2.0, you can create an identity broker application to provide single-sign on (SSO) access to the AWS for your users.

E. If your corporate directory is not compatible with SAML 2.0, you cannot create an identity broker application to provide single-sign on (SSO) access to the AWS Management Console for your users.

Q36.You are planning to use a third party product to monitor your AWS accounts and its resources for optimization. To enable this you are planning to use roles to delegate access to them. What information third party must provide to you to create a role that they can assume? Choose 3.

A. The third party's AWS account ID which you will specify as the principal when you define the trust policy for the role.

B. The third party's AWS account root user id which you will specify as the principal when you define the trust policy for the role.

C. An external ID to uniquely associate with the role. You will specify this ID when you define the trust policy for the role. The third party then must provide this ID when they assume the role.

D. The access keys of third party account to uniquely associate with the role. You will specify these keys when you define the trust policy for the role. The third party then must provide these keys when they assume the role.

E. The permissions that the third party requires to work with your AWS resources. You must specify these permissions when defining the role's permission policy

Q37. What are the scenarios when you should create an IAM 'role' instead of a 'user'? Choose 3.

A. You're creating an application that runs on an Amazon Elastic Compute Cloud (Amazon EC2) instance and that application makes requests to other AWS resources.

B. You created an AWS account and you're the only person who works in your account.

C. Other people in your group need to work in your AWS account, and your group is using no other identity mechanism.

D. You want to use the command-line interface (CLI) to work with AWS.

E. Users in your company are authenticated in your corporate network and want to be able to use AWS without having to sign in again.

F. You're creating an app that runs on a mobile phone and that makes requests to AWS.

Q38. What are the best practices for managing IAM user access keys? Choose 4.

A. Remove (or Don't Generate) Account Access Key.

B. Use Temporary Security Credentials (IAM Roles) Instead of Long-Term Access Keys

C. Don't embed access keys directly into code.

D.   Rotate access keys periodically.

E.   Embed access keys directly into code for better security.

Q39. What are the steps you will follow to create an administrator user following IAM best practices? Choose 3.

A.   Create an Administrators group and give the group permission to access all AWS account's resources.

B.   Create an Administrators role and give the group permission to access all AWS account's resources.

C.   Create a user and add that user to the Administrators group.

D.   Create a role and add that role to the Administrators group.

E.   Create a password for the user to sign in to the AWS Management Console.

Q40. Soma is founder of an Artificial Intelligence product start up. Upon starting the company, she created her own AWS account and used AWS services by herself. Then as company expanded she hired developers, admins, testers, managers, and system administrators. What steps would you advice for Soma based on IAM best practices to manage user access? Choose 3.

A.   Using AWS account root user credentials she should create a user for herself called Soma, and a group called Admins. Add user Soma to group Admins.

B.   She should share her root credentials with Sysadmin to make the job of user management easier.

C.   She should create groups called Developers, Testers, Managers and SysAdmins. Employee's userid should be created by admins, and put them in their respective groups.

D.   She should continue using the root credentials to create users and groups.

Q41. You have an application running on EC2 instance which has to access AWS resources. How can you grant permission to application so that it can access the AWS resources following the best practices?

A.   Define an IAM role that has appropriate permissions for your application and launch the Amazon EC2 instance with roles for EC2.

B.   Pass an access key to the application.

C.   Embed the access key in the application

D.   Have the application read a key from a source such as an Amazon S3 encrypted bucket

Q42. Federated users don't have permanent identities in your AWS account the way that IAM users do. How do you assign permissions to federated users? Choose 2.

A.   Create an entity referred to as a role and define permissions for the role

B.   When a federated user signs in to AWS, the user is associated with the role and is granted the permissions that are defined in the role.

C. Create an entity referred to as a group and define permissions for the group

D. When a federated user signs in to AWS, the user is associated with the group and is granted the permissions that are defined in the group.

Q43. A principal can be an AWS account root user, an IAM user, or a role which can perform actions and access resources. How you can grant permissions to a principal to access a resource? Choose 2.

A. You can attach a trust policy to a user (directly, or indirectly through a group) or to a role.

B. You can attach a permissions policy to a user (directly, or indirectly through a group) or to a role.

C. For those services that support resource-based policies, you can identify the principal in the Principal element of a policy attached to the resource.

D. You can only attach a managed policy to a user (directly, or indirectly through a group) or to a role.

Q44. You are building a mobile app car racing game where user data such as scores and profiles is stored in Amazon S3 and Amazon DynamoDB. You know that for security and maintenance reasons, long-term AWS security credentials should not be distributed with the game. You do not want to create new user identities in IAM for each player because the game will have large number of users. You have designed the game in such a way so that users can sign in using an identity that they've already established with well-known external identity provider (IdP), such as Amazon, Facebook, Google, or any OpenID Connect (OIDC)-compatible IdP What is the process to configure your app to enable user login using their external identity provider user id and password?

A. Sign up as a developer with Login with Amazon, Facebook, Google, or any other OpenID Connect (OIDC) compatible IdP and configure one or more apps with the provider.

B. Create identity pool in Amazon Cognito to have IAM role for authenticated identities

C. Download and integrate the AWS SDK for iOS or the AWS SDK for Android with your app, and import the files required to use Amazon Cognito.

D. Create an instance of the Amazon Cognito credentials provider, passing the identity pool ID, your AWS account number, and the Amazon Resource Name (ARN) of the roles that you associated with the identity pool.

E. All of the above

Q45. You have a mobile app which access backend resources in AWS. You are using external identity provider (IdP), Amazon, for users to sign in and authenticate them. Arrange the following 5 steps in right sequence which mirrors the execution steps?

a) A customer starts your app on a mobile device. The app asks the user to sign in.

b) The app requests temporary security credentials from AWS STS, passing the Cognito token.

c) The app uses Login with Amazon resources to accept the user's credentials.

d) The temporary security credentials can be used by the app to access any AWS resources required by the app to operate. The role associated with the temporary security credentials and its assigned policies determines what can be accessed.

e) The app uses Cognito API operations to exchange the Login with Amazon ID token for a Cognito token.

A. a, b, c, d, e

B. a c, d, b, e

C. a, c, e, b, d

D. a, d, c, e, b

E. a, e, b, d, c

Q46. Which of the following AWS services allow you to attach a policy directly to a resource (instead of using a role as a proxy)? Choose 4.

A. Amazon RDS

B. Amazon Simple Storage Service (S3) buckets

C. Glacier vaults

D. Amazon Simple Notification Service (SNS) topics

E. Simple Queue Service (SQS) queues

F. Amazon EC2

Q47. When you want to configure web identity federation with an external identity provider (IdP) service, what you should create in IAM to inform AWS about the IdP and its configuration and also establishes "trust" between your AWS account and the IdP ?

A. IAM Role

B. IAM User

C. IAM Service linked Role

D. IAM identity provider

Q48. What are the features of AWS IAM Managed policies? Choose 4.

A. It is a standalone policy that is created and administered by AWS having its own Amazon Resource Name (ARN) that includes the policy name.

B. You cannot change the permissions defined in AWS managed policies.

C. One particularly useful category of AWS managed policies are those designed for job functions.

D. AWS managed policies are designed to provide permissions for many common use cases.

E. You can modify a managed policy and save it as your own account version.

Q49. You have created an IAM user named Austin with a permission boundary as shown below so that he should be allowed to manage only Amazon S3, Amazon CloudWatch, and Amazon EC2.

```
{
    "Version": "2012-10-17",
    "Statement": [
        {
            "Effect": "Allow",
            "Action": [
                "s3:*",
                "cloudwatch:*",
                "ec2:*"
            ],
            "Resource": "*"
        }
    ]
}
```

After that you attached following policy to Austin user:

```
{
    "Version": "2012-10-17",
    "Statement": {
    "Effect": "Allow",
    "Action": "iam:CreateUser",
    "Resource": "*"
    }
}
```

This policy allows creating a user in IAM. What will happen when Austin tries to create a user in IAM?

    A.   He will be able to create a user as per permission given in second policy.

    B.   It fails because the permissions boundary does not allow the iam:CreateUser operation.

    C.   You cannot attach two policies to an IAM user.

    D.   He will be able to create a user who has permission to resources in first policy only.

Q50. Which AWS service acts as an identity broker and does much of the federation work for you to enable your users to sign in directly with a user name and password, or through a third party such as Facebook, Amazon, or Google ?

    A.   AWS IAM

    B.   AWS Cognito

    C.   AWS WAF

    D.   AWS Inspector

Q51. What are the features of Amazon Cognito? Choose 3.
  A.  Encryption Key management
  B.  Social and enterprise identity federation
  C.  Access control for AWS resources
  D.  Standards-based authentication using common identity management standards including OpenID Connect, OAuth 2.0, and SAML 2.0

Q52. Which of the following statement is not correct about policies and IAM root user?
  A.  You cannot attach identity-based policies to the root user.
  B.  You cannot set the permissions boundary for the root user.
  C.  You can attach identity-based policies to the root user.
  D.  You can specify the root user as the principal in a resource-based policy or an ACL.
  E.  As a member of an account, the root user is affected by any SCPs for the account.

Q53. What are the two main components of Amazon Cognito?
  A.  Password Pools
  B.  User pools
  C.  IAM Pools
  D.  Identity Pools

Q54. What are the features of Amazon Cognito User Pools? Choose 3.
  A.  Sign-up and sign-in services. A built-in, customizable web UI to sign in users.
  B.  Social sign-in with Facebook, Google, and Login with Amazon, as well as sign-in with SAML identity providers from your user pool.
  C.  Obtain temporary, limited-privilege AWS credentials to access other AWS services.
  D.  User directory management and user profiles. Security features such as multi-factor authentication (MFA), checks for compromised credentials, account takeover protection, and phone and email verification.

Q55. What are the features of Amazon Identity User Pools? Choose 2.
  A.  User Identity directory management and user profiles.
  B.  Enable you to create unique identities for your users and federate them with identity providers.
  C.  Sign-up and sign-in services.
  D.  You can obtain temporary, limited-privilege AWS credentials to access other AWS services.

Q56. Which are the identity providers supported by Amazon Identity pool?
  A.  Login with Amazon (Identity Pools), Facebook (Identity Pools), Google (Identity Pools).
  B.  Amazon Cognito User Pools

C. Open ID Connect Providers (Identity Pools), SAML Identity Providers (Identity Pools)

D. All of the above

Q57. You are developing a mobile application that will enable user to login using their userids in Facebook, Amazon and Google. In the cloud backend you will have Serverless architecture. For backend application data storage you want to use a RDBMS database. What is the minimum set of AWS services you will need for your mobile application and backend cloud application?

A. Lambda, Cognito, API Gateway, DynamoDB
B. Lambda, Cognito, API Gateway, Aurora Serverless
C. Elastic Beanstalk, Cognito, API Gateway, Aurora
D. Lambda, Fargate, API Gateway, DynamoDB

Q58. Your company is adopting AWS cloud by migrating majority of existing on-premise application to cloud and retaining some of them on premise. Currently they use Microsoft Active Directory in the corporate network for centralized resource management and single sign on for users. As a solution architect you have recommended to use AWS Managed Microsoft AD. Which of the following is not a use cases possible by using AWS Managed Microsoft AD? Choose 2.

A. Sign In to AWS Applications and Services with AD Credentials.
B. Centrally manage your Amazon EC2 for Windows or Linux instances by joining your instances to your AWS Managed Microsoft AD domain.
C. Provision, manage, and deploy public and private Secure Sockets Layer/Transport Layer Security (SSL/TLS) certificates for use with AWS services and your internal connected resources.
D. Provide Directory Services to Your AD-Aware Workloads.
E. Provide SSO to Office 365 and Other Cloud Applications.
F. Extend Your On-Premises AD to the AWS Cloud.
G. Create and manage cryptographic keys and control their use across a wide range of AWS services and in your applications.

Q59. Which of the following is not a benefit provided by AD Connector?

A. Your end users and IT administrators can use their existing corporate credentials to log on to AWS applications such as Amazon WorkSpaces, Amazon WorkDocs, or Amazon WorkMail.
B. You can manage AWS resources like Amazon EC2 instances or Amazon S3 buckets through IAM role-based access to the AWS Management Console.
C. You can consistently enforce existing security policies (such as password expiration, password history, and account lockouts) whether users or IT administrators are accessing resources in your on-premises infrastructure or in the AWS Cloud.

D. You can use AD Connector to enable multi-factor authentication by integrating with your existing RADIUS-based MFA infrastructure to provide an additional layer of security when users access AWS applications.

E. None of the above

Q60. Which of the following is not true regarding AWS shared responsibility model?
A. AWS responsibility "Security of the Cloud" - AWS is responsible for protecting the infrastructure that runs all of the services offered in the AWS Cloud.
B. Shared responsibility model also extends to IT controls.
C. Shared responsibility model is limited to security only and doesn't extends to IT controls.
D. Customer is responsible for "Security in the Cloud" – Customer responsibility will be determined by the AWS Cloud services that a customer selects.

Q61. All AWS customers get access to the seven core Trusted Advisor checks to help increase the security and performance of the AWS environment. Choose 3 from below.
A. Security : S3 Bucket Permissions, Security Groups - Specific Ports Unrestricted, IAM Use
B. Security :MFA on Root Account, EBS Public Snapshots, RDS Public Snapshots
C. Service Limits
D. Amazon EC2 Reserved instance optimization

Q62. AWS Trusted Advisor offers a rich set of best practice checks and recommendations across five categories. Which of the following security checks are done? Choose 3.
A. Security Groups Unrestricted Access
B. Amazon Redshift Security Group
C. IAM Password policy, IAM Access key rotation
D. ELB Security groups and listener security

Q63. Which AWS online tool provides you real time guidance to help you provision your resources following AWS best practices in five categories of Cost optimization, performance, security, fault tolerance and service limits?
A. AWS System Manager
B. AWS Well architected Tool
C. AWS Trusted Advisor
D. AWS Organizations

Q64. Which of the following are cost optimization best practices checks performed by Trusted Advisor? Choose 3.
A. Lambda Optimization
B. Amazon EC2 Reserved Instances Optimization
C. Low utilization Amazon EC2 Instances

D.    Underutilized Amazon EBS volumes and Amazon Redshift Clusters

Q65. Which type of IAM Identity policy you can embed in a principal entity (a user, group, or role) and is an inherent part of the principal entity?
A.    AWS Managed Policies
B.    Inline Policies
C.    Customer Managed Policies
D.    Managed Policies

Q66. Which of the following statement is not correct about IAM Access Control Policies (ACLs)?
A.    ACLs are service policies that allow you to control which principals in another account can access a resource.
B.    ACLs cannot be used to control access for a principal within the same account.
C.    ACLs can be used to control access for a principal within the same account.
D.    ACLs are similar to resource-based policies, although they are the only policy type that does not use the JSON policy document format.
E.    Amazon S3, AWS WAF, and Amazon VPC are examples of services that support ACLs.

Q67 Soma is founder of an Artificial Intelligence product start up. Upon starting the company, she created her own AWS account and used AWS products by herself. Then as company expanded she hired developers, admins, testers, managers, and system administrators. Using AWS account root user credentials she created a user for herself called *Soma*, and a group called *Admins*. She added user *Soma* to group *Admins*. She also created groups called *Developers*, *Testers*, *Managers* and *SysAdmins*. She created users for each of her employees, and puts the users in their respective groups. What IAM best practice she should follow so that she can easily apply any account-wide permissions to all users in the AWS account?
A.    Create a customer managed policy and attach to each user.
B.    Any account wide permission can be updated in each of the group's permission (*Developers, Testers, Managers* and *SysAdmins*) are attached to.
C.    She should create a group called *AllUsers* and add all users to that group so that she can easily apply any account-wide permissions to all users in the AWS account..
D.    Create a customer managed policy and attach to each group.

Q68. Assume that a principal sends a request to AWS to access a resource in the same account as the principal's entity. Choose the correct statements which aligns with how IAM policy evaluation logic works? Choose 4.
A.    By default, all requests are implicitly allowed.
B.    By default, all requests are implicitly denied.
C.    An explicit allow in an identity-based or resource-based policy overrides implicit deny.

D.  An explicit allow in an identity-based or resource-based policy overrides implicit allow.

E.  If a permissions boundary, Organizations SCP, or session policy is present, it might override the allow with an implicit deny.

F.  An explicit deny in any policy overrides any allows.

Q69-70 are based on diagram below:

The administrator of the 123456789012 account attached identity-based policies to the users JohnSmith, CarlosSalazar, and MaryMajor. The administrator also added resource-based policies to Resource X, Resource Y, and Resource Z.

### Account Id : 123456789012

**Identity Based Policies**

**John Smith**
Can List, Read On Resource X

**Carlos Salazar**
Can List, Read On Resource Y, Z

**Mary Major**
Can List, Read, Write On Resource X, Y, Z

**Zhang Wei**
No Policy

**Resource Based Policies**

**Resource X**
John Smith : Can List, Read
Mary Major: Can List, Read

**Resource Y**
Carlos Salazar : Can List, Write
Zhang Wei: Can List, Read

**Resource Z**
Carlos Salazar : Denied Access
Zhang Wei: Allowed Full Access

Q69. Which of the following statements are correct about actions that can be performed by Mary Major and John Smith as per above identity and resource policies? Choose 2.

A.  John can perform list and read actions on Resource X.

B.  Mary can list, Read only on Resource X.

C.  Mary can perform list, read, and write operations on Resource X, Resource Y, and Resource Z.

D.  John can perform list and read actions on Resource Z.

Q70. Which of the following statements are correct about actions that can be performed by Carlos Salazar and Zhang Wei as per above identity and resource policies? Choose 2.

A.  Zhang has no access to Resource Z.

B.  Carlos can perform list, read, and write actions on Resource Y, Z.

C.  Carlos can perform list, read, and write actions on Resource Y, but is denied access to Resource Z.

D.  Zhang has full access to Resource Z.

Q71. What is the format of an IAM Policy?

A. XML
B. CSV
C. JSON
D. All of the above

Q72. You have created an IAM user for a new employee but she is not able to do actions. Which of the following is correct reason?
A. A newly created user becomes active after 24 hours.
B. By default, a brand new IAM user has no permissions to do anything.
C. Your account IAM service may be disabled.
D. AWS IAM service may be down.

Q73. Your company is adopting AWS cloud by migrating majority of existing on-premise application to cloud and retaining some of them on premise. Currently they use on-premises AD to administer user accounts, manage group memberships, and control access to on-premises resources. You want to enable your users to sign in to the AWS Management Console using on-premises AD credentials to manage AWS resources such as Amazon EC2, Amazon RDS, and Amazon S3. How can you achieve this? Choose 2.
A. Connect Your On-Premises Active Directory to AWS Simple AD for federated AWS Management Console access.
B. Connect Your On-Premises Active Directory to AWS Using AD Connector for federated AWS Management Console access.
C. By using an AD trust between AWS Microsoft AD and your on-premises AD, you can assign your on-premises AD users and groups to IAM roles for AWS Management Console access.
D. By using an AD trust between AWS Simple AD and your on-premises AD, you can assign your on-premises AD users and groups to IAM roles for AWS Management Console access.

Q74. Your company has headquarter in Los Angeles CA and have deployed their internal applications in US-West region. They are going to open a new office in Frankfurt Germany and are planning to transfer few employees as well. To comply with European regulations some of the applications will be replicated in a new AWS account created in EU-Central region. How will you manage the IAM users and roles being used by employees who will be transferred to Frankfurt?
A. IAM is a global service, users and roles are not region specific. You don't need to create new one for EU-Central region.
B. You will need to create new IAM users and roles for EU-Central region.
C. IAM users is a global service, roles are region specific. You don't need to create new users but will need to create new roles for EU-Central region.
D. IAM roles is a global service, users are region specific. You don't need to create new roles but will need to create new users for EU-Central region.

Q75. Which of the following is not an element in an IAM JSON Policy? Choose 2.
- A. Statement
- B. Effect
- C. Ip address
- D. Principal
- E. Encryption
- F. Action
- G. Resource

Q76. What Is IAM Access Analyzer? Choose 3.
- A. Informs you which resources in your account that you are sharing with external principals.
- B. Analyzes the policies applied to all of the supported resources in your account.
- C. Identifies policies that grants access to an external principal that isn't within your zone of trust, it generates a finding.
- D. Identify resources that are not encrypted at transit.

Q77. What are the features of IAM roles for EC2 instances? Choose 4
- A. AWS temporary security credentials to use when making requests from running EC2 instances to AWS services.
- B. Define cross account permission of EC2 instances.
- C. Automatic rotation of the AWS temporary security credentials.
- D. Granular AWS service permissions for applications running on EC2 instances.
- E. Simplifies management and deployment of AWS access keys to EC2 instances.

Q78. What are the benefits of temporary security credentials? Choose 3.
- A. Encrypt in transit data.
- B. Extend your internal user directories to enable federation to AWS, enabling your employees and applications to securely access AWS service APIs without needing to create an AWS identity for them.
- C. Request temporary security credentials for an unlimited number of federated users.
- D. Configure the time period after which temporary security credentials expire, offering improved security when accessing AWS service APIs through mobile devices where there is a risk of losing the device.

Q79. Your company is adopting AWS cloud by migrating majority of existing on-premise application to cloud and retaining some of them on premise. Currently they use on-premises AD to administer user accounts, manage group memberships, and control access to on-premises resources. You want to enable your users to sign in to the AWS Management Console using on-premises AD credentials to manage AWS resources such as Amazon EC2,

Amazon RDS, and Amazon S3. How can you achieve this without using AWS Directory services?

A. SAML Federation
B. Trust relationship between AD and IAM
C. Web Identity Federation
D. All of the above

Q80. What are the benefits of using AWS Key Management Service (AWS KMS)? Choose 3.

A. Centrally manage the encryption keys that control access to your data.
B. Manage encryption for AWS services, digitally sign data and encrypt data in your applications
C. Provision, manage, and deploy public and private Secure Sockets Layer/Transport Layer Security (SSL/TLS) certificates for use with AWS services and your internal connected resources.
D. Highly secure and built-in auditing to record all API requests, including key management actions and usage of your keys.

Q81. Which of the following keys never leave AWS KMS unencrypted? Choose 2.

A. Data Keys
B. Symmetric CMKs
C. Private keys of asymmetric CMKs
D. Public keys of asymmetric CMKs

Q82. Which strategy KMS uses to encrypt data and also protect your encryption key?

A. Encryption Context
B. Symmetric keys
C. Asymmetric keys
D. Envelope Encryption

Q83. Which of the following statements are correct when using Data key to encrypt large data within your application? Choose 3.

A. Data key creation: call the GenerateDataKey operation, AWS KMS uses the CMK that you specify to return a plaintext copy of the data key.
B. Data key creation: call the GenerateDataKey operation, AWS KMS uses the CMK that you specify to return a plaintext copy of the data key and a copy of the data key encrypted under the CMK
C. Data encryption: use the plaintext data key to encrypt data, remove it from memory as soon as possible. Safely store the encrypted data key with the encrypted data so it is available to decrypt the data.
D. Data encryption: use the plaintext data key to encrypt data, remove it from memory as soon as possible. Safely store the data key with the encrypted data so it is available to decrypt the data.

E.   Decrypting Data: pass the encrypted data key to the Decrypt operation, AWS KMS uses your CMK to decrypt the data key and then it returns the plaintext data key. Use the plaintext data key to decrypt your data and then remove the plaintext data key from memory as soon as possible.

F.   Decrypting Data: Use the plaintext data key to decrypt your data and then remove the plaintext data key from memory as soon as possible.

Q84. Which of the following statements are not correct about AWS KMS cryptographic operations encryption context? Choose 2.

A.   You cannot specify an encryption context in a cryptographic operation with an asymmetric CMK.

B.   All AWS KMS cryptographic operations that use symmetric CMKs accept an encryption context.

C.   All AWS KMS cryptographic operations that use symmetric or asymmetric CMKs accept an encryption context.

D.   When you include an encryption context in an encryption request, it is cryptographically bound to the ciphertext such that the same encryption context is required to decrypt (or decrypt and re-encrypt) the data

E.   An encryption context can consist of any keys and values in simple literal string.

F.   The key and value in an encryption context pair can be strings, integers or objects.

Q85.   Your company follows very strict access policy with regard to access to production environment deployed on AWS. There has been an outage in the production environment. To debug the issues you want to give ready only access to a software engineer so that she can view all resources in the Amazon EC2 console. She does have access to development and QA environment. Currently she doesn't have any access to production environment VPC deployed in the same AWS account. Which of the following is the best way to provide this short term access?

A.   Create a new IAM user with necessary access, provide the credentials to her and delete the user after the issue is fixed.

B.   Create a new IAM role with access policies which can be attached to her IAM user. Detach the role after the issue is fixed.

C.   Give the AWS account root user access to her temporarily.

D.   Share the IAM user credentials of an existing production support engineer, change the password after the issue is fixed.

Q86. As per AWS shared responsibility model which of the following are responsibility of the customer? Choose 2.

A.   For Amazon EC2 instance deployment, customer are responsible for management of the guest operating system (including updates and security patches), any application software or utilities installed by the customer on the instances, and the configuration of the AWS-provided firewall (called a security group) on each instance.

B. For services such as Amazon S3 and Amazon DynamoDB, customer should operate the infrastructure layer, the operating system, and platforms.
C. Customer is responsible for configuring or programming encryption of data in transit or rest.
D. Protecting the infrastructure that runs all of the services offered in the AWS Cloud.

Q87. Where can you upload and import an SSL certificate in AWS?
A. AWS Key Management Service (KMS)
B. AWS IAM
C. AWS Certificate Manager (ACM)
D. AWS CloudHSM

Q88. You are using Amazon Cognito authentication, authorization, and user management for your web and mobile apps. How can you increases security for your app by adding another authentication method, and not relying solely on user name and password?
A. Adding Multi-Factor Authentication (MFA) to Cognito User Pool
B. Allow sign in through a third party such as Facebook, Amazon, Google or Apple.
C. Add biometric authentication to Cognito user pool.
D. Add Captcha image capture to authentication.

Q89. Which AWS managed service is a cloud-based hardware security module (HSM) that allows you to easily add secure key storage and high-performance crypto operations to your AWS applications?
A. AWS Key Management Service (KMS)
B. AWS IAM
C. AWS Certificate Manager (ACM)
D. AWS CloudHSM

Q90. Which of the following is not a reason to use AWS CloudHSM instead of AWS KMS?
A. Store keys in dedicated, third-party validated hardware security modules under your exclusive control.
B. FIPS 140-2 compliance.
C. Use and manage encryption keys in multi-tenant managed service.
D. Integration with applications using PKCS#11, Java JCE, or Microsoft CNG interfaces.
E. High-performance in-VPC cryptographic acceleration (bulk crypto).

Q91. When you use an HSM from AWS CloudHSM, which of the following cryptographic tasks you cannot perform? Choose 2
A. Generate, store, import, export, and manage cryptographic keys, including symmetric keys and asymmetric key pairs.

B.  Provision, manage, and deploy public and private Secure Sockets Layer/Transport Layer Security (SSL/TLS) certificates for use with AWS services.
C.  Use symmetric and asymmetric algorithms to encrypt and decrypt data.
D.  Use cryptographic hash functions to compute message digests and hash-based message authentication codes (HMACs).
E.  Use it as managed service for creating and controlling your encryption keys, but you don't want or need to operate your own HSM.
F.  Cryptographically sign data (including code signing) and verify signatures.
G.  Generate cryptographically secure random data.

Q92. How can you set up a highly available and load balanced AWS HSM? Choose 2.
A.  Have at least two HSMs in your CloudHSM Cluster.
B.  Use Application Load Balancer or Network Load Balancer
C.  Create the HSMs in same AWS Availability Zones.
D.  Create the HSMs in different AWS Availability Zones.

Q93. Which AWS security service uses machine learning to automatically discover, classify, and protect sensitive data such as personally identifiable information (PII) or intellectual property.
A.  AWS WAF
B.  AWS Shield
C.  Amazon GuardDuty
D.  Amazon Macie

Q94. What data sources Amazon Macie supports?
A.  AWS CloudTrail event logs, including Amazon S3 object-level API activity
B.  Amazon S3
C.  VPC Flow Logs
D.  Cloudwatch

Q95: Which of the following is not an examples of suspicious activity that Amazon Macie can detect?
A.  Compromised user accounts enumerating and downloading large amounts of sensitive content from unusual IP addresses
B.  Download of large quantities of source code by a user account that typically does not access this type of sensitive content.
C.  Detection of large quantities of high-risk documents shared publically or to the entire company, such as files containing personally identifiable information (PII), protected health information (PHI), intellectual properties (IP), legal or financial data.
D.  None of the above

# Chapter 9 Developer Tools, Management & Governance

Q1. Which AWS service helps you enable governance, compliance, and operational and risk auditing of your AWS account and also records as events actions taken by a user, role, or an AWS service?
- A.  AWS Cloudwatch
- B.  AWS WAF
- C.  AWS Shield
- D.  AWS Cloudtrail

Q2. Where is Cloudtrail event logs stored?
- A.  EBS
- B.  RDS
- C.  Redshift
- D.  S3
- E.  EMR

Q3. Which AWS service you will use for continuous integration and continuous delivery for fast and reliable application and infrastructure updates?
- A.  AWS CodePipeline
- B.  AWS CodeBuild
- C.  AWS CodeDeploy
- D.  AWS CodeStar
- E.  AWS CloudFormation

Q4. Which AWS service is a fully managed build service that compiles source code, runs tests, and produces software packages that are ready to deploy?
- A.  AWS CodePipeline
- B.  AWS CodeBuild
- C.  AWS CodeDeploy
- D.  AWS CodeStar
- E.  AWS CloudFormation

Q5. Which AWS service automates code deployments to any instance, including Amazon EC2 instances and on-premises servers?
- A.  AWS CodePipeline
- B.  AWS CodeBuild
- C.  AWS CodeDeploy
- D.  AWS CodeStar
- E.  AWS CloudFormation

Q6. Which AWS service allows to model your entire infrastructure in a text file?
- A.  AWS CodePipeline
- B.  AWS CodeBuild

C.  AWS CodeDeploy
D.  AWS CodeStar
E.  AWS CloudFormation

Q7.  Which AWS configuration management service uses Chef?
A.  AWS CodePipeline
B.  AWS CodeBuild
C.  AWS CodeDeploy
D.  AWS OpsWorks
E.  AWS CloudFormation

Q8. Which AWS service helps you to continuously monitor and record configuration changes of your AWS resources and also inventory your AWS resources?
A.  AWS Cloudwatch
B.  AWS Config
C.  AWS SystemManager
D.  AWS OpsWorks
E.  AWS CloudFormation

Q9. Which AWS service will you use to collect and track metrics, collect and monitor log files, set alarms, and automatically react to changes in your AWS resources?
A.  AWS Cloudwatch
B.  AWS Config
C.  AWS SystemManager
D.  AWS Cloudwatch
E.  AWS CloudFormation

Q10. As a developer which AWS service you will use to analyze and debug production, distributed applications built using a microservices architecture?
A.  AWS Cloudwatch
B.  AWS Config
C.  AWS SystemManager
D.  AWS Cloudwatch
E.  AWS X-Ray

Q11.  Which of the following format can be used to write CloudFormation 'infrastructure as a code' scripts?
A.  JSON only
B.  YAML only
C.  JSON and YAML
D.  JSON and XML
E.  XML Only

Q12. You want to centralize operational data from multiple AWS services and automate tasks across your AWS resources. Which AWS service you should use?
  A.  AWS Account Dashboard
  B.  AWS System Manager
  C.  AWS Trusted Advisor
  D.  AWS Cloud Trail

Q13. Which of the following use case is not enabled by Cloudtrail?
  A.  IT and Security administrators can perform security analysis
  B.  DevOps engineers can model and provision AWS and third party application resources in your cloud environment
  C.  IT Administrators and DevOps engineers can track changes to AWS resources
  D.  DevOps engineers can troubleshoot operations issues
  E.  IT Auditors can use log files as compliance aid

Q14. What are the different use cases for AWS Config? Choose 4.
  A.  To exercise better governance over your resource configurations and to detect resource misconfigurations.
  B.  To have visibility and control of your infrastructure on AWS.
  C.  Auditing and Compliance for data that requires frequent audits to ensure compliance with internal policies and best practices.
  D.  Managing and Troubleshooting Configuration Changes.
  E.  Detailed historical information about your AWS resource configurations to analyze potential security weaknesses.

Q15. By default, what is the periodic interval in which Amazon EC2 sends metric data to CloudWatch?
  A.  1-minute
  B.  3-minute
  C.  5-minute
  D.  4-minute

Q16. What you should do to send metric data for your instance to CloudWatch in 1-minute periods?
  A.  Disable detailed monitoring
  B.  Enable detailed monitoring
  C.  Write a lambda program to process CloudWatch events
  D.  Change the value in Cloudwatch for periodic interval to 1 minute

Q17. You are the cloud infrastructure administrator for your company. The VPC created by different business unit development team have to following security guidelines:

- No security group should ingress from 0.0.0.0/0 to port 22
- VPC flow logs should be enabled
- Default security group of every VPC should restricts all traffic.

How can you ensure that you are notified whenever there is a change in existing VPC or a new VPC is created which violates the above rules?

A. Use AWS Cloudtrail and have a custom log analyzer to capture the settings and changes.

B. Use Amazon Inspector to capture the settings and changes.

C. Use Amazon Cloudwatch to capture the settings and changes.

D. Use AWS Config to create above compliance rules for VPC

Q18. What are differences between AWS Config and AWS CloudTrail? Choose 2.

A. AWS CloudTrail records user API activity on your account and allows you to access information about this activity. AWS Config records point-in-time configuration details for your AWS resources as Configuration Items (CIs).

B. AWS CloudTrail get full details about API actions, such as identity of the caller, the time of the API call, the request parameters, and the response elements returned by the AWS service. You can use AWS Config to answer "What did my AWS resource look like?" at a point in time. You can use AWS CloudTrail to answer "Who made an API call to modify this resource?"

C. AWS Config get full details about API actions, such as identity of the caller, the time of the API call, the request parameters, and the response elements returned by the AWS service. You can use AWS CloudTrail CI to answer "What did my AWS resource look like?" at a point in time. You can use AWS CloudTrail to answer "Who made an API call to modify this resource?"

D. AWS Config records user API activity on your account and allows you to access information about this activity. AWS CloudTrail records point-in-time configuration details for your AWS resources as Configuration Items (CIs).

Q19. Which AWS service enables you to monitor your complete stack (applications, infrastructure, and services) and leverage alarms, logs, and events data to take automated actions?

A. Account Dashboard

B. Flow Logs

C. CloudWatch

D. Cloud Trail

Q20. You are the solution architect for a Healthcare Application developed on AWS platform. Because of the regulatory requirements you want an email to be sent to a distribution list whenever there is configuration changes that involve security groups and Network Access Control List (ACL). How can you achieve this?

A. Configure VPC flow logs with CloudWatch Logs to monitor your trail logs and be notified when activity occurs through SNS email.

B. Configure CloudTrail with CloudWatch Logs to monitor your trail logs and be notified when activity occurs through SNS email.

C. Configure CloudTrail notify when activity occurs through SNS email.

D. Configure CloudWatch to monitor and be notified when activity occurs through SNS email.

Q21. What are the benefits of CloudFormation? Choose 3.

A. Simplifies Infrastructure Management. AWS CloudFormation is a service that helps you model and set up your Amazon Web Services resources.

B. Quickly Replicate Your Infrastructure. You can reuse your template to set up your resources consistently and repeatedly.

C. Easily Control and Track Changes to Your Infrastructure.

D. Provides an environment to easily deploy and run applications in the cloud.

Q22. You are maintaining three environment for your web application in the US-East region: Production, Staging and QA. Production environment has 4 EC2 instances. Your DevOps team uses CloudFormation to manage the environment infrastructure provisioning. To do performance testing in a secluded environment you have requested your DevOps team to spin off another environment in US-East region which is replica of Production environment. The DevOps mentions that they will cross the EC2 instance quota for the region if they create 4 EC2 instances but will meet the total quota if they provision 3 instances. What will happen if the DevOps team executes the CloudFormation template to provision 4 instances?

A. All four EC2 instances will be provisioned irrespective of regional total count exceeding the quota.

B. The template execution will fail and not a single EC2 instance will be provisioned.

C. The template execution will throw a warning, but provision three EC2 instance which will make the total equal to region quota.

D. The template execution will provision three EC2 instance and raise AWS support request automatically for provision of one more EC2 instance.

Q23. What are the features of AWS X-Ray? Choose 4.

A. Simplifies your compliance audits by automatically recording and storing event logs for actions made within your AWS account.

B. You can analyze simple asynchronous event calls, three-tier web applications, or complex microservices applications consisting of thousands of services.

C. Traces user requests as they travel through your entire application

D. You can glean insights into how your application is performing identify performance bottlenecks and discover root causes.

E. Can automatically highlight bugs or errors in your application code by analyzing the response code for each request made to your application.

285

Q24. You company's Cloud Center of Excellence has defined security policies for AWS services used for deployed applications. You have been tasked to create solution that will detect, inform and automatically react to non-compliant configuration changes within application microservices architecture. For example if a member of the development team has made a change to the API Gateway for a microservice to allow the endpoint to accept inbound HTTP traffic, rather than only allowing HTTPS requests. Your solution should identifies this change as a security violation, and performs two actions: creates a log of the detected change for auditing and send a notification. Which AWS services you will use to tackle this scenario so that it is scalable, reliable and cost effective?

    A.   AWS Config, Amazon SNS, Amazon SQS, AWS Lambda
    B.   AWS Config, Amazon SNS, Amazon SQS, Amazon EC2
    C.   AWS Config,  Amazon SQS, AWS Lambda
    D.   AWS Config, Amazon SNS, Amazon SQS
    E.   AWS Config, Amazon SNS

Q25. Choose two correct statements regarding Cloudwatch metrics?

    A.   Standard resolution, with data having a one-minute granularity
    B.   High resolution, with data at a granularity of one second
    C.   Standard resolution, with data having a one-second granularity
    D.   High resolution, with data at a granularity of one minute

Q26. Your company has deployed lot of web applications on AWS running on Auto Scaling EC2 instances. You want to monitor the EC2 service limits continuously and also to be proactively notified when your AWS account has reached 60% of the EC2 On-Demand instance limit. How can you achieve this? Choose 2.

    A.   Use the AWS Trusted Advisor Service Limits check to monitor service limits.
    B.   Configure alarm in Cloudwatch using TrustedAdvisor servicelimit metrics.
    C.   Configure alarm in Cloudtrail using TrustedAdvisor servicelimit metrics.
    D.   Use the AWS System Manager to monitor service limits.

Q27. Which AWS services will help your company to enable compliance, and operational and risk auditing of your AWS account? Choose 2.

    A.   CloudTrail
    B.   CloudWatch
    C.   Config
    D.   CloudFormation

Q28. You are using AWS Config to keep track of the configuration of your S3 bucket ACLs and policies for violations which allows public read or public write access. If AWS Config finds a policy violation for noncompliant S3 bucket, how can you ensure it is remediated automatically?

A. With AWS Config, use Amazon CloudWatch, Amazon SNS, and Lambda to overwrite a public bucket ACL.

B. There is not automatic option in AWS Config to remediate a non-compliant resource.

C. Use AWS Config auto remediation feature for AWS Config rules using existing S3 documents or custom S3 documents.

D. Use AWS Config auto remediation feature for AWS Config rules using existing SSM documents or custom SSM documents.

Q29. Your company has deployed applications on AWS across regions. As per audit requirements they want to monitor API activity for resources across all regions and also for any future regions as well. How can achieve this?

A. Turn on CloudTrail for each desired region. For future region create it separately using console.

B. Specify that a trail will apply to all regions and CloudTrail will automatically create the same trail in each region. Future region trail will be automatically created.

C. Turn on CloudTrail for each desired region. For future region create it separately using CloudFormation.

D. Turn on CloudTrail for each desired region. For future region create it separately using AWS CLI.

Q30. Which of the following provides an automated way to send log data to CloudWatch Logs from Amazon EC2 instances?

A. VPC Flow Logs

B. Cloudtrail

C. CloudWatch Logs Agent

D. Cloudtrail Logs Agent

Q31. Which of the following statement is not correct about Amazon CloudWatch Events?

A. Delivers a near real-time stream of system events that describe changes in Amazon Web Services (AWS) resources.

B. Using simple rules that you can quickly set up, you can match events and route them to one or more target functions or streams.

C. A rule matches incoming events and routes them to targets for processing.

D. A single rule can route to only a single target.

Q32. Which of the following you cannot configure as targets for CloudWatch Events?

A. Amazon EC2 instances, AWS Lambda functions, Amazon Kinesis Data Streams, Amazon Kinesis Data Firehose

B. Log groups in Amazon CloudWatch Logs, Amazon ECS tasks, Pipelines in CodePipeline

C. Amazon SNS topics, Amazon SQS queues, AWS Batch jobs, Step Functions state machines
D. S3, EBS, EFS, RDS, DynamoDB

Q33. Which of the following is incorrect about CloudFormation Stack?
A. A collection of AWS resources that you can manage as a single unit.
B. You can create, update, or delete a collection of resources by creating, updating, or deleting stacks.
C. If a resource cannot be created, AWS CloudFormation doesn't rolls the stack back.
D. All the resources in a stack are defined by the stack's AWS CloudFormation template.

Q34. You have used CloudFormation to create a stack comprising of EC2 instance, ELB and RDS. After few weeks you want to update the instances' AMI ID. How can you update it using CloudFormation? Choose 2.
A. Direct update, you submit a template or input parameters that specify updates to the resources in the stack, and AWS CloudFormation will immediately deploy them.
B. Updating Stack Using Change Sets which allow you to preview how proposed changes to a stack might impact your running resources.
C. You cannot update a running stack using CloudFormation.
D. Create a new stack and delete the existing resources.

Q35. When you submit an update, AWS CloudFormation updates resources based on differences between what you submit and the stack's current template. Resources that have not changed run without disruption during the update process. Which of the following is update behavior used by AWS CloudFormation for updated resources?
A. Update with No Interruption
B. Updates with Some Interruption
C. Replacement
D. All of the above

Q36. What are the recommendations provided by Cost Explorer? Choose 2.
A. Reserved Instance Recommendations
B. Budget Recommendations
C. EC2 Rightsizing recommendations
D. RD S Rightsizing recommendations

Q37. Your organization use multiple accounts for business units, applications, and developers. They often create separate accounts for development, testing, staging, and production on a per-application basis. They build global applications that span two or more regions, implement sophisticated multi-region disaster recovery models, replicate S3, Aurora, PostgreSQL, and

MySQL data in real time, and choose locations for storage and processing of sensitive data in accord with national and regional regulations.
Which feature of CloudFormation you can use that can make rolling out stacks across accounts in different region easy and consistent?

    A.  CloudFormation StackSet which extends the functionality of stacks by enabling you to create, update, or delete stacks across multiple accounts and regions with a single operation.
    B.  Use separate CloudFormation template for every region in each account.
    C.  Use third party tools provided by AWS partners to manage CloudFormation templates across regions and accounts.
    D.  Create a good designed parameter driven CloudFormation template which can be reused across account and regions.

Q38. Which AWS service records AWS API calls for your account and delivers log files to you?

    A.  AWS Cloudwatch
    B.  AWS Config
    C.  AWS Cloudtrail
    D.  AWS Cloudwatch
    E.  AWS X-Ray

Q39. Your company is using AWS CloudFormation to create, manage, and update a collection of AWS resources (a "stack") in a controlled, predictable manner. Currently to update a stack the process followed is to edit their existing template (or create a new one) and then use CloudFormation's Update Stack operation to activate the changes. Recently you have been asked by your DevOps head for additional insight into the changes that CloudFormation is planning to perform when there is an update to a stack. You should be able to preview the changes, verify that they are in line with their expectations, and proceed with the update. How can you achieve this?

    A.  There is no preview feature of update stack in CloudFormation.
    B.  Create a change set by submitting changes against the stack you want to update. CloudFormation compares the stack to the new template and/or parameter values and produces a change set that you can review and then choose to apply (execute).
    C.  Create a preview set by submitting changes against the stack you want to update. CloudFormation compares the stack to the new template and/or parameter values and produces a change set that you can review and then choose to apply (execute).
    D.  Create a test update set by submitting changes against the stack you want to update. CloudFormation compares the stack to the new template and/or parameter values and produces a change set that you can review and then choose to apply (execute).

Q40. You have been using 'infrastructure as code' by leveraging CloudFormation templates to deploy stacks for your web applications. You have a load balancer configuration that you use

for most of your stacks. Your manager asked you if there is a way to avoid copying and pasting the same configurations into your templates. What will be your answer?
- A. Use Reuse Stacks
- B. Use Parent-child Stacks
- C. Use Changed set stacks
- D. Use Nested Stacks

Q41. You are a solution architect for a multinational company which wants to migrate all their existing applications to AWS cloud platform. They want to create separate AWS account based on each country where they have regional headquarters. They also want to centrally manage billing; control access, compliance, and security; and share resources across AWS accounts. If you want to define your own custom multi-account environment with advanced governance and management capabilities which AWS service you will use?
- A. AWS Organizations
- B. AWS System Manager
- C. AWS Control Tower
- D. AWS Service Catalog

Q42. Which of the following central governance and management capabilities does AWS Organizations does not enable? Choose 2.
- A. Centralized management of all of your AWS accounts
- B. Consolidated billing for all member accounts
- C. Hierarchical grouping of your accounts to meet your budgetary, security, or compliance needs
- D. A landing zone which is a well-architected, multi-account AWS environment that's based on security and compliance best practices.
- E. Control over the AWS services and API actions that each account can access
- F. An Account Factory which is a configurable account template that helps to standardize the provisioning of new accounts with pre-approved account configurations.

Q43. Which of the following are components of setting up AWS Organizations? Choose 4.
- A. Root
- B. AWS Account
- C. IAM Policies
- D. Organization Unit (OU)
- E. Service control policies (SCPs)

Q44. AWS Trusted Advisor analyzes your environment on which of the following five categories?
- A. Cost Optimization
- B. Performance

C.  Security
D.  Reliability
E.  Fault Tolerance
F.  Service Limits

Q45. Your company uses AWS, it is looking to be more agile with deployments and enable developers to focus more on writing code instead of devoting time on managing servers, databases, networking, security etc. Which of the following three services can help you in achieving this goal?
A.  AWS CodeCommit
B.  AWS CodePipeline
C.  AWS Elastic Beanstalk
D.  AWS CloudFormation

Q46. Which of the following is not a use case for AWS Organizations?
A.  Implement and enforce corporate security, audit, and compliance policies
B.  Share resources across accounts
C.  Automate the deployment of AWS workloads
D.  Automate the creation of AWS accounts and categorize workloads

Q47. Which of the following statements are correct about AWS Organization Service control policies (SCPs)? Choose 4.
A.  SCPs aren't available if your Organization has enabled only the consolidated billing features.
B.  SCPs are available if your Organization has enabled only the consolidated billing features.
C.  SCPs are not available in an Organization that has all features enabled.
D.  SCPs are available only in an Organization that has all features enabled.
E.  SCPs are necessary but not sufficient for granting access in the accounts in your organization. You still need to attach IAM policies to users and roles in your organization's accounts to actually grant permissions to them.
F.  SCPs are sufficient for granting access in the accounts in your Organization. You don't need to attach IAM policies to users and roles in your Organization's accounts to actually grant permissions to them.
G.  An SCP never grants permissions. Instead, SCPs are JSON policies that specify the maximum permissions for an Organization or Organization Unit (OU).

Q48. The diagram below depicts the configuration in an AWS Organization setup for a company. Services whitelisted (allowed) for each group by the organization's SCP are in filled circle, and IAM policies allowing access to particular services are in without filled circle. The IAM user Bob is part of the Dev OU, and the IAM policy associated with Bob allows full access to the Amazon S3 and Amazon EC2 services. The SCP associated with the Dev OU and Sales OU allows the use of the S3 service. David user doesn't have any IAM policy attached to it. Which of the following statements are correct? Choose 2.

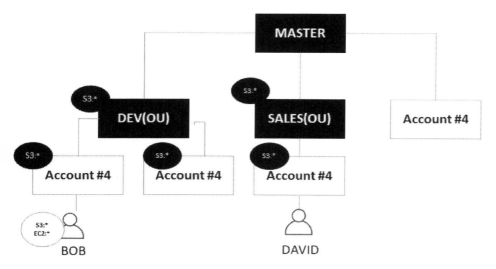

A. Bob cannot use EC2.
B. Bob can use EC2.
C. David can access S3.
D. David cannot access S3.

Q49. Which AWS service is for creating, managing, and working with software development projects on AWS and helps in quickly develop, build, and deploying applications?
A. AWS OpsWorks
B. AWS CodeStar
C. AWS SystemManager
D. AWS CloudFormation

Q50. Which AWS service can be used to set up CI/CD process?
A. Aws CodePipeline
B. Aws CodeCommit
C. Aws CodeBuild
D. Aws CodeDeploy

Q51. You are the solution architect for an online store application hosted on Amazon EC2 and using serverless technologies like Amazon API Gateway, AWS Lambda, and Amazon DynamoDB. Which AWS service you will use to analyze and debug production, distributed applications, such as those built using a microservices architecture?
A. AWS Cloudtrail

B. AWS Cloudwatch
C. AWS Config
D. AWS X-Ray

Q52. Which AWS service automates and simplifies the task of repeatedly and predictably creating groups of related resources of your applications as 'Infrastructure as Code'?
A. AWS CodePipeline
B. AWS CodeCommit
C. AWS CloudFormation
D. AWS CodeDeploy

Q53. Which of the following statements are correct about CloudFormation Template? Choose 4.
A. AWS CloudFormation templates are JSON or YAML-formatted text files.
B. A stack is a collection of resources that result from instantiating a template.
C. You create a stack by supplying a template and any required parameters to AWS CloudFormation.
D. A stack is collection of templates to create resources.
E. Based on the template and any dependencies specified in it, AWS CloudFormation determines what AWS resources need to be created and in what order.
F. AWS CloudFormation templates can be written using java, .net or python.

Q54. Your company's devops team wants to use CloudFormation for provisioning and configuring the resources required for a web application for test and production environment. Though the resources required are same for both environment but there will be difference in configuration. For example following configuration will be different for two environments: Amazon RDS database size, EC2 instance type, security groups. Load balancer. Which of the following statements is correct?
A. As the configuration of resources in two environment is different, devops team have to create two separate CloudFormation template.
B. Devops team can use one template for both environments by using parameters to customize configuration specific to an environment at the runtime.
C. CloudFormation parameter supports EC2 but not RDS configuration during runtime.
D. CloudFormation parameter supports RDS but not EC2 configuration during runtime.

Q55. Your devops team uses CloudFormation template to provision resources for web application running on Amazon EC2 instance and Amazon RDS Aurora. For the initial beta release they have deployed the web application on a production environment running on t1.micro Amazon EC2 instance. Next week they are planning to roll out the web application to wider set of users and expecting more traffic. To handle the increase in the traffic they want to change the production environment EC2 instance from t1.micro to m1.small Amazon EC2 instance type. How can they make this change using CloudFormation template?

A.  They have to create a new stack and delete the old one.
B.  Submit a support request to AWS for updating the stack.
C.  They can simply modify the existing stack's template.
D.  None of the above.

Q56. Which of the following statements are correct about CloudFormation stack deletion? Choose 3.

A.  When you delete a stack, you specify the stack to delete, and AWS CloudFormation deletes the stack and all the resources in that stack.
B.  If you want to delete a stack but want to retain some resources in that stack, you can use a deletion policy to retain those resources.
C.  You cannot retain resources from a stack which you want to delete.
D.  If AWS CloudFormation cannot delete a resource, the stack will not be deleted.

Q57. Which of the following are correct regarding CloudFormation best practices?

A.  Use input parameters to pass in information whenever you create or update a stack, using the NoEcho property to obfuscate the parameter value.
B.  Use dynamic parameters in the stack template to reference sensitive information that is stored and managed outside of CloudFormation, such as in the Systems Manager Parameter Store or Secrets Manager.
C.  Use input parameters to pass in information whenever you create or update a stack, using the Echo property to obfuscate the parameter value.
D.  When you launch stacks, you can install and configure software applications on Amazon EC2 instances by using the cfn-init helper script and the AWS:: CloudFormation::Init resource.

Q58. Your company has migrated all existing on-premise application to AWS cloud platform. All the application's stack primarily consists of EC2 instances, Application Load Balancer, RDS, kinesis streams and S3 buckets in VPCs. Which AWS service you will use so that you are able to do following tasks?

•   Group AWS resources together by any purpose or activity you choose, such as application, environment, region, project, campaign, business unit, or software lifecycle.
•   Centrally define the configuration options and policies for your managed instances.
•   Centrally view, investigate, and resolve operational work items related to AWS resources.
•   Automate or schedule a variety of maintenance and deployment tasks.

A.  AWS Managed Services
B.  AWS Systems Manager
C.  AWS CloudFormation
D.  AWS OpsWorks

Q59. What are the operating systems supported by AWS Systems Manager? Choose 3.
  A. MacOS
  B. Windows Server
  C. Linux
  D. Raspbian

Q60. Which of the following is not a feature of AWS Systems Manager Documents?
  A. Defines the actions that Systems Manager performs on your managed instances.
  B. Documents use JavaScript Object Notation (JSON) or YAML
  C. Types of Document: Command, Automation, Package, Session, Policy, Change Calendar
  D. Blueprints for building your AWS resources.

Q61. Your company has migrated all existing on premise application to AWS cloud platform. All the application's stack primarily consists of EC2 instances. Your company's cloud security team has laid down very strict guidelines not to open inbound ports, maintain bastion hosts, or manage SSH keys for logging into instance for management and administrative tasks. Which feature of System Manager you will use to gain secure access to instance as per guidelines? Choose 2.
  A. Patch Manager
  B. Session Manager
  C. Run Command
  D. OpsCenter

Q62. Which of the following are features of AWS Systems Manager? Choose 4
  A. AWS AppConfig helps you deploy application configuration in a managed and a monitored way just like code deployments
  B. Inventory: collects information about your instances and the software installed on them.
  C. Automation: allows you to safely automate common and repetitive IT operations and management tasks.
  D. AWS Config is a service that enables you to assess, audit, and evaluate the configurations of your AWS resources.
  E. Patch Manager: helps you select and deploy operating system and software patches automatically across large groups of Amazon EC2 or on-premises instances.

Q63. An SCP attached to the organization root allows permissions A, B, and C. The organization root contains an organizational unit (OU), and an SCP that allows C, D, and E is attached to that OU.

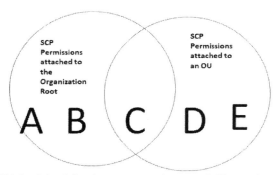

Which of the following statement is correct? Choose 2.
- A.  A or B permissions are blocked for the OU and any of its child OUs or accounts.
- B.  D or E permission cannot be used by any OUs or accounts in the organization.
- C.  OU and its children account can use A, B, C, D, E permission.
- D.  OU and its children account can use C, D or E permission.

Q64. What are the different services you can use for cost management? Choose 3.
- A.  AWS Budgets
- B.  AWS Cost & Usage reports
- C.  AWS Cloudwatch
- D.  AWS Cost Explorer

Q65. Which AWS tool enables you to view and analyze your costs and usage?
- A.  AWS System Manager
- B.  AWS Well architected Tool
- C.  AWS Trusted Advisor
- D.  AWS Billing and Cost Management

Q66. Your company has been using AWS for different kind of workloads running on EC2 instances for more than a year. As part of companywide cost optimization drive you been asked to look at how you can optimize the EC2 instances cost. Which AWS service you will use to analyze the current EC2 instances both from cost optimization and performance bottleneck identification so as to:
- •  Get downsizing recommendations within or across instance families.
- •  Get upsizing recommendations to remove performance bottlenecks.
- •  Understand the performance risks and how your workload would perform on various EC2 instance options to evaluate the price-performance trade-off for your workloads.
- A.  AWS Compute Optimizer
- B.  AWS Cost Explorer
- C.  AWS EC2 optimizer
- D.  AWS Budget

Q67. What are the five pillars of AWS well architected framework?
A. Operational Excellence
B. Security
C. Reliability
D. Performance Efficiency
E. Cost Optimization
F. Resiliency

Q68. Which of the following you can do in AWS Billing and Cost Management service? Choose 5.
A. Estimate and forecast your AWS cost and usage
B. Instance Performance report
C. Receive notifications when you exceed your budgeted thresholds
D. Assess your biggest investments in AWS resources
E. Analyze your spend and usage data
F. Reserved Instance Utilization Report & Reserved Instance Coverage Report

Q69. What are the default Cost Explorer reports available? Choose 2.
A. EC2 Performance Reports
B. Cost and Usage Reports
C. Reserved Instance Reports
D. Budget Reports

Q70. You are the solution architect for your company which is using AWS Organization features for setting up the accounts. You have created multiple AWS accounts mapped to each country where your company has office. These country specific regional AWS accounts are linked to master (payer) account. You are contemplating whether to use the consolidated billing feature in AWS Organizations to consolidate billing and payment for multiple AWS accounts. What are the benefits? Choose 3.
A. One bill – You get one bill for multiple accounts.
B. Easy tracking – You can track the charges across multiple accounts and download the combined cost and usage data.
C. Capacity Reservations – You will be able to reserve capacities for different AWS services.
D. Combined usage – You can combine the usage across all accounts in the organization to share the volume pricing discounts, Reserved Instance discounts, and Savings Plans. This can result in a lower charge for your project, department, or company than with individual standalone accounts.

# PRACTICE EXAM 1

Q1. You have a corporate intranet web application that required 500GB of block storage at 1000 IOPS throughout the day apart from 40 minutes at night when you run a schedule batch process to generate reports during which you require 3000 IOPS. Which Amazon EBS volume will be cost effective?
  A. General Purpose SSD (gp2)
  B. Provisioned IOPS SSD (io1)
  C. Throughput Optimized HDD (st1)
  D. Cold HDD (sc1)

Q2. Rama creates a S3 bucket 'mywestwebsite' in 'us-west-1' region. Which of these are correct url to access this bucket? Choose 3.
  A. https://amazonaws. s3.us-west-1.com/mywestwebsite
  B. https://s3.us-west-1.amazonaws.com/mywestwebsite
  C. https://s3.amazonaws.com/mywestwebsite
  D. https://mywestwebsite.s3.amazonaws.com
  E. https://mywestwebsite.s3.us-west-1.amazonaws.com

Q3. You have developed a web application and plan to deploy it in your VPC in us-west region. Your VPC has three subnets mapped to three availability zones: us-west-1a, us-west-1b, us-west-1c. Your application requires in normal scenario nine servers but can run on a minimum 66 percent capacity. How many web server instances should you deploy in each of three AZ so that you can meet the above availability requirements in a cost effective way?
  A. Six in us-west-1a, six in us-west-1b, six in us-west-1c.
  B. Two in us-west-1a, two in us-west-1b, four in us-west-1c.
  C. Four in us-west-1a, four in us-west-1b, four in us-west-1c.
  D. Three in us-west-1a, three in us-west-1b, three in us-west-1c.

Q4. Your company is planning to use WordPress hosted on AWS for corporate website. You are planning to run your WordPress site using an auto scaling group of Amazon EC2 instances and database layer on Amazon RDS Aurora. Which Amazon service you should use to store shared, unstructured WordPress data like php files, config themes, plugin etc. This storage service should be accessible by multiple WordPress EC2 instances.
  A. Amazon S3
  B. Amazon RDS
  C. Amazon EFS
  D. Amazon EBS

Q5. You have deployed a fleet of EC2 instances using an auto scaling group based on target tracking dynamic scaling. Recently you notice that scaling policy is launching, terminating and relaunching many instances in an hour. This has led to increased cost as you are getting billed for every instance which is getting launched for few seconds to few minutes. What should you do so that frequency of launching and termination of instances is optimized? Choose 2

A. Scale out quickly but scale in slowly. Increase the duration of cooldown period.
B. Scale out slowly and scale in quickly. Decrease the duration of cooldown period.
C. Change the target tracking scaling metric.
D. Analyze and change the target tracking metric target value.

Q6. Which AWS service you will use to direct your users to application based on their geographic location, application health, and weights that you can configure. You also want to use static IP addresses that are globally unique for your application so that there is no need to update clients as your application scales. Your application has Application Load Balancers.
A. CloudFront
B. Route53
C. Application Load Balancer
D. Global Accelerator

Q7. You have purchased an a1.large Linux Standard Reserved Instance in us-west-1a. Which of the following ways you can modify the reservation? Choose 3.
A. Change it into windows instance
B. Change it in a1.xlarge
C. Change the region to us-east and AZ to us-east-1a
D. Change the AZ to us-west-1b
E. Change it into two a1.medium instances.

Q8. Which of the following statements is incorrect as the suitable scenario for using ENI vs EN vs EFA?
A. Use ENI when you need basic networking and want to create a separate management network at low cost.
B. Use ENI when you need to accelerate High Performance Computing and machine learning application.
C. Use EN (Enhanced Networking) when you need speeds between 10GBps and 100 GBps with high throughput.
D. Use EFA when you need to accelerate High Performance Computing and machine learning application

Q9.You are migrating your on premise Windows-based custom build .Net applications to AWS cloud platform using Lift-and-Shift strategy. These applications require shared file storage provided by Windows-based file systems (NTFS) and that uses the SMB protocol. Which AWS services you will use? Choose 2.
A. Lambda
B. EFS
C. EBS
D. EC2
E. FSx for Windows File Server

Q10. You recently launched your website to your global users. After few hours you got to know that some of the static images you are distributing through Cloudfront needs to be changed as they are of older version. You know that default expiration of content served from Cloudfront edge server is 24 hours. What should you do so that new version of images are immediately reflected in user requests? Choose 2.
   A. Invalidate the file from edge caches.
   B. Validate the file from edge caches.
   C. Replace the files in the origin servers with new files having same name.
   D. Use file versioning to serve a different version of the file that has a different name.

Q11. You have a web app that provides video transcoding services. The videos uploaded by the users are first stored in a S3 bucket where you have configured "An object created event" notification to a SQS queue. There are fleet of EC2 instances which picks up the videos from the queue and places it in another S3 bucket after transcoding the file. These consumer fleet of EC2 instance also has dynamic auto scaling policy based on custom metric 'backlog per instance'. Which type of EC2 instances you will use which will be most cost effective given that you don't have defined duration in which you have to complete the transcoding for an uploaded file?
   A. Reserved Instances
   B. On-demand Instances
   C. Saving plans Instances
   D. Spot Instances

Q12. Which Amazon EBS volume type you will use for
   • Streaming workloads requiring consistent, fast throughput at a low price
   • Big data or Data warehouses
   • Log processing
   A. General Purpose SSD (gp2)
   B. Provisioned IOPS SSD (io1)
   C. Throughput Optimized HDD (st1)
   D. Cold HDD (sc1)

Q13. You are using Amazon SQS in your ecommerce application to send order confirmation email asynchronously. You have created a program which polls the SQS queue frequently for new order message and then sends the email after fetching new order message from the queue. You observe that at times the program is getting empty response to the *ReceiveMessage* request. What should you do to eliminate empty responses to reduce cost?
   A. Create a delay queue.
   B. Increase the duration of visibility timeout value to higher number.

C. Make wait time for the ReceiveMessage API action is greater than 0 to effect long polling.
D. Make wait time for the ReceiveMessage API action is greater than 0 to effect short polling.

Q14. You are developing a mobile application that will enable user to login using their userids in Facebook, Amazon and Google. In the cloud backend you will have Serverless architecture. For backend application data storage you want to use a RDBMS database. What is the minimum set of AWS services you will need for your mobile application and backend cloud application?
A. Lambda, Cognito, API Gateway, DynamoDB
B. Lambda, Cognito, API Gateway, Aurora Serverless
C. Elastic Beanstalk, Cognito, API Gateway, Aurora
D. Lambda, Fargate, API Gateway, DynamoDB

Q15. You are solution architect for a Stock Trading web application provider company. Financial regulation mandates them to keep the trading data for five years. From analysis of past internal and customer access behavior you are certain that data more than two year old is unlikely to be accessed, data less than two year old but more than six months old is infrequently accessed. Any data less than six months old will need to have faster access. Currently 150 TB data are stored in in-premise data storage which company is planning to move to AWS cloud storage to save cost. Which is the most cost effective option?
A. Store the data on Amazon S3 with lifecycle policy that change the storage class from Standard to Standard-IA in six months, from Standard-IA to Glacier in 1.5 years and expiration in 3.5 years.
B. Store the data on Amazon S3 with lifecycle policy that change the storage class from Standard to Standard-IA in six months, from Standard-IA to Glacier in two year and expiration in five years.
C. Store all the data in Redshift data warehouse
D. Store all the data in EBS general purpose volume attached to EC2 cheapest instance

Q16. Which AWS service lets you monitor the HTTP and HTTPS requests that are forwarded to an Amazon API Gateway, Amazon CloudFront or an Application Load Balancer and gives you control over which traffic to allow or block to your web applications by defining customizable web security rules?
A. AWS Shield
B. AWS Cloudtrail
C. AWS Cloudwatch
D. AWS WAF

Q17. What are the two steps you will take regarding your instances if your application requirement is low network latency, high network throughput, majority of the network traffic is between the instances in the group and require highest packet-per-second network Performance? Choose 2.
   A.  Use Cluster placement groups
   B.  Use Spread Placement groups
   C.  Choose an instance type that supports enhanced networking
   D.  Choose an instance type that supports performance networking

Q18. You are the architect of a payment gateway provider and anticipating a fivefold increase in traffic in the upcoming shopping season. You are using RDS with MySQL as database engine. During load testing you notice a decrease in query performance with increase in traffic. Which of the following options you could do immediately to increase database performance?
   A.  Instead of MySQL use Oracle or SQL Server.
   B.  Instead of MySQL use DynamoDB.
   C.  Use Multi-AZ deployment option to increase read and write performance.
   D.  Use Read Replicas and redirect read queries to those replicas.

Q19. John hosts his personal blog website as static website on S3. The bucket name he uses to store his website files is 'west-bucket' in 'us-west-2' region. The photos are uploaded under the main bucket folder using the S3 console. What is the url of john's static website?
A. http:// s3-us-west-2.amazonaws.com/ west-bucket
B. http://west-bucket.s3-us-west-2.amazonaws.com/
C. http://west-bucket.s3-website-us-west-2.amazonaws.com/
D. http:// s3-website-us-west-2.amazonaws.com/west-bucket

Q20. You are creating proof of concept web application and want to quickly deploy and manage applications in the AWS Cloud without having to learn about the infrastructure that runs those applications. You don't want to handle the details of capacity provisioning, load balancing, scaling, and application health monitoring. Which AWS services you should leverage?
   A.  EC2, ELB, Auto Scaling
   B.  AWS Elastic Beanstalk
   C.  Lambda, ELB, Auto Scaling
   D.  EC2, S3, ELB, Auto Scaling
   E.  Lambda, ELB, Auto Scaling, CloudFormation

Q21. You are running the following On-Demand Instances in account A:
   •  4 x m3.large Linux, default tenancy instances in Availability Zone us-east-1a
   •  2 x m4.xlarge Amazon Linux, default tenancy instances in Availability Zone us-east-1b
   •  1 x c4.xlarge Amazon Linux, default tenancy instances in Availability Zone us-east-1c

You purchase the following Reserved Instances in account A:

- 4 x m3.large Linux, default tenancy Reserved Instances in Availability Zone us-east-1a (capacity is reserved)
- 4 x m4.large Amazon Linux, default tenancy Reserved Instances in Region us-east-1
- 1 x c4.large Amazon Linux, default tenancy Reserved Instances in Region us-east-1

How the reserved instances are applied? Choose 3.

A. reservation of the four m3.large zonal Reserved Instances is used by the four m3.large instances
B. m4.large regional Reserved Instances billing discount applies to 100% usage of 2 x m4.xlarge Amazon Linux, default tenancy
C. m4.large regional Reserved Instances billing discount applies to 50% usage 2 x m4.xlarge Amazon Linux, default tenancy
D. c4.large regional Reserved Instance billing discount applies to 50% of c4.xlarge usage.
E. c4.large regional Reserved Instance billing discount applies to 100% of c4.xlarge usage.

Q22. A law firm has an internal tablet/mobile application used by employees to download large word documents in their devices for offline review. These document's size are in the range of 10-20 MB. The employees save the document in local device storage, edit it in offline mode and then use the feature in app to upload file to cloud storage. Most of the time users are expected to be in area of high mobile bandwidth of LTE or WIFI but some time they may be in area using a slow speed network (EDGE) or 3G with lots of fluctuations. The files are stored in AWS S3 buckets. What approach should the architect recommend for file upload in application?

A. Use Single PUT operation to upload the files to S3
B. Use Multipart upload to upload the files to S3
C. Use Amazon S3 Transfer Acceleration to upload the files
D. Use Single POST operation to upload the files to S3

Q23. Because of a new regulatory compliance requirement you have to encrypt all your encrypted existing application RDS DB instances. You know that in AWS RDS DB instance you can only enable encryption for an Amazon RDS DB instance when you create it, not after the DB instance is created. What steps you should take to meet the compliance requirements? Choose 2.

A. Step1: You create a new DB instance with encryption enabled
B. Step 2: Copy data from the old DB instance to new encrypted DB instance
C. Step1: You can create a snapshot of your DB instance, and then create an encrypted copy of that snapshot.
D. Step2: You can then restore a DB instance from the encrypted snapshot, and thus you have an encrypted copy of your original DB instance.

Q24. When should you use EFS vs FSx for Windows vs FSx for Lustre? Choose 3.
    A. Use EFS, for Windows Applications and Windows instances when you need simple, scalable, fully managed elastic NFS file.
    B. Use FSx for Windows File Server, for Linux based application when you need centralized storage having native support for POSIX file system features and support for network access through industry-standard Server Message Block (SMB) protocol.
    C. Use EFS, for Linux Applications and Linux instances when you need simple, scalable, fully managed elastic NFS file.
    D. Use FSx for Windows File Server, for Windows based application when you need centralized storage having native support for Windows file system features and support for network access through industry-standard Server Message Block (SMB) protocol.
    E. Use FSx for Lustre, when you need to launch and run the popular, high-performance Lustre file system for workloads where speed matters, such as machine learning, high performance computing (HPC), video processing, and financial modeling.

Q25. Your Amazon ECS service can optionally be configured to use Elastic Load Balancing to distribute traffic evenly across the tasks in your service.
    A. TRUE
    B. FALSE

Q26. What is a 'fan out 'scenario?
    A. A publisher sends same message to multiple SNS topics or SQS queues
    B. Amazon SNS message is sent to a topic and then replicated and pushed to multiple Amazon SQS queues, HTTP endpoints, or email addresses.
    C. Message is sent to a SQS queue and then replicated and pushed to multiple Amazon SNS topics.
    D. Message is sent to a SQS queue and then replicated and pushed to multiple Amazon SQS queues.

Q27. Your company is planning to store their important documents in S3 storage. The compliance unit wants to be intimated when documents are created or deleted along with the user name. You know that S3 has the feature of event notification for object events like s3: ObjectCreated:*, s3: ObjectRemoved:*. What are the destination where S3 can publish events? Choose3.
    A. Amazon SES
    B. Amazon Simple Notification Service (Amazon SNS) topic
    C. Amazon Simple Queue Service (Amazon SQS) queue
    D. AWS Lambda

Q28. You have three VPCs A, B, C. How many peer connection you need to configure so all the VPCs can access the resource of one another?
    A.   Two peer configuration. A-B and B-C peer configuration needs to be done. A-C transitive peering configuration will be automatically done.
    B.   Three peer configuration. A-B, B-C and C-A.
    C.   Two peer configuration. A-C and B-C peer configuration needs to be done. A-B transitive peering configuration will be automatically done.
    D.   None of the above.

Q29. You have a photo upload application and use S3 to store the uploaded images. After an image is uploaded you want to create a thumbnail version of it. Which of the following option will be most scalable and cost effective?
    A.   Create a Lambda function that Amazon S3 can invoke when objects are created. Then, the Lambda function can read the image object from the source bucket and create a thumbnail image target bucket.
    B.   Have a fleet of EC2 instances running a program which continuously reads the most latest object uploaded in S3 and converts into thumbnail.
    C.   S3 posts new image upload event notification as JSON to a SQS queue from which a fleet of EC2 servers will process the image.
    D.   S3 posts new image upload event notification as JSON to a SNS topic from which a fleet of EC2 servers will process the image.

Q30. You want to run a public-facing web application, while maintaining back-end servers that aren't publicly accessible. You will have to set up security and routing so that the web servers can communicate with the MySQL database servers. You also need to ensure that database servers can connect to the Internet for software updates but the Internet cannot establish connections to the database servers. How will you set up your VPC configuration? Choose 3.
    A.   Set up web servers in a public subnet and the database servers in a private subnet.
    B.   The DB instances in the private subnet can access the Internet by using a network address translation (NAT) gateway that resides in the public subnet.
    C.   Security Group attached with DB Instance should only allow read or write database requests from the web servers by configuring source as web server's security group.
    D.   The DB instances in the private subnet can access the Internet by using a web server EC2 instance that resides in the public subnet.

Q31. You are the solution architect for a global financial services company providing banking and stock market trading to its customers. Because of compliance and regulatory reasons the application must be hosted in respective country of the users. For example a U.S citizen request must be routed to application hosted in US-East region and for a European Union user it must be routed to application hosted in EU-Central region. Which routing policy you will configure in the Route 53 to achieve this requirement?
    A.   Geolocation Routing

B. Geoproximity Routing
C. User Location Routing
D. User Profile Routing

Q32. A building construction company's architects use CAD software installed in their workstation to design architecture blueprints. These blueprint files are very large. The company started using S3 and AWS Storage gateway for file storage and back up. After a while as number of users increased after rolling it out across different global office locations, it was found that transferring/fetching large data files speed was slow. What should they do to decrease the amount of time required to transfer data in a cost effective way?
A. Increase the bandwidth with your Internet service provider.
B. Create VPN connection with AWS resources.
C. Use AWS Direct Connect to connect with AWS resources.
D. Use AWS Transit Gateway to connect with AWS resources.

Q33. You are a solution architect for a multinational company which wants to migrate all their existing applications to AWS cloud platform. They want to create separate AWS account based on each country where they have regional headquarters. They also want to centrally manage billing; control access, compliance, and security; and share resources across AWS accounts. If you want to define your own custom multi-account environment with advanced governance and management capabilities which AWS service you will use?
A. AWS Organizations
B. AWS System Manager
C. AWS Control Tower
D. AWS Service Catalog

Q34. You are using DynamoDB to host a discussion forum website on AWS topics (S3, VPC, ELB....). Users can subscribe to notification whenever there is a new discussion thread or post on topics they have chosen. For example user Smith has chosen to be notified for (RDS, EC2, ECS). How can you achieve this?
A. Use Lambda with DynamoDB stream to capture the new post or topic record insertion in the table, function will have logic to query the list of users subscribed to that discussion topic then it will send notification to subscribed users through SNS.
B. Use Cloudwatch with DynamoDB stream to capture the new post or topic record insertion in the table, trigger a Lambda to query the list of users subscribed to that discussion topic then it will send notification to subscribed users through SNS.
C. Use Cloudtrail with DynamoDB stream to capture the new post or topic record insertion in the table, trigger a Lambda to query the list of users subscribed to that discussion topic then it will send notification to subscribed users through SNS.
D. Use a scheduled job running in an EC2 server to continuously read the DynamoDB table and send the notification to subscribed users through SNS.

Q35. You have configured a VPC with public and private subnet as shown in the diagram below with:
Public subnet: web server instance, NAT instance for private subnet instances to access the internet.
Private subnet: RDS instances, fleet of EC2 instances in an auto scaling group. These instances access internet through NAT instance in the public subnet for software updates.

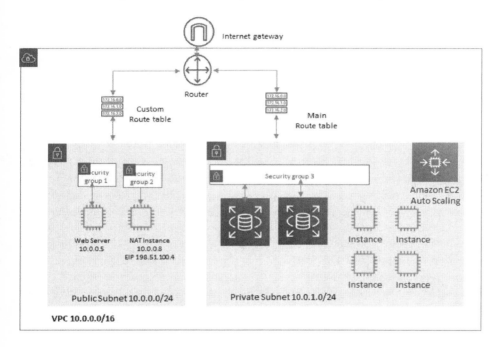

The software updates for instances in the private subnet is schedule to run every night from 11 pm – 1am. You observe recently that these updates has become very slow and some of the updates are getting time out before the maintenance window of two hours. You identify the bottleneck is NAT instance network bandwidth. What architecture changes you can do to resolve this problem?

A. Increase the number of NAT instances and change its instance type to one having more bandwidth.
B. Use NAT gateway instead of NAT instance.
C. Place NAT instance in the private subnet to increase network performance.
D. Change the maintenance window of private subnet instances so as not to overlap with one another.

Q36. Which strategy KMS uses to encrypt data and also protect your encryption key?

A. Encryption Context
B. Symmetric keys
C. Asymmetric keys
D. Envelope Encryption

Q37. You are the solution architect for a law firm which is using S3 to store numerous documents related to cases handled by their lawyers. Recently one of the employee inadvertely deleted few important documents stored in bucket. Luckily another employee had the local copy in his computer and you were able to restore the document in the bucket. You have been asked to do configuration changes in S3 so that such unintentional mistakes can be avoided and even if it happens there should be easier way to recover form it ?Choose 3.

A. Set S3 object lock
B. Enable S3 cross region replication
C. Enable bucket versioning
D. Enable MFA delete on a bucket

Q38. You run an online photo editing website for two type of members: free members and fee paying premium members. The set of editing requests and photos is placed asynchronously in a SQS queue which is then process by worked EC2 instances in an auto scaling group. The architecture has two SQS queues, one for premium members and one for free members editing task. You have on-demand EC2 instances in an auto scale group to process the messages in the premium members queue and spot instances for processing the message from free member queue. At times spot instances are terminated by AWS. What will happen to messages which are in-process by those terminated instances?

A. The message will be deleted by SQS.
B. The message will be deleted by the terminated instance and will not appear in the queue.
C. The message will be visible immediately in the queue and picked up for processing by other live spot instance.
D. The message will be visible in the queue after the visibility time is over and picked up for processing by other live spot instance.

Q39. You are designing an online gaming application for users across the world. As the game comprise of augmented reality, high performance and very low latency is one of the important criteria for providing best gaming experience. Because of this reason you want to design a multiregional architecture using DynamoDB as the database. Which of the following will you use in the application to meet these design criteria? Choose 2.

A. Use Cloudfront with DynamoDB as origin
B. Enable DynamoDB Accelerator (DAX) and DynamoDB auto scaling
C. Use DynamoDB Global Tables
D. Enable DynamoDB Adaptive Capacity

Q40. How many IP addresses in each subnet CIDR block are not available for you to use, and cannot be assigned to an instance?
    A.  2
    B.  3
    C.  4
    D.  5

Q41. You have developed your own blog website 'www.mycloudblogs.com' in which you write about AWS, Cloud and Digital topics. It also has other features of discussion forums and ability for the user to take mock tests. You have deployed it in a VPC, web server on EC2 instances with Auto Scaling group and an Application Load Balancer (ALB) in the front. The domain name 'www.mycloudblogs.com' will be pointing to the ALB. You are also using Route 53 to manage DNS Which record types will you create in Route 53 assuming you have configured your VPC and ALB to route only IPv4 traffic?
    A.  'AAAA' Alias record with Alias Target as the ALB
    B.  'A' Alias record with Alias Target as the ALB
    C.  'A' Non Alias record with Alias Target as the ALB
    D.  'AAAA' Non Alias record with Alias Target as the ALB
    E.  CNAME record with Alias Target as the ALB

Q42. Your company is migrating two existing applications to AWS. Application portfolio has one internet application which will be accessed by its customers and one intranet application which will be accessed only by employees from corporate network. Your plan is to create one VPC and deploy each application instances individually in a separate subnet. You also want to ensure that whole design is fault tolerant and services should not be hampered in case one of AWS AZ goes down? How many minimum subnets should you create?
    A.  2 subnets
    B.  4 subnets
    C.  1 subnets
    D.  6 subnets

Q43. How are the rules evaluated in a security group (SG) and network ACLs? Choose 2.
    A.  Network ACLs evaluate all rules before deciding whether to allow traffic
    B.  SG evaluate all rules before deciding whether to allow traffic
    C.  Network ACLs process rules in number order when deciding whether to allow traffic
    D.  SG process rules in number order when deciding whether to allow traffic

Q44. You were doing a PoC for a web application using a simple three tier architecture as shown below.

Users

Amazon Route 53

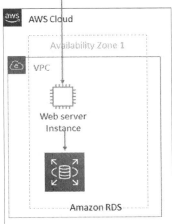

Now you want to leverage other AWS services and features to change this architecture for production environment for global user base. The key architecture criteria are:
- It should be resilient.
- It should be elastic to grow for handling the increased load.
- Reduce latency for global user base and high performance.
- Though application is stateless, it should be able to track user session.
- Storage for static assets and backups.

What services you will use to meet above criteria?

A.  Application Load Balancer, RDS Multi-AZ & Read Replica, Web EC2 Instance Auto Scale Multi AZ, ElastiCache, Cloudfront, S3

B.  Application Load Balancer, RDS , Web EC2 Instance Auto Scale Multi AZ, DynamoDB, ElastiCache, Cloudfront, S3

C.  Application Load Balancer, RDS Multi-AZ & Read Replica, Web EC2 Instance Auto Scale Multi AZ, S3

D.  Application Load Balancer, RDS, Web EC2 Instance Auto Scale Multi AZ, DynamoDB, ElastiCache, Cloudfront, S3


Q45. You are the solution architect for a SaaS application in which you provide different domain to each tenant. How will you configure multiple certificates for different domains

311

using Elastic Load Balancing (ELB) so that multi-tenant SaaS applications can run behind the same load balancer? Choose 2.

A. Use a Subject Alternative Name (SAN) certificate to validate multiple domains behind the load balancer, including wildcard domains, with AWS Certificate Manager (ACM).

B. Use an Application Load Balancer (ALB), which supports multiple SSL certificates and smart certificate selection using Server Name Indication (SNI).

C. It is not possible.

D. Use a Classic Load Balancer, which supports multiple SSL certificates and smart certificate selection using Server Name Indication (SNI).

Q46. You are solution architect for a sports media company that hosts its websites on AWS. Most of the users visits the website for reading latest news, videos and articles on different sports available on the website, only minority of users write reviews or comments. Website server runs on Amazon EC2 auto scale enabled instances along with single EC2 instance for MySQL. With increase in the popularity of the website you have been tasked to make it more resilient and improve the performance. How can you do that? Choose 2.

A. Migrate MySQL to Amazon RDS with Multi-AZ for performance.

B. Migrate MySQL to Amazon RDS with Multi-AZ for resiliency.

C. Enable Read Replicas on Amazon RDS and distribute read traffic for performance improvement.

D. Enable Read Replicas on Amazon RDS and distribute read traffic for resiliency.

Q47. What is Recovery Time Objective (RTO)?

A. The time it takes after a disruption to restore a database to its service level, as defined by the operational level agreement (OLA).

B. The acceptable amount of performance loss measured in time.

C. The time it takes after a disruption to restore a business process to its service level, as defined by the operational level agreement (OLA).

D. The acceptable amount of data loss measured in time.

Q48. What are available retrieval options when restoring an archived object from S3 in Glacier and Deep Archive storage? Choose 3.

A. Expedited

B. Standard

C. Urgent

D. Bulk

E. Immediate

Q49. You are solution architect for a new global tennis sports news web site. Web site will be hosted on a fleet of EC2 instances. Which AWS services you can use to ensure that when load on website increases, users will not experience slow response? Choose 3.

A.   Amazon ElastiCache as in memory data store for web caching.
B.   AWS Auto Scaling for web site resources.
C.   CloudFormation to deploy the application in AWS region with maximum online users.
D.   AWS CloudFront with website as the custom origin.

Q50. How can you ensure that the load balancer stops sending requests to instances that are deregistering or unhealthy while keeping the existing session connection open so as to complete the in-flight requests to these instances ?
A.   Programmatically keep sending requests to the same instance till session completes.
B.   Enable sticky sessions.
C.   Enable connection draining.
D.   All of the above.

Q51. Which AWS security service uses machine learning to automatically discover, classify, and protect sensitive data such as personally identifiable information (PII) or intellectual property.
A.   AWS WAF
B.   AWS Shield
C.   Amazon GuardDuty
D.   Amazon Macie

Q52. . How can you protect data at rest in S3? Choose 2.
A.   Using server side encryption
B.   Using client side encryption
C.   Using SSL between client and S3

Q53. Which AWS database service will you choose for Online Analytical Processing (OLAP)?
A.   Amazon RDS
B.   Amazon Redshift
C.   Amazon Glacier
D.   Amazon DynamoDB

Q54. Soma is founder of an Artificial Intelligence product start up. Upon starting the company, she created her own AWS account and used AWS products by herself. Then as company expanded she hired developers, admins, testers, managers, and system administrators. Using AWS account root user credentials she created a user for herself called *Soma*, and a group called *Admins*. She added user *Soma* to group *Admins*. She also created groups called *Developers*, *Testers*, *Managers* and *SysAdmins*. She created users for each of her employees, and puts the users in their respective groups. What IAM best practice she should follow so that she can easily apply any account-wide permissions to all users in the AWS account?
A.   Create a customer managed policy and attach to each user.

B.   Any account wide permission can be updated in each of the group's permission (*Developers*, *Testers*, *Managers* and *SysAdmins*) are attached to.

C.   She should create a group called *AllUsers* and add all users to that group so that she can easily apply any account-wide permissions to all users in the AWS account..

D.   Create a customer managed policy and attach to each group.

Q55. Your company is adopting AWS cloud by migrating majority of existing on-premise application to cloud and retaining some of them on premise. Currently they use on-premises AD to administer user accounts, manage group memberships, and control access to on-premises resources. You want to enable your users to sign in to the AWS Management Console using on-premises AD credentials to manage AWS resources such as Amazon EC2, Amazon RDS, and Amazon S3. How can you achieve this? Choose 2.

A.   Connect Your On-Premises Active Directory to AWS Simple AD for federated AWS Management Console access.

B.   Connect Your On-Premises Active Directory to AWS Using AD Connector for federated AWS Management Console access.

C.   By using an AD trust between AWS Microsoft AD and your on-premises AD, you can assign your on-premises AD users and groups to IAM roles for AWS Management Console access.

D.   By using an AD trust between AWS Simple AD and your on-premises AD, you can assign your on-premises AD users and groups to IAM roles for AWS Management Console access.

Q56. You are the solution architect for a gaming company which has a website from which user can download PC games after online payment. The game executable files are stored in Amazon S3 buckets and distribution is configured in CloudFront. How can you ensure that your users can access your files using only CloudFront URL and not through Amazon S3 URLs? Choose 2.

A.   Require that your users access your private files by using special CloudFront signed URLs.

B.   Require that your users access your private files by using signed cookies.

C.   Create an origin access identity, which is a special CloudFront user, and associate the origin access identity with your distribution

D.   Change the permissions either on your Amazon S3 bucket or on the files in your bucket so that only the origin access identity has read permission (or read and download permission).

Q57. Which AWS service you will use for real time analytics of streaming data such as IoT telemetry data, application logs, and website clickstreams. ?

A.   Amazon Athena

B.   Amazon Kinesis

C.   Amazon Elasticsearch Service

D.  Amazon QuickSight

Q58. Your company has headquarter in Los Angeles CA and have deployed their internal applications in US-West region. They are going to open a new office in Frankfurt Germany and are planning to transfer few employees as well. To comply with European regulations some of the applications will be replicated in a new AWS account created in EU-Central region. How will you manage the IAM users and roles being used by employees who will be transferred to Frankfurt?

A.  IAM is a global service, users and roles are not region specific. You don't need to create new one for EU-Central region.
B.  You will need to create new IAM users and roles for EU-Central region.
C.  IAM users is a global service, roles are region specific. You don't need to create new users but will need to create new roles for EU-Central region.
D.  IAM roles is a global service, users are region specific. You don't need to create new roles but will need to create new users for EU-Central region.

Q59. Which AWS service enables developers to manage and synchronize mobile app data in real time across devices and users, but still allows the data to be accessed and altered when the mobile device is in an offline state?

A.  Amazon API Gateway
B.  Amazon Cognito
C.  AWS DataSync
D.  AWS AppSync

Q60. Which of the following statements are true regarding security groups (SG) and network ACLs? Choose 2.

A.  SG operates at instance level and network ACLs operates at subnet level.
B.  SG supports allow rules only and network ACLs support allow and deny rules.
C.  Network ACLs operates at instance level and SG operates at subnet level.
D.  Network ACLs supports allow rules only and SG support allow and deny rules.

Q61. Which of the following statements are true regarding security groups (SG) and network ACLs? Choose 2.

A.  Network ACLs is stateful: Return traffic is automatically allowed, regardless of any rules.
B.  SG is stateful: Return traffic is automatically allowed, regardless of any rules.
C.  Network ACLs is stateless: Return traffic must be explicitly allowed by rules
D.  SG is stateless: Return traffic must be explicitly allowed by rules.

Q62. Your company first project in AWS cloud is an internal web application to be used by employees only. You want to provide single sign on where employee can use their existing corporate sign on identities. You don't want to a have separate user management module in the new application which will require your employees to have a separate authentication userid/password. Essentially this will enable your employees to have single sign on to new web application using existing corporate identities. You found that AWS supports this by way of user federation for authenticating using existing corporate identities. Which of the following consideration have to be kept in mind to use this user federation feature? Choose 3.

A. Existing corporate Identity Provider should be compatible with Security Assertion Markup Language 2.0 (SAML 2.0) to provide single-sign on (SSO) access.

B. If your corporate Identity Provider is Microsoft Active Directory Federation Service (AD FS), you cannot configure SSO.

C. If your corporate Identity Provider is Microsoft Active Directory Federation Service (AD FS), you can configure SSO.

D. If your corporate directory is not compatible with SAML 2.0, you can create an identity broker application to provide single-sign on (SSO) access to the AWS for your users.

E. If your corporate directory is not compatible with SAML 2.0, you cannot create an identity broker application to provide single-sign on (SSO) access to the AWS Management Console for your users.

Q63. Which are the two service provided by AWS for workflow implementation?

A. Simple Workflow Service (SWF)

B. Step Functions

C. API Gateway

D. SQS

Q64. Which load balancer you should use if you need extreme performance and static IP is needed for your application?

A. Application Load Balancers

B. Classic Load Balancers

C. Database Load Balancers

D. Network Load Balancers

Q65. Your company is exploring AWS Storage Gateway for extending their on-premise storage. One of the key criteria is to have AWS as the primary storage but still there should be fast and low latency access to frequently accessed data. Which Storage Gateway option will meet this criteria? Choose 2.

A. Tape Gateway

B. File Gateway

C. Volume Stored Gateway

D. Volume Cached Gateway

# PRACTICE EXAM 2

Q1. Which EBS RAID configuration you will use when I/O performance is more important than fault tolerance; for example, as in a heavily used database (where data replication is already set up separately)?
- A.  RAID 0
- B.  RAID 1
- C.  RAID 5
- D.  RAID 6

Q2. What are the reasons to enable cross region replication on your S3 buckets?
- A.  Comply with compliance requirements
- B.  Minimize latency
- C.  Increase operational efficiency
- D.  Maintain object copies under different ownership
- E.  All of the above

Q3. You purchased a t2.medium default tenancy Amazon Linux/Unix Reserved Instance in the US East (N. Virginia) region and you have two running t2.small instances in your account in that Region. How will the reserved instance billing benefit applied?
- A.  You will not get any benefit as you don't have running instance type matching to reserved instance type bought.
- B.  You will get benefit applied to usage of only one running t2.small.
- C.  You will get benefit applied to usage of both running t2.small
- D.  You will get benefit applied to 75% usage of both running t2.small

Q4. You are the solution architect for a media company which is planning to migrate on-premise applications to AWS. You are analyzing the workflows like video editing, studio production, broadcast processing, sound design, and rendering which uses an existing shared storage to process large files. Which Amazon service you will use that provides a:
- strong data consistency model with high throughput
- scale on demand to petabytes without disrupting applications
- growing and shrinking automatically as you add and remove files
- shared file access which can cut the time it takes to perform these jobs
- ability to consolidate multiple local file repositories into a single location accessible by application deployed on multiple EC2 instances
- A.  Amazon EFS
- B.  Amazon EBS
- C.  Amazon S3
- D.  Amazon RDS

Q5. Your company has an intranet application for employees to fill up their weekly timesheet. Usage pattern analysis depicts a surge in traffic on Friday evening and Wednesday evening from 4-6 pm. Which auto scaling policy would you use to add and remove instances?

A. Schedule based auto scaling policy
B. Demand based auto scaling policy
C. Maintain current instance levels at all times
D. Manual Scaling by specifying change in the max, min and desired capacity

Q6. What are two ways that you can customize how AWS Global Accelerator sends traffic to your endpoints?
A. Change the traffic dial to limit the traffic for one or more endpoint groups.
B. Change the traffic dial to limit the traffic for endpoints in a group.
C. Specify weights to change the proportion of traffic to the endpoint group.
D. Specify weights to change the proportion of traffic to the endpoints in a group.

Q7. Your online gaming application gets steady traffic apart from first three days of month when you run promotion giving discounts and bonus points to gamers. During those three days the traffic triples because of new users joining and existing users playing more. Currently you have six instances on which your application runs. What is the cost effective way to plan your instances to handle this periodic traffic surge?
A. Run 6 on demand instances then add 12 more on-demand only for first three days of the month
B. Run 6 on demand instances then add 12 more as spot instances
C. Use 18 reserved instances i.e. three time the normal demand all the time
D. Run 6 reserved instance and then add 12 on demand instances for three days every month.

Q8. Select the features of Elastic Fabric Adapter (EFA)? Choose 3.
A. Brings the scalability, flexibility, and elasticity of cloud to tightly-coupled High Performance Computing (HPC) applications and machine learning applications.
B. Tightly-coupled HPC applications have access to lower and more consistent latency and higher throughput than traditional TCP channels, enabling them to scale better.
C. Provide all ENA devices functionalities plus a new OS bypass hardware interface that allows user-space applications to communicate directly with the hardware-provided reliable transport functionality.
D. EFA and ENA are same.

Q9. Which of the following are correct statements as when should you use Amazon FSx Windows File Servers vs. Amazon EFS vs. Amazon FSx for Lustre? Choose 3.
A. For Windows-based applications, Amazon FSx provides fully managed Windows file servers with features and performance optimized for "lift-and-shift" business-critical application workloads including home directories (user shares), media workflows, and ERP applications via SMB protocol.

B. If you have Linux-based applications, Amazon EFS is a cloud-native fully managed file system that provides simple, scalable, elastic file storage accessible from Linux instances via the NFS protocol.

C. For compute-intensive and fast processing workloads, like high performance computing (HPC), machine learning, EDA, and media processing, Amazon FSx for Lustre, provides a file system that's optimized for performance, with input and output stored on Amazon S3.

D. If you have Windows-based applications, Amazon EFS is a cloud-native fully managed file system that provides simple, scalable, elastic file storage accessible from EC2 windows instances via the NFS protocol

Q10. You need to prevent users in specific countries from accessing your content stored in S3 and distributed through CloudFront. How can you achieve this?

A. Use the S3 geo restriction feature.

B. Use the CloudFront geo restriction feature.

C. Use the CloudFront ip restriction feature.

D. You cannot restrict the access based on countries.

Q11. You have launched a new instance for a test environment using Amazon Linux 2, with a public DNS name that is reachable from the internet. You plan to use this server to deploy a dynamic PHP application that reads and writes information to a database. You did following procedures to install an Apache web server with PHP and MariaDB (a community-developed fork of MySQL) support on your Amazon Linux 2 instance (sometimes called a LAMP web server or LAMP stack).

- Update the distribution software packages.
- Installed the necessary web server, php, and mariadb packages.
- Start httpd service and turned on via systemctl.
- Add ec2-user to the apache group.
- The appropriate ownership and file permissions are set for the web directory and the files contained within it.
- A simple web page is created to test the web server and PHP engine.

How can you automate the above steps when you launch instances for QA, Integration and production environment?

A. Convert the tasks into a shell script and a set of cloud-init directives that executes when the instance launches using instance meta data.

B. Convert the tasks into a shell script and a set of cloud-init directives that executes when the instance launches using user data.

C. Convert the tasks into a shell script and a set of cloud-init directives that executes when the instance launches using AWS Config.

D. Convert the tasks into a shell script and a set of cloud-init directives that executes when the instance launches using AWS CloudFormation.

Q12. What is the main characteristics of two SSD based EBS volume? Choose 2.
   A.   General purpose SSD volume balances price and performance for a wide variety of workloads
   B.   Provisioned IOPS SSD is highest-performance SSD volume for mission-critical low-latency or high-throughput workloads
   C.   Provisioned IOPS SSD volume balances price and performance for a wide variety of workloads
   D.   General purpose is highest-performance SSD volume for mission-critical low-latency or high-throughput workloads

Q13. You are the solution architect of a financial services company. You are planning to use Amazon SQS while designing a distributed trading application. Key functional requirements pertaining to message queue are: processing of the messages in a sequential order, message should be processed only once and there should not be duplicate messages in the queue. How will you ensure the above requirements? Choose 3 options.
   A.   Use SQS Standard Queues.
   B.   Use SQS FIFO queues.
   C.   Use SWF FIFO.
   D.   Enable content-based deduplication.
   E.   Explicitly provide the message deduplication ID (or view the sequence number) for the message.

Q14. You have a blog site that is only used for a few minutes several times per day. You want to design the application on Serverless architecture so that you consume resources on usage basis. You also don't want to compromise on scalability and performance. Which AWS services you will use? Choose 2
   A.   Lambda
   B.   Aurora Serverless
   C.   S3
   D.   RDS MySQL

Q15. Agrim uses S3 to store all his personal photos. He has a bucket name "personalgallery" in us-east-1 region. After he came back from a vacation in Alaska, he uploads all camera snaps in his laptop desktop folder "alaskaphotos". The photos have file name photo1.jpg, photo2.jpg etc. He logs into his AWS account and opens the S3 console. He then drags the desktop folder "alaskaphotos" inside the "personalgallery" bucket to upload files. Which of the following is correct? Choose 2.
   A.   All the snap files photo1.jpg, photo2.jpg etc. will be visible in the S3 console inside the main bucket folder "personalgallery"

B. All the snap files photo1.jpg, photo2.jpg etc. will be visible in the S3 console inside another folder "alaskaphotos" under the main bucket folder "personalgallery"
C. The key name of the photos files will be "photo1.jpg" "photo2.jpg" etc.
D. The key name of the photos files will be "/alaskaphotos/photo1.jpg" "/alaskaphotos/photo2.jpg" etc.

Q16. What protection AWS Shield provide?
    A. Block common attack patterns, such as SQL injection or cross-site scripting
    B. Protection against Distributed Denial of Service (DDoS) attacks
    C. Protection against In-Transit data spoofing
    D. Protection against EC2 hacking
    E. Protection against encryption key loss

Q17. Your web application is hosted on EC2 instances inside a VPC. You are writing a shell scrip which will run in the instance based on following instance attributes:
VPC id, Subnet id, private ip address, public ip address, security groups, public hostname.
How will your script get this information?
    A. Using cURL to get instance meta data information from http://169.254.169.254/latest/user-data/
    B. Using Cloudtrail
    C. Using cURL to get instance meta data information from http://169.254.169.254/latest/meta-data/
    D. Using CloudWatch

Q18. How can you encrypt your Amazon RDS DB instances and snapshots at rest? Choose 2.
    A. No configuration required as Amazon RDS always encrypts the data at rest.
    B. You can encrypt data in RDS DB instance but cannot encrypt snapshots.
    C. Enabling the encryption option for your Amazon RDS DB instances while creation.
    D. While database creation supply the AWS KMS key identifier for your encryption key otherwise Amazon RDS uses your default encryption key for your new DB instance.

Q19. John hosts his personal blog website as static website on S3. The bucket name he uses to store his website files is 'west-bucket' in 'us-west-2' region. The photos are uploaded under the main bucket folder using the S3 console. What is the url of john's static website?
A. http:// s3-us-west-2.amazonaws.com/ west-bucket
B. http://west-bucket.s3-us-west-2.amazonaws.com/
C. http://west-bucket.s3-website-us-west-2.amazonaws.com/
D. http:// s3-website-us-west-2.amazonaws.com/west-bucket

Q20. Your solution architect has configured following scaling policy in the auto scaling group for your web server instances:

- Scaling policy to keep the average aggregate CPU utilization of your Auto Scaling group at 40 percent.
- Scaling policy to keep the request count per target of your Elastic Load Balancing target group at 1000 for your Auto Scaling group.

Which type of dynamic scaling policy is this?
   A. Cloudwatch Scaling
   B. Target tracking scaling
   C. Step scaling
   D. Simple scaling

Q21. What are the two types of Enhanced Networking Types?
   A. AMD 82599 Virtual Function (VF) interface
   B. Elastic Network Adapter (ENA)
   C. Intel 82599 Virtual Function (VF) interface
   D. Elastic Network Interface (ENI)

Q22. You are a solution architect for a global steel manufacturing company having plants across the globe. Recently an analytical and reporting application was launched in us-west region which involves each manufacturing plant uploading their weekly production data across the globe to a S3 bucket in us-west-1 region. The size of weekly production data file ranges from gigabytes to petabytes. After the first week of release feedback came from plants in countries other than US that they are experiencing slow upload times. How can you make the process of uploading the files to S3 faster?
   A. Use S3 multipart upload
   B. Change you design to first upload the data in region closest to the plan , then replicate it to us-west-1 central bucket using cross-region replication.
   C. Use S3 Transfer Acceleration
   D. Use Amazon Cloudfront

Q23. Your company has SaaS product which provides different kind of reports to various subscribed customers. The reports ranges from adhoc, daily and monthly on various metrics. This is resulting in very high read traffic to underlying Amazon RDS MySQL instance. What can you do to improve the performance without affecting the user experience?
   A. Ensure that underlying RDS MySQL instance is Multi-AZ enabled.
   B. Create a read replica for underlying RDS MySQL.
   C. Change the RDS instance from MySQL to PostgreSQL.
   D. Analyze and improve the performance of read queries.

Q24. You are planning a strategy to migrate over 600 terabytes (TB) of data from on-premises storage system to Amazon S3 and Amazon EFS. You don't want to use other AWS offline data transfer services. You need to move data from their on-premises storage to AWS via

Direct Connect or VPN, without traversing the public internet, to further increase the security of the copied data. Which AWS service you will use?

A. AWS Snowball
B. AWS Snowball Edge
C. AWS Snowmobile
D. AWS DataSync
E. AWS AppSync

Q25. What are the different IAM Roles you have to create for your ECS to work properly? Choose 5.

A. Amazon ECS Task Execution IAM Role
B. Amazon ECS Container Instance IAM Role
C. Amazon ECS Instance Agent IAM Role
D. Amazon ECS CodeDeploy IAM Role
E. Amazon ECS CloudWatch Events IAM Role
F. Amazon ECS Cluster IAM Role

Q26. You have on-premise distributed applications connected through message broker supporting JMS APIs and AMQP/ MQTT Protocols. You are planning to migrate the whole application portfolio to AWS and re-develop using native AWS services. Which AWS service should you use to replace the message broker architecture layer?

A. Amazon Message Broker
B. Amazon SQS
C. Amazon SWF
D. Amazon MQ

Q27. As a solution architect you want to ensure that Amazon Simple Storage Service (Amazon S3) buckets and objects are secure. The resources that needs to be private must be private. What are the ways to limit permission to Amazon S3 resources? Choose 4.

A. Writing AWS Identity and Access Management (IAM) user policies that specify the users that can access specific buckets and objects.
B. Writing bucket policies that define access to specific buckets and objects.
C. Using Client side encryption
D. Using Amazon S3 Block Public Access as a centralized way to limit public access.
E. Using server side encryption
F. Setting access control lists (ACLs) on your buckets and objects.

Q28. Which of the following three statements are correct about VPC peering connections?

A. Transitive peering relationships is supported.
B. A VPC peering connection is a one to one relationship between two VPCs.
C. A VPC can peer with multiple VPCs in one to many relationships.
D. Transitive peering relationships are not supported.

Q29. You are creating a test web app based on serverless architecture. The main functionality of the app is to process the photos uploaded by the user and execute following steps:
- Extract meta data such as geolocation, time, size, format.
- create a thumbnail version
- use image recognition to tag objects in the photo

Which AWS services you will use?
- A. Amazon S3, AWS Lambda, AWS Step Functions, Amazon Rekognition, Amazon DynamoDB
- B. Amazon S3, EC2, AWS Step Functions, Amazon Rekognition, Amazon DynamoDB
- C. Amazon RDS , EC2, AWS Step Functions, Amazon Rekognition, Amazon DynamoDB
- D. Amazon RDS, AWS Lambda, AWS Step Functions, Amazon Rekognition, Amazon DynamoDB

Q30. Which are the features provided by Amazon Virtual Private Cloud that you can use to increase and monitor the security for your virtual private cloud (VPC)? Choose 3.
- A. Security groups
- B. Network access control lists (ACLs)
- C. Flow logs
- D. Cloudwatch

Q31. You have a website www.example.com which has its static images stored in S3. The domain name of distribution you have created in the CloudFront for S3 as origin is: d111111abcdef8.cloudfront.net. You don't want to use CloudFront domain name for your files. For example the URL for a file called /images/image.jpg will be:

http://d111111abcdef8.cloudfront.net/images/image.jpg

Your solution architect told you that you can use your own domain name, www.example.com, instead of the cloudfront.net domain name by adding 'www.example.com 'as an alternate domain name to your distribution setting. Which of the following steps are required to use alternate domain name? Choose 4.
- A. 'www.example.com 'should be registered domain name with Route 53 or another domain provider.
- B. Add a certificate from an authorized certificate authority (CA) to CloudFront that covers the 'www.example.com 'domain name to validate that you are authorized to use the domain.
- C. Update the 'Alternate Domain Name (CNAME) 'distribution settings field with 'www.example.com'.
- D. There is no need to configure the DNS service for the domain to route traffic for the domain 'www.example.com', to the CloudFront domain name for your distribution 'd111111abcdef8.cloudfront.net'.

E.   Configure the DNS service for the domain to route traffic for the domain 'www.example.com', to the CloudFront domain name for your distribution 'd111111abcdef8.cloudfront.net'.

Q32. Which component of site to site VPN is on the AWS VPC side?
   A.   Direct Connect
   B.   Virtual Private Gateway
   C.   AWS Transit Gateway
   D.   Customer Gateway

Q33. The diagram below depicts the configuration in an AWS Organization setup for a company. Services whitelisted (allowed) for each group by the organization's SCP are in filled circle, and IAM policies allowing access to particular services are in without filled circle. The IAM user Bob is part of the Dev OU, and the IAM policy associated with Bob allows full access to the Amazon S3 and Amazon EC2 services. The SCP associated with the Dev OU and Sales OU allows the use of the S3 service. David user doesn't have any IAM policy attached to it. Which of the following statements are correct? Choose 2.

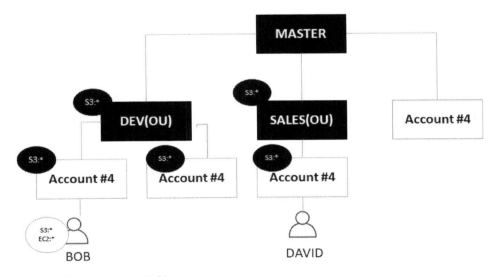

   A.   Bob cannot use EC2.
   B.   Bob can use EC2.
   C.   David can access S3.
   D.   David cannot access S3.

Q34. Which two secondary indexes you can create on a DynamoDB table? Choose 2.
   A.   Global secondary index – An index with a partition key and sort key that can be different from those on the table.

327

B. Local secondary index – An index that has the same partition key as the table, but a different sort key.

C. Global secondary index – An index with a partition key and sort key that can be same as those on the table.

D. Local secondary index – An index that has the same partition key as the table, but two different sort key.

Q35. What you must do to enable access to or from the internet for instances in a VPC subnet? Choose 4.

A. Attach an internet gateway to your VPC.

B. Attach a Transit Gateway or VPN Gateway to your VPC.

C. Ensure that your subnet's route table points to the internet gateway.

D. Ensure that instances in your subnet have a globally unique IP address (public IPv4 address, Elastic IP address, or IPv6 address).

E. Ensure that your network access control and security group rules allow the relevant traffic to flow to and from your instance.

Q36. AWS Trusted Advisor analyzes your environment on which of the following five categories?

A. Cost Optimization

B. Performance

C. Security

D. Reliability

E. Fault Tolerance

F. Service Limits

Q37. Which of the following two statements are correct about data archiving storage classes in S3? Choose 2.

A. GLACIER—used for archives where portions of the data might need to be retrieved in minutes.

B. DEEP_ARCHIVE —used for archives where portions of the data might need to be retrieved in minutes.

C. GLACIER —Use for archiving data that rarely needs to be accessed.

D. DEEP_ARCHIVE—Use for archiving data that rarely needs to be accessed.

Q38. You run an online photo editing website for two type of members: free members and fee paying premium members. The set of editing requests and photos is placed asynchronously in a SQS queue which is then processed by EC2 instances in an auto scaling group. How can you modify the architecture to ensure that your premium members editing upload get higher request than free member photo uploads?

328

A.  Set the *message timer* attribute for free member's message so that those category messages are delayed for processing.
B.  Create two queues, one for premium members and one for free members editing task. EC2 processing program should poll premium member's queue first and only if message request is empty then it should poll the free member's queue.
C.  Set the priority in a message attribute and EC2 program will process the message accordingly.
D.  Create a separate delay queue for free member's messages.

Q39. Which of the following DynamoDB table partition key schemes will result in better provisioned throughput efficiency? Choose 2.
A.  User ID, where the application has many users.
B.  Status code, where there are only a few possible status codes.
C.  Item creation date, rounded to the nearest time period (for example, day, hour, or minute).
D.  Device ID, where each device accesses data at relatively similar intervals.
E.  Device ID, where even if there are many devices being tracked, one is by far more popular than all the others.

Q40. You are the solution architect for a mortgage broker who has a web application running on an on-demand EC2 instance in a public subnet of VPC. The database servers are in the private subnet. This web application is for end customers to log in and check their application status. You are using security group to manage the user request reaching your instances in public and private subnet. Your IT monitoring team notice a brute force attack from an ip address outside the company network. How can you block the ip address so that request doesn't reach your web servers?
A.  Create a rule in security group attached to web server instance to block the ip address.
B.  Create a rule in Network Access Control attached to web server instance to deny access to ip address.
C.  Move the web servers instance from public subnet to private subnet.
D.  Create a rule to block the ip address in the internet gateway.

Q41. In your route 53 hosted zone, you have created two record sets associated with one DNS name—one with weight 3 and one with weight 1. Which of the following is true.
A.  30% of the time Route 53 will return the record set with weight 1 and 10% of the time Route 53 will return the record set with weight 3
B.  30% of the time Route 53 will return the record set with weight 3 and 10% of the time Route 53 will return the record set with weight 1
C.  75% of the time Route 53 will return the record set with weight 1 and 25% of the time Route 53 will return the record set with weight 3

D.    75% of the time Route 53 will return the record set with weight 3 and 25% of the time Route 53 will return the record set with weight 1

Q42. You have created a VPC with public and private subnet with instances in both the subnet. To provide internet access to instances in private subnet you are using NAT gateway. The private subnet instance daily stores and fetches data from S3 which is nearly 1 TB of size every day. This request and data is passed through the NAT gateway. You notice in your month's billing that this is one of the major cost as NAT gateway is billed both in Price per NAT gateway as $/hour as well as Price per GB data processed ($). How can you minimize the data transfer cost?
   A.    There is no alternate way as instance in private subnet can access internet over NAT gateway only.
   B.    Use VPC Gateway Endpoint which supports Amazon S3.
   C.    Use Amazon S3 Gateway.
   D.    Use Customer Gateway

Q43. What are components of site to site VPN? Choose 3.
   A.    Direct Connect
   B.    Virtual Private Gateway
   C.    AWS Transit Gateway
   D.    Customer Gateway

Q44. You are using Amazon ElastiCache for Memcache to cache queries of your web application RDS MySQL. You have just released the web application to beta users with minimum number of nodes in the ElastiCache cluster. As the number of users will increase you will need to increase the number of cluster nodes. What you should do minimize the changes in your caching when scale out is done?
   A.    On adding new nodes, update the list of cache node endpoints manually in the configuration file and re-initialize the application by restarting it.
   B.    Auto Discovery capable client must be used to connect to Amazon ElastiCache Cluster.
   C.    Auto Discovery capable server must be used to connect to Amazon ElastiCache Cluster.
   D.    None of the above

Q45. You are the solution architect for a financial services company who is migrating their in-house application to AWS. Because of the sensitive financial data and security requirement you are planning to house the application instances in private subnet that are not publicly reachable. Your architecture consists of
   •    A public-facing load balancer to distribute the load across the instances in the private subnets.

- Two tier: Application and Database tiers. Application tier consists of EC2 instances in auto scaling group. Database tier using RDS in a Multi-AZ deployment.
- Application and Database tiers should be in separate private subnets.
- Application which should be highly available and scalable.

How many minimum subnets you will need to create?
   A.  Total 4. Across Two AZs, each with two private subnets.
   B.  Total 6. Across Two AZs, each having one public subnet and two private subnets.
   C.  Total 6. One AZ, having two public subnet and four private subnets.
   D.  Total 5. One AZ, having one public subnet and four private subnets.

Q46. Amazon RDS read replicas complement Multi-AZ deployments. While both features maintain a second copy of your data, choose two differences from the following list.
   A.  In Read Replicas only database engine on primary instance is active while in Multi-AZ all replicas are accessible and can be used for read scaling.
   B.  Multi-AZ Deployments have synchronous replication and is highly durable while Read Replicas have Asynchronous replication and is highly scalable.
   C.  In Multi-AZ only database engine on primary instance is active while in Read Replicas all read replicas are accessible and can be used for read scaling.
   D.  Read Replicas have synchronous replication and is highly durable while Multi-AZ have Asynchronous replication and is highly scalable.

Q47. You are an IT administrator of a company which has a SaaS product developed using AWS platform. You have enabled multi-AZ deployment for the product RDS database. Few days after the release you get an alert from DB event notification on your mobile phone that your primary Amazon RDS instance has failed. What should you do ensure that your production environment is available to users by ensuring a fast seamless failover to secondary instance?
   A.  Update the DB connection string used by application server to secondary database instance.
   B.  Create a new primary instance by making a copy from the secondary instance.
   C.  No need to do anything, Amazon RDS handles failovers automatically so you can resume database operations as quickly as possible without administrative intervention.
   D.  Update the DNS record of the DB instance to point to the standby DB instance.

Q48. You have created a static blog website using S3. The name of the bucket is 'mycloudblogs.com' created in us-west-2 region. The website is available at the following Amazon S3 website endpoint:
http://mycloudblogs.com.s3-website-us-west-2.amazonaws.com/

Your website also has JavaScript on the webpages that are stored in this bucket to be able to make authenticated GET and PUT requests against the same bucket by using the Amazon S3 API endpoint for the bucket:

mycloudblogs.com.s3-us-west-2.amazonaws.com

You have also created the alias record for mycloudblogs.com in Route 53 so that your user can access the website by using the url http://mycloudblogs.com.

When you tested the website by invoking the website endpoint url on your browser you are getting following error:
'No 'Access-Control-Allow-Origin' header is present on the requested resource'.

What could be the reason?
    A.   You need to pass a unique header value from browser to Amazon S3 for every request.
    B.   You need to pass a unique header value from Amazon S3 to browser for every request.
    C.   Need to configure your CORS Settings for your bucket on amazon S3 console.
    D.   Need to configure your CORS Settings for your bucket in Route 53 record.

Q49. How can you restrict access to content like documents, business data, media streams, or content that is intended for selected users when you are securely serving these private content through CloudFront? Choose 2.
    A.   Require that your users access your private content by using special CloudFront signed URLs or signed cookies.
    B.   Require that content is always encrypted.
    C.   Require that your users access content by using CloudFront URLs, not URLs that access content directly on the origin server (for example, Amazon S3 or a private HTTP server).
    D.   Require that it is always through HTTPS.

Q50. You have created an online event ticket platform in which users can buy tickets for county and state fairs. The platform supports user request originating from multiple channels of desktop web, mobile web and native mobile app in iOS/Android. You have designed and deployed your instances in such a way that there are different instances to serve the request based on source channel. The request URL when user starts to buy a ticket are:

Web: www.statefair.com/web/buytickets
Mobile Web: www.statefair.com/mobileweb/buytickets
Native mobile app: www.statefair.com/mobileapp/buytickets

Your architecture has one application load balancer to serve the requests originating from different channels. How can you configure the load balancer so that request are served by their respective instances?

A. Replace your application load balancer with network load balancer and configure path based routing in your application load balancer to route request to different target group of instances.

B. Replace your application load balancer with network load balancer and configure host based routing in your application load balancer to route request to different target group of instances.

C. Configure path based routing in your application load balancer to route request to different target group of instances.

D. Configure host based routing in your application load balancer to route request to different target group of instances.

Q51. Which Amazon service offers threat detection that enables you to continuously monitor and protect your AWS accounts and workloads by continuously analyzing streams of meta-data generated from your account and network activity found in AWS CloudTrail Events, Amazon VPC Flow Logs, and DNS Logs?

A. AWS WAF

B. AWS Shield

C. Amazon GuardDuty

D. Amazon Macie

Q52. A company wants to use S3 to store the paid invoices by its customers. These paid invoices are accessed by various departments from finance, sales, and department heads and customer representatives for 30 days. The invoices that are paid more than 30 days before are infrequently accessed only by accounting department for auditing purpose. After the financial year these invoices are rarely accessed by any one and even if accessed, fast retrieval is not a consideration. How the solution architect of the company should plan on using different storage tiers in most cost effective way?

A. Use STANDARD tier for storing paid invoice for first 30 days. Configure lifecycle rule to move the invoice to ONEZONE_IA after 30 days and to GLACIER after the financial year is over.

B. Use STANDARD tier for storing paid invoice for first 30 days. Configure lifecycle rule to move the invoice to STANDARD _IA after 30 days and to GLACIER after the financial year is over.

C. Use STANDARD tier for storing paid invoice for first 30 days. Configure lifecycle rule to move the invoice to STANDARD _IA after 30 days and to DEEP_ARCHIVE after the financial year is over.

D. Use STANDARD tier for storing paid invoice for first 30 days. Configure lifecycle rule to move the invoice to STANDARD _IA after 30 days and to DEEP_ARCHIVE after the financial year is over.

Q53. You are building an ETL solution for daily sales report analysis. All the regional headquarter in the country upload their sales data between 7pm-11pm to a S3 bucket. Upon upload each file should be transformed and loaded into a data warehouse. What services you will use to design this solution in a most cost effective way? Choose 2.

A. Configure S3 event notification to trigger a lambda function which will kick start ETL job whenever a file is uploaded.
B. Use AWS Glue for ETL and Redshift for Data warehouse
C. Use AWS Data Pipeline for ETL and Redshift for Data warehouse
D. Use AWS Glue for ETL and Amazon EMR for Data warehouse

Q54. What are the features of IAM roles for EC2 instances? Choose 4
A. AWS temporary security credentials to use when making requests from running EC2 instances to AWS services.
B. Define cross account permission of EC2 instances.
C. Automatic rotation of the AWS temporary security credentials.
D. Granular AWS service permissions for applications running on EC2 instances.
E. Simplifies management and deployment of AWS access keys to EC2 instances.

Q55. How is web identity federation i.e. providing access to externally authenticated users supported in AWS? Choose 3.
A. Using Amazon Cognito as an identity broker which does much of the federation work.
B. If you are creating a mobile app or web-based app it blocks users who have Login with Amazon, Facebook, Google, or any OpenID Connect (OIDC) compatible identity provider.
C. You can create a mobile app or web-based app that can let users identify themselves through an Internet identity provider like Login with Amazon, Facebook, Google, or any OpenID Connect (OIDC) compatible identity provider, the app can use federation to access AWS.
D. Using Web Identity Federation API Operations for Mobile Apps

Q56. You have a S3 bucket named Photos with versioning enabled. You do following steps:
1. PUT a new object photo.gif which gets version ID = 111111
2. PUT a new version of photo.gif.
3. DELETE photo.gif
Which of the following two statements are correct?

A. After Step2, Amazon S3 generates a new version ID (121212), and adds the newer version to the bucket retaining the older version with ID=111111.There is two versions of photo.gif.

B. After Step2, Amazon S3 overwrites the older version with ID=111111 and grants it new ID. There is only one version of photo.gif.

C. After Step 3, when you DELETE an object, all versions remain in the bucket and Amazon S3 inserts a delete marker.

D. After Step 3, when you DELETE an object, all versions are deleted from the bucket.

Q57. You want to leverage AWS native components to do Clickstream analytics by collecting, analyzing, and reporting aggregate data about which webpages someone visits and in what order in your website. The clickstream analytics solution should provide these capabilities:

- Streaming data ingestion, which can process millions of website clicks (clickstream data) a day from global websites.

- Near real-time visualizations and recommendations, with web usage metrics that include events per hour, visitor count, web/HTTP user agents (e.g., a web browser), abnormal events, aggregate event count, referrers, and recent events. You want to build a recommendation engine on a data warehouse.

- Analysis and visualizations of your clickstream data both real time and analytical.

Which AWS native services you will use to build this solution?

A. Amazon IoT core, Amazon Elasticsearch Amazon S3, Amazon RDS, Amazon Redshift, Amazon Quicksight, Amazon Athena

B. Amazon Kinesis Data Firehose, Amazon Elasticsearch Amazon S3, Amazon Redshift, Amazon Quicksight, Amazon Athena

C. Amazon IoT core, Amazon Elasticsearch Amazon S3, Amazon DynamoDB, Amazon Redshift, Amazon Quicksight, Amazon Athena

D. Amazon EC2, Amazon Elasticsearch Amazon S3, Amazon Redshift, Amazon Quicksight, Amazon Athena

Q58. What are the best practices for managing IAM user access keys? Choose 4.

A. Remove (or Don't Generate) Account Access Key.

B. Use Temporary Security Credentials (IAM Roles) Instead of Long-Term Access Keys

C. Don't embed access keys directly into code.

D. Rotate access keys periodically.

E. Embed access keys directly into code for better security.

Q59. Your company has been using AWS for different kind of workloads running on EC2 instances for more than a year. As part of companywide cost optimization drive you been asked to look at how you can optimize the EC2 instances cost. Which AWS service you will use to analyze the current EC2 instances both from cost optimization and performance bottleneck identification so as to:

- Get downsizing recommendations within or across instance families.
- Get upsizing recommendations to remove performance bottlenecks.
- Understand the performance risks and how your workload would perform on various EC2 instance options to evaluate the price-performance trade-off for your workloads.
  A. AWS Compute Optimizer
  B. AWS Cost Explorer
  C. AWS EC2 optimizer
  D. AWS Budget

Q60. Your organization has adopted AWS and hosts applications that spans hundreds of VPCs. Which AWS service can minimize the operations burden of managing such a vast distributed network, Connecting and managing hundreds of VPCs via peering requiring massive route tables which is difficult to deploy, manage and can be error prone ?
  A. AWS Direct Connect
  B. AWS Site to Site VPN
  C. AWS VPN Gateway
  D. AWS Transit Gateway

Q61. Based on the figure below of a network ACL configured for a subnet, how the rules will be evaluated for a packet destined for the SSL port (443)?

**Inbound**

| Rule # | Type | Protocol | Port Range | Source | Allow/Deny |
|---|---|---|---|---|---|
| 100 | HTTP | TCP | 80 | 0.0.0.0/0 | ALLOW |
| 110 | HTTPS | TCP | 443 | 0.0.0.0/0 | ALLOW |
| 120 | SSH | TCP | 22 | 192.0.2.0/24 | ALLOW |
| 130 | RDP | TCP | 3389 | 192.0.2.0/24 | ALLOW |
| 140 | Custom TCP | TCP | 1024-65535 | 0.0.0.0/0 | ALLOW |
| * | All traffic | All | All | 0.0.0.0/0 | DENY |

**Outbound**

| Rule # | Type | Protocol | Port Range | Destination | Allow/Deny |
|---|---|---|---|---|---|
| 100 | HTTP | TCP | 80 | 0.0.0.0/0 | ALLOW |
| 110 | HTTPS | TCP | 443 | 0.0.0.0/0 | ALLOW |
| 120 | Custom TCP | TCP | 1024-65535 | 0.0.0.0/0 | ALLOW |
| * | All traffic | All | All | 0.0.0.0/0 | DENY |

  A. Rule 110 will be directly matched and inbound packet will be allowed.

B.   First the lower number rule 100 will be evaluated and then next 110 will be evaluated which matches.

C.   All the six rule will be evaluated at once and packet match with a rule will be done.

D.   Rules will be evaluated in descending order i.e. 140, 130, 120, 110 till the match.

Q62. . Your company has around 3000 users and want to use Microsoft Active Directory compatible features to manage their EC2 instances running Windows and other AWS applications such as Amazon workspaces, Amazon Workdocs or Amazon WorkMail. You don't want to set a trust relationship with on-premise AD. Which AWS service will you use?

A.   AWS Managed Microsoft AD

B.   AD Connector

C.   Amazon Cloud Directory

D.   Simple AD

Q63. You are learning AWS by watching tutorial videos which are in English. To test your learning you want to create a PoC application which will take a video file as an input and generate subtitles in Spanish. The system will receive a video input, extract the audio track, transcribe it, and generate different subtitle files for your video. Your initial core design is to use:

- Amazon Elastic Transcoder to extract the audio from the video
- Amazon Transcribe to convert the audio to text
- Amazon Translate to achieve fast, high-quality language translation

You will also include a workflow management component which will coordinate components and steps through the functions of your application. What are other services you will use to design a cost optimized PoC application?

A.   S3, Lambda, Cognito, DynamoDB

B.   S3, Lambda, Step functions, Cognito, DynamoDB

C.   S3, EC2, Step functions, Cognito, DynamoDB

D.   S3, ECS, Step functions, Cognito, DynamoDB

Q64. You have configured an application load balancer listening on port 80 and mapped it to a target group of EC2 instances also listening on port 80. When a client request reaches load balancer with correct protocol and port, how many connection load balancer maintains between client and target EC2 instance?

A.   1

B.   2

C.   3

D.   4

Q65. You are the solution architect for a pharmaceutical company which has been using a client application to manage their on-premise data backup and archival. The application uses iSCSI protocol to transfer data between application and on-premise storage. The on-premise storage currently store TBs of data and is reaching near capacity. The company doesn't want to invest in expanding the on-premise storage capacity. Which AWS service company should leverage so that there is minimum or no change to existing backup & archiving application as well as low latency is provided for frequently used data?

A. Use AWS Tape Gateway.

B. Use AWS Volume Storage Gateway.

C. Use AWS File Gateway.

D. Use AWS Volume Cached Gateway

# Answer Chapter 1 Compute: Amazon EC2, Auto Scaling, AWS Lambda, AWS Elastic Beanstalk, Amazon Elastic Container Service, AWS Fargate

Answer Q1. D

Answer Q2. B, D
AWS Documentation Reference:
https://docs.aws.amazon.com/AWSEC2/latest/UserGuide/instance-types.html
When you launch an instance, the instance type that you specify determines the hardware of the host computer used for your instance. Each instance type offers different compute, memory, and storage capabilities and are grouped in instance families based on these capabilities.
https://docs.aws.amazon.com/AWSEC2/latest/UserGuide/ec2-instances-and-amis.html
https://docs.aws.amazon.com/AWSEC2/latest/UserGuide/AMIs.html
An Amazon Machine Image (AMI) is a template that contains a software configuration (for example, an operating system, an application server, and applications). From an AMI, you launch an instance, which is a copy of the AMI running as a virtual server in the cloud. An Amazon Machine Image (AMI) provides the information required to launch an instance.
An AMI includes the following:
- One or more EBS snapshots, or, for instance-store-backed AMIs, a template for the root volume of the instance (for example, an operating system, an application server, and applications).
- Launch permissions that control which AWS accounts can use the AMI to launch instances.
- A block device mapping that specifies the volumes to attach to the instance when it's launched.

Answer Q3. B, C, D
AWS Documentation Reference:
https://docs.aws.amazon.com/AWSEC2/latest/UserGuide/AMIs.html
An Amazon Machine Image (AMI) provides the information required to launch an instance.
An AMI includes the following:
- One or more EBS snapshots, or, for instance-store-backed AMIs, a template for the root volume of the instance (for example, an operating system, an application server, and applications).
- Launch permissions that control which AWS accounts can use the AMI to launch instances.
- A block device mapping that specifies the volumes to attach to the instance when it's launched.
A is wrong as Instance Type is selected by the user separately.

Answer Q4. B, C
AWS Documentation Reference:
https://docs.aws.amazon.com/AWSEC2/latest/UserGuide/RootDeviceStorage.html

When you launch an instance, the root device volume contains the image used to boot the instance. You can choose between AMIs backed by Amazon EC2 instance store and AMIs backed by Amazon EBS.

Answer Q5. A, B
AWS Documentation Reference: Amazon EC2 Root Device Volume
https://docs.aws.amazon.com/AWSEC2/latest/UserGuide/RootDeviceStorage.html
Instance store backed AMI: Data on any instance store volumes persists only during the life of the instance
EBS backed AMI: By default, the root volume is deleted when the instance terminates.
By default, Amazon EBS-backed instance root volumes have the DeleteOnTermination flag set to true. Change this flag so that the volume persists after termination. Data on any other Amazon EBS volumes persists after instance termination by default.

Answer Q6. D
AWS Documentation Reference: Changing the Root Device Volume to Persist
https://docs.aws.amazon.com/AWSEC2/latest/UserGuide/RootDeviceStorage.html#Using_RootDeviceStorage
EBS backed AMI: By default, the root volume is deleted when the instance terminates. By default, Amazon EBS-backed instance root volumes have the DeleteOnTermination flag set to true. Change this flag so that the volume persists after termination. Data on any other Amazon EBS volumes persists after instance termination by default.

Answer Q7. A, D
AWS Documentation Reference:
https://docs.aws.amazon.com/AWSEC2/latest/UserGuide/ComponentsAMIs.html
You can select an AMI to use based on the following characteristics:
• Region
• Operating system
• Architecture (32-bit or 64-bit)
• Launch Permissions
• Storage for the Root Device

Answer Q8. A, B, C
AWS Documentation Reference: Launch Permissions
https://docs.aws.amazon.com/AWSEC2/latest/UserGuide/ComponentsAMIs.html#launch-permissions
There is no 'private' launch permission

Answer Q9. A. True
AWS Documentation Reference:
https://docs.aws.amazon.com/AWSEC2/latest/UserGuide/Using_ConvertingS3toEBS.html

You can convert an instance store-backed Linux AMI that you own to an Amazon EBS-backed Linux AMI

Answer Q10. B. False
AWS Documentation Reference:
https://docs.aws.amazon.com/AWSEC2/latest/UserGuide/Using_ConvertingS3toEBS.html
You can't convert an instance store-backed Windows AMI to an Amazon EBS-backed Windows AMI and you cannot convert an AMI that you do not own.

Answer Q11. A, B, C
AWS Documentation Reference:
https://docs.aws.amazon.com/AWSEC2/latest/UserGuide/AMIEncryption.html
By default, without explicit encryption parameters, a RunInstances action maintains the existing encryption state of an AMI's source snapshots while restoring EBS volumes from them. If encryption by default is enabled, all volumes created from the AMI (whether from encrypted or unencrypted snapshots) will be encrypted. If encryption by default is not enabled, then the instance maintains the encryption state of the AMI.

Answer Q12. A, B, C
AWS Documentation Reference:
https://docs.aws.amazon.com/AWSEC2/latest/UserGuide/AMIEncryption.html

Answer Q13. B, C
AWS Documentation Reference:
https://docs.aws.amazon.com/AWSEC2/latest/UserGuide/AMIEncryption.html

Answer Q14. D
AWS Documentation Reference: Encryption and Copying
https://docs.aws.amazon.com/AWSEC2/latest/UserGuide/CopyingAMIs.html
You cannot copy an encrypted snapshot to yield an unencrypted one.

Answer Q15. B
The key criteria is to deploy minimum servers to meet the fault tolerance requirement of at least six servers being available when on AZ goes down. Though option A and D will ensure availability of at least six servers when one of the AZ goes down but total number of servers is more that option B.

Answer Q16. B, C, D
AWS Documentation Reference:
https://docs.aws.amazon.com/AWSEC2/latest/UserGuide/enhanced-networking.html
Enhanced networking uses single root I/O virtualization (SR-IOV) to provide high-performance networking capabilities on supported instance types. SR-IOV is a method of

device virtualization that provides higher I/O performance and lower CPU utilization when compared to traditional virtualized network interfaces. Enhanced networking provides higher bandwidth, higher packet per second (PPS) performance, and consistently lower inter-instance latencies. There is no additional charge for using enhanced networking.

## Answer Q17. D
AWS Documentation Reference:
https://docs.aws.amazon.com/AWSEC2/latest/UserGuide/placement-groups.html
You can use placement groups to influence the placement of a group of interdependent instances to meet the needs of your workload. You can create a placement group using one of the following placement strategies:

- Cluster – packs instances close together inside an Availability Zone.
- Partition – spreads your instances across logical partitions such that groups of instances in one partition do not share the underlying hardware with groups of instances in different partitions.
- Spread – strictly places a small group of instances across distinct underlying hardware to reduce correlated failures.

## Answer Q18. A, C
There is no option of performance networking for instances.
AWS Documentation Reference:
https://docs.aws.amazon.com/AWSEC2/latest/UserGuide/placement-groups.html#placement-groups-cluster
A cluster placement group is a logical grouping of instances within a single Availability Zone. Cluster placement groups are recommended for applications that benefit from low network latency, high network throughput, or both. They are also recommended when the majority of the network traffic is between the instances in the group. To provide the lowest latency and the highest packet-per-second network performance for your placement group, choose an instance type that supports enhanced networking.

## Answer Q19. C
AWS Documentation Reference:
https://docs.aws.amazon.com/AWSEC2/latest/UserGuide/placement-groups.html#placement-groups-partition
Partition placement groups can be used to deploy large distributed and replicated workloads, such as HDFS, HBase, and Cassandra, across distinct racks. Partition placement groups help reduce the likelihood of correlated hardware failures for your application. When using partition placement groups, Amazon EC2 divides each group into logical segments called partitions. Each partition comprises multiple instances. Amazon EC2 ensures that each partition within a placement group has its own set of racks. Each rack has its own network and power source. No two partitions within a placement group share the same racks, allowing you to isolate the impact of hardware failure within your application.

Answer Q20.  B
AWS Documentation Reference:
https://docs.aws.amazon.com/AWSEC2/latest/UserGuide/placement-groups.html#placement-groups-spread
Spread placement groups are recommended for applications that have a small number of critical instances that should be kept separate from each other. It is a group of Instances that are each placed on distinct racks, with each rack having its own network and power source.

Answer Q21. A, B, C
AWS Documentation Reference:
https://docs.aws.amazon.com/AWSEC2/latest/UserGuide/AccessingInstances.html
You cannot connect from Linux local computer using putty to your Linux EC2 instance.

Answer Q22.B, C
AWS Documentation Reference:
https://docs.aws.amazon.com/AWSEC2/latest/UserGuide/Stop_Start.html

Answer Q23.A, B
AWS Documentation Reference:
https://docs.aws.amazon.com/AWSEC2/latest/UserGuide/Stop_Start.html

Answer Q24. A, C, D
AWS Documentation Reference:
https://docs.aws.amazon.com/AWSEC2/latest/UserGuide/elastic-ip-addresses-eip.html
An Elastic IP address is a static IPv4 address designed for dynamic cloud computing. An Elastic IP address is a public IPv4 address, which is reachable from the internet. If your instance does not have a public IPv4 address, you can associate an Elastic IP address with your instance to enable communication with the internet.

Answer Q25. A, C, D, E
AWS Documentation Reference:
https://docs.aws.amazon.com/AWSEC2/latest/UserGuide/elastic-ip-addresses-eip.html
Back to Q25

Answer Q26. D
The key criteria is to deploy minimum servers to meet the fault tolerance requirement of availability of at least six servers (66% of total 9) when on AZ goes down and also meeting requirement of at least nine servers for normal scenario.
Though A and C will ensure availability of at least six servers when one of the AZ goes down but total number of servers is more than that of option D.

Answer Q27. B, C, D, E
AWS Documentation Reference:
https://docs.aws.amazon.com/AWSEC2/latest/UserGuide/Hibernate.html#instance_hibern
ate

Answer Q28. A, C, D
AWS Documentation Reference:
https://docs.aws.amazon.com/AWSEC2/latest/UserGuide/using-eni.html
An elastic network interface is a logical networking component in a VPC that represents a
virtual network card.

Answer Q29. D
AWS Documentation Reference:
https://docs.aws.amazon.com/AWSEC2/latest/UserGuide/viewing_metrics_with_cloudwatc
h.html

Answer Q30. D
AWS Documentation Reference:
https://docs.aws.amazon.com/AWSEC2/latest/UserGuide/MultipleIP.html
You can specify multiple private IPv4 and IPv6 addresses for your instances.

Answer Q31.A, C
AWS Documentation Reference:
https://docs.aws.amazon.com/AWSEC2/latest/UserGuide/ComponentsAMIs.html#storage-
for-the-root-device
All AMIs are categorized as either backed by Amazon EBS or backed by instance store. The
former means that the root device for an instance launched from the AMI is an Amazon EBS
volume created from an Amazon EBS snapshot. The latter means that the root device for an
instance launched from the AMI is an instance store volume created from a template stored in
Amazon S3.

Answer Q32. C
AWS Documentation Reference:
https://docs.aws.amazon.com/en_pv/AWSEC2/latest/UserGuide/InstanceStorage.html
An instance store provides temporary block-level storage for your instance. This storage is
located on disks that are physically attached to the host computer. Instance store is ideal for
temporary storage of information that changes frequently, such as buffers, caches, scratch data,
and other temporary content, or for data that is replicated across a fleet of instances, such as a
load-balanced pool of web servers.

Answer Q33. D
AWS Documentation Reference: Instance Store Lifetime

https://docs.aws.amazon.com/AWSEC2/latest/UserGuide/InstanceStorage.html#instance-store-lifetime

The data in an instance store persists only during the lifetime of its associated instance. If an instance reboots (intentionally or unintentionally), data in the instance store persists. However, data in the instance store is lost under any of the following circumstances:

* The underlying disk drive fails
* The instance stops
* The instance terminates

Answer Q34. D
AWS Documentation Reference:
https://docs.aws.amazon.com/AWSEC2/latest/UserGuide/AccessingInstancesLinux.html
In a terminal window, use the ssh command to connect to the instance. You specify the private key (.pem) file and user_name@public_dns_name. For example, if you used Amazon Linux 2 or the Amazon Linux AMI, the user name is ec2-user.
ssh -i /path/my-key-pair.pem ec2-user@ec2-198-51-100-1.compute-1.amazonaws.com

Answer Q35. D
AWS Documentation Reference:
https://docs.aws.amazon.com/AWSEC2/latest/UserGuide/CopyingAMIs.html
There are no charges for copying an AMI. However, standard storage and data transfer rates apply.
Answer Q36. A
AWS Documentation Reference:
https://docs.aws.amazon.com/AWSEC2/latest/UserGuide/ec2-security-groups.html#security-group-rules
If there is more than one rule for a specific port, AWS applies the most permissive rule. For example, if you have a rule that allows access to TCP port 22 (SSH) from IP address 203.0.113.1 and another rule that allows access to TCP port 22 from everyone, everyone has access to TCP port 22.

Answer Q37. B, C, D
AWS Documentation Reference:
https://aws.amazon.com/blogs/aws/the-floodgates-are-open-increased-network-bandwidth-for-ec2-instances/
Make sure that you are using the latest, ENA-enabled AMIs on current-generation EC2 instances. ENA-enabled AMIs are available for Amazon Linux, Ubuntu 14.04 & 16.04, RHEL 7.4, SLES 12, and Windows Server (2008 R2, 2012, 2012 R2, and 2016).The ENA gives you high throughput and low latency, while minimizing the load on the host processor. It is designed to work well in the presence of multiple vCPUs, with intelligent packet routing backed up by multiple transmit and receive queues.

https://docs.aws.amazon.com/AWSEC2/latest/UserGuide//enhanced-networking.html
Enhanced networking provides higher bandwidth, higher packet per second (PPS) performance, and consistently lower inter-instance latencies.

Cluster placement groups are recommended for applications that benefit from low network latency, high network throughput, or both, and if the majority of the network traffic is between the instances in the group. To provide the lowest latency and the highest packet-per-second network performance for your placement group, choose an instance type that supports enhanced networking.

Answer Q38. A, B
AWS Documentation Reference:
https://docs.aws.amazon.com/AWSEC2/latest/UserGuide/AMIEncryption.html
AMIs that are backed by Amazon EBS snapshots can take advantage of Amazon EBS encryption. Snapshots of both data and root volumes can be encrypted and attached to an AMI. You can launch instances and copy images with full EBS encryption support included. Encryption parameters for these operations are supported in all Regions where AWS KMS is available.

Answer Q39. A, B, C
AWS Documentation Reference: Image-Copying Scenarios
https://docs.aws.amazon.com/AWSEC2/latest/UserGuide/AMIEncryption.html

Answer Q40. A, C, D
AWS Documentation Reference: Image-Copying Scenarios
https://docs.aws.amazon.com/AWSEC2/latest/UserGuide/AMIEncryption.html

Answer Q41. B, D
AWS Documentation Reference: Image-Copying Scenarios
https://docs.aws.amazon.com/AWSEC2/latest/UserGuide/AMIEncryption.html

Answer Q42. A, B, D
AWS Documentation Reference:
https://docs.aws.amazon.com/AWSEC2/latest/UserGuide/using-instance-addressing.html#concepts-private-addresses
An instance receives a primary private IP address from the IPv4 address range of the subnet. A private IPv4 address is an IP address that's not reachable over the Internet. You can use private IPv4 addresses for communication between instances in the same VPC. Each instance is also given an internal DNS hostname that resolves to the primary private IPv4 address; for example, ip-10-251-50-12.ec2.internal. You can use the internal DNS hostname for communication between instances in the same VPC, but AWS can't resolve the internal DNS hostname outside of the VPC.

Answer Q43. A, C, D
AWS Documentation Reference:
https://docs.aws.amazon.com/AWSEC2/latest/UserGuide/using-instance-addressing.html#concepts-private-addresses
Each instance has a default network interface (eth0) that is assigned the primary private IPv4 address. You can also specify additional private IPv4 addresses, known as secondary private IPv4 addresses. Unlike primary private IP addresses, secondary private IP addresses can be reassigned from one instance to another.

Answer Q44.A, B, C, D
E is incorrect, Standard RIs can only be modified. Convertible RIs can be exchanged as well as modified.
AWS Documentation Reference:
https://docs.aws.amazon.com/AWSEC2/latest/UserGuide/ri-modifying.html#ri-modification-limits
You can modify these attributes as follows:

| Modifiable attribute | Supported platforms | Limitations |
| --- | --- | --- |
| Change Availability Zones within the same Region | Linux and Windows | - |
| Change the scope from Availability Zone to Region and vice versa | Linux and Windows | If you change the scope from Availability Zone to Region, you lose the capacity reservation benefit. If you change the scope from Region to Availability Zone, you lose Availability Zone flexibility and instance size flexibility (if applicable). |
| Change the instance size within the same instance family | Linux only | The reservation must use default tenancy. Some instance families are not supported, because there are no other sizes available.. |
| Change the network from EC2-Classic to Amazon VPC and vice versa | Linux and Windows | The network platform must be available in your AWS account. If you created your AWS account after 2013-12-04, it does not support EC2-Classic. |

Answer Q45.A, B, D, E
C is wrong as you don't need AWS IAM user to access your instance through SSH from your local home computer or corporate computer.
AWS Documentation Reference:
https://docs.aws.amazon.com/AWSEC2/latest/UserGuide/connection-prereqs.html
https://docs.aws.amazon.com/AWSEC2/latest/UserGuide/AccessingInstancesLinux.html

- Get the public DNS name or Elastic ip address of the instance: You can get the public DNS or elastic ip address for your instance using the Amazon EC2 console.

- Get the default user name for the AMI that you used to launch your instance: For Amazon Linux 2 or the Amazon Linux AMI, the user name is ec2-user.

- Enable inbound SSH traffic from your IP address to your instance. Ensure that the security group associated with your instance allows incoming SSH traffic from your IP address. The default security group for the VPC does not allow incoming SSH traffic by default. The security group created by the launch instance wizard enables SSH traffic by default.

- Locate the private key and verify permissions: Get the fully-qualified path to the location on your computer of the .pem file for the key pair that you specified when you launched the instance.

- To connect to your instance using SSH. In a terminal window, use the ssh command to connect to the instance. You specify the private key (.pem) file, the user name for your AMI, and the public DNS name for your instance. For example, if you used Amazon Linux 2 or the Amazon Linux AMI, the user name is ec2-user.

Answer Q46. C

AWS Documentation Reference:

https://docs.aws.amazon.com/AWSEC2/latest/UserGuide/using-instance-addressing.html#concepts-public-addresses

AWS releases your instance's public IP address when you associate an Elastic IP address with it. When you disassociate the Elastic IP address from your instance, it receives a new public IP address.

Answer Q47. C, D, E

A is wrong because you cannot modify the operating system.

B is wrong because instance size footprint of a1.large and a1.xlarge is not same as shown in table below.

| Instance size | Normalization factor |
|---|---|
| medium | 2 |
| large | 4 |
| xlarge | 8 |

AWS Documentation Reference:

https://docs.aws.amazon.com/AWSEC2/latest/UserGuide/ri-modifying.html#ri-modification-limits

You can modify these attributes as follows:

| Modifiable attribute | Supported platforms | Limitations |
|---|---|---|
| Change Availability Zones within the same Region | Linux and Windows | - |
| Change the scope from Availability Zone to Region and vice versa | Linux and Windows | If you change the scope from Availability Zone to Region, you lose the capacity reservation benefit. If you change the scope from Region to Availability Zone, you lose Availability Zone flexibility and instance size flexibility (if applicable). |
| Change the instance size within the same instance family | Linux only | The reservation must use default tenancy. Some instance families are not supported, because there are no other sizes available.. |
| Change the network from EC2-Classic to Amazon VPC and vice versa | Linux and Windows | The network platform must be available in your AWS account. If you created your AWS account after 2013-12-04, it does not support EC2-Classic. |

Answer Q48. B, C, E, F
AWS Documentation Reference:
https://aws.amazon.com/ec2/pricing/
Amazon EC2 provides the following purchasing options for instances:

- On-Demand Instances where you pay for the instances that you use by the second, with no long-term commitments or upfront payments.
- Reserved Instances where you make a low, one-time, up-front payment for an instance, reserve it for a one- or three-year term, and pay a significantly lower hourly rate for these instances.
- Spot Instances where you request unused EC2 instances, which can lower your costs significantly.
- Savings Plans are a flexible pricing model that offer low prices on EC2 and Fargate usage, in exchange for a commitment to a consistent amount of usage (measured in $/hour) for a 1 or 3 year term.

Answer Q49. B, C
AWS Documentation Reference:
https://docs.aws.amazon.com/AWSEC2/latest/UserGuide/ec2-reserved-instances.html
Reserved Instances provide you with significant savings on your Amazon EC2 costs compared to On-Demand Instance pricing. Reserved Instances are not physical instances, but rather a billing discount applied to the use of On-Demand Instances in your account. These On-Demand Instances must match certain attributes, such as instance type and Region, in order to benefit from the billing discount.

Answer Q50. D
AWS Documentation Reference:

https://docs.aws.amazon.com/AWSEC2/latest/UserGuide/ec2-reserved-instances.html
As reserved instance attributes matches only to existing T2 instance, therefore billing benefit
will be immediately applied to it. As you don't have any C4 server instance which matches the
attribute of purchase reserved instance hence its benefits is not applied.

Answer Q51. A, B, C, E
AWS Documentation Reference:
https://docs.aws.amazon.com/AWSEC2/latest/UserGuide/ec2-reserved-instances.html
D is not correct as hardware memory and CPU is already factored in instance type. For
example: m4.large

Answer Q52. A, C, D
AWS Documentation Reference:
https://docs.aws.amazon.com/AWSEC2/latest/UserGuide/reserved-instances-types.html

Answer Q53. A, D
AWS Documentation Reference:
https://docs.aws.amazon.com/AWSEC2/latest/UserGuide/reserved-instances-types.html

Answer Q54. A, B, D
AWS Documentation Reference:
https://docs.aws.amazon.com/AWSEC2/latest/UserGuide/ri-convertible-exchange.html#ri-merge-convertible
If you merge two or more Convertible Reserved Instances, the term of the new Convertible
Reserved Instance must be the same as the original Convertible Reserved Instances, or the
highest of the original Convertible Reserved Instances. The expiration date for the new
Convertible Reserved Instance is the expiration date that's furthest in the future.
- You can merge aaaa1111 and bbbb2222 and exchange them for a 1-year Convertible
  Reserved Instance. You cannot exchange them for a 3-year Convertible Reserved
  Instance. The expiration date of the new Convertible Reserved Instance is 2018-12-31.
- You can merge bbbb2222 and cccc3333 and exchange them for a 3-year Convertible
  Reserved Instance. You cannot exchange them for a 1-year Convertible Reserved
  Instance. The expiration date of the new Convertible Reserved Instance is 2018-07-31.
- You can merge cccc3333 and dddd4444 and exchange them for a 3-year Convertible
  Reserved Instance. You cannot exchange them for a 1-year Convertible Reserved
  Instance. The expiration date of the new Convertible Reserved Instance is 2019-12-31.

C is wrong because the expiration date for the new Convertible Reserved Instance is the
expiration date that's furthest in the future. In this case it should be 3 years.

Answer Q55. A, D
AWS Documentation Reference:

https://aws.amazon.com/ec2/faqs/#Spot_Instances

While running, Spot Instances are exactly the same as On-Demand or Reserved instances. The main differences are that Spot Instances typically offer a significant discount off the On-Demand prices, your instances can be interrupted by Amazon EC2 for capacity requirements with a 2-minute notification.

Answer Q56. A, B

AWS Documentation Reference:

https://docs.aws.amazon.com/whitepapers/latest/cost-optimization-leveraging-ec2-spot-instances/when-to-use-spot-instances.html

Spot Instances are a cost-effective choice if you can be flexible about when your applications run and if your applications can be interrupted. Take advantage of Spot Instances to run and scale applications such as stateless web services, image rendering, big data analytics, and massively parallel computations. Spot Instances are typically used to supplement On-Demand Instances, where appropriate, and are not meant to handle 100% of your workload. However, you can use all Spot Instances for any stateless, non-production application, such as development and test servers, where occasional downtime is acceptable. They are not a good choice for sensitive workloads or databases.

Answer Q57. B, C, D

AWS Documentation Reference:

https://docs.aws.amazon.com/AWSEC2/latest/UserGuide/spot-interruptions.html#interruption-reasons

The following are the possible reasons that Amazon EC2 might interrupt your Spot Instances:

Price – The Spot price is greater than your maximum price.

Capacity – If there are not enough unused EC2 instances to meet the demand for Spot Instances, Amazon EC2 interrupts Spot Instances. The order in which the instances are interrupted is determined by Amazon EC2.

Constraints – If your request includes a constraint such as a launch group or an Availability Zone group, these Spot Instances are terminated as a group when the constraint can no longer be met.

Answer Q58.A, C, D

AWS Documentation Reference:

https://docs.aws.amazon.com/AWSEC2/latest/UserGuide/spot-fleet.html

A Spot Fleet is a collection, or fleet, of Spot Instances, and optionally On-Demand Instances.

The Spot Fleet attempts to launch the number of Spot Instances and On-Demand Instances to meet the target capacity that you specified in the Spot Fleet request. The request for Spot Instances is fulfilled if there is available capacity and the maximum price you specified in the request exceeds the current Spot price. The Spot Fleet also attempts to maintain its target capacity fleet if your Spot Instances are interrupted.

You can also set a maximum amount per hour that you're willing to pay for your fleet, and Spot Fleet launches instances until it reaches the maximum amount. When the maximum amount you're willing to pay is reached, the fleet stops launching instances even if it hasn't met the target capacity.

Answer Q59. A, B, C
AWS Documentation Reference:
https://aws.amazon.com/premiumsupport/knowledge-center/understand-convertible-ris/
Standard RIs can only be modified. You can modify a Standard RI to change the following attributes:
- Availability Zone or scope
- Network platform (EC2-Classic or VPC)
- Instance size

Convertible RIs can be exchanged as well as modified. You can exchange the RI for comparable RIs depending on their value, which gives you more flexibility to change the instances that your RIs will apply to later.
https://docs.aws.amazon.com/AWSEC2/latest/UserGuide/reserved-instances-types.html

Answer Q60. B, C
AWS Documentation Reference:
https://docs.aws.amazon.com/AWSEC2/latest/UserGuide/reserved-instances-scope.html

Answer Q61. A, D
AWS Documentation Reference:
https://docs.aws.amazon.com/AWSEC2/latest/UserGuide/reserved-instances-scope.html

Answer Q62. B, C, D
AWS Documentation Reference: How Regional Reserved Instances Are Applied
https://docs.aws.amazon.com/AWSEC2/latest/UserGuide/apply_ri.html
A is not correct as instance size flexibility is applied in case of reserved instance for a region. Instance size flexibility only applies to Reserved Instances that use the Amazon Linux/Unix platform with default tenancy.

Answer Q63. C
AWS Documentation Reference:
https://docs.aws.amazon.com/AWSEC2/latest/UserGuide/apply_ri.html
Regional Reserved Instances provide instance size flexibility where the Reserved Instance discount applies to instance usage within the instance family, regardless of size. Instance size flexibility is determined by the normalization factor of the instance size. The discount applies either fully or partially to running instances of the same instance family, depending on the instance size of the reservation, in any Availability Zone in the Region. The only attributes that must be matched are the instance family, tenancy, and platform. Instance size flexibility is

applied from the smallest to the largest instance size within the instance family based on the normalization factor.

A t2.medium instance has a normalization factor of 2 and t2.small has a normalization factor of 1. Therefore you will get benefit applicable to both running t2.small instances. 2/ (2x1) =100%

Answer Q64. B

AWS Documentation Reference:

https://docs.aws.amazon.com/AWSEC2/latest/UserGuide/apply_ri.html

Regional Reserved Instances provide instance size flexibility where the Reserved Instance discount applies to instance usage within the instance family, regardless of size. Instance size flexibility is determined by the normalization factor of the instance size. The discount applies either fully or partially to running instances of the same instance family, depending on the instance size of the reservation, in any Availability Zone in the Region. The only attributes that must be matched are the instance family, tenancy, and platform. Instance size flexibility is applied from the smallest to the largest instance size within the instance family based on the normalization factor.

A t2.large instance has a normalization factor of 4 and t2.medium has a normalization factor of 2. Therefore you will get benefit applicable to 2/4=50% usage.

Answer Q65. A, B, C, D

AWS Documentation Reference:

https://docs.aws.amazon.com/AWSEC2/latest/UserGuide/ri-modifying.html

Answer Q66. B, D

AWS Documentation Reference:

https://docs.aws.amazon.com/AWSEC2/latest/UserGuide/ri-modifying.html

Each Reserved Instance has an instance size footprint, which is determined by the normalization factor of the instance type and the number of instances in the reservation. When you modify a Reserved Instance, the footprint of the target configuration must match that of the original configuration, otherwise the modification request is not processed.

t2.large normalization factor is 4.

t2.medium normalization factor is 2.

t2.large normalization factor is 1.

Therefor you can divide a reservation for one t2.large (1 x 4) instance into four t2.small (4 x 1) instances or two t2.medium instance (2x2) resulting in same footprint.

Answer Q67. A, C, D

AWS Documentation Reference:

https://docs.aws.amazon.com/AWSEC2/latest/UserGuide/ec2-scheduled-instances.html

Answer Q68. E

AWS Documentation Reference:

https://docs.aws.amazon.com/AWSEC2/latest/UserGuide/dedicated-hosts-overview.html
An Amazon EC2 Dedicated Host is a physical server with EC2 instance capacity fully dedicated to your use. Dedicated Hosts allow you to use your existing per-socket, per-core, or per-VM software licenses, including Windows Server, Microsoft SQL Server, SUSE, Linux Enterprise Server, and so on.

Answer Q69. A, B, D
AWS Documentation Reference: Dedicated Instance Basics
https://docs.aws.amazon.com/AWSEC2/latest/UserGuide/dedicated-instance.html
There is no tenancy attribute called 'shared'.

Answer Q70. A, C, D
AWS Documentation Reference:
https://docs.aws.amazon.com/AWSEC2/latest/UserGuide/dedicated-instance.html

Answer Q71. C
AWS Documentation Reference: How Zonal Reserved Instances Are Applied
https://docs.aws.amazon.com/AWSEC2/latest/UserGuide/apply_ri.html
Reserved Instances assigned to a specific Availability Zone provide the Reserved Instance discount to matching instance usage in that Availability Zone. You have purchased two c4.xlarge default tenancy Linux/Unix Standard Reserved Instances in Availability Zone us-east-1a, then up to two c4.xlarge default tenancy Linux/Unix instances running in the Availability Zone us-east-1a can benefit from the Reserved Instance discount. The attributes (tenancy, platform, Availability Zone, instance type, and instance size) of the running instances must match that of the Reserved Instances.

Answer Q72.A, B, D
AWS Documentation Reference: Examples of Applying Reserved Instances
https://docs.aws.amazon.com/AWSEC2/latest/UserGuide/apply_ri.html
The Reserved Instance benefits are applied in the following way:
- The discount and capacity reservation of the four m3.large zonal Reserved Instances is used by the four m3.large instances because the attributes (instance size, Region, platform, tenancy) between them match.
- The m4.large regional Reserved Instances provide Availability Zone and instance size flexibility, because they are regional Amazon Linux Reserved Instances with default tenancy.
- An m4.large is equivalent to 4 normalized units/hour.
- You've purchased four m4.large regional Reserved Instances, and in total, they are equal to 16 normalized units/hour (4x4). Account A has two m4.xlarge instances running, which is equivalent to 16 normalized units/hour (2x8). In this case, the four m4.large regional Reserved Instances provide the billing benefit to an entire hour of usage of the two m4.xlarge instances.

- The c4.large regional Reserved Instance in us-east-1 provides Availability Zone and instance size flexibility, because it is a regional Amazon Linux Reserved Instance with default tenancy, and applies to the c4.xlarge instance. A c4.large instance is equivalent to 4 normalized units/hour and a c4.xlarge is equivalent to 8 normalized units/hour.

- In this case, the c4.large regional Reserved Instance provides partial benefit to c4.xlarge usage. This is because the c4.large Reserved Instance is equivalent to 4 normalized units/hour of usage, but the c4.xlarge instance requires 8 normalized units/hour. Therefore, the c4.large Reserved Instance billing discount applies to 50% of c4.xlarge usage. The remaining c4.xlarge usage is charged at the On-Demand rate.

## Answer Q73.A, C, D
AWS Documentation Reference:
https://docs.aws.amazon.com/AWSEC2/latest/UserGuide/ri-modifying.html
You can allocate your reservations into different instance sizes across the same instance family, for example, across the T2 instance family, as long as the instance size footprint of your reservation remains the same.

- You can combine a reservation for two t2.small (2x1) instances into one t2.medium (1x2) instance.
- You can divide a reservation for one t2.large (1 x 4) instance into four t2.small (4 x 1) instances
- You can combine a reservation for four t2.small (4x1) instances into one t2.large (1x4) instance.

However, you cannot change your reservation for two t2.small (2 x 1) instances into one t2.large (1 x 4) instance. This is because the existing instance size footprint of your current reservation is smaller than the proposed reservation.

## Answer Q74. D
AWS Documentation Reference:
https://docs.aws.amazon.com/AWSEC2/latest/UserGuide/spot-fleet.html#spot-fleet-allocation-strategy
The allocation strategy for the Spot Instances in your Spot Fleet determines how it fulfills your Spot Fleet request from the possible Spot Instance pools represented by its launch specifications. The following are the allocation strategies that you can specify in your Spot Fleet request:
lowestPrice : The Spot Instances come from the pool with the lowest price. This is the default strategy.
Diversified :The Spot Instances are distributed across all pools.
capacityOptimized:The Spot Instances come from the pool with optimal capacity for the number of instances that are launching.
InstancePoolsToUseCount :The Spot Instances are distributed across the number of Spot pools that you specify. This parameter is valid only when used in combination with lowestPrice.

Answer Q75. D

Having 6 reserved instances will give the best cost benefit and adding 12 on-demand instances only for those three days gives the flexibility.

A is not cost optimized, having all 18 instances on-demand will be most costly.

B having 8 spot instances, there is risk that not all of them may be provisioned or there may be early termination of instances.

C having 18 reserved instances is not an optimized strategy as it will be applicable only for three days and you will be paying for 18 instances for rest of the days of month when you are using only 6 instances.

Answer Q76.A, B

AWS Documentation Reference:

https://docs.aws.amazon.com/AWSEC2/latest/UserGuide/ri-modifying.html

You have a reservation with two t2.micro instances (giving you a footprint of 1) and a reservation with one t2.small instance (giving you a footprint of 1). You can merge both reservations to a single reservation with one t2.medium instance (1x 2) or two t2.small (2x 1) —the combined instance size footprint of the two original reservations equals the footprint of the modified reservation.

Answer Q77. A, B, D, E

AWS Documentation Reference: Whitepaper: serverless-architectures-with-aws-lambda

Introduction - What Is Serverless?

For service or platform to be considered serverless, it should provide the following capabilities:

• No server management – You don't have to provision or maintain any servers. There is no software or runtime to install, maintain, or administer.

• Flexible scaling – You can scale your application automatically or by adjusting its capacity through toggling the units of consumption (for example, throughput, memory) rather than units of individual servers.

• High availability – Serverless applications have built-in availability and fault tolerance. You don't need to architect for these capabilities because the services running the application provide them by default.

• No idle capacity – You don't have to pay for idle capacity. There is no need to pre-provision or over-provision capacity for things like compute and storage. There is no charge when your code isn't running.

Answer Q78. B, C, D

AWS Documentation Reference:

https://docs.aws.amazon.com/lambda/latest/dg/lambda-services.html

Services That Lambda Reads Events From

• Amazon Kinesis
• Amazon DynamoDB

- Amazon Simple Queue Service

Amazon API Gateway service invokes Lambda functions synchronously.

Answer Q79. B

Your fixed requirement for the year is at least 2*3=6 instances, 2 for each environment. For these you can purchase reserved instances. For rest of instance need you should avail spot instances for maximum cost benefit.

Answer Q80. A, B, C

D is incorrect Lambda cannot be directly integrated with RDS, ECS or Auto scaling.

AWS Documentation Reference:

https://docs.aws.amazon.com/lambda/latest/dg/lambda-services.html

Answer Q81. D

AWS Documentation Reference:

https://docs.aws.amazon.com/lambda/latest/dg/lambda-services.html

AWS Lambda integrates with other AWS services to invoke functions. You can configure triggers to invoke a function in response to resource lifecycle events, respond to incoming HTTP requests, consume events from a queue, or run on a schedule.

Answer Q82. A, B

AWS Documentation Reference:

https://docs.aws.amazon.com/lambda/latest/dg/resource-model.html

You can modify the following settings for your lambda function:

Memory– The amount of memory available to the function during execution. Choose an amount between 128 MB and 3,008 MB in 64-MB increments. Lambda allocates CPU power linearly in proportion to the amount of memory configured. At 1,792 MB, a function has the equivalent of one full vCPU (one vCPU-second of credits per second).

Timeout – The amount of time that Lambda allows a function to run before stopping it. The default is 3 seconds. The maximum allowed value is 900 seconds.

https://aws.amazon.com/about-aws/whats-new/2017/11/set-concurrency-limits-on-individual-aws-lambda-functions/

Option C and D are incorrect because concurrency is subject to a Regional limit that is shared by all functions in a Region. You can now set a concurrency limit on individual AWS Lambda functions. The concurrency limit you set will reserve a portion of your account level concurrency limit for a given function. This feature allows you to throttle a given function if it reaches a maximum number of concurrent executions allowed, which you can choose to set. In the given scenario throttling is not an issues, lambda tasks are getting terminated.

Answer Q83. D

AWS Documentation Reference:

https://docs.aws.amazon.com/AWSEC2/latest/UserGuide/user-data.html

When you launch an instance in Amazon EC2, you have the option of passing user data to the instance that can be used to perform common automated configuration tasks and even run scripts after the instance starts. You can write commands for executing all the above options in a user data shell scripts which will be executed during launch of instance.

Answer Q84. C

AWS Documentation Reference:

https://aws.amazon.com/iot-core/

AWS IoT Core is a managed cloud service that lets connected devices easily and securely interact with cloud applications and other devices. AWS IoT Core can support billions of devices and trillions of messages, and can process and route those messages to AWS endpoints and to other devices reliably and securely. With AWS IoT Core, your applications can keep track of and communicate with all your devices, all the time, even when they aren't connected.

AWS IoT Core also makes it easy to use AWS and Amazon services like AWS Lambda, Amazon Kinesis, Amazon S3, Amazon SageMaker, Amazon DynamoDB, Amazon CloudWatch, AWS CloudTrail, Amazon QuickSight, and Alexa Voice Service to build IoT applications that gather, process, analyze and act on data generated by connected devices, without having to manage any infrastructure.

Answer Q85. B

AWS Documentation Reference:

https://docs.aws.amazon.com/IAM/latest/UserGuide/id_roles_use_switch-role-ec2.html

Applications that run on an EC2 instance must include AWS credentials in their AWS API requests. You could have your developers store AWS credentials directly within the EC2 instance and allow applications in that instance to use those credentials. But developers would then have to manage the credentials and ensure that they securely pass the credentials to each instance and update each EC2 instance when it's time to rotate the credentials. That's a lot of additional work.

Instead, you can and should use an IAM role to manage temporary credentials for applications that run on an EC2 instance. When you use a role, you don't have to distribute long-term credentials (such as a user name and password or access keys) to an EC2 instance. Instead, the role supplies temporary permissions that applications can use when they make calls to other AWS resources. When you launch an EC2 instance, you specify an IAM role to associate with the instance. Applications that run on the instance can then use the role-supplied temporary credentials to sign API requests.

Answer Q86. D

AWS Documentation Reference:

https://docs.aws.amazon.com/lambda/latest/dg//env_variables.html

The first time you create or update Lambda functions that use environment variables in a region, a default service key is created for you automatically within AWS KMS. This key is used to encrypt environment variables.

It is not best secure encryption option because all the environment variables you've specified are encrypted by default after, but not during, the deployment process. They are then decrypted automatically by AWS Lambda when the function is invoked. If you need to store sensitive information in an environment variable, AWS strongly suggest you encrypt that information before deploying your Lambda function

The Lambda console makes that easier for you by providing encryption helpers that leverage AWS Key Management Service to store that sensitive information as Ciphertext. You can check the Enable helpers for encryption in transit checkbox and supply a custom key. The Lambda console also provides decryption helper code to decrypt that information for use in your in Lambda function code.

Creating your own key gives you more flexibility, including the ability to create, rotate, disable, and define access controls, and to audit the encryption keys used to protect your data.

Answer Q87. A, E
AWS Documentation Reference:
Here you have to meet two criteria: ensuring the availability of instances as well optimizing the cost.
B is incorrect as Spot instance will be less cost but availability is not guaranteed.
C is incorrect as Reserved instances is billing discount, it doesn't provide instances.
D is incorrect as On-demand instances though will ensure instance availability but it will be costlier than scheduled reserved instances.

https://docs.aws.amazon.com/AWSEC2/latest/UserGuide/ec2-scheduled-instances.html
Scheduled Reserved Instances (Scheduled Instances) enable you to purchase capacity reservations that recur on a daily, weekly, or monthly basis, with a specified start time and duration, for a one-year term. You reserve the capacity in advance, so that you know it is available when you need it. You pay for the time that the instances are scheduled, even if you do not use them.

Scheduled Instances are a good choice for workloads that do not run continuously, but do run on a regular schedule. Scheduled reserved instances prices are at discount to on-demand prices.

https://aws.amazon.com/savingsplans/
Savings Plans offer significant savings over On Demand, just like EC2 Reserved Instances, in exchange for a commitment to use a specific amount of compute power (measured in $/hour) for a one or three year period. You can sign up for Savings Plans for a 1- or 3-year term and easily manage your plans by taking advantage of recommendations, performance reporting and budget alerts in the AWS Cost Explorer.

Answer Q88. B
AWS Documentation Reference:
https://docs.aws.amazon.com/AWSEC2/latest/UserGuide/ec2-instance-metadata.html
To view all categories of instance metadata from within a running instance, use the following URI:
http://169.254.169.254/latest/meta-data/
The IP address 169.254.169.254 is a link-local address and is valid only from the instance.

Answer Q89. A, B, C, F, G
AWS Documentation Reference:
https://docs.aws.amazon.com/whitepapers/latest/microservices-on-aws/serverless-microservices.html
Microservice based on AWS Serverless services will meet the architecture criteria:
- the complete service is built out of managed services
- eliminates the architectural burden to design for scale and high availability
- eliminates the operational efforts of running and monitoring the underlying infrastructure.
EC2 and Amazon RDS are not serverless services.

Answer Q90. B, C, I
AWS Documentation Reference: Whitepaper: Fault-Tolerant Components on AWS
https://d1.awsstatic.com/whitepapers/aws-building-fault-tolerant-applications.pdf

In addition to AWS Lambda, other AWS serverless technologies include:
- AWS Fargate—a serverless compute engine for containers
- Amazon DynamoDB—a fast and flexible NoSQL database
- Amazon Aurora Serverless—a MySQL compatible relational database
- Amazon API Gateway—a service to create, publish, monitor and secure APIs
- Amazon S3—a secure, durable and highly scalable object storage
- Amazon Elastic File System—a simple, scalable, elastic file storage
- Amazon SNS—a fully managed pub/sub messaging service
- Amazon SQS—a fully managed message queuing service

Answer Q91. D
Since 'cost' is the most important criteria, spot instances pricing provides least pricing compared to other purchasing options.
AWS Documentation Reference:
https://docs.aws.amazon.com/AWSEC2/latest/UserGuide/using-spot-instances.html
A Spot Instance is an unused EC2 instance that is available for less than the On-Demand price. Because Spot Instances enable you to request unused EC2 instances at steep discounts, you can lower your Amazon EC2 costs significantly. Spot Instances are a cost-effective choice

if you can be flexible about when your applications run and if your applications can be interrupted.

Answer Q92. B
AWS Documentation Reference:
https://docs.aws.amazon.com/AWSEC2/latest/UserGuide/ec2-instance-metadata.html
To retrieve user data from within a running instance, use the following URI:
http://169.254.169.254/latest/user-data

Answer Q93. A, B, D
AWS Documentation Reference:
https://docs.aws.amazon.com/AWSEC2/latest/UserGuide/dedicated-hosts-overview.html#dedicated-hosts-dedicated-instances

Answer Q94. C
AWS Documentation Reference:
https://docs.aws.amazon.com/elasticbeanstalk/latest/dg/Welcome.html
With Elastic Beanstalk, you can quickly deploy and manage applications in the AWS Cloud without having to learn about the infrastructure that runs those applications. Elastic Beanstalk reduces management complexity without restricting choice or control. You simply upload your application, and Elastic Beanstalk automatically handles the details of capacity provisioning, load balancing, scaling, and application health monitoring.

https://docs.aws.amazon.com/elasticbeanstalk/latest/dg/create_deploy_docker.html    Elastic Beanstalk supports the deployment of web applications from Docker containers. With Docker containers, you can define your own runtime environment. You can choose your own platform, programming language, and any application dependencies (such as package managers or tools), that aren't supported by other platforms. Docker containers are self-contained and include all the configuration information and software your web application requires to run. All environment variables defined in the Elastic Beanstalk console are passed to the containers.

By using Docker with Elastic Beanstalk, you have an infrastructure that automatically handles the details of capacity provisioning, load balancing, scaling, and application health monitoring. You can manage your web application in an environment that supports the range of services that are integrated with Elastic Beanstalk, including but not limited to VPC, RDS, and IAM.

Option B is incorrect because ECS also provides features of capacity provisioning, load balancing, scaling, and application health monitoring; but these features are not automatically enabled by default unlike Elastic Beanstalk.

Option A is incorrect as AWS CodeDeploy is a fully managed deployment service that automates software deployments to a variety of compute services such as Amazon EC2, AWS Fargate, AWS Lambda, and your on-premises servers.

Answer Q95. A, B
C is not a suitable use case for Docker as it is primarily designed for mainly isolated containers. D is not a suitable use case because an application designed to run in a Docker container on Windows can't run on Linux, and vice versa.
AWS Documentation Reference:
https://docs.aws.amazon.com/AmazonECS/latest/developerguide/common_use_cases.html
Containers are optimal for running small, decoupled services, and they offer the following advantages:

- Containers make services easy to model in an immutable image with all of your dependencies.
- Containers can use any application and any programming language.
- The container image is a versioned artifact, so you can track your container images to the source they came from.
- You can test your containers locally, and deploy the same artifact to scale.

Docker containers are particularly suited for batch job workloads. Batch jobs are often short-lived and embarrassingly parallel. You can package your batch processing application into a Docker image so that you can deploy it anywhere, such as in an Amazon ECS task.

Answer Q96. D
You are not charged for using VPC.
AWS Documentation Reference:
https://aws.amazon.com/premiumsupport/knowledge-center/ebs-charge-stopped-instance/
You are charged for EBS storage for the amount of storage provisioned to your account, measured in "gigabyte-months." EC2 instances accrue charges only while they're running, but EBS volumes attached to instances continue to retain information and accrue charges, even when the instance is stopped.

Answer Q97.A, B

Answer Q98. D
AWS Documentation Reference:
https://docs.aws.amazon.com/vpc/latest/userguide/VPC_ElasticNetworkInterfaces.html

Answer Q99.C
AWS Documentation Reference:
https://aws.amazon.com/about-aws/whats-new/2019/04/bring-your-own-ip-for-amazon-virtual-private-cloud-is-now-available-in-four-additional-regions/
https://docs.aws.amazon.com/AWSEC2/latest/UserGuide/ec2-byoip.html

BYOIP allows you to bring your own publicly-routable IP address prefixes to AWS and advertise them on the internet. You can create Elastic IP addresses from your BYOIP address prefix and use them with AWS resources such as EC2 instances, Network Load Balancers, and NAT gateways. The Elastic IP addresses you create from BYOIP address prefixes work the same way as Elastic IP addresses you get from AWS. BYOIP also allows you to minimize your downtime during migration by simultaneously advertising your IP address prefix from AWS and withdrawing it from the current location.

If your applications are using trusted IP addresses that your partners and customers have whitelisted in their firewalls, you can now move these applications to AWS without requiring your partners and customers to change their IP address whitelists. BYOIP is also useful for applications that rely on IP address reputation to allow traffic from your endpoints to reach intended recipients, such as commercial email services. Some legacy applications have hard-coded IP address dependencies. Bring Your Own IP enables you to migrate such applications to AWS with minimal disruptions.

### Answer Q100. A, B
AWS Documentation Reference:
https://docs.aws.amazon.com/AWSEC2/latest/UserGuide//TroubleshootingInstancesConnecting.html#TroubleshootingInstancesConnectingPuTTY
Error: Server refused our key or No supported authentication methods available
If you use PuTTY to connect to your instance and get either of the following errors, Error: Server refused our key or Error: No supported authentication methods available, verify that you are connecting with the appropriate user name for your AMI. Type the user name in User name in the PuTTY Configuration window.

The appropriate user names are as follows:
* For Amazon Linux 2 or the Amazon Linux AMI, the user name is ec2-user.
* For an Ubuntu AMI, the user name is ubuntu.
You should also verify that your private key (.pem) file has been correctly converted to the format recognized by PuTTY (.ppk).

### Answer Q101. E
AWS Documentation Reference:
https://docs.aws.amazon.com/autoscaling/ec2/userguide/create-launch-config.html
When you create a launch configuration, you must specify information about the EC2 instances to launch. Include the Amazon Machine Image (AMI), instance type, key pair, security groups, and block device mapping.

### Answer Q102. A, B, C
AWS Documentation Reference:
https://docs.aws.amazon.com/autoscaling/ec2/userguide/auto-scaling-benefits.html

When you use Amazon EC2 Auto Scaling, your applications gains following benefits:

Better fault tolerance: Amazon EC2 Auto Scaling can detect when an instance is unhealthy, terminate it, and launch an instance to replace it. You can also configure Amazon EC2 Auto Scaling to use multiple Availability Zones. If one Availability Zone becomes unavailable, Amazon EC2 Auto Scaling can launch instances in another one to compensate.

Better availability: Amazon EC2 Auto Scaling helps ensure that your application always has the right amount of capacity to handle the current traffic demand.

Better cost management: Amazon EC2 Auto Scaling can dynamically increase and decrease capacity as needed. Because you pay for the EC2 instances you use, you save money by launching instances when they are needed and terminating them when they aren't.

Auto scaling doesn't improves performance but it ensures that performance and availability of application is not compromised by rebalancing the number of instances.

Answer Q103. C

Answer Q104. A, B, C, E, F
AWS Documentation Reference:
https://docs.aws.amazon.com/autoscaling/ec2/userguide/scaling_plan.html
Maintain current instance levels at all times: You can configure your Auto Scaling group to maintain a specified number of running instances at all times.
Manual scaling: Manual scaling is the most basic way to scale your resources, where you specify only the change in the maximum, minimum, or desired capacity of your Auto Scaling group
Scale based on a schedule: Scaling by schedule means that scaling actions are performed automatically as a function of time and date.
Scale based on demand: A more advanced way to scale your resources, using scaling policies, lets you define parameters that control the scaling process

There is no account based scaling.

Answer Q105. C
AWS Documentation Reference:
https://docs.aws.amazon.com/autoscaling/ec2/userguide/scaling_plan.html
Scale based on demand: A more advanced way to scale your resources, using scaling policies, lets you define parameters that control the scaling process. When you configure dynamic scaling, you define how to scale the capacity of your Auto Scaling group in response to changing demand. For example, you have a web application that currently runs on two instances and you want the CPU utilization of the Auto Scaling group to stay at around 50 percent when the load on the application changes.

https://docs.aws.amazon.com/autoscaling/ec2/userguide/as-scale-based-on-demand.html

Answer Q106. A, C, D
AWS Documentation Reference:
https://docs.aws.amazon.com/autoscaling/ec2/userguide/what-is-amazon-ec2-auto-scaling.html
The key components of Amazon EC2 Auto Scaling.
Auto Scaling Groups: Your EC2 instances are organized into groups so that they can be treated as a logical unit for the purposes of scaling and management. When you create a group, you can specify its minimum, maximum, and, desired number of EC2 instances.

Configuration templates: Your group uses a launch template or a launch configuration as a configuration template for its EC2 instances. You can specify information such as the AMI ID, instance type, key pair, security groups, and block device mapping for your instances.

Scaling options: Amazon EC2 Auto Scaling provides several ways for you to scale your Auto Scaling groups. For example, you can configure a group to scale based on the occurrence of specified conditions (dynamic scaling) or on a schedule.

Answer Q107. A, C
AWS Documentation Reference:
https://docs.aws.amazon.com/autoscaling/ec2/userguide/auto-scaling-benefits.html
An Auto Scaling group can contain EC2 instances in one or more Availability Zones within the same Region. However, Auto Scaling groups cannot span multiple Regions.
For Auto Scaling groups in a VPC, the EC2 instances are launched in subnets. You select the subnets for your EC2 instances when you create or update the Auto Scaling group. You can select one or more subnets per Availability Zone.

Answer Q108. B
AWS Documentation Reference:
https://docs.aws.amazon.com/autoscaling/ec2/userguide/LaunchConfiguration.html
https://docs.aws.amazon.com/autoscaling/ec2/userguide/change-launch-config.html
A launch configuration is an instance configuration template that an Auto Scaling group uses to launch EC2 instances. When you create a launch configuration, you specify information for the instances. Include the ID of the Amazon Machine Image (AMI), the instance type, a key pair, one or more security groups, and a block device mapping.

An Auto Scaling group is associated with one launch configuration at a time, and you can't modify a launch configuration after you've created it. To change the launch configuration for an Auto Scaling group, use an existing launch configuration as the basis for a new launch configuration. Then, update the Auto Scaling group to use the new launch configuration.

You don't need to first terminate the existing instances based on old AMI. After you change the launch configuration for an Auto Scaling group, any new instances are launched using the new configuration options, but existing instances are not affected. If you want all the instances to be based on new AMI, you can terminate existing instances in the Auto Scaling group to force a new instance to launch that uses the new configuration. Or, you can allow automatic scaling to gradually replace older instances with newer instances based on your termination policies.

Answer Q109. B, C
AWS Documentation Reference: Distributing Instances Across Availability Zones
https://docs.aws.amazon.com/autoscaling/ec2/userguide/auto-scaling-benefits.html
Amazon EC2 Auto Scaling attempts to distribute instances evenly between the Availability Zones that are enabled for your Auto Scaling group. Amazon EC2 Auto Scaling does this by attempting to launch new instances in the Availability Zone with the fewest instances. If the attempt fails, however, Amazon EC2 Auto Scaling attempts to launch the instances in another Availability Zone until it succeeds.

Answer Q110. B
https://aws.amazon.com/blogs/compute/building-loosely-coupled-scalable-c-applications-with-amazon-sqs-and-amazon-sns/
In the given scenario, the application is responsible for handling and persisting the order data, as well as dealing with increases in traffic for popular items.
One potential point of vulnerability in the order processing workflow is in saving the order in the database. As stated the key business requirement is that every order has to be persisted into the database. However, any potential deadlock, race condition, or network issue could cause the persistence of the order to fail. Then, the order is lost with no recourse to restore the order.
With good logging capability, you may be able to identify when an error occurred and which customer order failed. This wouldn't allow you to "restore" the transaction, and by that stage, your customer is no longer your customer.
As illustrated in the following diagram, introducing an SQS queue helps improve your ordering application. Using the queue isolates the processing logic into its own component and runs it in a separate process from the web application. This, in turn, allows the system to be more resilient to spikes in traffic, while allowing work to be performed only as fast as necessary in order to manage costs.

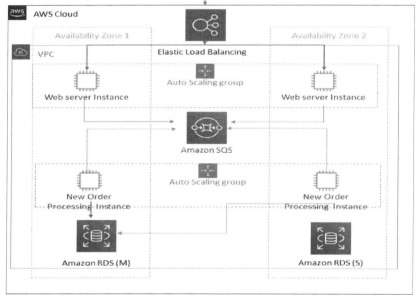

Answer Q111. B, C, D

AWS Documentation Reference:

https://docs.aws.amazon.com/autoscaling/ec2/userguide/AutoScalingGroup.html

To configure Amazon EC2 instances that are launched by your Auto Scaling group, you can specify a launch template, a launch configuration, or an EC2 instance.

Answer Q112. A, B, D

AWS Documentation Reference:

https://docs.aws.amazon.com/autoscaling/ec2/userguide/AutoScalingGroup.html

C is wrong as you cannot specify reserved instance as purchase option for instances.

Answer Q113.B

https://docs.aws.amazon.com/autoscaling/ec2/userguide/schedule_time.html

To configure your Auto Scaling group to scale based on a schedule, you create a scheduled action. The scheduled action tells Amazon EC2 Auto Scaling to perform a scaling action at specified times. To create a scheduled scaling action, you specify the start time when the scaling action should take effect, and the new minimum, maximum, and desired sizes for the scaling action. At the specified time, Amazon EC2 Auto Scaling updates the group with the values for minimum, maximum, and desired size specified by the scaling action.

There is no need to create a new auto scaling group.

Answer Q114. C, D

https://aws.amazon.com/ec2/autoscaling/faqs/

Amazon EC2 Auto Scaling cannot scale past the Amazon EC2 limit of instances that you can run. Amazon Elastic Compute Cloud (Amazon EC2) limit per region for spot instances is 20 for an account.

Also if maximum size of auto scaling group is reached no new instance will be launched.

Answer Q115. B, C, D

AWS Documentation Reference:

https://docs.aws.amazon.com/autoscaling/ec2/userguide/as-scale-based-on-demand.html#as-scaling-types

Amazon EC2 Auto Scaling supports the following types of scaling policies:

Target tracking scaling—Increase or decrease the current capacity of the group based on a target value for a specific metric. This is similar to the way that your thermostat maintains the temperature of your home – you select a temperature and the thermostat does the rest.

Step scaling—Increase or decrease the current capacity of the group based on a set of scaling adjustments, known as step adjustments, that vary based on the size of the alarm breach.

Simple scaling—Increase or decrease the current capacity of the group based on a single scaling adjustment.

Answer Q116.  A, C

AWS Documentation Reference:

https://docs.aws.amazon.com/autoscaling/ec2/userguide/attach-load-balancer-asg.html

Amazon EC2 Auto Scaling integrates with Elastic Load Balancing to enable you to attach one or more load balancers to an existing Auto Scaling group. After you attach the load balancer, it automatically registers the instances in the group and distributes incoming traffic across the instances.

B is incorrect because an auto scaling group can be mapped to more than one load balancer.

Answer Q117.A, B, C

AWS Documentation Reference:

https://docs.aws.amazon.com/autoscaling/ec2/userguide/Cooldown.html
The cooldown period ensures that your Auto Scaling group doesn't launch or terminate additional instances before the previous scaling activity takes effect. You can configure the length of time based on your instance warm-up period or other application needs.

Answer Q118. A
AWS Documentation Reference:
https://docs.aws.amazon.com/autoscaling/ec2/userguide/as-add-elb-healthcheck.html
If you configure the EC2 Auto Scaling group to use Elastic Load Balancing health checks, it considers the instance unhealthy if it fails either the EC2 status checks or the load balancer health checks.

Answer Q119. B
AWS Documentation Reference:
https://docs.aws.amazon.com/autoscaling/ec2/userguide/as-add-elb-healthcheck.html
If you attach multiple load balancers to an Auto Scaling group, all of them must report that the instance is healthy in order for it to consider the instance healthy. If one load balancer reports an instance as unhealthy, the Auto Scaling group replaces the instance, even if other load balancers report it as healthy.

Answer Q120. A, D
AWS Documentation Reference:
https://docs.aws.amazon.com/autoscaling/ec2/userguide/as-add-availability-zone.html
You can take advantage of the safety and reliability of geographic redundancy by spanning your Auto Scaling group across multiple Availability Zones within a Region and then attaching a load balancer to distribute incoming traffic across those zones. Incoming traffic is distributed equally across all Availability Zones enabled for your load balancer.

Answer Q121. A
Schedule based auto scaling policy allows you to scale out or in at a specific time.

Answer Q122. A, B
AWS Documentation Reference:
https://docs.aws.amazon.com/AmazonECS/latest/APIReference/API_StartTask.html
https://docs.aws.amazon.com/AmazonECS/latest/APIReference/API_RunTask.html

Answer Q123. A, D
AWS Documentation Reference:
https://docs.aws.amazon.com/autoscaling/ec2/userguide/as-scaling-target-tracking.html
https://docs.aws.amazon.com/autoscaling/ec2/userguide/Cooldown.html
A recommended best practice is to scale out quickly when needed but scale in slowly to avoid having to relaunch if there is workload fluctuation up and down more frequently.

It will also be better to analyze what should be the value of the metric which would reduce the fluctuation of scaling up and down.

Answer Q124. A

AWS Documentation Reference:

https://docs.aws.amazon.com/autoscaling/ec2/userguide/as-maintain-instance-levels.html

If a fixed number of instances are needed, this can be achieved by setting the same value for minimum, maximum, and desired capacity. If there are no other scaling conditions attached to the Auto Scaling group, the group maintains this number of running instances even if an instance becomes unhealthy.

To maintain the same number of instances, Amazon EC2 Auto Scaling performs a periodic health check on running instances within an Auto Scaling group. When it finds that an instance is unhealthy, it terminates that instance and launches a new one. If you stop or terminate a running instance, the instance is considered to be unhealthy and is replaced.

Answer Q125. A, B, C

AWS Documentation Reference:

https://docs.aws.amazon.com/autoscaling/ec2/userguide/as-manual-scaling.html

At any time, you can change the size of an existing Auto Scaling group manually. You can either update the desired capacity of the Auto Scaling group, or update the instances that are attached to the Auto Scaling group. Manually scaling your group can be useful when automatic scaling is not needed or when you need to hold capacity at a fixed number of instances.

Answer Q126. B

AWS Documentation Reference:

https://docs.aws.amazon.com/elasticbeanstalk/latest/dg/Welcome.html

With Elastic Beanstalk, you can quickly deploy and manage applications in the AWS Cloud without having to learn about the infrastructure that runs those applications. Elastic Beanstalk reduces management complexity without restricting choice or control. You simply upload your application, and Elastic Beanstalk automatically handles the details of capacity provisioning, load balancing, scaling, and application health monitoring.

Answer Q127. E

AWS Documentation Reference:

https://docs.aws.amazon.com/elasticbeanstalk/latest/dg/Welcome.html

Elastic Beanstalk supports applications developed in Go, Java, .NET, Node.js, PHP, Python, and Ruby. When you deploy your application, Elastic Beanstalk builds the selected supported platform version and provisions one or more AWS resources, such as Amazon EC2 instances, to run your application.

Answer Q128. A, B, D

AWS Documentation Reference:

https://docs.aws.amazon.com/autoscaling/ec2/userguide/attach-instance-asg.html
The instance to attach must meet the following criteria:

- The instance is in the running state.
- The AMI used to launch the instance must still exist.
- The instance is not a member of another Auto Scaling group.
- The instance is launched into one of the Availability Zones defined in your Auto Scaling group.
- If the Auto Scaling group has an attached load balancer, the instance and the load balancer must both be in EC2-Classic or the same VPC. If the Auto Scaling group has an attached target group, the instance and the load balancer must both be in the same VPC.

Answer Q129. A, B, D
AWS Documentation Reference:
https://docs.aws.amazon.com/autoscaling/ec2/userguide/detach-instance-asg.html
When you detach instances, you have the option of decrementing the desired capacity for the Auto Scaling group by the number of instances you are detaching. If you choose not to decrement the capacity, Amazon EC2 Auto Scaling launches new instances to replace the ones that you detached. If you decrement the capacity but detach multiple instances from the same Availability Zone, Amazon EC2 Auto Scaling can rebalance the Availability Zones unless you suspend the AZRebalance process.

Answer Q130. C, D
A is incorrect because, as for beta users the configuration is 'single instance' with no load balancing and auto scaling, Elastic Beanstalk will not scale as per performance requirements.
B is incorrect because simply changing the instance type from micro to large may not be enough to meet performance needs.
C, D steps will be required to ensure that Elastic Beanstalk automatically scales as per application performance needs.

AWS Documentation Reference:
https://docs.aws.amazon.com/en_pv/elasticbeanstalk/latest/dg/environments-create-wizard.html
You can fine-tune configuration options in your environment.

- You can configure the Amazon EC2 instances that serve requests in your environment. You have the option of choosing Instance type, AMI ID and ability to specify the type, size, and input/output operations per second (IOPS) for your root volume.
- You can configure the compute capacity of your environment and Auto Scaling group settings to optimize the number of instances as per your needs. You have the ability to configure a scaling trigger based on a metric that lets Amazon EC2 Auto Scaling know when to scale the number of instances in your environment.

- Elastic Beanstalk supports several types of load balancer. Use the Modify load balancer configuration page to select a load balancer type and to configure settings for it.

Answer Q131. B
AWS Documentation Reference:
https://docs.aws.amazon.com/autoscaling/ec2/userguide/as-instance-termination.html
The default termination policy is designed to help ensure that your instances span Availability Zones evenly for high availability. The default policy is kept generic and flexible to cover a range of scenarios.
The default termination policy behavior is as follows:
1.  Determine which Availability Zones have the most instances, and at least one instance that is not protected from scale in.
2.  Determine which instances to terminate so as to align the remaining instances to the allocation strategy for the On-Demand or Spot Instance that is terminating. This only applies to an Auto Scaling group that specifies allocation strategies.
3.  Determine whether any of the instances use the oldest launch template or configuration:

    [For Auto Scaling groups that use a launch template]
    Determine whether any of the instances use the oldest launch template unless there are instances that use a launch configuration. Amazon EC2 Auto Scaling terminates instances that use a launch configuration before instances that use a launch template.

    [For Auto Scaling groups that use a launch configuration]
    Determine whether any of the instances use the oldest launch configuration.

4.  After applying all of the above criteria, if there are multiple unprotected instances to terminate, determine which instances are closest to the next billing hour. If there are multiple unprotected instances closest to the next billing hour, terminate one of these instances at random.

Answer Q132. B
AWS Documentation Reference:
https://docs.aws.amazon.com/autoscaling/ec2/userguide/as-scale-based-on-demand.html
If you are scaling based on a utilization metric that increases or decreases proportionally to the number of instances in an Auto Scaling group, AWS recommends that you use target tracking scaling policies otherwise, you use step scaling policies.

Answer Q133. B
AWS Documentation Reference:
https://docs.aws.amazon.com/autoscaling/ec2/userguide/as-scale-based-on-demand.html#multiple-scaling-policy-resolution

When there are multiple policies in force at the same time, there's a chance that each policy could instruct the Auto Scaling group to scale out (or in) at the same time. When these situations occur, Amazon EC2 Auto Scaling chooses the policy that provides the largest capacity for both scale out and scale in.

Suppose, for example, that the policy for CPU utilization launches one instance, while the policy for the SQS queue launches two instances. If the scale-out criteria for both policies are met at the same time, Amazon EC2 Auto Scaling gives precedence to the SQS queue policy. This results in the Auto Scaling group launching two instances.

The approach of giving precedence to the policy that provides the largest capacity applies even when the policies use different criteria for scaling in. For example, if one policy terminates three instances, another policy decreases the number of instances by 25 percent, and the group has eight instances at the time of scale in, Amazon EC2 Auto Scaling gives precedence to the policy that provides the largest number of instances for the group. This results in the Auto Scaling group terminating two instances (25% of 8 = 2). The intention is to prevent Amazon EC2 Auto Scaling from removing too many instances.

Answer Q134. B
AWS Documentation Reference:
https://docs.aws.amazon.com/autoscaling/ec2/userguide/as-scaling-target-tracking.html
With target tracking scaling policies, you select a scaling metric and set a target value. Amazon EC2 Auto Scaling creates and manages the CloudWatch alarms that trigger the scaling policy and calculates the scaling adjustment based on the metric and the target value. The scaling policy adds or removes capacity as required to keep the metric at, or close to, the specified target value. In addition to keeping the metric close to the target value, a target tracking scaling policy also adjusts to the changes in the metric due to a changing load pattern.

Answer Q135. A, C, D
AWS Documentation Reference: Choosing Metrics
https://docs.aws.amazon.com/autoscaling/ec2/userguide/as-scaling-target-tracking.html
Keep the following in mind when choosing a metric:
Not all metrics work for target tracking. This can be important when you are specifying a customized metric. The metric must be a valid utilization metric and describe how busy an instance is. The metric value must increase or decrease proportionally to the number of instances in the Auto Scaling group. That's so the metric data can be used to proportionally scale out or in the number of instances.

For example, the CPU utilization of an Auto Scaling group (that is, the Amazon EC2 metric CPUUtilization with the metric dimension AutoScalingGroupName) works, if the load on the Auto Scaling group is distributed across the instances.

The following metrics do not work for target tracking:

- The number of requests received by the load balancer fronting the Auto Scaling group (that is, the Elastic Load Balancing metric RequestCount). The number of requests received by the load balancer doesn't change based on the utilization of the Auto Scaling group.

- Load balancer request latency (that is, the Elastic Load Balancing metric Latency). Request latency can increase based on increasing utilization, but doesn't necessarily change proportionally.

- The CloudWatch SQS queue metric ApproximateNumberOfMessagesVisible. The number of messages in a queue may not change proportionally to the size of the Auto Scaling group that processes messages from the queue. However, a customized metric that measures the number of messages in the queue per EC2 instance in the Auto Scaling group can work.

Answer Q136. B, C, D, E
AWS Documentation Reference:
https://docs.aws.amazon.com/en_pv/elasticbeanstalk/latest/dg/Welcome.html
With Elastic Beanstalk, you can quickly deploy and manage applications in the AWS Cloud without having to learn about the infrastructure that runs those applications. Elastic Beanstalk reduces management complexity without restricting choice or control. You simply upload your application, and Elastic Beanstalk automatically handles the details of capacity provisioning, load balancing, scaling, and application health monitoring.

By default, Elastic Beanstalk does defines a security group, which allows everyone to connect using port 80 (HTTP).

A is not correct because Elastic Beanstalk doesn't manage data at rest and data in transit encryption.

Answer Q137. A, C, D
AWS Documentation Reference:
https://docs.aws.amazon.com/en_pv/elasticbeanstalk/latest/dg/concepts.platforms.html
Elastic Beanstalk provides platforms for programming languages (Go, Java, Node.js, PHP, Python, Ruby), application servers (Tomcat, Passenger, Puma), and Docker containers.

Answer Q138. F
AWS Documentation Reference:
https://aws.amazon.com/elasticbeanstalk/faqs/

Answer Q139. B, C
AWS Documentation Reference:
https://docs.aws.amazon.com/autoscaling/ec2/userguide/as-scaling-target-tracking.html

You can have multiple target tracking scaling policies for an Auto Scaling group, provided that each of them uses a different metric. The intention of Amazon EC2 Auto Scaling is to always prioritize availability, so its behavior differs depending on whether the target tracking policies are ready for scale out or scale in. It will scale out the Auto Scaling group if any of the target tracking policies are ready for scale out, but will scale in only if all of the target tracking policies (with the scale-in portion enabled) are ready to scale in.

You can disable the scale-in portion of a target tracking scaling policy. This feature provides you with the flexibility to scale in your Auto Scaling group using a different method. For example, you can use a different scaling policy type for scale in while using a target tracking scaling policy for scale out.

Answer Q140. C
AWS Documentation Reference: Scaling Adjustment Types
https://docs.aws.amazon.com/autoscaling/ec2/userguide/as-scaling-simple-step.html
Amazon EC2 Auto Scaling supports the following adjustment types for step scaling and simple scaling:

ChangeInCapacity—Increase or decrease the current capacity of the group by the specified number of instances. A positive value increases the capacity and a negative adjustment value decreases the capacity.
ExactCapacity—Change the current capacity of the group to the specified number of instances. Specify a positive value with this adjustment type.
PercentChangeInCapacity—Increment or decrement the current capacity of the group by the specified percentage. A positive value increases the capacity and a negative value decreases the capacity. If the resulting value is not an integer, it is rounded as follows:

- Values greater than 1 are rounded down. For example, 12.7 is rounded to 12.
- Values between 0 and 1 are rounded to 1. For example, .67 is rounded to 1.
- Values between 0 and -1 are rounded to -1. For example, -.58 is rounded to -1.
- Values less than -1 are rounded up. For example, -6.67 is rounded to -6.

Answer Q141. A, B, C, E

Answer Q142. A, C

Answer Q143. C, D
Lambda does not support React.js and Angular.

Answer Q144. B
AWS Documentation Reference:
https://aws.amazon.com/lambda/

https://docs.aws.amazon.com/AWSSimpleQueueService/latest/SQSDeveloperGuide/sqs-configure-lambda-function-trigger.html
You can configure an existing Amazon SQS queue to trigger an AWS Lambda function when new messages arrive in a queue. Lambda functions let you run code without provisioning or managing a server. You pay only for the compute time you consume - there is no charge when your code is not running. Just upload your code and Lambda takes care of everything required to run and scale your code with high availability

Answer Q145. A
Lambda function can be configured as S3 event notification target.
AWS Documentation Reference:
https://aws.amazon.com/lambda/
AWS Lambda lets you run code without provisioning or managing servers. You pay only for the compute time you consume - there is no charge when your code is not running. Just upload your code and Lambda takes care of everything required to run and scale your code with high availability
Answer Q146. B, C, D
AWS Documentation Reference: Whitepaper: Big_Data_Analytics_Options_on_AWS
B: Real-time File Processing – You can trigger Lambda to invoke a process where a file has been uploaded to Amazon S3 or modified. For example, to change an image from color to gray scale after it has been uploaded to Amazon S3.

C: Real-time Stream Processing – You can use Kinesis Data Streams and Lambda to process streaming data for click stream analysis, log filtering, and social media analysis.

D: Extract, Transform, Load – You can use Lambda to run code that transforms data and loads that data into one data repository to another.

A is not correct.
Dynamic Websites – While it is possible to run a static website with AWS Lambda, running a highly dynamic and large volume website can be performance prohibitive. Utilizing Amazon EC2 and Amazon CloudFront would be a recommended use-case.

Answer Q147. A, C
AWS Documentation Reference: Step Adjustments
https://docs.aws.amazon.com/autoscaling/ec2/userguide/as-scaling-simple-step.html
If the metric value gets to 60, the desired capacity of the group increases by 1 instance, to 11 instances, based on the second step adjustment of the scale-out policy (add 10 percent of 10 instances). After the new instance is running and its specified warm-up time has expired, the current capacity of the group increases to 11 instances. If the metric value rises to 70 even after this increase in capacity, the desired capacity of the group increases by another 3 instances, to

14 instances, based on the third step adjustment of the scale-out policy (add 30 percent of 11 instances, 3.3 instances, rounded down to 3 instances).

Answer Q148. B, C

AWS Documentation Reference: Step Adjustments

https://docs.aws.amazon.com/autoscaling/ec2/userguide/as-scaling-simple-step.html

This is continuation of scenario in previous question after the metric value has reached 70 and number of instances has been adjusted to 14.

If the metric value gets to 40, the desired capacity of the group decreases by 1 instance, to 13 instances, based on the second step adjustment of the scale-in policy (remove 10 percent of 14 instances, 1.4 instances, rounded down to 1 instance). If the metric value falls to 30 even after this decrease in capacity, the desired capacity of the group decreases by another 3 instances, to 10 instances, based on the third step adjustment of the scale-in policy (remove 30 percent of 13 instances, 3.9 instances, rounded down to 3 instances).

Answer Q149. A, B, C, F

AWS Documentation Reference: Step Adjustments

https://docs.aws.amazon.com/autoscaling/ec2/userguide/as-scaling-simple-step.html

There are a few rules for the step adjustments for your policy:

- The ranges of your step adjustments can't overlap or have a gap.
- Only one step adjustment can have a null lower bound (negative infinity). If one step adjustment has a negative lower bound, then there must be a step adjustment with a null lower bound.
- Only one step adjustment can have a null upper bound (positive infinity). If one step adjustment has a positive upper bound, then there must be a step adjustment with a null upper bound.
- The upper and lower bound can't be null in the same step adjustment.
- If the metric value is above the breach threshold, the lower bound is inclusive and the upper bound is exclusive. If the metric value is below the breach threshold, the lower bound is exclusive and the upper bound is inclusive.

Answer Q150. A, B, D

AWS Documentation Reference:

https://docs.aws.amazon.com/autoscaling/ec2/userguide/healthcheck.html

Amazon EC2 Auto Scaling can determine the health status of an instance using one or more of the following:

- Status checks provided by Amazon EC2 to identify hardware and software issues that may impair an instance. This includes both instance status checks and system status checks.
- Health checks provided by Elastic Load Balancing.
- Your custom health checks.

Answer Q151. B
AWS Documentation Reference:
https://docs.aws.amazon.com/AWSEC2/latest/UserGuide/security-group-rules-reference.html
To connect to your instance, your security group must have inbound rules that allow SSH access (for Linux instances) or RDP access (for Windows instances) from public IPv4 address of your computer, or a range of IP addresses in your local network. If your VPC is enabled for IPv6 and your instance has an IPv6 address, you can enter an IPv6 address or range.

Answer Q152. A, B, D
AWS Documentation Reference:
https://docs.aws.amazon.com/lambda/latest/dg/limits.html

Answer Q153. A, C, D
AWS Documentation Reference:
https://docs.aws.amazon.com/autoscaling/ec2/userguide/as-add-elb-healthcheck.html
The load balancer periodically sends pings, attempts connections, or sends requests to test the EC2 instances. These tests are called health checks.

Answer Q154. A, B
AWS Documentation Reference:
https://docs.aws.amazon.com/autoscaling/ec2/userguide/as-add-elb-healthcheck.html
If you configured the Auto Scaling group to use Elastic Load Balancing health checks, it considers the instance unhealthy if it fails either the EC2 status checks or the load balancer health checks.

Answer Q155. B, C
AWS Documentation Reference:
https://docs.aws.amazon.com/autoscaling/ec2/userguide/as-add-elb-healthcheck.html
If you attach multiple load balancers to an Auto Scaling group, all of them must report that the instance is healthy in order for it to consider the instance healthy. If one load balancer reports an instance as unhealthy, the Auto Scaling group replaces the instance, even if other load balancers report it as healthy.

Answer Q156. D
AWS Documentation Reference:
https://aws.amazon.com/blogs/iot/building-connected-vehicle-solutions-on-the-aws-cloud/
The bedrock of any successful cloud-based connected vehicle solution is the secure and scalable ingestion and rapid processing of connected vehicle data. To accomplish this, you can use AWS IoT, a managed cloud platform that lets connected devices easily and securely interact with cloud applications and other devices.

Once you've delivered your connected vehicle data into the AWS Cloud, you need a reliable way to store it. Because connected vehicle solutions can store sensitive data from hundreds of thousands of vehicles from all over the world, your storage solution must be secure, scalable, and globally available. Amazon S3 meets all of these requirements and is designed to provide 99.99% availability and 99.999999999% durability of data.

Amazon Kinesis Firehose is used to move connected vehicle data from AWS IoT to an Amazon S3 bucket. It is a managed and scalable data delivery service capable of capturing, transforming, compressing, and encrypting terabytes of streaming data before delivering it to Amazon S3. This makes connected vehicle data storage as simple as specifying Amazon Kinesis Firehose as a destination in the AWS IoT rules engine.

It is important to consistently load batches of raw data from AWS IoT to Amazon S3 so it can later be queried, analyzed, and replayed. But, certain events, such as warnings or anomalies, require real-time processing. For these use cases, you can leverage Amazon Kinesis Analytics and Amazon Kinesis Streams.

The SaaS application should be developed based on microservices architecture. AWS Lambda functions which natively enable event-driven, on-demand data processing and automatically scale to meet the demand of your connected vehicle data. Additionally, since Lambda functions are serverless, you can run your code without provisioning or managing servers.

DynamoDB and RDS to store nosql and relation data.

API gateway for retrieving this data for a variety of mobile, web, or in-vehicle applications.

Answer Q157. A
AWS Documentation Reference: Image recognition & processing
https://aws.amazon.com/serverless/resources/?serverless.sort-by=item.additionalFields.createdDate&serverless.sort-order=desc#Reference_architectures
https://github.com/aws-samples/lambda-refarch-imagerecognition
The architecture is depicted in the diagram below.
1. An image is uploaded to the S3 bucket
2. The S3 upload event triggers the Lambda function, which kicks off an execution of the state machine in AWS Step Functions, passing in the S3 bucket and object key as input parameters.
3. The state machine has the following sub-steps:
   a. Read the file from S3 and extract image metadata
   b. Based on output from previous step, validate if the file uploaded is a supported file format (png or jpg). If not, throw NotSupportedImageType error and end execution.
   c. Store the extracted metadata in the DynamoDB table.
   d. In parallel, kick off two processes simultaneously:
      i. Call Amazon Rekognition to detect objects in the image file. If detected, store the tags in the DynamoDB table

ii.    Generate a thumbnail and store it under the S3 bucket

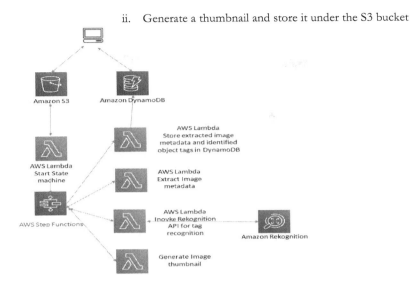

## Answer Q158. D
AWS Documentation Reference:

https://docs.aws.amazon.com/lambda/latest/dg/configuration-vpc.html

You can configure a function to connect to private subnets in a virtual private cloud (VPC) in your account. Use Amazon Virtual Private Cloud (Amazon VPC) to create a private network for resources such as databases, cache instances, or internal services. Connect your function to the VPC to access private resources during execution. When you connect a function to a VPC, Lambda creates an elastic network interface for each combination of security group and subnet in your function's VPC configuration.

https://docs.aws.amazon.com/lambda/latest/dg/services-rds-tutorial.html

## Answer Q159. B, D
AWS Documentation Reference:

https://aws.amazon.com/docker/

Amazon ECS is a highly scalable, high-performance container orchestration service to run Docker containers on the AWS cloud.

Elastic Beanstalk supports the deployment of web applications from Docker containers.

EC2 instance directly doesn't support Docker, you have to instance Docker engine on it.

## Answer Q160. C
AWS Documentation Reference:

https://docs.aws.amazon.com/whitepapers/latest/microservices-on-aws/simple-microservices-architecture-on-aws.html

Amazon Elastic Container Service (Amazon ECS) is a fully managed container orchestration service.

Answer Q161. A, B, C, D
Lambda is not a compute engine for ECS.
AWS Documentation Reference:
https://aws.amazon.com/ecs/faqs/
https://aws.amazon.com/fargate/

Answer Q162. A, C
AWS Documentation Reference:
https://docs.aws.amazon.com/AmazonECS/latest/developerguide/launch_types.html
An Amazon ECS launch type determines the type of infrastructure on which your tasks and services are hosted.
The Fargate launch type allows you to run your containerized applications without the need to provision and manage the backend infrastructure. Just register your task definition and Fargate launches the container for you.
The EC2 launch type allows you to run your containerized applications on a cluster of Amazon EC2 instances that you manage.
Amazon ECS supports Fargate technology and customers will be able to choose AWS Fargate to launch their containers without having to provision or manage EC2 instances. AWS Fargate is the easiest way to launch and run containers on AWS. Customers who require greater control of their EC2 instances to support compliance and governance requirements or broader customization options can choose to use ECS without Fargate to launch EC2 instances.

Answer Q163. B, C
AWS Documentation Reference:
https://aws.amazon.com/fargate/

Answer Q164. A
AWS Documentation Reference:
https://aws.amazon.com/blogs/compute/implementing-safe-aws-lambda-deployments-with-aws-codedeploy/
https://docs.aws.amazon.com/serverless-application-model/latest/developerguide/automating-updates-to-serverless-apps.html
If you use AWS SAM to create your serverless application, it comes built-in with CodeDeploy to help ensure safe Lambda deployments. With just a few lines of configuration, AWS SAM does the following for you:

- Deploys new versions of your Lambda function, and automatically creates aliases that point to the new version.
- Gradually shifts customer traffic to the new version until you're satisfied that it's working as expected, or you roll back the update.

- Defines pre-traffic and post-traffic test functions to verify that the newly deployed code is configured correctly and your application operates as expected.
- Rolls back the deployment if CloudWatch alarms are triggered.

The different deployment options are:

Canary: Traffic is shifted in two increments. You can choose from predefined canary options. The options specify the percentage of traffic that's shifted to your updated Lambda function version in the first increment, and the interval, in minutes, before the remaining traffic is shifted in the second increment.

Linear: Traffic is shifted in equal increments with an equal number of minutes between each increment. You can choose from predefined linear options that specify the percentage of traffic that's shifted in each increment and the number of minutes between each increment.

All-at-once: All traffic is shifted from the original Lambda function to the updated Lambda function version at once.

Answer Q165. D
RDS MySQL, RDS MS-SQL, RDS Oracle, EC2 are not serverless services.

AWS Documentation Reference:  Whitepaper: AWS Serverless Multi-Tier Architectures

Presentation Tier: Amazon S3 allows you to serve static websites, such as single page applications (SPAs), directly from an S3 bucket without requiring provision of a web server. You can use Amazon CloudFront as a managed content delivery network (CDN) to improve performance and enable SSL/TL using managed or custom certificates.

Logic tier: Amazon API Gateway with AWS Lambda to expose and create services. You can define a Lambda function that implements a custom authorization scheme that uses a bearer token strategy (for example, OAuth, SAML) or uses request parameters to identify users.
Data tier:  Amazon DynamoDB is used for the API lambda services. Amazon S3 is used to host static content used by the /info service.

Answer Q166. B
AWS Documentation Reference:  Whitepaper:
Serverless Streaming Architectures and Best Practices
https://d1.awsstatic.com/whitepapers/Serverless_Streaming_Architecture_Best_Practices.pdf

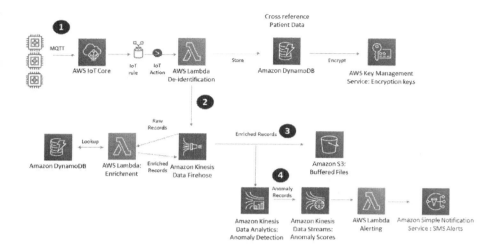

In Point 1 of Figure, one or more medical devices ("IoT sensors") are wired to a patient in a hospital. The devices transmit sensor data to the hospital IoT gateway which are then forwarded securely using the MQTT protocol to the AWS IoT gateway service for processing.

Next, the data must be de-identified in order to be processed in an anonymized way. AWS IoT is configured with an IoT Rule that selects measurements for a specific set of patients and an IoT Action that delivers these selected measurements to a Lambda de-identification function. The Lambda performs three tasks.

- First the function removes PHI and PII attributes (Patient Name and Patient DOB) from the records.

- Second for the purpose of future cross-reference the function encrypts and stores the Patient Name and Patient DOB attributes in a DynamoDB table along with the Patient ID.

- And finally the function sends the de-identified records to a Kinesis Data Firehose delivery stream (Point 2 in Figure).

After sensor data has been ingested, it may need to be enriched or modified with simple transformations such as field level substitutions and data enrichment from relatively small and static data sets.

The solution introduces a Lambda function that is invoked by Kinesis Data Firehose as records are received by the delivery stream. The Lambda function looks up information about each device from a DynamoDB table and adds these as fields to the measurement records. Firehose then buffers and sends the modified records to the configured destinations (Point 3 in Figure). A copy of the source records is saved in S3 as a backup and for future analysis.

Using AWS Lambda functions for transformations in this pattern removes the conventional hassle of setting up and maintaining infrastructure. Lambda runs more copies of the function in parallel in response to concurrent transformation invocations, and scales precisely with the size of the workload down to the individual request. As a result, the problem of idle infrastructure and wasted infrastructure cost is eliminated.

Copies of the enriched records from the prior pattern (Point 4 in Figure) are delivered to a Kinesis Data Analytics application that detects anomalies in the measurements across all devices for a manufacturer. The anomaly scores (Point 5 in Figure) are sent to a Kinesis Data Stream and processed by a Lambda function. A sample record with the added anomaly score is shown below:

{ "timestamp": "2018-01-27T05:11:50", "device_id": "device8401", "patient_id": "patient2605", "temperature": 100.3, "pulse": 108.6, "oxygen_percent": 48.4, "systolic": 110.2, "diastolic": 75.6, "manufacturer": "Manufacturer 09", "model": "Model 02", "anomaly_score": 0.9845 }

Based on a range or threshold of anomalies detected, the Lambda function sends a notification to the manufacturer with the model number and device id and a set of measurements that caused the anomaly.

Answer Q167.A, B
AWS Documentation Reference:
https://docs.aws.amazon.com/AWSEC2/latest/UserGuide//TroubleshootingInstancesConn ecting.html#TroubleshootingInstancesConnectingSSH
If you connect to your instance using SSH and get any of the following errors, Host key not found in [directory], Permission denied (publickey), or Authentication failed, permission denied, verify that you are connecting with the appropriate user name for your AMI and that you have specified the proper private key (.pem) file for your instance.

Answer Q168. C
AWS Documentation Reference:
https://docs.aws.amazon.com/solutions/latest/instance-scheduler/overview.html
The AWS Instance Scheduler is a solution that automates the starting and stopping of Amazon Elastic Compute Cloud (Amazon EC2) and Amazon Relational Database Service (Amazon RDS) instances. The solution is easy to deploy and can help reduce operational costs.
AWS doesn't charge for stopped EC2 instance. For example, an organization can use the Instance Scheduler in a production environment to automatically stop instances every day, outside of business hours. For customers who leave all of their instances running at full utilization, this solution can result in up to 70% cost savings for those instances that are only necessary during regular business hours (weekly utilization reduced from 168 hours to 50 hours).
While your database instance is stopped, you are charged for provisioned storage, manual snapshots and automated backup storage within your specified retention window, but not for database instance hours.

Answer Q169. A

AWS Documentation Reference:

https://docs.aws.amazon.com/AmazonCloudWatch/latest/events/WhatIsCloudWatchEvents.html

Amazon CloudWatch Events delivers a near real-time stream of system events that describe changes in Amazon Web Services (AWS) resources. Using simple rules that you can quickly set up, you can match events and route them to one or more target functions or streams.

Answer Q170. B, C, D

AWS Documentation Reference:

https://docs.aws.amazon.com/AWSEC2/latest/UserGuide/instancedata-data-categories.html

To view all categories of instance metadata from within a running instance, use the following URI.http://169.254.169.254/latest/meta-data/

The IP address 169.254.169.254 is a link-local address and is valid only from the instance.

You will not get information on instance Route table, NACL configuration and SSL certificate.

Answer Q171.B

AWS Documentation Reference:

https://docs.aws.amazon.com/AWSEC2/latest/UserGuide/user-data.html

When you launch an instance in Amazon EC2, you have the option of passing user data to the instance that can be used to perform common automated configuration tasks and even run scripts after the instance starts. You can pass two types of user data to Amazon EC2: shell scripts and cloud-init directives. You can also pass this data into the launch wizard as plain text, as a file (this is useful for launching instances using the command line tools), or as base64-encoded text (for API calls).

Answer Q172. A

AWS Documentation Reference:

https://aws.amazon.com/premiumsupport/knowledge-center/copy-ami-region/

To create a copy of your AMI in another AWS Region, follow these steps:

- Create an AMI of your EC2 instance.
- Copy the AMI of your EC2 instance to another AWS Region:

After the copy operation completes, launch a new EC2 instance from your AMI in the new AWS Region.

https://docs.aws.amazon.com/AWSEC2/latest/UserGuide/CopyingAMIs.html

AWS does not copy launch permissions, user-defined tags, or Amazon S3 bucket permissions from the source AMI to the new AMI. After the copy operation is complete, you can apply launch permissions, user-defined tags, and Amazon S3 bucket permissions to the new AMI.

B is wrong because AMI are region specific.

C is wrong because there is no feature of EC2 cloning.

Answer Q173. D

AWS Documentation Reference:

https://docs.aws.amazon.com/AWSEC2/latest/UserGuide/iam-roles-for-amazon-ec2.html

Applications must sign their API requests with AWS credentials. Instead of storing security credentials in the EC2 instances, use IAM roles so that your applications can securely make API requests from your instances, without requiring you to manage the security credentials that the applications use. Instead of creating and distributing your AWS credentials, you can delegate permission to make API requests using IAM roles as follows:

- Create an IAM role.

- Define which accounts or AWS services can assume the role.

- Define which API actions and resources the application can use after assuming the role.

- Specify the role when you launch your instance, or attach the role to an existing instance. Have the application retrieve a set of temporary credentials and use them.

You cannot attach multiple IAM roles to a single instance, but you can attach a single IAM role to multiple instances.

Answer Q174. A, B, D

AWS Documentation Reference:

https://aws.amazon.com/blogs/aws/elb-connection-draining-remove-instances-from-service-with-care/

When Connection Draining is enabled and configured, the process of deregistering an instance from an Elastic Load Balancer gains an additional step. For the duration of the configured timeout, the load balancer will allow existing, in-flight requests made to an instance to complete, but it will not send any new requests to the instance. During this time, the API will report the status of the instance as InService, along with a message stating that "Instance deregistration currently in progress." Once the timeout is reached, any remaining connections will be forcibly closed.

https://docs.aws.amazon.com/autoscaling/ec2/userguide/healthcheck.html

After an instance has been marked unhealthy because of an Amazon EC2 or Elastic Load Balancing health check, it is almost immediately scheduled for replacement. Amazon EC2 Auto Scaling creates a new scaling activity for terminating the unhealthy instance and then terminates it. Later, another scaling activity launches a new instance to replace the terminated instance. When your instance is terminated, any associated Elastic IP addresses are disassociated and are not automatically associated with the new instance. You must associate these Elastic IP addresses with the new instance manually. Similarly, when your instance is terminated, its attached EBS volumes are detached. You must attach these EBS volumes to the new instance manually.

Answer Q175. A, B, C, D

AWS Documentation Reference:

https://aws.amazon.com/getting-started/projects/build-serverless-web-app-lambda-apigateway-s3-dynamodb-cognito/

Amazon S3 hosts static web resources including HTML, CSS, JavaScript, and image files which are loaded in the user's browser.

Amazon Cognito provides user management and authentication functions to secure the backend API.

JavaScript executed in the browser sends and receives data from a public backend API built using Lambda and API Gateway.

For persistence layer you can choose DynamoDB where data can be stored by the API's Lambda function.

Lambda is more cost effective than EC2.

Answer Q176. D

AWS Documentation Reference:

https://docs.aws.amazon.com/AmazonECS/latest/developerguide/Welcome.html

https://aws.amazon.com/blogs/compute/building-blocks-of-amazon-ecs/

Cluster: An ECS cluster is a grouping of (container) instances* (or tasks in Fargate) that lie within a single region, but can span multiple Availability Zones – it's even a good idea for redundancy.

An ECS container instance is an EC2 instance running the agent, has a specifically defined IAM policy and role, and has been registered into your cluster.

The Amazon ECS container agent is a Go program that runs in its own container within each EC2 instance that you use with ECS. The agent is the intermediary component that takes care of the communication between the scheduler and your instances.

The task definition is a text file, in JSON format, that describes one or more containers, up to a maximum of ten, that form your application.

A task is the instantiation of a task definition within a cluster. After you have created a task definition for your application within Amazon ECS, you can specify the number of tasks that will run on your cluster. When you want to start a container, it has to be part of a task. Therefore, you have to create a task first. Succinctly, tasks are a logical grouping of 1 to N containers that run together on the same instance, with N defined by you, up to 10. Let's say you want to run a custom blog engine. You could put together a web server, an application server, and an in-memory cache, each in their own container. Together, they form a basic frontend unit.

The Amazon ECS task scheduler is responsible for placing tasks within your cluster. Scheduler is the component that decides what (which containers) gets to run where (on which instances), according to a number of constraints.

Answer Q177. A, B, D, E
AWS Documentation Reference:
https://docs.aws.amazon.com/AmazonECS/latest/developerguide/task_execution_IAM_rol
e.html
The Amazon ECS container agent makes calls to the Amazon ECS API on your behalf, so it
requires an IAM policy and role for the service to know that the agent belongs to you. This
IAM role is referred to as a task execution IAM role. You can have multiple task execution
roles for different purposes associated with your account.
The following are common use cases for a task execution IAM role:
Your task uses the Fargate launch type and

- is pulling a container image from Amazon ECR.
- uses the awslogs log driver.

Your tasks uses either the Fargate or EC2 launch type and

- is using private registry authentication.
- the task definition is referencing sensitive data using Secrets Manager secrets or AWS
  Systems Manager Parameter Store parameters.

https://docs.aws.amazon.com/AmazonECS/latest/developerguide/instance_IAM_role.html
The Amazon ECS container agent makes calls to the Amazon ECS API on your behalf.
Container instances that run the agent require an IAM policy and role for the service to know
that the agent belongs to you. Before you can launch container instances and register them into
a cluster, you must create an IAM role for those container instances to use when they are
launched.

https://docs.aws.amazon.com/AmazonECS/latest/developerguide/codedeploy_IAM_role.ht
ml
Before you can use the CodeDeploy blue/green deployment type with Amazon ECS, the
CodeDeploy service needs permissions to update your Amazon ECS service on your behalf.
These permissions are provided by the CodeDeploy IAM role (ecsCodeDeployRole).

https://docs.aws.amazon.com/AmazonECS/latest/developerguide/CWE_IAM_role.html
Before you can use Amazon ECS scheduled tasks with CloudWatch Events rules and targets,
the CloudWatch Events service needs permissions to run Amazon ECS tasks on your behalf.
These permissions are provided by the CloudWatch Events IAM role (ecsEventsRole).

Answer Q178. A, B, C
AWS Documentation Reference: Elastic Fabric Adapter (EFA)
https://docs.aws.amazon.com/AWSEC2/latest/UserGuide/efa.html
An Elastic Fabric Adapter (EFA) is a network device that you can attach to your Amazon EC2
instance to accelerate High Performance Computing (HPC) and machine learning applications.

EFA enables you to achieve the application performance of an on-premises HPC cluster, with the scalability, flexibility, and elasticity provided by the AWS Cloud.

EFA provides lower and more consistent latency and higher throughput than the TCP transport traditionally used in cloud-based HPC systems. It enhances the performance of inter-instance communication that is critical for scaling HPC and machine learning applications. It is optimized to work on the existing AWS network infrastructure and it can scale depending on application requirements.
https://aws.amazon.com/ec2/faqs/
High Performance Computing (HPC) applications distribute computational workloads across a cluster of instances for parallel processing. Examples of HPC applications include computational fluid dynamics (CFD), crash simulations, and weather simulations. HPC applications are generally written using the Message Passing Interface (MPI) and impose stringent requirements for inter-instance communication in terms of both latency and bandwidth. Applications using MPI and other HPC middleware which supports the libfabric communication stack can benefit from EFA.
EFA brings the scalability, flexibility, and elasticity of cloud to tightly-coupled HPC applications. With EFA, tightly-coupled HPC applications have access to lower and more consistent latency and higher throughput than traditional TCP channels, enabling them to scale better.
An ENA ENI provides traditional IP networking features necessary to support VPC networking. An EFA ENI provides all the functionality of an ENA ENI, plus hardware support for applications to communicate directly with the EFA ENI without involving the instance kernel (OS-bypass communication) using an extended programming interface.

Answer Q179.C
AWS Documentation Reference:
https://docs.aws.amazon.com/AWSEC2/latest/UserGuide/instancedata-data-retrieval.html
To view all categories of instance metadata from within a running instance, use the following URI.
http://169.254.169.254/latest/meta-data/
The IP address 169.254.169.254 is a link-local address and is valid only from the instance.

Answer Q180. B
AWS Documentation Reference: Whitepaper: Big Data Analytics Options on AWS
Capturing and Analyzing Sensor Data

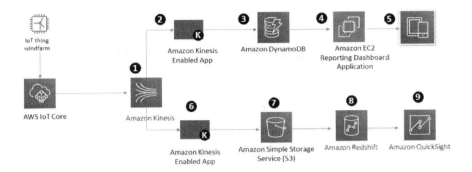

When AWS IoT ingests data from connected devices, an AWS IoT rule sends the data to a Kinesis data delivery stream.

1. The process begins with each unit providing a constant data stream to Amazon Kinesis Data Streams. This provides an elastic and durable interface the units can talk to that can be scaled seamlessly as more and more turbine units are sold and brought online.

2. Using the Amazon Kinesis Data Streams provided tools such as the Kinesis Client Library or SDK, a simple application is built on Amazon EC2 to read data as it comes into Amazon Kinesis Data Streams, analyze it, and determine if the data warrants an update to the real-time dashboard. It looks for changes in system operation, temperature fluctuations, and any errors that the units encounter.

3. This data flow needs to occur in near real time so that customers and maintenance teams can be alerted as quickly as possible if there is an issue with the unit. The data in the dashboard does have some aggregated trend information, but it is mainly the current state as well as any system errors. So, the data needed to populate the dashboard is relatively small. Additionally, there will be lots of potential access to this data from the following sources:

• Customers checking on their system via a mobile device or browser
• Maintenance teams checking the status of its fleet
• Data and intelligence algorithms and analytics in the reporting platform spot trends that can be then sent out as alerts

DynamoDB was chosen to store this near real-time data set because it is both highly available and scalable; throughput to this data can be easily scaled up or down to meet the needs of its consumers as the platform is adopted and usage grows.

4. The reporting dashboard is a custom web application that is built on top of this data set and run on Amazon EC2. It provides content based on the system status and trends as well as alerting customers and maintenance crews of any issues that may come up with the unit

5. The customer accesses the data from a mobile device or a web browser to get the current status of the system and visualize historical trends.

The data flow (steps 2-5) that was just described is built for near real-time reporting of information to human consumers. It is built and designed for low latency and can scale very quickly to meet demand. The data flow (steps 6-9) that is depicted in the lower part of the diagram does not have such stringent speed and latency requirements. This allows the architect to design a different solution stack that can hold larger amounts of data at a much smaller cost per byte of information and choose less expensive compute and storage resources.

6. To read from the Amazon Kinesis stream, there is a separate Amazon Kinesis-enabled application that probably runs on a smaller EC2 instance that scales at a slower rate. While this application is going to analyze the same data set as the upper data flow, the ultimate purpose of this data is to store it for long-term record and to host the data set in a data warehouse. This data set ends up being all data sent from the systems and allows a much broader set of analytics to be performed without the near real-time requirements.

7. The data is transformed by the Amazon Kinesis-enabled application into a format that is suitable for long-term storage, for loading into its data warehouse, and storing on Amazon S3. The data on Amazon S3 not only serves as a parallel ingestion point to Amazon Redshift, but is durable storage that will hold all data that ever runs through this system; it can be the single source of truth. It can be used to load other analytical tools if additional requirements arise. Amazon S3 also comes with native integration with Amazon Glacier, if any data needs to be cycled into long-term, low-cost storage.

8. Amazon Redshift is used as the data warehouse for the larger data set. It can scale easily when the data set grows larger, by adding another node to the cluster.

9. For visualizing the analytics, one of the many partner visualization platforms can be used via the OBDC/JDBC connection to Amazon Redshift. This is where the reports, graphs, and ad hoc analytics can be performed on the data set to find certain variables and trends that can lead to A/C units underperforming or breaking.

This architecture can start off small and grow as needed. Additionally, by decoupling the two different work streams from each other, they can grow at their own rate without upfront commitment, allowing the manufacturer to assess the viability of this new offering without a large initial investment.

Answer Q181. A
AWS Documentation Reference:
https://docs.aws.amazon.com/IAM/latest/UserGuide/id_roles_use_switch-role-ec2.html

An instance profile is a container for an IAM role that you can use to pass role information to an EC2 instance when the instance starts.

Using roles to grant permissions to applications that run on EC2 instances requires a bit of extra configuration. An application running on an EC2 instance is abstracted from AWS by the virtualized operating system. Because of this extra separation, an additional step is needed to assign an AWS role and its associated permissions to an EC2 instance and make them available to its applications. This extra step is the creation of an instance profile that is attached to the instance. The instance profile contains the role and can provide the role's temporary credentials to an application that runs on the instance. Those temporary credentials can then be used in the application's API calls to access resources and to limit access to only those resources that the role specifies.

Answer Q182. B, C
AWS Documentation Reference:
https://docs.aws.amazon.com/AWSEC2/latest/UserGuide/enhanced-networking.html
Enhanced networking uses single root I/O virtualization (SR-IOV) to provide high-performance networking capabilities on supported instance types. SR-IOV is a method of device virtualization that provides higher I/O performance and lower CPU utilization when compared to traditional virtualized network interfaces. Enhanced networking provides higher bandwidth, higher packet per second (PPS) performance, and consistently lower inter-instance latencies.

https://docs.aws.amazon.com/AWSEC2/latest/UserGuide/enhanced-networking.html#supported_instances
Depending on your instance type, enhanced networking can be enabled using one of the following mechanisms:
Elastic Network Adapter (ENA)
The Elastic Network Adapter (ENA) supports network speeds of up to 100 Gbps for supported instance types.
Intel 82599 Virtual Function (VF) interface
The Intel 82599 Virtual Function interface supports network speeds of up to 10 Gbps for supported instance types.

Answer Q183. B

# Answer Chapter 2: Networking :Amazon Virtual Private Cloud (VPC), Elastic Load Balancing, Amazon API Gateway, AWS App Mesh, AWS Direct Connect, AWS PrivateLink, AWS Global Accelerator, AWS Transit Gateway, AWS VPN

Answer Q1. A, B, D

AWS Documentation Reference:

https://docs.aws.amazon.com/vpc/latest/userguide/VPC_SecurityGroups.html#VPCSecurit
yGroups

A security group acts as a virtual firewall for your instance to control inbound and outbound
traffic.

Answer Q2. A, C, D

AWS Documentation Reference:

https://docs.aws.amazon.com/vpc/latest/userguide/VPC_SecurityGroups.html#VPCSecurit
yGroups

Answer Q3. A, C, D

AWS Documentation Reference:

https://docs.aws.amazon.com/vpc/latest/userguide/VPC_SecurityGroups.html#DefaultSecu
rityGroup

Your VPC automatically comes with a default security group. If you don't specify a different
security group when you launch the instance, AWS associates the default security group with
your instance.

Answer Q4. C, D

AWS Documentation Reference:

https://docs.aws.amazon.com/vpc/latest/userguide/VPC_SecurityGroups.html#VPCSecurit
yGroups

When you create a security group, it has no inbound rules. Therefore, no inbound traffic
originating from another host to your instance is allowed until you add inbound rules to the
security group.

By default, a security group includes an outbound rule that allows all outbound traffic. You can
remove the rule and add outbound rules that allow specific outbound traffic only. If your
security group has no outbound rules, no outbound traffic originating from your instance is
allowed.

Answer Q5. A, B, C, E

AWS Documentation Reference:

https://docs.aws.amazon.com/vpc/latest/userguide/getting-started-ipv4.html

The diagram below represents an example configuration. The steps to be followed are:

Step 1: Create the VPC

Use the Amazon VPC wizard in the Amazon VPC console to create a VPC. The wizard
performs the following steps for you:

    A.    Creates a VPC with a /16 IPv4 CIDR block (a network with 65,536 private IP
        addresses).

    B.    Attaches an Internet gateway to the VPC.

C.     Creates a size /24 IPv4 subnet (a range of 256 private IP addresses) in the VPC.

D.     Creates a custom route table, and associates it with your subnet, so that traffic can flow between the subnet and the Internet gateway.

Step 2: Create a Security Group

A security group acts as a virtual firewall to control the traffic for its associated instances. To use a security group, you add the inbound rules to control incoming traffic to the instance, and outbound rules to control the outgoing traffic from your instance. To associate a security group with an instance, you specify the security group when you launch the instance. Add the inbound rules yourself. The outbound rule is a default rule that allows all outbound communication to anywhere

Internet gateway

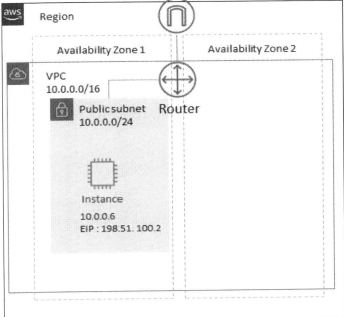

Custom Route Table

| Destination | Target |
|---|---|
| 10.0.0.0/16 | Local |
| 0.0.0.0/0 | Igw-id |

Inbound Security Group

| Source IP | Protocol | Port | Comments |
|---|---|---|---|
| 0.0.0.0/0 | TCP | 80 | HTTP access |
| 0.0.0.0/0 | TCP | 443 | HTTPS access |
| Home network address range | TCP | 22 | SSH access |

Outbound Security Group

| Source IP | Protocol | Port | Comments |
|---|---|---|---|
| 0.0.0.0/0 | All | All | Default outbound |

Step 3: Launch an Instance into Your VPC

When you launch an EC2 instance into a VPC, you must specify the subnet in which to launch the instance. In this case, you'll launch an instance into the public subnet of the VPC you created. Attach the custom security group created in step 2.

Step 4: Assign an Elastic IP Address to Your Instance

In the previous step, you launched your instance into a public subnet — a subnet that has a route to an Internet gateway. However, the instance in your subnet also needs a public IPv4 address to be able to communicate with the Internet. By default, an instance in a nondefault VPC is not assigned a public IPv4 address. In this step, you'll allocate an Elastic IP address to your account, and then associate it with your instance.

Answer Q6. A, B

AWS Documentation Reference:

https://docs.aws.amazon.com/vpc/latest/userguide/VPC_Subnets.html

A VPC spans all the Availability Zones in the region. After creating a VPC, you can add one or more subnets in each Availability Zone. When you create a subnet, you specify the CIDR block for the subnet, which is a subset of the VPC CIDR block. Each subnet must reside entirely within one Availability Zone and cannot span zones.

Answer Q7. A

AWS Documentation Reference:

https://docs.aws.amazon.com/vpc/latest/userguide/VPC_Subnets.html#vpc-subnet-basics

If a subnet's traffic is routed to an internet gateway, the subnet is known as a public subnet. In this diagram, subnet 1A is a public subnet. In the route table destination 0.0.0.0/0 is mapped to internet gateway.

Answer Q8. B

AWS Documentation Reference:

https://docs.aws.amazon.com/vpc/latest/userguide/VPC_Subnets.html#vpc-subnet-basics

If a subnet doesn't have a route to the internet gateway, the subnet is known as a private subnet. In this diagram, subnet 2A is a private subnet.

Answer Q9. C

AWS Documentation Reference:

https://docs.aws.amazon.com/vpc/latest/userguide/VPC_Subnets.html#vpc-subnet-basics

If a subnet doesn't have a route to the internet gateway, but has its traffic routed to a virtual private gateway for a Site-to-Site VPN connection, the subnet is known as a VPN-only subnet. In this diagram, subnet 3A is a VPN-only subnet.

Answer Q10. A, D

AWS Documentation Reference:

https://docs.aws.amazon.com/vpc/latest/userguide/VPC_Subnets.html#vpc-subnet-basics
The CIDR block of a subnet can be the same as the CIDR block for the VPC (for a single subnet in the VPC), or a subset of the CIDR block for the VPC (for multiple subnets).

Answer Q11. A, B
AWS Documentation Reference:
https://docs.aws.amazon.com/vpc/latest/userguide/VPC_Subnets.html#vpc-sizing-ipv4
The allowed block size is between a /28 netmask (16 IP addresses) and /16 netmask (65,536 IP addresses). If you create more than one subnet in a VPC, the CIDR blocks of the subnets cannot overlap.

Answer Q12. D
AWS Documentation Reference:
https://docs.aws.amazon.com/vpc/latest/userguide/VPC_Subnets.html#vpc-sizing-ipv4
The first four IP addresses and the last IP address in each subnet CIDR block are not available for you to use, and cannot be assigned to an instance. For example, in a subnet with CIDR block 10.0.0.0/24, the following five IP addresses are reserved:
10.0.0.0: Network address.
10.0.0.1: Reserved by AWS for the VPC router.
10.0.0.2: Reserved by AWS.
10.0.0.3: Reserved by AWS for future use.
10.0.0.255: Network broadcast address.

Answer Q13. A, B, C
D is incorrect.
https://docs.aws.amazon.com/vpc/latest/userguide/VPC_Subnets.html#vpc-sizing-ipv4

Answer Q14. B
AWS Documentation Reference:
https://docs.aws.amazon.com/vpc/latest/userguide/VPC_Subnets.html#SubnetSecurity
AWS provides two features that you can use to increase security in your VPC: security groups and network ACLs. Security groups control inbound and outbound traffic for your instances, and network ACLs control inbound and outbound traffic for your subnets. In most cases, security groups can meet your needs; however, you can also use network ACLs if you want an additional layer of security for your VPC

Answer Q15. B, C
AWS Documentation Reference:
https://docs.aws.amazon.com/vpc/latest/userguide/VPC_Subnets.html
If you have an IPv4 address prefix in your VPC that overlaps with one of your networks' prefixes, any traffic to the network's prefix is dropped.

Answer Q16. B, C, D

AWS Documentation Reference:

https://docs.aws.amazon.com/vpc/latest/userguide/default-vpc.html

Answer Q17. C

AWS Documentation Reference:

https://docs.aws.amazon.com/vpc/latest/userguide/vpc-ip-addressing.html

By default, Amazon EC2 and Amazon VPC use the IPv4 addressing protocol. When you create a VPC, you must assign it an IPv4 CIDR block (a range of private IPv4 addresses). Private IPv4 addresses are not reachable over the Internet. To connect to your instance over the Internet, or to enable communication between your instances and other AWS services that have public endpoints, you can assign a globally-unique public IPv4 address to your instance.

Answer Q18. B

AWS Documentation Reference:

https://docs.aws.amazon.com/vpc/latest/userguide/vpc-ip-addressing.html

You can optionally associate an IPv6 CIDR block with your VPC and subnets, and assign IPv6 addresses from that block to the resources in your VPC.

Answer Q19. B, C

AWS Documentation Reference:

https://docs.aws.amazon.com/vpc/latest/userguide/vpc-ip-addressing.html

Your VPC will operate in dual-stack mode: your resources can communicate over IPv4, or IPv6, or both. IPv4 and IPv6 addresses are independent of each other; you must configure routing and security in your VPC separately for IPv4 and IPv6.

Answer Q20. A, C, D

AWS Documentation Reference:

https://docs.aws.amazon.com/vpc/latest/userguide/VPC_DHCP_Options.html

The Amazon EC2 instances you launch into a nondefault VPC are private by default; they're not assigned a public IPv4 address unless you specifically assign one during launch, or you modify the subnet's public IPv4 address attribute. By default, all instances in a nondefault VPC receive an unresolvable host name that AWS assigns (for example, ip-10-0-0-202). You can assign your own domain name to your instances, and use up to four of your own DNS servers. To do that, you must specify a special set of DHCP options to use with the VPC.

Answer Q21. C, D

AWS Documentation Reference:

You can control whether your instance receives a public IP address by doing the following:
Modifying the public IP addressing attribute of your subnet.

https://docs.aws.amazon.com/vpc/latest/userguide/vpc-ip-addressing.html#subnet-public-ip

Enabling or disabling the public IP addressing feature during instance launch, which overrides the subnet's public IP addressing attribute.

https://docs.aws.amazon.com/vpc/latest/userguide/vpc-ip-addressing.html#vpc-public-ip

Answer Q22. A, B, C

AWS Documentation Reference:

https://docs.aws.amazon.com/vpc/latest/userguide/VPC_Security.html

Amazon Virtual Private Cloud provides features that you can use to increase and monitor the security for your virtual private cloud (VPC):

Security groups — Act as a firewall for associated Amazon EC2 instances, controlling both inbound and outbound traffic at the instance level

Network access control lists (ACLs) — Act as a firewall for associated subnets, controlling both inbound and outbound traffic at the subnet level

Flow logs — Capture information about the IP traffic going to and from network interfaces in your VPC

The following diagram illustrates the layers of security provided by security groups and network ACLs. For example, traffic from an Internet gateway is routed to the appropriate subnet using the routes in the routing table. The rules of the network ACL associated with the subnet control which traffic is allowed to the subnet. The rules of the security group associated with an instance control which traffic is allowed to the instance.

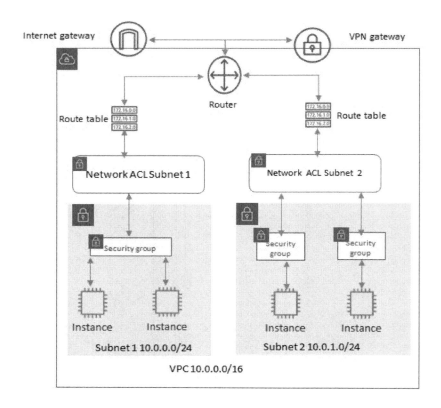

Answer Q23. A, B
AWS Documentation Reference:
https://docs.aws.amazon.com/vpc/latest/userguide/VPC_Security.html

Answer Q24. B
AWS Documentation Reference:
https://docs.aws.amazon.com/vpc/latest/userguide/vpc-dns.html
If both attributes are set to true, the following occurs:

• Instances with a public IP address receive corresponding public DNS hostnames.

• The Amazon-provided DNS server can resolve Amazon-provided private DNS hostnames.

If either or both of the attributes is set to false, the following occurs:

• Instances with a public IP address do not receive corresponding public DNS hostnames.

• The Amazon-provided DNS server cannot resolve Amazon-provided private DNS hostnames.

- Instances receive custom private DNS hostnames if there is a custom domain name in the DHCP options set. If you are not using the Amazon-provided DNS server, your custom domain name servers must resolve the hostname as appropriate.

By default, both attributes are set to true in a default VPC or a VPC created by the VPC wizard. By default, only the enableDnsSupport attribute is set to true in a VPC created any other way.

Answer Q25. B
Any changes to the security group is applied immediately to all the instances in that group.

Answer Q26. B, C
AWS Documentation Reference: Comparison of Security Groups and Network ACLs
https://docs.aws.amazon.com/vpc/latest/userguide/VPC_Security.html

Answer Q27. C
AWS Documentation Reference:
https://docs.aws.amazon.com/vpc/latest/userguide/VPC_SecurityGroups.html
When you launch an instance in a VPC, you can assign up to five security groups to the instance.

Answer Q28. A
AWS Documentation Reference:
https://docs.aws.amazon.com/vpc/latest/userguide/VPC_SecurityGroups.html
Instances associated with a security group can't talk to each other unless you add rules allowing it in the security group. (Exception: the default security group has these rules by default). Add inbound rule:
Source: The security group ID (sg-xxxxxxxx)
Protocol: all
Port range: all
Comments: Allow inbound traffic from instances assigned to the same security group.

Answer Q29.A
AWS Documentation Reference:
https://docs.aws.amazon.com/vpc/latest/userguide/vpc-network-acls.html
Your VPC automatically comes with a modifiable default network ACL. By default, it allows all inbound and outbound IPv4 traffic and, if applicable, IPv6 traffic.

Answer Q30.D
AWS Documentation Reference:
https://docs.aws.amazon.com/vpc/latest/userguide/vpc-network-acls.html

You can create a custom network ACL and associate it with a subnet. By default, each custom network ACL denies all inbound and outbound traffic until you add rules.

Answer Q31.A, C
AWS Documentation Reference:
https://docs.aws.amazon.com/vpc/latest/userguide/vpc-network-acls.html
Each subnet in your VPC must be associated with a network ACL. If you don't explicitly associate a subnet with a network ACL, the subnet is automatically associated with the default network ACL.

Answer Q32.D
AWS Documentation Reference:
https://docs.aws.amazon.com/vpc/latest/userguide/vpc-network-acls.html
A subnet can be associated with only one network ACL at a time. When you associate a network ACL with a subnet, the previous association is removed.

Answer Q33.A
AWS Documentation Reference:
https://docs.aws.amazon.com/vpc/latest/userguide/vpc-network-acls.html
You can associate a network ACL with multiple subnets.

Answer Q34.B, C
AWS Documentation Reference:
https://docs.aws.amazon.com/vpc/latest/userguide/VPC_SecurityGroups.html
https://docs.aws.amazon.com/vpc/latest/userguide/vpc-network-acls.html
SG evaluate all rules before deciding whether to allow traffic.
Network ACL process rules in number order when deciding whether to allow traffic.

Answer Q35. B
Key considerations are:
• VPC is mapped to one region but can span AZs
• A subnet is mapped to on AZ in VPC's region
• Both the application will be inside the same VPC but in different subnet of their own.
• To achieve fault tolerance in case one AZ goes down, each application should have one instances in two subnets which are mapped to two different AZs.

For example if you are deploying INTERNETApp and INTRANETApp by creating a VPC in us-east-1 region. Your network topology can be
• Subnet1, us-east-1a AZ having INTERNETApp instance.
• Subnet2, us-east-1b AZ having INTERNETApp instance.
• Subnet3 us-east-1c AZ having INTRANETApp instance.

- Subnet4, us-east-1d AZ having INTRANETApp instance.

This ensures that in case one AZ goes down, user request can be served by instance in subnet mapped to other active AZ.

## Answer Q36. A, B, E
AWS Documentation Reference:

https://aws.amazon.com/privatelink/

AWS PrivateLink enables you to securely connect your VPCs to supported AWS services, to your own services on AWS, to services hosted by other AWS accounts, and to third-party services on AWS Marketplace. Since traffic between your VPC and any one of these services does not leave the Amazon network, an Internet gateway, NAT device, public IP address, or VPN connection is no longer needed to communicate with the service.

To use AWS PrivateLink, create an interface VPC endpoint for a service in your VPC. This creates an Elastic Network Interface (ENI) in your subnet with a private IP address that serves as an entry point for traffic destined to the service. Service endpoints available over AWS PrivateLink will appear as ENIs with private IPs in your VPCs.

## Answer Q37. A, D
AWS Documentation Reference:

https://docs.aws.amazon.com/vpc/latest/userguide/vpc-network-acls.html

Rules are evaluated starting with the lowest numbered rule. As soon as a rule matches traffic, it's applied regardless of any higher-numbered rule that may contradict it.

## Answer Q38. B
AWS Documentation Reference:

https://docs.aws.amazon.com/vpc/latest/userguide/vpc-network-acls.html

The following is an example default network ACL for a VPC that supports IPv4 only.

| Inbound | | | | | |
|---------|------|----------|------------|-----------|------------|
| Rule # | Type | Protocol | Port Range | Source | Allow/Deny |
| 100 | All IPv4 traffic | All | All | 0.0.0.0/0 | ALLOW |
| * | All IPv4 traffic | All | All | 0.0.0.0/0 | DENY |
| Outbound | | | | | |
| Rule # | Type | Protocol | Port Range | Destination | Allow/Deny |
| 100 | All IPv4 traffic | All | All | 0.0.0.0/0 | ALLOW |
| * | All IPv4 traffic | All | All | 0.0.0.0/0 | DENY |

## Answer Q39. A, D, E
AWS Documentation Reference:

https://aws.amazon.com/privatelink/

Maintain regulatory compliance: Preventing personally identifiable information (PII) from traversing the Internet helps maintain compliance with regulations such as HIPAA or PCI. With AWS PrivateLink you can confidentially share PII by connecting your AWS resources with AWS services or VPCs from third-party organizations. PII traffic between VPCs and AWS services doesn't traverse the Internet where it could become compromised. You can share your data offline over AWS PrivateLink and continue to enforce your regulatory compliance.

Securely access saas applications: SaaS providers are collecting data from their enterprise customers and using the data for log analysis, security scans, or performance management. SaaS providers will install agents or clients in their customers' VPCs to generate and send data back to the provider. When using SaaS applications, customers have to choose between allowing Internet access from their VPC, which puts the VPC resources at risk, and not using these applications at all. With AWS PrivateLink, you can connect your VPCs to AWS services and SaaS applications in a secure and scalable manner.

Migrate to hybrid cloud: Easily migrate services from on-premises locations to the AWS cloud. On-premises applications can connect to service endpoints in Amazon VPC over AWS Direct Connect or AWS VPN. Service endpoints will direct the traffic to AWS services over AWS PrivateLink, while keeping the network traffic within the AWS network. AWS PrivateLink enables SaaS providers to offer services that will look and feel like they are hosted directly on a private network. These services are securely accessible both from the cloud and from premises via AWS Direct Connect and AWS VPN, in a highly available and scalable manner.

Answer Q40. B
AWS Documentation Reference:
https://docs.aws.amazon.com/vpc/latest/userguide/vpc-network-acls.html
As a packet comes to the subnet, network ACL evaluate it against the ingress rules of the ACL the subnet is associated with (starting at the top of the list of rules, and moving to the bottom). Here's how the evaluation goes if the packet is destined for the SSL port (443). The packet doesn't match the first rule evaluated (rule 100). It does match the second rule (110), which allows the packet into the subnet.

Answer Q41. C
AWS Documentation Reference:
https://docs.aws.amazon.com/vpc/latest/userguide/vpc-network-acls.html
Each network ACL includes a default rule whose rule number is an asterisk. This rule ensures that if a packet doesn't match any of the other rules, it's denied. You can't modify or remove this rule. The packet had been destined for port 139 (NetBIOS), it doesn't match any of the rules, and the * rule ultimately denies the packet.

Answer Q42. A, B

AWS Documentation Reference:

https://docs.aws.amazon.com/vpc/latest/userguide/vpc-network-acls.html

To cover the different types of clients that might initiate traffic to public-facing instances in your VPC, you can open ephemeral ports 1024-65535. The client that initiates the request chooses the ephemeral port range. The range varies depending on the client's operating system. Many Linux kernels (including the Amazon Linux kernel) use ports 32768-61000. Requests originating from Elastic Load Balancing use ports 1024-65535. Windows operating systems through Windows Server 2003 use ports 1025-5000. Windows Server 2008 and later versions use ports 49152-65535. A NAT gateway uses ports 1024-65535. For example, if a request comes into a web server in your VPC from a Windows XP client on the Internet, your network ACL must have an outbound rule to enable traffic destined for ports 1025-5000.

If an instance in your VPC is the client initiating a request, your network ACL must have an inbound rule to enable traffic destined for the ephemeral ports specific to the type of instance (Amazon Linux, Windows Server 2008, and so on).

Answer Q43. C

AWS Documentation Reference:

https://docs.aws.amazon.com/vpc/latest/userguide/flow-logs.html

Flow logs can help you with a number of tasks; for example, to troubleshoot why specific traffic is not reaching an instance, which in turn helps you diagnose overly restrictive security group rules. You can also use flow logs as a security tool to monitor the traffic that is reaching your instance.

Answer Q44 A, B, C

AWS Documentation Reference:

https://docs.aws.amazon.com/vpc/latest/userguide/flow-logs.html

You can create a flow log for a VPC, a subnet, or a network interface. If you create a flow log for a subnet or VPC, each network interface in the VPC or subnet is monitored.

You can create flow logs for network interfaces that are created by other AWS services; for example, Elastic Load Balancing, Amazon RDS, Amazon ElastiCache, Amazon Redshift, and Amazon WorkSpaces.

Answer Q45. C, D

AWS Documentation Reference:

https://docs.aws.amazon.com/vpc/latest/userguide/flow-logs.html

Security groups are stateful — this means that responses to allowed traffic are also allowed, even if the rules in your security group do not permit it. Conversely, network ACLs are stateless, therefore responses to allowed traffic are subject to network ACL rules.

Your security group's inbound rules allow ICMP traffic and the outbound rules do not allow ICMP traffic; however, because security groups are stateful, the response ping from your instance is allowed. Your network ACL permits inbound ICMP traffic but does not permit

outbound ICMP traffic. Because network ACLs are stateless, the response ping is dropped and does not reach your home computer. In a flow log, this is displayed as two flow log records: An ACCEPT record for the originating ping that was allowed by both the network ACL and the security group, and therefore was allowed to reach your instance.
A REJECT record for the response ping that the network ACL denied.

Answer Q46. C, D
AWS Documentation Reference:
https://docs.aws.amazon.com/vpc/latest/userguide/flow-logs.html

Answer Q47.A
AWS Documentation Reference:
https://docs.aws.amazon.com/vpc/latest/userguide/flow-logs.html
Your security group denies inbound ICMP traffic, the flow log displays a single REJECT record, because the traffic was not permitted to reach your instance.

Answer Q48. A, C, D
AWS Documentation Reference:
https://docs.aws.amazon.com/vpc/latest/peering/what-is-vpc-peering.html

Answer Q49. B, C, D
AWS Documentation Reference:
https://docs.aws.amazon.com/vpc/latest/peering/what-is-vpc-peering.html

Answer Q50. E
AWS Documentation Reference:
https://docs.aws.amazon.com/vpc/latest/peering/what-is-vpc-peering.html

Answer Q51. A, B, C
AWS Documentation Reference: VPC Peering Basics
https://docs.aws.amazon.com/vpc/latest/peering/vpc-peering-basics.html
You will need to update the security group rules that are associated with your instance to ensure that traffic to and from the peer VPC is not restricted. If both VPCs are in the same region, you can reference a security group from the peer VPC as a source or destination for ingress or egress rules in your security group rules.

Answer Q52.B, C, D
AWS Documentation Reference: VPC Peering Limitations
https://docs.aws.amazon.com/vpc/latest/peering/vpc-peering-basics.html

Answer Q53. C
AWS Documentation Reference:

https://docs.aws.amazon.com/AWSEC2/latest/UserGuide/using-network-security.html
When multiple security groups are associated with an instance, the rules from each security group are effectively aggregated to create one set of rules. This aggregate set of rules is then used to determine whether to allow access.

## Answer Q54. A
AWS Documentation Reference:
https://docs.aws.amazon.com/AWSEC2/latest/UserGuide/using-network-security.html
When multiple security groups are associated with an instance, the rules from each security group are effectively aggregated to create one set of rules. This aggregate set of rules is then used to determine whether to allow access.
If there is more than one rule for a specific port, the most permissive rule is applied. Here you have a rule that allows access to TCP port 22 (SSH) from IP address 204.0.223.0/24 and another rule that allows access to TCP port 22 from everyone, hence everyone will have access to TCP port 22.

## Answer Q55. A, B
AWS Documentation Reference:
https://docs.aws.amazon.com/vpc/latest/userguide/VPC_Route_Tables.html
Each subnet in your VPC must be associated with a route table; the table controls the routing for the subnet. A subnet can only be associated with one route table at a time, but you can associate multiple subnets with the same route table.

## Answer Q56. B, C
AWS Documentation Reference:
https://docs.aws.amazon.com/vpc/latest/userguide/VPC_Route_Tables.html#RouteTableDetails

## Answer Q57. E
AWS Documentation Reference:
https://docs.aws.amazon.com/vpc/latest/userguide/VPC_Internet_Gateway.html

## Answer Q58. A, B
AWS Documentation Reference:
https://docs.aws.amazon.com/vpc/latest/userguide/VPC_Internet_Gateway.html
An internet gateway is a horizontally scaled, redundant, and highly available VPC component that allows communication between instances in your VPC and the internet. It therefore imposes no availability risks or bandwidth constraints on your network traffic.

An internet gateway serves two purposes: to provide a target in your VPC route tables for internet-routable traffic, and to perform network address translation (NAT) for instances that have been assigned public IPv4 addresses.

An internet gateway supports IPv4 and IPv6 traffic.

To use an internet gateway, your subnet's route table must contain a route that directs internet-bound traffic to the internet gateway. You can scope the route to all destinations not explicitly known to the route table (0.0.0.0/0 for IPv4 or :/0 for IPv6), or you can scope the route to a narrower range of IP addresses.

To enable access to or from the internet for instances in a VPC subnet, you must do the following:

- Attach an internet gateway to your VPC.

- Add a route to your subnet's route table that directs internet-bound traffic to the internet gateway. If a subnet is associated with a route table that has a route to an internet gateway, it's known as a public subnet. If a subnet is associated with a route table that does not have a route to an internet gateway, it's known as a private subnet.

- Ensure that instances in your subnet have a globally unique IP address (public IPv4 address, Elastic IP address, or IPv6 address).

- Ensure that your network access control lists and security group rules allow the relevant traffic to flow to and from your instance.

Answer Q59. B

AWS Documentation Reference:

https://docs.aws.amazon.com/vpc/latest/userguide/egress-only-internet-gateway.html

An egress-only Internet gateway is a horizontally scaled, redundant, and highly available VPC component that allows outbound communication over IPv6 from instances in your VPC to the Internet, and prevents the Internet from initiating an IPv6 connection with your instances.

Answer Q60. C, D

AWS Documentation Reference:

https://docs.aws.amazon.com/vpc/latest/userguide/vpc-nat-gateway.html
https://docs.aws.amazon.com/vpc/latest/userguide/VPC_NAT_Instance.html

You can use a network address translation (NAT) gateway to enable instances in a private subnet to connect to the internet or other AWS services, but prevent the internet from initiating a connection with those instances.

You can use a network address translation (NAT) instance in a public subnet in your VPC to enable instances in the private subnet to initiate outbound IPv4 traffic to the Internet or other AWS services, but prevent the instances from receiving inbound traffic initiated by someone on the Internet.

Answer Q61. A, C

AWS Documentation Reference:

https://docs.aws.amazon.com/vpc/latest/userguide/egress-only-internet-gateway.html

An egress-only Internet gateway is stateful: it forwards traffic from the instances in the subnet to the Internet or other AWS services, and then sends the response back to the instances.

Answer Q62. A, B, C
AWS Documentation Reference:
https://aws.amazon.com/blogs/security/how-to-record-ssh-sessions-established-through-a-bastion-host/

Answer Q63. A, C
B is not possible because you cannot create a VPC peering connection between VPCs with matching or overlapping IPv4 CIDR blocks.
AWS Documentation Reference: VPC
https://docs.aws.amazon.com/vpc/latest/peering/invalid-peering-configurations.html
Answer Q64. A, C
AWS Documentation Reference: VPC
https://docs.aws.amazon.com/vpc/latest/peering/invalid-peering-configurations.html
If the VPCs have multiple IPv4 CIDR blocks, you cannot create a VPC peering connection if any of the CIDR blocks overlap (regardless of whether you intend to use the VPC peering connection for communication between the non-overlapping CIDR blocks only).

Answer Q65. A, C
AWS Documentation Reference:
If you have an IPv4 address prefix in your VPC that overlaps with one of your networks' prefixes, any traffic to the network's prefix is dropped.
In the given scenario when instances in the VPC try to talk to hosts in the 10.0.37.0/24 address space, the traffic is dropped because 10.0.37.0/24 is part of the larger prefix assigned to the VPC (10.0.0.0/16). The instances can talk to hosts in the 10.1.38.0/24 space because that block isn't part of 10.0.0.0/16.

Answer Q66. A, B, C
AWS Documentation Reference:
https://docs.aws.amazon.com/vpc/latest/userguide/VPC_Scenario2.html
The configuration for this scenario includes a virtual private cloud (VPC) with a public subnet and a private subnet as shown below.

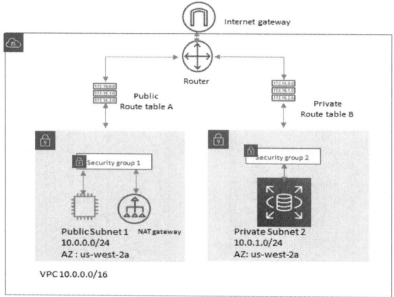

The web servers is in a public subnet and the database servers in a private subnet. You can set up security and routing so that the web servers can communicate with the database servers. The instances in the public subnet can send outbound traffic directly to the Internet, whereas the instances in the private subnet can't. Instead, the instances in the private subnet can access the Internet by using a network address translation (NAT) gateway that resides in the public subnet. The database servers can connect to the Internet for software updates using the NAT gateway, but the Internet cannot establish connections to the database servers.

The configuration for this scenario includes the following:

- A VPC with a size /16 IPv4 CIDR block (example: 10.0.0.0/16).
- A public subnet with a size /24 IPv4 CIDR block (example: 10.0.0.0/24)
- A private subnet with a size /24 IPv4 CIDR block (example: 10.0.1.0/24).
- An Internet gateway. This connects the VPC to the Internet and to other AWS services.
- Instances in the public subnet with Elastic IPv4 addresses, which are public IPv4 addresses that enable them to be reached from the Internet. The instances can have public IP addresses assigned at launch instead of Elastic IP addresses. Instances in the private subnet are back-end servers that don't need to accept incoming traffic from the Internet and therefore do not have public IP addresses; however, they can send requests to the Internet using the NAT gateway (see the next bullet).
- A NAT gateway with its own Elastic IPv4 address. Instances in the private subnet can send requests to the Internet through the NAT gateway over IPv4 (for example, for software updates).
- A custom route table' Public Route Table A' associated with the public subnet. This route table contains an entry that enables instances in the subnet to communicate with other

instances in the VPC over IPv4, and an entry that enables instances in the subnet to communicate directly with the Internet over IPv4.

- The main route table 'Private Route Table B' associated with the private subnet. The route table contains an entry that enables instances in the subnet to communicate with other instances in the VPC over IPv4, and an entry that enables instances in the subnet to communicate with the Internet through the NAT gateway over IPv4.

ROUTING:

DB Private Route Table B:

The first entry is the default entry for local routing in the VPC; this entry enables the instances in the VPC to communicate with each other. The second entry sends all other subnet traffic to the NAT gateway

| Destination | Target |
|---|---|
| 10.0.0.0/16 | Local |
| 0.0.0.0/0 | Nat-gw-id |

Web Server Public Route Table A:

The first entry is the default entry for local routing in the VPC; this entry enables the instances in this VPC to communicate with each other. The second entry routes all other subnet traffic to the Internet over the Internet gateway

| Destination | Target |
|---|---|
| 10.0.0.0/16 | Local |
| 0.0.0.0/0 | Igw-id |

SECURITY GROUPS:

Create the following security groups instead of using the default security group:
Web Server Security Group 1: Specify this security group when you launch the web servers in the public subnet. This allows the web servers to receive Internet traffic, as well as SSH traffic from your home network. The web servers can also initiate read and write requests to the database servers in the private subnet, and send traffic to the Internet; for example, to get software updates.
Inbound Table

| Source IP | Protocol | Port | Comments |
|---|---|---|---|
| 0.0.0.0/0 | TCP | 80 | HTTP access |
| 0.0.0.0/0 | TCP | 443 | HTTPS access |
| Home network IP address range | TCP | 22 | SSH access |

Outbound Table

| Source IP | Protocol | Port | Comments |
|---|---|---|---|
| ID of DB Security Group | TCP | 3306 | Access to DB servers in this SG |
| 0.0.0.0/0 | TCP | 443 | Outbound HTTPS access |
| 0.0.0.0/0 | TCP | 80 | Outbound HTTP access |

DB Server Security Group 2: Specify this security group when you launch the database servers in the private subnet. The following table describes the recommended rules for the security group, which allow read or write database requests from the web servers. The database servers can also initiate traffic bound for the Internet (the route table sends that traffic to the NAT gateway, which then forwards it to the Internet over the Internet gateway).

Inbound Table

| Source IP | Protocol | Port | Comments |
|---|---|---|---|
| Id of web server security group | TCP | 3306 | Allow inbound MySQL Server access from the web servers associated with the Web Server security group. |

Outbound table

| Source IP | Protocol | Port | Comments |
|---|---|---|---|
| 0.0.0.0/0 | TCP | 443 | Outbound HTTPS access |
| 0.0.0.0/0 | TCP | 80 | Outbound HTTP access |

Answer Q67. A, B, C
AWS Documentation Reference: Public IPv4 Addresses
https://docs.aws.amazon.com/vpc/latest/userguide/vpc-ip-addressing.html

A public IP address is assigned from Amazon's pool of public IP addresses; it's not associated with your account. When a public IP address is disassociated from your instance, it's released back into the pool, and is no longer available for you to use. You cannot manually associate or disassociate a public IP address. Instead, in certain cases, AWS releases the public IP address from your instance, or assign it a new one. If you require a persistent public IP address allocated to your account that can be assigned to and removed from instances as you require, use an Elastic IP address instead.

Answer Q68. B, C, D

AWS Documentation Reference:

https://aws.amazon.com/rds/faqs/

*How do I connect to an RDS DB Instance in VPC?*

DB Instances deployed within a VPC can be accessed by EC2 Instances deployed in the same VPC. If these EC2 Instances are deployed in a public subnet with associated Elastic IPs, you can access the EC2 Instances via the internet.

DB Instances deployed within a VPC can be accessed from the Internet or from EC2 Instances outside the VPC via VPN or bastion hosts that you can launch in your public subnet, or using Amazon RDS's Publicly Accessible option:

- To use a bastion host, you will need to set up a public subnet with an EC2 instance that acts as a SSH Bastion. This public subnet must have an internet gateway and routing rules that allow traffic to be directed via the SSH host, which must then forward requests to the private IP address of your RDS DB instance.

- To use public connectivity, simply create your DB Instances with the Publicly Accessible option set to yes. With Publicly Accessible active, your DB Instances within a VPC will be fully accessible outside your VPC by default. This means you do not need to configure a VPN or bastion host to allow access to your instances.

You can also set up a VPN Gateway that extends your corporate network into your VPC, and allows access to the RDS DB instance in that VPC.

Answer Q69. A, C

AWS Documentation Reference:

https://aws.amazon.com/vpn/faqs/

https://docs.aws.amazon.com/vpc/latest/userguide/vpc-nat.html

Instances without public IP addresses can access the internet in one of two ways:

1. Instances without public IP addresses can route their traffic through a network address translation (NAT) gateway or a NAT instance to access the internet. These instances use the public IP address of the NAT gateway or NAT instance to traverse the internet. The NAT gateway or NAT instance allows outbound communication but doesn't allow machines on the internet to initiate a connection to the privately addressed instances.

2. For Amazon VPCs with a Site-to-Site VPN connection or Direct Connect connection, instances can route their Internet traffic down the virtual private gateway to your existing datacenter. From there, it can access the Internet via your existing egress points and network security/monitoring devices.

Answer Q70.A, B, C

AWS Documentation Reference:

https://docs.aws.amazon.com/vpc/latest/userguide/vpc-nat.html

You can use a NAT device to enable instances in a private subnet to connect to the internet (for example, for software updates) or other AWS services, but prevent the internet from initiating connections with the instances. A NAT device forwards traffic from the instances in the private subnet to the internet or other AWS services, and then sends the response back to the instances. When traffic goes to the internet, the source IPv4 address is replaced with the NAT device's address and similarly, when the response traffic goes to those instances, the NAT device translates the address back to those instances' private IPv4 addresses.

NAT devices are not supported for IPv6 traffic—use an egress-only Internet gateway instead.

Answer Q71. C, D

AWS Documentation Reference:

https://docs.aws.amazon.com/vpc/latest/userguide/vpc-nat.html

Answer Q72. B, C, D

A is wrong.

Type and size: NAT Gateway: Uniform offering; you don't need to decide on the type or size. NAT instances: Choose a suitable instance type and size, according to your predicted workload.

AWS Documentation Reference:

https://docs.aws.amazon.com/vpc/latest/userguide/vpc-nat-comparison.html

Answer Q73. A, B, D, E

C, doesn't matter as NAT gateway is for providing internet access to instances in private subnet.

AWS Documentation Reference:

https://docs.aws.amazon.com/vpc/latest/userguide/nat-gateway-troubleshooting.html

Following checks needs to be done.

Check that the NAT gateway is in the Available state. If the NAT gateway is in a failed state, there may have been an error when it was created.

Check that you've configured your route tables correctly:

- The NAT gateway must be in a public subnet with a route table that routes internet traffic to an internet gateway.

- Your instance must be in a private subnet with a route table that routes internet traffic to the NAT gateway.
- Check that there are no other route table entries that route all or part of the internet traffic to another device instead of the NAT gateway.

Ensure that your security group rules for your private instance allow outbound internet traffic. For the ping command to work, the rules must also allow outbound ICMP traffic. The NAT gateway itself allows all outbound traffic and traffic received in response to an outbound request (it is therefore stateful).

Ensure that the network ACLs that are associated with the private subnet and public subnets do not have rules that block inbound or outbound internet traffic. For the ping command to work, the rules must also allow inbound and outbound ICMP traffic.

You can enable flow logs to help you diagnose dropped connections because of network ACL or security group rules.

If you are using the ping command, ensure that you are pinging a website that has ICMP enabled. If ICMP is not enabled, you will not receive reply packets. To test this, perform the same ping command from the command line terminal on your own computer.

Check that your instance is able to ping other resources, for example, other instances in the private subnet (assuming that security group rules allow this).

Ensure that your connection is using a TCP, UDP, or ICMP protocol only.

Answer Q74. C
AWS Documentation Reference: Disabling Source/Destination Checks
https://docs.aws.amazon.com/vpc/latest/userguide/VPC_NAT_Instance.html#EIP_Disable_SrcDestCheck
Each EC2 instance performs source/destination checks by default. This means that the instance must be the source or destination of any traffic it sends or receives. However, a NAT instance must be able to send and receive traffic when the source or destination is not itself. Therefore, you must disable source/destination checks on the NAT instance.

Answer Q75. A
A NAT instance can be used as a bastion server.

Answer Q76. A, B, C, E
AWS Documentation Reference:
https://docs.aws.amazon.com/vpc/latest/userguide/VPC_NAT_Instance.html

The configuration for this scenario includes a virtual private cloud (VPC) with a public subnet and a private subnet as shown below.

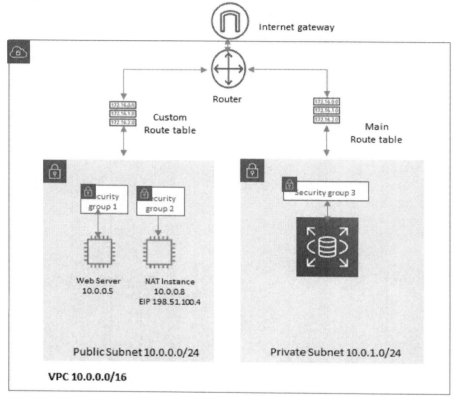

The web servers is in a public subnet and the database servers in a private subnet. You can set up security and routing so that the web servers can communicate with the database servers. The instances in the public subnet can send outbound traffic directly to the Internet, whereas the instances in the private subnet can't. Instead, the instances in the private subnet can access the Internet by using a network address translation (NAT) instance that resides in the public subnet. The database servers can connect to the Internet for software updates using the NAT instance, but the Internet cannot establish connections to the database servers.

The configuration for this scenario includes the following:

- A VPC with a size /16 IPv4 CIDR block (example: 10.0.0.0/16).
- A public subnet with a size /24 IPv4 CIDR block (example: 10.0.0.0/24)
- A private subnet with a size /24 IPv4 CIDR block (example: 10.0.1.0/24).
- An Internet gateway. This connects the VPC to the Internet and to other AWS services.

- Instances in the public subnet with Elastic IPv4 addresses, which are public IPv4 addresses that enable them to be reached from the Internet. The instances can have public IP addresses assigned at launch instead of Elastic IP addresses. Instances in the private subnet are back-end servers that don't need to accept incoming traffic from the Internet and therefore do not have public IP addresses; however, they can send requests to the Internet using the NAT instance (see the next bullet).
- A NAT instance with its own Elastic IPv4 address. Instances in the private subnet can send requests to the Internet through the NAT instance over IPv4 (for example, for software updates).
- A custom route table is associated with the public subnet. This route table contains an entry that enables instances in the subnet to communicate with other instances in the VPC over IPv4, and an entry that enables instances in the subnet to communicate directly with the Internet over IPv4.
- The main route table is associated with the private subnet. The route table contains an entry that enables instances in the subnet to communicate with other instances in the VPC over IPv4, and an entry that enables instances in the private subnet to communicate with the Internet through the NAT instance over IPv4.

ROUTING:
The main route table associated with database server private subnet is

| Destination | Target |
|---|---|
| 10.0.0.0/16 | Local |
| 0.0.0.0/0 | Nat-instance-id |

The first entry is the default entry for local routing in the VPC; this entry enables the instances in the VPC to communicate with each other. The second entry sends all other subnet traffic to the NAT instance.

The custom route table associated with web server and NAT instance in public subnet is

| Destination | Target |
|---|---|
| 10.0.0.0/16 | Local |
| 0.0.0.0/0 | Igw-id |

The first entry is the default entry for local routing in the VPC; this entry enables the instances in this VPC to communicate with each other. The second entry routes all other subnet traffic to the Internet over the Internet gateway

SECURITY GROUPS:

Create the following security groups instead of using the default security group:

Web Server Security Group 1: Specify this security group when you launch the web servers in the public subnet. This allows the web servers to receive Internet traffic, as well as SSH traffic from your home network. The web servers can also initiate read and write requests to the database servers in the private subnet, and send traffic to the Internet; for example, to get software updates.

Inbound Table

| Source IP | Protocol | Port | Comments |
|---|---|---|---|
| 0.0.0.0/0 | TCP | 80 | HTTP access |
| 0.0.0.0/0 | TCP | 443 | HTTPS access |
| Home network IP address range | TCP | 22 | SSH access |

Outbound Table

| Source IP | Protocol | Port | Comments |
|---|---|---|---|
| ID of DB Security Group | TCP | 3306 | Access to DB servers in this SG |
| 0.0.0.0/0 | TCP | 443 | Outbound HTTPS access |
| 0.0.0.0/0 | TCP | 80 | Outbound HTTP access |

NAT instance security group:

Define the NATSG security group as described in the following table to enable your NAT instance to receive Internet-bound traffic from instances in a private subnet, as well as SSH traffic from your network. The NAT instance can also send traffic to the Internet, which enables the instances in the private subnet to get software updates.

Inbound Table

| Source IP | Protocol | Port | Comments |
|---|---|---|---|
| 10.0.1.0/24 | TCP | 80 | Inbound HTTP access from private subnet server |
| 10.0.1.0/24 | TCP | 443 | Inbound HTTPS access from private subnet server |
| Home network IP address range | TCP | 22 | SSH access to NAT instance from home |

Outbound Table

| Source IP | Protocol | Port | Comments |
|-----------|----------|------|----------|
| 0.0.0.0/0 | TCP | 443 | Outbound HTTPS access to internet |
| 0.0.0.0/0 | TCP | 80 | Outbound HTTP access to internet |

DB Server Security Group 2: Specify this security group when you launch the database servers in the private subnet. The following table describes the recommended rules for the security group, which allow read or write database requests from the web servers. The database servers can also initiate traffic bound for the Internet (the route table sends that traffic to the NAT gateway, which then forwards it to the Internet over the Internet gateway).

NAT instance act as a bastion host in your public subnet to use as a proxy for SSH traffic from your home network to your private subnet, add a rule to the DB security group that allows inbound SSH or RDP traffic from the NAT instance or its associated security group.

Inbound Table

| Source IP | Protocol | Port | Comments |
|-----------|----------|------|----------|
| Id of web server security group | TCP | 3306 | Allow inbound MySQL Server access from the web servers associated with the Web Server security group. |
| 10.0.0.8 | TCP | 22 | allows inbound SSH traffic from the NAT instance acting as bastion instance |

Outbound table

| Source IP | Protocol | Port | Comments |
|-----------|----------|------|----------|
| 0.0.0.0/0 | TCP | 443 | Outbound HTTPS access |
| 0.0.0.0/0 | TCP | 80 | Outbound HTTP access |

Answer Q77.A, B
AWS Documentation Reference:
https://docs.aws.amazon.com/vpc/latest/userguide/VPC_Scenario4.html
The instances in your VPC subnet 3A can't reach the Internet directly; any Internet-bound traffic must first traverse the virtual private gateway to your network, where the traffic is then subject to your firewall and corporate security policies. If the instances send any AWS-bound traffic (for example, requests to Amazon S3 or Amazon EC2), the requests must go over the virtual private gateway to your network and then to the Internet before reaching AWS.

Answer Q78. A, C, D, E
AWS Documentation Reference:
https://docs.aws.amazon.com/vpc/latest/userguide/VPC_Internet_Gateway.html

To enable access to or from the internet for instances in a VPC subnet, you must do the following:

- Attach an internet gateway to your VPC.
- Ensure that your subnet's route table points to the internet gateway.
- Ensure that instances in your subnet have a globally unique IP address (public IPv4 address, Elastic IP address, or IPv6 address).
- Ensure that your network access control and security group rules allow the relevant traffic to flow to and from your instance.

Answer Q79. B
AWS Documentation Reference:
https://docs.aws.amazon.com/vpc/latest/userguide/vpc-nat-comparison.html
Most appropriate solution is to use NAT gateway instead of NAT instance. Its bandwidth can scale up to 45 Gbps and software is optimized for handling NAT traffic.

Answer Q80. B, C, E
A is not an answer as S3, Lambda, EC2, RDS are resources you place inside the VPC.
D is not an answer as these services are external to VPC.

Answer Q81. A, B
Limits for Amazon VPC resources per Region for your AWS account for number of VPC is 5.
You can request an increase for these limits using the Amazon VPC limits form.
When you create a VPC, you must specify an IPv4 CIDR block for the VPC. The allowed block size is between a /16 netmask (65,536 IP addresses) and /28 netmask (16 IP addresses).

Answer Q82. B, C, D
AWS Documentation Reference:
https://docs.aws.amazon.com/vpc/latest/userguide/what-is-amazon-vpc.html

Answer Q83. B
A is wrong as security group doesn't have option to create DENY rules.
C is wrong as this is an internet application you cannot move it private subnet.
D is wrong as internet gateway doesn't have option to create DENY rules.
AWS Documentation Reference:
https://docs.aws.amazon.com/vpc/latest/userguide/vpc-network-acls.html
A network access control list (ACL) is an optional layer of security for your VPC that acts as a firewall for controlling traffic in and out of one or more subnets. You might set up network ACLs with rules similar to your security groups in order to add an additional layer of security to your VPC. A network ACL has separate inbound and outbound rules, and each rule can either allow or deny traffic

https://docs.aws.amazon.com/vpc/latest/userguide/VPC_SecurityGroups.html

In a security group you can specify allow rules, but not deny rules.

Answer Q84. A, B
AWS Documentation Reference:
https://docs.aws.amazon.com/vpc/latest/peering/vpc-peering-routing.html
To send private IPv4 traffic from an instance in one VPC to an instance in a peer VPC, you must add a route to the route table that's associated with subnet in which instance resides. The route points to the CIDR block (or portion of the CIDR block) of the peer VPC in the VPC peering connection.

Answer Q85. D
AWS Documentation Reference:
https://docs.aws.amazon.com/vpc/latest/userguide/vpc-endpoints.html

Answer Q86.A, D
AWS Documentation Reference:
https://docs.aws.amazon.com/vpc/latest/userguide/vpc-endpoints.html
An interface endpoint is an elastic network interface with a private IP address from the IP address range of your subnet that serves as an entry point for traffic destined to a supported service.
A gateway endpoint is a gateway that you specify as a target for a route in your route table for traffic destined to a supported AWS service.

Answer Q87. A, B
AWS Documentation Reference: Gateway Endpoints
https://docs.aws.amazon.com/vpc/latest/userguide/vpc-endpoints.html

Answer Q88.A
AWS Documentation Reference:
https://docs.aws.amazon.com/vpc/latest/peering/vpc-peering-routing.html
https://docs.aws.amazon.com/vpc/latest/peering/peering-configurations-full-access.html
To send private IPv4 traffic from an instance in one VPC to an instance in a peer VPC, you must add a route to the route table that's associated with subnet in which instance resides. The route points to the CIDR block (or portion of the CIDR block) of the peer VPC in the VPC peering connection.
The owner of the other VPC in the peering connection must also add a route to their subnet's route table to direct traffic back to your VPC. The route tables for each VPC point to the relevant VPC peering connection to access the entire CIDR block of the peer VPC.
There has to be entry in the route table of both the VPCs.

Answer Q89. B
A, C are wrong because transitive peering connection is not supported.

AWS Documentation Reference: Three VPCs Peered Together

https://docs.aws.amazon.com/vpc/latest/peering/peering-configurations-full-access.html

Answer Q90. C

Transitive peering connection is not supported, so you have to calculate possible number of unique pairs possible. The mathematical formula is. C (n, 2). Here n =7.

$7!/(5!)(2!)$

$(7*6*5*4*3*2*1)/( (5*4*3*2*1)( 2*1)$

$(7*6)/(2*1)$

21

Answer Q91. A, B

AWS Documentation Reference: Edge to Edge Routing Through a Gateway or Private Connection

https://docs.aws.amazon.com/vpc/latest/peering/invalid-peering-configurations.html

If either VPC in a peering relationship has one of the following connections, you cannot extend the peering relationship to that connection:

- A VPN connection or an AWS Direct Connect connection to a corporate network
- An internet connection through an internet gateway
- An internet connection in a private subnet through a NAT device
- A VPC endpoint to an AWS service; for example, an endpoint to Amazon S3.
- (IPv6) A ClassicLink connection. You can enable IPv4 communication between a linked EC2-Classic instance and instances in a VPC on the other side of a VPC peering connection. However, IPv6 is not supported in EC2-Classic, so you cannot extend this connection for IPv6 communication.

Answer Q92. A, B, D

AWS Documentation Reference: Interface Endpoints

https://docs.aws.amazon.com/vpc/latest/userguide/vpc-endpoints.html

Answer Q93. B, C

Edge to edge routing is not supported.

AWS Documentation Reference: Edge to Edge Routing Through a Gateway or Private Connection

https://docs.aws.amazon.com/vpc/latest/peering/invalid-peering-configurations.html

Answer Q94. B, C

Edge to edge routing is not supported.

AWS Documentation Reference: Edge to Edge Routing Through a Gateway or Private Connection

https://docs.aws.amazon.com/vpc/latest/peering/invalid-peering-configurations.html

Answer Q95. A, D
Edge to edge routing is not supported.
AWS Documentation Reference: Edge to Edge Routing Through a Gateway or Private Connection
https://docs.aws.amazon.com/vpc/latest/peering/invalid-peering-configurations.html

Answer Q96. B
Using VPC Endpoints for S3 calls is the solution. There is no additional charge for using endpoints.
AWS Documentation Reference:
https://docs.aws.amazon.com/vpc/latest/userguide/vpce-gateway.html
A VPC endpoint enables you to privately connect your VPC to supported AWS services and VPC endpoint services powered by PrivateLink without requiring an internet gateway, NAT device, VPN connection, or AWS Direct Connect connection. Instances in your VPC do not require public IP addresses to communicate with resources in the service. Traffic between your VPC and the other service does not leave the Amazon network.

Answer Q97. B, C, D
AWS Documentation Reference:
https://docs.aws.amazon.com/vpc/latest/userguide/VPC_Route_Tables.html#route-tables-priority
AWS uses the most specific route in your route table that matches the traffic to determine how to route the traffic (longest prefix match).
In the given example, the VPC A subnet route table has a route for IPv4 internet traffic (0.0.0.0/0) that points to an internet gateway, and a route for 172.31.0.0/16 IPv4 traffic that points to a peering connection (pcx-11223344556677889). Any traffic from the subnet that's destined for the 172.31.0.0/16 IP address range uses the peering connection, because this route is more specific than the route for internet gateway. Any traffic destined for a target within the VPC (10.0.0.0/16) is covered by the Local route, and therefore is routed within the VPC. All other traffic from the subnet uses the internet gateway.

Answer Q98. D
Using VPC Endpoints for DynamoDB calls is the solution. There is no additional charge for using endpoints.
AWS Documentation Reference:
https://docs.aws.amazon.com/vpc/latest/userguide/vpce-gateway.html
A VPC endpoint enables you to privately connect your VPC to supported AWS services and VPC endpoint services powered by PrivateLink without requiring an internet gateway, NAT device, VPN connection, or AWS Direct Connect connection. Instances in your VPC do not require public IP addresses to communicate with resources in the service. Traffic between your VPC and the other service does not leave the Amazon network.

Answer Q99. B

AWS Documentation Reference: Peering Two or More VPCs to Provide Full Access to Resources

https://docs.aws.amazon.com/vpc/latest/peering/peering-scenarios.html

Answer Q100. B

AWS Documentation Reference: Peering Two or More VPCs to Provide Full Access to Resources

https://docs.aws.amazon.com/vpc/latest/peering/peering-scenarios.html

Answer Q101. B, C, D

AWS Documentation Reference:

https://docs.aws.amazon.com/vpn/latest/s2svpn/how_it_works.html

Answer Q102. B

AWS Documentation Reference:

https://docs.aws.amazon.com/vpn/latest/s2svpn/how_it_works.html

A virtual private gateway is the VPN concentrator on the Amazon side of the Site-to-Site VPN connection. You create a virtual private gateway and attach it to the VPC from which you want to create the Site-to-Site VPN connection.

Answer Q103. D

AWS Documentation Reference:

https://docs.aws.amazon.com/vpn/latest/s2svpn/how_it_works.html

A customer gateway is a resource in AWS that provides information to AWS about your Customer Gateway Device. To use Amazon VPC with a Site-to-Site VPN connection, you or your network administrator must also configure the customer gateway device or application in your remote network.

Answer Q104. C

AWS Documentation Reference:

https://docs.aws.amazon.com/vpn/latest/s2svpn/how_it_works.html

A transit gateway is a transit hub that you can use to interconnect your virtual private clouds (VPC) and on-premises networks.

Answer Q105. D

Site-to-Site VPN supports Internet Protocol security (IPsec) VPN connections.

Answer Q106. B

A Site-to-Site VPN connection offers two VPN tunnels between a virtual private gateway or transit gateway on the AWS side and a customer gateway on the remote (customer) side.

Answer Q107. D

AWS Documentation Reference:

https://aws.amazon.com/transit-gateway/

AWS Transit Gateway is a service that enables customers to connect their Amazon Virtual Private Clouds (VPCs) and their on-premises networks to a single gateway. As you grow the number of workloads running on AWS, you need to be able to scale your networks across multiple accounts and Amazon VPCs to keep up with the growth.

With AWS Transit Gateway, you only have to create and manage a single connection from the central gateway in to each Amazon VPC, on-premises data center, or remote office across your network. Transit Gateway acts as a hub that controls how traffic is routed among all the connected networks which act like spokes. This hub and spoke model significantly simplifies management and reduces operational costs because each network only has to connect to the Transit Gateway and not to every other network. Any new VPC is simply connected to the Transit Gateway and is then automatically available to every other network that is connected to the Transit Gateway. This ease of connectivity makes it easy to scale your network as you grow.

Answer Q108. D

AWS Documentation Reference:

https://docs.aws.amazon.com/vpc/latest/userguide/flow-logs-cwl.html#process-records-cwl

VPC Flow Logs is a feature that enables you to capture information about the IP traffic going to and from network interfaces in your VPC. Flow logs can publish flow log data directly to Amazon CloudWatch.

In this example, you have a flow log for VPC. You want to create an alarm that alerts you if there have been 10 or more rejected attempts to connect to your instance over TCP port 22 (SSH) within a 1-hour time period. First, you must create a metric filter that matches the pattern of the traffic for which to create the alarm. Then, you can create an alarm for the metric filter.

https://docs.aws.amazon.com/vpc/latest/userguide/flow-logs.html

https://docs.aws.amazon.com/vpc/latest/userguide/flow-logs-cwl.html

Q109. A

AWS Documentation Reference:

https://docs.aws.amazon.com/vpc/latest/userguide/egress-only-internet-gateway.html

IPv6 addresses are globally unique, and are therefore public by default. If you want your instance to be able to access the Internet, but you want to prevent resources on the Internet from initiating communication with your instance, you can use an egress-only Internet gateway. To do this, create an egress-only Internet gateway in your VPC, and then add a route to your route table that points all IPv6 traffic (::/0) or a specific range of IPv6 address to the egress-only Internet gateway. IPv6 traffic in the subnet that's associated with the route table is routed to the egress-only Internet gateway.

An egress-only Internet gateway is a horizontally scaled, redundant, and highly available VPC component that allows outbound communication over IPv6 from instances in your VPC to the Internet, and prevents the Internet from initiating an IPv6 connection with your instances. An egress-only Internet gateway is stateful: it forwards traffic from the instances in the subnet to the Internet or other AWS services, and then sends the response back to the instances.

NAT Gateway and NAT Instance though used for providing private subnet access to internet doesn't support IPv6 traffic.

## Q110. A, B, C
Subnet is not created by default when you create a custom VPC.

## Q111. A, B, C
Elb doesn't directly improves the performance of servers.
AWS Documentation Reference:
https://docs.aws.amazon.com/elasticloadbalancing/latest/userguide/what-is-load-balancing.html
A load balancer distributes workloads across multiple compute resources, such as virtual servers. Using a load balancer increases the availability and fault tolerance of your applications.
You can add and remove compute resources from your load balancer as your needs change, without disrupting the overall flow of requests to your applications.
You can configure health checks, which are used to monitor the health of the compute resources so that the load balancer can send requests only to the healthy ones. You can also offload the work of encryption and decryption to your load balancer so that your compute resources can focus on their main work.
Use Amazon Virtual Private Cloud (Amazon VPC) to create and manage security groups associated with load balancers to provide additional networking and security options. You can also create an internal (non-internet-facing) load balancer.
Elastic Load Balancing provides integrated certificate management and SSL/TLS decryption, allowing you the flexibility to centrally manage the SSL settings of the load balancer and offload CPU intensive work from your application.

## Q112. A, C, D
AWS Documentation Reference:
https://docs.aws.amazon.com/elasticloadbalancing/latest/userguide/what-is-load-balancing.html

## Q113. A
AWS Documentation Reference: Product comparisons
https://aws.amazon.com/elasticloadbalancing/features/?nc=sn&loc=2

## Q114. B
AWS Documentation Reference: Product comparisons

https://aws.amazon.com/elasticloadbalancing/features/?nc=sn&loc=2

Q115. C
AWS Documentation Reference: Product comparisons
https://aws.amazon.com/elasticloadbalancing/features/?nc=sn&loc=2

Q116. A

Q117.C

Q118.D

Q119. A

Q120. B, C
AWS Documentation Reference: Cross-Zone Load Balancing
https://docs.aws.amazon.com/elasticloadbalancing/latest/userguide/how-elastic-load-balancing-works.html
When you enable an Availability Zone for your load balancer, Elastic Load Balancing creates a load balancer node in the Availability Zone. The nodes for your load balancer distribute requests from clients to registered targets. When cross-zone load balancing is enabled, each load balancer node distributes traffic across the registered targets in all enabled Availability Zones. When cross-zone load balancing is disabled, each load balancer node distributes traffic across the registered targets in its Availability Zone only.

Q121. B
AWS Documentation Reference: Cross-Zone Load Balancing
https://docs.aws.amazon.com/elasticloadbalancing/latest/userguide/how-elastic-load-balancing-works.html
When you enable an Availability Zone for your load balancer, Elastic Load Balancing creates a load balancer node in the Availability Zone. The nodes for your load balancer distribute requests from clients to registered targets. When cross-zone load balancing is enabled, each load balancer node distributes traffic across the registered targets in all enabled Availability Zones. When cross-zone load balancing is disabled, each load balancer node distributes traffic only across the registered targets in its Availability Zone.
There are two enabled Availability Zones, with 2 targets in Availability Zone A and 8 targets in Availability Zone B. Clients send requests, and Amazon Route 53 responds to each request with the IP address of one of the load balancer nodes. This distributes traffic such that each load balancer node receives 50% of the traffic from the clients. Each load balancer node distributes its share of the traffic across the registered targets in its scope.
If cross-zone load balancing is enabled, each of the 10 targets receives 10% of the traffic. This is because each load balancer node can route its 50% of the client traffic to all 10 targets.

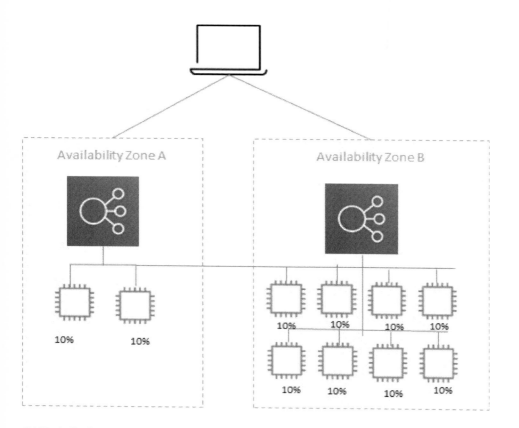

Q122. A, B, C
AWS Documentation Reference: Application Load Balancer Components
https://docs.aws.amazon.com/elasticloadbalancing/latest/application/introduction.html
A load balancer serves as the single point of contact for clients. The load balancer distributes incoming application traffic across multiple targets, such as EC2 instances, in multiple Availability Zones. This increases the availability of your application. You add one or more listeners to your load balancer.

A listener checks for connection requests from clients, using the protocol and port that you configure. The rules that you define for a listener determine how the load balancer routes requests to its registered targets. Each rule consists of a priority, one or more actions, and one or more conditions. When the conditions for a rule are met, then its actions are performed. You must define a default rule for each listener, and you can optionally define additional rules.

Each target group routes requests to one or more registered targets, such as EC2 instances, using the protocol and port number that you specify. You can register a target with multiple target groups. You can configure health checks on a per target group basis. Health checks are performed on all targets registered to a target group that is specified in a listener rule for your load balancer.

## Q123. A, B, D
AWS Documentation Reference: Load Balancer Scheme
https://docs.aws.amazon.com/elasticloadbalancing/latest/userguide/how-elastic-load-balancing-works.html#request-routing

Before a client sends a request to your load balancer, it resolves the load balancer's domain name using a Domain Name System (DNS) server. The DNS entry is controlled by Amazon, because your load balancers are in the amazonaws.com domain. The Amazon DNS servers return one or more IP addresses to the client. These are the IP addresses of the load balancer nodes for your load balancer. When you enable an Availability Zone for your load balancer, Elastic Load Balancing creates a load balancer node in the Availability Zone.

With Network Load Balancers, Elastic Load Balancing creates a network interface for each Availability Zone that you enable. Each load balancer node in the Availability Zone uses this network interface to get a static IP address. You can optionally associate one Elastic IP address with each network interface when you create the load balancer.

When you create a load balancer, you must choose whether to make it an internal load balancer or an Internet-facing load balancer. The nodes of an Internet-facing load balancer have public IP addresses. The DNS name of an Internet-facing load balancer is publicly resolvable to the public IP addresses of the nodes. Therefore, Internet-facing load balancers can route requests from clients over the Internet.

The nodes of an internal load balancer have only private IP addresses. The DNS name of an internal load balancer is publicly resolvable to the private IP addresses of the nodes. Therefore, internal load balancers can only route requests from clients with access to the VPC for the load balancer.

Both internet-facing and internal load balancers route requests to your targets using private IP addresses. Therefore, your targets do not need public IP addresses to receive requests from an internal or an internet-facing load balancer.

## Q124. C
AWS Documentation Reference: Cross-Zone Load Balancing
https://docs.aws.amazon.com/elasticloadbalancing/latest/userguide/how-elastic-load-balancing-works.html

When you enable an Availability Zone for your load balancer, Elastic Load Balancing creates a load balancer node in the Availability Zone. The nodes for your load balancer distribute requests from clients to registered targets. When cross-zone load balancing is enabled, each load balancer node distributes traffic across the registered targets in all enabled Availability

Zones. When cross-zone load balancing is disabled, each load balancer node distributes traffic only across the registered targets in its Availability Zone.

There are two enabled Availability Zones, with 2 targets in Availability Zone A and 8 targets in Availability Zone B. Clients send requests, and Amazon Route 53 responds to each request with the IP address of one of the load balancer nodes. This distributes traffic such that each load balancer node receives 50% of the traffic from the clients. Each load balancer node distributes its share of the traffic across the registered targets in its scope.

If cross-zone load balancing is disabled, each of the 2 targets in Availability Zone A receives 25% of the traffic and each of the 8 targets in Availability Zone B receives 6.25% of the traffic. This is because each load balancer node can route its 50% of the client traffic only to targets in its Availability Zone.

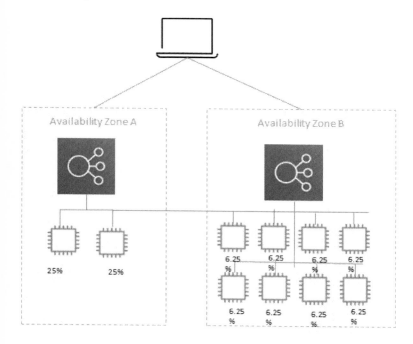

Q125. B, C, D

AWS Documentation Reference: Load Balancer Scheme

https://docs.aws.amazon.com/elasticloadbalancing/latest/userguide/how-elastic-load-balancing-works.html#request-routing

When you create a load balancer, you must choose whether to make it an internal load balancer or an Internet-facing load balancer. The nodes of an internal load balancer have only private IP addresses. The DNS name of an internal load balancer is publicly resolvable to the private IP addresses of the nodes. Therefore, internal load balancers can only route requests from clients with access to the VPC for the load balancer.

## Q126. D
AWS Documentation Reference:
https://aws.amazon.com/elasticloadbalancing/faqs/
*How do I decide which load balancer to select for my application?*
Elastic Load Balancing supports three types of load balancers. You can select the appropriate load balancer based on your application needs. If you need to load balance HTTP requests, AWS recommend you to use Application Load Balancer. For network/transport protocols (layer4 – TCP, UDP) load balancing, and for extreme performance/low latency applications AWS recommend using Network Load Balancer. If your application is built within the EC2 Classic network then you should use Classic Load Balancer.

## Q127. B, C
AWS Documentation Reference: Load Balancer Scheme
https://docs.aws.amazon.com/elasticloadbalancing/latest/userguide/how-elastic-load-balancing-works.html#request-routing
Both Internet-facing and internal load balancers route requests to your targets using private IP addresses. Therefore, your targets do not need public IP addresses to receive requests from an internal or an Internet-facing load balancer.

## Q128. A, B
AWS Documentation Reference: Load Balancer Scheme
https://docs.aws.amazon.com/elasticloadbalancing/latest/userguide/how-elastic-load-balancing-works.html#request-routing
If your application has multiple tiers, for example web servers that must be connected to the Internet and database servers that are only connected to the web servers, you can design an architecture that uses both internal and Internet-facing load balancers. Create an Internet-facing load balancer and register the web servers with it. Create an internal load balancer and register the database servers with it. The web servers receive requests from the Internet-facing load balancer and send requests for the database servers to the internal load balancer. The database servers receive requests from the internal load balancer.

## Q129. D
AWS Documentation Reference: Benefits of Migrating from a Classic Load Balancer
https://docs.aws.amazon.com/elasticloadbalancing/latest/application/introduction.html

## Q130. C, D
AWS Documentation Reference: Subnets for Your Load Balancer
https://docs.aws.amazon.com/elasticloadbalancing/latest/application/application-load-balancers.html

When you create a load balancer, you must specify one public subnet from at least two Availability Zones. You can specify only one public subnet per Availability Zone.

To ensure that your load balancer can scale properly, verify that each subnet for your load balancer has a CIDR block with at least a /27 bitmask (for example, 10.0.0.0/27) and has at least 8 free IP addresses. Your load balancer uses these IP addresses to establish connections with the targets.

### Q131. A, B, D

For target type, you can select Instance to register targets by instance ID, IP to register IP addresses, and Lambda function to register a Lambda function

### Q132. B, C

AWS Documentation Reference:

https://docs.aws.amazon.com/elasticloadbalancing/latest/application/load-balancer-subnets.html

You can enable or disable the Availability Zones for your load balancer at any time. After you enable an Availability Zone, the load balancer starts routing requests to the registered targets in that Availability Zone. After you disable an Availability Zone, the targets in that Availability Zone remain registered with the load balancer, but the load balancer will not route requests to them.

### Q133. A, C, D

AWS Documentation Reference:

https://docs.aws.amazon.com/elasticloadbalancing/latest/application/load-balancer-listeners.html

Before you start using your Application Load Balancer, you must add one or more listeners. A listener is a process that checks for connection requests, using the protocol and port that you configure. The rules that you define for a listener determine how the load balancer routes requests to the targets in one or more target groups.

### Q134. A, B

### Q135. C, D

### Q136. A

AWS Documentation Reference:

https://docs.aws.amazon.com/elasticloadbalancing/latest/application/load-balancer-target-groups.html

Each target group is used to route requests to one or more registered targets. When you create each listener rule, you specify a target group and conditions. When a rule condition is met, traffic is forwarded to the corresponding target group. You can create different target groups for different types of requests.

Q137. B, C, D

AWS Documentation Reference: Target Type

https://docs.aws.amazon.com/elasticloadbalancing/latest/application/load-balancer-target-groups.html

When the target type is ip, you can specify IP addresses from one of the following CIDR blocks:

- The subnets of the VPC for the target group
- 10.0.0.0/8 (RFC 1918)
- 100.64.0.0/10 (RFC 6598)
- 172.16.0.0/12 (RFC 1918)
- 192.168.0.0/16 (RFC 1918)

You can't specify publicly routable IP addresses.

Q138. B

AWS Documentation Reference: Sticky Sessions

https://docs.aws.amazon.com/elasticloadbalancing/latest/application/load-balancer-target-groups.html

Sticky sessions are a mechanism to route requests to the same target in a target group. This is useful for servers that maintain state information in order to provide a continuous experience to clients. To use sticky sessions, the clients must support cookies. When a load balancer first receives a request from a client, it routes the request to a target, generates a cookie named AWSALB that encodes information about the selected target, encrypts the cookie, and includes the cookie in the response to the client. The client should include the cookie that it receives in subsequent requests to the load balancer. When the load balancer receives a request from a client that contains the cookie, if sticky sessions are enabled for the target group and the request goes to the same target group, the load balancer detects the cookie and routes the request to the same target.

Q139. C

AWS Documentation Reference:

https://aws.amazon.com/about-aws/whats-new/2014/03/20/elastic-load-balancing-supports-connection-draining/

https://aws.amazon.com/blogs/aws/elb-connection-draining-remove-instances-from-service-with-care/

When you enable Connection Draining on a load balancer, any back-end instances that you deregister will complete requests that are in progress before deregistration. Likewise, if a back-end instance fails health checks, the load balancer will not send any new requests to the unhealthy instance but will allow existing requests to complete.

This means that you can perform maintenance such as deploying software upgrades or replacing back-end instances without impacting your customers' experience.

Connection Draining is also integrated with Auto Scaling, making it even easier to manage the capacity behind your load balancer. When Connection Draining is enabled, Auto Scaling will wait for outstanding requests to complete before terminating instances.

Q140. A

AWS Documentation Reference:

https://docs.aws.amazon.com/elasticloadbalancing/latest/application/target-group-health-checks.html

Your Application Load Balancer periodically sends requests to its registered targets to test their status. These tests are called health checks.

Q141. A, C, D

AWS Documentation Reference:

https://docs.aws.amazon.com/elasticloadbalancing/latest/application/target-group-health-checks.html

Each load balancer node routes requests only to the healthy targets in the enabled Availability Zones for the load balancer. Each load balancer node checks the health of each target, using the health check settings for the target groups with which the target is registered. After your target is registered, it must pass one health check to be considered healthy. After each health check is completed, the load balancer node closes the connection that was established for the health check.

If a target group contains only unhealthy registered targets, the load balancer nodes route requests across its unhealthy targets.

Health checks do not support WebSockets.

Q142.A, B, C

AWS Documentation Reference:

https://docs.aws.amazon.com/elasticloadbalancing/latest/application/load-balancer-listeners.html#listener-rules

Each listener has a default rule, and you can optionally define additional rules. Each rule consists of a priority, one or more actions, and one or more conditions. When you create a listener, you define actions for the default rule. Default rules can't have conditions. If the conditions for none of a listener's rules are met, then the action for the default rule is performed. Each rule has a priority. Rules are evaluated in priority order, from the lowest value to the highest value. The default rule is evaluated last. You can change the priority of a nondefault rule at any time. You cannot change the priority of the default rule.

Q143. D

You can use application load balancers for your containers as well as micro services. Load balancers gives you better availability and fault tolerance of your application instances.

Q144. E

AWS Documentation Reference: A registered target is not in service

https://docs.aws.amazon.com/elasticloadbalancing/latest/application/load-balancer-troubleshooting.html

If a target is taking longer than expected to enter the InService state, it might be failing health checks. Your target is not in service until it passes one health check.

A: The security group associated with an instance must allow traffic from the load balancer using the health check port and health check protocol. You can add a rule to the instance security group to allow all traffic from the load balancer security group. Also, the security group for your load balancer must allow traffic to the instances.

B: The network ACL associated with the subnets for your instances must allow inbound traffic on the health check port and outbound traffic on the ephemeral ports (1024-65535). The network ACL associated with the subnets for your load balancer nodes must allow inbound traffic on the ephemeral ports and outbound traffic on the health check and ephemeral ports.

C: If the availability zone C is not enabled for the load balancer, request will not be routed to new instances.

D: Create a target page for the health check and specify its path as the ping path.

Q145. B, C, D

AWS Documentation Reference: Clients cannot connect to an Internet-facing load balancer

https://docs.aws.amazon.com/elasticloadbalancing/latest/application/load-balancer-troubleshooting.html

If the load balancer is not responding to requests, check for the following:

- Your Internet-facing load balancer is attached to a private subnet: Verify that you specified public subnets for your load balancer. A public subnet has a route to the Internet Gateway for your virtual private cloud (VPC).

- A security group or network ACL does not allow traffic: The security group for the load balancer and any network ACLs for the load balancer subnets must allow inbound traffic from the clients and outbound traffic to the clients on the listener ports.

- Internet facing load balancer has to be attached to a public subnet.

Q146. A, C

Q147. D

Q148. E

AWS Documentation Reference: Benefits of Migrating from a Classic Load Balancer

https://docs.aws.amazon.com/elasticloadbalancing/latest/network/introduction.html

Q149. A, B

AWS Documentation Reference: Listener Configuration

https://docs.aws.amazon.com/elasticloadbalancing/latest/network/load-balancer-listeners.html

Q150. A, B

AWS Documentation Reference: Target Type

https://docs.aws.amazon.com/elasticloadbalancing/latest/network/load-balancer-target-groups.html

Q151. B

AWS Documentation Reference: Source IP Preservation

https://docs.aws.amazon.com/elasticloadbalancing/latest/network/load-balancer-target-groups.html

If you specify targets using an instance ID, the source IP addresses of the clients are preserved and provided to your applications.

Q152. A

AWS Documentation Reference: Source IP Preservation

https://docs.aws.amazon.com/elasticloadbalancing/latest/network/load-balancer-target-groups.html

If you specify targets by IP address, the source IP addresses are the private IP addresses of the load balancer nodes. If you need the IP addresses of the clients, enable Proxy Protocol and get the client IP addresses from the Proxy Protocol header.

Q153. A, B

AWS Documentation Reference:

https://aws.amazon.com/blogs/aws/new-application-load-balancer-sni/

https://aws.amazon.com/premiumsupport/knowledge-center/acm-add-domain-certificates-elb/

To add multiple certificates for different domains to a load balancer, do one of the following:

- Use a Subject Alternative Name (SAN) certificate to validate multiple domains behind the load balancer, including wildcard domains, with AWS Certificate Manager (ACM).
- Use an Application Load Balancer (ALB), which supports multiple SSL certificates and smart certificate selection using Server Name Indication (SNI).

The Subject Alternative Name (SAN) is an extension to the X.509 specification that allows users to specify additional host names for a single SSL certificate.

SNI stands for Server Name Indication. It is an extension of the TLS protocol. It denotes which domain name the browser is trying to connect at the beginning of the handshake process. This technology allows a server to present multiple SSL Certificates to one IP address and port. Hence allows multiple secure (HTTPS) websites (or any other service over TLS) to be served by the same IP address without requiring all those sites to use the same certificate.

SNI is automatically enabled when you associate more than one TLS certificate with the same secure listener on an application load balancer. Similarly, SNI mode for a secure listener is automatically disabled when you have only one certificate associated to a secure listener.

Q154. A, B, C

A allows inbound traffic on the load balancer listener port.

B Allow outbound traffic to instances on the instance listener port.

C Allow traffic from the load balancer on the instance listener port.

D is not required as by default as security group is stateful and will allow outbound traffic to ELB.

AWS Documentation Reference:

https://docs.aws.amazon.com/AWSEC2/latest/UserGuide/security-group-rules-reference.html

https://docs.aws.amazon.com/elasticloadbalancing/latest/application/load-balancer-update-security-groups.html

Q155. B, C, D

A is wrong as it allows inbound traffic on the load balancer listener port from internet.

B allows inbound traffic originating within the servers in VPC.

C allows outbound traffic to instances on the instance listener port.

D allows traffic from the load balancer on the instance listener port.

E is not required as by default as security group is stateful and will allow outbound traffic to ELB.

AWS Documentation Reference:

https://docs.aws.amazon.com/AWSEC2/latest/UserGuide/security-group-rules-reference.html

https://docs.aws.amazon.com/elasticloadbalancing/latest/application/load-balancer-update-security-groups.html

Q156. B

For network/transport protocols (layer4 – TCP, UDP) load balancing, and for extreme performance/low latency applications AWS recommends using Network Load Balancer.

Q157.C

AWS Documentation Reference:

https://docs.aws.amazon.com/elasticloadbalancing/latest/application/load-balancer-listeners.html#listener-rules

Each listener rule action has a type, an order, and the information required to perform the action. The following are supported action types for a rule:

- Authenticate-cognito: [HTTPS listeners] Use Amazon Cognito to authenticate users.
- Authenticate-oidc: [HTTPS listeners] Use an identity provider that is compliant with OpenID Connect (OIDC) to authenticate users.

- Fixed-response: Return a custom HTTP response.
- Forward: Forward requests to the specified target groups.
- Redirect: Redirect requests from one URL to another.

## Q158.D
AWS Documentation Reference:

https://docs.aws.amazon.com/elasticloadbalancing/latest/application/load-balancer-listeners.html#listener-rules

The following are the supported condition types for a rule:

- Host-header: Route based on the host name of each request. For more information, see Host Conditions.
- Http-header: Route based on the HTTP headers for each request.
- Http-request-method: Route based on the HTTP request method of each request.
- Path-pattern: Route based on path patterns in the request URLs.
- Query-string: Route based on key/value pairs or values in the query strings.
- Source-ip: Route based on the source IP address of each request.

## Q159. B
AWS Documentation Reference:

https://docs.aws.amazon.com/elasticloadbalancing/latest/application/application-load-balancers.html#connection-idle-timeout

For each request that a client makes through a load balancer, the load balancer maintains two connections. A front-end connection is between a client and the load balancer, and a back-end connection is between the load balancer and a target. The load balancer manages an idle timeout that is triggered when no data is sent over a front-end connection for a specified time period. If no data has been sent or received by the time that the idle timeout period elapses, the load balancer closes the connection.

## Q160. B
AWS Documentation Reference:

https://aws.amazon.com/about-aws/whats-new/2014/03/20/elastic-load-balancing-supports-connection-draining/

https://docs.aws.amazon.com/autoscaling/ec2/userguide/attach-load-balancer-asg.html

https://docs.aws.amazon.com/elasticloadbalancing/latest/classic/config-conn-drain.html

When you enable Connection Draining on a load balancer, any back-end instances that you deregister will complete requests that are in progress before deregistration. Likewise, if a back-end instance fails health checks, the load balancer will not send any new requests to the unhealthy instance but will allow existing requests to complete. This means that you can perform maintenance such as deploying software upgrades or replacing back-end instances without impacting your customers' experience. Connection Draining is also integrated with Auto Scaling, making it even easier to manage the capacity behind your load balancer. When

Connection Draining is enabled, Auto Scaling will wait for outstanding requests to complete before terminating instances.

## Q161. C

AWS Documentation Reference: Availability Zones and Load Balancer Nodes
https://docs.aws.amazon.com/elasticloadbalancing/latest/userguide/how-elastic-load-balancing-works.html
When you enable an Availability Zone for your load balancer, Elastic Load Balancing creates a load balancer node in the Availability Zone. If you register targets in an Availability Zone but do not enable the Availability Zone, these registered targets do not receive traffic.

## Q162. A, C, D

AWS Documentation Reference:
https://docs.aws.amazon.com/elasticloadbalancing/latest/application/load-balancer-update-security-groups.html#security-group-recommended-rules
A: to allow all inbound traffic on the load balancer listener port
B: to allow outbound traffic to instances on the instance listener port
C: to allow outbound traffic to instances on the health check port

## Q163. A, C, D

AWS Documentation Reference:
https://docs.aws.amazon.com/elasticloadbalancing/latest/application/load-balancer-update-security-groups.html#security-group-recommended-rules
A: to allow inbound traffic from the VPC CIDR on the load balancer listener port
B: to allow outbound traffic to instances on the instance listener port
C: to allow outbound traffic to instances on the health check port

## Q164. D

AWS Documentation Reference:
https://docs.aws.amazon.com/waf/latest/developerguide/web-acl.html
A WAF web access control list (web ACL) gives you fine-grained control over the web requests that your Amazon CloudFront distribution, Amazon API Gateway API, or Application Load Balancer responds to. You can use criteria like the following to allow or block requests:

- IP address origin of the request
- Country of origin of the request
- String match or regular expression (regex) match in a part of the request
- Size of a particular part of the request
- Detection of malicious SQL code or scripting

You can also test for any combination of these conditions. You can block or count web requests that not only meet the specified conditions, but also exceed a specified number of requests in any 5-minute period. You can combine conditions using logical operators.

This criteria is provided inside the rules that you include in your web ACL and in rule groups that you use in the web ACL.

Q165.B

Q166. A, C

Q167. D
AWS Documentation Reference: Cross-Zone Load Balancing
https://docs.aws.amazon.com/elasticloadbalancing/latest/userguide/how-elastic-load-balancing-works.html
When you enable an Availability Zone for your load balancer, Elastic Load Balancing creates a load balancer node in the Availability Zone. The nodes for your load balancer distribute requests from clients to registered targets. When cross-zone load balancing is enabled, each load balancer node distributes traffic across the registered targets in all enabled Availability Zones. When cross-zone load balancing is disabled, each load balancer node distributes traffic across the registered targets in its Availability Zone only.

Q168.B, C, D
AWS Documentation Reference:
https://aws.amazon.com/blogs/aws/new-application-load-balancing-via-ip-address-to-aws-on-premises-resources/
Application Load Balancers can distribute traffic to AWS resources using their IP addresses as targets in addition to the instance IDs. You can also load balance to resources outside the VPC hosting the load balancer using their IP addresses as targets. This includes resources in peered VPCs, EC2-Classic, and on-premises locations reachable over AWS Direct Connect or a VPN connection.
Alternatively, you can use DNS based weighted load balancing across AWS and on-premises resources using two load balancers i.e. one load balancer for AWS and other for on-premises resources. In the scenario where application-A back-ends are in VPC and application-B back-ends are in on-premises locations then you can put back-ends for each application in different target groups and use content based routing to route traffic to each target group.

Q169.D
AWS Documentation Reference:
https://docs.aws.amazon.com/elasticloadbalancing/latest/application/load-balancer-cloudwatch-metrics.html

Q170.B
AWS Documentation Reference:
https://docs.aws.amazon.com/elasticloadbalancing/latest/application/load-balancer-access-logs.html

Elastic Load Balancing provides access logs that captures detailed information about requests sent to your load balancer. Each log contains information such as the time the request was received, the client's IP address, latencies, request paths, and server responses. You can use these access logs to analyze traffic patterns and troubleshoot issues.

## Q171. B
AWS Documentation Reference:
https://docs.aws.amazon.com/elasticloadbalancing/latest/network/load-balancer-monitoring.html
You can use VPC Flow Logs to capture detailed information about the traffic going to and from your Network Load Balancer.

## Q172. A
AWS Documentation Reference:
https://docs.aws.amazon.com/elasticloadbalancing/latest/network/load-balancer-access-logs.html
Elastic Load Balancing provides access logs that capture detailed information about the TLS requests sent to your Network Load Balancer. You can use these access logs to analyze traffic patterns and troubleshoot issues. Access logs are created only if the load balancer has a TLS listener and they contain information only about TLS requests.

## Q173. C
To receive a history of Application Load Balancing API calls made on your account, use AWS CloudTrail.

## Q174. C
AWS Documentation Reference:
https://aws.amazon.com/directconnect/

## Q175 A, C, D
B defines AWS VPN.
AWS Documentation Reference:
https://aws.amazon.com/directconnect/

## Q176 A, B, D, E
AWS Documentation Reference: Cost Optimization Pillar
https://aws.amazon.com/architecture/well-architected/
Appropriately Provisioned and Right Sizing: You need to set and monitor capacity attributes so that your excess capacity is kept to a minimum and performance is maximized for end users. Right sizing is using the lowest cost resource that still meets the technical specifications of a specific workload.

In AWS, there are a number of different purchasing models that allow you to use services and resources in the most cost-effective way that suits your business needs. The following section describes each purchasing model:
• On demand
• Spot Instances
• Reserved Instances/Capacity
• EC2 Fleet

You want to select the geographic location that minimizes your costs. The AWS Cloud infrastructure is built around Regions and Availability Zones. Each AWS Region operates within local market conditions, and resource pricing can be different in each Region. Choose a specific Region to operate a component of or your entire solution so that you can run at the lowest possible price globally.

In the cloud, managed services remove the operational burden of maintaining servers for tasks like sending email or managing databases. Since managed services operate at cloud scale, they can offer a lower cost per transaction or service.

Architecting for data transfer ensures that you minimize data transfer costs. This may involve using content delivery networks to locate data closer to users, or using dedicated network links from your premises to AWS.

### Q177. C, D

AWS Documentation Reference: Cost Optimization Pillar: Optimize Data Transfer
https://aws.amazon.com/architecture/well-architected/

Architecting for data transfer ensures that you minimize data transfer costs. This may involve using content delivery networks to locate data closer to users, or using dedicated network links from your premises to AWS.

Amazon CloudFront is a global content delivery network that delivers data with low latency and high transfer speeds. It caches data at edge locations across the world, which reduces the load on your resources. By using CloudFront, you can reduce the administrative effort in delivering content to large numbers of users globally, with minimum latency.

AWS Direct Connect allows you to establish a dedicated network connection from your premises to AWS. This can reduce network costs, increase bandwidth, and provide a more consistent network experience than internet-based connections.

### Q178. C

AWS Documentation Reference:
https://aws.amazon.com/directconnect/features/?nc=sn&loc=2

Transferring large data sets over the Internet can be time consuming and expensive. When you use the cloud, you can find that transferring large data sets can be slow because your business critical network traffic is contending for bandwidth with your other Internet usage. To decrease the amount of time required to transfer your data, you could increase the bandwidth to your Internet service provider, which frequently requires a costly contract renewal and a minimum commitment. With AWS Direct Connect, you can transfer your business critical data directly from your datacenter, office, or colocation environment into and from AWS bypassing your Internet service provider and removing network congestion. Further, AWS Direct Connect's simple pay as-you-go pricing, and no minimum commitment means you pay only for the network ports you use and the data you transfer over the connection, which can greatly reduce your networking costs.

Q179. A, B, C
AWS Documentation Reference:
https://aws.amazon.com/directconnect/features/?nc=sn&loc=2
Working with Large Data Sets: Transferring large data sets over the Internet can be time consuming and expensive. With AWS Direct Connect, you can transfer your business critical data directly from your datacenter, office, or colocation environment into and from AWS bypassing your Internet service provider and removing network congestion.

Real-time Data Feeds: Applications that use real-time data feeds can also benefit from using AWS Direct Connect. For example, applications such as voice and video perform best when network latency remains constant. Network latency over the Internet can vary given that the Internet is constantly changing how data gets from point A to B. With AWS Direct Connect, you control how your data is routed, which can provide a more consistent network experience over Internet-based connections.

Hybrid Environments: AWS Direct Connect can help you build hybrid environments that satisfy regulatory requirements requiring the use of private connectivity. Hybrid environments allow you to combine the elasticity and economic benefits of AWS with the ability to utilize other infrastructure that you already own.

Q180. D
AWS Documentation Reference:
https://aws.amazon.com/transit-gateway/
AWS Transit Gateway is a service that enables customers to connect their Amazon Virtual Private Clouds (VPCs) and their on-premises networks to a single gateway. As you grow the number of workloads running on AWS, you need to be able to scale your networks across multiple accounts and Amazon VPCs to keep up with the growth. Today, you can connect pairs of Amazon VPCs using peering. However, managing point-to-point connectivity across many Amazon VPCs, without the ability to centrally manage the connectivity policies, can be operationally costly and cumbersome. For on-premises connectivity, you need to attach your AWS VPN to each individual Amazon VPC. This solution can be time consuming to build and hard to manage when the number of VPCs grows into the hundreds.

With AWS Transit Gateway, you only have to create and manage a single connection from the central gateway in to each Amazon VPC, on-premises data center, or remote office across your network. Transit Gateway acts as a hub that controls how traffic is routed among all the connected networks which act like spokes. This hub and spoke model significantly simplifies management and reduces operational costs because each network only has to connect to the Transit Gateway and not to every other network. Any new VPC is simply connected to the Transit Gateway and is then automatically available to every other network that is connected to the Transit Gateway. This ease of connectivity makes it easy to scale your network as you grow.

## Q181. A
AWS Documentation Reference:
https://docs.aws.amazon.com/vpc/latest/userguide/VPC_Subnets.html
The subnet with CIDR block 10.0.0.0/28 provides 16 ip addresses. The first four IP addresses and the last IP address in each subnet CIDR block are not available for you to use, and cannot be assigned to an instance. Therefore you can use 16-5=11 ip addresses for instances in the subnet.
There are many tools available to help you calculate subnet CIDR blocks; for example, see

http://www.subnet-calculator.com/cidr.php

## Q182. B
AWS Documentation Reference:
https://docs.aws.amazon.com/vpc/latest/userguide/VPC_Subnets.html
There are many tools available to help you calculate subnet CIDR blocks; for example, see http://www.subnet-calculator.com/cidr.php.

You have to keep in mind that the first four IP addresses and the last IP address in each subnet CIDR block are not available for you to use, and cannot be assigned to an instance. In effect your CIDR block should have at least 16+5=21 total ip addresses.
10.0.0.0/27 = 32 total ip addresses
10.0.0.0/28 = 16 total ip addresses
10.0.0.0/29 = 8 total ip addresses
10.0.0.0/30 = 4 total ip addresses

## Q183. A, B

## Q184.D
AWS Documentation Reference:
https://aws.amazon.com/premiumsupport/knowledge-center/public-load-balancer-private-ec2/
*How do I connect a public-facing load balancer to EC2 instances that have private IP addresses?*
You must create public subnets in the same Availability Zones as the private subnets that are used by your private instances. Then associate these public subnets to the internet-facing load balancer.

1. List the Availability Zones that have the instances you want to attach to the load balancer.

2. Create an equal number of public subnets in the same Availability Zones where your private instances exist. To ensure that the load balancer can scale properly, verify that each subnet for the load balancer has a CIDR block with at least a /27 bitmask (for example, 10.0.0.0/27) and has at least 8 free IP addresses. Your load balancer uses these IP addresses to establish connections with the backend instances; for more information, see VPCs and Subnets.

E. If you have more than one private subnet in the same Availability Zone that contains instances that need to be registered with the load balancer, you only need to create one public subnet. You need only one public subnet per Availability Zone; you can add the private instances in all the private subnets that reside in that particular Availability Zone.

3. From the Amazon EC2 console, create a load balancer and associate the newly created public subnets with it.

4. Add the private instances to the load balancer.

## Q185. B
Application tier and Database tier need to be in separate private subnet. For fault tolerance and availability they should be redundantly deployed in two separate AZs. Therefor you will need two private subnet in two separate AZs.

To use elastic load balancer you must create public subnets in the same Availability Zones as the private subnets that are used by your private instances. Hence you will need to create one public subnet in each of the two AZ.

AZ-1: public subnet-a -> Load balancer, private subnet-a -> application tier, private subnet-b -> database tier

AZ-2: public subnet-b -> Load balancer, private subnet-c -> application tier, private subnet-d -> database tier

## Q186 A, B, C
AWS Documentation Reference:
https://docs.aws.amazon.com/vpc/latest/userguide/VPC_Subnets.html
There are many tools available to help you calculate subnet CIDR blocks; for example, see
http://www.subnet-calculator.com/cidr.php

If you create a VPC with CIDR block 10.0.0.0/24, it supports 256 IP addresses. You can break this CIDR block into two subnets, each supporting 128 IP addresses. One subnet uses CIDR block 10.0.0.0/25 (for addresses 10.0.0.0 - 10.0.0.127) and the other uses CIDR block 10.0.0.128/25 (for addresses 10.0.0.128 - 10.0.0.255).
The first four IP addresses and the last IP address in each subnet CIDR block are not available for you to use, and cannot be assigned to an instance.

Q187. C
AWS Documentation Reference:
https://docs.aws.amazon.com/AWSEC2/latest/UserGuide/security-group-rules-reference.html#sg-rules-ping
The ping command is a type of ICMP traffic. To ping your instance, you must add the following inbound ICMP rule.

Q188. C
AWS Documentation Reference:
https://docs.aws.amazon.com/elasticloadbalancing/latest/application/load-balancer-listeners.html#path-conditions
https://aws.amazon.com/blogs/aws/new-host-based-routing-support-for-aws-application-load-balancers/
You can use path conditions to define rules that route requests based on the URL in the request (also known as path-based routing).

The path pattern is applied only to the path of the URL, not to its query parameters.

A path pattern is case-sensitive, can be up to 128 characters in length, and can contain any of the following characters.

A–Z, a–z, 0–9

_ - . $ / ~ " ' @ : +

& (using &amp;)

* (matches 0 or more characters)

? (matches exactly 1 character)

In the given scenario you can create path pattern as
www.statefair.com/web/*
www.statefair.com/mobileweb/*
www.statefair.com/mobileapp/*

Network load balancer doesn't support path based routing.

Q189. D
AWS Documentation Reference:

https://aws.amazon.com/blogs/aws/new-host-based-routing-support-for-aws-application-load-balancers/

You can use host conditions to define rules that route requests based on the host name in the host header (also known as host-based routing). This enables you to support multiple domains using a single load balancer.

A hostname is not case-sensitive, can be up to 128 characters in length, and can contain any of the following characters:

A–Z, a–z, 0–9

- .

* (matches 0 or more characters)

? (matches exactly 1 character)

You must include at least one "." character. You can include only alphabetical characters after the final "." character.

Q190. A, C
AWS Documentation Reference:
https://docs.aws.amazon.com/elasticloadbalancing/latest/application/tutorial-target-ecs-containers.html

You can use a microservices architecture to structure your application as services that you can develop and deploy independently. You can install one or more of these services on each EC2 instance, with each service accepting connections on a different port. You can use a single Application Load Balancer to route requests to all the services for your application. When you register an EC2 instance with a target group, you can register it multiple times; for each service, register the instance using the port for the service.

Q191.A
AWS Documentation Reference:
https://docs.aws.amazon.com/AmazonECS/latest/developerguide/service-load-balancing.html

Your Amazon ECS service can optionally be configured to use Elastic Load Balancing to distribute traffic evenly across the tasks in your service.

Amazon ECS services support the Application Load Balancer, Network Load Balancer, and Classic Load Balancer load balancer types. Application Load Balancers are used to route HTTP/HTTPS (or Layer 7) traffic. Network Load Balancers and Classic Load Balancers are used to route TCP (or Layer 4) traffic.

Application Load Balancers offer several features that make them attractive for use with Amazon ECS services:

- Each service can serve traffic from multiple load balancers and expose multiple load balanced ports by specifying multiple target groups.
- They are supported by tasks using both the Fargate and EC2 launch types.
- Application Load Balancers allow containers to use dynamic host port mapping (so that multiple tasks from the same service are allowed per container instance).
- Application Load Balancers support path-based routing and priority rules (so that multiple services can use the same listener port on a single Application Load Balancer).

Q192. B

AWS Documentation Reference:

https://aws.amazon.com/about-aws/global-infrastructure/localzones/

AWS Local Zones are a new type of AWS infrastructure deployment that places AWS compute, storage, database, and other select services closer to large population, industry, and IT centers where no AWS Region exists today. With AWS Local Zones, you can easily run latency-sensitive portions of applications local to end-users and resources in a specific geography, delivering single-digit millisecond latency for use cases such as media & entertainment content creation, real-time gaming, reservoir simulations, electronic design automation, and machine learning.

Each AWS Local Zone location is an extension of an AWS Region where you can run your latency-sensitive applications using AWS services such as Amazon Elastic Compute Cloud, Amazon Virtual Private Cloud, Amazon Elastic Block Store, Amazon FSx, and Amazon Elastic Load Balancing in geographic proximity to end-users. AWS Local Zones provide a high-bandwidth, secure connection between local workloads and those running in the AWS Region, allowing you to seamlessly connect back to your other workloads running in AWS and to the full range of in-region services through the same APIs and tool sets.

Q193. A

AWS Documentation Reference:

https://docs.aws.amazon.com/vpc/latest/userguide/vpc-nat-gateway.html

You can use a network address translation (NAT) gateway to enable instances in a private subnet to connect to the internet or other AWS services, but prevent the internet from initiating a connection with those instances.

C and D are wrong as to create a NAT gateway, you must specify the public subnet in which the NAT gateway should reside.

Here the key criteria mention as 'which option is highly available' .Option B will not be a 'highly available' solution because all web servers in three AZ connect to one single NAT gateway. If the AZ of NAT gateway is down, all three web servers will not be able to connect to payment gateway. Therefore option A is correct choice.

Q194. D

AWS Documentation Reference:

https://docs.aws.amazon.com/directconnect/latest/UserGuide/WorkingWithVirtualInterface s.html

You must create one of the following virtual interfaces to begin using your AWS Direct Connect connection.

Private virtual interface: A private virtual interface should be used to access an Amazon VPC using private IP addresses.

Public virtual interface: A public virtual interface can access all AWS public services using public IP addresses.

Transit virtual interface: A transit virtual interface should be used to access one or more Amazon VPC Transit Gateways associated with Direct Connect gateways. You can use transit virtual interfaces with 1/2/5/10 Gbps AWS Direct Connect connections.

Q195. B, C, D

AWS Documentation Reference:

https://docs.aws.amazon.com/directconnect/latest/UserGuide/Troubleshooting.html#ts-routing

In the given situation your virtual interface is up and you've established a BGP peering session. If you cannot route traffic over the virtual interface, use the following steps to troubleshoot the issue:

1. Ensure that you are advertising a route for your on-premises network prefix over the BGP session. For a private virtual interface, this can be a private or public network prefix. For a public virtual interface, this must be your publicly routable network prefix.

2. For a private virtual interface, ensure that your VPC security groups and network ACLs allow inbound and outbound traffic for your on-premises network prefix.

3. For a private virtual interface, ensure that your VPC route tables have prefixes pointing to the virtual private gateway to which your private virtual interface is connected. For example, if you prefer to have all your traffic routed towards your on-premises network by default, you can add the default route (0.0.0.0/0 or ::/0) with the virtual private gateway as the target in your VPC route tables.

Alternatively, enable route propagation to automatically update routes in your route tables based on your dynamic BGP route advertisement. You can have up to 100 propagated routes per route table. This limit cannot be increased.

Q196.B, C, D
AWS Documentation Reference:
https://docs.aws.amazon.com/whitepapers/latest/aws-vpc-connectivity-options/network-to-amazon-vpc-connectivity-options.html
AWS Managed VPN: Amazon VPC provides the option of creating an IPsec VPN connection between remote customer networks and their Amazon VPC over the internet

AWS Direct Connect makes it easy to establish a dedicated network connection from your premises to your Amazon VPC or among Amazon VPCs. This option can potentially reduce network costs, increase bandwidth throughput, and provide a more consistent network experience than the other VPC-to-VPC connectivity options.

Transit VPC: A transit VPC is a common strategy for connecting multiple, geographically disperse VPCs and remote networks in order to create a global network transit center. One common strategy for connecting multiple VPCs with remote networks is to implement a hub-and-spoke network topology in each region that routes all traffic through a network transit center using AWS Transit Gateway or a transit VPC.

Q197. A, C, D
AWS Documentation Reference:
https://aws.amazon.com/premiumsupport/knowledge-center/elb-capture-client-ip-addresses/
Your access logs capture the IP address of your load balancer because the load balancer establishes the connection to your instances. You must perform additional configuration to capture the IP addresses of clients in your access logs.

- For Application Load Balancers and Classic Load Balancers with HTTP/HTTPS listeners, you must use X-Forwarded-For headers to capture client IP addresses. Then, you must print those client IP addresses in your access logs.
- For Classic Load Balancers with TCP/SSL listeners, you must enable Proxy Protocol support on the Classic Load Balancer and the target application. Be sure to configure Proxy Protocol support on both sides or your application might experience issues. You can also enable Proxy Protocol support using the AWS CLI.
- For Network Load Balancers, you can register your targets by instance ID to capture client IP addresses without additional web server configuration. For instructions, see Target Group Attributes instead of the following resolutions.

## Q198. D

AWS Documentation Reference:

https://aws.amazon.com/answers/networking/aws-multiple-region-multi-vpc-connectivity/

Inter-region VPC Peering: Inter-region VPC peering connections allow secure communication between VPC resources in different AWS Regions. All network traffic between regions is encrypted, stays on the AWS global network backbone, and never traverses the public internet, thereby reducing threat vectors, such as common exploits and DDoS attacks. VPC peering is appropriate for many scenarios, for example, to provide VPCs full access to each other's resources or to provide a set of VPCs partial access to resources in a central VPC. You can configure peering connections to provide access to part of a CIDR block or to an entire CIDR block of the peer VPC.

## Q199. A, D

AWS Documentation Reference:

https://aws.amazon.com/about-aws/global-infrastructure/regions_az/

AWS has the concept of a Region, which is a physical location around the world where it has cluster of data centers. Each group of logical data centers is called an Availability Zone. Each AWS Region consists of multiple, isolated, and physically separate AZ's within a geographic area. Unlike other cloud providers, who often define a region as a single data center, the multiple AZ design of every AWS Region offers advantages for customers. Each AZ has independent power, cooling, and physical security and is connected via redundant, ultra-low-latency networks. AWS customers focused on high availability can design their applications to run in multiple AZ's to achieve even greater fault-tolerance. AWS infrastructure Regions meet the highest levels of security, compliance, and data protection.

https://aws.amazon.com/about-aws/global-infrastructure/regions_az/

AWS Local Zones place compute, storage, database, and other select AWS services closer to end-users. With AWS Local Zones, you can easily run highly-demanding applications that require single-digit millisecond latencies to your end-users such as media & entertainment content creation, real-time gaming, reservoir simulations, electronic design automation, and machine learning.

Each AWS Local Zone location is an extension of an AWS Region where you can run your latency sensitive applications using AWS services such as Amazon Elastic Compute Cloud, Amazon Virtual Private Cloud, Amazon Elastic Block Store, Amazon File Storage, and Amazon Elastic Load Balancing in geographic proximity to end-users. AWS Local Zones provide a high-bandwidth, secure connection between local workloads and those running in the AWS Region, allowing you to seamlessly connect to the full range of in-region services through the same APIs and tool sets.

## Q200.D

AWS Documentation Reference:

https://aws.amazon.com/about-aws/global-infrastructure/regions_az/

AWS Local Zones place compute, storage, database, and other select AWS services closer to end-users. With AWS Local Zones, you can easily run highly-demanding applications that require single-digit millisecond latencies to your end-users such as media & entertainment content creation, real-time gaming, reservoir simulations, electronic design automation, and machine learning.

Each AWS Local Zone location is an extension of an AWS Region where you can run your latency sensitive applications using AWS services such as Amazon Elastic Compute Cloud, Amazon Virtual Private Cloud, Amazon Elastic Block Store, Amazon File Storage, and Amazon Elastic Load Balancing in geographic proximity to end-users. AWS Local Zones provide a high-bandwidth, secure connection between local workloads and those running in the AWS Region, allowing you to seamlessly connect to the full range of in-region services through the same APIs and tool sets.

## Q201.A, C
AWS Documentation Reference:
https://aws.amazon.com/about-aws/global-infrastructure/regions_az/
An Availability Zone (AZ) is one or more discrete data centers with redundant power, networking, and connectivity in an AWS Region. AZ's give customers the ability to operate production applications and databases that are more highly available, fault tolerant, and scalable than would be possible from a single data center. All AZ's in an AWS Region are interconnected with high-bandwidth, low-latency networking, over fully redundant, dedicated metro fiber providing high-throughput, low-latency networking between AZ's. All traffic between AZ's is encrypted. The network performance is sufficient to accomplish synchronous replication between AZ's. AZ's make partitioning applications for high availability easy. If an application is partitioned across AZ's, companies are better isolated and protected from issues such as power outages, lightning strikes, tornadoes, earthquakes, and more. AZ's are physically separated by a meaningful distance, many kilometers, from any other AZ, although all are within 100 km (60 miles) of each other.

## Q202. A, B, E
AWS Documentation Reference:
https://aws.amazon.com/premiumsupport/knowledge-center/autoscaling-fault-tolerance-load-balancer/
If you have a preexisting Elastic Load Balancing load balancer, you can create an Auto Scaling group to automatically terminate unhealthy instances and launch new, healthy ones. In addition to improving the fault tolerance of your application, Auto Scaling can be configured to dynamically scale up your application in response to demand.

You can create an Auto Scaling group that launches copies of instances you've already configured, or create a launch configuration that uses an Amazon Machine Image (AMI) instead. After you create the Auto Scaling group, attach your load balancer to it.

Make sure to create your Auto Scaling group in the same region and Availability Zone as your load balancer.

Q203. D
None of the other options provide static ip address.
AWS Documentation Reference:
https://aws.amazon.com/global-accelerator/features/
https://aws.amazon.com/blogs/aws/new-aws-global-accelerator-for-availability-and-performance/

AWS Global Accelerator uses AWS's vast, highly available and congestion-free global network to direct internet traffic from your users to your applications running in AWS regions. With AWS Global Accelerator, your users are directed to your workload based on their geographic location, application health, and weights that you can configure. AWS Global Accelerator also allocates static Anycast IP addresses that are globally unique for your application and do not change, thus removing the need to update clients as your application scales. You can get started by provisioning your Accelerator and associating it with your applications running on: Network Load Balancers, Application Load Balancers, or Elastic IP addresses. AWS Global Accelerator then allocates two static Anycast IP addresses from the AWS network which serve as an entry point for your workloads. AWS Global Accelerator supports both TCP and UDP protocols, health checking of your target endpoints and will route traffic away from unhealthy applications. You can use an Accelerator in one or more AWS regions, providing increased availability and performance for your end users.

Q204. B, C, D
AWS Documentation Reference:
https://docs.aws.amazon.com/global-accelerator/latest/dg/introduction-components.html

Static IP addresses: AWS Global Accelerator provides you with a set of two static IP addresses that are anycast from the AWS edge network. The IP addresses serve as single fixed entry points for your clients. If you already have Elastic Load Balancing load balancers, EC2 instances, or Elastic IP address resources set up for your applications, you can easily add those to Global Accelerator. This allows Global Accelerator to use static IP addresses to access the resources.

Accelerator: An accelerator directs traffic to optimal endpoints over the AWS global network to improve the availability and performance of your internet applications. Each accelerator includes one or more listeners.

DNS name: Global Accelerator assigns each accelerator a default Domain Name System (DNS) name, similar to a1234567890abcdef.awsglobalaccelerator.com, that points to the static

IP addresses that Global Accelerator assigns to you. Depending on the use case, you can use your accelerator's static IP addresses or DNS name to route traffic to your accelerator, or set up DNS records to route traffic using your own custom domain name.

Listener: A listener processes inbound connections from clients to Global Accelerator, based on the port (or port range) and protocol that you configure. Global Accelerator supports both TCP and UDP protocols. Each listener has one or more endpoint groups associated with it, and traffic is forwarded to endpoints in one of the groups. You associate endpoint groups with listeners by specifying the Regions that you want to distribute traffic to. Traffic is distributed to optimal endpoints within the endpoint groups associated with a listener.

Endpoint group: Each endpoint group is associated with a specific AWS Region. Endpoint groups include one or more endpoints in the Region.

Endpoint: Endpoints can be Network Load Balancers, Application Load Balancers, EC2 instances, or Elastic IP addresses. An Application Load Balancer endpoint can be an internet-facing or internal.

Q205. A, B
C is the feature of Amazon CloudFront. D is the features of AWS PrivateLink.
AWS Documentation Reference:
https://docs.aws.amazon.com/global-accelerator/latest/dg/introduction-benefits-of-migrating.html
Use cases are:
Acceleration for latency-sensitive applications: Many applications, especially in areas such as gaming, media, mobile apps, and financials, require very low latency for a great user experience. To improve the user experience, Global Accelerator directs user traffic to the application endpoint that is nearest to the client, which reduces internet latency and jitter. Global Accelerator routes traffic to the closest edge location by using Anycast, and then routes it to the closest regional endpoint over the AWS global network.

Scale for increased application utilization: When application usage grows, the number of IP addresses and endpoints that you need to manage also increases. Global Accelerator enables you to scale your network up or down. It lets you associate regional resources, such as load balancers and EC2 instances, to two static IP addresses. You whitelist these addresses just once in your client applications, firewalls, and DNS records. With Global Accelerator, you can add or remove endpoints in AWS Regions, run blue/green deployment, and do A/B testing without having to update the IP addresses in your client applications. This is particularly useful for IoT, retail, media, automotive, and healthcare use cases in which you can't easily update client applications frequently.

Q206. B, C

AWS Documentation Reference:

https://aws.amazon.com/global-accelerator/faqs/

AWS Global Accelerator and Amazon CloudFront are separate services that use the AWS global network and its edge locations around the world. CloudFront improves performance for both cacheable content (such as images and videos) and dynamic content (such as API acceleration and dynamic site delivery). Global Accelerator improves performance for a wide range of applications over TCP or UDP by proxying packets at the edge to applications running in one or more AWS Regions. Global Accelerator is a good fit for non-HTTP use cases, such as gaming (UDP), IoT (MQTT), or Voice over IP, as well as for HTTP use cases that specifically require static IP addresses or deterministic, fast regional failover. Both services integrate with AWS Shield for DDoS protection.

Q207.A, D

AWS Documentation Reference:

https://docs.aws.amazon.com/global-accelerator/latest/dg/introduction-how-it-works.html

There are two ways that you can customize how AWS Global Accelerator sends traffic to your endpoints:

- Change the traffic dial to limit the traffic for one or more endpoint groups
- Specify weights to change the proportion of traffic to the endpoints in a group

You configure traffic dials for endpoint groups. The traffic dial lets you cut off a percentage of traffic—or all traffic—to the group, by "dialing down" traffic that the accelerator has already directed to it based on other factors, such as proximity.

You use weights, on the other hand, to set values for individual endpoints within an endpoint group. Weights provide a way to divide up traffic within the endpoint group. For example, you can use weights to do performance testing for specific endpoints in a Region.

Q208. A, B

AWS Documentation Reference:

https://docs.aws.amazon.com/global-accelerator/latest/dg/about-endpoint-groups-traffic-dial.html

For each endpoint group, you can set a traffic dial to control the percentage of traffic that is directed to the group. The percentage is applied only to traffic that is already directed to the endpoint group, not to all listener traffic. Now, say you have 100 requests coming to your accelerator, with 50 from the East Coast of the United States and 50 from the West Coast. The accelerator directs the traffic as follows:

- The first 25 requests on each coast (50 requests in total) are served from their nearby endpoint group. That is, 25 requests are directed to the endpoint group in us-west-2 and 25 are directed to the endpoint group in us-east-1.
- The next 50 requests are directed to the opposite Regions. That is, the next 25 requests from the East Coast are served by us-west-2, and the next 25 requests from the West Coast are served by us-east-1.

The result in this scenario is that both endpoint groups serve the same amount of traffic. However, each one receives a mix of traffic from both Regions.

Q209. B, C, D
AWS Documentation Reference:
https://docs.aws.amazon.com/global-accelerator/latest/dg/preserve-client-ip-address.html
Your options for preserving and accessing the client IP address for AWS Global Accelerator depend on the endpoints that you've set up with your accelerator. There are two types of endpoints that can preserve the source IP address of the client in incoming packets: Application Load Balancers and EC2 instances.

- When you use an internet-facing Application Load Balancer as an endpoint with Global Accelerator, you can choose to preserve the source IP address of the original client for packets that arrive at the load balancer by enabling client IP address preservation.

- When you use an internal Application Load Balancer or an EC2 instance with Global Accelerator, the endpoint always has client IP address preservation enabled.

Global Accelerator does not support client IP address preservation for Network Load Balancer and Elastic IP address endpoints.

# Answer Chapter 3 Storage: Amazon Simple Storage Services (S3), EBS, EFS, Storage Gateway

Q1. A, B, C.
D is not possible as S3 cannot be attached to an EC2 instance.

Q2. A, B, C.
Elastic File System, Elastic Block Storage and Storage Gateway are different AWS services.
AWS Documentation Reference:
https://aws.amazon.com/s3/storage-classes/
Amazon S3 offers a range of storage classes designed for different use cases. These include S3 Standard for general-purpose storage of frequently accessed data; S3 Intelligent-Tiering for data with unknown or changing access patterns; S3 Standard-Infrequent Access (S3 Standard-IA) and S3 One Zone-Infrequent Access (S3 One Zone-IA) for long-lived, but less frequently accessed data; and Amazon S3 Glacier (S3 Glacier) and Amazon S3 Glacier Deep Archive (S3 Glacier Deep Archive) for long-term archive and digital preservation.

Q3. B, C, D, E
S3 cannot be mounted to an EC2 instance.

Q4. D.
Here one of the key requirement is to have files in network folder used by the existing collaboration application.
AWS Documentation Reference:
https://aws.amazon.com/storagegateway/faqs/
File Gateway is a configuration of the AWS Storage Gateway service that provides your applications a file interface to seamlessly store files as objects in Amazon S3, and access them using industry standard file protocols. The file gateway enables you to store and retrieve objects in Amazon S3 using file protocols, such as NFS. Objects written through file gateway can be directly accessed in S3.
C and D will not be correct as the volume gateway (cached or stored) provides block storage to your applications using the iSCSI protocol.
A is not correct because storing the files as objects directly in S3 will not meet the requirement of network file sharing.

Q5. E. All of the above
AWS Documentation Reference:
https://docs.aws.amazon.com/AmazonS3/latest/dev/Introduction.html#ConsistencyModel
Amazon S3 provides read-after-write consistency for PUTS of new objects in your S3 bucket in all regions with one caveat. The caveat is that if you make a HEAD or GET request to the key name (to find if the object exists) before creating the object, Amazon S3 provides eventual consistency for read-after-write.

Amazon S3 offers eventual consistency for overwrite PUTS and DELETES in all regions.

Updates to a single key are atomic. For example, if you PUT to an existing key, a subsequent read might return the old data or the updated data, but it will never return corrupted or partial data. If a PUT request is successful, your data is safely stored. Amazon S3 achieves high availability by replicating data across multiple servers within Amazon's data centers. "
This propagation can take some time, hence the listed behavior.

Q6. B, D, E
AWS Documentation Reference:
https://docs.aws.amazon.com/AmazonS3/latest/dev/UsingBucket.html#access-bucket-intro
Amazon S3 supports both virtual-hosted–style and path-style URLs to access a bucket.
In a virtual-hosted–style URL, the bucket name is part of the domain name in the URL. For example:

http://*bucket*.s3.*aws-region*.amazonaws.com.
http://*bucket*.s3.amazonaws.com

In a virtual-hosted–style URL, you can use either of these endpoints. If you make a request to the http://bucket.s3.amazonaws.com endpoint, the DNS has sufficient information to route your request directly to the Region where your bucket resides.
Virtual style url that will work are
https://mywestwebsite.s3.amazonaws.com
https://mywestwebsite.s3.us-west-1.amazonaws.com
https://mywestwebsite.s3-us-west-1.amazonaws.com
For
https://s3.amazonaws.com/mywestwebsite
it will throw an error with suggested endpoint "mywestwebsite.s3.amazonaws.com"

In a path-style URL, the bucket name is not part of the domain. For example:

Region-specific endpoint, http://s3.*aws-region*.amazonaws.com/*bucket*

Valid endpoint names for this west region:
s3.us-west-1.amazonaws.com

For a bucket in the region us-west-1

Path url that will work are:
https://s3.us-west-1.amazonaws.com/mywestwebsite
https://s3-us-west-1.amazonaws.com/mywestwebsite

Q7. B, C, D, E

Please refer to explanation of previous question. Only difference is based on the us-east-1 region endpoint the path url will follow the format:

http://s3.amazonaws.com/*bucket*

Valid endpoint names for this region:

s3.amazonaws.com
s3.us-east-1.amazonaws.com

Hence
https://s3.amazonaws.com/myeastwebsite
Will not throw error.

Q8. A, B
AWS Documentation Reference:
https://docs.aws.amazon.com/AmazonS3/latest/user-guide/using-folders.html
Amazon S3 console supports displaying objects stored in the buckets in form of folders. The console treats all objects that have a forward slash "/" character as the last (trailing) character in the key name as a folder. In this scenario the bucket name is "mywestwebsite" and as per the virtual style url naming object key name is "photos/whale.jpg". As there is a "/" character in the object key name , in the S3 console there will be folder "photos" inside the bucket "mywestwebsite" and under that folder you will see the file "whale.jpg"

Q9. C
S3 provides eventual consistency for overwrite PUTS and DELETES in all regions.
On replacing an existing object and immediately attempting to read it, S3 might return the prior data until the change is fully propagated.
D is not correct. As object existed and it was updated, S3 will return an object on GET.

Q10. B, D
AWS Documentation Reference:
https://docs.aws.amazon.com/AmazonS3/latest/user-guide/using-folders.html
For the sake of organizational simplicity, the Amazon S3 console supports the folder concept as a means of grouping objects. Amazon S3 does this by using a shared name prefix for objects (that is, objects that have names that begin with a common string). Object names are also referred to as key names.

Amazon S3 console supports displaying objects stored in the buckets in form of folders. The console treats all objects that have a forward slash "/" character as the last (trailing) character in the key name as a folder.
In the given scenario all the files have 'alaskaphotos/*.jpg' in their key name, hence there is a folder 'alaskaphotos' inside the bucket in the S3 console.

You can have folders within folders, but not buckets within buckets. You can upload and copy objects directly into a folder. Folders can be created, deleted, and made public, but they cannot be renamed. Objects can be copied from one folder to another.

## Q11. C

AWS Documentation Reference links:

https://docs.aws.amazon.com/AmazonS3/latest/dev/WebsiteHosting.html
https://docs.aws.amazon.com/AmazonS3/latest/dev/WebsiteEndpoints.html
https://docs.aws.amazon.com/general/latest/gr/rande.html#s3_website_region_endpoints

After configuring a S3 bucket for website hosting, website content are uploaded to the bucket. The bucket must have public read access. The website is then available at the AWS Region-specific website endpoint of the bucket, which is in one of the following formats:

<bucket-name>.s3-website-<AWS-region>.amazonaws.com
<bucket-name>.s3-website. <AWS-region>.amazonaws.com

Which format is used for the endpoint depends on what Region the bucket is in.

In the given scenario the website endpoint for us-west-2 regions is
's3-website-us-west-2.amazonaws.com' therefore the url for the website will be
http://west-bucket.s3-website-us-west-2.amazonaws.com/

## Q12. B

AWS Documentation Reference links:

https://docs.aws.amazon.com/AmazonS3/latest/dev/WebsiteHosting.html
https://docs.aws.amazon.com/AmazonS3/latest/dev/WebsiteEndpoints.html
https://docs.aws.amazon.com/general/latest/gr/rande.html#s3_website_region_endpoints

After configuring a S3 bucket for website hosting, website content are uploaded to the bucket. The bucket must have public read access. The website is then available at the AWS Region-specific website endpoint of the bucket, which is in one of the following formats:

<bucket-name>.s3-website-<AWS-region>.amazonaws.com
<bucket-name>.s3-website. <AWS-region>.amazonaws.com

Which format is used for the endpoint depends on what Region the bucket is in.

In the given scenario the website endpoint for eu-central-1regions is
's3-website.eu-central-1.amazonaws.com' therefore the url for the website will be
http://eu-bucket.s3-website.eu-central-1.amazonaws.com/

Q13. B, D
AWS Documentation Reference URL:
https://docs.aws.amazon.com/AmazonS3/latest/dev/website-hosting-custom-domain-walkthrough.html#root-domain-walkthrough-s3-tasks
Registering a domain name is not essential   you can use the S3 website end point.  However you can use your own domain, such as example.com to serve your content.
It is not required to enable HTTP on the bucket.

Q14. B
All of the storage classes except for ONEZONE_IA are designed to be resilient to simultaneous complete data loss in a single Availability Zone and partial loss in another Availability Zone.

Q15. A, B
AWS Documentation Reference: Storage Classes for Infrequently Accessed Objects
https://docs.aws.amazon.com/AmazonS3/latest/dev/storage-class-intro.html#sc-infreq-data-access
The STANDARD_IA and ONEZONE_IA storage classes are designed for long-lived and infrequently accessed data. (IA stands for infrequent access.) STANDARD_IA and ONEZONE_IA objects are available for millisecond access (similar to the STANDARD storage class).
For example, you might choose the STANDARD_IA and ONEZONE_IA storage classes:
* For storing backups.
* For older data that is accessed infrequently, but that still requires millisecond access.

Q16. True.
The GLACIER and DEEP_ARCHIVE storage classes are designed for low-cost data archiving. These storage classes offer the same durability and resiliency as the STANDARD storage class.

Q17. A, B, D
AWS Documentation Reference:
https://aws.amazon.com/storagegateway/
AWS Storage Gateway is a hybrid cloud storage service that gives you on-premises access to virtually unlimited cloud storage. Customers use Storage Gateway to simplify storage management and reduce costs for key hybrid cloud storage use cases. These include moving tape backups to the cloud, reducing on-premises storage with cloud-backed file shares, providing low latency access to data in AWS for on-premises applications, as well as various migration, archiving, processing, and disaster recovery use cases.

To support these use cases, the service provides three different types of gateways – Tape Gateway, File Gateway, and Volume Gateway – that seamlessly connect on-premises applications to cloud storage, caching data locally for low-latency access. Your applications connect to the service through a virtual machine or hardware gateway appliance using standard storage protocols, such as NFS, SMB, and iSCSI. The gateway connects to AWS storage services, such as Amazon S3, Amazon S3 Glacier, Amazon S3 Glacier Deep Archive, Amazon EBS, and AWS Backup, providing storage for files, volumes, snapshots, and virtual tapes in AWS. The service includes a highly-optimized data transfer mechanism, with bandwidth management, automated network resilience, and efficient data transfer.

Q18. A, B, C
AWS Documentation Reference:
https://aws.amazon.com/storagegateway/features/
AWS Storage Gateway supports three storage interfaces: file, volume, and tape. Each gateway you have can provide one type of interface.

The file gateway enables you to store and retrieve objects in Amazon S3 using file protocols, such as NFS. Objects written through file gateway can be directly accessed in S3.

The volume gateway provides block storage to your applications using the iSCSI protocol. Data on the volumes is stored in Amazon S3. To access your iSCSI volumes in AWS, you can take EBS snapshots which can be used to create EBS volumes.

The tape gateway provides your backup application with an iSCSI virtual tape library (VTL) interface, consisting of a virtual media changer, virtual tape drives, and virtual tapes. Virtual tape data is stored in Amazon S3 or can be archived to Amazon Glacier.

Q19. B

Q20. A

Q21. B

Q22. B
The key point to consider here is file size in the range of 10-20 MB and upload resiliency in low speed network.
C is not suitable because Amazon S3 transfer acceleration is used mainly when:
- You have to upload to a centralized bucket from all over the world.
- You have to transfer gigabytes to terabytes of data on a regular basis across continents.

A is feasible as you can upload up to 5 GB object size in one PUT operation to S3 bucket. But using single put operation may not be suitable in low bandwidth scenario.

Correct answer is B, to use multipart upload api to upload the files to S3. If you're uploading over a spotty network, multipart uploading increases resiliency to network errors by avoiding upload restarts. Multipart upload can be used for file sizes greater than 5 MB.

Q23. B, D
AWS Documentation Reference:
https://docs.aws.amazon.com/AmazonS3/latest/dev/UploadingObjects.html
Multipart upload API is designed to upload larger objects, hence option A is not correct where it mentions 'any size objects'.        You can use a multipart upload for objects from 5 MB to 5 TB in size.
C is not correct because on a stable high bandwidth network there will be no need to increase resiliency to network errors.

B, D are the correct answers.
In case of spotty networks when using multipart uploading, you need to retry uploading only parts that are interrupted during the upload. You don't need to restart uploading your object from the beginning.

Q24. A, C
AWS Documentation Reference:
https://docs.aws.amazon.com/AmazonS3/latest/dev/transfer-acceleration.html
Amazon S3 Transfer Acceleration enables fast, easy, and secure transfers of files over long distances between your client and an S3 bucket. Transfer Acceleration takes advantage of Amazon CloudFront's globally distributed edge locations. As the data arrives at an edge location, data is routed to Amazon S3 over an optimized network path.

Q25. C
As it is an AWS error message hence A and B are ruled out.
S3 bucket can store object size from 0 bytes to 5 TB, so D is not a correct answer.
C is the correct answer because maximum size of object that can be uploaded to S3 in single PUT operation is 5 GB.

Q26. C
AWS recommends to use multi part upload api when your object size reaches 100 MB. You can upload objects in parts. These object parts can be uploaded independently, in any order, and in parallel. You can use a multipart upload for objects from 5 MB to 5 TB in size.

Q27. A, B
AWS Documentation Reference:
https://docs.aws.amazon.com/AmazonS3/latest/dev/transfer-acceleration.html#transfer-acceleration-why-use

You might want to use Transfer Acceleration on a bucket for various reasons, including the following:

• You have customers that upload to a centralized bucket from all over the world.

• You transfer gigabytes to terabytes of data on a regular basis across continents.

• You are unable to utilize all of your available bandwidth over the Internet when uploading to Amazon S3.

Q28. A

Q29. B, C, D

AWS Documentation Reference:

https://docs.aws.amazon.com/AmazonS3/latest/dev/NotificationHowTo.html#notification-how-to-event-types-and-destinations

Amazon S3 supports the following destinations where it can publish events:

• Amazon Simple Notification Service (Amazon SNS) topic

• Amazon Simple Queue Service (Amazon SQS) queue

• AWS Lambda

Q30. A, B, D, E

AWS Documentation Reference:

https://docs.aws.amazon.com/AmazonS3/latest/dev/website-hosting-custom-domain-walkthrough.html

The name of the bucket must be same as the custom domain name www.mycloudblog.com.

You create the alias records that you add to the hosted zone for your domain maps www.mycloudblog.com to the corresponding S3 buckets. Instead of using IP addresses, the alias records use the Amazon S3 website endpoints. Amazon Route 53 maintains a mapping between the alias records and the IP addresses where the Amazon S3 buckets reside.

You will need to configure the bucket for static website hosting and making it read accessible for everyone.

Enabling HTTP on the bucket is not required.

Q31. B, D

AWS Documentation Reference:

https://docs.aws.amazon.com/AmazonS3/latest/dev/Versioning.html

Versioning is a means of keeping multiple versions/copies of an object in the same bucket.

In bucket , for example, you can have two objects with the same key, but different version IDs, such as whale.jpeg (version 1) and whale.jpeg (version 2).

Q32. D

AWS Documentation Reference:

https://docs.aws.amazon.com/AmazonS3/latest/dev/Versioning.html
Objects that are stored in your bucket before you set the versioning state have a version ID of null.

Q33. B, C
AWS Documentation Reference:
https://docs.aws.amazon.com/AmazonS3/latest/dev/Versioning.html
Once you enable versioning on a bucket, Amazon S3 automatically adds a unique version ID to every object stored (using PUT, POST or DELETE) in the bucket.

When versioning is enabled, a simple DELETE doesn't permanently delete an object.
Instead, Amazon S3 inserts a delete marker in the bucket, and that marker becomes the current version of the object with a new ID. You can GET the previous version of the object by the version id or recover it from the console.

When versioning is enable a simple GET request retrieves the current version of an object. To retrieve a specific version, you have to specify its version ID.

Q34. A, C, E
Buckets can be in one of three states: unversioned (the default), versioning-enabled, or versioning-suspended. Once you version-enable a bucket, it can never return to an unversioned state. You can, however, suspend versioning on that bucket.

Q35. A, C
AWS Documentation Reference:
https://docs.aws.amazon.com/AmazonS3/latest/dev/Versioning.html
When versioning is enabled, a simple DELETE doesn't permanently delete an object.
Instead, Amazon S3 inserts a delete marker in the bucket, and that marker becomes the current version of the object with a new ID. You can GET the previous version of the object by the version id or recover it from the console.

MFA adds another layer of security which requires additional authentication for either of the following operations:
• Change the versioning state of your bucket or permanently delete an object version.
• It ensures that data in your bucket cannot be accidentally deleted

MFA Delete requires two forms of authentication together:
• Your security credentials
• The concatenation of a valid serial number, a space, and the six-digit code displayed on an approved authentication device

Q36. C

AWS Documentation Reference:

https://docs.aws.amazon.com/AmazonS3/latest/dev/replication.html

Cross-region replication (CRR) enables automatic, asynchronous copying of objects across buckets in different AWS Regions. Buckets configured for cross-region replication can be owned by the same AWS account or by different accounts.

Q37. D

AWS Documentation Reference:

https://docs.aws.amazon.com/AmazonS3/latest/dev/replication.html

Although Amazon S3 stores your data across multiple geographically distant Availability Zones by default, compliance requirements might dictate that you store data at even greater distances. Cross-region replication allows you to replicate data between distant AWS Regions to satisfy these requirements.

This also minimizes latency in accessing objects by maintaining object copies in AWS Regions that are geographically closer to your users.

If you have compute clusters in two different AWS Regions that analyze the same set of objects, you might choose to maintain object copies in those Regions. This will help to increase operational efficiency.

Q38. A, B, C, D

AWS Documentation Reference:

https://docs.aws.amazon.com/AmazonS3/latest/dev/replication.html

Q39. B

Q40. B, C, D

AWS Documentation Reference:

https://docs.aws.amazon.com/AmazonS3/latest/dev/replication-what-is-isnot-replicated.html

A is wrong as object inherent file type doesn't matter when it is stored in S3.

E is wrong because objects encrypted using Amazon S3 managed keys (SSE-S3) are replicated.

B is correct, Amazon S3 doesn't replicate objects retroactively.

C is correct, only objects in the source bucket for which the bucket owner has permissions to read objects and access control lists (ACLs) are replicated.

D is correct, objects created with server-side encryption using customer-provided (SSE-C) encryption keys are not replicated. Also, by default, Amazon S3 does not replicate objects created with server-side encryption using AWS KMS–managed encryption (SSE-KMS) keys. . However, you can explicitly enable replication of these objects in the replication configuration

Q41. B

You can replicate objects from a source bucket to only one destination bucket. After Amazon S3 replicates an object, the object can't be replicated again. S3 does not replicate objects in the source bucket that are replicas that were created by another cross-region replication.

Q42. A, B
AWS Documentation Reference:
https://docs.aws.amazon.com/AmazonS3/latest/dev/object-lifecycle-mgmt.html
You can define when objects transition to another storage class. For example, you might choose to transition objects to the STANDARD_IA storage class 30 days after you created them, or archive objects to the GLACIER storage class one year after creating them.

You can define when objects expire. Amazon S3 deletes expired objects on your behalf.
With lifecycle configuration rules, you can tell Amazon S3 to transition objects to less expensive storage classes, or archive or delete them.

Q43. A, C, D

Q44. B, D
AWS Documentation Reference:
https://docs.aws.amazon.com/AmazonS3/latest/dev/lifecycle-transition-general-considerations.html
You can transition from:
- The STANDARD storage class to any other storage class.
- Any storage class to the S3 Glacier or S3 Glacier Deep Archive storage classes.
- The STANDARD_IA storage class to the INTELLIGENT_TIERING or ONEZONE_IA storage classes.
- The INTELLIGENT_TIERING storage class to the ONEZONE_IA storage class.
- The S3 Glacier storage class to the S3 Glacier Deep Archive storage class.

Q45. A, C, E
AWS Documentation Reference:
https://docs.aws.amazon.com/AmazonS3/latest/dev/lifecycle-transition-general-considerations.html

Q46. A, C, D, E
AWS Documentation Reference:
https://docs.aws.amazon.com/AmazonS3/latest/dev/lifecycle-transition-general-considerations.html
You can't transition from:

- Any storage class to the STANDARD storage class.
- Any storage class to the REDUCED_REDUNDANCY storage class.

- The INTELLIGENT_TIERING storage class to the STANDARD_IA storage class.
- The ONEZONE_IA storage class to the STANDARD_IA or INTELLIGENT_TIERING storage classes.
- Transition from the DEEP_ARCHIVE storage class to any other storage class.

## Q47.C
AWS Documentation Reference:
https://docs.aws.amazon.com/storagegateway/latest/userguide/WhatIsStorageGateway.html
AWS Storage Gateway is a hybrid cloud storage service that gives you on-premises access to virtually unlimited cloud storage. Customers use Storage Gateway to simplify storage management and reduce costs for key hybrid cloud storage use cases. These include moving tape backups to the cloud, reducing on-premises storage with cloud-backed file shares, providing low latency access to data in AWS for on-premises applications, as well as various migration, archiving, processing, and disaster recovery use cases.

## Q48. B
AWS Documentation Reference:
https://docs.aws.amazon.com/storagegateway/latest/userguide/WhatIsStorageGateway.html
A volume gateway provides cloud-backed storage volumes that you can mount as Internet Small Computer System Interface (iSCSI) devices from your on-premises application servers.

## Q49. C
Bucket names must be unique across all existing bucket names in Amazon S3.

## Q50. A
AWS Documentation Reference:
https://docs.aws.amazon.com/storagegateway/latest/userguide/WhatIsStorageGateway.html
A file gateway supports a file interface into Amazon Simple Storage Service (Amazon S3) and combines a service and a virtual software appliance. By using this combination, you can store and retrieve objects in Amazon S3 using industry-standard file protocols such as Network File System (NFS) and Server Message Block (SMB). The software appliance, or gateway, is deployed into your on-premises environment as a virtual machine (VM) running on VMware ESXi or Microsoft Hyper-V hypervisor.

## Q51. A, B
AWS Documentation Reference:
https://docs.aws.amazon.com/storagegateway/latest/userguide/WhatIsStorageGateway.html
Cached volumes – You store your data in Amazon Simple Storage Service (Amazon S3) and retain a copy of frequently accessed data subsets locally. Cached volumes offer a substantial cost savings on primary storage and minimize the need to scale your storage on-premises. You also retain low-latency access to your frequently accessed data.

Stored volumes – If you need low-latency access to your entire dataset, first configure your on-premises gateway to store all your data locally. Then asynchronously back up point-in-time snapshots of this data to Amazon S3. This configuration provides durable and inexpensive offsite backups that you can recover to your local data center or Amazon EC2. For example, if you need replacement capacity for disaster recovery, you can recover the backups to Amazon EC2.

Q52. A, B, C, D
AWS Documentation Reference:
https://docs.aws.amazon.com/AmazonS3/latest/dev/uploadobjusingmpu.html
https://docs.aws.amazon.com/AmazonS3/latest/dev/qfacts.html
You can use multipart api to upload object sizes from 5 MB to 5 TB. Hence E is not correct.

Q53. A, B, D
AWS Documentation Reference:
https://docs.aws.amazon.com/storagegateway/latest/userguide/WhatIsStorageGateway.html
You can run Storage Gateway either on-premises as a VM appliance, or as hardware appliance or in AWS as an Amazon EC2 instance.

Q54. A, B, D
AWS Documentation Reference:
https://docs.aws.amazon.com/storagegateway/latest/userguide/StorageGatewayConcepts.html

Q55. B
AWS Documentation Reference:
https://docs.aws.amazon.com/AmazonS3/latest/dev/storage-class-intro.html#sc-freq-data-access
For performance-sensitive use cases (those that require millisecond access time) and frequently accessed data, Amazon S3 provides the following storage classes:

STANDARD—the default storage class. If you don't specify the storage class when you upload an object, Amazon S3 assigns the STANDARD storage class.

REDUCED_REDUNDANCY—The Reduced Redundancy Storage (RRS) storage class is designed for noncritical, reproducible data that can be stored with less redundancy than the STANDARD storage class.
Q56. D
AWS Storage Gateway is a hybrid cloud storage service that gives you on-premises access to virtually unlimited cloud storage. The service provides three different types of gateways – Tape Gateway, File Gateway, and Volume Gateway – that seamlessly connect on-premises

applications to cloud storage, caching data locally for low-latency access. Your applications connect to the service through a virtual machine or hardware gateway appliance using standard storage protocols, such as NFS, SMB, and iSCSI.

Q57. B, C, D
AWS Documentation Reference:
https://aws.amazon.com/blogs/storage/aws-storage-gateway-in-2019/
Use case B: Move backups to the cloud
You can use cloud storage for on-premises data backups to reduce infrastructure and administration costs. You can use all three types of gateways for backup. This enables you to backup files, applications, databases, and volumes, either directly to Amazon S3, to EBS snapshots, or to virtual tape libraries.

Use Case C: Shift on-premises storage to cloud-backed file shares
A number of AWS customers have on-premises applications that need easy-to-use, cost-effective, scalable file storage. However, they often run out of capacity on their on-premises storage arrays, and face expensive hardware replacement cycles every three-to-five years. Many on-premises file workloads (for example, web servers, logging, and database backups) do not need expensive storage arrays. Instead, you can use File Gateway, which gives on-premises access to virtually unlimited cloud storage for files stored as Amazon S3 objects. It provides on-premises Windows and Linux applications easy integration to durable storage in Amazon S3 using SMB or NFS interfaces. You simply point applications to write to the gateway and the data seamlessly arrives in AWS.

Using the File Gateway in such a way allows you to keep using your existing applications, but reduce the amount of storage you must provision on-premises. The cache provides low-latency access to the working dataset and you get the elasticity of cloud storage. The data is stored as S3 objects and you can access it using the S3 API. You can use the 'Notify-When-Uploaded' event to know when your data has arrived in AWS, and automatically trigger an AWS Lambda function for further processing data in AWS. This enables you to easily manage distributed data pipelines. File Gateway thus allows you to replace your entry-level and midrange on-premises NAS with cloud backed storage, with the additional benefit of getting access to data in the cloud for further processing. You can now access your data through NFS or SMB on-premises and through the S3 API in AWS.

Use Case D: Low latency access to data in AWS for on-premises applications
The first two use cases shows how Storage Gateway allows you to store data to AWS, either for backups or as a replacement to your on-premises file servers. There is a third use case where customers have data in the cloud that they want to share and distribute with remote locations. For example, data may be generated through a genomics application in AWS, and also must be accessed from on-premises by researchers. In other cases, a media archive or geospatial dataset may have been moved from on-premises for archival in AWS using services

such as AWS Snowball or AWS DataSync, but customers want to have "on-demand" access to this data from existing on-premises applications.

With File Gateway, customers have on-demand, low-latency access to data stored in AWS for application workflows that can span the globe. You can use features such as cache refresh to refresh data in geographically distributed locations so content can be easily shared across your offices.

Q58. D
AWS Documentation Reference:
https://docs.aws.amazon.com/AmazonS3/latest/dev/serv-side-encryption.html

Q59. A, C, D
AWS Documentation Reference:
https://docs.aws.amazon.com/storagegateway/latest/userguide/StorageGatewayConcepts.html
Tape Gateway offers a durable, cost-effective solution to archive your data in the AWS Cloud. With its virtual tape library (VTL) interface, you use your existing tape-based backup infrastructure to store data on virtual tape cartridges that you create on your tape gateway. Each tape gateway is preconfigured with a media changer and tape drives. These are available to your existing client backup applications as iSCSI devices.

Q60. B, C
AWS Documentation Reference:
https://docs.aws.amazon.com/AmazonS3/latest/dev/storage-class-intro.html#sc-infreq-data-access
The STANDARD_IA and ONEZONE_IA storage classes are designed for long-lived and infrequently accessed data. (IA stands for infrequent access.) STANDARD_IA and ONEZONE_IA objects are available for millisecond access (similar to the STANDARD storage class).
STANDARD_IA—Use for your primary or only copy of data that can't be recreated.
ONEZONE_IA—Use if you can recreate the data if the Availability Zone fails, and for object replicas when setting cross-region replication (CRR).

These storage classes differ as follows:
• STANDARD_IA—Amazon S3 stores the object data redundantly across multiple geographically separated Availability Zones (similar to the STANDARD storage class). STANDARD_IA objects are resilient to the loss of an Availability Zone. This storage class offers greater availability and resiliency than the ONEZONE_IA class.
• ONEZONE_IA—Amazon S3 stores the object data in only one Availability Zone, which makes it less expensive than STANDARD_IA. However, the data is not resilient to the physical loss of the Availability Zone resulting from disasters, such as earth quakes and

floods. The ONEZONE_IA storage class is as durable as STANDARD_IA, but it is less available and less resilient.

Q61. B

Q62. B, D
File Gateway and Volume Cached Gateway maintain local copy of frequently accessed data.

Q63. D
Amazon S3 is a REST service, so you can use SSL to protect the data in transit if you are using the S3 API or use client side encryption if you are using the AWS SDK. A and B are options to use client side encryption before uploading data to S3.

Q64. A, B, C
AWS Documentation Reference:
https://docs.aws.amazon.com/AmazonS3/latest/dev/Introduction.html#ConsistencyModel
Amazon S3 offers eventual consistency for overwrite PUTS and DELETES in all Regions. Amazon S3 achieves high availability by replicating data across multiple servers within AWS data centers. If a PUT request is successful, your data is safely stored. However, information about the changes must replicate across Amazon S3, which can take some time, and so you might observe the following behaviors:
* A process replaces an existing object and immediately tries to read it. Until the change is fully propagated, Amazon S3 might return the previous data.
In this case original value is 'yellow', so you may get any value 'yellow', 'red' or 'ruby'.
Amazon S3 does not currently support object locking. If two PUT requests are simultaneously made to the same key, the request with the latest timestamp wins.

Q65. A, B
By using Server-Side Encryption, you request Amazon S3 to encrypt your object before saving it on disks in its data centers and decrypt it when you download the objects.

By using Client-Side Encryption, you can encrypt data client-side and upload the encrypted data to Amazon S3. In this case, you manage the encryption process, the encryption keys, and related tools.

SSL connection given data in transit encryption.

Q66. A, B, C
AWS Documentation Reference:
https://docs.aws.amazon.com/AmazonS3/latest/dev/access-control-block-public-access.html
The Amazon S3 Block Public Access feature provides settings for access points, buckets, and accounts to help you manage public access to Amazon S3 resources. You can enable block

public access settings only for access points, buckets, and AWS accounts. Amazon S3 doesn't support block public access settings on a per-object basis.

When Amazon S3 evaluates whether an operation is prohibited by a block public access setting, it rejects any request that violates an access point, bucket, or account setting.

Q67. A, C

AWS Documentation Reference:

https://docs.aws.amazon.com/AmazonS3/latest/dev/ObjectVersioning.html

When you PUT an object in a versioning-enabled bucket, the noncurrent version is not overwritten. The following figure shows that when a new version of photo.gif is PUT into a bucket that already contains an object with the same name, the original object (ID = 111111) remains in the bucket, Amazon S3 generates a new version ID (222222), and adds the newer version to the bucket.

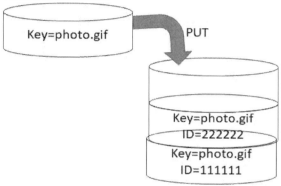

When you DELETE an object, all versions remain in the bucket and Amazon S3 inserts a delete marker, as shown in the following figure. The delete marker becomes the current version of the object.

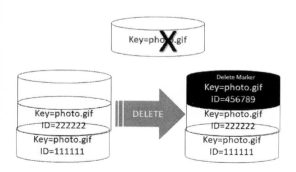

Q68. A, B, D, F

C, E are ways to encrypt data in transit and data at rest in S3.

AWS Identity and Access Management (IAM) user policies can be defined in way so as to specify the users that can access specific buckets and objects.

You can use a bucket policy to grant access across AWS accounts, grant public or anonymous permissions, and allow or block access based on certain conditions.

Q69. A, B, C, D
AWS Documentation Reference:
https://docs.aws.amazon.com/AmazonS3/latest/dev/access-policy-alternatives-guidelines.html
E is incorrect because if the AWS account that owns the object also owns the bucket, then it can write a bucket policy to manage the object permissions.

The following are the scenarios when you use object ACLs to manage object permissions.

- An object ACL is the only way to manage access to objects not owned by the bucket owner – An AWS account that owns the bucket can grant another AWS account permission to upload objects. The bucket owner does not own these objects. The AWS account that created the object must grant permissions using object ACLs.
  A bucket owner cannot grant permissions on objects it does not own. For example, a bucket policy granting object permissions applies only to objects owned by the bucket owner. However, the bucket owner, who pays the bills, can write a bucket policy to deny access to any objects in the bucket, regardless of who owns it. The bucket owner can also delete any objects in the bucket.

- Permissions vary by object and you need to manage permissions at the object level – You can write a single policy statement granting an AWS account read permission on millions of objects with a specific key name prefix. For example, grant read permission on objects starting with key name prefix "logs". However, if your access permissions vary by object, granting permissions to individual objects using a bucket policy may not be practical. Also the bucket policies are limited to 20 KB in size.
- Object ACLs control only object-level permissions – There is a single bucket policy for the entire bucket, but object ACLs are specified per object.
- An AWS account that owns a bucket can grant another AWS account permission to manage access policy. It allows that account to change anything in the policy. To better manage permissions, you may choose not to give such a broad permission, and instead grant only the READ-ACP and WRITE-ACP permissions on a subset of objects. This limits the account to manage permissions only on specific objects by updating individual object ACLs.

The only recommended use case for the bucket ACL is to grant write permission to the Amazon S3 Log Delivery group to write access log objects to your bucket (see Amazon S3 Server Access Logging). If you want Amazon S3 to deliver access logs to your bucket, you will need to grant write permission on the bucket to the Log Delivery group. The only way you can grant necessary permissions to the Log Delivery group is via a bucket ACL.

Q70.C
AWS Documentation Reference:
https://docs.aws.amazon.com/AmazonS3/latest/dev/ObjectVersioning.html
When you DELETE an object, all versions remain in the bucket and Amazon S3 inserts a delete marker, as shown in the following figure. The delete marker becomes the current version of the object.

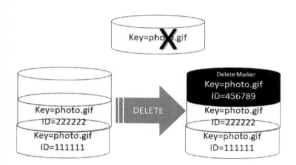

The delete marker becomes the current version of the object. By default, GET requests retrieve the most recently stored version. Performing a simple GET Object request when the current version is a delete marker returns a 404 Not Found error.

Q71. False
By default, all S3 buckets are private and can be accessed only by users that are explicitly granted access.

Q72. A, B
AWS Documentation Reference:
https://docs.aws.amazon.com/AmazonS3/latest/dev/ObjectVersioning.html
You can, however, GET a noncurrent version of an object by specifying its version ID. In the following figure, we GET a specific object version, 111111. Amazon S3 returns that object version even though it's not the current version.

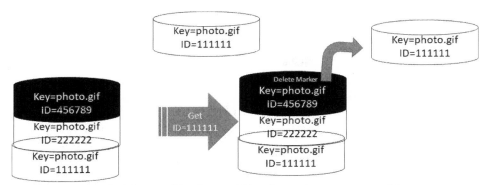

You can permanently delete an object by specifying the version you want to delete.

## Q73. C
AWS Documentation Reference:
https://docs.aws.amazon.com/AmazonS3/latest/dev/object-lifecycle-mgmt.html
You should define lifecycle configuration rules for objects that have a well-defined lifecycle.
In case of daily raw data, it will be transformed or deleted after the process every day which can be implemented as part of ETL process itself.

## Q74. A, B, D
AWS Documentation Reference:
https://aws.amazon.com/blogs/security/iam-policies-and-bucket-policies-and-acls-oh-my-controlling-access-to-s3-resources/
You can manage permissions by creating users and managing permissions individually by attaching policies to users (or user groups).

B because If you're more interested in "What can this user do in AWS?" then IAM policies is the better option. You can answer this by looking up an IAM user and then examining their IAM policies to see what rights they have.

A and D:
Assuming requirement is to control access to other AWS services as well apart from S3. IAM policies will be easier to manage since you can centrally manage all of your permissions in IAM, instead of spreading them between IAM and S3.

Assuming scenario where you have numerous S3 buckets each with different permissions requirements. IAM policies will be easier to manage since you don't have to define a large number of S3 bucket policies and can instead rely on fewer, more detailed IAM policies.

## Q75. D
AWS Documentation Reference:

https://docs.aws.amazon.com/AmazonS3/latest/dev/how-s3-evaluates-access-control.html
In order to determine whether the requester has permission to perform the specific operation, Amazon S3 does the following, in order, when it receives a request:

1. Converts all the relevant access policies (user policy, bucket policy, ACLs) at run time into a set of policies for evaluation.

2. Evaluates the resulting set of policies in the following steps. In each step, Amazon S3 evaluates a subset of policies in a specific context, based on the context authority.

- User context – In the user context, the parent account to which the user belongs is the context authority. Amazon S3 evaluates a subset of policies owned by the parent account. This subset includes the user policy that the parent attaches to the user. If the parent also owns the resource in the request (bucket, object), Amazon S3 also evaluates the corresponding resource policies (bucket policy, bucket ACL, and object ACL) at the same time. A user must have permission from the parent account to perform the operation. This step applies only if the request is made by a user in an AWS account. If the request is made using root credentials of an AWS account, Amazon S3 skips this step.
- Bucket context – In the bucket context, Amazon S3 evaluates policies owned by the AWS account that owns the bucket. If the request is for a bucket operation, the requester must have permission from the bucket owner. If the request is for an object, Amazon S3 evaluates all the policies owned by the bucket owner to check if the bucket owner has not explicitly denied access to the object. If there is an explicit deny set, Amazon S3 does not authorize the request.
- Object context – If the request is for an object, Amazon S3 evaluates the subset of policies owned by the object owner.

Q76. A
AWS Documentation Reference: Example 3: Bucket Operation Requested by an IAM Principal Whose Parent AWS Account Is Also the Bucket Owner
https://docs.aws.amazon.com/AmazonS3/latest/dev/access-control-auth-workflow-bucket-operation.html
Amazon S3 performs the following context evaluation:

Because the request is from an IAM principal, in the user context, Amazon S3 evaluates all policies that belong to the parent AWS account to determine if Jill has permission to perform the operation.

1. In this example, parent AWS account 1111-1111-1111, to which the principal belongs, is also the bucket owner. As a result, in addition to the user policy, Amazon S3 also evaluates the bucket policy and bucket ACL in the same context, because they belong to the same account.

2. Because Amazon S3 evaluated the bucket policy and bucket ACL as part of the user context, it does not evaluate the bucket context.

## Q77. B, C, D, E
AWS Documentation Reference:
https://aws.amazon.com/blogs/security/iam-policies-and-bucket-policies-and-acls-oh-my-controlling-access-to-s3-resources/

## Q78. B
AWS Documentation Reference: Example 4: Bucket Operation Requested by an IAM Principal Whose Parent AWS Account Is Not the Bucket Owner
https://docs.aws.amazon.com/AmazonS3/latest/dev/access-control-auth-workflow-bucket-operation.html
In this example, the request is sent by Jill, an IAM user whose parent AWS account is 1111-1111-1111, but the bucket is owned by another AWS account, 2222-2222-2222.
Jill will need permissions from both the parent AWS account and the bucket owner. Amazon S3 evaluates the context as follows:

Because the request is from an IAM principal, Amazon S3 evaluates the user context by reviewing the policies authored by the account to verify that Jill has the necessary permissions. If Jill has permission, then Amazon S3 moves on to evaluate the bucket context; if not, it denies the request.

In the bucket context, Amazon S3 verifies that bucket owner 2222-2222-2222 has granted Jill (or her parent AWS account) permission to perform the requested operation. If she has that permission, Amazon S3 grants the request and performs the operation; otherwise, Amazon S3 denies the request.

## Q79.A, B, D, E
AWS Documentation Reference:
https://docs.aws.amazon.com/AmazonS3/latest/dev/S3_ACLs_UsingACLs.html
Access control lists (ACLs) are one of the resource-based access policy options that you can use to manage access to your buckets and objects. You can use ACLs to grant basic read/write permissions to other AWS accounts. There are limits to managing permissions using ACLs. For example, you can grant permissions only to other AWS accounts; you cannot grant permissions to users in your account. You cannot grant conditional permissions, nor can you explicitly deny permissions. ACLs are suitable for specific scenarios. For example, if a bucket owner allows other AWS accounts to upload objects, permissions to these objects can only be managed using object ACL by the AWS account that owns the object.
https://docs.aws.amazon.com/AmazonS3/latest/dev/acl-overview.html#specifying-grantee

When using ACLs, a grantee can be an AWS account or one of the predefined Amazon S3 groups. However, the grantee cannot be an IAM user.

Q80. D
AWS Documentation Reference:
https://docs.aws.amazon.com/AmazonS3/latest/dev/example-bucket-policies.html#example-bucket-policies-use-case-3/

For the option A, following is an example of bucket policy having ipaddress in the condition block:

```
{
 "Version": " 2012-10-17",
 "Id": "S3PolicyId",
 "Statement": [
  {
   "Sid": "IPAllow",
   "Effect": "Allow",
   "Principal": "*",
   "Action": "s3:*",
   "Resource": "arn:aws:s3:::projectbucket/*",
   "Condition": {
     "IpAddress": {"aws:SourceIp": "65.350.234.0/16"}
        }
  }
 ]
}
```

The Condition block uses the IpAddress and NotIpAddress conditions and the aws:SourceIp condition key, which is an AWS-wide condition key.

Option B and C, policy that denies access to all AWS actions in the account when the request comes from outside the specified IP range.
For option B

```
{
  "Version": "2012-10-17",
  "Statement": {
   "Effect": "Deny",
   "Action": "*",
   "Resource": "*",
   "Condition": {
     "NotIpAddress": {
       "aws:SourceIp": [
```

```
        "65.350.234.0/16"


            ]
        }
      }
    }
}
For option C
{
    "Version": "2012-10-17",
    "Statement": {
      "Effect": "Allow",
      "Action": "*",
      "Resource": "*",
      "Condition": {
        "IpAddress": {
          "aws:SourceIp": [
            "65.350.234.0/16"


          ]
        }
      }
    }
}
```

Q81. B
AWS Documentation Reference:
https://docs.aws.amazon.com/storagegateway/latest/userguide/WhatIsStorageGateway.html
A volume gateway provides cloud-backed storage volumes that you can mount as Internet Small Computer System Interface (iSCSI) devices from your on-premises application servers. The gateway supports the following volume configurations:

Cached volumes – You store your data in Amazon Simple Storage Service (Amazon S3) and retain a copy of frequently accessed data subsets locally. Cached volumes offer a substantial cost savings on primary storage and minimize the need to scale your storage on-premises. You also retain low-latency access to your frequently accessed data.

Stored volumes – If you need low-latency access to your entire dataset, first configure your on-premises gateway to store all your data locally. Then asynchronously back up point-in-time snapshots of this data to Amazon S3. This configuration provides durable and inexpensive offsite backups that you can recover to your local data center or Amazon Elastic Compute

Cloud (Amazon EC2). For example, if you need replacement capacity for disaster recovery, you can recover the backups to Amazon EC2.

Q82. C
AWS Documentation Reference:
https://docs.aws.amazon.com/AmazonS3/latest/dev/intro-lifecycle-rules.html
Lifecycle Rules: Based on an Object's Age:
You can specify a time period, in number of days from the creation (or modification) of the objects, when Amazon S3 can take the action.
When you specify the number of days in the Transition and Expiration actions in a lifecycle configuration, note the following:
It is the number of days since object creation when the action will occur.
Amazon S3 calculates the time by adding the number of days specified in the rule to the object creation time and rounding the resulting time to the next day midnight UTC. For example, if an object was created at 1/15/2020 10:30 AM UTC and you specify 3 days in a transition rule, then the transition date of the object would be calculated as 1/19/2020 00:00 UTC.

Q83. C
AWS Documentation Reference:
https://docs.aws.amazon.com/AmazonS3/latest/dev/ShareObjectPreSignedURL.html
Amazon S3 Pre-Signed URLs Allow application users to download files from your private Amazon S3 buckets without giving access to buckets.
All objects by default are private. Only the object owner has permission to access these objects. However, the object owner can optionally share objects with others by creating a presigned URL, using their own security credentials, to grant time-limited permission to download the objects. You can generate presigned URL programmatically using the AWS SDK for Java and .NET.

When you create a presigned URL for your object, you must provide your security credentials, specify a bucket name, an object key, specify the HTTP method (GET to download the object) and expiration date and time. The presigned URLs are valid only for the specified duration.

Anyone who receives the presigned URL can then access the object.

A is not right choice as making the folder public will make it accessible to everyone.
B bucket policy can be used to give access to AWS account IAM user or roles only and not website registered users.
D the registered users in the website are external users and should not have IAM user access.

Q84. A
AWS Documentation Reference:
https://aws.amazon.com/getting-started/projects/replace-tape-with-cloud/

The AWS Storage Gateway service offers a Tape Gateway configuration that gives you an alternative to physical backup tapes that fits seamlessly into your existing backup process.

The simplest approach is to run Storage Gateway on-premises as a virtual machine (VM). This will provide you the ability to create virtual tapes in your gateway's Virtual Tape Library. Virtual tapes are stored in Amazon S3 and available to your backup software through the VTL interface. This replaces tape and tape automation, so you can start using the cloud as a backup target with minimal disruption to existing systems and processes.

Tape Gateway enables backups to the cloud and preserves your existing software licensing investment, backup jobs, and catalogs.

You will be able to reduce your costs with long-term archival storage using Amazon S3 Glacier and Amazon S3 Glacier Deep Archive. You can use your backup software to move a virtual tape into Amazon S3 Glacier or Amazon S3 Glacier Deep Archive for further cost reductions.

Q85.D
Volume Gateway works with your existing applications through the industry-standard iSCSI protocol. The Cache Volume Gateway maintains on-premises of recently accessed data

Q86. A
AWS Documentation Reference:
https://docs.aws.amazon.com/AmazonS3/latest/dev/storage-class-intro.html#sc-dynamic-data-access
INTELLIGENT_TIERING delivers automatic cost savings by moving data on a granular object level between two access tiers, a frequent access tier and a lower-cost infrequent access tier, when access patterns change. The INTELLIGENT_TIERING storage class is ideal if you want to optimize storage costs automatically for long-lived data when access patterns are unknown or unpredictable.

Q87. B
AWS Documentation Reference:
https://docs.aws.amazon.com/storagegateway/latest/userguide/StorageGatewayConcepts.html#storage-gateway-stored-volume-concepts
By using stored volumes, you can store your primary data locally, while asynchronously backing up that data to AWS. Stored volumes provide your on-premises applications with low-latency access to their entire datasets. At the same time, they provide durable, offsite backups. You can create storage volumes and mount them as iSCSI devices from your on-premises application servers. Data written to your stored volumes is stored on your on-premises storage hardware. This data is asynchronously backed up to Amazon S3 as Amazon Elastic Block Store (Amazon EBS) snapshots.

Q88. A, B, C

AWS Documentation Reference:

https://docs.aws.amazon.com/AmazonS3/latest/dev/intro-lifecycle-rules.html

Lifecycle Rules: Based on a Specific Date

When specifying an action in a lifecycle rule, you can specify a date when you want Amazon S3 to take the action. When the specific date arrives, S3 applies the action to all qualified objects (based on the filter criteria).

If you specify a lifecycle action with a date that is in the past, all qualified objects become immediately eligible for that lifecycle action. The date-based action is not a one-time action. S3 continues to apply the date-based action even after the date has passed, as long as the rule status is Enabled.

When you specify a date-based Expiration action to delete all objects (assume no filter specified in the rule). On the specified date, S3 expires all the objects in the bucket. S3 also continues to expire any new objects you create in the bucket. To stop the lifecycle action, you must remove the action from the lifecycle configuration, disable the rule, or delete the rule from the lifecycle configuration.

Q89. C, D

AWS Documentation Reference:

https://docs.aws.amazon.com/AmazonS3/latest/dev/storage-class-intro.html#sc-glacier

The GLACIER and DEEP_ARCHIVE storage classes are designed for low-cost data archiving. These storage classes offer the same durability and resiliency as the STANDARD storage class.

Q90. C

AWS Documentation Reference:

https://docs.aws.amazon.com/AmazonS3/latest/dev/cors.html

https://docs.aws.amazon.com/sdk-for-javascript/v2/developer-guide/cors.html

Cross-origin resource sharing (CORS) defines a way for client web applications that are loaded in one domain to interact with resources in a different domain.

Cross-origin resource sharing, or CORS, is a security feature of modern web browsers. It enables web browsers to negotiate which domains can make requests of external websites or services. CORS is an important consideration when developing browser applications with the AWS SDK for JavaScript because most requests to resources are sent to an external domain, such as the endpoint for a web service. In this case S3 web service.

In the simplest case, your browser script makes a GET request for a resource from a server in another domain. Depending on the CORS configuration of that server, if the request is from a domain that's authorized to submit GET requests, the cross-origin server responds by returning the requested resource.

If either the requesting domain or the type of HTTP request is not authorized, the request is denied.

Amazon S3 buckets require CORS configuration before you can perform operations on them.

To configure your bucket to allow cross-origin requests, you create a CORS configuration, which is an XML document with rules that identify the origins that you will allow to access your bucket, the operations (HTTP methods) that will support for each origin, and other operation-specific information. When Amazon S3 receives a preflight request from a browser, it evaluates the CORS configuration for the bucket and uses the first CORSRule rule that matches the incoming browser request to enable a cross-origin request.

Q91.C.
AWS Documentation Reference:
https://docs.aws.amazon.com/storagegateway/latest/userguide/WhatIsStorageGateway.html
AWS Storage Gateway's file interface, or file gateway, offers you a seamless way to connect to the cloud in order to store application data files and backup images as durable objects on Amazon S3 cloud storage. File gateway offers SMB or NFS-based access to data in Amazon S3 with local caching.

Q92. D
For first 30 days as there are lot of users frequently accessing the data, therefore STANDARD class will be most appropriate.
After 30 days as there is infrequent access so STANDARD_IA will be more appropriate.
After 30 days as it is rarely accessed and retrieval time is not a criteria, so most cost effective storage will be DEEP_ARCHIVE.

DEEP_ARCHIVE is used for archiving data that rarely needs to be accessed. Storage costs for DEEP_ARCHIVE are less expensive than using the GLACIER storage class.

Q93. A, D
AWS Documentation Reference:
https://docs.aws.amazon.com/AmazonS3/latest/dev/storage-class-intro.html#sc-glacier
GLACIER—Use for archives where portions of the data might need to be retrieved in minutes.
DEEP_ARCHIVE—Use for archiving data that rarely needs to be accessed.

Q94.C, D
AWS Documentation Reference:
https://docs.aws.amazon.com/AmazonS3/latest/dev/lifecycle-transition-general-considerations.html
Restoring Archived Objects:
Archived objects are not accessible in real time. You must first initiate a restore request and then wait until a temporary copy of the object is available for the duration that you specify in the request.

Q95. B, C

AWS Documentation Reference:

https://docs.aws.amazon.com/AmazonS3/latest/dev/how-to-set-lifecycle-configuration-intro.html

When you add a lifecycle configuration to a bucket, the configuration rules apply to both existing objects and objects that you add later. For example, if you add a lifecycle configuration rule today with an expiration action that causes objects with a specific prefix to expire 30 days after creation, Amazon S3 will queue for removal any existing objects that are more than 30 days old.

### Q96. A, C

AWS Documentation Reference:

https://docs.aws.amazon.com/AmazonS3/latest/dev/qfacts.html

Part size can be from 5 MB to 5 GB, last part can be < 5 MB.

### Q97. C

AWS Documentation Reference:

https://docs.aws.amazon.com/AmazonS3/latest/dev/DeletingObjects.html

If your bucket is version-enabled, then multiple versions of the same object can exist in the bucket. When working with version-enabled buckets, the delete API enables the following options:

Specify a non-versioned delete request—That is, you specify only the object's key, and not the version ID. In this case, Amazon S3 creates a delete marker and returns its version ID in the response. This makes your object disappear from the bucket.

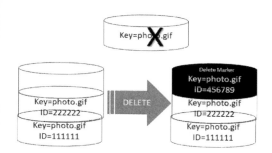

Specify a versioned delete request—That is, you specify both the key and also a version ID. In this case the following two outcomes are possible:

- If the version ID maps to a specific object version, then Amazon S3 deletes the specific version of the object.

- If the version ID maps to the delete marker of that object, Amazon S3 deletes the delete marker. This makes the object reappear in your bucket.

## Q98. B
AWS Documentation Reference:
https://docs.aws.amazon.com/AmazonS3/latest/dev/how-to-set-lifecycle-configuration-intro.html
Based on the requirement S3 is the most cost effective storage giving different storage options based on the accessibility and life duration time based requirements. Hence C and D is not correct. You didn't need Redshift data warehouse to store for this requirement. EBS provides block storage and is specifically meant for EC2 (Elastic Computing Cloud) instances and is not accessible unless mounted to one

S3 lifecycle rules are applied based on object creation date. Hence A is not correct.

Option B provides the appropriate transition of data based on the life time from creation date to right S3 storage tier.

## Q99.C, D
AWS Documentation Reference:
https://docs.aws.amazon.com/AmazonS3/latest/dev/DeletingObjects.html
If your bucket is version-enabled, then multiple versions of the same object can exist in the bucket. When working with version-enabled buckets, the delete API enables the following options: That is, you specify both the key and also a version ID. In this case the following two outcomes are possible:
- If the version ID maps to a specific object version, then Amazon S3 deletes the specific version of the object.
- If the version ID maps to the delete marker of that object, Amazon S3 deletes the delete marker. This makes the object reappear in your bucket.

## Q100. B
AWS Documentation Reference:
https://docs.aws.amazon.com/AmazonS3/latest/dev/selecting-content-from-objects.html
With Amazon S3 Select, you can use simple structured query language (SQL) statements to filter the contents of Amazon S3 objects and retrieve just the subset of data that you need. By using Amazon S3 Select to filter this data, you can reduce the amount of data that Amazon S3 transfers, which reduces the cost and latency to retrieve this data.

Amazon S3 Select works on objects stored in CSV, JSON, or Apache Parquet format. It also works with objects that are compressed with GZIP or BZIP2 (for CSV and JSON objects only), and server-side encrypted objects. You can specify the format of the results as either CSV or JSON, and you can determine how the records in the result are delimited.

https://aws.amazon.com/blogs/aws/s3-glacier-select/

## Q101. B, C

The instance store is ideal for temporary storage, because the data stored in instance store volumes is not persistent through instance stops, terminations, or hardware failures.

For data to retain longer use EBS volumes. EBS volumes preserve their data through instance stops and terminations, can be easily backed up with EBS snapshots, can be removed from one instance and reattached to another, and support full-volume encryption.

## Q102. A, D

AWS Documentation Reference:

https://docs.aws.amazon.com/AWSEC2/latest/UserGuide/EBSVolumeTypes.html

## Q103. A, B

AWS Documentation Reference:

https://docs.aws.amazon.com/AWSEC2/latest/UserGuide/EBSVolumeTypes.html

## Q104. A, C, D, E

AWS Documentation Reference:

https://docs.aws.amazon.com/AWSEC2/latest/UserGuide/AmazonEBS.html

## Q105. B

AWS Documentation Reference:

https://docs.aws.amazon.com/en_pv/AWSEC2/latest/UserGuide/EBSVolumeTypes.html

## Q106. B.

AWS Documentation Reference:

https://docs.aws.amazon.com/en_pv/AWSEC2/latest/UserGuide/EBSVolumeTypes.html

## Q107. C.

AWS Documentation Reference:

https://docs.aws.amazon.com/en_pv/AWSEC2/latest/UserGuide/EBSVolumeTypes.html

## Q108. A

AWS Documentation Reference: General Purpose SSD (gp2) Volumes: I/O Credits and Burst Performance

https://docs.aws.amazon.com/en_pv/AWSEC2/latest/UserGuide/EBSVolumeTypes.html

General Purpose SSD (gp2) volumes offer between a minimum of 100 IOPS (at 33.33 GiB and below) and a maximum of 16,000 IOPS (at 5,334 GiB and above), baseline performance scales linearly at 3 IOPS per GiB of volume size. The 500 GB gp2 storage will have baseline performance of 500*3 = 1500 IOPS. As the volume uses fewer I/O credits of 1000 IPS than it earns 1500 IOPS in a second, unused I/O credits are added to the I/O credit balance.

When your volume requires 3000 IOPS which is more than the baseline performance I/O level of 1500 IOPS, it draws on I/O credits in the credit balance to burst to the required performance level

Q109. A, C
AWS Documentation Reference: Restoring an Amazon EBS Volume from a Snapshot
https://docs.aws.amazon.com/en_pv/AWSEC2/latest/UserGuide/ebs-restoring-volume.html
New volumes created from existing EBS snapshots load lazily in the background. This means that after a volume is created from a snapshot, there is no need to wait for all of the data to transfer from Amazon S3 to your EBS volume before your attached instance can start accessing the volume and all its data. If your instance accesses data that hasn't yet been loaded, the volume immediately downloads the requested data from Amazon S3, and then continues loading the rest of the volume data in the background.

Q110. A, C, D
AWS Documentation Reference:
https://docs.aws.amazon.com/en_pv/AWSEC2/latest/UserGuide/EBSPerformance.html
Use EBS-Optimized Instances
On instances without support for EBS-optimized throughput, network traffic can contend with traffic between your instance and your EBS volumes; on EBS-optimized instances, the two types of traffic are kept separate.

Be Aware of the Performance Penalty When Initializing Volumes from Snapshots
There is a significant increase in latency when you first access each block of data on a new EBS volume that was restored from a snapshot. You can avoid this performance hit by accessing each block prior to putting the volume into production. This process is called initialization (formerly known as pre-warming).

Use RAID 0 to Maximize Utilization of Instance Resources
Some instance types can drive more I/O throughput than what you can provision for a single EBS volume. You can join multiple gp2, io1, st1, or sc1 volumes together in a RAID 0 configuration to use the available bandwidth for these instances

Q111. B
AWS Documentation Reference: RAID Configuration Options
https://docs.aws.amazon.com/en_pv/AWSEC2/latest/UserGuide/raid-config.html

Q112. A
AWS Documentation Reference: RAID Configuration Options
https://docs.aws.amazon.com/en_pv/AWSEC2/latest/UserGuide/raid-config.html

## Q113. C, D

AWS Documentation Reference: RAID Configuration Options

https://docs.aws.amazon.com/en_pv/AWSEC2/latest/UserGuide/raid-config.html

RAID 0 can stripe multiple volumes together; for on-instance redundancy, RAID 1 can mirror two volumes together.

The resulting size of a RAID 0 array is the sum of the sizes of the volumes within it, and the bandwidth is the sum of the available bandwidth of the volumes within it. The resulting size and bandwidth of a RAID 1 array is equal to the size and bandwidth of the volumes in the array. For example, two 500 GiB Amazon EBS io1 volumes with 4,000 provisioned IOPS each will create a 1000 GiB RAID 0 array with an available bandwidth of 8,000 IOPS and 1,000 MiB/s of throughput or a 500 GiB RAID 1 array with an available bandwidth of 4,000 IOPS and 500 MiB/s of throughput.

## Q114. B, C

AWS Documentation Reference:

https://docs.aws.amazon.com/en_pv/AWSEC2/latest/UserGuide/ebs-io-characteristics.html

On a given volume configuration, certain I/O characteristics drive the performance behavior for your EBS volumes.

SSD-backed volumes—General Purpose SSD (gp2) and Provisioned IOPS SSD (io1)—deliver consistent performance whether an I/O operation is random or sequential.

HDD-backed volumes—Throughput Optimized HDD (st1) and Cold HDD (sc1)—deliver optimal performance only when I/O operations are large and sequential.

## Q115. C, D

AWS Documentation Reference:

https://docs.aws.amazon.com/AWSEC2/latest/UserGuide/raid-config.html

https://docs.aws.amazon.com/AWSEC2/latest/UserGuide/enhanced-networking.html

A is not correct because RAID1 does not provide a write performance improvement; it will require more Amazon EC2 to Amazon EBS bandwidth than non-RAID configurations because the data is written to multiple volumes simultaneously. It is pertinent when fault tolerance is more important than I/O performance; for example, as in a critical application. RAID 1 can mirror two volumes together.

B is not correct because placement group helps in instance to instance to communication. Enhanced networking does provides higher I/O performance and lower CPU utilization when compared to traditional virtualized network interfaces. Enhanced networking provides higher bandwidth, higher packet per second (PPS) performance, and consistently lower inter-instance latencies.

C is correct because RAID 0 can stripe multiple volumes together. I/O is distributed across the volumes in a stripe. If you add a volume, you get the straight addition of throughput.

RAID 0 can stripe multiple volumes together. The resulting size of a RAID 0 array is the sum of the sizes of the volumes within it, and the bandwidth is the sum of the available bandwidth of the volumes within it. The resulting size and bandwidth of a RAID 1 array is equal to the size and bandwidth of the volumes in the array. For example, two 500 GiB Amazon EBS io1 volumes with 4,000 provisioned IOPS each will create a 1000 GiB RAID 0 array with an available bandwidth of 8,000 IOPS and 1,000 MiB/s of throughput or a 500 GiB RAID 1 array with an available bandwidth of 4,000 IOPS and 500 MiB/s of throughput.

D is also another way of improving performance because EBS optimized instance keeps network traffic and traffic between instance and EBS separate.

Q116. A, B
AWS Documentation Reference: RAID Configuration Options
https://docs.aws.amazon.com/en_pv/AWSEC2/latest/UserGuide/raid-config.html
RAID 5 and RAID 6 are not recommended for Amazon EBS because the parity write operations of these RAID modes consume some of the IOPS available to your volumes.

Q117. A, D
AWS Documentation Reference: Creating New Empty Volumes with Encryption
https://docs.aws.amazon.com/en_pv/AWSEC2/latest/UserGuide/EBSEncryption.html
When you create a new, empty EBS volume, you can encrypt it by enabling encryption for the specific volume creation operation. If you enabled EBS encryption by default, the volume is automatically encrypted. By default, the volume is encrypted to your default key for EBS encryption. Alternatively, you can specify a different CMK for the specific volume creation operation. The volume is encrypted by the time it is first available, so your data is always secured.

Q118. A, B, E
AWS Documentation Reference: Encryption Support for Snapshots
https://docs.aws.amazon.com/en_pv/AWSEC2/latest/UserGuide/EBSSnapshots.html

Q119. C, D
AWS Documentation Reference: Encryption Support for Snapshots
https://docs.aws.amazon.com/en_pv/AWSEC2/latest/UserGuide/EBSSnapshots.html

Q120. E
AWS Documentation Reference: How EBS Encryption Works
https://docs.aws.amazon.com/en_pv/AWSEC2/latest/UserGuide/EBSEncryption.html

Q121. A
AWS Documentation Reference:

https://docs.aws.amazon.com/AWSEC2/latest/UserGuide/snapshot-lifecycle.html

You can use Amazon Data Lifecycle Manager to automate the creation, retention, and deletion of snapshots taken to back up your Amazon EBS volumes. Automating snapshot management helps you to:

- Protect valuable data by enforcing a regular backup schedule.
- Retain backups as required by auditors or internal compliance.
- Reduce storage costs by deleting outdated backups.

## Q122. B, C

AWS Documentation Reference:

https://docs.aws.amazon.com/en_pv/AWSEC2/latest/UserGuide/EBSEncryption.html

## Q123. A, D

AWS Documentation Reference:

https://docs.aws.amazon.com/AWSEC2/latest/UserGuide/ebs-creating-snapshot.html

Snapshots occur asynchronously; the point-in-time snapshot is created immediately, but the status of the snapshot is pending until the snapshot is complete (when all of the modified blocks have been transferred to Amazon S3), which can take several hours for large initial snapshots or subsequent snapshots where many blocks have changed. While it is completing, an in-progress snapshot is not affected by ongoing reads and writes to the volume.

You can take a snapshot of an attached volume that is in use. However, snapshots only capture data that has been written to your Amazon EBS volume at the time the snapshot command is issued. This might exclude any data that has been cached by any applications or the operating system. If you can pause any file writes to the volume long enough to take a snapshot, your snapshot should be complete. However, if you can't pause all file writes to the volume, you should unmount the volume from within the instance, issue the snapshot command, and then remount the volume to ensure a consistent and complete snapshot. You can remount and use your volume while the snapshot status is pending.

## Q124. C, D, E

AWS Documentation Reference: Creating New Empty Volumes with Encryption

https://docs.aws.amazon.com/en_pv/AWSEC2/latest/UserGuide/EBSEncryption.html

When you create a new, empty EBS volume, you can encrypt it by enabling encryption for the specific volume creation operation. If you enabled EBS encryption by default, the volume is automatically encrypted. By default, the volume is encrypted to your default key for EBS encryption. Alternatively, you can specify a different CMK for the specific volume creation operation.

When you create an encrypted EBS volume and attach it to a supported instance type, the following types of data are encrypted:

- Data at rest inside the volume
- All data moving between the volume and the instance

- All snapshots created from the volume
- All volumes created from those snapshots

A is not the most efficient way of achieving the desired functionality.

B is incorrect as IAM doesn't provide you services to encrypt EBS volume.

## Q125. B

AWS Documentation Reference:

https://aws.amazon.com/efs/

S3 is object based storage, EBS is block based storage and RDS is a relational database.

Here key words to focus is on 'files' and 'parallel shared access to multiple Amazon EC2 instances'.

Amazon Elastic File System (Amazon EFS) provides a simple, scalable, fully managed elastic NFS file system for use with AWS Cloud services and on-premises resources. It is built to scale on demand to petabytes without disrupting applications, growing and shrinking automatically as you add and remove files, eliminating the need to provision and manage capacity to accommodate growth.

Amazon EFS offers two storage classes: the Standard storage class, and the Infrequent Access storage class (EFS IA). EFS IA provides price/performance that's cost-optimized for files not accessed every day. By simply enabling EFS Lifecycle Management on your file system, files not accessed according to the lifecycle policy you choose will be automatically and transparently moved into EFS IA.

Amazon EFS is designed to provide massively parallel shared access to thousands of Amazon EC2 instances, enabling your applications to achieve high levels of aggregate throughput and IOPS with consistent low latencies.

Amazon EFS is well suited to support a broad spectrum of use cases from home directories to business-critical applications. Customers can use EFS to lift-and-shift existing enterprise applications to the AWS Cloud. Other use cases include: big data analytics, web serving and content management, application development and testing, media and entertainment workflows, database backups, and container storage.

## Q126. A, B

AWS Documentation Reference:

https://docs.aws.amazon.com/AWSEC2/latest/UserGuide/EBSVolumeTypes.html

## Q127. C

AWS Documentation Reference: Data availability

https://docs.aws.amazon.com/AWSEC2/latest/UserGuide/ebs-volumes.html#EBSFeatures

When you create an EBS volume in an Availability Zone, it is automatically replicated within that zone to prevent data loss due to failure of any single hardware component. After you create a volume, you can attach it to any EC2 instance in the same Availability Zone.

## Q128. A

AWS Documentation Reference:
https://docs.aws.amazon.com/en_pv/AWSEC2/latest/UserGuide/EBSVolumeTypes.html

## Q129. D

Here the key decision criteria is giving the similar level of 'performance' to premium and free members in most cost optimized way.

AWS Documentation Reference:
https://aws.amazon.com/s3/storage-classes/

For premium member use S3-Standard as it delivers low latency and high throughput.
S3 One Zone-IA doesn't provide availability and resilience of S3 Standard but offers the same high durability, high throughput, and low latency of S3 Standard, with a low per GB storage price and per GB retrieval fee.

## Q130. C

AWS Documentation Reference:
https://docs.aws.amazon.com/en_pv/AWSEC2/latest/UserGuide/EBSVolumeTypes.html

## Q131. A, B, C

AWS Documentation Reference: Amazon S3 Data Consistency Model
https://docs.aws.amazon.com/AmazonS3/latest/dev/Introduction.html

Amazon S3 offers eventual consistency for overwrite PUTS and DELETES in all Regions.
Amazon S3 provides read-after-write consistency for PUTS of new objects in your S3 bucket in all Regions with one caveat. The caveat is that if you make a HEAD or GET request to the key name (to find if the object exists) before creating the object, Amazon S3 provides eventual consistency for read-after-write. Amazon S3 achieves high availability by replicating data across multiple servers within AWS data centers. If a PUT request is successful, your data is safely stored. However, information about the changes must replicate across Amazon S3, which can take some time, and so you might observe the following behaviors:

- A process writes a new object to Amazon S3 and immediately lists keys within its bucket. Until the change is fully propagated, the object might not appear in the list.

- A process replaces an existing object and immediately tries to read it. Until the change is fully propagated, Amazon S3 might return the previous data.

- A process deletes an existing object and immediately tries to read it. Until the deletion is fully propagated, Amazon S3 might return the deleted data.

- A process deletes an existing object and immediately lists keys within its bucket. Until the deletion is fully propagated, Amazon S3 might list the deleted object.

## Q132. D

AWS Documentation Reference:
https://docs.aws.amazon.com/en_pv/AWSEC2/latest/UserGuide/EBSVolumeTypes.html

Q133. A, C, D

Cross region replication doesn't protect against object deletion, it enables automatic, asynchronous copying of objects across Amazon S3 buckets.

AWS Documentation Reference:

https://docs.aws.amazon.com/AmazonS3/latest/dev/object-lock.html

With Amazon S3 object lock, you can store objects using a write-once-read-many (WORM) model. You can use it to prevent an object from being deleted or overwritten for a fixed amount of time or indefinitely. Amazon S3 object lock helps you meet regulatory requirements that require WORM storage, or simply add another layer of protection against object changes and deletion.

https://aws.amazon.com/blogs/security/securing-access-to-aws-using-mfa-part-3/

https://docs.aws.amazon.com/AmazonS3/latest/dev/DeletingObjectVersions.html

Versioning keeps multiple versions of an object in the same bucket. When you enable it on a bucket, Amazon S3 automatically adds a unique version ID to every object stored in the bucket. At that point, a simple DELETE action does not permanently delete an object version; it merely associates a delete marker with the object. If you want to permanently delete an object version, you must specify its version ID in your DELETE request.

https://docs.aws.amazon.com/AmazonS3/latest/dev/UsingMFADelete.html

You can add another layer of protection by enabling MFA Delete on a versioned bucket. Once you do so, you must provide your AWS account's access keys and a valid code from the account's MFA device in order to permanently delete an object version or suspend or reactivate versioning on the bucket.

Q134. D

AWS Documentation Reference:

https://docs.aws.amazon.com/en_pv/AWSEC2/latest/UserGuide/snapshot-lifecycle.html

You can use Amazon Data Lifecycle Manager (Amazon DLM) to automate the creation, retention, and deletion of snapshots taken to back up your Amazon EBS volumes. Automating snapshot management helps you to:

- Protect valuable data by enforcing a regular backup schedule.
- Retain backups as required by auditors or internal compliance.
- Reduce storage costs by deleting outdated backups.

Q135. A

AWS Documentation Reference:

https://docs.aws.amazon.com/AmazonS3/latest/user-guide/access-analyzer.html

https://aws.amazon.com/blogs/storage/protect-amazon-s3-buckets-using-access-analyzer-for-s3/?nc1=b_rp

Access Analyzer for S3 evaluates your bucket access policies and enables you to discover and swiftly remediate buckets with potentially unintended access. Access Analyzer for Amazon S3 alerts you to S3 buckets that are configured to allow access to anyone on the internet or other AWS accounts, including AWS accounts outside of your organization. For each public or shared bucket, you receive findings into the source and level of public or shared access. For example, Access Analyzer for S3 might show that a bucket has read or write access provided through bucket access control lists (ACLs), bucket policies, or both. Armed with this knowledge, you can take immediate and precise corrective action to restore your bucket access to what you intended.

Q136. A, B, D
AWS Documentation Reference:
https://docs.aws.amazon.com/AmazonS3/latest/dev/restoring-objects.html
The following table summarizes the archival retrieval options.

| Storage Class | Expedited | Standard | Bulk |
|---|---|---|---|
| GLACIER | 1–5 minutes | 3–5 hours | 5–12 hours |
| DEEP_ARCHIVE | Not available | Within 12 hours | Within 48 hours |

Q137. B, C, D
AWS Documentation Reference:
https://docs.aws.amazon.com/AmazonS3/latest/dev/website-hosting-custom-domain-walkthrough.html
If you already have a registered domain name example.com with Route 53 following steps needs to be done:

1.   Create and Configure Buckets and Upload Website Content
To support requests for both the root domain (example.com) and subdomain (www.example.com), you create two buckets. You will host your content out of the root domain bucket (example.com), and you will create a redirect request for the subdomain bucket (www.example.com). The redirect request redirects users who try to access www.example.com to the root domain. In other words, if someone enters www.example.com in their browser, they are redirected to example.com and see the content that is hosted in the Amazon S3 bucket with that name
After you've configured your root domain bucket for website hosting and your subdomain bucket for redirect, you can upload your index document and optional website content to your root domain bucket. The content can be text files, family photos, videos—whatever you want.

2.   Edit Block Public Access Settings
The bucket that you use to host a website must have public read access. It is intentional that everyone in the world will have read access to this bucket. By default, Amazon S3 blocks public access to your account and buckets. To grant public read access, you must disable block

public access for the bucket and write a bucket policy that allows public read access. In this example, example.com contains the website content. Therefore, you need to make this bucket publically readable.

3.  Add Alias Records for example.com and www.example.com
Figure out your website endpoints. If the example.com domain bucket resides in the US West (Oregon) Region, the Amazon S3 website endpoint would be as follows:
http://example.com.s3-website-us-west-2.amazonaws.com/

If the www.example.com subdomain bucket resides in the same Region, the endpoint would be as follows:
http://www.example.com.s3-website-us-west-2.amazonaws.com/

Create the alias records that you add to the hosted zone for your domain maps example.com and www.example.com. Instead of using IP addresses, the alias records use the above Amazon S3 website endpoints.

Q138. A
AWS Documentation Reference:
https://aws.amazon.com/blogs/storage/protecting-data-with-amazon-s3-object-lock/
https://docs.aws.amazon.com/AmazonS3/latest/dev/object-lock.html
Amazon S3 Object Lock is an Amazon S3 feature that allows you to store objects using a write once, read many (WORM) model. You can use WORM protection for scenarios where it is imperative that data is not changed or deleted after it has been written.
Amazon S3 Object Lock provides two ways to manage object retention. The first is retention periods and the second is legal holds.

*   A retention period specifies a fixed period of time during which an object remains locked. During this period, your object is WORM-protected and can't be overwritten or deleted. You apply a retention period either in number of days or number of years with the minimum being 1-day and no maximum limit.
*   A legal hold provides the same protection as a retention period, but it has no expiration date. Instead, a legal hold remains in place until you explicitly remove it.

When setting a retention period for your objects or buckets, you can choose the retention mode you wish to apply to your objects. You can choose either the Governance mode or the Compliance mode for your objects.

You should use the Governance mode if you want to protect objects from being deleted by most users during a pre-defined retention period, but at the same time want some users with special permissions to have the flexibility to alter the retention settings or delete the objects. Users with the s3:BypassGovernanceRetention permission can override or remove governance-mode retention settings. Most customers will use the Governance mode since they don't have compliant storage requirements.

You should use the Compliance mode if you have a requirement to store compliant data. You should only use the Compliance mode if you never want any user, including the root user in your AWS account, to be able to delete the objects during a pre-defined retention period. The only way to delete an object under the Compliance mode before its retention date expires is to delete the associated AWS account.

Q139. A, B, E, F, G
AWS Documentation Reference:
https://docs.aws.amazon.com/AmazonS3/latest/dev/NotificationHowTo.html
Currently, Amazon S3 can publish notifications for the following events:

New object created events — Amazon S3 supports multiple APIs to create objects. You can request notification when only a specific API is used (for example, s3:ObjectCreated:Put), or you can use a wildcard (for example, s3:ObjectCreated:*) to request notification when an object is created regardless of the API used.

Object removal events —You can request notification when an object is deleted or a versioned object is permanently deleted by using the s3:ObjectRemoved:Delete event type. Or you can request notification when a delete marker is created for a versioned object by using s3:ObjectRemoved:DeleteMarkerCreated. You can also use a wildcard s3:ObjectRemoved:* to request notification anytime an object is deleted.

Restore object events — Amazon S3 supports the restoration of objects archived to the GLACIER storage class. You request to be notified of object restoration completion by using s3:ObjectRestore:Completed. You use s3:ObjectRestore:Post to request notification of the initiation of a restore.

Reduced Redundancy Storage (RRS) object lost events — Amazon S3 sends a notification message when it detects that an object of the RRS storage class has been lost.

Replication events — Amazon S3 sends event notifications for replication configurations that have S3 Replication Time Control (S3 RTC) enabled. It sends these notifications when an object fails replication, when an object exceeds the 15-minute threshold, when an object is replicated after the 15-minute threshold, and when an object is no longer tracked by replication metrics. It publishes a second event when that object replicates to the destination Region.

Q140. A, D
AWS Documentation Reference:
https://docs.aws.amazon.com/AmazonS3/latest/dev/replication.html

You can replicate objects between different AWS Regions or within the same AWS Region. Cross-Region replication (CRR) is used to copy objects across Amazon S3 buckets in different AWS Regions.

Same-Region replication (SRR) is used to copy objects across Amazon S3 buckets in the same AWS Region.

Q141. A, B, D, E

C is incorrect because S3 service is not under user VPC.

AWS Documentation Reference:

https://docs.aws.amazon.com/AmazonS3/latest/dev/replication.html

Replication can help you do the following:

Replicate objects while retaining metadata — you can use replication to make copies of your objects that retain all metadata, such as the original object creation time and version IDs. This capability is important if you need to ensure that your replica is identical to the source object

Replicate objects into different storage classes — you can use replication to directly put objects into Glacier, DEEP ARCHIVE, or another storage class in the destination bucket. You can also replicate your data to the same storage class and use lifecycle policies on the destination bucket to move your objects to a colder storage class as it ages.

Maintain object copies under different ownership — Regardless of who owns the source object, you can tell Amazon S3 to change replica ownership to the AWS account that owns the destination bucket. This is referred to as the owner override option. You can use this option to restrict access to object replicas.

Replicate objects within 15 minutes — you can use S3 Replication Time Control (S3 RTC) to replicate your data in the same AWS Region or across different Regions in a predictable time frame. S3 RTC replicates 99.99 percent of new objects stored in Amazon S3 within 15 minutes (backed by a service level agreement).

Q142. D

D is a use case for CRR where global users latency can be reduced by replicating data in different AWS regions.

AWS Documentation Reference:

https://docs.aws.amazon.com/AmazonS3/latest/dev/replication.html

Same-Region replication can help you do the following:

Aggregate logs into a single bucket — if you store logs in multiple buckets or across multiple accounts, you can easily replicate logs into a single, in-Region bucket. This allows for simpler processing of logs in a single location.

Configure live replication between production and test accounts — if you or your customers have production and test accounts that use the same data, you can replicate objects between those multiple accounts, while maintaining object metadata, by implementing SRR rules.

Abide by data sovereignty laws — you might be required to store multiple copies of your data in separate AWS accounts within a certain Region. Same-Region replication can help you automatically replicate critical data when compliance regulations don't allow the data to leave your country.

## Q143. B, C, D
AWS Documentation Reference:
https://docs.aws.amazon.com/AmazonS3/latest/dev/replication-what-is-isnot-replicated.html

## Q144. D
AWS Documentation Reference:
https://docs.aws.amazon.com/AmazonS3/latest/dev/replication-what-is-isnot-replicated.html
You can replicate objects from a source bucket to only one destination bucket. After Amazon S3 replicates an object, the object can't be replicated again. In this case, objects in bucket B that are replicas of objects in bucket A are not replicated to bucket C.

## Q145. B
AWS Documentation Reference:
https://docs.aws.amazon.com/AmazonS3/latest/dev/replication-what-is-isnot-replicated.html
How Delete Operations Affect Replication
If you delete an object from the source bucket, the following occurs:

a. If you specify an object version ID to delete in a DELETE request, Amazon S3 deletes that object version in the source bucket. But it doesn't replicate the deletion in the destination bucket. In other words, it doesn't delete the same object version from the destination bucket. This protects data from malicious deletions.

b. If you make a DELETE request without specifying an object version ID, Amazon S3 adds a delete marker. Amazon S3 deals with the delete marker as follows:

* If you are using the latest version of the replication configuration (that is, you specify the Filter element in a replication configuration rule), Amazon S3 does not replicate the delete marker.

- If you don't specify the Filter element, Amazon S3 assumes that the replication configuration is an earlier version V1. In the earlier version, Amazon S3 handled replication of delete markers differently.

## Q146. C
AWS Documentation Reference:
https://aws.amazon.com/efs/

## Q147. C
AWS Documentation Reference: Web serving & content management
https://aws.amazon.com/efs/
Amazon EFS provides a durable, high throughput file system for content management systems and web serving applications that store and serve information for a range of applications like websites, online publications, and archives. Since Amazon EFS adheres to the expected file system directory structure, file naming conventions, and permissions that web developers are accustomed to, it can easily integrate with web applications

## Q148. D

## Q149. A
AWS Documentation Reference:
https://aws.amazon.com/efs/
Amazon Elastic File System (Amazon EFS) provides a simple, scalable, fully managed elastic NFS file system for use with AWS Cloud services and on-premises resources. It is built to scale on demand to petabytes without disrupting applications, growing and shrinking automatically as you add and remove files, eliminating the need to provision and manage capacity to accommodate growth.
Media workflows like video editing, studio production, broadcast processing, sound design, and rendering often depend on shared storage to manipulate large files. Amazon EFS provides a strong data consistency model with high throughput and shared file access which can cut the time it takes to perform these jobs and consolidate multiple local file repositories into a single location for all users.

## Q150. D
AWS Documentation Reference:
https://docs.aws.amazon.com/AmazonS3/latest/dev/ServerLogs.html#server-access-logging-overview
Server access logging provides detailed records for the requests that are made to a bucket. Each access log record provides details about a single access request, such as the requester, bucket name, request time, request action, response status, and an error code, if relevant.

## Q151. B, C, D

AWS Documentation Reference:

https://aws.amazon.com/premiumsupport/knowledge-center/read-access-objects-s3-bucket/
You should not have any Block Public Access settings on the bucket that prevents you from making the objects public. By default, Block Public Access settings are set to True on new S3 buckets. After that you can enable public read access in one of these ways:

- Update the object's access control list (ACL) using the Amazon S3 console
- Update the object's ACL using the AWS Command Line Interface (AWS CLI)
- Use a bucket policy that grants public read access to a specific object tag

Q152. C
AWS Documentation Reference:
https://docs.aws.amazon.com/snowball/latest/ug/whatissnowball.html
Snowball is intended for transferring large amounts of data. If you want to transfer less than 10 TB of data between your on-premises data centers and Amazon S3, Snowball might not be your most economical choice.

Q153. A, D
AWS Documentation Reference:
https://docs.aws.amazon.com/snowball/latest/ug/device-differences.html
Each device has different storage capacities, as follows:

| Storage capacity (usable capacity) | Snowball | Snowball Edge |
|---|---|---|
| 50 TB (42 TB) - US regions only | ✓ | |
| 80 TB (72 TB) | ✓ | |
| 100 TB (83 TB) | | ✓ |
| 100 TB Clustered (45 TB per node) | | ✓ |

Q154. C
AWS Documentation Reference:
https://aws.amazon.com/storagegateway/faqs/
When should I consider using Snowball instead of the Internet?
https://aws.amazon.com/snowball-edge/pricing/
https://aws.amazon.com/snowball/pricing/
https://docs.aws.amazon.com/snowball/latest/ug/device-differences.html
We need to consider three data points

1. Net usable storage provided by different Snowball and Snowball Edge options

| Storage capacity (usable capacity) | Snowball | Snowball Edge |
|---|---|---|
| 50 TB (42 TB) - US regions only | ✓ | |
| 80 TB (72 TB) | ✓ | |
| 100 TB (83 TB) | | ✓ |
| 100 TB Clustered (45 TB per node) | | ✓ |

2. The price comparison between Snowball and Snowball edge for different options

| | Snowball 50 TB (42 TB) | Snowball 80 TB (72 TB) | Snowball Edge Storage Optimized 100 TB (83 TB) |
|---|---|---|---|
| Service Fee per Job | $200 | $250 | $300 |
| Extra Day Charge | $15 | $15 | $30 |

3. Theoretical Min. Number of Days to Transfer 80TB at 80% Network Utilization will be nearly 100 days.

Given all the three factors above Snowball Edge 100 TB with net storage of 83 TB is the right option.

Q155. B
AWS Documentation Reference:
https://aws.amazon.com/storagegateway/faqs/
*Q: What is the relationship between files and objects?*
The object key is derived from the file path within the file system. In the given scenario, if you have a gateway with hostname *file.amazon.com* and have mapped it to S3 bucket *my-bucket*, then file gateway will expose a mount point called *file.amazon.com:/export/my-bucket*. If you then mount this locally on */mnt/my-bucket* and create a file named file.html in a directory */mnt/my-bucket/dir* this file will be stored as an object in the bucket *my-bucket* with a key of *dir/file.html*.

Q156. B, C
AWS Documentation Reference:
https://docs.aws.amazon.com/AmazonS3/latest/dev/ServerLogs.html#server-access-logging-overview
To enable access logging, you must do the following:
- Turn on the log delivery by adding logging configuration on the bucket for which you want Amazon S3 to deliver access logs. We refer to this bucket as the source bucket.
- Grant the Amazon S3 Log Delivery group write permission on the bucket where you want the access logs saved. We refer to this bucket as the target bucket.

Q157. A, B

AWS Documentation Reference: *How are Amazon S3 and Amazon S3 Glacier designed to achieve 99.999999999% durability?*
https://aws.amazon.com/s3/faqs/
Amazon S3 Standard, S3 Standard-IA, and S3 Glacier storage classes redundantly store your objects on multiple devices across a minimum of three Availability Zones (AZs) in an Amazon S3 Region before returning SUCCESS. The S3 One Zone-IA storage class stores data redundantly across multiple devices within a single AZ. These services are designed to sustain concurrent device failures by quickly detecting and repairing any lost redundancy, and they also regularly verify the integrity of your data using checksums.

Q158. B, D
AWS Documentation Reference:
https://docs.aws.amazon.com/amazonglacier/latest/dev/downloading-an-archive-two-steps.html

The two S3 storage class for archiving data is Glacier and Deep Archive. The following table summarizes the archival retrieval options

| Storage Class | Expedited | Standard | Bulk |
|---|---|---|---|
| GLACIER | 1–5 minutes | 3–5 hours | 5–12 hours |
| DEEP_ARCHIVE | Not available | Within 12 hours | Within 48 hours |

Given the required retrieval time of 1-5 minutes, Glacier will be the appropriate
You should purchase provisioned retrieval capacity if your workload requires highly reliable and predictable access to a subset of your data in minutes. Without provisioned capacity Expedited retrievals are accepted, except for rare situations of unusually high demand. However, if you require access to Expedited retrievals under all circumstances, you must purchase provisioned retrieval capacity.

Q159. B, C
AWS Documentation Reference: IOPS
https://docs.aws.amazon.com/AWSEC2/latest/UserGuide/ebs-io-characteristics.html
IOPS are a unit of measure representing input/output operations per second. The operations are measured in KiB, and the underlying drive technology determines the maximum amount of data that a volume type counts as a single I/O. I/O size is capped at 256 KiB for SSD volumes and 1,024 KiB for HDD volumes because SSD volumes handle small or random I/O much more efficiently than HDD volumes.

Q160. D
AWS Documentation Reference: IOPS
https://docs.aws.amazon.com/AWSEC2/latest/UserGuide/ebs-io-characteristics.html
When small I/O operations are physically contiguous, Amazon EBS attempts to merge them into a single I/O operation up to the maximum size. For example, for SSD volumes, a single

1,024 KiB I/O operation counts as 4 operations (1,024÷256=4), while 8 contiguous I/O operations at 32 KiB each count as 1 operation (8×32=256). However, 8 random I/O operations at 32 KiB each count as 8 operations. Each I/O operation under 32 KiB counts as 1 operation.

Q161. C
AWS Documentation Reference: I/O size and volume throughput limits
https://docs.aws.amazon.com/AWSEC2/latest/UserGuide/ebs-io-characteristics.html
A gp2 volume 1000 GiB with burst credits available has an IOPS limit of 3,000 and a volume throughput limit of 250 MiB/s. If you are using a 256 KiB I/O size, your volume reaches its throughput limit at 1000 IOPS (1000 x 256 KiB = 250 MiB). For smaller I/O sizes (such as 16 KiB), this same volume can sustain 3,000 IOPS because the throughput is well below 250 MiB/s.
3000 *16KiB=48MiB

Q162. D
AWS Documentation Reference: Provisioned IOPS SSD (io1) Volumes
https://docs.aws.amazon.com/AWSEC2/latest/UserGuide/ebs-volume-types.html
The maximum ratio of provisioned IOPS to requested volume size (in GiB) is 50:1. A 100 GiB volume can be provisioned with up to 5,000 IOPS.

Q163. A, B
AWS Documentation Reference: Throughput Credits and Burst Performance
https://docs.aws.amazon.com/AWSEC2/latest/UserGuide/ebs-volume-types.html
Like gp2, st1 uses a burst-bucket model for performance. Volume size determines the baseline throughput of your volume, which is the rate at which the volume accumulates throughput credits. Volume size also determines the burst throughput of your volume, which is the rate at which you can spend credits when they are available. For a 1-TiB st1 volume, burst throughput is limited to 250 MiB/s, the bucket fills with credits at 40 MiB/s, and it can hold up to 1 TiB-worth of credits.

C and D are incorrect because st2 doesn't provide I/O credits and burst.

Q164. B
AWS Documentation Reference:
https://aws.amazon.com/blogs/storage/taking-crash-consistent-snapshots-across-multiple-amazon-ebs-volumes-on-an-amazon-ec2-instance/
https://aws.amazon.com/premiumsupport/knowledge-center/snapshot-ebs-raid-array/
Previously when you combined multiple EBS volumes to meet your application or performance needs (such as RAID), you followed a multi-step process. This process ensured that the backups of all EBS volumes were in sync relative to each other. You had to pause I/O or stop the instance to temporarily disable write access, create snapshots for each of your volumes, and then resume I/O. This added complexity to your backup process. Now, you can

simplify your backup process with a one-click solution to take exact point-in-time backups across multiple EBS volumes attached to an EC2 instance.

To create snapshots for Amazon EBS volumes that are configured in a RAID array, use the multi-volume snapshot feature of your instance. The multi-volume snapshot feature is a one-click solution that takes individual, point-in-time backups of all Amazon EBS volumes attached to your instance. This process makes sure that the backup of your Amazon EBS volumes attached to the instance are in sync relative to each other, resulting in an accurate restore of the Amazon EBS volumes in RAID.

Q165. C
AWS Documentation Reference:
https://docs.aws.amazon.com/AmazonS3/latest/dev/transfer-acceleration.html
Amazon S3 Transfer Acceleration enables fast, easy, and secure transfers of files over long distances between your client and an S3 bucket. Transfer Acceleration takes advantage of Amazon CloudFront's globally distributed edge locations. As the data arrives at an edge location, data is routed to Amazon S3 over an optimized network path.
You might want to use Transfer Acceleration on a bucket for various reasons, including the following:

- You have customers that upload to a centralized bucket from all over the world.

- You transfer gigabytes to terabytes of data on a regular basis across continents.

- You are unable to utilize all of your available bandwidth over the Internet when uploading to Amazon S3.

Q166. A
AWS Documentation Reference: Cold HDD (sc1) Volumes
https://docs.aws.amazon.com/AWSEC2/latest/UserGuide/ebs-volume-types.html
Cold HDD (sc1) volumes provide low-cost magnetic storage that defines performance in terms of throughput rather than IOPS. With a lower throughput limit than st1, sc1 is a good fit for large, sequential cold-data workloads. If you require infrequent access to your data and are looking to save costs, sc1 provides inexpensive block storage. Bootable sc1 volumes are not supported.
Cold HDD (sc1) volumes, though similar to Throughput Optimized HDD (st1) volumes, are designed to support infrequently accessed data.
This volume type is optimized for workloads involving large, sequential I/O, and AWS recommend that customers with workloads performing small, random I/O use gp2.

Q167. B
AWS Documentation Reference: Throughput Optimized HDD (st1) Volumes
https://docs.aws.amazon.com/AWSEC2/latest/UserGuide/ebs-volume-types.html
Throughput Optimized HDD (st1) volumes provide low-cost magnetic storage that defines performance in terms of throughput rather than IOPS. This volume type is a good fit for large,

sequential workloads such as Amazon EMR, ETL, data warehouses, and log processing. Bootable st1 volumes are not supported.

Throughput Optimized HDD (st1) volumes, though similar to Cold HDD (sc1) volumes, are designed to support frequently accessed data.

This volume type is optimized for workloads involving large, sequential I/O, and AWS recommend that customers with workloads performing small, random I/O use gp2.

Q168. C
AWS Documentation Reference:
https://docs.aws.amazon.com/AWSEC2/latest/UserGuide/ebs-volume-types.html
SSD-backed volumes optimized for transactional workloads involving frequent read/write operations with small I/O size, where the dominant performance attribute is IOPS
Provisioned IOPS SSD (io1) can have Max IOPS per Volume of 64,000.Maximum IOPS and throughput are guaranteed only on Nitro-based Instances. Other instances guarantee up to 32,000 IOPS and 500 MiB/s.

General Purpose SSD (gp2) can have Max IOPS per Volume of 16,000.

Q169. B
AWS Documentation Reference:
https://docs.aws.amazon.com/AmazonS3/latest/dev/PresignedUrlUploadObject.html
All objects and buckets by default are private. The presigned URLs are useful if you want your user/customer to be able to upload a specific object to your bucket, but you don't require them to have AWS security credentials or permissions. The presigned URLs are valid only for the specified duration.

Q170.E, G
AWS Documentation Reference:
https://aws.amazon.com/s3/storage-classes/

Q171. A
AWS Documentation Reference:
https://aws.amazon.com/s3/storage-classes/

The S3 Intelligent-Tiering storage class is designed to optimize costs by automatically moving data to the most cost-effective access tier, without performance impact or operational overhead. It works by storing objects in two access tiers: one tier that is optimized for frequent access and another lower-cost tier that is optimized for infrequent access. For a small monthly monitoring and automation fee per object, Amazon S3 monitors access patterns of the objects in S3 Intelligent-Tiering, and moves the ones that have not been accessed for 30 consecutive days to the infrequent access tier. If an object in the infrequent access tier is accessed, it is automatically moved back to the frequent access tier. There are no retrieval fees when using the S3 Intelligent-Tiering storage class, and no additional tiering fees when objects are moved between access tiers.

It is the ideal storage class for long-lived data with access patterns that are unknown or unpredictable. S3 Storage Classes can be configured at the object level and a single bucket can contain objects stored in S3 Standard, S3 Intelligent-Tiering, S3 Standard-IA, and S3 One Zone-IA. You can upload objects directly to S3 Intelligent-Tiering, or use S3 Lifecycle policies to transfer objects from S3 Standard and S3 Standard-IA to S3 Intelligent-Tiering.

Q172. C
AWS Documentation Reference:
https://aws.amazon.com/glacier/features/?nc=sn&loc=2
Data stored in Amazon S3 Glacier is immutable, meaning that after an archive is created it cannot be updated. This ensures that data such as compliance and regulatory records cannot be altered after they have been archived.

Data is stored in Amazon S3 Glacier in "archives." An archive can be comprised of any data such as photos, videos, or documents. You can upload a single file as an archive or aggregate multiple files into a TAR or ZIP file and upload as one archive. A single archive can be as large as 40 terabytes. You can store an unlimited number of archives and an unlimited amount of data in Amazon S3 Glacier.

Amazon S3 Glacier uses "vaults" as containers to store archives. You can view a list of your vaults in the AWS Management Console and use the AWS SDKs to perform a variety of vault operations such as create vault, delete vault, lock vault, list vault metadata, retrieve vault inventory, tag vaults for filtering and configure vault notifications. You can also set access policies for each vault to grant or deny specific activities to users.

Amazon S3 Glacier Vault Lock allows you to easily deploy and enforce compliance controls on individual S3 Glacier vaults via a lockable policy. You can specify controls such as "Write Once Read Many" (WORM) in a Vault Lock policy and lock the policy from future edits. Once locked, the policy becomes immutable and Amazon S3 Glacier will enforce the prescribed controls to help achieve your compliance objectives.

Uploading an archive is a synchronous operation.

Downloading an archive is an asynchronous operation.

To delete an archive you need to use the Amazon S3 Glacier REST API or the AWS SDKs and specify the archive ID.

Q173. A, B
AWS Documentation Reference:
https://aws.amazon.com/storagegateway/file/
File gateway enables your existing file-based applications, devices, and workflows to use Amazon S3, without modification. File gateway supports Amazon S3 Standard, S3 Standard - Infrequent Access (S3 Standard - IA) and S3 One Zone - IA. File gateway supports Linux clients connecting to the gateway using Network File System (NFS) versions 3 and 4.1 for Linux clients, and supports Windows clients connecting to the gateway using Server Message Block (SMB) versions 2 and 3. You can create an NFS or SMB file share using the AWS Management Console or service API and associate the file share with a new or existing Amazon S3 bucket. To access the file share from your applications, you mount it from your application using standard UNIX or Windows commands.

https://docs.aws.amazon.com/efs/latest/ug/whatisefs.html
https://aws.amazon.com/blogs/aws/amazon-efs-update-on-premises-access-via-direct-connect-vpc/

Amazon Elastic File System (Amazon EFS) provides a simple, scalable, fully managed elastic NFS file system for use with AWS Cloud services and on-premises resources. To use this feature for migration, you simply attach an EFS file system to your on-premises servers, copy your data to it, and then process it in the cloud as desired, leaving your data in AWS for the long term. Amazon EFS offers two storage classes: the Standard storage class, and the Infrequent Access storage class (EFS IA).

Q174. A
AWS Documentation Reference:
https://aws.amazon.com/s3/faqs/
*How much data can I store in Amazon S3?*
The total volume of data and number of objects you can store are unlimited. Individual Amazon S3 objects can range in size from a minimum of 0 bytes to a maximum of 5 terabytes. The largest object that can be uploaded in a single PUT is 5 gigabytes. For objects larger than 100 megabytes, customers should consider using the Multipart Upload capability.

Q175. B

Q176. A, D

AWS Documentation Reference:
https://docs.aws.amazon.com/AmazonS3/latest/dev/Introduction.html#ConsistencyModel
Amazon S3 offers eventual consistency for overwrite PUTS and DELETES in all Regions.

Q177. B

AWS Documentation Reference:

https://docs.aws.amazon.com/AmazonS3/latest/dev/Introduction.html#ConsistencyModel
Amazon S3 provides read-after-write consistency for PUTS of new objects in your S3 bucket
in all Regions with one caveat. The caveat is that if you make a HEAD or GET request to a
key name before the object is created, then create the object shortly after that, a subsequent
GET might not return the object due to eventual consistency.

Q178. C, D

AWS Documentation Reference:

https://docs.aws.amazon.com/AmazonS3/latest/dev/Versioning.html#MultiFactorAuthentic
ationDelete
You can optionally add another layer of security by configuring a bucket to enable MFA
(multi-factor authentication) Delete, which requires additional authentication for either of the
following operations:
- Change the versioning state of your bucket
- Permanently delete an object version

Q179. A, B, D

AWS Documentation Reference:

https://aws.amazon.com/ebs/
Amazon EBS lets you scale easily with additional volumes to support growing file systems.
https://aws.amazon.com/efs/
Amazon Elastic File System (Amazon EFS) provides a simple, scalable, fully managed elastic
NFS file system for use with AWS Cloud services and on-premises resources.
https://aws.amazon.com/s3/
S3 can store files as objects.

Q180. B

AWS Documentation Reference:

https://aws.amazon.com/s3/faqs/
*How secure is my data in Amazon S3?*
You can securely upload/download your data to Amazon S3 via SSL endpoints using the
HTTPS protocol.

Q181. A, B, D

Storage class of the object has no impact on upload/download latency.
AWS Documentation Reference:

https://aws.amazon.com/premiumsupport/knowledge-center/s3-troubleshoot-slow-
downloads-uploads/
The location of the client making requests: You can test the impact of geographical distance
between the client and the S3 bucket. For example, you can launch an Amazon Elastic

Compute Cloud (Amazon EC2) instance in the same AWS Region as the bucket, and then launch another instance in another Region. Test an upload and download of the same file using both instances, and then compare the throughput between the two Regions.

The client resources: There might be latency introduced in your application or how your host that's making the requests is handling the requests sent and responses received. As a best practice, confirm that there's no resource contention within the host (for example, CPU, memory, or network bandwidth) that might be contributing to the overall latency.

Request rate to Amazon S3: By default, S3 buckets can support thousands of requests per second per prefix. If a client is getting HTTP 5xx error responses from Amazon S3, this can indicate that the supported request rate per prefix is exceeded.

Q182. B, C, D, E
A is incorrect as Amazon S3 Transfer Acceleration enables fast, easy, and secure transfers of files over long distances between your client and an S3 bucket by taking advantage of Amazon CloudFront's globally distributed edge locations. It is not used for caching.

F is the benefit of S3 Transfer Acceleration and not CloudFront.

AWS Documentation Reference:
https://docs.aws.amazon.com/AmazonS3/latest/dev/optimizing-performance-design-patterns.html

Using Caching for Frequently Accessed Content: Many applications that store data in Amazon S3 serve a "working set" of data that is repeatedly requested by users. If a workload is sending repeated GET requests for a common set of objects, you can use a cache such as Amazon CloudFront, Amazon ElastiCache, or AWS Elemental MediaStore to optimize performance. Successful cache adoption can result in low latency and high data transfer rates. Applications that use caching also send fewer direct requests to Amazon S3, which can help reduce request costs.

Timeouts and Retries for Latency-Sensitive Applications: If an application generates high request rates (typically sustained rates of over 5,000 requests per second to a small number of objects), it might receive HTTP 503 slowdown responses.
Amazon S3 automatically scales in response to sustained new request rates, dynamically optimizing performance. While Amazon S3 is internally optimizing for a new request rate, you will receive HTTP 503 request responses temporarily until the optimization completes. After Amazon S3 internally optimizes performance for the new request rate, all requests are generally served without retries. For latency-sensitive applications, Amazon S3 advises tracking and aggressively retrying slower operations.

Horizontal Scaling and Request Parallelization for High Throughput: Amazon S3 is a very large distributed system. To help you take advantage of its scale, AWS encourages to horizontally scale parallel requests to the Amazon S3 service endpoints. In addition to distributing the requests within Amazon S3, this type of scaling approach helps distribute the load over multiple paths through the network. For high-throughput transfers, Amazon S3 advises using applications that use multiple connections to GET or PUT data in parallel.

Q183. C
AWS Documentation Reference:
https://aws.amazon.com/premiumsupport/knowledge-center/s3-object-prefix-naming/
https://docs.aws.amazon.com/AmazonS3/latest/dev/optimizing-performance.html
Previously Amazon S3 performance guidelines recommended randomizing prefix naming with hashed characters to optimize performance for frequent data retrievals. You no longer have to randomize prefix naming for performance, and can use sequential date-based naming for your prefixes.

https://docs.aws.amazon.com/AmazonS3/latest/dev/optimizing-performance-guidelines.html
Combine Amazon S3 (Storage) and Amazon EC2 (Compute) in the Same AWS Region:
Although S3 bucket names are globally unique, each bucket is stored in a Region that you select when you create the bucket. To optimize performance, AWS recommends that you access the bucket from Amazon EC2 instances in the same AWS Region when possible. This helps reduce network latency and data transfer costs.

Use Byte-Range Fetches: Using the Range HTTP header in a GET Object request, you can fetch a byte-range from an object, transferring only the specified portion. You can use concurrent connections to Amazon S3 to fetch different byte ranges from within the same object. This helps you achieve higher aggregate throughput versus a single whole-object request. Fetching smaller ranges of a large object also allows your application to improve retry times when requests are interrupted.

Amazon S3 Transfer Acceleration manages fast, easy, and secure transfers of files over long geographic distances between the client and an S3 bucket.

Q184. C, F
AWS Documentation Reference:
https://docs.aws.amazon.com/AWSEC2/latest/UserGuide/placement-groups.html
Cluster placement groups are recommended for applications that benefit from low network latency, high network throughput, or both, and if the majority of the network traffic is between the instances in the group. This will not directly influence the transfer speed between EC2 instance and S3.

https://docs.aws.amazon.com/AmazonS3/latest/dev/optimizing-performance-guidelines.html
To optimize performance, AWS recommends that you access the bucket from Amazon EC2 instances in the same AWS Region when possible. This helps reduce network latency and data transfer costs.
https://aws.amazon.com/premiumsupport/knowledge-center/s3-transfer-data-bucket-instance/

Q185. A, B, C
AWS Documentation Reference:
https://docs.aws.amazon.com/AmazonS3/latest/dev/batch-ops.html
You can use Amazon S3 batch operations to perform large-scale batch operations on Amazon S3 objects. Amazon S3 batch operations can execute a single operation on lists of Amazon S3 objects that you specify. A single job can perform the specified operation on billions of objects containing exabytes of data. Amazon S3 tracks progress, sends notifications, and stores a detailed completion report of all actions, providing a fully managed, auditable, serverless experience. You can use Amazon S3 batch operations through the AWS Management Console, AWS CLI, AWS SDKs, or REST API.

Use Amazon S3 batch operations to copy objects and set object tags or access control lists (ACLs). You can also initiate object restores from Amazon S3 Glacier or invoke an AWS Lambda function to perform custom actions using your objects. You can perform these operations on a custom list of objects, or you can use an Amazon S3 inventory report to make generating even the largest lists of objects easy. Amazon S3 batch operations use the same Amazon S3 APIs that you already use with Amazon S3, so you'll find the interface familiar.

Q186. B, C, D, E
AWS Documentation Reference:
https://aws.amazon.com/premiumsupport/knowledge-center/s3-access-file-folder/
Check the following permissions for any settings that are denying your access to the prefix or object:

Ownership of the prefix or object: By default, an S3 object is owned by the AWS account that uploaded it. This is true even when the bucket is owned by another account. You can use a bucket policy to require that other accounts grant you ownership of objects they upload to your bucket.

Restrictions in the bucket policy: Modify the bucket policy to edit or remove any "Effect": "Deny" statements that are incorrectly denying you access to the prefix or object.

Restrictions in your AWS Identity and Access Management (IAM) user policy: In the JSON policy documents, search for policies related to Amazon S3 access. Then, search those policies for any "Effect": "Deny" statements that are blocking your access to the prefix or object.

Permissions to object encrypted by AWS Key Management Service (AWS KMS): If an object is encrypted with an AWS KMS key, then you need permissions to both the object and the key.

Q187. A, D
AWS Documentation Reference:
https://aws.amazon.com/premiumsupport/knowledge-center/s3-existing-objects-default-encryption/

Enabling default encryption doesn't change the encryption of objects that are already in the bucket. After you enable default encryption, the encryption that you set applies only to future uploads. For example, if you enable server-side encryption with AWS KMS (SSE-KMS) on the bucket, then any unencrypted objects already in the bucket remain unencrypted. Additionally, any objects already encrypted using Amazon S3-managed keys (SSE-S3) remain encrypted with SSE-S3.
To change the encryption of an existing object to SSE-KMS, you must re-upload the object. Or, you can copy the object over itself.

Q188. A, C, E
AWS Documentation Reference:
https://docs.aws.amazon.com/AmazonS3/latest/dev/WebsiteEndpoints.html#WebsiteRestEndpointDiff

Q189. A, D, E
AWS Documentation Reference:
https://docs.aws.amazon.com/efs/latest/ug/performance.html

Q190. C
AWS Documentation Reference:
https://docs.aws.amazon.com/efs/latest/ug/performance.html
AWS recommend the General Purpose performance mode for the majority of your Amazon EFS file systems. General Purpose is ideal for latency-sensitive use cases, like web serving environments, content management systems, home directories, and general file serving. If you don't choose a performance mode when you create your file system, Amazon EFS selects the General Purpose mode for you by default.

Q191. B
AWS Documentation Reference:
https://docs.aws.amazon.com/efs/latest/ug/performance.html

File systems in the Max I/O mode can scale to higher levels of aggregate throughput and operations per second. This scaling is done with a tradeoff of slightly higher latencies for file metadata operations. Highly parallelized applications and workloads, such as big data analysis, media processing, and genomics analysis, can benefit from this mode.

Q192. B, C
AWS Documentation Reference:
https://docs.aws.amazon.com/efs/latest/ug/performance.html
There are two throughput modes to choose from for your file system, Bursting Throughput and Provisioned Throughput. With Bursting Throughput mode, throughput on Amazon EFS scales as the size of your file system in the standard storage class grows.

Q193. A, D

Q194. D, E
EC2 instance with windows based AMI along with Amazon FSx for Windows File Server to provide the environment similar to on-premise

AWS Documentation Reference:
https://aws.amazon.com/fsx/windows/
Amazon FSx is built on Windows Server and provides you with the native Windows file system features and performance that your applications need from a file store. By providing fully managed native Windows file shares with features like Microsoft AD integration and automatic backups, you can easily migrate Windows-based applications to AWS. Amazon FSx supports Windows-native file system features such as Access Control Lists (ACLs), shadow copies, and user quotas to help you move your applications to AWS with minimal disruption. Amazon FSx provides NTFS file systems that can be accessed from up to thousands of compute instances using the SMB protocol. Amazon FSx works with Microsoft Active Directory (AD) to easily integrate your file system with your Windows environments.

Q195. A, B, C
AWS Documentation Reference:
https://aws.amazon.com/fsx/windows/faqs/?nc=sn&loc=7
*When should I use Amazon FSx Windows File Servers vs. Amazon EFS vs. Amazon FSx for Lustre?*
For Windows-based applications, Amazon FSx provides fully managed Windows file servers with features and performance optimized for "lift-and-shift" business-critical application workloads including home directories (user shares), media workflows, and ERP applications. It is accessible from Windows and Linux instances via the SMB protocol.

If you have Linux-based applications, Amazon EFS is a cloud-native fully managed file system that provides simple, scalable, elastic file storage accessible from Linux instances via the NFS protocol.

For compute-intensive and fast processing workloads, like high performance computing (HPC), machine learning, EDA, and media processing, Amazon FSx for Lustre, provides a file system that's optimized for performance, with input and output stored on Amazon S3.

Q196. B, C, D
AWS Documentation Reference:
https://aws.amazon.com/fsx/windows/
By supporting the SMB protocol, Amazon FSx can connect your file system to Amazon EC2, VMware Cloud on AWS, Amazon WorkSpaces, and Amazon AppStream 2.0 instances. Amazon FSx supports all Windows versions starting from Windows Server 2008 and Windows 7, and current versions of Linux. Amazon FSx also supports on-premises access via AWS Direct Connect or AWS VPN, and access from multiple VPCs, accounts, and regions using VPC Peering or AWS Transit Gateway.

Q197. A, C, D
FSx doesn't have feature of read replicas like RDS.
AWS Documentation Reference:
https://docs.aws.amazon.com/fsx/latest/WindowsGuide/high-availability-multiAZ.html
https://aws.amazon.com/fsx/windows/faqs/?nc=sn&loc=7

To ensure high availability and durability, Amazon FSx automatically replicates your data within an Availability Zone (AZ) to protect it from component failure, continuously monitors for hardware failures, and automatically replaces infrastructure components in the event of a failure. You can also create a Multi-AZ file system, which provides redundancy across multiple AZs. Amazon FSx also takes highly durable backups (stored in S3) of your file system daily using Windows's Volume Shadow Copy Service, and allows you to take additional backups at any point.

Q198. E
AWS Documentation Reference:
https://docs.aws.amazon.com/fsx/latest/WindowsGuide/high-availability-multiAZ.html
Choosing Single AZ or Multi-AZ File System Deployment
Multi-AZ file systems support all the availability and durability features of Single-AZ file systems, and in addition, are designed to provide continuous availability to data, even in the event that an AZ is unavailable. In a Multi-AZ deployment, Amazon FSx automatically provisions and maintains a standby file server in a different Availability Zone. Any changes written to disk in your file system are synchronously replicated across AZs to the standby. Using Amazon FSx Multi-AZ deployments can enhance availability during planned system maintenance, and help protect your data against instance failure and Availability Zone disruption. In the event of planned file system maintenance or unplanned service disruption,

Amazon FSx automatically fails over to the secondary file server, allowing you to continue accessing your data without manual intervention

Q199. B, C, D
AWS Documentation Reference:
https://docs.aws.amazon.com/fsx/latest/WindowsGuide/high-availability-multiAZ.html
Failover Process for Amazon FSx for Windows File Server
Multi-AZ file systems automatically fail over from the preferred file server to the standby file server if any of the following conditions occur:
- An Availability Zone outage occurs.
- The preferred file server becomes unavailable.
- The preferred file server undergoes planned maintenance.

When failing over from one file server to another, the new active file server automatically begins serving all file system reads and write requests. Once the resources in the preferred subnet are available, Amazon FSx automatically fails back to the preferred file server in the preferred subnet.

Q200. A, B, D
AWS Documentation Reference:
https://docs.aws.amazon.com/fsx/latest/WindowsGuide/high-availability-multiAZ.html
Failover Experience on Windows Clients
When failing over from one file server to another, the new active file server automatically begins serving all file system read and write requests. After the resources in the preferred subnet are available, Amazon FSx automatically fails back to the preferred file server in the preferred subnet. Because the file system's DNS name remains the same, failovers are transparent to Windows applications, which resume file system operations without manual intervention.

Failover Experience on Linux Clients
Linux clients do not support automatic DNS-based failover. Therefore, they don't automatically connect to the standby file server during a failover. They will automatically resume file system operations after the Multi-AZ file system has failed back to the file server in the preferred subnet.

Q201. B, C
AWS Documentation Reference:
https://docs.aws.amazon.com/fsx/latest/WindowsGuide/aws-ad-integration-fsxW.html
Amazon FSx provides you with two options for using your Amazon FSx for Windows File Server file system with Active Directory: Using Amazon FSx with AWS Directory Service for Microsoft Active Directory and Using Amazon FSx with Your Self-Managed Microsoft Active Directory.

Q202. A

AWS Documentation Reference:

https://docs.aws.amazon.com/fsx/latest/WindowsGuide/using-data-dedup.html

Large datasets often have redundant data, which increases the data storage costs. For example, with user file shares, multiple users can store many copies or versions of the same file. With software development shares, many binaries remain unchanged from build to build.

You can reduce your data storage costs by turning on data deduplication for your file system. Data deduplication reduces or eliminates redundant data by storing duplicated portions of the dataset only once. After data deduplication is enabled, it continually and automatically scans and optimizes your file system in the background.

The storage savings that you can achieve with data deduplication depends on the nature of your dataset, including how much duplication exists across files. Typical savings average 50–60 percent for general-purpose file shares. Within shares, savings range from 30–50 percent for user documents to 70–80 percent for software development datasets.

Q203. D

Q204. B

AWS Documentation Reference:

https://docs.aws.amazon.com/fsx/latest/WindowsGuide/group-file-systems.html

Amazon FSx for Windows File Server supports the use of Microsoft's Distributed File System (DFS) Namespaces. You can use DFS Namespaces to group file shares on multiple file systems into one common folder structure (a namespace) that you use to access the entire file dataset. DFS Namespaces can help you to organize and unify access to your file shares across multiple file systems. DFS Namespaces can also help to scale file data storage beyond what each file system supports (64 TB) for large file datasets—up to hundreds of petabytes.

Q205. B, C

A is benefit of Storage Gateway and D is benefit of Snowball.

AWS Documentation Reference:

https://aws.amazon.com/datasync/

Benefits of DataSync are:

Simplify and automate transfers: AWS DataSync makes it easy for you to move data over the network between on-premises storage and AWS. DataSync automates both the management of data transfer processes and the infrastructure required for high-performance, secure data transfer. The service also includes automatic encryption and data.

Move data 10x faster: Transfer data rapidly over the network into AWS, up to 10 times faster than is common with open-source tooling.

Q206. A, B, C

D is the use case for AWS Storage Gateway.

AWS Documentation Reference:
https://docs.aws.amazon.com/datasync/latest/userguide/what-is-datasync.html

Main use cases for AWS DataSync:

Data migration – Move active datasets rapidly over the network into Amazon S3, Amazon EFS, or Amazon FSx for Windows File Server. DataSync includes automatic encryption and data integrity validation to help make sure that your data arrives securely, intact, and ready to use.

Data movement for timely in-cloud processing – Move data into or out of AWS for processing when working with systems that generate data on-premises. This approach can speed up critical hybrid cloud workflows across many industries. These include video production in media and entertainment, seismic research in oil and gas, machine learning in life science, and big data analytics in finance.

Data archiving – Move cold data from expensive on-premises storage systems directly to durable and secure long-term storage such as Amazon S3 Glacier or S3 Glacier Deep Archive. By doing this, you can free up on-premises storage capacity and shut down legacy storage systems.

Q207. D
AWS Documentation Reference:
https://aws.amazon.com/blogs/storage/transferring-files-from-on-premises-to-aws-and-back-without-leaving-your-vpc-using-aws-datasync/
AWS DataSync is a service to simplify, automate, and accelerate data transfer between on-premises storage and AWS, such as Amazon Elastic File System (EFS) and Amazon S3. DataSync can be leveraged to migrate on-premises storage to AWS, in order to shut down entire data centers, or move cold data to more cost-effective storage. DataSync adheres to high standards of information security: all data transferred between the source and destination is encrypted via TLS, data is never persisted by DataSync, and access to AWS storage locations is entirely in your control. DataSync is also managed by standard AWS tools such as IAM (for S3) and security groups (for EFS). In addition to these security measures, data can be moved from on-premises storage to AWS via Direct Connect or VPN, without traversing the public internet, to further increase the security of the copied data.
https://aws.amazon.com/blogs/storage/migrating-storage-with-aws-datasync/

Q208. C, D
AWS Documentation Reference:
https://aws.amazon.com/blogs/storage/transferring-files-from-on-premises-to-aws-and-back-without-leaving-your-vpc-using-aws-datasync/

DataSync allows you to configure a source storage location (NFS or SMB share) on-premises, and a destination in AWS storage services (Amazon S3 or Amazon EFS). It uses a purpose-built network protocol and scale-out architecture to accelerate the transfer of data to AWS. To operate the service and to transfer your files, you can either utilize public service endpoints in their respective AWS Regions (such as datasync.us-east-1.amazonaws.com), or transfer files via your Direct Connect or VPN utilizing private IP addresses accessible only from within your VPC.

When using only private IPs, you can ensure that your VPC is not reachable over the internet, and prevent any packets from entering or exiting the network. This means that you can eliminate all internet access from your on-premises, but still use DataSync for data transfers to and from AWS using Private IP addresses.

DataSync uses an agent to transfer data from your on-premises storage. The agent is deployed as a virtual machine that should be deployed on-premises in the same LAN as your source storage to minimize the distance traveled via protocols, such as NFS. Once deployed, the agent acts as an extension of the DataSync service, and is managed seamlessly by AWS. Using DataSync with VPC endpoints means that your agent can communicate with the DataSync service endpoints using private IPs. In configuring this setup, you'll place a private VPC endpoint in your VPC that connects to the DataSync service. This endpoint will be used for communication between your agent and the DataSync service.

Q209. A, B
AWS Documentation Reference:
https://aws.amazon.com/datasync/faqs/
AWS DataSync is ideal for online data transfers. You can use DataSync to migrate active data to AWS, transfer data to the cloud for analysis and processing, archive data to free up on-premises storage capacity, or replicate data to AWS for business continuity.

AWS Snowball Edge is suitable for offline data transfers, for customers who are bandwidth constrained, or transferring data from remote, disconnected, or austere environments.

Q210. B
AWS Documentation Reference:
https://aws.amazon.com/datasync/faqs/
If your applications are already integrated with the Amazon S3 API, and you want higher throughput for transferring large files to S3, you can use S3 Transfer Acceleration.

Q211. A
AWS Documentation Reference: IOPS
https://docs.aws.amazon.com/AWSEC2/latest/UserGuide/ebs-io-characteristics.html
For HDD-backed volumes, both a single 1,024 KiB I/O operation and 8 sequential 128 KiB operations would count as one operation. However, 8 random 128 KiB I/O operations would count as 8 operations.

Q212. B, C, D
AWS Documentation Reference:
https://aws.amazon.com/fsx/lustre/
Amazon FSx for Lustre makes it easy and cost effective to launch and run the world's most popular high-performance file system. Use it for workloads where speed matters, such as machine learning, high performance computing (HPC), video processing, and financial modeling.

The open source Lustre file system is designed for applications that require fast storage – where you want your storage to keep up with your compute. Lustre was built to quickly and cost effectively process the fastest-growing data sets in the world, and it's the most widely used file system for the 500 fastest computers in the world. It provides sub-millisecond latencies, up to hundreds of gigabytes per second of throughput, and millions of IOPS.

Now as a fully managed service, Amazon FSx enables you to use Lustre file systems for any workload where storage speed matters. It eliminates the traditional complexity of setting up and managing Lustre file systems, allowing you to spin up a high-performance file system in minutes. It also provides multiple deployment options to optimize cost.

Amazon FSx for Lustre integrates natively with Amazon S3, making it easy to process your cloud data sets in S3 with a high-performance POSIX interface. When linked to an S3 bucket, FSx for Lustre transparently presents S3 objects as files. FSx for Lustre tracks changes and enables you to write changed and new data on the file system back to your S3 bucket at any time.

Amazon FSx for Lustre is POSIX-compliant, so you can use your current Linux-based applications without having to make any changes. FSx for Lustre provides a native file system interface and works as any file system does with your Linux operating system. It also provides read-after-write consistency and supports file locking. You can control access to your FSx for Lustre file systems with POSIX permissions and Amazon Virtual Private Cloud (VPC) rules. You can access your file systems from Amazon EC2 instances, and from on-premises computers using AWS Direct Connect or AWS VPN.

Q213. A, B, C, E, F, G
AWS Documentation Reference:
https://aws.amazon.com/fsx/lustre/
Suitable use cases for using Amazon FSx for Lustre :
- Media data processing workflows, like video rendering, visual effects, and media production, need the compute and storage resources to handle the massive amounts of data being created. FSx for Lustre provides the high performance and low latencies needed for processing, distributing, and analyzing digital media files.

- Machine learning workloads use massive amounts of training data. These workloads often use shared file storage because multiple compute instances need to process the training datasets concurrently. FSx for Lustre is optimal for machine learning workloads, because it provides shared file storage with high throughput and consistent, low latencies to process the ML training datasets. FSx for Lustre is also integrated with Amazon SageMaker, allowing you to accelerate your training jobs.

- High performance computing (HPC) enables scientists and engineers to solve complex, compute-intensive problems. HPC workloads, like oil & gas discovery, and genome analysis, process massive amounts of data that need to be accessed by multiple compute instances with high levels of throughput. FSx for Lustre is ideal for HPC and scientific computing workloads because it provides a file system that's optimized for the performance and costs of high-performance workloads, with file system access across thousands of EC2 instances. FSx for Lustre also integrates with AWS ParallelCluster and AWS Batch, making it easy to use with your HPC workloads.

- Customers developing autonomous vehicle systems often test models by running simulations and training on massive amounts of vehicle sensor and camera data to ensure vehicle safety. FSx for Lustre enables you to access that data simultaneously from thousands of nodes with high levels of performance, allowing you to more easily run simulations at scale and to accelerate model development.

- EDA is a high-performance application used to simulate performance and failures during the design phase of silicon chip production. FSx for Lustre provides the performance and flexibility that enables you to innovate faster, design and verify new products, and scale to meet demand.

Q214. C, D, E
AWS Documentation Reference:
https://docs.aws.amazon.com/efs/latest/ug/whatisefs.html
Amazon Elastic File System (Amazon EFS) provides a simple, scalable, fully managed elastic NFS file system for use with AWS Cloud services and on-premises resources. It is built to scale on demand to petabytes without disrupting applications, growing and shrinking automatically as you add and remove files, eliminating the need to provision and manage capacity to accommodate growth.
Using Amazon EFS with Microsoft Windows–based Amazon EC2 instances is not supported.
Amazon EFS supports the Network File System version 4 (NFSv4.1 and NFSv4.0) protocol, so the applications and tools that you use today work seamlessly with Amazon EFS. Multiple Amazon EC2 instances can access an Amazon EFS file system at the same time, providing a common data source for workloads and applications running on more than one instance or server.
https://docs.aws.amazon.com/fsx/latest/WindowsGuide/what-is.html
Amazon FSx for Windows File Server provides fully managed Microsoft Windows file servers, backed by a fully native Windows file system. Amazon FSx has native support for Windows

file system features and for the industry-standard Server Message Block (SMB) protocol to access file storage over a network.

https://docs.aws.amazon.com/fsx/latest/LustreGuide/what-is.html

Amazon FSx for Lustre makes it easy and cost-effective to launch and run the popular, high-performance Lustre file system. You use Lustre for workloads where speed matters, such as machine learning, high performance computing (HPC), video processing, and financial modeling. Amazon FSx for Lustre is POSIX-compliant, so you can use your current Linux-based applications without having to make any changes. Amazon FSx for Lustre provides a native file system interface and works as any file system does with your Linux operating system.

# Answer Chapter 4: Databases: Amazon RDS, Amazon Aurora, Amazon DynamoDB, Amazon ElastiCache, Amazon DocumentDB

Q1. B
AWS Documentation Reference:
https://docs.aws.amazon.com/AmazonRDS/latest/UserGuide/Concepts.MultiAZ.html
Amazon RDS provides high availability and failover support for DB instances using Multi-AZ deployments.

Q2. A, C
AWS Documentation Reference:
https://docs.aws.amazon.com/AmazonRDS/latest/UserGuide/Concepts.MultiAZ.html
In a Multi-AZ deployment, Amazon RDS automatically provisions and maintains a synchronous standby replica in a different Availability Zone. The primary DB instance is synchronously replicated across Availability Zones to a standby replica to provide data redundancy, eliminate I/O freezes, and minimize latency spikes during system backups. Running a DB instance with high availability can enhance availability during planned system maintenance, and help protect your databases against DB instance failure and Availability Zone disruption.

Q3. B
AWS Documentation Reference:
https://aws.amazon.com/rds/
Amazon Relational Database Service (Amazon RDS) is a managed service that makes it easy to set up, operate, and scale a relational database in the cloud. It provides cost-efficient and resizable capacity, while managing time-consuming database administration tasks, freeing you up to focus on your applications and business. Amazon RDS gives you access to the capabilities of a familiar MySQL, MariaDB, Oracle, SQL Server, or PostgreSQL database along with Amazon Aurora. Amazon Aurora is a MySQL and PostgreSQL-compatible relational database.

Q4. A

Q5. A, B, C
AWS Documentation Reference:
https://docs.aws.amazon.com/AmazonRDS/latest/UserGuide/Concepts.DBInstanceClass.html#Concepts.DBInstanceClass.Types
Amazon RDS supports three types of instance classes: Standard, Memory Optimized, and Burstable Performance.

Q6. A, B, D, E
AWS Documentation Reference:
https://docs.aws.amazon.com/AmazonRDS/latest/UserGuide/MonitoringOverview.html
You can use the following automated monitoring tools to watch Amazon RDS and report when something is wrong:

Amazon RDS Events – Subscribe to Amazon RDS events to be notified when changes occur with a DB instance, DB snapshot, DB parameter group, or DB security group.

Database log files – View, download, or watch database log files using the Amazon RDS console or Amazon RDS API operations. You can also query some database log files that are loaded into database tables.

Amazon RDS Enhanced Monitoring — Look at metrics in real time for the operating system.

Amazon RDS integrates with Amazon CloudWatch for additional monitoring capabilities

Q7. A, B

AWS Documentation Reference:

https://aws.amazon.com/rds/faqs/

Amazon RDS manages the work involved in setting up a relational database: from provisioning the infrastructure capacity you requested to installing the database software. Once your database is up and running, Amazon RDS automates common administrative tasks such as performing backups and patching the software that powers your database. With optional Multi-AZ deployments, Amazon RDS also manages synchronous data replication across Availability Zones with automatic failover. Since Amazon RDS provides native database access, you interact with the relational database software as you normally would. This means you're still responsible for managing the database settings that are specific to your application. You'll need to build the relational schema that best fits your use case and are responsible for any performance tuning to optimize your database for your application's workflow.

Q8. A, D

AWS Documentation Reference:

https://docs.aws.amazon.com/AmazonRDS/latest/UserGuide/Concepts.MultiAZ.html

If you have a DB instance in a Single-AZ deployment and you modify it to be a Multi-AZ deployment (for engines other than SQL Server or Amazon Aurora), Amazon RDS takes primarily two steps. First, Amazon RDS takes a snapshot of the primary DB instance from your deployment and then restores the snapshot into another Availability Zone. Amazon RDS then sets up synchronous replication between your primary DB instance and the new instance.

Q9. A, B, C

AWS Documentation Reference: Failover Process for Amazon RDS

https://docs.aws.amazon.com/AmazonRDS/latest/UserGuide/Concepts.MultiAZ.html

Q10. C

AWS Documentation Reference: Failover Process for Amazon RDS

https://docs.aws.amazon.com/AmazonRDS/latest/UserGuide/Concepts.MultiAZ.html

In the event of a planned or unplanned outage of your DB instance, Amazon RDS automatically switches to a standby replica in another Availability Zone if you have enabled Multi-AZ. The failover mechanism automatically changes the DNS record of the DB instance to point to the standby DB instance.

Q11. B
All Amazon RDS database engine supports multi-AZ deployment.

Q12. C
A manual failover of the DB instance can be initiated by rebooting the primary instance.

Q13 A, B
AWS Documentation Reference:
https://aws.amazon.com/rds/details/multi-az/

Q14. A, B, D
AWS Documentation Reference:
https://aws.amazon.com/rds/details/multi-az/
Unlike Single-AZ deployments, I/O activity is not suspended on your primary during backup for Multi-AZ deployments for the MySQL, MariaDB, Oracle, and PostgreSQL engines, because the backup is taken from the standby. However, note that you may still experience elevated latencies for a few minutes during backups for Multi-AZ deployments.

Q15. A, D
AWS Documentation Reference:
https://aws.amazon.com/rds/details/multi-az/
On instance failure in Amazon Aurora deployments, Amazon RDS uses RDS Multi-AZ technology to automate failover to one of up to 15 Amazon Aurora Replicas you have created in any of three Availability Zones. If no Amazon Aurora Replicas have been provisioned, in the case of a failure, Amazon RDS will attempt to create a new Amazon Aurora DB instance for you automatically.

Q16.A, B, C
AWS Documentation Reference:
https://aws.amazon.com/rds/aurora/details/mysql-details/?nc=sn&loc=2&dn=1
Each 10GB chunk of your database volume is replicated six ways, across three Availability Zones. Amazon Aurora storage is fault-tolerant, transparently handling the loss of up to two copies of data without affecting database write availability and up to three copies without affecting read availability. Amazon Aurora storage is also self-healing; data blocks and disks are continuously scanned for errors and replaced automatically

Q17. C, D
AWS Documentation Reference:
https://aws.amazon.com/rds/aurora/
https://docs.aws.amazon.com/AmazonRDS/latest/AuroraUserGuide/Aurora.Overview.Stor
ageReliability.html

Aurora MySQL gives 5X the throughput of standard MySQL. This performance is on par with commercial databases, at 1/10th the cost. Aurora cluster volumes automatically grow as the amount of data in your database increases. An Aurora cluster volume can grow to a maximum size of 64 tebibytes (TiB).

https://aws.amazon.com/rds/aurora/serverless/

Amazon Aurora Serverless is an on-demand, auto-scaling configuration for Amazon Aurora (MySQL-compatible and PostgreSQL-compatible editions), where the database will automatically start up, shut down, and scale capacity up or down based on your application's needs. It enables you to run your database in the cloud without managing any database instances. It's a simple, cost-effective option for infrequent, intermittent, or unpredictable workloads.

Q18. B

Q19. D

AWS Documentation Reference:

https://aws.amazon.com/rds/aurora/details/mysql-details/?nc=sn&loc=2&dn=1

Each 10GB chunk of your database volume is replicated six ways, across three Availability Zones.

Q20. A, C

AWS Documentation Reference:

https://docs.aws.amazon.com/AmazonRDS/latest/AuroraUserGuide/aurora-global-database.html

An Aurora global database consists of one primary AWS Region where your data is mastered, and one read-only, secondary AWS Region. Aurora replicates data to the secondary AWS Region with typical latency of under a second. The Aurora cluster in the primary AWS Region where your data is mastered performs both read and write operations. The cluster in the secondary region enables low-latency reads. You can scale up the secondary cluster independently by adding one or more DB instances (Aurora Replicas) to serve read-only workloads. For disaster recovery, you can remove and promote the secondary cluster to allow full read and write operations

Q21. B

AWS Documentation Reference: Backup Retention Period

https://docs.aws.amazon.com/AmazonRDS/latest/UserGuide/USER_WorkingWithAutomatedBackups.html

The default backup retention period is seven days if you create the DB instance using the console.

Q22. A

AWS Documentation Reference: Backup Retention Period

https://docs.aws.amazon.com/AmazonRDS/latest/UserGuide/USER_WorkingWithAutoma
tedBackups.html
The default backup retention period is one day if you create the DB instance using the
Amazon RDS API or the AWS CLI.

Q23. C
AWS Documentation Reference: Backup Retention Period
https://docs.aws.amazon.com/AmazonRDS/latest/UserGuide/USER_WorkingWithAutoma
tedBackups.html
Setting the backup retention period to 0 disables automated backups.

Q24. A, B.D
AWS Documentation Reference: Working With Backups
https://docs.aws.amazon.com/AmazonRDS/latest/UserGuide/USER_WorkingWithAutoma
tedBackups.html

Q25. A, B
AWS Documentation Reference:
https://aws.amazon.com/rds/faqs/
*What happens during Multi-AZ failover and how long does it take?*
Failover is automatically handled by Amazon RDS so that you can resume database operations
as quickly as possible without administrative intervention. When failing over, Amazon RDS
simply flips the canonical name record (CNAME) for your DB instance to point at the
standby, which is in turn promoted to become the new primary. AWS encourage you to follow
best practices and implement database connection retry at the application layer.

Q26. D
AWS Documentation Reference: Working With Backups
https://docs.aws.amazon.com/AmazonRDS/latest/UserGuide/USER_WorkingWithAutoma
tedBackups.html

Q27. B
AWS Documentation Reference: Backup Window
https://docs.aws.amazon.com/AmazonRDS/latest/UserGuide/USER_WorkingWithAutoma
tedBackups.html
If you don't specify a preferred backup window when you create the DB instance, Amazon
RDS assigns a default 30-minute backup window. This window is selected at random from an
8-hour block of time for each AWS Region.

Q28. A, B, D
AWS Documentation Reference: Backup Window

https://docs.aws.amazon.com/AmazonRDS/latest/UserGuide/USER_WorkingWithAutoma
tedBackups.html

## Q29. D
AWS Documentation Reference: Backup Window: Backup Storage
https://docs.aws.amazon.com/AmazonRDS/latest/UserGuide/USER_WorkingWithAutoma
tedBackups.html
If you chose to retain automated backups when you delete a DB instance, the automated
backups are saved for the full retention period. If you don't choose Retain automated backups
when you delete a DB instance, all automated backups are deleted with the DB instance. After
they are deleted, the automated backups can't be recovered. If you choose to have Amazon
RDS create a final DB snapshot before it deletes your DB instance, you can use that to recover
your DB instance. Or you can use a previously created manual snapshot. Manual snapshots are
not deleted.

## Q30. C, D
AWS Documentation Reference: Backup Window:
https://docs.aws.amazon.com/AmazonRDS/latest/UserGuide/USER_WorkingWithParamG
roups.html
https://docs.aws.amazon.com/AmazonRDS/latest/UserGuide/USER_WorkingWithOption
Groups.html

## Q31.C

## Q32.D
## Q33. A, B

## Q34. C
Amazon RDS DB snapshots and automated backups are stored in S3.

## Q35. B
AWS Documentation Reference:
https://docs.aws.amazon.com/AmazonRDS/latest/UserGuide/CHAP_Storage.html
DB instances for Amazon RDS for MySQL, MariaDB, PostgreSQL, Oracle, and Microsoft
SQL Server use Amazon Elastic Block Store (Amazon EBS) volumes for database and log
storage.

## Q36. A
AWS Documentation Reference: White paper: Using AWS for Disaster Recovery
Recovery time objective (RTO) is the time it takes after a disruption to restore a business
process to its service level, as defined by the operational level agreement (OLA). If a disaster

occurs at 12:00 PM (noon) and the RTO is eight hours, the DR process should restore the business process to the acceptable service level by 8:00 PM.

Q37. B
AWS Documentation Reference: White paper: Using AWS for Disaster Recovery
Recovery point objective (RPO) is the acceptable amount of data loss measured in time. If a disaster occurs at 12:00 PM (noon) and the RPO is one hour, the system should recover all data that was in the system before 11:00 AM. Data loss will span only one hour, between 11:00 AM and 12:00 PM (noon).

Q38 A.
AWS Documentation Reference:
https://docs.aws.amazon.com/AmazonRDS/latest/UserGuide/CHAP_Storage.html
DB instances for Amazon RDS for MySQL, MariaDB, PostgreSQL, Oracle, and Microsoft SQL Server use Amazon Elastic Block Store (Amazon EBS) volumes for database and log storage. Depending on the amount of storage requested, Amazon RDS automatically stripes across multiple Amazon EBS volumes to enhance performance.

Q39. B, C, D
AWS Documentation Reference:
https://docs.aws.amazon.com/AmazonRDS/latest/UserGuide/CHAP_Storage.html
Amazon RDS provides three storage types: General Purpose SSD (also known as gp2), Provisioned IOPS SSD (also known as io1), and magnetic.

Q40 C
AWS Documentation Reference:
https://docs.aws.amazon.com/AmazonRDS/latest/UserGuide/CHAP_Storage.html
For production application that requires fast and consistent I/O performance, AWS recommend Provisioned IOPS (input/output operations per second) storage

Q41. A, B, C
AWS Documentation Reference:
https://docs.aws.amazon.com/AmazonRDS/latest/UserGuide/CHAP_Storage.html
D is false, Provisioned IOPS storage is a storage type that delivers predictable performance, and consistently low latency. Provisioned IOPS storage is optimized for online transaction processing (OLTP) workloads that have consistent performance requirements. For production application that requires fast and consistent I/O performance, AWS recommend Provisioned IOPS (input/output operations per second) storage.

Q42. D
AWS Documentation Reference: Factors That Affect Storage Performance
https://docs.aws.amazon.com/AmazonRDS/latest/UserGuide/CHAP_Storage.html

Q43. B

AWS Documentation Reference:

https://aws.amazon.com/rds/faqs/?nc=sn&loc=6

Amazon Aurora: All DB clusters.

Amazon RDS for MySQL: All DB instances support creation of read replicas. Automatic backups must be and remain enabled on the source DB instance for read replica operations. Automatic backups on the replica are supported only for Amazon RDS read replicas running MySQL 5.6 and later, not 5.5.

Amazon RDS for PostgreSQL: DB instances with PostgreSQL version 9.3.5 or newer support creation of read replicas. Existing PostgreSQL instances prior to version 9.3.5 need to be upgraded to PostgreSQL version 9.3.5 to take advantage of Amazon RDS read replicas.

Amazon RDS for MariaDB: All DB instances support creation of read replicas. Automatic backups must be and remain enabled on the source DB Instance for read replica operations.

Amazon RDS for Oracle: Supported for Oracle version 12.1.0.2.v12 and higher and for all 12.2 versions using the Bring Your Own License model with Oracle Database Enterprise Edition and licensed for the Active Data Guard Option.

Q44. A, B

AWS Documentation Reference:

https://docs.aws.amazon.com/AmazonRDS/latest/UserGuide/USER_ReadRepl.html

Deploying one or more Read Replicas for a given source DB instance might make sense in a variety of scenarios, including the following:

Scaling beyond the compute or I/O capacity of a single DB instance for read-heavy database workloads. You can direct this excess read traffic to one or more Read Replicas.

Serving read traffic while the source DB instance is unavailable. In some cases, your source DB instance might not be able to take I/O requests, for example due to I/O suspension for backups or scheduled maintenance. In these cases, you can direct read traffic to your Read Replicas. For this use case, keep in mind that the data on the Read Replica might be "stale" because the source DB instance is unavailable.

Q45. A, C

AWS Documentation Reference:

https://docs.aws.amazon.com/AmazonRDS/latest/UserGuide/USER_ReadRepl.html

Deploying one or more Read Replicas for a given source DB instance might make sense in a variety of scenarios, including the following:

Business reporting or data warehousing scenarios where you might want business reporting queries to run against a Read Replica, rather than your primary, production DB instance.

Implementing disaster recovery. You can promote a Read Replica to a standalone instance as a disaster recovery solution if the source DB instance fails.

Q46. A, D

AWS Documentation Reference:

https://docs.aws.amazon.com/AmazonRDS/latest/UserGuide/USER_ReadRepl.html

When you create a Read Replica, you first specify an existing DB instance as the source. Then Amazon RDS takes a snapshot of the source instance and creates a read-only instance from the snapshot. Amazon RDS then uses the asynchronous replication method for the DB engine to update the Read Replica whenever there is a change to the source DB instance.

Q47. C, D

AWS Documentation Reference:

https://docs.aws.amazon.com/AmazonRDS/latest/UserGuide/USER_ReadRepl.html

The Read Replica operates as a DB instance that allows only read-only connections. Applications connect to a Read Replica the same way they do to any DB instance. Amazon RDS replicates all databases in the source DB instance.

Q48. B, D are false.

AWS Documentation Reference:

https://docs.aws.amazon.com/AmazonRDS/latest/UserGuide/USER_ReadRepl.html

Amazon RDS doesn't support circular replication.

Read Replica can resides in a different AWS Region than its source DB instance. With Amazon RDS, you can create a MariaDB, MySQL, or PostgreSQL Read Replica in a different AWS Region than the source DB instance.

Q49. C

AWS Documentation Reference:

https://docs.aws.amazon.com/AmazonRDS/latest/AuroraUserGuide/CHAP_AuroraOvervi ew.html

Amazon Aurora (Aurora) is a fully managed relational database engine that's compatible with MySQL and PostgreSQL.

Q50. A, C, D

AWS Documentation Reference:

https://docs.aws.amazon.com/AmazonRDS/latest/AuroraUserGuide/CHAP_AuroraOvervi ew.html

B is not correct because Aurora automatically fails over to an Aurora Replica in case the primary DB instance becomes unavailable.

Q51. A, B, D

There is no end point called Write endpoint.

AWS Documentation Reference:

https://docs.aws.amazon.com/AmazonRDS/latest/AuroraUserGuide/Aurora.Overview.End points.html

When you connect to an Aurora cluster, the host name and port that you specify point to an intermediate handler called an endpoint. Aurora uses the endpoint mechanism to abstract these connections. Thus, you don't have to hardcode all the hostnames or write your own logic for load-balancing and rerouting connections when some DB instances aren't available.

A cluster endpoint for an Aurora DB cluster connects to the current primary DB instance for that DB cluster. This endpoint is the only one that can perform write operations such as DDL statements.

A reader endpoint for an Aurora DB cluster connects to one of the available Aurora Replicas for that DB cluster. Each Aurora DB cluster has one reader endpoint. If there is more than one Aurora Replica, the reader endpoint directs each connection request to one of the Aurora Replicas.

A custom endpoint for an Aurora cluster represents a set of DB instances that you choose. When you connect to the endpoint, Aurora performs load balancing and chooses one of the instances in the group to handle the connection. You define which instances this endpoint refers to, and you decide what purpose the endpoint serves.

An instance endpoint connects to a specific DB instance within an Aurora cluster. Each DB instance in a DB cluster has its own unique instance endpoint. So there is one instance endpoint for the current primary DB instance of the DB cluster, and there is one instance endpoint for each of the Aurora Replicas in the DB cluster.

Using endpoints, you can map each connection to the appropriate instance or group of instances based on your use case. For example, to perform DDL statements you can connect to whichever instance is the primary instance. To perform queries, you can connect to the reader endpoint, with Aurora automatically performing load-balancing among all the Aurora Replicas. For clusters with DB instances of different capacities or configurations, you can connect to custom endpoints associated with different subsets of DB instances. For diagnosis or tuning, you can connect to a specific instance endpoint to examine details about a specific DB instance.

Q52. A, B, D
AWS Documentation Reference:
https://docs.aws.amazon.com/AmazonRDS/latest/AuroraUserGuide/Aurora.Overview.Stor ageReliability.html
Aurora data is stored in the cluster volume, which is a single, virtual volume that uses solid state drives (SSDs). A cluster volume consists of copies of the data across multiple Availability Zones in a single AWS Region. Because the data is automatically replicated across Availability Zones, your data is highly durable with less possibility of data loss. This replication also ensures that your database is more available during a failover. It does so because the data copies already exist in the other Availability Zones and continue to serve data requests to the DB instances in your DB cluster.

Aurora cluster volumes automatically grow as the amount of data in your database increases. An Aurora cluster volume can grow to a maximum size of 64 tebibytes (TiB).

Q53. D
Multi-AZ deployment doesn't improve performance.

Q54. A

Q55. C

Q56. A
AWS Documentation Reference:
https://docs.aws.amazon.com/AmazonRDS/latest/UserGuide/USER_ReadRepl.html
The primary purpose is improving performance by scaling beyond the compute or I/O capacity of a single DB instance for read-heavy database workloads. You can direct excess read traffic to one or more Read Replicas.

Q57. B, C
AWS Documentation Reference: Increased Availability
https://aws.amazon.com/rds/details/read-replicas/
Read replicas in Amazon RDS for MySQL, MariaDB, PostgreSQL, and Oracle provide a complementary availability mechanism to Amazon RDS Multi-AZ Deployments. You can promote a read replica if the source DB instance fails. This functionality complements the synchronous replication, automatic failure detection, and failover provided with Multi-AZ deployments.

Q58. A, B
AWS Documentation Reference:
https://aws.amazon.com/rds/details/read-replicas/
You can combine Multi-AZ deployments and read replicas to enjoy the benefits of each. For example, you can configure a source database as Multi-AZ for high availability and create a read replica (in Single-AZ) for read scalability.

Q59. B
AWS Documentation Reference:
https://aws.amazon.com/rds/details/read-replicas/
With RDS for MySQL, MariaDB, PostgreSQL, and Oracle you can also set the read replica as Multi-AZ, allowing you to use the read replica as a DR target. When you promote the read replica to be a standalone database, it will already be Multi-AZ enabled.
https://aws.amazon.com/rds/features/multi-az/

Q60. B, C
AWS Documentation Reference: Read Replicas and Multi-AZ Deployments
https://aws.amazon.com/rds/details/read-replicas/
https://aws.amazon.com/rds/features/multi-az/

Q61. A, D

AWS Documentation Reference: Read Replicas and Multi-AZ Deployments

https://aws.amazon.com/rds/details/read-replicas/

https://aws.amazon.com/rds/features/multi-az/

Q62. A, D

AWS Documentation Reference: Read Replicas and Multi-AZ Deployments

https://aws.amazon.com/rds/details/read-replicas/

https://aws.amazon.com/rds/features/multi-az/

Q63. A

C is wrong, as that applies to Multi-AZ deployment.

During the backup window, storage I/O may be briefly suspended while the backup process initializes (typically under a few seconds) and you may experience a brief period of elevated latency. There is no I/O suspension for Multi-AZ DB deployments, since the backup is taken from the standby.

Q64. B

AWS Documentation Reference:

https://docs.aws.amazon.com/AmazonRDS/latest/UserGuide/USER_ReadRepl.html

You can reduce the load on your source DB instance by routing read queries from your applications to the Read Replica. Using Read Replicas, you can elastically scale out beyond the capacity constraints of a single DB instance for read-heavy database workloads.

Q65. B

AWS Documentation Reference:

https://aws.amazon.com/rds/faqs/

When you delete a DB instance, you can create a final DB snapshot upon deletion; if you do, you can use this DB snapshot to restore the deleted DB instance at a later date. Amazon RDS retains this final user-created DB snapshot along with all other manually created DB snapshots after the DB instance is deleted.

Automated backups are deleted when the DB instance is deleted. Only manually created DB Snapshots are retained after the DB Instance is deleted.

Q66. A, C

B is not a correct answer because Redshift is applicable for creating a data warehouse.

D is not correct because S3 is more appropriate for object storage and it provides eventual consistency for read-after-write which doesn't meet the typical design consideration for session management.

AWS Documentation Reference:

https://aws.amazon.com/caching/session-management/

Sticky Sessions with Local Session Caching: Sticky sessions, also known as session affinity, allow you to route a site user to the particular web server that is managing that individual user's session. The session's validity can be determined by a number of methods, including a client-side cookies or via configurable duration parameters that can be set at the load balancer which routes requests to the web servers.

Distributed Session Management: In order to address scalability and to provide a shared data storage for sessions that can be accessible from any individual web server, you can abstract the HTTP sessions from the web servers themselves. A common solution to for this is to leverage an In-Memory Key/Value store such as Redis and Memcached. Other options are DynamoDB and RDS.

Q67. A, B, D

AWS Documentation Reference:

https://aws.amazon.com/rds/faqs/

A DB Subnet Group is a collection of subnets that you may want to designate for your RDS DB Instances in a VPC. Each DB Subnet Group should have at least one subnet for every Availability Zone in a given Region. When creating a DB Instance in VPC, you will need to select a DB Subnet Group. Amazon RDS then uses that DB Subnet Group and your preferred Availability Zone to select a subnet and an IP address within that subnet. Amazon RDS creates and associates an Elastic Network Interface to your DB Instance with that IP address. For Multi-AZ deployments, defining a subnet for all Availability Zones in a Region will allow Amazon RDS to create a new standby in another Availability Zone should the need arise. You need to do this even for Single-AZ deployments, just in case you want to convert them to Multi-AZ deployments at some point.

Q68. B, C

AWS Documentation Reference:

https://aws.amazon.com/rds/faqs/

You can create a read replica with a Multi-AZ DB instance deployment as its source. Since Multi-AZ DB instances address a different need than read replicas, it makes sense to use the two in conjunction for production deployments and to associate a read replica with a Multi-AZ DB Instance deployment. The "source" Multi AZ-DB instance provides you with enhanced write availability and data durability, and the associated read replica would improve read traffic scalability.

Amazon RDS for MySQL, MariaDB, PostgreSQL, and Oracle allow you to enable Multi-AZ configuration on read replicas to support disaster recovery and minimize downtime from engine upgrades.

Q69. B

AWS Documentation Reference:

https://aws.amazon.com/rds/faqs/

In the event of Multi-AZ failover, any associated and available read replicas will automatically resume replication once failover has completed (acquiring updates from the newly promoted primary).

Q70. A, C

AWS Documentation Reference:

https://aws.amazon.com/rds/faqs/

A database parameter group (DB Parameter Group) acts as a "container" for engine configuration values that can be applied to one or more DB Instances. If you create a DB Instance without specifying a DB Parameter Group, a default DB Parameter Group is used. This default group contains engine defaults and Amazon RDS system defaults optimized for the DB Instance you are running. However, if you want your DB Instance to run with your custom-specified engine configuration values, you can simply create a new DB Parameter Group, modify the desired parameters, and modify the DB Instance to use the new DB Parameter Group. Once associated, all DB Instances that use a particular DB Parameter Group get all the parameter updates to that DB Parameter Group.

Q71. A, B, D, E

AWS Documentation Reference: Monitoring storage performance

https://docs.aws.amazon.com/AmazonRDS/latest/UserGuide/CHAP_Storage.html

The following metrics are useful for monitoring storage for your DB instance:

IOPS – The number of I/O operations completed each second. This metric is reported as the average IOPS for a given time interval. Amazon RDS reports read and write IOPS separately on 1-minute intervals. Total IOPS is the sum of the read and write IOPS. Typical values for IOPS range from zero to tens of thousands per second.

Latency – The elapsed time between the submission of an I/O request and its completion. This metric is reported as the average latency for a given time interval. Amazon RDS reports read and write latency separately on 1-minute intervals in units of seconds. Typical values for latency are in the millisecond (ms). For example, Amazon RDS reports 2 ms as 0.002 seconds.

Throughput – The number of bytes each second that are transferred to or from disk. This metric is reported as the average throughput for a given time interval. Amazon RDS reports read and write throughput separately on 1-minute intervals using units of megabytes per second (MB/s). Typical values for throughput range from zero to the I/O channel's maximum bandwidth.

Queue Depth – The number of I/O requests in the queue waiting to be serviced. These are I/O requests that have been submitted by the application but have not been sent to the device because the device is busy servicing other I/O requests. Time spent waiting in the queue is a component of latency and service time (not available as a metric). This metric is reported as the average queue depth for a given time interval. Amazon RDS reports queue depth in 1-minute intervals. Typical values for queue depth range from zero to several hundred.

Q72. D

AWS Documentation Reference: Factors That Affect Storage Performance

https://docs.aws.amazon.com/AmazonRDS/latest/UserGuide/CHAP_Storage.html

Both system activities and database workload can affect storage performance.

The following system-related activities consume I/O capacity and might reduce database instance performance while in progress:

- Multi-AZ standby creation
- Read replica creation
- Changing storage types

In some cases your database or application design results in concurrency issues, locking, or other forms of database contention.

To get the most performance out of your Amazon RDS database instance, choose a current generation instance type with enough bandwidth to support your storage type. For example, you can choose EBS-optimized instances and instances with 10-gigabit network connectivity.

Q73. A

AWS Documentation Reference:

https://docs.aws.amazon.com/AmazonRDS/latest/UserGuide/UsingWithRDS.SSL.html

https://docs.aws.amazon.com/AmazonRDS/latest/UserGuide/CHAP_MySQL.html#MySQL.Concepts.SSLSupport

You can use Secure Socket Layer (SSL) or Transport Layer Security (TLS) from your application to encrypt a connection to a DB instance running MySQL, MariaDB, SQL Server, Oracle, or PostgreSQL. Each DB engine has its own process for implementing SSL/TLS. Amazon RDS automatically creates a Secure Sockets Layer (SSL) certificate for each RDS database to enable client connections over SSL. Use RDS SSL certificates specific to your AWS Region or Regions to ensure that your applications are connecting to the RDS instance in the correct AWS Region.

B is incorrect as by default connection between EC2 instances and RDS databases are not encrypted.

C is incorrect as this step applies to Using SSL with a Microsoft SQL Server DB Instance.

https://docs.aws.amazon.com/AmazonRDS/latest/UserGuide/SQLServer.Concepts.General.SSL.Using.html

D is incorrect as this step applied to using SSL with an Oracle DB Instance.
https://docs.aws.amazon.com/AmazonRDS/latest/UserGuide/CHAP_Oracle.html#Oracle.
Concepts.SSL

Q74. C, D

AWS Documentation Reference:

https://docs.aws.amazon.com/AmazonRDS/latest/UserGuide/Overview.Encryption.html

You can only enable encryption for an Amazon RDS DB instance when you create it, not after the DB instance is created. However, because you can encrypt a copy of an unencrypted DB snapshot, you can effectively add encryption to an unencrypted DB instance. That is, you can create a snapshot of your DB instance, and then create an encrypted copy of that snapshot. You can then restore a DB instance from the encrypted snapshot, and thus you have an encrypted copy of your original DB instance

Q75. B

Amazon RDS encrypted DB instances use the industry standard AES-256 encryption algorithm to encrypt your data on the server that hosts your Amazon RDS DB instances.

Q76. A, B, D

AWS Documentation Reference:

https://docs.aws.amazon.com/AmazonRDS/latest/UserGuide/Overview.Encryption.html

When you create an encrypted DB instance, you can also supply the AWS KMS key identifier for your encryption key. If you don't specify an AWS KMS key identifier, then Amazon RDS uses your default encryption key for your new DB instance. AWS KMS creates your default encryption key for Amazon RDS for your AWS account. Your AWS account has a different default encryption key for each AWS Region. Once you have created an encrypted DB instance, you can't change the type of encryption key used by that DB instance.

Q77. A, B, C

AWS Documentation Reference:

https://docs.aws.amazon.com/AmazonRDS/latest/UserGuide/Overview.RDSSecurityGroup
s.html

A DB security group controls access to EC2-Classic DB instances that are not in a VPC.
A VPC security group controls access to DB instances and EC2 instances inside a VPC.
An EC2 security group controls access to an EC2 instance.

Q78. A, C, D

AWS Documentation Reference:

https://docs.aws.amazon.com/AmazonRDS/latest/UserGuide/Overview.RDSSecurityGroup
s.html

Q79.B, C

AWS Documentation Reference:

https://docs.aws.amazon.com/AmazonRDS/latest/UserGuide/USER_WorkingWithAutoma
tedBackups.html

After you create a DB instance, you can modify the backup retention period. You can set the backup retention period to between 0 and 35 days. Setting the backup retention period to 0 disables automated backups.

Disabling automated backups disables point-in-time recovery. Disabling automatic backups for a DB instance deletes all existing automated backups for the instance. If you disable and then re-enable automated backups, you are only able to restore starting from the time you re-enabled automated backups.

Q80. B
AWS Documentation Reference:
https://docs.aws.amazon.com/AmazonRDS/latest/UserGuide/USER_PIT.html
You can restore a DB instance to a specific point in time, creating a new DB instance. When you restore a DB instance to a point in time, the default DB security group is applied to the new DB instance.

Q81. C, D
AWS Documentation Reference:
https://docs.aws.amazon.com/AmazonRDS/latest/UserGuide/Overview.Encryption.html#
Overview.Encryption.Enabling
To enable encryption for a new DB instance, choose Enable encryption on the Amazon RDS console. If you use the create-db-instance AWS CLI command to create an encrypted DB instance, set the --storage-encrypted parameter to true. If you use the CreateDBInstance API operation, set the StorageEncrypted parameter to true.

When you create an encrypted DB instance, you can also supply the AWS KMS key identifier for your encryption key. If you don't specify an AWS KMS key identifier, then Amazon RDS uses your default encryption key for your new DB instance. AWS KMS creates your default encryption key for Amazon RDS for your AWS account. Your AWS account has a different default encryption key for each AWS Region.

On a database instance running with Amazon RDS encryption, data stored at rest in the underlying storage is encrypted, as are its automated backups, read replicas, and snapshots. Encryption and decryption are handled transparently.

Q82. A
AWS Documentation Reference:
https://docs.aws.amazon.com/AmazonRDS/latest/UserGuide/USER_Monitoring.OS.html
Amazon RDS provides metrics in real time for the operating system (OS) that your DB instance runs on. You can view the metrics for your DB instance using the console, or

consume the Enhanced Monitoring JSON output from Amazon CloudWatch Logs in a monitoring system of your choice.

## Q83.B

AWS Documentation Reference:

https://aws.amazon.com/rds/reserved-instances/

Reserved Instances can also provide significant cost savings for mission critical applications that run on Multi-AZ database deployments for higher availability and data durability.

Amazon RDS Reserved Instances provide size flexibility for the MySQL, MariaDB, PostgreSQL, and Amazon Aurora database engines as well as the "Bring your own license" (BYOL) edition of the Oracle database engine. With size flexibility, your RI's discounted rate will automatically apply to usage of any size in the instance family (using the same database engine). Size flexibility does not apply to Microsoft SQL Server and the License Included (LI) edition of Oracle.

For example, let's say you purchased a db.m4.2xlarge MySQL RI in US East (N. Virginia). The discounted rate of this RI can automatically apply to 2 db.m4.xlarge MySQL instances without you needing to do anything.

The RI discounted rate will also apply to usage to both Single-AZ and Multi-AZ configurations for the same database engine and instance family. For example, let's say you purchased a db.r3.large PostgreSQL Single-AZ RI in EU (Frankfurt). The discounted rate of this RI can automatically apply to 50% of the usage of a db.r3.large PostgreSQL Multi-AZ instance in the same region.

## Q84.C, D

AWS Documentation Reference:

https://aws.amazon.com/rds/mysql/pricing/?pg=pr&loc=2

- Data transferred between Amazon RDS and Amazon EC2 Instances in the same Availability Zone is free.
- Data transferred between Availability Zones for replication of Multi-AZ deployments is free.
- Amazon RDS DB Instances outside VPC: For data transferred between an Amazon EC2 instance and Amazon RDS DB Instance in different Availability Zones of the same Region, there is no Data Transfer charge for traffic in or out of the Amazon RDS DB Instance. You are only charged for the Data Transfer in or out of the Amazon EC2 instance, and standard Amazon EC2 Regional Data Transfer charges apply.
- Amazon RDS DB Instances inside VPC: For data transferred between an Amazon EC2 instance and Amazon RDS DB Instance in different Availability Zones of the same Region, Amazon EC2 Regional Data Transfer charges apply on both sides of transfer.

- DB Snapshot Copy is charged for the data transferred to copy the snapshot data across regions. Once the snapshot is copied, standard database snapshot charges will apply to store it in the destination region.

## Q85. A, B
AWS Documentation Reference:
https://docs.aws.amazon.com/AmazonRDS/latest/AuroraUserGuide/aurora-serverless.html
Amazon Aurora Serverless is an on-demand, autoscaling configuration for Amazon Aurora

## Q86. B, C, D
AWS Documentation Reference:
https://docs.aws.amazon.com/AmazonRDS/latest/AuroraUserGuide/aurora-serverless.html

Infrequently used applications: You have an application that is only used for a few minutes several times per day or week, such as a low-volume blog site.

New applications: You are deploying a new application and are unsure about which instance size you need. With Aurora Serverless, you can create a database endpoint and have the database autoscale to the capacity requirements of your application.

Variable workloads: You're running a lightly used application, with peaks of 30 minutes to several hours a few times each day, or several times per year. Examples are applications for human resources, budgeting, and operational reporting applications. With Aurora Serverless, you no longer need to provision to either peak or average capacity.

Unpredictable workloads: You're running workloads where there is database usage throughout the day, but also peaks of activity that are hard to predict. An example is a traffic site that sees a surge of activity when it starts raining. With Aurora Serverless, your database autoscales capacity to meet the needs of the application's peak load and scales back

## Q87. A
B is not correct, you will be charged for both EC2 and DB instance if they are running.
C & D option you will save money to a certain extent compared to having EC2 and DB instance all the time. But not most optimized.

AWS Documentation Reference:
https://docs.aws.amazon.com/AmazonRDS/latest/UserGuide/CHAP_Tutorials.RestoringFromSnapshot.html
When the survey is done, the EC2 instance can be stopped and the DB instance can be deleted after a final DB snapshot is created. When you need to conduct another survey, you can restart the EC2 instance and restore the DB instance from the DB snapshot. For stopped EC2 instances, AWS does not charge for any instance usage fees.

Q88. C

AWS Documentation Reference:

https://docs.aws.amazon.com/AmazonRDS/latest/UserGuide/CHAP_Storage.html

General Purpose SSD, also called gp2, volumes offer cost-effective storage that is ideal for a broad range of workloads.

Q89. D

AWS Documentation Reference: I/O Credits and Burst Performance

https://docs.aws.amazon.com/AmazonRDS/latest/UserGuide/CHAP_Storage.html

General Purpose SSD storage offers cost-effective storage that is acceptable for most database workloads. Baseline I/O performance for General Purpose SSD storage is 3 IOPS for each GiB. This relationship means that larger volumes have better performance. Volumes below 1 TiB in size also have ability to burst to 3,000 IOPS for extended periods of time.

General Purpose SSD storage performance is governed by volume size, which dictates the base performance level of the volume and how quickly it accumulates I/O credits. Larger volumes have higher base performance levels and accumulate I/O credits faster. I/O credits represent the available bandwidth that your General Purpose SSD storage can use to burst large amounts of I/O when more than the base level of performance is needed. The more I/O credits your storage has for I/O, the more time it can burst beyond its base performance level and the better it performs when your workload requires more performance.

When your storage requires more than the base performance I/O level, it uses I/O credits in the I/O credit balance to burst to the required performance level. Such a burst goes to a maximum of 3,000 IOPS. Storage larger than 1,000 GiB has a base performance that is equal or greater than the maximum burst performance.

Q90. C, D

AWS Documentation Reference:

https://aws.amazon.com/rds/faqs/

When you purchase a reserved instance, you can select the Multi-AZ option in the DB instance configuration available for purchase. In addition, if you are using a DB engine and license model that supports reserved instance size-flexibility, a Multi-AZ reserved instance will cover usage for two Single-AZ DB instances.

A DB instance reservation can be applied to a read replica, provided the DB instance class and Region are the same.

Q91. B, D

AWS Documentation Reference:

https://docs.aws.amazon.com/AmazonRDS/latest/AuroraUserGuide/USER_PIT.html

You can restore a DB cluster to a specific point in time, creating a new DB cluster.

https://docs.aws.amazon.com/AmazonRDS/latest/AuroraUserGuide/AuroraMySQL.Managi
ng.Backtrack.html
https://aws.amazon.com/blogs/aws/amazon-aurora-backtrack-turn-back-time/
With Amazon Aurora MySQL compatibility, you can backtrack a DB cluster to a specific time,
without restoring data from a backup.

Q92. A, B, C
AWS Documentation Reference:
https://docs.aws.amazon.com/AmazonRDS/latest/UserGuide/MonitoringOverview.html
You can use the following automated monitoring tools to watch Amazon RDS and report
when something is wrong:

- Amazon RDS Events – Subscribe to Amazon RDS events to be notified when changes
  occur with a DB instance, DB snapshot, DB parameter group, or DB security group.
- Database log files – View, download, or watch database log files using the Amazon RDS
  console or Amazon RDS API operations. You can also query some database log files that
  are loaded into database tables.
- Amazon RDS Enhanced Monitoring — Look at metrics in real time for the operating
  system.
- In addition, Amazon RDS integrates with Amazon CloudWatch for additional monitoring
  capabilities:
- Amazon CloudWatch Metrics – Amazon RDS automatically sends metrics to
  CloudWatch every minute for each active database.
- Amazon CloudWatch Alarms – You can watch a single Amazon RDS metric over a
  specific time period, and perform one or more actions based on the value of the metric
  relative to a threshold you set.
- Amazon CloudWatch Logs – Most DB engines enable you to monitor, store, and access
  your database log files in CloudWatch Logs.

Q93. A, B, D
AWS Documentation Reference:
https://docs.aws.amazon.com/AmazonRDS/latest/UserGuide/USER_PerfInsights.html
Performance Insights expands on existing Amazon RDS monitoring features to illustrate your
database's performance and help you analyze any issues that affect it. With the Performance
Insights dashboard, you can visualize the database load and filter the load by waits, SQL
statements, hosts, or users.
The central metric for Performance Insights is DB Load, which represents the average number
of active sessions for the DB engine. The DB Load metric is collected every second. An active
session is a connection that has submitted work to the DB engine and is waiting for a response
from it. For example, if you submit a SQL query to the DB engine, the database session is
active while the DB engine is processing that query.

Q94. B, C, D, E, F, G

AWS Documentation Reference:

https://aws.amazon.com/premiumsupport/knowledge-center/rds-cannot-connect/

https://aws.amazon.com/premiumsupport/knowledge-center/rds-connectivity-instance-subnet-vpc/

Publicly Accessible property of the Amazon RDS instance should be set to Yes.

Be sure that your instance is in the available state: If you recently launched or rebooted your DB instance, confirm that the instance is in the available state in the Amazon RDS console. Depending on the size of your DB instance, it can take up to 20 minutes for the instance to become available for network connections.

Be sure that your DB instance allows connections:

Be sure that traffic from the source connecting to your DB instance isn't gated by one or more of the following:

- Any Amazon Virtual Private Cloud (Amazon VPC) security groups associated with the DB instance. If necessary, add rules to the security group associated with the VPC that allow traffic related to the source in and out of the DB instance. You can specify an IP address, a range of IP addresses, or another VPC security group.

- Any DB security group associated with the DB instance. If the DB instance isn't in a VPC, it might be using a DB security group to gate traffic. Update your DB security group to allow traffic from the IP address range, Amazon Elastic Compute Cloud (Amazon EC2) security group, or EC2 Classic instance that you use to connect.

- Connections outside a VPC. Be sure that the instance is publicly accessible and that the instance is associated with a public subnet (the route table allows access from an internet gateway). Publicly Accessible property of the instance is set to Yes.

- Network access control lists (ACLs). Network ACLs act as a firewall for resources in a specific subnet in a VPC. If you use ACLs in your VPC, be sure that they have rules that allow inbound and outbound traffic to and from the DB instance.

- Network or local firewalls. Check with your network administrator to determine if your network allows traffic to and from the ports the DB instance uses for inbound and outbound communication.

- Amazon RDS doesn't accept internet control message protocol (ICMP) traffic, including ping.

Troubleshoot potential DNS name or endpoint issues: When connecting to your DB instance, you use a DNS name (endpoint) provided by the Amazon RDS console. Be sure that you use the correct endpoint, and that you provide the endpoint in the correct format to the client you use to connect to the DB instance.

Check the route tables associated with your Multi-AZ deployment: When you create a Multi-AZ deployment, you launch multiple replica DB instances in different Availability Zones to improve the fault tolerance of your application. Be sure that the subnets associated with each instance are associated with the same or similar route tables. Otherwise, if your primary instance fails over to a standby replica, and the standby replica is associated with a different route table, traffic that was previously routed to your DB instance might no longer be routed correctly.

Verify the connectivity: Verify your connection by running one of the following commands:
telnet <RDS endpoint> <port number>
nc <RDS endpoint> <port number>
If either the telnet or nc commands succeed, it indicates that a network connection was established, and the issue is likely caused by the user authentication to the database, such as user name and password.

## Q95 B, C
AWS Documentation Reference:
https://docs.aws.amazon.com/AmazonRDS/latest/UserGuide/Concepts.MultiAZ.html
Amazon RDS provides high availability and failover support for DB instances using Multi-AZ deployments. In a Multi-AZ deployment, Amazon RDS automatically provisions and maintains a synchronous standby replica in a different Availability Zone. The primary DB instance is synchronously replicated across Availability Zones to a standby replica to provide data redundancy, eliminate I/O freezes, and minimize latency spikes during system backups. Running a DB instance with high availability can enhance availability during planned system maintenance, and help protect your databases against DB instance failure and Availability Zone disruption.
The high-availability feature is not a scaling solution for read-only scenarios; you cannot use a standby replica to serve read traffic.
https://aws.amazon.com/rds/details/read-replicas/
To service read-only traffic, you should use a Read Replica. Amazon RDS Read Replicas provide enhanced performance and durability for database (DB) instances. This feature makes it easy to elastically scale out beyond the capacity constraints of a single DB instance for read-heavy database workloads. You can create one or more replicas of a given source DB Instance and serve high-volume application read traffic from multiple copies of your data, thereby increasing aggregate read throughput.

## Q96. B, C, D, E, F
A is incorrect as EBS is block level storage and doesn't provide data caching feature.

AWS Documentation Reference:
https://aws.amazon.com/caching/aws-caching/

Amazon ElastiCache is a web service that makes it easy to deploy, operate, and scale an in-memory data store and cache in the cloud. The service improves the performance of web applications by allowing you to retrieve information from fast, managed, in-memory data stores, instead of relying entirely on slower disk-based databases.

Amazon DynamoDB Accelerator (DAX) is a fully managed, highly available, in-memory cache for DynamoDB that delivers up to a 10x performance improvement – from milliseconds to microseconds – even at millions of requests per second. DAX does all the heavy lifting required to add in-memory acceleration to your DynamoDB tables, without requiring developers to manage cache invalidation, data population, or cluster management.

Amazon CloudFront is a global content delivery network (CDN) service that accelerates delivery of your websites, APIs, video content or other web assets. Amazon CloudFront can be used to deliver your entire website, including dynamic, static, streaming, and interactive content using a global network of edge locations. Requests for your content are automatically routed to the nearest edge location, so content is delivered with the best possible performance.

AWS Greengrass is software that lets you run local compute, messaging & data caching for connected devices in a secure way. With AWS Greengrass, connected devices can run AWS Lambda functions, keep device data in sync, and communicate with other devices securely – even when not connected to the Internet.

Amazon Route 53 is a highly available and scalable cloud Domain Name System (DNS) web service providing Domain Name System (DNS) Caching. Every domain request made on the internet essentially queries DNS cache servers in order to resolve the IP address associated with the domain name. DNS caching can occur on many levels including on the OS, via ISPs and DNS servers.

Q97. B, C, E
AWS Documentation Reference:
https://aws.amazon.com/sqs/faqs/
*How reliable is the storage of my data in Amazon SQS?*
Amazon SQS stores all message queues and messages within a single, highly-available AWS region with multiple redundant Availability Zones (AZs), so that no single computer, network, or AZ failure can make messages inaccessible.
https://docs.aws.amazon.com/amazondynamodb/latest/developerguide/Introduction.html
In DynamoDB all of your data is stored on solid-state disks (SSDs) and is automatically replicated across multiple Availability Zones in an AWS Region, providing built-in high availability and data durability.
https://aws.amazon.com/s3/faqs/
*How are Amazon S3 and Amazon S3 Glacier designed to achieve 99.999999999% durability?*

Amazon S3 Standard, S3 Standard-IA, and S3 Glacier storage classes redundantly store your objects on multiple devices across a minimum of three Availability Zones (AZs) in an Amazon S3 Region before returning SUCCESS. The S3 One Zone-IA storage class stores data redundantly across multiple devices within a single AZ. These services are designed to sustain concurrent device failures by quickly detecting and repairing any lost redundancy, and they also regularly verify the integrity of your data using checksums.

Q98. B, G
EBS and S3 doesn't provide reservation model.
AWS Documentation Reference:
https://aws.amazon.com/rds/reserved-instances/
Amazon RDS Reserved Instances give you the option to reserve a DB instance for a one or three year term and in turn receive a significant discount compared to the On-Demand Instance pricing for the DB instance.
https://aws.amazon.com/ec2/pricing/reserved-instances/
Amazon EC2 Reserved Instances (RI) provide a significant discount (up to 75%) compared to On-Demand pricing and provide a capacity reservation when used in a specific Availability Zone.
https://aws.amazon.com/elasticache/reserved-cache-nodes/
Amazon ElastiCache Reserved Nodes give you the option to make a low, one-time payment for each cache node you want to reserve and in turn receive a significant discount on the hourly charge for that Node.
https://docs.aws.amazon.com/redshift/latest/mgmt/purchase-reserved-node-instance.html
If you intend to keep your Amazon Redshift cluster running continuously for a prolonged period, you should consider purchasing reserved node offerings. These offerings provide significant savings over on-demand pricing, but they require you to reserve compute nodes and commit to paying for those nodes for either a one-year or three-year duration.

Q99. D
AWS Documentation Reference:
https://docs.aws.amazon.com/amazondynamodb/latest/developerguide/Introduction.html
DynamoDB automatically spreads the data and traffic for your tables over a sufficient number of servers to handle your throughput and storage requirements, while maintaining consistent and fast performance. All of your data is stored on solid-state disks (SSDs) and is automatically replicated across multiple Availability Zones in an AWS Region, providing built-in high availability and data durability.

Q100.C
AWS Documentation Reference:
https://aws.amazon.com/dynamodb/
Here the key words to consider are 'no servers to provision', 'automatically scales tables up and down to adjust for capacity and maintain performance' and 'in-memory caching'.

DynamoDB provides these features.

Amazon DynamoDB is a key-value and document database that delivers single-digit millisecond performance at any scale. It's a fully managed, multiregion, multimaster, durable database with built-in security, backup and restore, and in-memory caching for internet-scale applications.

DynamoDB is serverless with no servers to provision, patch, or manage and no software to install, maintain, or operate. DynamoDB automatically scales tables up and down to adjust for capacity and maintain performance. Availability and fault tolerance are built in, eliminating the need to architect your applications for these capabilities. DynamoDB provides both provisioned and on-demand capacity modes so that you can optimize costs by specifying capacity per workload, or paying for only the resources you consume.

D is incorrect as Redshift is a data warehouse service. A is incorrect as ElastiCache is a caching service. C is incorrect because for RDS you will need to choose underlying EBS storage, storage size, it doesn't automatically scales tables up and down to adjust for capacity and maintain performance' nor it has in-memory caching service.

Q101. D

Q102. A, B, C
AWS Documentation Reference:
https://aws.amazon.com/dynamodb/features/

Q103. B, C, D
AWS Documentation Reference:
https://docs.aws.amazon.com/amazondynamodb/latest/developerguide/HowItWorks.CoreComponents.html#HowItWorks.CoreComponents.PrimaryKey
Each primary key attribute must be a scalar (meaning that it can hold only a single value). The only data types allowed for primary key attributes are string, number, or binary. There are no such restrictions for other, non-key attributes.

Q104. A, B, D
AWS Documentation Reference:
https://docs.aws.amazon.com/amazondynamodb/latest/developerguide/Introduction.html

Q105. B, C
AWS Documentation Reference:
https://docs.aws.amazon.com/amazondynamodb/latest/developerguide/HowItWorks.ReadConsistency.html
DynamoDB supports eventually consistent and strongly consistent reads.

Eventually Consistent Reads: When you read data from a DynamoDB table, the response might not reflect the results of a recently completed write operation. The response might include some stale data. If you repeat your read request after a short time, the response should return the latest data.

Strongly Consistent Reads : When you request a strongly consistent read, DynamoDB returns a response with the most up-to-date data, reflecting the updates from all prior write operations that were successful. Consistent reads are not supported on global secondary indexes (GSI).

Q106. B, C
AWS Documentation Reference:
https://docs.aws.amazon.com/amazondynamodb/latest/developerguide/HowItWorks.ReadWriteCapacityMode.html
DynamoDB has two read/write capacity modes for processing reads and writes on your tables: On-demand and Provisioned

Q107. B, C, D
AWS Documentation Reference:
https://docs.aws.amazon.com/amazondynamodb/latest/developerguide/HowItWorks.ReadWriteCapacityMode.html

Q108. A, B, D
AWS Documentation Reference:
https://docs.aws.amazon.com/amazondynamodb/latest/developerguide/HowItWorks.ReadWriteCapacityMode.html

Q109.A
AWS Documentation Reference:
https://aws.amazon.com/documentdb/
Amazon DocumentDB is a fast, scalable, highly available, and fully managed document database service that supports MongoDB workloads.

Q110. A, C
AWS Documentation Reference:
https://docs.aws.amazon.com/amazondynamodb/latest/developerguide/HowItWorks.ReadWriteCapacityMode.html

https://docs.aws.amazon.com/amazondynamodb/latest/developerguide/ProvisionedThroughput.html#ItemSizeCalculations.Reads

Q111. A, C, D

The total number of read capacity units required depends on the item size, and whether you want an eventually consistent or strongly consistent read. For example, if your item size is 8 KB, you require 2 read capacity units to sustain one strongly consistent read per second, 1 read capacity unit if you choose eventually consistent reads, or 4 read capacity units for a transactional read request.

AWS Documentation Reference:

https://docs.aws.amazon.com/amazondynamodb/latest/developerguide/HowItWorks.Read
WriteCapacityMode.html

https://docs.aws.amazon.com/amazondynamodb/latest/developerguide/ProvisionedThroug
hput.html#ItemSizeCalculations.Reads

## Q112. C, D

AWS Documentation Reference:

https://docs.aws.amazon.com/amazondynamodb/latest/developerguide/HowItWorks.Read
WriteCapacityMode.html

The total number of write capacity units required depends on the item size. For example, if your item size is 2 KB, you require 2 write capacity units to sustain one write request per second or 4 write capacity units for a transactional write request

## Q113. B

## Q114. A, C, D

A, C: because one read capacity unit represents one strongly consistent read per second, or two eventually consistent reads per second, for an item up to 4 KB in size.

$6*4= 24$

$6*2*4= 48$

D: Transactional read requests require two read capacity units to perform one read per second for items up to 4 KB.

AWS Documentation Reference:

https://docs.aws.amazon.com/amazondynamodb/latest/developerguide/HowItWorks.Read
WriteCapacityMode.html#HowItWorks.ProvisionedThroughput.Manual

One read request unit represents one strongly consistent read request, or two eventually consistent read requests, for an item up to 4 KB in size. Transactional read requests require 2 read request units to perform one read for items up to 4 KB. If you need to read an item that is larger than 4 KB, DynamoDB needs additional read request units. The total number of read request units required depends on the item size, and whether you want an eventually consistent or strongly consistent read. For example, if your item size is 8 KB, you require 2 read request units to sustain one strongly consistent read, 1 read request unit if you choose eventually consistent reads, or 4 read request units for a transactional read request

## Q115. A, D

One write capacity unit represents one write per second for an item up to 1 KB in size.
A: 1 KB × 6 write capacity units

D: Transactional write requests require 2 write capacity units to perform one write per second for items up to 1 KB.
AWS Documentation Reference:
https://docs.aws.amazon.com/amazondynamodb/latest/developerguide/HowItWorks.Read
WriteCapacityMode.html#HowItWorks.ProvisionedThroughput.Manual
One write capacity unit represents one write per second for an item up to 1 KB in size. If you need to write an item that is larger than 1 KB, DynamoDB must consume additional write capacity units. Transactional write requests require 2 write capacity units to perform one write per second for items up to 1 KB. The total number of write capacity units required depends on the item size. For example, if your item size is 2 KB, you require 2 write capacity units to sustain one write request per second or 4 write capacity units for a transactional write request

Q116. A
Eventually consistent reads is by default.

Q117. C
DynamoDB being a NoSQL database is the pertinent choice here because of ability to store the data as key value pairs. Using DynamoDB for session storage alleviates issues that occur with session handling in a distributed web application by moving sessions off of the local file system and into a shared location. DynamoDB is fast, scalable, easy to set up, and handles replication of your data automatically.

Q118. A, D
AWS Documentation Reference:
https://docs.aws.amazon.com/amazondynamodb/latest/developerguide/HowItWorks.CoreC
omponents.html
Partition key – A simple primary key, composed of one attribute known as the partition key.
Partition key and sort key – Referred to as a composite primary key, this type of key is composed of two attributes. The first attribute is the partition key, and the second attribute is the sort key.
There is no global secondary or local secondary primary key.

Q119. A, B
AWS Documentation Reference:
https://docs.aws.amazon.com/amazondynamodb/latest/developerguide/HowItWorks.CoreC
omponents.html

Q120. C

DynamoDB being a NoSQL database is the pertinent choice here because of high volume and velocity of data coming every 5 minutes from many hundreds of devices.

Q121. A, C, D
AWS Documentation Reference:
https://docs.aws.amazon.com/amazondynamodb/latest/developerguide/bp-general-nosql-design.html
B is not a best practice for NoSQL design, in RDBMS, you design for flexibility without worrying about implementation details or performance.
In DynamoDB, you design your schema specifically to make the most common and important queries as fast and as inexpensive as possible. Your data structures are tailored to the specific requirements of your business use cases.

Q122. A, B
Option C is incorrect because adding a load balancer at the front of DynamoDB will not improve performance of DynamoDB.
Option D is incorrect because EC2 auto scaling is for EC2 instances only.
AWS Documentation Reference:
https://docs.aws.amazon.com/amazondynamodb/latest/developerguide/AutoScaling.html
Option A is correct because Amazon DynamoDB auto scaling uses the AWS Application Auto Scaling service to dynamically adjust provisioned throughput capacity on your behalf, in response to actual traffic patterns. This enables a table or a global secondary index to increase its provisioned read and write capacity to handle sudden increases in traffic, without throttling. When the workload decreases, Application Auto Scaling decreases the throughput so that you don't pay for unused provisioned capacity.
https://aws.amazon.com/dynamodb/dax/
Option B is correct as DAX is a DynamoDB-compatible caching service that enables you to benefit from fast in-memory performance for demanding applications.

Q123.A, B, C
AWS Documentation Reference:
https://docs.aws.amazon.com/amazondynamodb/latest/developerguide/ProvisionedThroughput.html#ProvisionedThroughput.CapacityUnits.InitialSettings

Every application has different requirements for reading and writing from a database. When you are determining the initial throughput settings for a DynamoDB table, take the following inputs into consideration:

Item sizes. Some items are small enough that they can be read or written using a single capacity unit. Larger items require multiple capacity units. By estimating the sizes of the items that will be in your table, you can specify accurate settings for your table's provisioned throughput.

Expected read and write request rates. In addition to item size, you should estimate the number of reads and writes you need to perform per second.

Read consistency requirements. Read capacity units are based on strongly consistent read operations, which consume twice as many database resources as eventually consistent reads. You should determine whether your application requires strongly consistent reads, or whether it can relax this requirement and perform eventually consistent reads instead. (Read operations in DynamoDB are eventually consistent, by default. You can request strongly consistent reads for these operations if necessary.)

There is no concept of 'write consistency'.

Q124. B
AWS Documentation Reference:
https://docs.aws.amazon.com/amazondynamodb/latest/developerguide/bp-partition-key-uniform-load.html
Most of the time you will be querying for messages for given employeeid sorted by timestamp. If a single table has only a small number of partition key values, distributing your write operations across more distinct partition key values for improved performance. Partition key having distinct values helps in optimized partitions where values are stored.

Q125.B
AWS Documentation Reference:
https://docs.aws.amazon.com/amazondynamodb/latest/developerguide/Streams.html
DynamoDB Streams captures a time-ordered sequence of item-level modifications in any DynamoDB table and stores this information in a log for up to 24 hours.

Q126. D
AWS Documentation Reference:
https://docs.aws.amazon.com/amazondynamodb/latest/developerguide/Streams.html
DynamoDB Streams is an optional feature that captures data modification events in DynamoDB tables. DynamoDB Streams writes a stream record whenever one of the following events occurs:

- A new item is added to the table: The stream captures an image of the entire item, including all of its attributes.
- An item is updated: The stream captures the "before" and "after" image of any attributes that were modified in the item.
- An item is deleted from the table: The stream captures an image of the entire item before it was deleted.

All other user cases apart from D will use one or all of above three events of data items to execute the business functionality. You can use DynamoDB Streams together with AWS Lambda to create a trigger code that executes automatically whenever an event of interest appears in a stream. For example, for option F you will have a Customers table that contains customer information for a company. To send a "welcome" email to each new customer, you could enable a stream on that table, and then associate the stream with a Lambda function. The Lambda function would execute whenever a new stream record appears, but only process new items added to the Customers table. For any item that has an EmailAddress attribute, the Lambda function would invoke Amazon Simple Email Service (Amazon SES) to send an email to that address.

## Q127. C, D
AWS Documentation Reference:
https://docs.aws.amazon.com/amazondynamodb/latest/developerguide/ProvisionedThroughput.html#ProvisionedThroughput.CapacityUnits.InitialSettings
The items are 3 KB in size, and you want strongly consistent reads. For this scenario, each read requires one provisioned read capacity unit. To determine this number, you divide the item size of the operation by 4 KB, and then round up to the nearest whole number, as in this example:

3 KB / 4 KB = 0.75, or 1 read capacity unit.

A read capacity unit represents one strongly consistent read per second for an item up to 4 KB in size.

For this scenario, you have to set the table's provisioned read throughput to 80 read capacity units:
1 read capacity unit per item × 80 reads per second = 80 read capacity units

## Q128. A, C
AWS Documentation Reference:
https://docs.aws.amazon.com/amazondynamodb/latest/developerguide/bp-indexes-general.html

https://docs.aws.amazon.com/amazondynamodb/latest/developerguide/SecondaryIndexes.html
Global secondary index—an index with a partition key and a sort key that can be different from those on the base table. A global secondary index is considered "global" because queries on the index can span all of the data in the base table, across all partitions. A global secondary index has no size limitations and has its own provisioned throughput settings for read and write activity that are separate from those of the table.

Local secondary index—an index that has the same partition key as the base table, but a different sort key. A local secondary index is "local" in the sense that every partition of a local secondary index is scoped to a base table partition that has the same partition key value. As a result, the total size of indexed items for any one partition key value can't exceed 10 GB. Also, a local secondary index shares provisioned throughput settings for read and write activity with the table it is indexing.

## Q129. A, C, D, E
AWS Documentation Reference:
https://docs.aws.amazon.com/amazondynamodb/latest/developerguide/SecondaryIndexes.html

## Q130. C, D
AWS Documentation Reference:
https://docs.aws.amazon.com/amazondynamodb/latest/developerguide/ProvisionedThroughput.html#ProvisionedThroughput.CapacityUnits.InitialSettings
For this scenario, each write requires one provisioned write capacity unit. To determine this number, you divide the item size of the operation by 1 KB, and then round up to the nearest whole number:

512 bytes / 1 KB = 0.5, or 1 write capacity unit.

A write capacity unit represents one write per second, for an item up to 1 KB in size.

For this scenario, you would want to set the table's provisioned write throughput to 100 write capacity units:

1 write capacity unit per item × 100 writes per second = 100 write capacity units.

## Q131. A, C, D
AWS Documentation Reference:
https://docs.aws.amazon.com/amazondynamodb/latest/developerguide/DAX.html

## Q132. A, C
AWS Documentation Reference:
https://docs.aws.amazon.com/amazondynamodb/latest/developerguide/Query.html
The Query operation in Amazon DynamoDB finds items based on primary key values. You can query any table or secondary index that has a composite primary key (a partition key and a sort key). The query operation based on primary key like userid which has more unique values will be efficient.
As the Gamescore is not part of composite key, and data retrieval needs to scan all the data.

## Q133. B
AWS Documentation Reference:
https://docs.aws.amazon.com/amazondynamodb/latest/developerguide/GSI.html

To make the new leaderboards you will have to retrieve data from GameScores based on non-partition key attribute GameTitle, it would need to use a Scan operation. This will become inefficient as the data grows. To speed up queries on non-key attributes, you can create a global secondary index. Global secondary index is an index with a partition key and sort key that can be different from those on the table. You could create a global secondary index named GameTitleIndex, with a partition key of GameTitle and a sort key of TopScore. The base table's primary key attributes are always projected into an index, so the UserId attribute is also present. The following diagram shows what GameTitleIndex index would look like.

| GameTitle | TopScore | UserId |
|---|---|---|
| Aliens | 200 | 102 |
| Battleships | 0 | 102 |
| Battleships | 10 | 103 |
| Battleships | 6000 | 101 |
| FighterPlane | 1000 | 101 |
| FighterPlane | 2000 | 103 |
| Forumla1 | 1000 | 103 |
| StarGate | 50 | 103 |
| StarGate | 100 | 101 |

Now you can query GameTitleIndex and easily obtain the scores based on an individual game. The results are ordered by the sort key values, TopScore. If you set the ScanIndexForward parameter to false, the results are returned in descending order, so the highest score is returned first.

Q134. C
AWS Documentation Reference:
https://docs.aws.amazon.com/amazondynamodb/latest/developerguide/AutoScaling.html
DynamoDB auto scaling enables a table or a global secondary index to increase its provisioned read and write capacity to handle sudden increases in traffic, without throttling.
When the workload decreases, Application Auto Scaling decreases the throughput so that you don't pay for unused provisioned capacity. With Application Auto Scaling, you create a scaling policy for a table or a global secondary index. The scaling policy specifies whether you want to

scale read capacity or write capacity (or both), and the minimum and maximum provisioned capacity unit settings for the table or index.

The scaling policy also contains a target utilization the percentage of consumed provisioned throughput at a point in time. Application Auto Scaling uses a target tracking algorithm to adjust the provisioned throughput of the table (or index) upward or downward in response to actual workloads, so that the actual capacity utilization remains at or near your target utilization.

Q135.A, B, D

AWS Documentation Reference:

https://docs.aws.amazon.com/amazondynamodb/latest/developerguide/HowItWorks.CoreComponents.html

DynamoDB Streams is an optional feature that captures data modification events in DynamoDB tables.

Q136. A, B, D, E

AWS Documentation Reference:

https://docs.aws.amazon.com/amazondynamodb/latest/developerguide/DAX.html

Q137. A, B

AWS Documentation Reference: Attribute Projections

https://docs.aws.amazon.com/amazondynamodb/latest/developerguide/GSI.html#GSI.Projections

A projection is the set of attributes that is copied from a table into a secondary index. The partition key and sort key of the table are always projected into the index; you can project other attributes to support your application's query requirements. When you query an index, Amazon DynamoDB can access any attribute in the projection as if those attributes were in a table of their own.

When you create a secondary index, you need to specify the attributes that will be projected into the index. DynamoDB provides three different options for this:

KEYS_ONLY – Each item in the index consists only of the table partition key and sort key values, plus the index key values. The KEYS_ONLY option results in the smallest possible secondary index.

INCLUDE – In addition to the attributes described in KEYS_ONLY, the secondary index will include other non-key attributes that you specify.

ALL – The secondary index includes all of the attributes from the source table. Because all of the table data is duplicated in the index, an ALL projection results in the largest possible secondary index.

Q138. C

Amazon ElastiCache provides support for two engines: Memcached and Redis

Q139. A

AWS Documentation Reference:

https://docs.aws.amazon.com/amazondynamodb/latest/developerguide/howitworks-ttl.html

When Time to live is enabled on a table, a background job checks the TTL attribute of items to see if they are expired. You can mark on attribute as TTL attribute.

Q140. A, B, C, D

AWS Documentation Reference:

https://docs.aws.amazon.com/amazondynamodb/latest/developerguide/DAX.html

E is a suitable use case as DAX provides access to eventually consistent data from DynamoDB tables, with microsecond latency.

Q141. A

Q142. B, C, D

AWS Documentation Reference:

https://aws.amazon.com/elasticache/redis-vs-memcached/?nc=sn&loc=3&dn=3

Redis supports transactions which let you execute a group of commands as an isolated and atomic operation.

Q143. A

AWS Documentation Reference:

https://docs.aws.amazon.com/AmazonElastiCache/latest/red-ug/elasticache-use-cases.html#elasticache-for-redis-use-cases-gaming

Redis sorted sets move the computational complexity associated with leaderboards from your application to your Redis cluster. Leaderboards, such as the Top 10 scores for a game, are computationally complex, especially with a large number of concurrent players and continually changing scores. Redis sorted sets guarantee both uniqueness and element ordering. Using Redis sorted sets, each time a new element is added to the sorted set it's reranked in real time. It's then added to the set in its appropriate numeric position.

Q144. A, B, D

AWS Documentation Reference:

https://docs.aws.amazon.com/AmazonElastiCache/latest/mem-ug/elasticache-use-cases.html

Q145. A, B, D

AWS Documentation Reference:

https://docs.aws.amazon.com/AmazonElastiCache/latest/red-ug/Strategies.html

Lazy loading is a caching strategy that loads data into the cache only when necessary. Lazy loading allows for stale data, but won't fail with empty nodes.

The write through strategy adds data or updates data in the cache whenever data is written to the database. Write through ensures that data is always fresh, but may fail with empty nodes and may populate the cache with superfluous data.

By adding a time to live (TTL) value to each write, you will be able to enjoy the advantages of each strategy and largely avoid cluttering up the cache with superfluous data.

Q146. A, C, D

AWS Documentation Reference:

https://docs.aws.amazon.com/AmazonElastiCache/latest/red-ug/SelectEngine.html

Q147.D

AWS Documentation Reference:

https://docs.aws.amazon.com/amazondynamodb/latest/developerguide/LSI.html

Without a local secondary index, the application would have to Scan the entire Thread table and discard any posts that were not within the specified time frame. With a local secondary index, a Query operation could use LastPostDateTime as a sort key and find the data quickly. In this example, the partition key is ForumName and the sort key of the local secondary index is LastPostDateTime. In addition, the sort key value from the base table (in this example, Subject) is projected into the index, but it is not a part of the index key.

| ForumName | LastPostDateTime | Subject |
|-----------|------------------|---------|
| S3 | 2019-01-01:08:14:35 | bbb |
| S3 | 2019-04-18:08:26:21 | ddd |
| S3 | 2019-11-12:22:24:23 | ccc |
| S3 | 2019-12-12:15:24:03 | aaa |
| EC2 | 2019-07-05:18:06:12 | yyy |
| EC2 | 2019-09-09:11:55:01 | zzz |
| RDS | 2019-02-28:28:06:02 | ttt |
| RDS | 2019-10-25:12:32:23 | rrr |
| RDS | 2019-12-30:16:26:07 | sss |

Q148. A, D

AWS Documentation Reference:

https://docs.aws.amazon.com/amazondynamodb/latest/developerguide/bp-partition-key-uniform-load.html

The partition key portion of a table's primary key determines the logical partitions in which a table's data is stored. This in turn affects the underlying physical partitions. Provisioned I/O capacity for the table is divided evenly among these physical partitions. Therefore a partition key design that doesn't distribute I/O requests evenly can create "hot" partitions that result in throttling and use your provisioned I/O capacity inefficiently.

It does mean that the more distinct partition key values that your workload accesses, the more those requests will be spread across the partitioned space.

Option A and D will result in more distinct values.

Q149 B

AWS Documentation Reference:

https://aws.amazon.com/getting-started/projects/boosting-mysql-database-performance-with-amazon-elasticache-for-redis/

You can boost the performance of your applications by adding an in-memory caching layer to your relational database. You will implement a cache-aside strategy using Amazon ElastiCache for Redis on top of a MySQL database. The cache-aside strategy is one of the most popular options for boosting database performance. When an application needs to read data from a database, it first queries the cache. If the data is not found, the application queries the database and populates the cache with the result.

A is incorrect, it is the feature of RDS read replica.
C is incorrect, it is the feature of DynamoDB DAX.
D is incorrect, it is the feature of CDN.

Q150. A

AWS Documentation Reference:

https://docs.aws.amazon.com/amazondynamodb/latest/developerguide/Streams.Lambda.html

Amazon DynamoDB is integrated with AWS Lambda so that you can create triggers—pieces of code that automatically respond to events in DynamoDB Streams. With triggers, you can build applications that react to data modifications in DynamoDB tables.

If you enable DynamoDB Streams on a table, you can associate the stream Amazon Resource Name (ARN) with an AWS Lambda function that you write. Immediately after an item in the table is modified, a new record appears in the table's stream. AWS Lambda polls the stream and invokes your Lambda function synchronously when it detects new stream records.

The Lambda function can perform any actions you specify, such as sending a notification or initiating a workflow.

Q151. A, B, C
AWS Documentation Reference:
https://docs.aws.amazon.com/AmazonElastiCache/latest/red-ug/SelectEngine.html

Q152. B, C, D
AWS Documentation Reference:
https://docs.aws.amazon.com/AmazonElastiCache/latest/red-ug/SelectEngine.html

Q153. A, B, D, E
AWS Documentation Reference:
https://docs.aws.amazon.com/AmazonElastiCache/latest/red-ug/WhatIs.html

Q154. A, B, C
AWS Documentation Reference:
https://docs.aws.amazon.com/AmazonElastiCache/latest/red-ug/WhatIs.Components.html
A node is the smallest building block of an ElastiCache deployment. A node can exist in isolation from or in some relationship to other nodes. A node is a fixed-size chunk of secure, network-attached RAM. Each node runs an instance of the engine and version that was chosen when you created your cluster.
A Redis shard (called a node group in the API and CLI) is a grouping of one to six related nodes.
A Redis cluster is a logical grouping of one or more ElastiCache for Redis Shards. Data is partitioned across the shards in a Redis (cluster mode enabled) cluster.

Q155. A
AWS Documentation Reference: ElastiCache for Redis Shards
https://docs.aws.amazon.com/AmazonElastiCache/latest/red-ug/WhatIs.Components.html
A Redis (cluster mode disabled) cluster always has one shard.

Q156. D
AWS Documentation Reference: ElastiCache for Redis Shards
https://docs.aws.amazon.com/AmazonElastiCache/latest/red-ug/WhatIs.Components.html
A Redis (cluster mode enabled) cluster can have 1–90 shards.

Q157. A, C
AWS Documentation Reference:
https://docs.aws.amazon.com/amazondynamodb/latest/developerguide/bp-partition-key-design.html
You should design your application for uniform activity across all logical partition keys in the table and its secondary indexes. You can determine the access patterns that your application

requires, and estimate the total read capacity units (RCU) and write capacity units (WCU) that each table and secondary index requires.

Adaptive capacity is a feature that enables DynamoDB to run imbalanced workloads indefinitely. It minimizes throttling due to throughput exceptions. It also helps you reduce costs by enabling you to provision only the throughput capacity that you need.

Adaptive capacity is enabled automatically for every DynamoDB table, at no additional cost. You don't need to explicitly enable or disable it.

https://aws.amazon.com/blogs/database/amazon-dynamodb-auto-scaling-performance-and-cost-optimization-at-any-scale/

With on-demand, DynamoDB instantly allocates capacity as it is needed. But as the cost optimization is also one of the design criteria, Auto scaling with reserved capacity will be right choice. Auto scaling responds quickly and simplifies capacity management, which lowers costs by scaling your table's provisioned capacity and reducing operational overhead.

Q158.B, C

AWS Documentation Reference:

https://docs.aws.amazon.com/amazondynamodb/latest/developerguide/GlobalTables.html

Amazon DynamoDB global tables provide a fully managed solution for deploying a multiregion, multi-master database, without having to build and maintain your own replication solution. DynamoDB global tables are ideal for massively scaled applications with globally dispersed users. In such an environment, users expect very fast application performance. Global tables provide automatic multi-master replication to AWS Regions worldwide. They enable you to deliver low-latency data access to your users no matter where they are located.

https://aws.amazon.com/dynamodb/dax/

Amazon DynamoDB Accelerator (DAX) is a fully managed, highly available, in-memory cache for DynamoDB that delivers up to a 10x performance improvement – from milliseconds to microseconds – even at millions of requests per second.

https://docs.aws.amazon.com/amazondynamodb/latest/developerguide/AutoScaling.html

Amazon DynamoDB auto scaling uses the AWS Application Auto Scaling service to dynamically adjust provisioned throughput capacity on your behalf, in response to actual traffic patterns. This enables a table or a global secondary index to increase its provisioned read and write capacity to handle sudden increases in traffic, without throttling. When the workload decreases, Application Auto Scaling decreases the throughput so that you don't pay for unused provisioned capacity.

https://docs.aws.amazon.com/amazondynamodb/latest/developerguide/bp-partition-key-design.html#bp-partition-key-partitions-adaptive

Adaptive capacity is enabled automatically for every DynamoDB table, at no additional cost. You don't need to explicitly enable or disable it. Adaptive capacity is a feature that enables DynamoDB to run imbalanced workloads indefinitely. It minimizes throttling due to throughput exceptions. It also helps you reduce costs by enabling you to provision only the throughput capacity that you need.

Q159. D, E
AWS Documentation Reference:
https://docs.amazonaws.cn/en_us/AmazonRDS/latest/UserGuide/USER_VPC.WorkingWit
hRDSInstanceinaVPC.html
Your VPC must have at least two subnets. These subnets must be in two different Availability Zones in the AWS Region where you want to deploy your DB instance. A subnet is a segment of a VPC's IP address range that you can specify and that lets you group instances based on your security and operational needs.

If you want your DB instance in the VPC to be publicly accessible, you must enable the VPC attributes DNS hostnames and DNS resolution.

Your VPC must have a DB subnet group that you create (for more information, see the next section). You create a DB subnet group by specifying the subnets you created. Amazon RDS uses that DB subnet group and your preferred Availability Zone to choose a subnet and an IP address within that subnet to assign to your DB instance.

Your VPC must have a VPC security group that allows access to the DB instance.

The CIDR blocks in each of your subnets must be large enough to accommodate spare IP addresses for Amazon RDS to use during maintenance activities, including failover and compute scaling.

A VPC can have an instance tenancy attribute of either default or dedicated. All default VPCs have the instance tenancy attribute set to default, and a default VPC can support any DB instance class.

If you choose to have your DB instance in a dedicated VPC where the instance tenancy attribute is set to dedicated, the DB instance class of your DB instance must be one of the approved Amazon EC2 dedicated instance types. For example, the m3.medium EC2 dedicated instance corresponds to the db.m3.medium DB instance class. For information about instance tenancy in a VPC, go to Using EC2 Dedicated Instances in the Amazon Virtual Private Cloud User Guide.

Q160. A, C, D
AWS Documentation Reference:
https://docs.aws.amazon.com/AmazonElastiCache/latest/red-ug/Shards.html

Q161. A, B
AWS Documentation Reference:
https://docs.aws.amazon.com/AmazonElastiCache/latest/red-ug/Replication.Redis.Groups.html

Redis implements replication in two ways:

With a single shard that contains all of the cluster's data in each node—Redis (cluster mode disabled)

With data partitioned across up to 90 shards—Redis (cluster mode enabled)

Q162. B, C

AWS Documentation Reference:

https://docs.aws.amazon.com/AmazonElastiCache/latest/red-ug/Replication.Redis.Groups.html

Each shard in a replication group has a single read/write primary node and up to 5 read-only replica nodes. You can create a cluster with higher number of shards and lower number of replicas totaling up to 90 nodes per cluster. This cluster configuration can range from 90 shards and 0 replicas to 15 shards and 5 replicas, which is the maximum number of replicas allowed.

Q163.A

AWS Documentation Reference: Whitepaper: Web Application Hosting in the AWS Cloud

https://d1.awsstatic.com/whitepapers/aws-web-hosting-best-practices.pdf

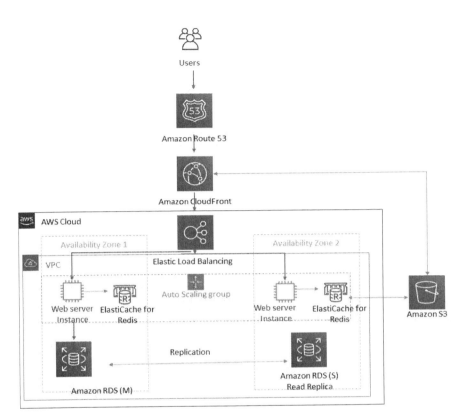

The above architecture achieves resiliency through failover based on multi-AZ architecture. The web EC2 instances are deployed across AZ, RDS is mutli-AZ enabled and Application Load Balancing with Elastic Load Balancing (ELB)/Application Load Balancer (ALB) – Allows you to spread load across multiple Availability Zones and Amazon EC2 Auto Scaling groups for redundancy and decoupling of services.

Caching with Amazon ElastiCache – Provides caching services with Redis or Memcached to remove load from the app and database, and lower latency for frequent requests. Also for storing session information.

Managed Database with Amazon RDS – Creates a highly available, Multi-AZ database architecture with six possible DB engines. Read Replica will improve read intensive transaction performance.

Edge Caching with Amazon CloudFront – Edge caches high-volume content to decrease the latency to customers.

Static Storage and Backups with Amazon S3 – Enables simple HTTP-based object storage for backups and static assets like images and video.

Q164. B

AWS Documentation Reference: Recommendation Data (Redis Hashes)
https://docs.aws.amazon.com/AmazonElastiCache/latest/red-ug/elasticache-use-cases.html
Using INCR or DECR in Redis makes compiling recommendations simple. Each time a user "likes" a product, you increment an item:productID:like counter. Each time a user "dislikes" a product, you increment an item:productID:dislike counter. Using Redis hashes, you can also maintain a list of everyone who has liked or disliked a product.

Q165. C, D
AWS Documentation Reference:
https://docs.aws.amazon.com/AmazonElastiCache/latest/red-ug/Replication.Redis.Groups.html
Redis implements replication in two ways:
With a single shard that contains all of the cluster's data in each node—Redis (cluster mode disabled)
With data partitioned across up to 90 shards—Redis (cluster mode enabled)
Each shard in a replication group has a single read/write primary node and up to 5 read-only replica nodes. You can create a cluster with higher number of shards and lower number of replicas totaling up to 90 nodes per cluster. This cluster configuration can range from 90 shards and 0 replicas to 15 shards and 5 replicas, which is the maximum number of replicas allowed.

Q166. A, B, C, D
AWS Documentation Reference: Redis (Cluster Mode Disabled)
https://docs.aws.amazon.com/AmazonElastiCache/latest/red-ug/Replication.Redis.Groups.html
A Redis (cluster mode disabled) cluster has a single shard, inside of which is a collection of Redis nodes; one primary read/write node and up to five secondary, read-only replica nodes. Each read replica maintains a copy of the data from the cluster's primary node. Asynchronous replication mechanisms are used to keep the read replicas synchronized with the primary. Applications can read from any node in the cluster. Applications can write only to the primary node. Read replicas improve read throughput and guard against data loss in cases of a node failure.

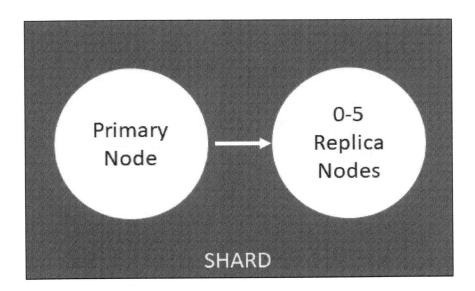

Q167. A, B, C, E

AWS Documentation Reference: Redis (Cluster Mode Enabled)

https://docs.aws.amazon.com/AmazonElastiCache/latest/red-ug/Replication.Redis.Groups.html

A Redis (cluster mode enabled) cluster is comprised of from 1 to 90 shards (API/CLI: node groups). Each shard has a primary node and up to five read-only replica nodes. The configuration can range from 90 shards and 0 replicas to 15 shards and 5 replicas, which is the maximum number or replicas allowed. Each read replica in a shard maintains a copy of the data from the shard's primary. Asynchronous replication mechanisms are used to keep the read replicas synchronized with the primary. Applications can read from any node in the cluster. Applications can write only to the primary nodes. Read replicas enhance read scalability and guard against data loss. Data is partitioned across the shards in a Redis (cluster mode enabled) cluster.

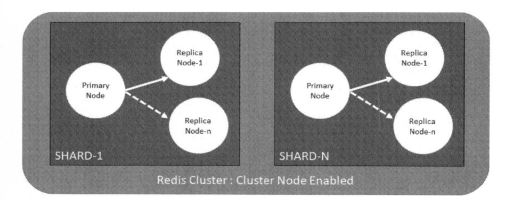

Redis Cluster : Cluster Node Enabled

Q168. B, C, D
AWS Documentation Reference: Which Should I Choose?
https://docs.aws.amazon.com/AmazonElastiCache/latest/red-ug/Replication.Redis-
RedisCluster.html
When choosing between Redis (cluster mode disabled) or Redis (cluster mode enabled),
consider the following factors:

Scaling v. partitioning – Business needs change. You need to either provision for peak demand
or scale as demand changes. Redis (cluster mode disabled) supports scaling. You can scale read
capacity by adding or deleting replica nodes, or you can scale capacity by scaling up to a larger
node type. Both of these operations take time.
Redis (cluster mode enabled) supports partitioning your data across up to 90 node groups. You
can dynamically change the number of shards as your business needs change. One advantage
of partitioning is that you spread your load over a greater number of endpoints, which reduces
access bottlenecks during peak demand. Additionally, you can accommodate a larger data set
since the data can be spread across multiple servers.

Node size v. number of nodes – Because a Redis (cluster mode disabled) cluster has only one
shard, the node type must be large enough to accommodate all the cluster's data plus necessary
overhead. On the other hand, because you can partition your data across several shards when
using a Redis (cluster mode enabled) cluster, the node types can be smaller, though you need
more of them.

Reads v. writes – If the primary load on your cluster is applications reading data, you can scale
a Redis (cluster mode disabled) cluster by adding and deleting read replicas. However, there is a
maximum of 5 read replicas. If the load on your cluster is write-heavy, you can benefit from
the additional write endpoints of a Redis (cluster mode enabled) cluster with multiple shards.

Q169. A

AWS Documentation Reference: Which Should I Choose?

https://docs.aws.amazon.com/AmazonElastiCache/latest/red-ug/Replication.Redis-RedisCluster.html

Redis (cluster mode disabled) will be appropriate as:

As you application data need is not huge Redis (cluster mode disabled) with only one shard and right node type will be large enough to accommodate all the cluster's data plus necessary overhead. The primary load on your cluster is applications reading data, you can scale a Redis (cluster mode disabled) cluster by adding and deleting read replicas. You can scale read capacity by adding or deleting replica nodes, or you can scale capacity by scaling up to a larger node type.

Q170. B

AWS Documentation Reference: Which Should I Choose?

https://docs.aws.amazon.com/AmazonElastiCache/latest/red-ug/Replication.Redis-RedisCluster.html

Redis (cluster mode enabled) will be appropriate as:

As you application data need is large, with Redis (cluster mode enabled) you can partition your data across up to 90 shards. You can dynamically change the number of shards as your business needs change. The load on your cluster is write-heavy, you can benefit from the additional write endpoints of a Redis (cluster mode enabled) cluster with multiple shards.

Q171. B, C

AWS Documentation Reference:

https://aws.amazon.com/nosql/

Q172. A

ElastiCache for Memcached clusters are comprised of 1 to 20 nodes

Q173. C, D

There is no primary node in Memcache cluster.

AWS Documentation Reference:

https://docs.aws.amazon.com/AmazonElastiCache/latest/mem-ug/AutoDiscovery.html

For clusters running the Memcached engine, ElastiCache supports Auto Discovery—the ability for client programs to automatically identify all of the nodes in a cache cluster, and to initiate and maintain connections to all of these nodes.

With Auto Discovery, your application does not need to manually connect to individual cache nodes; instead, your application connects to one Memcached node and retrieves the list of nodes. From that list your application is aware of the rest of the nodes in the cluster and can connect to any of them. You do not need to hard code the individual cache node endpoints in your application. All of the cache nodes in the cluster maintain a list of metadata about all of the other nodes. This metadata is updated whenever nodes are added or removed from the cluster.

Q174. A, C
AWS Documentation Reference:
https://aws.amazon.com/elasticache/faqs/
Amazon ElastiCache is protocol-compliant with Memcached. Therefore, you can use standard Memcached operations like get, set, incr and decr in exactly the same way as you would in your existing Memcached deployments. Amazon ElastiCache supports both the text and binary protocols. It also supports most of the standard stats results, which can also be viewed as graphs via CloudWatch.
As a result, you can switch to using Amazon ElastiCache without recompiling or re-linking your applications, the libraries you use will continue to work. To configure the cache servers your application accesses, all you will need to do is to update your application's Memcached config file to include the endpoints of the servers (nodes) AWS provision for you. You can simply use the "Copy Node Endpoints" option on the AWS Management Console or the "DescribeCacheClusters" API to get a list of the endpoints. As with any migration process, AWS recommend thorough testing of your new Amazon ElastiCache deployment before completing the cut over from your current solution. Amazon ElastiCache currently allows access only from the Amazon EC2 network, so in order to use the service, you should have your application servers in Amazon EC2.

Q175. B
AWS Documentation Reference: Auto Discovery
https://aws.amazon.com/elasticache/faqs/
Auto Discovery enables automatic discovery of cache nodes by clients when they are added to or removed from an Amazon ElastiCache cluster. To take advantage of Auto Discovery, an Auto Discovery capable client must be used to connect to an Amazon ElastiCache Cluster.
To use the Auto Discovery feature a client must be able to use a Configuration Endpoint and determine the cluster node endpoints. You may either use the Amazon ElastiCache Cluster Client or extend your existing Memcached client to include the Auto Discovery command set.
Upon initialization, the client will automatically determine the current members of the Amazon ElastiCache cluster using the Configuration Endpoint. When you make changes to your cache cluster by adding or removing nodes or if a node is replaced upon failure, the Auto Discovery client automatically determines the changes and you do not need to initialize your clients manually.
Q176. C
RDS is not a NoSQL database.
AWS Documentation Reference:
https://aws.amazon.com/nosql/
Types of NoSQL Databases in AWS :

Amazon DynamoDB: Key-value: Key-value databases are highly partitionable and allow horizontal scaling at scales that other types of databases cannot achieve. Use cases such as gaming, ad tech, and IoT lend themselves particularly well to the key-value data model.

Amazon DocumentDB :Document: In application code, data is represented often as an object or JSON-like document because it is an efficient and intuitive data model for developers. Document databases make it easier for developers to store and query data in a database by using the same document model format that they use in their application code. The flexible, semistructured, and hierarchical nature of documents and document databases allows them to evolve with applications' needs. The document model works well with catalogs, user profiles, and content management systems where each document is unique and evolves over time.

Amazon Neptune : Graph: A graph database's purpose is to make it easy to build and run applications that work with highly connected datasets. Typical use cases for a graph database include social networking, recommendation engines, fraud detection, and knowledge graphs.

Amazon ElastiCache: In-memory: Gaming and ad-tech applications have use cases such as leaderboards, session stores, and real-time analytics that require microsecond response times and can have large spikes in traffic coming at any time.

Search: Amazon Elasticsearch Service (Amazon ES) is purpose built for providing near-real-time visualizations and analytics of machine-generated data by indexing, aggregating, and searching semistructured logs and metrics. Amazon ES also is a powerful, high-performance search engine for full-text search use cases.

Q177. B
AWS Documentation Reference:
https://docs.aws.amazon.com/amazondynamodb/latest/developerguide/GlobalTables.html
Amazon DynamoDB global tables provide a fully managed solution for deploying a multiregion, multi-master database, without having to build and maintain your own replication solution. With global tables you can specify the AWS Regions where you want the table to be available. DynamoDB performs all of the necessary tasks to create identical tables in these Regions and propagate ongoing data changes to all of them.

Q178. A, B, C
AWS Documentation Reference:
https://aws.amazon.com/blogs/aws/amazon-rds-update-share-encrypted-snapshots-encrypt-existing-instances/
You can now add encryption at rest using KMS keys to a previously unencrypted database instance. This is a simple, multi-step process:

1. Create a snapshot of the unencrypted database instance.

2. Copy the snapshot to a new, encrypted snapshot. Enable encryption and specify the desired KMS key as you do so
3. Restore the encrypted snapshot to a new database instance
4. Update your application to refer to the endpoint of the new database instance

Q179. D
AWS Documentation Reference:
https://aws.amazon.com/premiumsupport/knowledge-center/fault-tolerance-elasticache/

Multi-AZ with Automatic Failover
Multi-AZ with Automatic Failover is the best option when data retention, minimal downtime, and application performance are a priority.

Daily automatic backups
You can schedule daily automatic backups at a time when you expect low resource utilization for your cluster. ElastiCache creates a backup of the cluster, and then writes all data from the cache to a Redis RDB file

Manual backups using Redis append-only file (AOF)
Manual backups using AOF are retained indefinitely and are useful for testing and archiving. You can schedule manual backups to occur up to 20 times per node within any 24-hour period. When AOF is enabled for Redis, whenever data is written to your Redis cluster, a corresponding transaction record is written to a Redis append only file (AOF). If your Redis process restarts, ElastiCache creates a replacement cluster and provisions it. You can then run the AOF against the cluster to repopulate it with data.

Q180. A, B, C, E
AWS Documentation Reference:
https://docs.aws.amazon.com/AmazonElastiCache/latest/red-ug/FaultTolerance.html#FaultTolerance.Redis.Cluster.Replication

When a read replica fails
- ElastiCache detects the failed read replica.
- ElastiCache takes the failed node off line.
- ElastiCache launches and provisions a replacement node in the same AZ.
- The new node synchronizes with the Primary node.
During this time your application can continue reading and writing using the other nodes.

Q181. A, D
AWS Documentation Reference:
https://docs.aws.amazon.com/AmazonElastiCache/latest/red-ug/FaultTolerance.html#FaultTolerance.Redis.Cluster.Replication

Redis Multi-AZ with Automatic Failover

You can enable Multi-AZ with automatic failover on your Redis replication groups. Whether you enable Multi-AZ with auto failover or not, a failed Primary will be detected and replaced automatically. How this takes place varies whether or not Multi-AZ is or is not enabled.

When Multi-AZ with Auto Failover is enabled

1. ElastiCache detects the Primary node failure.
2. ElastiCache promotes the read replica node with the least replication lag to primary node.
3. The other replicas sync with the new primary node.
4. ElastiCache spins up a read replica in the failed primary's AZ.
5. The new node syncs with the newly promoted primary.

Failing over to a replica node is generally faster than creating and provisioning a new Primary node. This means your application can resume writing to your Primary node sooner than if Multi-AZ were not enabled.

When Multi-AZ with Auto Failover is disabled
1. ElastiCache detects Primary failure.
2. ElastiCache takes the Primary offline.
3. ElastiCache creates and provisions a new Primary node to replace the failed Primary.
4. ElastiCache syncs the new Primary with one of the existing replicas.
5. When the sync is finished, the new node functions as the cluster's Primary node.

During this process, steps 1 through 4, your application can't write to the Primary node. However, your application can continue reading from your replica node

Q182. A, B

AWS Documentation Reference:

https://aws.amazon.com/nosql/document/

A document database is a type of nonrelational database that is designed to store and query data as JSON-like documents. Document databases make it easier for developers to store and query data in a database by using the same document-model format they use in their application code. The flexible, semistructured, and hierarchical nature of documents and document databases allows them to evolve with applications' needs. The document model works well with use cases such as catalogs, user profiles, and content management systems.

C and D are appropriate use cases for using Amazon ElastiCache.

Q183. A, C, D, F, G

AWS Documentation Reference:

https://aws.amazon.com/documentdb/features/

MongoDB 3.6 compatible :Amazon DocumentDB is compatible with MongoDB 3.6 drivers and tools. A vast majority of the applications, drivers, and tools that customers already use today with their MongoDB database can be used with Amazon DocumentDB with little or no change.

Storage that Automatically Scales :Amazon DocumentDB will automatically grow the size of your storage volume as your cluster storage needs grow. Your storage volume will grow in increments of 10 GB up to a maximum of 64 TB.

Low Latency Read Replicas :Increase read throughput to support high volume application requests by creating up to 15 database read replicas.

Multi-AZ Deployments with Read Replicas :On instance failure, Amazon DocumentDB automates failover to one of up to 15 Amazon DocumentDB replicas you have created in any of three Availability Zones. If no Amazon DocumentDB replicas have been provisioned, in the case of a failure, Amazon DocumentDB will attempt to create a new instance for you automatically.

Fault-tolerant and Self-healing Storage :Each 10GB portion of your storage volume is replicated six ways, across three Availability Zones. Amazon DocumentDB uses fault-tolerant storage that transparently handles the loss of up to two copies of data without affecting database write availability and up to three copies without affecting read availability.

Q184. A, D
AWS Documentation Reference:
https://docs.aws.amazon.com/documentdb/latest/developerguide/how-it-works.html

An Amazon DocumentDB cluster consists of two components:

- Cluster volume—Uses a cloud-native storage service to replicate data six ways across three Availability Zones, providing highly durable and available storage. An Amazon DocumentDB cluster has exactly one cluster volume, which can store up to 64 TB of data.
- Instances—Provide the processing power for the database, writing data to, and reading data from, the cluster storage volume. An Amazon DocumentDB cluster can have 0–16 instances.

Instances serve one of two roles:

- Primary instance—Supports read and write operations, and performs all the data modifications to the cluster volume. Each Amazon DocumentDB cluster has one primary instance.

- Replica instance—Supports only read operations. An Amazon DocumentDB cluster can have up to 15 replicas in addition to the primary instance. Having multiple replicas enables you to distribute read workloads. In addition, by placing replicas in separate Availability Zones, you also increase your cluster availability.

Q185. B, C
AWS Documentation Reference:
- https://docs.aws.amazon.com/documentdb/latest/developerguide/failover.html

Failover is automatically handled by Amazon DocumentDB so that your applications can resume database operations as quickly as possible without manual administrative intervention.

- If you have an Amazon DocumentDB replica, in the same or a different Availability Zone, when failing over, Amazon DocumentDB flips the canonical name record (CNAME) for your cluster endpoint to a healthy replica, which is in turn is promoted to become the new primary. Start-to-finish, failover typically completes within 30 seconds. Additionally, the read replicas endpoint doesn't require any CNAME updates during failover.

- If you do not have an Amazon DocumentDB Replica (i.e. single instance), Amazon DocumentDB will first attempt to create a new instance in the same Availability Zone as the original instance. If unable to do so, Amazon DocumentDB will attempt to create a new instance in a different Availability Zone. From start to finish, failover typically completes in under 15 minutes.

# Answer Chapter 5 Analytics: Amazon Athena, Amazon EMR, Amazon Kinesis, Amazon Redshift, AWS Glue, AWS Data Pipeline, Amazon Quicksight, AWS Lake Formation

Q1. B

AWS Documentation Reference:

https://aws.amazon.com/big-data/datalakes-and-analytics/

For real-time analytics, Amazon Kinesis makes it easy to collect, process and analyze streaming data such as IoT telemetry data, application logs, and website clickstreams. This enable you to process, and analyze data as it arrives in your data lake, and respond in real-time instead of having to wait until all your data is collected before the processing can begin.

Q2. A, B, C, E

AWS Documentation Reference:

https://aws.amazon.com/kinesis/?nc=sn&loc=1

- Amazon Kinesis Data Streams enables you to build custom applications that process or analyze streaming data.

- Amazon Kinesis Video Streams enables you to build custom applications that process or analyze streaming video.

- Amazon Kinesis Data Firehose enables you to deliver real-time streaming data to AWS destinations such as Amazon S3, Amazon Redshift, Amazon Kinesis Analytics, and Amazon Elasticsearch Service.

- Amazon Kinesis Data Analytics enables you to process and analyze streaming data with standard SQL.

Q3. A

Kinesis Data Streams can be used to collect log and event data from sources such as servers, desktops, and mobile devices. Here the key word is custom application to process stream data. You can build custom Kinesis Applications using Kinesis Client library to continuously process the data, generate metrics, power live dashboards, and emit aggregated data into stores such as Amazon S3.

Kinesis Data Firehose and Data Analytics are not appropriate to write a custom application to process streaming data.

Q4. A, C, D

AWS Documentation Reference: Whitepaper: Big_Data_Analytics_Options_on_AWS

A: Real-time data analytics –Kinesis Data Streams enables real-time data analytics on streaming data, such as analyzing website clickstream data and customer engagement analytics.

C: Log and data feed intake and processing – With Kinesis Data Streams, you can have producers push data directly into an Amazon Kinesis stream. For example, you can submit system and application logs to Kinesis Data Streams and access the stream for processing within seconds. This prevents the log data from being lost if the front-end or application server fails, and reduces local log storage on the source. Kinesis Data Streams provides accelerated data intake because you are not batching up the data on the servers before you submit it for intake.

D: Real-time metrics and reporting – You can use data ingested into Kinesis Data Streams for extracting metrics and generating KPIs to power reports and dashboards at real-time speeds. This enables data-processing application logic to work on data as it is streaming in continuously, rather than wait for data batches to arrive.

B and E are not ideal use case because:

B: Kinesis Data Streams is not suited for long-term data storage. By default, data is retained for 24 hours, and you can extend the retention period by up to 7 days. You can move any data that needs to be stored for longer than 7 days into another durable storage service such as Amazon S3, Amazon Glacier, Amazon Redshift, or DynamoDB.

E: For batch ETL jobs AWS data pipeline is more appropriate.

Q5. A, B, D

AWS Documentation Reference:

https://aws.amazon.com/redshift/faqs/

*Q: What is Amazon Redshift?*

Amazon Redshift is a fast, fully managed data warehouse that makes it simple and cost-effective to analyze all your data using standard SQL and your existing Business Intelligence (BI) tools.

It allows you to run complex analytic queries against petabytes of structured data using sophisticated query optimization, columnar storage on high-performance storage, and massively parallel query execution. Most results come back in seconds.

Amazon Redshift also includes Amazon Redshift Spectrum, allowing you to directly run SQL queries against exabytes of unstructured data in Amazon S3 data lakes. No loading or transformation is required, and you can use open data formats, including Avro, CSV, Ion, JSON, ORC, Parquet, and more. Redshift Spectrum automatically scales query compute capacity based on the data being retrieved, so queries against Amazon S3 run fast, regardless of data set size. Amazon Redshift not only significantly lowers the cost and operational overhead of a data warehouse, but with Redshift Spectrum, it also makes it easy to analyze large amounts of data in its native format without requiring you to load the data.

Q6. C

AWS Documentation Reference:

https://docs.aws.amazon.com/redshift/latest/mgmt/enhanced-vpc-routing.html

When you use Amazon Redshift Enhanced VPC Routing, Amazon Redshift forces all COPY and UNLOAD traffic between your cluster and your data repositories through your Amazon VPC.

If Enhanced VPC Routing is not enabled, Amazon Redshift routes traffic through the internet, including traffic to other services within the AWS network.

By using Enhanced VPC Routing, you can use standard VPC features, such as VPC security groups, network access control lists (ACLs), VPC endpoints, VPC endpoint policies, internet gateways, and Domain Name System (DNS) servers

## Q7. D
AWS Documentation Reference:
https://aws.amazon.com/big-data/datalakes-and-analytics/
For dashboards and visualizations, Amazon QuickSight provides you a fast, cloud-powered business analytics service, that that makes it easy to build stunning visualizations and rich dashboards that can be accessed from any browser or mobile device.

## Q8. C
Amazon Data Pipeline: for running ETL jobs
Amazon S3: for storing large volumes of data
Amazon EMR: for running Hadoop
Amazon Redshift: for data warehouse

AWS Data Pipeline is a web service that helps you reliably process and move data between different AWS compute and storage services, as well as on-premises data sources, at specified intervals. With AWS Data Pipeline, you can regularly access your data where it's stored, transform and process it at scale, and efficiently transfer the results to AWS services such as Amazon S3, Amazon RDS, Amazon DynamoDB, and Amazon EMR.

## Q9. A
Amazon Kinesis Data Streams to collect and process large streams of data records in real time. You can create data-processing applications, known as Kinesis Data Streams applications. A typical Kinesis Data Streams application reads data from a data stream as data records. These applications can use the Kinesis Client Library, and they can run on Amazon EC2 instances. You can send the processed records to dashboards, use them to generate alerts, dynamically change pricing and advertising strategies, or send data to a variety of other AWS services.

Amazon Kinesis Data Firehose is a fully managed service for delivering real-time streaming data to destinations such as Amazon Simple Storage Service (Amazon S3), Amazon Redshift, Amazon Elasticsearch Service (Amazon ES), and Splunk.

## Q10. A
AWS Documentation Reference: Whitepaper: Big_Data_Analytics_Options_on_AWS
Highly formatted canned Reports is not a scenario where Amazon Quicksight should be used. Amazon QuickSight is much more suited for ad hoc query, analysis and visualization of data. For highly formatted reports e.g. formatted financial statements consider using a different tool. Amazon QuickSight is an ideal Business Intelligence tool allowing end users to create visualizations that provide insight into their data to help them make better business decisions. Amazon QuickSight is a very fast, easy-to-use, cloud-powered business analytics service that

makes it easy for all employees within an organization to build visualizations, perform ad-hoc analysis, and quickly get business insights from their data, anytime, on any device. It can connect to a wide variety of data sources including flat files e.g. CSV and Excel, access on premise databases including SQL Server, MySQL and PostgreSQL., AWS resources like Amazon RDS databases, Amazon Redshift, Amazon Athena and Amazon S3. Amazon QuickSight enables organizations to scale their business analytics capabilities to hundreds of thousands of users, and delivers fast and responsive query performance by using a robust in-memory engine (SPICE).

Q11. B, C
B: solution powered by Amazon Elasticsearch Service provides you a highly available, turnkey environment to quickly begin logging and analyzing your AWS environment and applications.
C – Athena is a good tool for interactive one-time SQL queries against data on Amazon S3. For example, you could use Athena to run a query on web and application logs to troubleshoot a performance issue. You simply define a table for your data and start querying using standard SQL. Athena integrates with Amazon QuickSight for easy visualization.

Q12. . C
AWS Documentation Reference:
https://aws.amazon.com/redshift/
Amazon Redshift is a fast, scalable data warehouse that makes it simple and cost-effective to analyze all your data across your data warehouse and data lake.

Q13. B

Q14.C

Q15. E
AWS Documentation Reference: Whitepaper: Big Data Analytics Options on AWS
Small data sets – Amazon EMR is built for massive parallel processing; if your data set is small enough to run quickly on a single machine, in a single thread, the added overhead to map and reduce jobs may not be worth it for small data sets that can easily be processed in memory on a single system.
ACID transaction requirements – While there are ways to achieve ACID (atomicity, consistency, isolation, durability) or limited ACID on Hadoop, using another database, such as Amazon Relational Database Service (Amazon RDS) or a relational database running on Amazon EC2 may be a better option for workloads with stringent requirements.

Q16. A
AWS Documentation Reference:
https://aws.amazon.com/blogs/big-data/create-real-time-clickstream-sessions-and-run-analytics-with-amazon-kinesis-data-analytics-aws-glue-and-amazon-athena/

Data ingestion: You can use Kinesis Data Streams to build custom applications that process or analyze streaming data for specialized needs. Kinesis Data Streams can continuously capture and store terabytes of data per hour from hundreds of thousands of sources, such as website clickstreams, financial transactions, social media feeds, IT logs, and location-tracking events. Kinesis Firehose is not appropriate as it more suitable for storing the streaming data directly in to AWS storage.

Data sessionization: Kinesis Data Analytics is the easiest way to process streaming data in real time with standard SQL without having to learn new programming languages or processing frameworks. With Kinesis Data Analytics, you can query streaming data or build entire streaming applications using SQL, so that you can gain actionable insights and respond to your business and customer needs promptly.

To perform the sessionization in batch jobs, you could use a tool such as AWS Glue or Amazon EMR. But with daily schedules, queries and aggregation, it can take more resources and time because each aggregation involves working with large amounts of data. Performing sessionization in Kinesis Data Analytics takes less time and gives you a lower latency between the sessions generation.

Q17. B
AWS Documentation Reference:
https://aws.amazon.com/kinesis/data-firehose/
Amazon Kinesis Data Firehose is integrated with Amazon S3, Amazon Redshift, and Amazon Elasticsearch Service. From the AWS Management Console, you can point Kinesis Data Firehose to an Amazon S3 bucket, Amazon Redshift table, or Amazon Elasticsearch domain. You can then use your existing analytics applications and tools to analyze streaming data.

Q18. D
AWS Documentation Reference:
AWS re:INVENT 2017: Analyzing Streaming Data in Real Time with Amazon Kinesis
https://www.slideshare.net/AmazonWebServices/abd301analyzing-streaming-data-in-real-time-with-amazon-kinesis

Ingest and deliver raw data
- CloudTrail provides continuous account activity logging

- Events are sent in real time to Kinesis Data Firehose or Streams
- Each event includes a timestamp, IAM user, AWS service name, API call, response, and more

Compute Operational Metrics in real time
Amazon kinesis data analytics compute metrics using SQL in real time

Persist data for real time dashboards

- Use Kinesis Data Firehose to archive processed to in S3
- Use AWS Lambda to deliver data to DynamoDB (or another database)
- Open source or other tools to visualize the data

Q19. A, C, D, F
B and E are features of EMR File System (EMRFS).
AWS Documentation Reference: Work with Storage and File Systems
https://docs.aws.amazon.com/emr/latest/ManagementGuide/emr-plan-file-systems.html

HDFS is a distributed, scalable, and portable file system for Hadoop. An advantage of HDFS is data awareness between the Hadoop cluster nodes managing the clusters and the Hadoop cluster nodes managing the individual steps. HDFS is used by the master and core nodes. One advantage is that it's fast; a disadvantage is that it's ephemeral storage which is reclaimed when the cluster ends. It's best used for caching the results produced by intermediate job-flow steps.
https://docs.aws.amazon.com/emr/latest/ManagementGuide/emr-plan-storage.html

Instance store and/or EBS volume storage is used for HDFS data. Amazon EBS volumes attached to EMR clusters are ephemeral: the volumes are deleted upon cluster and instance termination (for example, when shrinking instance groups), so it's important that you not expect data to persist.

Q20.A, B
AWS Documentation Reference:
Whitepaper: Streaming Data Solutions on AWS with Amazon Kinesis
https://d0.awsstatic.com/whitepapers/whitepaper-streaming-data-solutions-on-aws-with-amazon-kinesis.pdf

You use Kinesis Streams if you want to do some custom processing with streaming data. Amazon Kinesis Firehose is the easiest way to load streaming data into AWS. It can capture, transform, and load streaming data into Amazon Kinesis Analytics, Amazon S3, Amazon Redshift, and Amazon Elasticsearch Service, enabling near real-time analytics with existing business intelligence tools and dashboards that you're already using today. In the given scenario the key requirement is to ingest streaming data into Redshift data warehouse without custom processing. You do not need to write applications or manage resources. You configure your data producers to send data to Kinesis Firehose, which automatically delivers the data to the destination that you specified. So Kinesis Firehose should be used to ingest the data as depicted in the figure below:

Currently, the data in the ABC Tolls data warehouse can be up to 24 hours old because of their daily batch process. Their current data warehouse solution is Amazon Redshift. Kinesis Firehose can receive a stream of data records and insert them into Amazon Redshift. You can create a Kinesis Firehose delivery stream and configure it so that it would copy data to their Amazon Redshift table every 15 minutes. Their current solution stores records to a file system as part of their batch process. As part of this new solution, they can use the Amazon Kinesis Agent on their servers to forward their log data to Kinesis Firehose. Since Kinesis Firehose uses Amazon S3 to store raw streaming data before it is copied to Amazon Redshift, ABC Tolls didn't need to build another solution to archive their raw data.

The Amazon Kinesis Agent is a stand-alone Java software application that offers an easy way to collect and send data to Kinesis Firehose. The agent continuously monitors a set of files and sends new data to stream. You can install the agent on Linux-based server environments such as web servers, log servers, and database servers. After installing the agent, configure it by specifying the files to monitor and the destination stream for the data. After the agent is configured, it durably collects data from the files and reliably sends it to the delivery stream. ABC Tolls were already creating log files, so forwarding the log entries to Kinesis Firehose was a simple installation and configuration of the agent. No additional code was needed to start streaming their data.

Q21. D
AWS Documentation Reference:
Whitepaper: Streaming Data Solutions on AWS with Amazon Kinesis
https://d0.awsstatic.com/whitepapers/whitepaper-streaming-data-solutions-on-aws-with-amazon-kinesis.pdf
To support the feature to send a notification when a spending threshold is breached, the ABC Tolls development team has created a mobile application and can use an Amazon DynamoDB table. The application will allow customers to set their threshold, and a specific database table

stores this value for each customer. The table will also store the cumulative amount spent by each customer, each month. To provide timely notifications, ABC Tolls needs to update the cumulative value in this table in a timely manner, and compare that value with the threshold to determine if a notification should be sent to the customer.

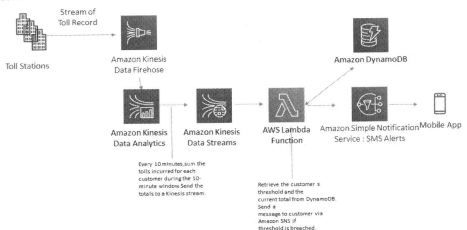

Toll transactions are already streaming through Kinesis Firehose, you can use this streaming data as the source for their aggregation and alerting. As Kinesis Analytics enables you to use SQL to aggregate the streaming data, it is an ideal solution to the problem. In this solution, Kinesis Analytics totals the value of the transactions for each customer over a 10-minute time period (window). At the end of the window, it sends the totals to a Kinesis stream. This stream is the event source for an AWS Lambda function. The Lambda function queries the DynamoDB table to retrieve the thresholds and current total spent by each customer represented in the output from Kinesis Analytics. For each customer, the Lambda function updates the current total in DynamoDB and also compares the total with the threshold. If the threshold has been exceeded, it uses the AWS SDK to tell Amazon Simple Notification Service (SNS) to send a notification to the customers.

Q22. A
AWS Documentation Reference:
https://aws.amazon.com/getting-started/projects/build-log-analytics-solution/
The following diagram represents the architecture for analyzing web server logs.

- Set up a Kinesis Agent on data sources to collect data and send it continuously to Amazon Kinesis Firehose.
- Create an end-to-end data delivery stream using Kinesis Firehose. The delivery stream will transmit your data from the agent to destinations including Amazon Kinesis Analytics, Amazon Redshift, Amazon Elasticsearch Service, and Amazon S3.
- Process incoming log data using SQL queries in Amazon Kinesis Analytics.

- Load processed data from Kinesis Analytics to Amazon Elasticsearch Service to index the data.
- Analyze and visualize the processed data using Kibana.

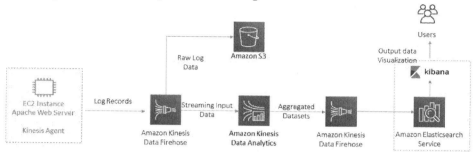

Amazon Kinesis Firehose is a fully managed service for delivering real-time streaming data to destinations such as Amazon S3, Amazon Redshift, or Amazon ES. With Firehose, you do not need to write any applications or manage any resources. You configure your data producers to send data to Firehose and it automatically delivers the data to the destination that you specified. In this solution, you will create two separate Amazon Kinesis Firehose delivery streams. One will receive the data from your Apache access log producer, and the other will receive the output from an Amazon Kinesis Analytics application.

Amazon Kinesis Analytics is the easiest way to process and analyze streaming data in real-time with ANSI standard SQL. It enables you to read data from Amazon Kinesis Streams and Amazon Kinesis Firehose, and build stream processing queries that filter, transform, and aggregate the data as it arrives. Amazon Kinesis Analytics automatically recognizes standard data formats, parses the data, and suggests a schema, which you can edit using the interactive schema editor. It provides an interactive SQL editor and stream processing templates so you can write sophisticated stream processing queries in just minutes. Amazon Kinesis Analytics runs your queries continuously, and writes the processed results to output destinations such as Amazon Kinesis Streams and Amazon Kinesis Firehose, which can deliver the data to Amazon S3, Amazon Redshift, and Amazon ES. Amazon Kinesis Analytics automatically provisions, deploys, and scales the resources required to run your queries.

Amazon ES is a popular open-source search and analytics engine for big data use cases such as log and click stream analysis. Amazon ES manages the capacity, scaling, patching, and administration of Elasticsearch clusters for you while giving you direct access to the Elasticsearch API. Amazon ES provides integrated and managed access to Kibana, a data visualization plugin for Elasticsearch. Customers can create a variety of Kibana charts and dashboards for large volumes of data, and can load and use dashboards developed by the Kibana and AWS user communities.

Amazon S3 provides secure, durable, and highly-scalable cloud storage for the objects that make up your application. Many organizations choose to export log data to Amazon S3.

Amazon S3 offers customers a durable, highly scalable location to store log data and to consolidate log files for custom processing and analysis. Amazon S3 is the best choice for long-term retention and archiving of log data, especially for organizations with compliance programs that require log data to be auditable in its native format.

Once log data is in an Amazon S3 bucket, define lifecycle rules to automatically enforce retention policies and move these objects to other, cost-effective storage classes, such as Amazon S3 Standard - Infrequent Access (Standard - IA) or Amazon Glacier.

Q23.B
AWS Documentation Reference:
https://aws.amazon.com/quickstart/architecture/clickstream-analytics/

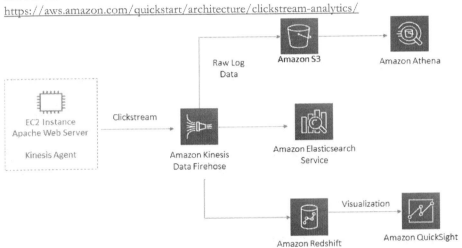

The clickstream data as users navigate through a website captured in the web server logs is sent to the Kinesis Data Firehose delivery stream using Kinesis Agent installed on the web servers.

Once the data is processed, the Kinesis Data Firehose delivery stream sends the data in near real-time to Amazon Redshift. You can build a recommendation engine with Amazon Redshift application programming interfaces (APIs).

Kinesis Data Firehose with an Amazon S3 destination persists managed feeds to a curated datasets bucket in Amazon S3.

Kinesis Data Firehose with an Amazon ES destination stores and indexes the dataset in Amazon ES.

Amazon CloudWatch metrics monitor the health of the services.

You can run ad-hoc queries on the data in Amazon S3 with Amazon Athena, create and share visualization dashboards on the Amazon Redshift data using Amazon QuickSight, and use Kibana to visualize the data in Amazon ES.

## Q24.B, C, D
AWS Documentation Reference: Work with Storage and File Systems
https://docs.aws.amazon.com/emr/latest/ManagementGuide/emr-plan-file-systems.html
EMRFS is an implementation of the Hadoop file system used for reading and writing regular files from Amazon EMR directly to Amazon S3. EMRFS provides the convenience of storing persistent data in Amazon S3 for use with Hadoop while also providing features like Amazon S3 server-side encryption, read-after-write consistency, and list consistency.

## Q25. C
AWS Documentation Reference
https://docs.aws.amazon.com/glue/latest/dg/what-is-glue.html
AWS Glue is a fully managed ETL (extract, transform, and load) service that makes it simple and cost-effective to categorize your data, clean it, enrich it, and move it reliably between various data stores. AWS Glue consists of a central metadata repository known as the AWS Glue Data Catalog, an ETL engine that automatically generates Python or Scala code, and a flexible scheduler that handles dependency resolution, job monitoring, and retries. AWS Glue is serverless, so there's no infrastructure to set up or manage.

## Q26. D
AWS Glue is a fully managed ETL (extract, transform, and load) service that makes it simple and cost-effective to categorize your data, clean it, enrich it, and move it reliably between various data stores. It doesn't have the feature of creating BI dashboard.

AWS Documentation Reference: When Should I Use AWS Glue?
https://docs.aws.amazon.com/glue/latest/dg/what-is-glue.html

You can use AWS Glue to build a data warehouse to organize, cleanse, validate, and format data. You can transform and move AWS Cloud data into your data store. You can also load data from disparate sources into your data warehouse for regular reporting and analysis.

You can use AWS Glue when you run serverless queries against your Amazon S3 data lake. AWS Glue can catalog your Amazon Simple Storage Service (Amazon S3) data, making it available for querying with Amazon Athena and Amazon Redshift Spectrum. With crawlers, your metadata stays in sync with the underlying data. Athena and Redshift Spectrum can directly query your Amazon S3 data lake using the AWS Glue Data Catalog.

You can create event-driven ETL pipelines with AWS Glue. You can run your ETL jobs as soon as new data becomes available in Amazon S3 by invoking your AWS Glue ETL jobs from an AWS Lambda function.

## Q27. A
https://docs.aws.amazon.com/streams/latest/dev/key-concepts.html
A shard is a uniquely identified sequence of data records in a stream. A stream is composed of one or more shards, each of which provides a fixed unit of capacity. Each shard can support up to 5 transactions per second for reads, up to a maximum total data read rate of 2 MB per second and up to 1,000 records per second for writes, up to a maximum total data write rate of 1 MB per second (including partition keys). The data capacity of your stream is a function of the number of shards that you specify for the stream. The total capacity of the stream is the sum of the capacities of its shards.
If your data rate increases, you can increase or decrease the number of shards allocated to your stream.
https://aws.amazon.com/blogs/big-data/scale-your-amazon-kinesis-stream-capacity-with-updateshardcount/

## Q28. A, B
AWS Documentation Reference:
https://aws.amazon.com/glue/
AWS Glue is a fully managed extract, transform, and load (ETL) service that makes it easy for customers to prepare and load their data for analytics.

C is incorrect because AWS Data Pipeline is a web service that helps you reliably process and move data between different AWS compute and storage services, as well as on-premises data sources, at specified intervals.

D is incorrect because EMR is not a data warehouse service but it Runs and Scales Apache Spark, Hadoop, HBase, Presto, Hive, and other Big Data Frameworks

## Q29. C
AWS Documentation Reference:
https://docs.aws.amazon.com/redshift/latest/mgmt/managing-clusters-vpc.html
When you request Amazon Redshift to create a cluster in your VPC, you must provide your VPC information by creating a cluster subnet group. A cluster subnet group allows you to specify a set of subnets in your VPC. When provisioning a cluster you provide the subnet group and Amazon Redshift creates the cluster on one of the subnets in the group.

## Q30. A, C, D
AWS Documentation Reference:
https://aws.amazon.com/glue/faqs/

*When should I use AWS Glue vs. AWS Data Pipeline?*

AWS Glue provides a managed ETL service that runs on a serverless Apache Spark environment. This allows you to focus on your ETL job and not worry about configuring and managing the underlying compute resources. AWS Glue takes a data first approach and allows you to focus on the data properties and data manipulation to transform the data to a form where you can derive business insights. It provides an integrated data catalog that makes metadata available for ETL as well as querying via Amazon Athena and Amazon Redshift Spectrum.

AWS Data Pipeline provides a managed orchestration service that gives you greater flexibility in terms of the execution environment, access and control over the compute resources that run your code, as well as the code itself that does data processing. AWS Data Pipeline launches compute resources in your account allowing you direct access to the Amazon EC2 instances or Amazon EMR clusters.

Furthermore, AWS Glue ETL jobs are Scala or Python based. If your use case requires you to use an engine other than Apache Spark or if you want to run a heterogeneous set of jobs that run on a variety of engines like Hive, Pig, etc., then AWS Data Pipeline would be a better choice.

Q31. A, B, D
AWS Documentation Reference:
https://docs.aws.amazon.com/datapipeline/latest/DeveloperGuide/what-is-datapipeline.html
AWS Data Pipeline is a web service that you can use to automate the movement and transformation of data. With AWS Data Pipeline, you can define data-driven workflows, so that tasks can be dependent on the successful completion of previous tasks. You define the parameters of your data transformations and AWS Data Pipeline enforces the logic that you've set up.

The following components of AWS Data Pipeline work together to manage your data:

* A pipeline definition specifies the business logic of your data management. For more information, see Pipeline Definition File Syntax.
* A pipeline schedules and runs tasks by creating Amazon EC2 instances to perform the defined work activities. You upload your pipeline definition to the pipeline, and then activate the pipeline. You can edit the pipeline definition for a running pipeline and activate the pipeline again for it to take effect. You can deactivate the pipeline, modify a data source, and then activate the pipeline again. When you are finished with your pipeline, you can delete it.
* Task Runner polls for tasks and then performs those tasks. For example, Task Runner could copy log files to Amazon S3 and launch Amazon EMR clusters. Task Runner is installed and runs automatically on resources created by your pipeline definitions. You can

write a custom task runner application, or you can use the Task Runner application that is provided by AWS Data Pipeline.

Q32. A, D
AWS Documentation Reference:
https://docs.aws.amazon.com/glue/latest/dg/components-overview.html
The different components of AWS Glue are:

AWS Glue Console
You use the AWS Glue console to define and orchestrate your ETL workflow. The console calls several API operations in the AWS Glue Data Catalog and AWS Glue Jobs system to perform the following tasks:

- Define AWS Glue objects such as jobs, tables, crawlers, and connections.
- Schedule when crawlers run.
- Define events or schedules for job triggers.
- Search and filter lists of AWS Glue objects.
- Edit transformation scripts.

AWS Glue Data Catalog
The AWS Glue Data Catalog is your persistent metadata store. It is a managed service that lets you store, annotate, and share metadata in the AWS Cloud in the same way you would in an Apache Hive metastore. The AWS Glue Data Catalog contains references to data that is used as sources and targets of your extract, transform, and load (ETL) jobs in AWS Glue. To create your data warehouse, you must catalog this data. The AWS Glue Data Catalog is an index to the location, schema, and runtime metrics of your data. You use the information in the Data Catalog to create and monitor your ETL jobs. Information in the Data Catalog is stored as metadata tables, where each table specifies a single data store. Typically, you run a crawler to take inventory of the data in your data stores, but there are other ways to add metadata tables into your Data Catalog.

AWS Glue Crawlers and Classifiers
AWS Glue also lets you set up crawlers that can scan data in all kinds of repositories, classify it, extract schema information from it, and store the metadata automatically in the AWS Glue Data Catalog. From there it can be used to guide ETL operations.

AWS Glue ETL Operations
Using the metadata in the Data Catalog, AWS Glue can autogenerate Scala or PySpark (the Python API for Apache Spark) scripts with AWS Glue extensions that you can use and modify to perform various ETL operations. For example, you can extract, clean, and transform raw data, and then store the result in a different repository, where it can be queried and analyzed. Such a script might convert a CSV file into a relational form and save it in Amazon Redshift.

The AWS Glue Jobs System

The AWS Glue Jobs system provides managed infrastructure to orchestrate your ETL workflow. You can create jobs in AWS Glue that automate the scripts you use to extract, transform, and transfer data to different locations. Jobs can be scheduled and chained, or they can be triggered by events such as the arrival of new data.

Q33. A, C, D

AWS Documentation Reference:

https://aws.amazon.com/athena/

https://aws.amazon.com/athena/faqs/?nc=sn&loc=6

Amazon Athena is an interactive query service that makes it easy to analyze data in Amazon S3 using standard SQL. Athena is serverless, so there is no infrastructure to setup or manage, and you can start analyzing data immediately. You don't even need to load your data into Athena, it works directly with data stored in S3. To get started, just log into the Athena Management Console, define your schema, and start querying. Amazon Athena uses Presto with full standard SQL support and works with a variety of standard data formats, including CSV, JSON, ORC, Apache Parquet and Avro. While Amazon Athena is ideal for quick, ad-hoc querying and integrates with Amazon QuickSight for easy visualization, it can also handle complex analysis, including large joins, window functions, and arrays.

Q34. D

AWS Documentation Reference:

https://docs.aws.amazon.com/quicksight/latest/user/supported-data-sources.html

# Answer Chapter 6 Content Delivery: Amazon Route 53, Amazon CloudFront,

Q1. A, C, D

B is not a service provided by Amazon Route 53.

AWS Documentation Reference:

https://docs.aws.amazon.com/en_pv/Route53/latest/DeveloperGuide/Welcome.html

Register domain names: Your website needs a name, such as example.com. Route 53 lets you register a name for your website or web application, known as a domain name.

Route internet traffic to the resources for your domain: When a user opens a web browser and enters your domain name (example.com) or subdomain name (acme.example.com) in the address bar, Route 53 helps connect the browser with your website or web application.

Check the health of your resources: Route 53 sends automated requests over the internet to a resource, such as a web server, to verify that it's reachable, available, and functional. You also can choose to receive notifications when a resource becomes unavailable and choose to route internet traffic away from unhealthy resources.

Q2. A, B, D

AWS Documentation Reference: Routing Traffic to Other AWS Resources

https://docs.aws.amazon.com/en_pv/Route53/latest/DeveloperGuide/integration-with-other-services.html

Amazon API Gateway: Amazon API Gateway lets you create, publish, maintain, monitor, and secure APIs at any scale. You can create APIs that access AWS or other web services, as well as data stored in the AWS Cloud. You can use Route 53 to route traffic to an API Gateway API.

Amazon CloudFront: To speed up delivery of your web content, you can use Amazon CloudFront, the AWS content delivery network (CDN). CloudFront can deliver your entire website—including dynamic, static, streaming, and interactive content—by using a global network of edge locations. CloudFront routes requests for your content to the edge location that gives your users the lowest latency. You can use Route 53 to route traffic for your domain to your CloudFront distribution.

Amazon EC2: When you launch an EC2 instance, EC2 automatically installs the operating system (Linux or Microsoft Windows) and additional software included in the AMI, such as web server or database software. If you host a website or run a web application on an EC2 instance, you can route traffic for your domain, such as example.com, to your server by using Route 53.

AWS Elastic Beanstalk: If you use AWS Elastic Beanstalk to deploy and manage applications in the AWS Cloud, you can use Route 53 to route DNS traffic for your domain, such as example.com, to an Elastic Beanstalk environment.

Elastic Load Balancing: If you host a website on multiple Amazon EC2 instances, you can distribute traffic to your website across the instances by using an Elastic Load Balancing (ELB) load balancer. The ELB service automatically scales the load balancer as traffic to your website changes over time. The load balancer also can monitor the health of its registered instances and route domain traffic only to healthy instances. You can use Route 53 to route traffic for your domain to your Classic, Application, or Network Load Balancer.

Amazon RDS :If you use an Amazon RDS database instance for data storage for your web application, the domain name that is assigned to your DB instance is a long, partially random, alphanumeric string, such as myexampledb.a1b2c3d4wxyz.us-west-2.rds.amazonaws.com. If you want to use a domain name that's easier to remember, you can use Route 53 to associate your domain name, such as productdata.example.com, with the domain name of your DB instance.

Amazon S3: Amazon Simple Storage Service (Amazon S3) provides secure, durable, highly scalable cloud storage. You can configure an S3 bucket to host a static website that can include web pages and client-side scripts. (S3 doesn't support server-side scripting.) You can use Route 53 to route traffic to an Amazon S3 bucket.

Amazon Virtual Private Cloud (Amazon VPC): An interface endpoint lets you connect to services that are powered by AWS PrivateLink. These services include some AWS services, services hosted by other AWS customers and partners in their own VPCs (referred to as endpoint services), and supported AWS Marketplace partner services. You can use Route 53 to route traffic to an interface endpoint.

Amazon WorkMail: If you're using Amazon WorkMail for your business email and you're using Route 53 as your DNS service, you can use Route 53 to route traffic to your Amazon WorkMail email domain.

Q3. D
AWS Documentation Reference:
https://docs.aws.amazon.com/en_pv/Route53/latest/DeveloperGuide/hosted-zones-working-with.html
There are two types of hosted zones: Public hosted zones contain records that specify how you want to route traffic on the internet. Private hosted zones contain records that specify how you want to route traffic in an Amazon VPC.
Q4. A, B, D, E
AWS Documentation Reference:
https://docs.aws.amazon.com/en_pv/Route53/latest/DeveloperGuide/hosted-zones-working-with.html
A hosted zone is a container for records, and records contain information about how you want to route traffic for a specific domain, such as example.com, and its subdomains

(acme.example.com, zenith.example.com). A hosted zone and the corresponding domain have the same name. There are two types of hosted zones:

Public hosted zones contain records that specify how you want to route traffic on the internet. Private hosted zones contain records that specify how you want to route traffic in an Amazon VPC.

## Q5. A, C, D
The name of each record in a hosted zone must end with the name of the hosted zone sharing the same suffix. In the given scenario each record must have 'example.com'.
B is wrong because it has suffix 'example.us' which is different from 'example.com'.
AWS Documentation Reference:
https://docs.aws.amazon.com/en_pv/Route53/latest/DeveloperGuide/rrsets-working-with.html

## Q6. A
AWS Documentation Reference: CNAME Record Type
https://docs.aws.amazon.com/en_pv/Route53/latest/DeveloperGuide/ResourceRecordTypes.html
The DNS protocol does not allow you to create a CNAME record for the top node of a DNS namespace, also known as the zone apex. If you register the DNS name example.com, the zone apex is example.com. You cannot create a CNAME record for example.com, but you can create CNAME records for www.example.com, newproduct.example.com, and so on.

## Q7. A
AWS Documentation Reference:
https://docs.aws.amazon.com/en_pv/Route53/latest/DeveloperGuide/ResourceRecordTypes.html#AFormat

## Q8. B
AWS Documentation Reference:
https://docs.aws.amazon.com/en_pv/Route53/latest/DeveloperGuide/ResourceRecordTypes.html#AAAAFormat
## Q9. C
AWS Documentation Reference:
https://docs.aws.amazon.com/en_pv/Route53/latest/DeveloperGuide/ResourceRecordTypes.html#CNAMEFormat

## Q10. D

## Q11. B
AWS Documentation Reference:

https://docs.aws.amazon.com/en_pv/Route53/latest/DeveloperGuide/ResourceRecordType
s.html#MXFormat

## Q12. A

AWS Documentation Reference:

https://docs.aws.amazon.com/en_pv/Route53/latest/DeveloperGuide/ResourceRecordType
s.html#SPFFormat

SPF records can be used to verify the identity of the sender of email messages.

## Q13. C

AWS Documentation Reference:

https://docs.aws.amazon.com/en_pv/Route53/latest/DeveloperGuide/ResourceRecordType
s.html#TXTFormat

## Q14. A, C

AWS Documentation Reference:

https://docs.aws.amazon.com/Route53/latest/DeveloperGuide/resource-record-sets-
choosing-alias-non-alias.html

An alias record can only redirect queries to selected AWS resources, such as the following:

- Amazon S3 buckets
- CloudFront distributions
- Another record in the Route 53 hosted zone that you're creating the alias record in.

For example, you can create an alias record named acme.example.com that redirects queries to an Amazon S3 bucket that is also named acme.example.com. You can also create an acme.example.com alias record that redirects queries to a record named zenith.example.com in the example.com hosted zone.

In most configurations, you can create an alias record that has the same name as the hosted zone (the zone apex). The one exception is when you want to redirect queries from the zone apex (such as example.com) to a record in the same hosted zone that has a type of CNAME (such as zenith.example.com). The alias record must have the same type as the record you're routing traffic to, and creating a CNAME record for the zone apex isn't supported even for an alias record.

## Q15. A, B, C

AWS Documentation Reference:

https://docs.aws.amazon.com/Route53/latest/DeveloperGuide/resource-record-sets-
choosing-alias-non-alias.html

## Q16. C

AWS Documentation Reference:

Amazon Route 53 offers a special type of record called an 'Alias' record that lets you map your zone apex (example.com) DNS name to the DNS name for your ELB load balancer (such as my-loadbalancer-1234567890.us-west-2.elb.amazonaws.com). IP addresses associated with load balancers can change at any time due to scaling up, scaling down, or software updates. Route 53 responds to each request for an Alias record with one or more IP addresses for the load balancer. Route 53 supports alias records for three types of load balancers: Application Load Balancers, Network Load Balancers, and Classic Load Balancers.

https://docs.aws.amazon.com/Route53/latest/DeveloperGuide/resource-record-sets-values-alias.html

You can create an alias record pointing to ELB load balancer with following record type.

A — IPv4 address or AAAA — IPv6 address


https://docs.aws.amazon.com/Route53/latest/DeveloperGuide/resource-record-sets-choosing-alias-non-alias.html

When you use an alias record to route traffic to an AWS resource, Route 53 automatically recognizes changes in the resource. For example, suppose an alias record for example.com points to an ELB load balancer at lb1-1234.us-east-2.elb.amazonaws.com. If the IP address of the load balancer changes, Route 53 automatically starts to respond to DNS queries using the new IP address.

Q17. D

AWS Documentation Reference:

https://docs.aws.amazon.com/Route53/latest/DeveloperGuide/routing-policy.html#routing-policy-weighted

Weighted routing lets you associate multiple resources with a single domain name (example.com) or subdomain name (acme.example.com) and choose how much traffic is routed to each resource. This can be useful for a variety of purposes, including load balancing and testing new versions of software.

To configure weighted routing, you create records that have the same name and type for each of your resources. You assign each record a relative weight that corresponds with how much traffic you want to send to each resource. Amazon Route 53 sends traffic to a resource based on the weight that you assign to the record as a proportion of the total weight for all records in the group:

Formula for how much traffic is routed to a given resource:

Weight for a specified record / sum of the weights for all records.

For example, if you want to send a tiny portion of your traffic to one resource and the rest to another resource, you might specify weights of 1 and 255. The resource with a weight of 1 gets 1/256th of the traffic (1/1+255), and the other resource gets 255/256ths (255/1+255). You can gradually change the balance by changing the weights. If you want to stop sending traffic to a resource, you can change the weight for that record to 0.

In the given scenario record with weight 3 will receive (3/4) i.e 75% of traffic and record with weight 1 will receive (1/4) i.e 25% of traffic.

Q18. A
AWS Documentation Reference:
https://docs.aws.amazon.com/Route53/latest/DeveloperGuide/routing-policy.html
Since the requirement here is routing based on 'location' of the user, the appropriate routing policy will be Geolocation Routing. Geoproximity routing policy is used when you want to route traffic based on the location of your resources and, optionally, shift traffic from resources in one location to resources in another.
There is no routing policy for C and D.

Q19. C
AWS Documentation Reference:
https://docs.aws.amazon.com/Route53/latest/DeveloperGuide/routing-policy.html
If your application is hosted in multiple AWS Regions, you can improve performance for your users by serving their requests from the AWS Region that provides the lowest latency.

Q20. D
Simple routing policy is used for a single resource.
There is no routing policy as A and B.
AWS Documentation Reference:
https://docs.aws.amazon.com/Route53/latest/DeveloperGuide/routing-policy.html#routing-policy-weighted
Weighted routing lets you associate multiple resources with a single domain name (example.com) or subdomain name (acme.example.com) and choose how much traffic is routed to each resource. This can be useful for a variety of purposes, including load balancing and testing new versions of software.

To configure weighted routing, you create records that have the same name and type for each of your resources. You assign each record a relative weight that corresponds with how much traffic you want to send to each resource. Amazon Route 53 sends traffic to a resource based on the weight that you assign to the record as a proportion of the total weight for all records in the group:
Formula for how much traffic is routed to a given resource:

weight for a specified record / sum of the weights for all records.

Q21. A, D
AWS Documentation Reference:
Geolocation Routing:

https://docs.aws.amazon.com/Route53/latest/DeveloperGuide/routing-policy.html#routing-policy-geo

Geolocation routing lets you choose the resources that serve your traffic based on the geographic location of your users, meaning the location that DNS queries originate from. For example, you might want all queries from Europe to be routed to an ELB load balancer in the Frankfurt region.

When you use geolocation routing, you can localize your content and present some or all of your website in the language of your users. You can also use geolocation routing to restrict distribution of content to only the locations in which you have distribution rights. Another possible use is for balancing load across endpoints in a predictable, easy-to-manage way, so that each user location is consistently routed to the same endpoint.

You can specify geographic locations by continent, by country, or by state in the United States. If you create separate records for overlapping geographic regions—for example, one record for North America and one for Canada—priority goes to the smallest geographic region. This allows you to route some queries for a continent to one resource and to route queries for selected countries on that continent to a different resource.

Geoproximity Routing:

https://docs.aws.amazon.com/Route53/latest/DeveloperGuide/routing-policy.html#routing-policy-geoproximity

Geoproximity routing lets Amazon Route 53 route traffic to your resources based on the geographic location of your users and your resources. You can also optionally choose to route more traffic or less to a given resource by specifying a value, known as a bias. A bias expands or shrinks the size of the geographic region from which traffic is routed to a resource.

To use Geoproximity routing, you must use Route 53 traffic flow. You create Geoproximity rules for your resources and specify one of the following values for each rule:

- If you're using AWS resources, the AWS Region that you created the resource in
- If you're using non-AWS resources, the latitude and longitude of the resource

## Q22. B

AWS Documentation Reference:

https://docs.aws.amazon.com/Route53/latest/DeveloperGuide/routing-policy.html#routing-policy-failover

Failover routing lets you route traffic to a resource when the resource is healthy or to a different resource when the first resource is unhealthy. The primary and secondary records can route traffic to anything from an Amazon S3 bucket that is configured as a website to a complex tree of records.

## Q23. C

AWS Documentation Reference:

https://docs.aws.amazon.com/Route53/latest/DeveloperGuide/routing-policy.html#routing-policy-multivalue

Multivalue answer routing lets you configure Amazon Route 53 to return multiple values, such as IP addresses for your web servers, in response to DNS queries. You can specify multiple values for almost any record, but multivalue answer routing also lets you check the health of each resource, so Route 53 returns only values for healthy resources. It's not a substitute for a load balancer, but the ability to return multiple health-checkable IP addresses is a way to use DNS to improve availability and load balancing.

To route traffic approximately randomly to multiple resources, such as web servers, you create one multivalue answer record for each resource and, optionally, associate a Route 53 health check with each record. Route 53 responds to DNS queries with up to eight healthy records and gives different answers to different DNS resolvers. If a web server becomes unavailable after a resolver caches a response, client software can try another IP address in the response.

## Q24. B

AWS Documentation Reference: Maximum Response Size

https://docs.aws.amazon.com/Route53/latest/DeveloperGuide/DNSBehavior.html

To comply with DNS standards, responses sent over UDP are limited to 512 bytes in size. Responses exceeding 512 bytes are truncated and the resolver must re-issue the request over TCP.

## Q25. B

AWS Documentation Reference:

As it is mentioned that VPC and ALB routes only IPv4 traffic and not IPv6, option A and D is not applicable as AAAA record type is for IPv6 addresses.

Option C is incorrect because a Non Alias A record type should map to an ip address. In this case the ip address of ALB can change over time.

The correct option is B.

https://docs.aws.amazon.com/Route53/latest/DeveloperGuide/routing-to-elb-load-balancer.html

https://docs.aws.amazon.com/Route53/latest/DeveloperGuide/resource-record-sets-choosing-alias-non-alias.html

https://docs.aws.amazon.com/Route53/latest/DeveloperGuide/ResourceRecordTypes.html#CNAMEFormat

Amazon Route 53 alias records provide a Route 53–specific extension to DNS functionality. Alias records lets you route traffic to selected AWS resources, such as ALB, CloudFront distributions and Amazon S3 buckets.

To route domain traffic to an ELB load balancer, use Amazon Route 53 to create an alias record that points to your load balancer. An alias record is a Route 53 extension to DNS.

When you use an alias record to route traffic to an AWS resource, Route 53 automatically recognizes changes in the resource. For example, suppose an alias record for 'www.mycloudblogs.com' points to an ELB load balancer at lb1-1234.us-east-2.elb.amazonaws.com. If the IP address of the load balancer changes, Route 53 automatically starts to respond to DNS queries using the new IP address.

It's similar to a CNAME record, but you can create an alias record both for the root domain, mycloudblogs.com, and for subdomains, such as www. mycloudblogs.com.

E is not correct because the DNS protocol does not allow you to create a CNAME record for the top node of a DNS namespace, also known as the zone apex. For example, if you register the DNS name mycloudblogs.com, the zone apex is mycloudblogs.com. You cannot create a CNAME record for mycloudblogs.com, but you can create CNAME records for www. mycloudblogs.com and so on.

## Q26. D
AWS Documentation Reference:
https://docs.aws.amazon.com/Route53/latest/DeveloperGuide/routing-policy.html#routing-policy-multivalue
Multivalue answer routing lets you configure Amazon Route 53 to return multiple values, such as IP addresses for your web servers, in response to DNS queries. You can specify multiple values for almost any record, but multivalue answer routing also lets you check the health of each resource, so Route 53 returns only values for healthy resources. It's not a substitute for a load balancer, but the ability to return multiple health-checkable IP addresses is a way to use DNS to improve availability and load balancing.

To route traffic approximately randomly to multiple resources, such as web servers, you create one multivalue answer record for each resource and, optionally, associate a Route 53 health check with each record. Route 53 responds to DNS queries with up to eight healthy records and gives different answers to different DNS resolvers. If a web server becomes unavailable after a resolver caches a response, client software can try another IP address in the response.

## Q27. A, B, E
AWS Documentation Reference:
https://docs.aws.amazon.com/Route53/latest/DeveloperGuide/traffic-flow.html
If you use multiple resources, such as web servers, in multiple locations, it can be a challenge to create records for a complex configuration that uses a combination of Amazon Route 53 routing policies—failover, geolocation, latency, multivalue answer, and weighted. You can create records one at a time, but it's hard to keep track of the relationships among the records when you're reviewing the settings in a table in the console.

If you're using the Route 53 console, Route 53 traffic flow provides a visual editor that helps you create complex trees in a fraction of the time with a fraction of the effort. You can save the configuration as a traffic policy and then associate the traffic policy with one or more domain names (such as example.com) or subdomain names (such as www.example.com), in the same hosted zone or in multiple hosted zones. (You can only use traffic flow to create configurations for public hosted zones.) You can also use the visual editor to quickly find resources that you need to update and apply the updates to one or more DNS names such as www.example.com. In addition, you can roll back the updates if the new configuration isn't performing as you expected it to.

Here's an overview of how traffic flow works:

You use the visual editor to create a traffic policy. A traffic policy includes information about the routing configuration that you want to create: the routing policies that you want to use and the resources that you want to route DNS traffic to, such as the IP address of each EC2 instance and the domain name of each ELB load balancer. You can also associate health checks with your endpoints so that Route 53 routes traffic only to healthy resources. (Traffic flow also lets you route traffic to non-AWS resources.)

You create a policy record. This is where you specify the hosted zone (such as example.com) in which you want to create the configuration that you defined in your traffic policy. It's also where you specify the DNS name (such as www.example.com) that you want to associate the configuration with. You can create more than one policy record in the same hosted zone or in different hosted zones by using the same traffic policy.

When you create a policy record, Route 53 creates a tree of records. The root record appears in the list of records for your hosted zone. The root record has the DNS name that you specified when you created the policy record. Route 53 also creates records for the entire rest of the tree, but it hides them from the list of records for your hosted zone.

When a user browses to www.example.com, Route 53 responds to the query based on the configuration in the traffic policy that you used to create the policy record.

Q28. A, C
AWS Documentation Reference:
Geoproximity Routing:
https://docs.aws.amazon.com/Route53/latest/DeveloperGuide/routing-policy.html#routing-policy-geoproximity
Geoproximity routing lets Amazon Route 53 route traffic to your resources based on the geographic location of your users and your resources. You can also optionally choose to route more traffic or less to a given resource by specifying a value, known as a bias. A bias expands or shrinks the size of the geographic region from which traffic is routed to a resource.

To optionally change the size of the geographic region from which Route 53 routes traffic to a resource, specify the applicable value for the bias:

- To expand the size of the geographic region from which Route 53 routes traffic to a resource, specify a positive integer from 1 to 99 for the bias. Route 53 shrinks the size of adjacent regions.

- To shrink the size of the geographic region from which Route 53 routes traffic to a resource, specify a negative bias of -1 to -99. Route 53 expands the size of adjacent regions.

## Q29. C, D

AWS Documentation Reference:

https://aws.amazon.com/cloudfront/features/

https://docs.aws.amazon.com/whitepapers/latest/aws-overview/global-infrastructure.html

## Q30. A, C

AWS Documentation Reference:

https://docs.aws.amazon.com/en_pv/AmazonCloudFront/latest/DeveloperGuide/Introduct ion.html

Amazon CloudFront is a web service that speeds up distribution of your static and dynamic web content, such as .html, .css, .js, and image files, to your users. CloudFront delivers your content through a worldwide network of data centers called edge locations. When a user requests content that you're serving with CloudFront, the user is routed to the edge location that provides the lowest latency (time delay), so that content is delivered with the best possible performance.

If the content is already in the edge location with the lowest latency, CloudFront delivers it immediately.

If the content is not in that edge location, CloudFront retrieves it from an origin that you've defined—such as an Amazon S3 bucket, a MediaPackage channel, or an HTTP server (for example, a web server) that you have identified as the source for the definitive version of your content.

CloudFront speeds up the distribution of your content by routing each user request through the AWS backbone network to the edge location that can best serve your content. Typically, this is a CloudFront edge server that provides the fastest delivery to the viewer. Using the AWS network dramatically reduces the number of networks that your users' requests must pass through, which improves performance. Users get lower latency the time it takes to load the first byte of the file and higher data transfer rates.

You also get increased reliability and availability because copies of your files (also known as objects) are now held (or cached) in multiple edge locations around the world.

## Q31. B, C, D

A is incorrect. S3 can be used for static website content storage use case.

AWS Documentation Reference:

https://docs.aws.amazon.com/en_pv/AmazonCloudFront/latest/DeveloperGuide/Introduct ionUseCases.html

Accelerate Static Website Content Delivery: CloudFront can speed up the delivery of your static content (for example, images, style sheets, JavaScript, and so on) to viewers across the globe. A simple approach for storing and delivering static content is to use an Amazon S3 bucket. Using S3 together with CloudFront has a number of advantages, including the option to use Origin Access Identity (OAI) to easily restrict access to your S3 content.

Serve On-Demand or Live Streaming Video: CloudFront offers several options for streaming your media to global viewers—both pre-recorded files and live events.

- For on-demand streaming, you can use CloudFront to stream in common formats such as MPEG DASH, Apple HLS, Microsoft Smooth Streaming, and CMAF, to any device.
- For broadcasting a live stream, you can cache media fragments at the edge, so that multiple requests for the manifest file that delivers the fragments in the right order can be combined, to reduce the load on your origin server.

Serve Private Content by using Lambda@Edge Customizations: Using Lambda@Edge can help you configure your CloudFront distribution to serve private content from your own custom origin, as an option to using signed URLs or signed cookies.

You can use several techniques to restrict access to your origin exclusively to CloudFront, including using whitelisting CloudFront IPs in your firewall and using a custom header to carry a shared secret.

Q32.A, C

AWS Documentation Reference:

https://docs.aws.amazon.com/AmazonCloudFront/latest/DeveloperGuide/GettingStarted.Si mpleDistribution.html

CloudFront can distribute almost any type of file for you using an Amazon S3 bucket as the source. For example, CloudFront can distribute text, images, and videos. You can create multiple buckets, and there is no limit to the amount of data that you can store on Amazon S3.

By default, your Amazon S3 bucket and all the files in it are private—only the AWS account that created the bucket has read/write permission to the files. If you want to allow anyone to access the files in your Amazon S3 bucket using CloudFront URLs, you must grant public read permissions to the objects. (This is one of the most common mistakes when working with CloudFront and Amazon S3. You must explicitly grant permissions to each object in an Amazon S3 bucket.)

Create a CloudFront distribution for Origin Domain Name, choose the Amazon S3 bucket that you created earlier.

Q33. A, B, D

You can't serve Adobe Flash multimedia content over HTTP or HTTPS, but you can serve it using a CloudFront RTMP distribution.
AWS Documentation Reference:
https://docs.aws.amazon.com/en_pv/AmazonCloudFront/latest/DeveloperGuide/distributi
on-overview.html
You can use distributions to serve the following content over HTTP or HTTPS:

- Static and dynamic download content, for example, .html, .css, .js, and image files, using HTTP or HTTPS.

- Video on demand in different formats, such as Apple HTTP Live Streaming (HLS) and Microsoft Smooth Streaming.

- You can't serve Adobe Flash multimedia content over HTTP or HTTPS, but you can serve it using a CloudFront RTMP distribution.

- A live event, such as a meeting, conference, or concert, in real time. For live streaming, you can create the distribution automatically by using an AWS CloudFormation stack.

Q34. A, B, D, E
You don't configure in Cloudfront CNAME DNS service registration of alternate domain name to Cloudfront domain name.

AWS Documentation Reference:
https://docs.aws.amazon.com/en_pv/AmazonCloudFront/latest/DeveloperGuide/CNAME
s.html

https://docs.aws.amazon.com/en_pv/AmazonCloudFront/latest/DeveloperGuide/distributi
on-overview.html
When you want to use CloudFront to distribute your content, you create a distribution and choose the configuration settings you want. For example:

- Your content origin—that is, the Amazon S3 bucket, MediaPackage channel, or HTTP server from which CloudFront gets the files to distribute. You can specify any combination of up to 25 Amazon S3 buckets, channels, and/or HTTP servers as your origins.

- Access—whether you want the files to be available to everyone or restrict access to some users.

- Security—whether you want CloudFront to require users to use HTTPS to access your content.

- Cookie or query-string forwarding—whether you want CloudFront to forward cookies or query strings to your origin.

- Geo-restrictions—whether you want CloudFront to prevent users in selected countries from accessing your content.

- Access logs—whether you want CloudFront to create access logs that show viewer activity.

Q35. A, B, C, F
AWS Documentation Reference:
https://docs.aws.amazon.com/en_pv/AmazonCloudFront/latest/DeveloperGuide/Downloa
dDistS3AndCustomOrigins.html
An origin is the location where you store the original version of your content. When
CloudFront gets a request for your files, it goes to the origin to get the files that it distributes at
edge locations. You can use any combination of Amazon S3 buckets and HTTP servers as
your origin servers.
https://docs.aws.amazon.com/en_pv/AmazonCloudFront/latest/DeveloperGuide/Downloa
dDistS3AndCustomOrigins.html#concept_CustomOrigin
A custom origin is an HTTP server, for example, a web server. The HTTP server can be an
Amazon Elastic Compute Cloud (Amazon EC2) instance or an HTTP server that you manage
privately. An Amazon S3 origin configured as a website endpoint is also considered a custom
origin.
https://docs.aws.amazon.com/en_pv/AmazonCloudFront/latest/DeveloperGuide/distributi
on-web-creating.html
When you create a distribution, you specify where CloudFront sends requests for the files.
CloudFront supports using several AWS resources as origins. For example, you can specify an
Amazon S3 bucket or a MediaStore container, a MediaPackage channel, or a custom origin,
such as an Amazon EC2 instance or your own HTTP web server.

Q36. A, C, E
B and D are not suitable use case because request will originate from single geographic location
or appear to come from single network location because of VPN. Cloudfront is more suitable
when request can originate from multiple regions where reducing latency and improving
performance is main criteria.

Q37 A, B, D
AWS Documentation Reference:
https://aws.amazon.com/caching/web-caching/
Caching web content helps improve upon the responsiveness of your websites by reducing the
load on backend resources and network congestion. Web caching is performed by retaining
HTTP responses and web resources in the cache for the purpose of fulfilling future requests
from cache rather than from the origin servers.
One form of server side web caching includes utilizing key/value stores such as Memcached
and Redis. A key/value object store can be used to cache any web content desired by the
application developer. The web content is retrieved typically by means of application code or
use of an application framework that can leverage the In-Memory data store. Another benefit
to using key/value stores for web caching is they are also commonly used for storing web
sessions and other cached content. This provides a single solution to serve various use cases.
Amazon ElastiCache offers fully managed Redis and Memcached.

https://aws.amazon.com/autoscaling/

AWS Auto Scaling monitors your applications and automatically adjusts capacity to maintain steady, predictable performance at the lowest possible cost. Using AWS Auto Scaling, it's easy to setup application scaling for multiple resources across multiple services in minutes. The service provides a simple, powerful user interface that lets you build scaling plans for resources including Amazon EC2 instances and Spot Fleets, Amazon ECS tasks, Amazon DynamoDB tables and indexes, and Amazon Aurora Replicas. AWS Auto Scaling makes scaling simple with recommendations that allow you to optimize performance, costs, or balance between them. If you're already using Amazon EC2 Auto Scaling to dynamically scale your Amazon EC2 instances, you can now combine it with AWS Auto Scaling to scale additional resources for other AWS services. With AWS Auto Scaling, your applications always have the right resources at the right time.

https://aws.amazon.com/blogs/networking-and-content-delivery/dynamic-whole-site-delivery-with-amazon-cloudfront/
https://aws.amazon.com/cloudfront/

Amazon CloudFront is a fast content delivery network (CDN) service that securely delivers data, videos, applications, and APIs to customers globally with low latency, high transfer speeds, all within a developer-friendly environment.

Amazon Elastic Compute Cloud (Amazon EC2) origins serving dynamic and/or static content using CloudFront because it offers a number of additional benefits including performance, security, and cost benefits.

Q38. A, B, E
The improved architecture will be as below

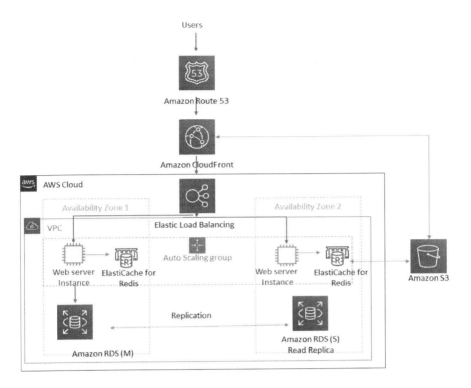

AWS Documentation Reference:
https://aws.amazon.com/blogs/networking-and-content-delivery/dynamic-whole-site-delivery-with-amazon-cloudfront/

It is a common practice to use Amazon CloudFront to accelerate the delivery of static web assets stored in Amazon Simple Storage Service (Amazon S3) or a web server to end users. CloudFront can cache content at edge locations closer to your viewers giving them greater performance, instant global reach, and higher platform availability. For Amazon Elastic Compute Cloud (Amazon EC2) origins serving dynamic and/or static content, you should also consider using CloudFront because it offers a number of additional benefits.

https://docs.aws.amazon.com/Route53/latest/DeveloperGuide/routing-policy.html#routing-policy-latency

If your application is hosted in multiple AWS Regions, you can improve performance for your users by serving their requests from the AWS Region that provides the lowest latency. To use latency-based routing, you create latency records for your resources in multiple AWS Regions. When Route 53 receives a DNS query for your domain or subdomain (example.com or acme.example.com), it determines which AWS Regions you've created latency records for, determines which region gives the user the lowest latency, and then selects a latency record for that region. Route 53 responds with the value from the selected record, such as the IP address for a web server.

https://aws.amazon.com/getting-started/projects/boosting-mysql-database-performance-with-amazon-elasticache-for-redis/

You can boost the performance of your applications by adding an in-memory caching layer to your relational database. You can implement a cache-aside strategy using Amazon ElastiCache for Redis on top of a RDS database. The cache-aside strategy is one of the most popular options for boosting database performance. When an application needs to read data from a database, it first queries the cache. If the data is not found, the application queries the database and populates the cache with the result.

Q39. A, B, C

AWS Documentation Reference:

https://docs.aws.amazon.com/Route53/latest/DeveloperGuide/health-checks-types.html

You can create three types of Amazon Route 53 health checks:

Health checks that monitor an endpoint: You can configure a health check that monitors an endpoint that you specify either by IP address or by domain name. At regular intervals that you specify, Route 53 submits automated requests over the internet to your application, server, or other resource to verify that it's reachable, available, and functional. Optionally, you can configure the health check to make requests similar to those that your users make, such as requesting a web page from a specific URL.

Health checks that monitor other health checks (calculated health checks):You can create a health check that monitors whether Route 53 considers other health checks healthy or unhealthy. One situation where this might be useful is when you have multiple resources that perform the same function, such as multiple web servers, and your chief concern is whether some minimum number of your resources are healthy. You can create a health check for each resource without configuring notification for those health checks. Then you can create a health check that monitors the status of the other health checks and that notifies you only when the number of available web resources drops below a specified threshold.

Health checks that monitor CloudWatch alarms: You can create CloudWatch alarms that monitor the status of CloudWatch metrics, such as the number of throttled read events for an Amazon DynamoDB database or the number of Elastic Load Balancing hosts that are considered healthy. After you create an alarm, you can create a health check that monitors the same data stream that CloudWatch monitors for the alarm.

Q40. A, B, D

C is one of the criteria as how Route 53 determines the status of health checks that monitor other health check.

AWS Documentation Reference:

https://docs.aws.amazon.com/Route53/latest/DeveloperGuide/dns-failover-determining-health-of-endpoints.html#dns-failover-determining-health-of-endpoints-monitor-endpoint

Each health checker evaluates the health of the endpoint based on two values:

- Response time. A resource can be slow to respond or can fail to respond to a health check request for a variety of reasons. For example, the resource is shut down for maintenance, it's under a distributed denial of service (DDoS) attack, or the network is down.

- Whether the endpoint responds to a number of consecutive health checks that you specify (the failure threshold)

Route 53 aggregates the data from the health checkers and determines whether the endpoint is healthy:

- If more than 18% of health checkers report that an endpoint is healthy, Route 53 considers it healthy.

- If 18% of health checkers or fewer report that an endpoint is healthy, Route 53 considers it unhealthy.

## Q41.F

You cannot configure RDS endpoint as origin for Cloudfront distribution.

AWS Documentation Reference:

https://docs.aws.amazon.com/en_pv/AmazonCloudFront/latest/DeveloperGuide/distribution-web-values-specify.html#DownloadDistValuesDomainName

The DNS domain name of the Amazon S3 bucket or HTTP server from which you want CloudFront to get objects for this origin, for example:

- Amazon S3 bucket – aws-s3-bucket1.s3.us-west-2.amazonaws.com
- Amazon S3 bucket configured as a website – https://bucket-name.s3-website.us-west-2.amazonaws.com
- MediaStore container – mymediastore.data.mediastore.us-west-1.amazonaws.com
- MediaPackage endpoint – mymediapackage.mediapackage.us-west-1.amazon.com
- Amazon EC2 instance – ec2-203-0-113-25.compute-1.amazonaws.com
- Elastic Load Balancing load balancer – my-load-balancer-1234567890.us-west-2.elb.amazonaws.com
- Your own web server – https://example.com

## Q42. A, D

AWS Documentation Reference: Adding CloudFront When You're Already Distributing Content from Amazon S3

https://docs.aws.amazon.com/en_pv/AmazonCloudFront/latest/DeveloperGuide/DownloadDistS3AndCustomOrigins.html

If you store your objects in an Amazon S3 bucket, you can either have users get your objects directly from S3, or you can configure CloudFront to get your objects from S3 and then distribute them to your users. Using CloudFront can be more cost effective if your users access your objects frequently because, at higher usage, the price for CloudFront data transfer is lower than the price for Amazon S3 data transfer. In addition, downloads are faster with CloudFront than with Amazon S3 alone because your objects are stored closer to your users.

## Q43. A, B, C, E
AWS Documentation Reference:
https://docs.aws.amazon.com/en_pv/AmazonCloudFront/latest/DeveloperGuide/CNAME s.html#alternate-domain-names-requirements

## Q44. A, D
B is incorrect as there no option called 'validating' the file.
C replacing the old file with new file having same name will not have effect of newer file getting served to user request. The new file will be served only after the expiration time setting.

AWS Documentation Reference:
https://docs.aws.amazon.com/en_pv/AmazonCloudFront/latest/DeveloperGuide/Removin gObjects.html
If you want to remove a file right away before it expires, you must do one of the following:

* Invalidate the file from edge caches. The next time a viewer requests the file, CloudFront returns to the origin to fetch the latest version of the file.
* Use file versioning. When you use versioning, different versions of a file have different names that you can use in your CloudFront distribution, to change which file is returned to viewers.

## Q45. A, B, C, D, F, G
AWS Documentation Reference:
https://docs.aws.amazon.com/en_pv/AmazonCloudFront/latest/DeveloperGuide/SecurityA ndPrivateContent.html

## Q46. A, C
AWS Documentation Reference:
https://docs.aws.amazon.com/en_pv/AmazonCloudFront/latest/DeveloperGuide/PrivateC ontent.html
Many companies that distribute content over the internet want to restrict access to documents, business data, media streams, or content that is intended for selected users, for example, users who have paid a fee. To securely serve this private content by using CloudFront, you can do the following:

* Require that your users access your private content by using special CloudFront signed URLs or signed cookies.

- Require that your users access your content by using CloudFront URLs, not URLs that access content directly on the origin server (for example, Amazon S3 or a private HTTP server). Requiring CloudFront URLs isn't necessary, but it is recommended to prevent users from bypassing the restrictions that you specify in signed URLs or signed cookies.

## Q47. C, D

AWS Documentation Reference:

https://docs.aws.amazon.com/en_pv/AmazonCloudFront/latest/DeveloperGuide/private-content-restricting-access-to-s3.html

CloudFront doesn't expose Amazon S3 URLs, but your users might have those URLs if your application serves any files directly from Amazon S3 or if anyone gives out direct links to specific files in Amazon S3. If users access your files directly in Amazon S3, they bypass the controls provided by CloudFront signed URLs or signed cookies, for example, control over the date and time that a user can no longer access your content and control over which IP addresses can be used to access content.

To ensure that your users access your files using only CloudFront URLs, regardless of whether the URLs are signed or signed cookies, do the following:

- Create an origin access identity, which is a special CloudFront user, and associate the origin access identity with your distribution. You associate the origin access identity with origins, so that you can secure all or just some of your Amazon S3 content. You can also create an origin access identity and add it to your distribution when you create the distribution.

- Change the permissions either on your Amazon S3 bucket or on the files in your bucket so that only the origin access identity has read permission (or read and download permission). When your users access your Amazon S3 files through CloudFront, the CloudFront origin access identity gets the files on behalf of your users. If your users request files directly by using Amazon S3 URLs, they're denied access. The origin access identity has permission to access files in your Amazon S3 bucket, but users don't.

## Q48. B

AWS Documentation Reference:

https://docs.aws.amazon.com/en_pv/AmazonCloudFront/latest/DeveloperGuide/georestrictions.html

When a user requests your content, CloudFront typically serves the requested content regardless of where the user is located. If you need to prevent users in specific countries from accessing your content, you can use the CloudFront geo restriction feature to do one of the following:

- Allow your users to access your content only if they're in one of the countries on a whitelist of approved countries.

- Prevent your users from accessing your content if they're in one of the countries on a blacklist of banned countries.

Q49. D

AWS Documentation Reference:

https://aws.amazon.com/lambda/edge/

Lambda@Edge is a feature of Amazon CloudFront that lets you run code closer to users of your application, which improves performance and reduces latency. With Lambda@Edge, you can enrich your web applications by making them globally distributed and improving their performance all with zero server administration. Lambda@Edge runs your code in response to events generated by the Amazon CloudFront content delivery network (CDN). Just upload your code to AWS Lambda, which takes care of everything required to run and scale your code with high availability at an AWS location closest to your end user.

Q50 .C

AWS Documentation Reference:

https://docs.aws.amazon.com/AmazonCloudFront/latest/DeveloperGuide/on-demand-video.html

https://aws.amazon.com/mediaconvert/

AWS Elemental MediaConvert is a file-based video transcoding service with broadcast-grade features. It allows you to easily create video-on-demand (VOD) content for broadcast and multiscreen delivery at scale. The service combines advanced video and audio capabilities with a simple web services interface and pay-as-you-go pricing. With AWS Elemental MediaConvert, you can focus on delivering compelling media experiences without having to worry about the complexity of building and operating your own video processing infrastructure.

Q51. A, D

AWS Documentation Reference:

https://docs.aws.amazon.com/AmazonCloudFront/latest/DeveloperGuide/live-streaming.html

To use AWS Media Services with CloudFront to deliver live content to a global audience, follow the guidance included in this section.

There are two main options for preparing and serving live streaming content:

- Convert your content into required formats, and then serve it: You can use AWS Elemental MediaPackage to convert your video content from a single format to multiple formats, and then package the content for different device types. MediaPackage lets you implement video features for viewers such as start-over, pause, rewind, and so on. MediaPackage can also protect your content from unauthorized copying by adding Digital Rights Management (DRM). For step-by-step instructions for using CloudFront to serve content that was formatted using MediaPackage.

- Store and serve your content using scalable origin: If your encoder already outputs content in the formats required by all of the devices that your viewers use, you can serve the content by using a highly-scalable origin like an AWS Elemental MediaStore container.

After you've set up your origin by using one of these options, you can distribute live streaming video to viewers by using CloudFront.

## Q52. C

AWS Documentation Reference:
https://docs.aws.amazon.com/AmazonCloudFront/latest/DeveloperGuide/lambda-cloudfront-trigger-events.html

When you associate a CloudFront distribution with a Lambda@Edge function, CloudFront intercepts requests and responses at CloudFront edge locations. You can execute Lambda functions when the following CloudFront events occur:

- When CloudFront receives a request from a viewer (viewer request)
- Before CloudFront forwards a request to the origin (origin request)
- When CloudFront receives a response from the origin (origin response)
- Before CloudFront returns the response to the viewer (viewer response)

## Q53. A, B, D, E, F

AWS Documentation Reference:
https://docs.aws.amazon.com/AmazonCloudFront/latest/DeveloperGuide/lambda-at-the-edge.html

The suitable use cases for Lambda@Edge processing are:

A Lambda function can inspect cookies and rewrite URLs so that users see different versions of a site for A/B testing.

CloudFront can return different objects to viewers based on the device they're using by checking the User-Agent header, which includes information about the devices. For example, CloudFront can return different images based on the screen size of their device. Similarly, the function could consider the value of the Referer header and cause CloudFront to return the images to bots that have the lowest available resolution.

Or you could check cookies for other criteria. For example, on a retail website that sells clothing, if you use cookies to indicate which color a user chose for a jacket, a Lambda function can change the request so that CloudFront returns the image of a jacket in the selected color.

A Lambda function can generate HTTP responses when CloudFront viewer request or origin request events occur.

A function can inspect headers or authorization tokens, and insert a header to control access to your content before CloudFront forwards the request to your origin.

A Lambda function can also make network calls to external resources to confirm user credentials, or fetch additional content to customize a response.

Q54. A, D, E

Rest of the services are created specific to a region.

Q55. A

AWS Documentation Reference: Updating Existing Content Using the Same File Names
https://docs.aws.amazon.com/en_pv/AmazonCloudFront/latest/DeveloperGuide/Updating
ExistingObjects.html

If you use the same names when you replace files, you can't control when CloudFront starts to serve the new files. If you update an existing file in your origin with a newer version that has the same name, an edge location won't get that new version from your origin until both of the following occur:

*   The old version of the file in the cache expires.
*   There's a user request for the file at that edge location.

Q56.B, C

AWS Documentation Reference:
https://docs.aws.amazon.com/Route53/latest/DeveloperGuide/dns-failover-determining-
health-of-endpoints.html

A health check can monitor the status of other health checks; this type of health check is known as a calculated health check. The health check that does the monitoring is the parent health check, and the health checks that are monitored are child health checks. One parent health check can monitor the health of up to 255 child health checks. Here's how the monitoring works:

*   Route 53 adds up the number of child health checks that are considered to be healthy.
*   Route 53 compares that number with the number of child health checks that must be healthy for the status of the parent health check to be considered healthy.

Q57. A, B

AWS Documentation Reference:
https://docs.aws.amazon.com/Route53/latest/DeveloperGuide/dns-failover-determining-
health-of-endpoints.html

When you create a health check that is based on a CloudWatch alarm, Route 53 monitors the data stream for the corresponding alarm instead of monitoring the alarm state. If the data stream indicates that the state of the alarm is OK, the health check is considered healthy. If the data stream indicates that the state is Alarm, the health check is considered unhealthy. If the data stream doesn't provide enough information to determine the state of the alarm, the health check status depends on the setting for Health check status: healthy, unhealthy, or last known status. (In the Route 53 API, this setting is InsufficientDataHealthStatus)

## Q58. B, C, D

AWS Documentation Reference:

https://docs.aws.amazon.com/Route53/latest/DeveloperGuide/dns-failover-simple-configs.html

If you created health checks, Route 53 periodically sends requests to the endpoint for each health check; it doesn't perform the health check when it receives a DNS query. Based on the responses, Route 53 decides whether the endpoints are healthy and uses that information to determine how to respond to queries.

When Route 53 receives a query for myawscertification.com, following steps are done:

1. Route 53 chooses a record based on the routing policy. In this case, it chooses a record based on weight.
2. It determines the current health of the selected record by checking the status of the health check for that record.
3. If the selected record is unhealthy, Route 53 chooses a different record. This time, the unhealthy record isn't considered.
4. When Route 53 finds a healthy record, it responds to the query with the applicable value, such as the IP address in an A record.

## Q59. B

AWS Documentation Reference:

https://docs.aws.amazon.com/Route53/latest/DeveloperGuide/dns-failover-simple-configs.html

When Route 53 determines that the third record is unhealthy, it responds to requests using the first record about 33% of the time, 10/ (10 + 20). It omits the weight of the third record from the calculation.

## Q60. B, D

AWS Documentation Reference: Restricting Access to Files on Custom Origins

https://docs.aws.amazon.com/en_pv/AmazonCloudFront/latest/DeveloperGuide/private-content-overview.html

If you use a web server as a custom origin, you can optionally set up custom headers to restrict access. For CloudFront to get your files from a custom origin, the files must be publicly accessible. But by using custom headers, you can restrict access to your content so that users can access it only through CloudFront, not directly.

To require that users access content through CloudFront, change the following settings in your CloudFront distributions:

- Origin Custom Headers: Configure CloudFront to forward custom headers to your origin.
- Viewer Protocol Policy: Configure your distribution to require viewers to use HTTPS to access CloudFront.

- Origin Protocol Policy: Configure your distribution to require CloudFront to use the same protocol as viewers to forward requests to the origin.

After you've made these changes, update your application on your custom origin to only accept requests that include these headers. The combination of Viewer Protocol Policy and Origin Protocol Policy ensure that your custom headers are encrypted between the viewer and your origin.

Q61. A, D
AWS Documentation Reference:
https://docs.aws.amazon.com/Route53/latest/DeveloperGuide/health-checks-how-route-53-chooses-records.html

Route 53 uses the following criteria when choosing a record:

Records without a health check are always healthy: If a record in a group of records that have the same name and type doesn't have an associated health check, Route 53 always considers it healthy and always includes it among possible responses to a query.

If no record is healthy, all records are healthy: If none of the records in a group of records are healthy, Route 53 needs to return something in response to DNS queries, but it has no basis for choosing one record over another. In this circumstance, Route 53 considers all the records in the group to be healthy and selects one based on the routing policy and on the values that you specify for each record.

Q62. C, D
AWS Documentation Reference:
https://docs.aws.amazon.com/Route53/latest/DeveloperGuide/health-checks-how-route-53-chooses-records.html

Weighted records that have a weight of 0: If you add health checks to all the records in a group of weighted records, but you give nonzero weights to some records and zero weights to others, health checks work the same as when all records have nonzero weights with the following exceptions:
- Route 53 initially considers only the nonzero weighted records, if any.
- If all the records that have a weight greater than 0 are unhealthy, then Route 53 considers the zero-weighted records.

Q63. A
AWS Documentation Reference:
https://docs.aws.amazon.com/Route53/latest/DeveloperGuide/dns-failover-types.html

You can use Route 53 health checking to configure active-active and active-passive failover configurations.

You configure active-active failover using any routing policy (or combination of routing policies) other than failover, and you configure active-passive failover using the failover routing policy.

Use Active-Active Failover configuration when you want all of your resources to be available the majority of the time. When a resource becomes unavailable, Route 53 can detect that it's unhealthy and stop including it when responding to queries. In active-active failover, all the records that have the same name, the same type (such as A or AAAA), and the same routing policy (such as weighted or latency) are active unless Route 53 considers them unhealthy. Route 53 can respond to a DNS query using any healthy record.

You use an active-passive failover configuration when you want a primary resource or group of resources to be available the majority of the time and you want a secondary resource or group of resources to be on standby in case all the primary resources become unavailable. When responding to queries, Route 53 includes only the healthy primary resources. If all the primary resources are unhealthy, Route 53 begins to include only the healthy secondary resources in response to DNS queries.

Q64. C, D
AWS Documentation Reference:
https://aws.amazon.com/premiumsupport/knowledge-center/cloudfront-access-to-amazon-s3/
To allow access to your Amazon S3 bucket only from a CloudFront distribution, first add an origin access identity (OAI) to your distribution. Then, review your bucket policy and Amazon S3 access control list (ACL) to be sure that:

- Only the OAI can access your bucket.
- CloudFront can access the bucket on behalf of requesters.
- Users can't access the objects in other ways, such as by using Amazon S3 URLs.

https://docs.aws.amazon.com/AmazonCloudFront/latest/DeveloperGuide/private-content-restricting-access-to-s3.html#private-content-granting-permissions-to-oai

Q65. A, B
AWS Documentation Reference:
https://docs.aws.amazon.com/AmazonCloudFront/latest/DeveloperGuide/high_availability_origin_failover.html
https://aws.amazon.com/about-aws/whats-new/2018/11/amazon-cloudfront-announces-support-for-origin-failover/
You can enable Origin Failover for your Amazon CloudFront distributions to improve the availability of content delivered to your end users.

With CloudFront's Origin Failover capability, you can setup two origins for your distributions - primary and secondary, such that your content is served from your secondary origin if CloudFront detects that your primary origin is unavailable. You can have two Amazon S3 buckets that serve as your origin that you independently upload your content to. If an object that CloudFront requests from your primary bucket is not present or if connection to your primary bucket times-out, CloudFront will request the object from your secondary bucket. So, you can configure CloudFront to trigger a failover in response to either HTTP 4xx or 5xx status codes.

## Q66. A, B, D
AWS Documentation Reference:
https://docs.aws.amazon.com/AmazonCloudFront/latest/DeveloperGuide/http-504-gateway-timeout.html
CloudFront will return an HTTP 504 status code if traffic is blocked to the origin by a firewall or security group, or if the origin isn't accessible on the internet. Check for those issues first. Then, if access isn't the problem, explore application delays and server timeouts to help you identify and fix the issues.

If the firewall on your origin server blocks CloudFront traffic, CloudFront returns an HTTP 504 status code, so it's good to make sure that isn't the issue before checking for other problems.
If your origin uses Elastic Load Balancing, review the ELB security groups and make sure that the security groups allow inbound traffic from CloudFront.
If CloudFront can't access your custom origin server because it isn't publicly available on the internet, CloudFront returns an HTTP 504 error. CloudFront edge locations connect to origin servers through the internet. If your custom origin is on a private network, CloudFront can't reach it. Because of this, you can't use private servers, including internal Classic Load Balancers, as origin servers with CloudFront.

## Q67. C, E
AWS Documentation Reference:
https://docs.aws.amazon.com/AmazonCloudFront/latest/DeveloperGuide/http-503-service-unavailable.html
C, E are the reasons for HTTP 503 Status Code (Service Unavailable). An HTTP 503 status code (Service Unavailable) typically indicates a performance issue on the origin server. In rare cases, it indicates that CloudFront temporarily can't satisfy a request because of limited resources at an edge location.
https://docs.aws.amazon.com/AmazonCloudFront/latest/DeveloperGuide/http-502-bad-gateway.html
A, B, D, F, G, H are reasons for HTTP 502 Status Code (Bad Gateway). An HTTP 502 status code (Bad Gateway) indicates that CloudFront wasn't able to serve the requested object because it couldn't connect to the origin server.

Q68. B

AWS Documentation Reference:

https://docs.aws.amazon.com/AmazonCloudFront/latest/DeveloperGuide/http-400-bad-request.html

Your CloudFront distribution might send error responses with HTTP status code 400 Bad Request, and a message similar to the following:

The authorization header is malformed; the region '<AWS Region>' is wrong; expecting '<AWS Region>'

For example:

The authorization header is malformed; the region 'us-east-1' is wrong; expecting 'us-west-2'

This problem can occur in the following scenario:

- Your CloudFront distribution's origin is an Amazon S3 bucket.
- You moved the S3 bucket from one AWS Region to another. That is, you deleted the S3 bucket, then later you created a new bucket with the same bucket name, but in a different AWS Region than where the original S3 bucket was located.

Q69.D

AWS Documentation Reference:

https://docs.aws.amazon.com/AmazonCloudFront/latest/DeveloperGuide/Expiration.html#ExpirationDownloadDist

D is incorrect and A is correct because: If the origin adds a Cache-Control max-age directive to objects and Minimum TTL = 0 Seconds, then CloudFront caches objects for the lesser of the value of the Cache-Control max-age directive or the value of the CloudFront maximum TTL. Here Maximum TTL to 5 minutes is less than Cache-Control max-age header 1 hour.

B is correct because when the origin adds an Expires header to objects and Minimum TTL = 0 Seconds, then CloudFront caches objects until the date in the Expires header or for the value of the CloudFront maximum TTL, whichever is sooner.

https://aws.amazon.com/premiumsupport/knowledge-center/cloudfront-cache-files-time/

Q70.C

AWS Documentation Reference:

https://docs.aws.amazon.com/AmazonCloudFront/latest/DeveloperGuide/Expiration.html#ExpirationDownloadDist

Q71.C

AWS Documentation Reference:

https://docs.aws.amazon.com/AmazonCloudFront/latest/DeveloperGuide/Expiration.html
#ExpirationDownloadDist

## Q72. A
AWS Documentation Reference:
https://docs.aws.amazon.com/AmazonCloudFront/latest/DeveloperGuide/QueryStringPara
meters.html
You can configure CloudFront to forward query strings to the origin and to cache based on
the language parameter. If you configure your web server to return the version of a given page
that corresponds with the selected language, CloudFront will cache each language version
separately, based on the value of the language query string parameter. CloudFront can cache
different versions of your content based on the values of query string parameters.

## Q73. B
AWS Documentation Reference:
https://docs.aws.amazon.com/AmazonCloudFront/latest/DeveloperGuide/Expiration.html
By default, each file automatically expires after 24 hours.

## Q74. A, B
AWS Documentation Reference:
https://aws.amazon.com/premiumsupport/knowledge-center/cloudfront-serving-outdated-
content-s3/
You can invalidate an S3 object to remove it from the CloudFront distribution's cache. After
the object is removed from the cache, the next request retrieves the object directly from
Amazon S3.

If you update content frequently, AWS recommend that you use object versioning to clear the
CloudFront distribution's cache. For frequent cache refreshes, using object versioning might
cost less than using invalidations.

# Answer Chapter 7 Application Integration: Amazon SQS, Amazon SNS, Amazon MQ, Amazon SWF, AWS Step Functions, Amazon EventBridge

Q1. A, B

AWS Documentation Reference:

https://aws.amazon.com/sqs/faqs/

Amazon SNS allows applications to send time-critical messages to multiple subscribers through a "push" mechanism, eliminating the need to periodically check or "poll" for updates. Amazon SQS is a message queue service used by distributed applications to exchange messages through a polling model, and can be used to decouple sending and receiving components.

SNS is a distributed publish-subscribe system. Messages are pushed to subscribers as and when they are sent by publishers to SNS.

SQS is distributed queuing system. Messages are NOT pushed to receivers. Receivers have to poll or pull messages from SQS.

Q2.D

AWS Documentation Reference:

https://docs.aws.amazon.com/amazon-mq/latest/developer-guide/welcome.html#difference-from-sqs-sns

Amazon MQ is a managed message broker service that provides compatibility with many popular message brokers. AWS recommend Amazon MQ for migrating applications from existing message brokers that rely on compatibility with APIs such as JMS or protocols such as AMQP, MQTT, OpenWire, and STOMP.

Q3. A, D

B and C are features of FIFO queues.

AWS Documentation Reference:

https://docs.aws.amazon.com/AWSSimpleQueueService/latest/SQSDeveloperGuide/standard-queues.html

A standard queue makes a best effort to preserve the order of messages, but more than one copy of a message might be delivered out of order.

Amazon SQS stores copies of your messages on multiple servers for redundancy and high availability. On rare occasions, one of the servers that stores a copy of a message might be unavailable when you receive or delete a message.

If this occurs, the copy of the message isn't deleted on that unavailable server, and you might get that message copy again when you receive messages. Design your applications to be idempotent (they should not be affected adversely when processing the same message more than once).

Q4. B

AWS Documentation Reference:

https://aws.amazon.com/sqs/faqs/

https://docs.aws.amazon.com/AWSSimpleQueueService/latest/SQSDeveloperGuide/FIFO-queues.html

FIFO (first-in-first-out) queues preserve the exact order in which messages are sent and received.

Standard queues provide a loose-FIFO capability that attempts to preserve the order of messages but receiving messages in the exact order they are sent is not guaranteed.

## Q5. B

Amazon SWF helps developers build, run, and scale background jobs that have parallel or sequential steps. You can think of Amazon SWF as a fully-managed state tracker and task coordinator in the Cloud.

## Q6. B

AWS Documentation Reference:

https://docs.aws.amazon.com/AWSSimpleQueueService/latest/SQSDeveloperGuide/sqs-visibility-timeout.html

When a consumer receives and processes a message from a queue, the message remains in the queue. Amazon SQS doesn't automatically delete the message. To prevent other consumers from processing the message again, Amazon SQS sets a visibility timeout, a period of time during which Amazon SQS prevents other consumers from receiving and processing the message.

## Q7. C

AWS Documentation Reference:

https://docs.aws.amazon.com/AWSSimpleQueueService/latest/SQSDeveloperGuide/sqs-delay-queues.html

Delay queues let you postpone the delivery of new messages to a queue for a number of seconds. If you create a delay queue, any messages that you send to the queue remain invisible to consumers for the duration of the delay period.

## Q8. A

AWS Documentation Reference:

https://docs.aws.amazon.com/AWSSimpleQueueService/latest/SQSDeveloperGuide/welcome.html

Unlimited Throughput – Standard queues support a nearly unlimited number of transactions per second (TPS) per action

At-Least-Once Delivery – A message is delivered at least once, but occasionally more than one copy of a message is delivered.

Best-Effort Ordering – Occasionally, messages might be delivered in an order different from which they were sent.

B is the design consideration for choosing FIFO queue.

C has opposing design consideration in Best effort ordering and FIFO ordering

D has opposing design consideration in At-least-once delivery and exactly once processing.

Q9. A
AWS Documentation Reference:
https://docs.aws.amazon.com/AWSSimpleQueueService/latest/SQSDeveloperGuide/sqs-limits.html

Q10. C
AWS Documentation Reference:
https://docs.aws.amazon.com/AWSSimpleQueueService/latest/SQSDeveloperGuide/sqs-limits.html

Q11. C
AWS Documentation Reference:
https://docs.aws.amazon.com/AWSSimpleQueueService/latest/SQSDeveloperGuide/sqs-delay-queues.html
When the wait time for the ReceiveMessage API action is greater than 0, long polling is in effect. Long polling helps reduce the cost of using Amazon SQS by eliminating the number of empty responses (when there are no messages available for a ReceiveMessage request) and false empty responses (when messages are available but aren't included in a response).

Long polling offers the following benefits:
- Eliminate empty responses by allowing Amazon SQS to wait until a message is available in a queue before sending a response. Unless the connection times out, the response to the ReceiveMessage request contains at least one of the available messages, up to the maximum number of messages specified in the ReceiveMessage action.
- Eliminate false empty responses by querying all—rather than a subset of—Amazon SQS servers

Q12. B
AWS Documentation Reference:
https://docs.aws.amazon.com/AWSSimpleQueueService/latest/SQSDeveloperGuide/sqs-delay-queues.html
Delay queues are similar to visibility timeouts because both features make messages unavailable to consumers for a specific period of time. The difference between the two is that, for delay queues, a message is hidden when it is first added to queue, whereas for visibility timeouts a message is hidden only after it is consumed from the queue.

Q13. B
AWS Documentation Reference:
https://docs.aws.amazon.com/AWSSimpleQueueService/latest/SQSDeveloperGuide/welcome.html
High Throughput – By default, FIFO queues support up to 3,000 messages per second with batching. To request a limit increase, file a support request. FIFO queues support up to 300

messages per second, per action (SendMessage, ReceiveMessage, or DeleteMessage) without batching.

Exactly-Once Processing – A message is delivered once and remains available until a consumer processes and deletes it. Duplicates aren't introduced into the queue.

First-In-First-Out Delivery – The order in which messages are sent and received is strictly preserved.

A is the design consideration for choosing standard queue.

C has opposing design consideration in Best effort ordering and FIFO ordering

D has opposing design consideration in At-least-once delivery and exactly once processing.

## Q14. A, D
AWS Documentation Reference:
https://docs.aws.amazon.com/AWSSimpleQueueService/latest/SQSDeveloperGuide/standard-queues.html

Amazon SQS stores copies of your messages on multiple servers for redundancy and high availability. On rare occasions, one of the servers that stores a copy of a message might be unavailable when you receive or delete a message.

If this occurs, the copy of the message isn't deleted on that unavailable server, and you might get that message copy again when you receive messages.

A standard queue makes a best effort to preserve the order of messages, but more than one copy of a message might be delivered out of order. If your system requires that order be preserved, AWS recommend using a FIFO (First-In-First-Out) queue or adding sequencing information in each message so you can reorder the messages when they're received.

## Q15. A, D
AWS Documentation Reference:
https://docs.aws.amazon.com/AWSSimpleQueueService/latest/SQSDeveloperGuide/sqs-limits.html

The minimum is 60 seconds (1 minute). The maximum is 1,209,600 seconds (14 days).

## Q16. C
AWS Documentation Reference:
https://docs.aws.amazon.com/AWSSimpleQueueService/latest/SQSDeveloperGuide/sqs-limits.html

The default visibility timeout for a message is 30 seconds.

## Q17. A, D
AWS Documentation Reference:
https://docs.aws.amazon.com/AWSSimpleQueueService/latest/SQSDeveloperGuide/sqs-limits.html

The minimum is 0 seconds. The maximum is 12 hours.

Q18. A, B
AWS Documentation Reference:
https://docs.aws.amazon.com/sns/latest/dg/welcome.html
C, D is incorrect as S3 and DynamoDB are not supported subscribers.
Q19. B
AWS Documentation Reference:
https://docs.aws.amazon.com/sns/latest/dg/sns-common-scenarios.html
The "fanout" scenario is when an Amazon SNS message is sent to a topic and then replicated and pushed to multiple Amazon SQS queues, HTTP endpoints, or email addresses. This allows for parallel asynchronous processing.

Q20. B, D, E
AWS Documentation Reference:
https://docs.aws.amazon.com/AWSSimpleQueueService/latest/SQSDeveloperGuide/FIFO-queues.html#FIFO-queues-exactly-once-processing

https://aws.amazon.com/es/blogs/aws/new-for-amazon-simple-queue-service-fifo-queues-with-exactly-once-delivery-deduplication/

SQS FIFO queue provides FIFO (First-In-First-Out) delivery and exactly-once processing:
- The order in which messages are sent and received is strictly preserved and a message is delivered once and remains available until a consumer processes and deletes it.
- Duplicates aren't introduced into the queue.

Unlike standard queues, FIFO queues don't introduce duplicate messages. FIFO queues help you avoid sending duplicates to a queue. If you retry the SendMessage action within the 5-minute deduplication interval, Amazon SQS doesn't introduce any duplicates into the queue.

To configure deduplication, you must do one of the following:
- Enable content-based deduplication. This instructs Amazon SQS to use a SHA-256 hash to generate the message deduplication ID using the body of the message—but not the attributes of the message.
- Explicitly provide the message deduplication ID (or view the sequence number) for the message.

Q21. C
AWS Documentation Reference:
https://docs.aws.amazon.com/AWSSimpleQueueService/latest/SQSDeveloperGuide/sqs-dead-letter-queues.html
Amazon SQS supports dead-letter queues, which other queues (source queues) can target for messages that can't be processed (consumed) successfully. Dead-letter queues are useful for

debugging your application or messaging system because they let you isolate problematic messages to determine why their processing doesn't succeed.

When you designate a queue to be a source queue, a dead-letter queue is not created automatically. You must first create a normal standard or FIFO queue before designating it a dead-letter queue.

Setting up a dead-letter queue allows you to do the following:

- Configure an alarm for any messages delivered to a dead-letter queue.

- Examine logs for exceptions that might have caused messages to be delivered to a dead-letter queue.

- Analyze the contents of messages delivered to a dead-letter queue to diagnose software or the producer's or consumer's hardware issues.

- Determine whether you have given your consumer sufficient time to process messages.

## Q22. D

Every user request results in a message being queued into the Amazon SQS "Request" queue. At the same time, the application stores the photos in Amazon S3. The message in the queue contains (among other things) the photo processing operation to be performed and a pointer to the location of the photos in Amazon S3. The Photo Processing Lambda reads messages from the queue, processes the request, and on completion, posts a status message to the "Response" queue.

## Q23. B

AWS Documentation Reference:
https://docs.amazonaws.cn/en_us/AWSSimpleQueueService/latest/SQSDeveloperGuide/sqs-visibility-timeout.html

Visibility timeout is a period of time during which Amazon SQS prevents other consumers from receiving and processing the message.

A is not correct. Increase visibility time out will not help as consumer program is not executing the downstream functionality and throwing exceptions.

D is not correct because FIFO queue has features which can be leveraged to ensure that duplicate messages are not there in the queue.

C is not correct as it is mentioned that consumer program is not executing the downstream functionality i.e. message is not getting process fully and throwing exception.

B is correct. Because message processing program is failing, message is not getting deleted and reappearing in the queue after visibility time out duration.

When a consumer receives and processes a message from a queue, the message remains in the queue. Amazon SQS doesn't automatically delete the message. The consumer must delete the message from the queue after receiving and processing it.

Q24. B

Q25 A, B, E, F
AWS Documentation Reference:
https://aws.amazon.com/message-queue/benefits/
Better Performance: Message queues enable asynchronous communication, which means that the endpoints that are producing and consuming messages interact with the queue, not each other. Producers can add requests to the queue without waiting for them to be processed. Consumers process messages only when they are available. No component in the system is ever stalled waiting for another, optimizing data flow.

Increased Reliability and Resiliency: Queues make your data persistent, and reduce the errors that happen when different parts of your system go offline. By separating different components with message queues, you create more fault tolerance. If one part of the system is ever unreachable, the other can still continue to interact with the queue. The queue itself can also be mirrored for even more availability.

Queues act as buffer for outstanding requests. Producer sends messages to the queue and consumers can scales up/down based on the message volume processing the messages asynchronously. Even if consumer is down or slow it does not affect the user experience.

Granular Scalability: Message queues make it possible to scale precisely where you need to. When workloads peak, multiple instances of your application can all add requests to the queue without risk of collision. As your queues get longer with these incoming requests, you can distribute the workload across a fleet of consumers. Producers, consumers and the queue itself can all grow and shrink on demand.

Simplified Decoupling: Message queues remove dependencies between components and significantly simplify the coding of decoupled applications. Software components aren't weighed down with communications code and can instead be designed to perform a discrete business function.
Message queues are an elegantly simple way to decouple distributed systems, whether you're using monolithic applications, microservices or serverless architectures.

Q26. C
AWS Documentation Reference:
https://docs.aws.amazon.com/AWSSimpleQueueService/latest/SQSDeveloperGuide/sqs-limits.html
By default messages in SQS are retained for only 4 days. After that SQS will automatically delete the messages. Since the EC2 application runs only every 7 days, messages which are

more than 4 days in the queue are not getting processed. To rectify this you can increase the maximum retention period to 7 days.

Q27. B, C
AWS Step Functions is a fully managed service that makes it easy to coordinate the components of distributed applications and microservices using visual workflows.
The Amazon Simple Workflow Service (Amazon SWF) makes it easy to build applications that coordinate work across distributed components.

Q28.C
AWS Documentation Reference:
https://docs.amazonaws.cn/en_us/AWSSimpleQueueService/latest/SQSDeveloperGuide/sqs-visibility-timeout.html
When a consumer receives and processes a message from a queue, the message remains in the queue. Amazon SQS doesn't automatically delete the message. Thus, the consumer must delete the message from the queue after receiving and processing it.

Q29. C
AWS Documentation Reference:
https://docs.aws.amazon.com/AWSSimpleQueueService/latest/SQSDeveloperGuide/working-with-messages.html
Processing Messages in a Timely Manner
A is incorrect. Low visibility time out can lead to duplicate message processing. If your application requires 10 seconds to process a message but you set the visibility timeout to only 2 seconds, a duplicate message is received by another consumer while the original consumer is still working on the message. In the given scenario this doesn't seems to be the case. If the processing time taken by consumer lambda program was more than visibility time out there would have been much more frequent case of duplication. As given in the question there has been only 'few' instances of duplicate processing.

B is incorrect. Though FIFO queue has features which can be leveraged to handle duplicate message scenario it will lead to lower throughput than provided by Standard Queue. It is mentioned in the question that current throughput cannot be reduced.

D is incorrect because delay queue doesn't have an effect on duplicate processing of messages.

https://docs.aws.amazon.com/AWSSimpleQueueService/latest/SQSDeveloperGuide/standard-queues.html

C is correct. In case of Standard queue consumer program may get duplicate message. It is the responsibility of consumer program to be idempotent (they should not be affected adversely when processing the same message more than once). Producer program will populate the message attribute with unique value. Consumer lambda program will use that message attribute value to keep track of them in a DynamoDB Table, establishing which are in progress, and which are complete. When a consumer lambda program receives a message it will check if the message attribute value exists in the table. If it does not exist, it will processes it. If it does exist, it will have logic to determine whether the message is a duplicate or it's a retry caused by previous processing failure.

## Q30. A, B, C
AWS Documentation Reference:
https://aws.amazon.com/message-queue/benefits/
Better Performance
Message queues enable asynchronous communication, which means that the endpoints that are producing and consuming messages interact with the queue, not each other. Producers can add requests to the queue without waiting for them to be processed. Consumers process messages only when they are available. No component in the system is ever stalled waiting for another, optimizing data flow.

Simplified Decoupling
Message queues remove dependencies between components and significantly simplify the coding of decoupled applications. Message queues are an elegantly simple way to decouple distributed systems, whether you're using monolithic applications, microservices or serverless architectures.

Increased Reliability
Queues make your data persistent, and reduce the errors that happen when different parts of your system go offline. By separating different components with message queues, you create more fault tolerance. If one part of the system is ever unreachable, the other can still continue to interact with the queue. The queue itself can also be mirrored for even more availability.

## Q31 C, D
AWS Documentation Reference:
https://docs.aws.amazon.com/autoscaling/ec2/userguide/as-using-sqs-queue.html
There are three main parts to this configuration:

- An Auto Scaling group to manage EC2 instances for the purposes of processing messages from an SQS queue.
- A custom metric to send to Amazon CloudWatch that measures the number of messages in the queue per EC2 instance in the Auto Scaling group.
- A target tracking policy that configures your Auto Scaling group to scale based on the custom metric and a set target value. CloudWatch alarms invoke the scaling policy.

The following diagram illustrates the architecture of this configuration.

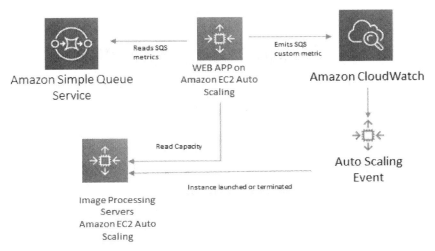

Option A and B are incorrect as the number of messages in your Amazon SQS queue does not solely define the number of instances needed. In fact, the number of instances in the fleet can be driven by multiple factors, including how long it takes to process a message and the acceptable amount of latency (queue delay).

The solution is to use a backlog per instance metric with the target value being the acceptable backlog per instance to maintain. You can calculate these numbers as follows:

Backlog per instance: To determine your backlog per instance, start with the Amazon SQS metric ApproximateNumberOfMessages to determine the length of the SQS queue (number of messages available for retrieval from the queue). Divide that number by the fleet's running capacity, which for an Auto Scaling group is the number of instances in the InService state, to get the backlog per instance.

Acceptable backlog per instance: To determine your target value, first calculate what your application can accept in terms of latency. Then, take the acceptable latency value and divide it by the average time that an EC2 instance takes to process a message.

Q32. A, B

Q33. B
AWS Documentation Reference:
https://aws.amazon.com/blogs/compute/implementing-serverless-video-subtitles/
Using Serverless managed services such as AWS Lambda and AWS Step Functions will be most appropriate for this PoC. A custom code base on Amazon EC2 would take too long to code and will be excessive computation for what is needed; a container with the code base on Amazon Elastic Container Service would be better, but still will be overkill from a compute

perspective. Step Functions would take care of coordinating the workflow of the application and the different Lambda functions. Set up an Amazon DynamoDB table to store the state of each file for further processing on the front end.

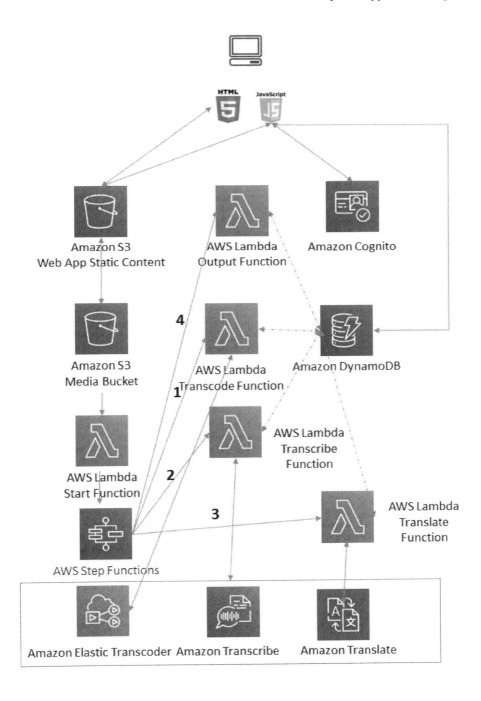

Backend

The solution consists of a Step Functions state machine that executes the following sequence triggered by an Amazon S3 event notification:

1. Transcode the file with Elastic Transcoder using its API. Wait two minutes, which is enough time for transcoding.
2. Submit the file to Amazon Transcribe and enter the following loop:
   1. Wait for 30 seconds.
   2. Check the API to know if transcription is over. If it is, go to step 4; otherwise, go back to step 3.1.
3. Process the transcript to become a VTT file, which goes to Amazon Translate several times to get a version of the file in another language.
4. Clean and wrap up.

Frontend

The front end's setup is easy: an Amazon S3 bucket with the static website feature on and a combination of HTML, AWS SDK for JavaScript in the Browser, and a JavaScript framework to handle calls to the AWS Platform. The sequence has the following steps:

1. Load HTML, CSS, and JavaScript from a bucket in Amazon S3.
2. Specific JavaScript for this project does the following:
   a. Sets up the AWS SDK
   b. Connects to Amazon Cognito against a predefined identity pool set up for anonymous users
   c. Loads a custom IAM role that gives access to an Amazon S3 bucket
3. The user uploads an MP4 file to the bucket, and the backend process starts.
4. A JavaScript loop checks the DynamoDB table where the state of the process is stored and do the following:
   a. Add a description of the video process and show the state of the process.
   b. Update the progress bar in the description block to inform the user what the process is doing
   c. Update the video links when the process is over.
5. When the process completes, the user can choose the list item to get an HTML5 video player with the VTT files loaded.

Q34. A, B, D

AWS Documentation Reference:

https://docs.aws.amazon.com/amazonswf/latest/developerguide/swf-dev-actors.html

In the course of its operations, Amazon SWF interacts with a number of different types of programmatic actors. Actors can be workflow starters, deciders, or activity workers. These actors communicate with Amazon SWF through its API. You can develop these actors in any programming language.

Q35. C
AWS Documentation Reference:
https://aws.amazon.com/blogs/compute/building-loosely-coupled-scalable-c-applications-with-amazon-sqs-and-amazon-sns/

In this example, the application is responsible for handling and persisting the order data, as well as dealing with increases in traffic for popular items.

One potential point of vulnerability in the order processing workflow is in saving the order in the database. The business expects that every order has been persisted into the database. However, any potential deadlock, race condition, or network issue could cause the persistence of the order to fail. Then, the order is lost with no recourse to restore the order.

With good logging capability, you may be able to identify when an error occurred and which customer order failed. This wouldn't allow you to "restore" the transaction, and by that stage, your customer is no longer your customer.

As illustrated in the following diagram, introducing an SQS queue helps improve your ordering application. Using the queue isolates the processing logic into its own component and runs it in a separate process from the web application. This in turn allows the system to be more resilient to spikes in traffic, while allowing work to be performed only as fast as necessary in order to manage costs.

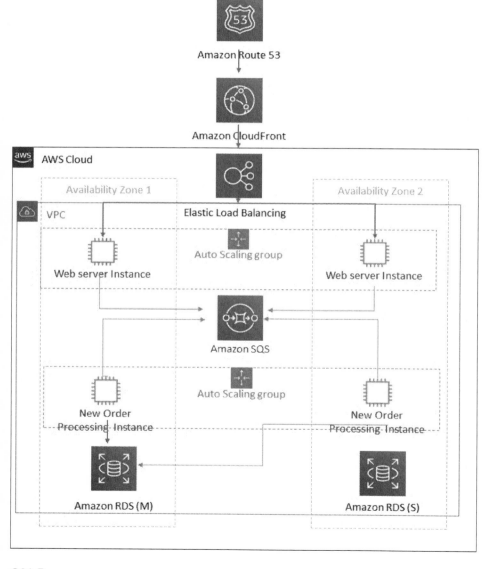

Q36. B

AWS Documentation Reference:

https://docs.aws.amazon.com/apigateway/latest/developerguide/welcome.html

Amazon API Gateway is an AWS service for creating, publishing, maintaining, monitoring, and securing REST and WebSocket APIs at any scale. API developers can create APIs that access AWS or other web services as well as data stored in the AWS Cloud. As an API Gateway API developer, you can create APIs for use in your own client applications (apps). Or you can make your APIs available to third-party app developers.

## Q37. D
AWS Documentation Reference:

https://docs.aws.amazon.com/amazonswf/latest/developerguide/swf-dev-domains.html

Domains provide a way of scoping Amazon SWF resources within your AWS account. All the components of a workflow, such as the workflow type and activity types, must be specified to be in a domain. It is possible to have more than one workflow in a domain; however, workflows in different domains can't interact with each other.

## Q38. B, C, D
AWS Documentation Reference:

https://docs.aws.amazon.com/amazonswf/latest/developerguide/swf-dev-tasks.html

There are three types of tasks in Amazon SWF:

Activity task – An Activity task tells an activity worker to perform its function, such as to check inventory or charge a credit card. The activity task contains all the information that the activity worker needs to perform its function.

Lambda task – A Lambda task is similar to an Activity task, but executes a Lambda function instead of a traditional Amazon SWF activity.

Decision task – A Decision task tells a decider that the state of the workflow execution has changed so that the decider can determine the next activity that needs to be performed. The decision task contains the current workflow history.

## Q39. A
AWS Documentation Reference:

https://docs.aws.amazon.com/amazonswf/latest/developerguide/swf-dev-adv-signals.html

For cases in which a workflow should be canceled—for example, the order itself was canceled by the customer—the RequestCancelWorkflowExecution action should be used rather than sending a signal to the workflow.

https://docs.aws.amazon.com/cli/latest/reference/swf/request-cancel-workflow-execution.html

RequestCancelWorkflowExecution action records a WorkflowExecutionCancelRequested event in the currently running workflow execution identified by the given domain, workflowId, and runId. This logically requests the cancellation of the workflow execution as a whole. It is up to the decider to take appropriate actions when it receives an execution history with this event.

## Q40. D
AWS Documentation Reference:
https://aws.amazon.com/appsync/faqs/
AWS AppSync is a service that enables developers to manage and synchronize mobile app data in real time across devices and users, but still allows the data to be accessed and altered when the mobile device is in an offline state.

The service further allows developers to optimize the user experience by selecting which data is automatically synchronized to each user's device when changes are made, minimizing storage and bandwidth requirements, with a query language called GraphQL.

Using these capabilities, developers can, in minutes, build real time collaborative experiences spanning browsers, mobile apps, Alexa skills, and IoT devices that remain usable when network connectivity is lost.

## Q41. B
B is correct. If you use only one queue there will be scenario where premium messages are far behind the free messages. Create two queues, one for premium members and one for free members editing task. EC2 processing program should poll premium member's queue first and only if message request is empty then it should poll the free member's queue.

A is incorrect. Message timers let you specify an initial invisibility period for a message added to a queue. For example, if you send a message with a 45-second timer, the message isn't visible to consumers for its first 45 seconds in the queue. But this will not have an effect on priority for processing.

C is incorrect as SQS doesn't provide a feature to set priority in individual messages.

D is incorrect as you cannot create a delay queue only for a subset of messages. Moreover delay queue will not have an effect on priority of message processing.

## Q42. A, B
AWS Documentation Reference:
https://docs.aws.amazon.com/step-functions/latest/dg/concepts-standard-vs-express.html
Standard Workflows are ideal for long-running, durable, and auditable workflows. They can run for up to a year and you can retrieve the full execution history using the Step Functions API, up to 90 days after your execution completes. Standard Workflows employ an at-most-once model, where your tasks and states are never executed more than once unless you have

specified Retry behavior in ASL. This makes them suited to orchestrating non-idempotent actions, such as starting an Amazon EMR cluster or processing payments. Standard Workflows executions are billed according to the number of state transitions processed.

Express Workflows are ideal for high-volume, event-processing workloads such as IoT data ingestion, streaming data processing and transformation, and mobile application backend. They can run for up to five minutes. Execution history is optionally available in Amazon CloudWatch Logs. Express Workflows employ an at-least-once model, where there is a possibility that an execution might be run more than once. This makes them ideal for orchestrating idempotent actions such as transforming input data and storing via PUT in Amazon DynamoDB. Express Workflow executions are billed by the number of executions, the duration of execution, and the memory consumed.

Q43. B, C, D
AWS Documentation Reference:
https://docs.aws.amazon.com/step-functions/latest/dg/concepts-states.html
States are elements in your state machine. A state is referred to by its name, which can be any string, but which must be unique within the scope of the entire state machine.
States can perform a variety of functions in your state machine:

- Do some work in your state machine (a Task state)
- Make a choice between branches of execution (a Choice state)
- Stop an execution with a failure or success (a Fail or Succeed state)
- Simply pass its input to its output or inject some fixed data (a Pass state)
- Provide a delay for a certain amount of time or until a specified time/date (a Wait state)
- Begin parallel branches of execution (a Parallel state)
- Dynamically iterate steps (a Map state)

Q44. B
AWS Documentation Reference:
https://docs.aws.amazon.com/step-functions/latest/dg/concepts-amazon-states-language.html
The Amazon States Language is a JSON-based, structured language used to define your state machine, a collection of states, that can do work (Task states), determine which states to transition to next (Choice states), stop an execution with an error (Fail states), and so on.

Q45. B
AWS Documentation Reference:
https://aws.amazon.com/ecs/features/
B is appropriate use case for Amazon ECS.
https://aws.amazon.com/step-functions/faqs/
What are some common AWS Step Functions use cases?

AWS Step Functions helps with any computational problem or business process that can be subdivided into a series of steps. It's also useful for creating end-to-end workflows to manage jobs with interdependencies. Common use cases include:

- Data processing: consolidate data from multiple databases into unified reports, refine and reduce large data sets into useful formats, or coordinate multi-step analytics and machine learning workflows

- DevOps and IT automation: build tools for continuous integration and continuous deployment, or create event-driven applications that automatically respond to changes in infrastructure

- E-commerce: automate mission-critical business processes, such as order fulfillment and inventory tracking

- Web applications: implement robust user registration processes and sign-on authentication

## Q46. C
AWS Documentation Reference:
https://aws.amazon.com/api-gateway/
https://aws.amazon.com/api-gateway/features/
With API Gateway, you can create RESTful APIs using either HTTP APIs (Preview) or REST APIs. HTTP APIs enable you to build high performance, cost effective APIs that only require API proxy functionality and are optimized for serverless workloads. REST APIs offer API proxy functionality and management features in a single solution.

## Q47. D
AWS Documentation Reference:
https://docs.aws.amazon.com/AWSSimpleQueueService/latest/SQSDeveloperGuide/sqs-visibility-timeout.html
When a consumer receives and processes a message from a queue, the message remains in the queue. To prevent other consumers from processing the message again, Amazon SQS sets a visibility timeout, a period of time during which Amazon SQS prevents other consumers from receiving and processing the message. Amazon SQS doesn't automatically delete the message. Thus, the consumer must delete the message from the queue after receiving and processing it.
In the given scenario as the processing is terminated before completion, the consumer program didn't deleted the message from the queue. Hence it will be visible again in the queue for other spot instance to receive it after the visibility time is over.

## Q48. B
AWS Documentation Reference:
https://aws.amazon.com/blogs/compute/new-express-workflows-for-aws-step-functions/
Step Functions Express Workflows type uses fast, in-memory processing for high-event-rate workloads of up to 100,000 state transitions per second, for a total workflow duration of up to 5 minutes. Express Workflows are suited to streaming data processing, IoT data ingestion,

mobile backend, and other high-throughput use-cases. Existing workflows in AWS Step Functions are now called Standard Workflows.

Q49. A
AWS Documentation Reference:
https://docs.aws.amazon.com/step-functions/latest/dg/concepts-standard-vs-express.html
Standard Workflows employ an at-most-once model, where your tasks and states are never executed more than once unless you have specified Retry behavior in ASL. This makes them suited to orchestrating non-idempotent actions, such as starting an Amazon EMR cluster or processing payments.

Q50. C, D
AWS Documentation Reference:
https://aws.amazon.com/step-functions/faqs/
*When should I use AWS Step Functions vs. Amazon Simple Workflow Service (SWF)?*
You should consider using AWS Step Functions for all your new applications, since it provides a more productive and agile approach to coordinating application components using visual workflows. If you require external signals to intervene in your processes, or you would like to launch child processes that return a result to a parent, then you should consider Amazon Simple Workflow Service (Amazon SWF). With Amazon SWF, instead of writing state machines in declarative JSON, you write a decider program to separate activity steps from decision steps. This provides you complete control over your orchestration logic, but increases the complexity of developing applications. You may write decider programs in the programming language of your choice, or you may use the Flow framework to use programming constructs that structure asynchronous interactions for you.

Q51. B, D
B is incorrect because this is a 'fan out' scenario. In a fanout scenario an Amazon SNS message is sent to a topic and then replicated and pushed to multiple Amazon SQS queues, HTTP endpoints, or email addresses.

D is incorrect because, SNS doesn't provide integration feature with Cognito for user authentication.

AWS Documentation Reference:
https://docs.aws.amazon.com/sns/latest/dg/sns-common-scenarios.html
The "fanout" scenario is when an Amazon SNS message is sent to a topic and then replicated and pushed to multiple Amazon SQS queues, HTTP endpoints, or email addresses. This allows for parallel asynchronous processing. For example, you could develop an application that sends an Amazon SNS message to a topic whenever an order is placed for a product. Then, the Amazon SQS queues that are subscribed to that topic would receive identical notifications for the new order. The Amazon EC2 server instance attached to one of the queues could handle

the processing or fulfillment of the order, while the other server instance could be attached to a data warehouse for analysis of all orders received.

Push email and text messaging are two ways to transmit messages to individuals or groups via email and/or SMS. For example, you could use Amazon SNS to push targeted news headlines to subscribers by email or SMS. Upon receiving the email or SMS text, interested readers could then choose to learn more by visiting a website or launching an application.

Mobile push notifications enable you to send messages directly to mobile apps. For example, you could use Amazon SNS for sending notifications to an app, indicating that an update is available. The notification message can include a link to download and install the update.

Q52. B
AWS Documentation Reference:
https://docs.aws.amazon.com/apigateway/latest/developerguide/api-gateway-caching.html
You can enable API caching in Amazon API Gateway to cache your endpoint's responses. With caching, you can reduce the number of calls made to your endpoint and also improve the latency of requests to your API. When you enable caching for a stage, API Gateway caches responses from your endpoint for a specified time-to-live (TTL) period, in seconds. API Gateway then responds to the request by looking up the endpoint response from the cache instead of making a request to your endpoint. The default TTL value for API caching is 300 seconds. The maximum TTL value is 3600 seconds. TTL=0 means caching is disabled.

Q53. A, C, E, F
AWS Documentation Reference:
https://docs.aws.amazon.com/sns/latest/dg/welcome.html
Amazon Simple Notification Service (Amazon SNS) is a web service that coordinates and manages the delivery or sending of messages to subscribing endpoints or clients. In Amazon SNS, there are two types of clients—publishers and subscribers—also referred to as producers and consumers. When using Amazon SNS, you (as the owner) create a topic and control access to it by defining policies that determine which publishers and subscribers can communicate with the topic. A publisher sends messages to topics that they have created or to topics they have permission to publish to. Instead of including a specific destination address in each message, a publisher sends a message to the topic. Amazon SNS matches the topic to a list of subscribers who have subscribed to that topic, and delivers the message to each of those subscribers. Each topic has a unique name that identifies the Amazon SNS endpoint for publishers to post messages and subscribers to register for notifications. Subscribers receive all messages published to the topics to which they subscribe, and all subscribers to a topic receive the same messages.

Q54. B

https://aws.amazon.com/blogs/compute/building-loosely-coupled-scalable-c-applications-with-amazon-sqs-and-amazon-sns/

In the given scenario, the application is responsible for handling and persisting the order data, as well as dealing with increases in traffic for popular items.

One potential point of vulnerability in the order processing workflow is in saving the order in the database. As stated the key business requirement is that every order has to be persisted into the database. However, any potential deadlock, race condition, or network issue could cause the persistence of the order to fail. Then, the order is lost with no recourse to restore the order.

With good logging capability, you may be able to identify when an error occurred and which customer order failed. This wouldn't allow you to "restore" the transaction, and by that stage, your customer is no longer your customer.

As illustrated in the following diagram, introducing an SQS queue helps improve your ordering application. Using the queue isolates the processing logic into its own component and runs it in a separate process from the web application. This, in turn, allows the system to be more resilient to spikes in traffic, while allowing work to be performed only as fast as necessary in order to manage costs.

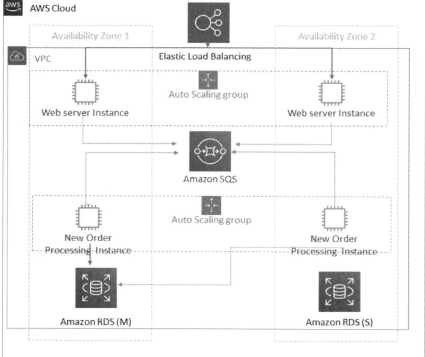

Q55.A, C
AWS Documentation Reference:
https://aws.amazon.com/sns/faqs/
Amazon Simple Queue Service (SQS) and Amazon SNS are both messaging services within AWS, which provide different benefits for developers. Amazon SNS allows applications to

send time-critical messages to multiple subscribers through a "push" mechanism, eliminating the need to periodically check or "poll" for updates.

Amazon SQS is a message queue service used by distributed applications to exchange messages through a polling model, and can be used to decouple sending and receiving components. Amazon SQS provides flexibility for distributed components of applications to send and receive messages without requiring each component to be concurrently available.

Q56.D

D is relevant use case for using Amazon Quicksight.

AWS Documentation Reference:

https://aws.amazon.com/appsync/faqs/

AWS AppSync can be used to build mobile apps that would benefit from being able to synchronize user and app data across devices, continue functioning when disconnected, and offer real-time collaboration experiences. There are applications across all verticals. Examples include:

- Gaming apps with real-time scoreboards
- News feeds and financial data
- Customer service dashboards
- Shared wallet, travel or itinerary tracking with offline usage
- Social Media with content feeds and search/discovery/messaging
- Dating apps with likes, messaging and geo/proximity awareness
- Field service apps that need to allow for querying and CRUD operations, even when disconnected
- Document collaboration
- 3D collaboration such as shared whiteboards
- AR/VR with multiple actors (doctors in surgery with observers, teachers and students)
- Multi-device (e.g., Alexa, mobile, web, IoT) and multi-modal applications (e.g., task list) that need to work offline yet reflect the same eventually consistent state
- Chat apps, including presence indicators and conversation history

Q57.D

AWS AppSync is a managed service that uses GraphQL to simplify application development by letting applications securely access, manipulate, and receive real-time updates from multiple data sources such as databases or APIs.

Q58. B, E

B and E are features of API Gateway.

AWS Documentation Reference:

https://aws.amazon.com/appsync/product-details/

Key features of AppSync are:

GraphQL: AWS AppSync uses GraphQL, a data language that enables client apps to fetch, change and subscribe to data from servers. In a GraphQL query, the client specifies how the data is to be structured when it is returned by the server. This makes it possible for the client to query only for the data it needs, in the format that it needs it in.

Real-time data access and updates: AWS AppSync lets you specify which portions of your data should be available in a real-time manner using GraphQL Subscriptions. GraphQL Subscriptions are simple statements in the application code that tell the service what data should be updated in real-time.

Offline data synchronization: The Amplify DataStore provides a queryable on-device DataStore for web, mobile and IoT developers with a local-first and familiar programming model to interact with data seamlessly whether you're online or offline.

Data querying, filtering, and search in apps: AWS AppSync gives client applications the ability to specify data requirements with GraphQL so that only the needed data is fetched, allowing for both server and client filtering.

Caching :AWS AppSync's server-side data caching capabilities reduce the need to directly access data sources by making data available in high speed in-memory managed caches, delivering data at low latency.

Q59. C
Amazon MQ is a managed message broker service for Apache ActiveMQ that makes it easy to set up and operate message brokers in the cloud.

# Answer Chapter 8 Security Identity and Compliance: AWS Identity and Access Management, AWS Artifact, AWS Certificate Manager, AWS CloudHSM, Amazon Cognito, AWS Directory Service, AWS Firewall Manager, Amazon GuardDuty, Amazon Inspector, AWS Key Management Service, Amazon Macie, AWS Security Hub, AWS Shield, AWS Single Sign-On, AWS WAF

Q1. B
AWS Documentation Reference:
https://aws.amazon.com/shield/

AWS Shield is a managed Distributed Denial of Service (DDoS) protection service that safeguards applications running on AWS. AWS Shield provides always-on detection and automatic inline mitigations that minimize application downtime and latency, so there is no need to engage AWS Support to benefit from DDoS protection. There are two tiers of AWS Shield - Standard and Advanced.

All AWS customers benefit from the automatic protections of AWS Shield Standard, at no additional charge. AWS Shield Standard defends against most common, frequently occurring network and transport layer DDoS attacks that target your web site or applications. When you use AWS Shield Standard with Amazon CloudFront and Amazon Route 53, you receive comprehensive availability protection against all known infrastructure (Layer 3 and 4) attacks.

For higher levels of protection against attacks targeting your applications running on Amazon Elastic Compute Cloud (EC2), Elastic Load Balancing (ELB), Amazon CloudFront, AWS Global Accelerator and Amazon Route 53 resources, you can subscribe to AWS Shield Advanced. In addition to the network and transport layer protections that come with Standard, AWS Shield Advanced provides additional detection and mitigation against large and sophisticated DDoS attacks, near real-time visibility into attacks, and integration with AWS WAF, a web application firewall. AWS Shield Advanced also gives you 24x7 access to the AWS DDoS Response Team (DRT) and protection against DDoS related spikes in your Amazon Elastic Compute Cloud (EC2), Elastic Load Balancing (ELB), Amazon CloudFront, AWS Global Accelerator and Amazon Route 53 charges.

Q2. A, D
AWS Documentation Reference:
https://aws.amazon.com/shield/

Q3. D
AWS Documentation Reference:
https://aws.amazon.com/waf/
AWS WAF is a web application firewall that lets you monitor the HTTP and HTTPS requests that are forwarded to an Amazon API Gateway, Amazon CloudFront or an Application Load Balancer. AWS WAF gives you control over which traffic to allow or block to your web applications by defining customizable web security rules.

Q4. A, B, C, E
AWS Documentation Reference:
https://docs.aws.amazon.com/en_pv/waf/latest/developerguide/how-aws-waf-works.html

Conditions define the basic characteristics that you want AWS WAF to watch for in web requests:

- Scripts that are likely to be malicious. Attackers embed scripts that can exploit vulnerabilities in web applications. This is known as cross-site scripting.
- IP addresses or address ranges that requests originate from.
- Country or geographical location that requests originate from.
- Length of specified parts of the request, such as the query string.
- SQL code that is likely to be malicious. Attackers try to extract data from your database by embedding malicious SQL code in a web request. This is known as SQL injection.
- Strings that appear in the request, for example, values that appear in the User-Agent header or text strings that appear in the query string. You can also use regular expressions (regex) to specify these strings.

## Q5. C
AWS Documentation Reference:
https://aws.amazon.com/guardduty/
Amazon GuardDuty is a threat detection service that continuously monitors for malicious activity and unauthorized behavior to protect your AWS accounts and workloads. The service uses machine learning, anomaly detection, and integrated threat intelligence to identify and prioritize potential threats. GuardDuty analyzes tens of billions of events across multiple AWS data sources, such as AWS CloudTrail, Amazon VPC Flow Logs, and DNS logs.

## Q6. B, C
AWS Documentation Reference:
https://docs.aws.amazon.com/waf/latest/developerguide/how-aws-waf-works.html
Rate-based rules are like regular rules with an added rate limit. A rate-based rule counts the requests that arrive from IP addresses that satisfy the rule's conditions. If the requests from an IP address exceed the rate limit in a five-minute period, the rule can trigger an action. This feature allows you to specify the number of web requests that are allowed by a client IP in a trailing, continuously updated, 5 minute period. If an IP address breaches the configured limit, new requests will be blocked until the request rate falls below the configured threshold.

## Q7. A, C, D
B is wrong because third-party auditors regularly test and verify the effectiveness of AWS security as part of the AWS compliance programs.
AWS Documentation Reference:
https://aws.amazon.com/compliance/shared-responsibility-model/

## Q8. A, C, D, F, G, H
AWS Documentation Reference: Policy Types
https://docs.aws.amazon.com/IAM/latest/UserGuide/access_policies.html

The following policy types, listed in order of frequency, are available for use in AWS.

Identity-based policies – Attach managed and inline policies to IAM identities (users, groups to which users belong, or roles). Identity-based policies grant permissions to an identity.

Resource-based policies – Attach inline policies to resources. The most common examples of resource-based policies are Amazon S3 bucket policies and IAM role trust policies. Resource-based policies grant permissions to a principal entity that is specified in the policy. Principals can be in the same account as the resource or in other accounts.

Permissions boundaries – Use a managed policy as the permissions boundary for an IAM entity (user or role). That policy defines the maximum permissions that the identity-based policies can grant to an entity, but does not grant permissions. Permissions boundaries do not define the maximum permissions that a resource-based policy can grant to an entity.

Organizations SCPs – Use an AWS Organizations service control policy (SCP) to define the maximum permissions for account members of an organization or organizational unit (OU). SCPs limit permissions that identity-based policies or resource-based policies grant to entities (users or roles) within the account, but do not grant permissions.

Access control lists (ACLs) – Use ACLs to control which principals in other accounts can access the resource to which the ACL is attached. ACLs are similar to resource-based policies, although they are the only policy type that does not use the JSON policy document structure. ACLs are cross-account permissions policies that grant permissions to the specified principal entity. ACLs cannot grant permissions to entities within the same account.

Session policies – Pass advanced session policies when you use the AWS CLI or AWS API to assume a role or a federated user. Session policies limit the permissions that the role or user's identity-based policies grant to the session. Session policies limit permissions for a created session, but do not grant permissions.

Q9.C
AWS Documentation Reference:
https://docs.aws.amazon.com/waf/latest/developerguide/how-aws-waf-works.html
Create a rate-based rule that includes the following conditions:
- The requests come from 192.0.2.44.
- They contain the value BadBot in the User-Agent header.

In this rate-based rule, you also define a rate limit. In this example you create a rate limit of 1,000. Requests that meet both of the preceding conditions and exceed 1,000 requests per five minutes trigger the rule's action (block or count), which is defined in the web ACL.

Q10. A

AWS Documentation Reference:

https://docs.aws.amazon.com/waf/latest/developerguide/how-aws-waf-works.html

By adding this rate-based rule to a web ACL, you could limit requests to your login page without affecting the rest of your site.

- The Part of the request to filter on is URI.
- The Match Type is Starts with.
- A Value to match is login.

Further, you specify a RateLimit of 1,000.

## Q11. C

AWS Documentation Reference:

https://docs.aws.amazon.com/waf/latest/developerguide/fms-chapter.html

AWS Firewall Manager simplifies your AWS WAF, AWS Shield Advanced, and Amazon VPC security groups administration and maintenance tasks across multiple accounts and resources. With Firewall Manager, you set up your AWS WAF firewall rules, Shield Advanced protections, and Amazon VPC security groups just once. The service automatically applies the rules and protections across your accounts and resources, even as you add new resources.

## Q12. D

AWS Documentation Reference:

https://docs.aws.amazon.com/directory-service/index.html#lang/en_us

## Q13. B

AWS Documentation Reference:

https://docs.aws.amazon.com/directoryservice/latest/admin-guide/what_is.html#choosing_an_option

AD Connector is a proxy service that provides an easy way to connect compatible AWS applications, such as Amazon WorkSpaces, Amazon QuickSight, and Amazon EC2 for Windows Server instances, to your existing on-premises Microsoft Active Directory. With AD Connector, you can simply add one service account to your Active Directory. AD Connector also eliminates the need of directory synchronization or the cost and complexity of hosting a federation infrastructure.

When you add users to AWS applications such as Amazon QuickSight, AD Connector reads your existing Active Directory to create lists of users and groups to select from. When users log in to the AWS applications, AD Connector forwards sign-in requests to your on-premises Active Directory domain controllers for authentication. AD Connector works with many AWS applications and services including Amazon WorkSpaces, Amazon WorkDocs, Amazon QuickSight, Amazon Chime, Amazon Connect, and Amazon WorkMail. You can also join your EC2 Windows instances to your on-premises Active Directory domain through AD Connector using seamless domain join. AD Connector also allows your users to access the AWS Management Console and manage AWS resources by logging in with their existing Active Directory credentials. With AD Connector, you continue to manage your Active

Directory as you do now. For example, you add new users and groups and update passwords using standard Active Directory administration tools in your on-premises Active Directory.

## Q14. A

AWS Documentation Reference:

https://docs.aws.amazon.com/directoryservice/latest/admin-guide/what_is.html#choosing_an_option

AWS Directory Service for Microsoft Active Directory is a feature-rich managed Microsoft Active Directory hosted on the AWS cloud. AWS Managed Microsoft AD is your best choice if you have more than 5,000 users and need a trust relationship set up between an AWS hosted directory and your on-premises directories.

All compatible applications work with user credentials that you store in AWS Managed Microsoft AD, or you can connect to your existing AD infrastructure with a trust and use credentials from an Active Directory running on-premises or on EC2 Windows. If you join EC2 instances to your AWS Managed Microsoft AD, your users can access Windows workloads in the AWS Cloud with the same Windows single sign-on (SSO) experience as when they access workloads in your on-premises network.

## Q15. D

AWS Documentation Reference:

https://docs.aws.amazon.com/directoryservice/latest/admin-guide/what_is.html#choosing_an_option

Simple AD is a Microsoft Active Directory–compatible directory from AWS Directory Service that is powered by Samba 4. Simple AD supports basic Active Directory features such as user accounts, group memberships, joining a Linux domain or Windows based EC2 instances. Simple AD is a standalone directory in the cloud, where you create and manage user identities and manage access to applications. You can use many familiar Active Directory–aware applications and tools that require basic Active Directory features. Simple AD is compatible with the following AWS applications: Amazon WorkSpaces, Amazon WorkDocs, Amazon QuickSight, and Amazon WorkMail. You can also sign in to the AWS Management Console with Simple AD user accounts and to manage AWS resources.

Simple AD does not support multi-factor authentication (MFA), trust relationships, DNS dynamic update, schema extensions, communication over LDAPS, PowerShell AD cmdlets, or FSMO role transfer.

You can use Simple AD as a standalone directory in the cloud to support Windows workloads that need basic AD features, compatible AWS applications, or to support Linux workloads that need LDAP service.

## Q16. A, C, D

AWS Documentation Reference:

https://docs.aws.amazon.com/IAM/latest/UserGuide/id_roles_providers_oidc.html

With web identity federation, you don't need to create custom sign-in code or manage your own user identities. Instead, users of your app can sign in using a well-known external identity provider (IdP), such as Login with Amazon, Facebook, Google, or any other OpenID Connect (OIDC)-compatible IdP. They can receive an authentication token, and then exchange that token for temporary security credentials in AWS that map to an IAM role with permissions to use the resources in your AWS account.

https://docs.aws.amazon.com/IAM/latest/UserGuide/id_roles_providers_oidc_cognito.html

For most scenarios, AWS recommends that you use Amazon Cognito because it acts as an identity broker and does much of the federation work for you.

https://docs.aws.amazon.com/IAM/latest/UserGuide/id_roles_providers_oidc_manual.html

If you don't use Amazon Cognito, then you must write code that interacts with a web IdP, such as Facebook, and then calls the AssumeRoleWithWebIdentity API to trade the authentication token you get from those IdPs for AWS temporary security credentials. If you have already used this approach for existing apps, you can continue to use it.

Q17. A, B

Q18. B, D
AWS Documentation Reference:
https://docs.aws.amazon.com/IAM/latest/UserGuide/introduction_access-management.html
Identity-based policies can be categorized into :

1.  Managed policies – Standalone identity-based policies that you can attach to multiple users, groups, and roles in your AWS account. You can use two types of managed policies

    a.  AWS managed policies – Managed policies that are created and managed by AWS.
    b.  Customer managed policies – Managed policies that you create and manage in your AWS account
    (Therefore answer is B and D)

2.  Inline policies – Policies that you create and manage and that are embedded directly into a single user, group, or role.

Q19. A, B
AWS Documentation Reference:
https://docs.aws.amazon.com/IAM/latest/UserGuide/intro-structure.html

Q20. A, C, D, E
AWS Documentation Reference:

https://docs.aws.amazon.com/IAM/latest/UserGuide/best-practices.html

Use Roles for Applications That Run on Amazon EC2 Instances: Applications that run on an Amazon EC2 instance need credentials in order to access other AWS services. To provide credentials to the application in a secure way, use IAM roles.
When you launch an EC2 instance, you can specify a role for the instance as a launch parameter. Applications that run on the EC2 instance can use the role's credentials when they access AWS resources. The role's permissions determine what the application is allowed to do. A role is an entity that has its own set of permissions, but that isn't a user or group. Roles also don't have their own permanent set of credentials the way IAM users do. In the case of Amazon EC2, IAM dynamically provides temporary credentials to the EC2 instance, and these credentials are automatically rotated for you.

Use Roles to Delegate Permissions: Don't share security credentials between accounts to allow users from another AWS account to access resources in your AWS account. Instead, use IAM roles. You can define a role that specifies what permissions the IAM users in the other account are allowed. You can also designate which AWS accounts have the IAM users that are allowed to assume the role.

Enable MFA for Privileged Users: For extra security, enable multi-factor authentication (MFA) for privileged IAM users (users who are allowed access to sensitive resources or API operations).

Do Not Share Access Keys: Access keys provide programmatic access to AWS. Do not embed access keys within unencrypted code or share these security credentials between users in your AWS account. For applications that need access to AWS, configure the program to retrieve temporary security credentials using an IAM role. To allow your users individual programmatic access, create an IAM user with personal access keys.

Q21. B, C, D

AWS Documentation Reference:
https://docs.aws.amazon.com/IAM/latest/UserGuide/id.html

A, E are scenarios when you should create a role.

B: It's possible to work with AWS using the root user credentials for your AWS account, but it is not recommended. Instead, it is strongly recommend that you create an IAM user for yourself and use the credentials for that user when you work with AWS

C: Create IAM users for the individuals who need access to your AWS resources, assign appropriate permissions to each user, and give each user his or her own credentials.

D: The CLI needs credentials that it can use to make calls to AWS. Create an IAM user and give that user permissions to run the CLI commands you need. Then configure the CLI on your computer to use the access key credentials associated with that IAM user.

Q22. A
True. An IAM user with administrator permissions is not the same thing as the AWS account root user.

Q23. A, B, C, D
E is wrong as PuTTY is an SSH and not telnet client.

AWS Documentation Reference:
https://docs.aws.amazon.com/IAM/latest/UserGuide/id_users.html
Access keys: A combination of an access key ID and a secret access key. You can assign two to a user at a time. These can be used to make programmatic calls to AWS. For example, you might use access keys when using the API for code or at a command prompt when using the AWS CLI or the AWS PowerShell tools.

Console password: A password that the user can type to sign in to interactive sessions such as the AWS Management Console.

SSH keys for use with CodeCommit: An SSH public key in the OpenSSH format that can be used to authenticate with CodeCommit.

Server certificates: SSL/TLS certificates that you can use to authenticate with some AWS services.

Q24. A, B, E, F
AWS Documentation Reference:
https://docs.aws.amazon.com/IAM/latest/UserGuide/id_users.html

Q25. B, D

Q26. D
AWS Documentation Reference:
https://docs.aws.amazon.com/IAM/latest/UserGuide/id_users_change-permissions.html
Add user to group – Make the user a member of a group. The policies from the group are attached to the user.
Copy permissions from existing user – Copy all group memberships, attached managed policies, inline policies, and any existing permissions boundaries from the source user.
Attach policies directly to user – Attach a managed policy directly to the user

Q27. A, B, D

Q28. A

A group is not truly an "identity" in IAM because it cannot be identified as a Principal in a permission policy

Q29. B

An IAM role is an IAM identity that you can create in your account that has specific permissions

Q30. E

Q31. A, C, D

AWS Documentation Reference:

https://docs.aws.amazon.com/IAM/latest/UserGuide/id_roles_terms-and-concepts.html

Q32. A, B, D

AWS Documentation Reference:

https://docs.aws.amazon.com/IAM/latest/UserGuide/id_roles_common-scenarios_aws-accounts.html

C is incorrect as creating separate identities and passwords for users who work in both accounts will lead to managing credentials for multiple accounts identity management difficult.

After the steps A, B, D are done:

The user requests switches to the role:

AWS console: The user chooses the account name on the navigation bar and chooses Switch Role. The user specifies the account ID (or alias) and role name. Alternatively, the user can click on a link sent in email by the administrator. The link takes the user to the Switch Role page with the details already filled in.

AWS API/AWS CLI: A user in the Developers group of the development account calls the AssumeRole function to obtain credentials for the role in production account. The user specifies the ARN of the role as part of the call.

Q33.B, D

Option B will be defense against the attack on DNS or Cloudfront.

Option D will be defense against attack on ALB endpoint. This will disable direct access to the endpoint of ALB.

AWS Documentation Reference:

https://aws.amazon.com/answers/networking/aws-ddos-attack-mitigation/

AWS Shield is a managed DDoS protection service that is available in two tiers: Standard and Advanced. AWS Shield Standard applies always-on detection and inline mitigation techniques, such as deterministic packet filtering and priority-based traffic shaping, to minimize application downtime and latency. AWS Shield Standard is included automatically and transparently to your Elastic Load Balancing load balancers, Amazon CloudFront distributions, and Amazon Route 53 resources at no additional cost. When you use these services that include AWS Shield Standard, you receive comprehensive availability protection against all known infrastructure layer attacks. Customers who have the technical expertise to manage their own monitoring and mitigation of application layer attacks can use AWS Shield together with AWS WAF rules to create a comprehensive DDoS attack mitigation strategy.

AWS WAF is a web application firewall that helps protect web applications from common web exploits that could affect application availability, compromise security, or consume excessive resources. You can use AWS WAF to define customizable web security rules that control which traffic accesses your web applications. If you use AWS Shield Advanced, you can use AWS WAF at no extra cost for those protected resources and can engage the DRT to create WAF rules.

AWS WAF rules use conditions to target specific requests and trigger an action, allowing you to identify and block common DDoS request patterns and effectively mitigate a DDoS attack. These include size constraint conditions to block a web request based on the length of its query string or request body, and geographic match conditions to implement geo restriction (also known as geoblocking) on requests that originate from specific countries. With AWS WAF, you can also create rate-based rules that automatically block requests from a single IP address if they exceed a customer-defined rate limit. One benefit of rate-based rules is that you can block requests from an IP address while it exceeds the threshold, and then automatically allow requests from that same client once they drop to an acceptable rate. This helps ensure that regular viewers are not held in a persistent block list. You can also combine the rate limit with conditions to trigger different actions for distinct scenarios.

Q34. A, B, D

AWS Documentation Reference:

https://docs.aws.amazon.com/IAM/latest/UserGuide/id_credentials_access-keys.html

Access keys are long-term credentials for an IAM user or the AWS account root user. You can use access keys to sign programmatic requests to the AWS CLI or AWS API (directly or using the AWS SDK). For more information, see Signing AWS API Requests in the Amazon Web Services General Reference.

Access keys consist of two parts: an access key ID (for example, AKIAIOSFODNN7EXAMPLE) and a secret access key (for example, wJalrXUtnFEMI/K7MDENG/bPxRfiCYEXAMPLEKEY). Like a user name and password, you must use both the access key ID and secret access key together to authenticate your requests. Manage your access keys as securely as you do your user name and password.

Q35. A, C, D
AWS Documentation Reference:
https://aws.amazon.com/single-sign-on/features/
If the users in your organization already have a way to be authenticated, such as by signing in to your corporate network, you don't have to create separate IAM users for them. Instead, you can federate those user identities into AWS.
https://docs.aws.amazon.com/IAM/latest/UserGuide/id_roles_providers_saml.html
AWS supports identity federation with SAML 2.0 (Security Assertion Markup Language 2.0), an open standard that many identity providers (IdPs) use. This feature enables federated single sign-on (SSO), so users can log into the AWS Management Console or call the AWS API operations without you having to create an IAM user for everyone in your organization. By using SAML, you can simplify the process of configuring federation with AWS, because you can use the IdP's service instead of writing custom identity proxy code.

You must configure your organization's IdP and your AWS account to trust each other. Inside your organization, you must have an IdP that supports SAML 2.0, like Microsoft Active Directory Federation Service (ADFS, part of Windows Server), Shibboleth, or another compatible SAML 2.0 provider.

https://docs.aws.amazon.com/IAM/latest/UserGuide/id_roles_providers_enable-console-saml.html
You can use a role to configure your SAML 2.0-compliant identity provider (IdP) and AWS to permit your federated users to access the AWS Management Console.

Q36. A, C, E
AWS Documentation Reference:
https://docs.aws.amazon.com/IAM/latest/UserGuide/id_roles_create_for-user_externalid.html

1. You hire Third Party Corp, so they create a unique customer identifier for you. They give you your unique customer ID and their AWS account number. You will use this information to create an IAM role.

2. You sign in to AWS to create an IAM role that gives Third Party Corp access to your resources. The role's trust policy specifies the AWS account number of Third Party Corp as the Principal. This allows identities from that account to assume the role. In addition, you add a Condition element to the trust policy which tests the ExternalId context key to ensure that it matches the unique customer ID from Third Party Corp. For example:

"Principal": {"AWS": "Example Corp's AWS Account ID"},
"Condition": {"StringEquals": {"sts:ExternalId": "Unique ID Assigned by Third Party Corp "}}

The permission policy for the role specifies what the role allows someone to do. For example, you could specify that the role allows someone to manage only your Amazon EC2 and S3 resources but not your IAM users or groups. After you create the role, you provide the Amazon Resource Name (ARN) of the role to Third Party Corp.

When they need to access your AWS resources, someone from the company calls the AWS sts:AssumeRole API. The call includes the ARN of the role to assume and the ExternalId parameter that corresponds to their customer ID.

If the request comes from someone using Third Party's AWS account, and if the role ARN and the external ID are correct, the request succeeds. It then provides temporary security credentials that Third Party Corp can use to access the AWS resources that your role allows.

Q37. A, E, F
AWS Documentation Reference:
https://docs.aws.amazon.com/IAM/latest/UserGuide/id.html

A: Don't create an IAM user and pass the user's credentials to the application or embed the credentials in the application. Instead, create an IAM role that you attach to the EC2 instance to give applications running on the instance temporary security credentials. The credentials have the permissions specified in the policies attached to the role.

E: Don't create IAM users. Configure a federation relationship between your enterprise identity system and AWS. You can do this in two ways:

- If your company's identity system is compatible with SAML 2.0, you can establish trust between your company's identity system and AWS.
- Create and use a custom proxy server that translates user identities from the enterprise into IAM roles that provide temporary AWS security credentials.

F: Don't create an IAM user and distribute the user's access key with the app. Instead, use an identity provider like Login with Amazon, Amazon Cognito, Facebook, or Google to authenticate users and map the users to an IAM role. The app can use the role to get temporary security credentials that have the permissions specified by the policies attached to the role.

B, C, D are scenarios when you should create a user instead or a role
Q38. A, B, C, D

AWS Documentation Reference:
https://docs.aws.amazon.com/general/latest/gr/aws-access-keys-best-practices.html

Remove (or Don't Generate) Account Access Key: Anyone who has the access key for your AWS account root user has unrestricted access to all the resources in your account, including billing information. You cannot restrict the permissions for your AWS account root user. One of the best ways to protect your account is to not have an access key for your AWS account root user. Unless you must have a root user access key (which is very rare), it is best not to generate one. Instead, the recommended best practice is to create one or more AWS Identity and Access Management (IAM) users, give them the necessary permissions, and use IAM users for everyday interaction with AWS.

Use Temporary Security Credentials (IAM Roles) Instead of Long-Term Access Keys
In many scenarios, you don't need a long-term access key that never expires (as you have with an IAM user). Instead, you can create IAM roles and generate temporary security credentials. Temporary security credentials consist of an access key ID and a secret access key, but they also include a security token that indicates when the credentials expire.

Don't embed access keys directly into code. The AWS SDKs and the AWS Command Line Tools allow you to put access keys in known locations so that you do not have to keep them in code. Put access keys in one of the following locations:
- The AWS credentials file. The AWS SDKs and AWS CLI automatically use the credentials that you store in the AWS credentials file.
- Environment variables. On a multitenant system, choose user environment variables, not system environment variables.

Rotate access keys periodically. Change access keys on a regular basis.

Q39. A, C, E

Q40. A, C
AWS Documentation Reference:
https://docs.aws.amazon.com/IAM/latest/UserGuide/best-practices.html

Q41.A
AWS Documentation Reference:
https://docs.aws.amazon.com/general/latest/gr/aws-access-keys-best-practices.html
https://docs.aws.amazon.com/IAM/latest/UserGuide/id_roles_use_switch-role-ec2.html
Do not pass an access key to the application, embed it in the application, or have the application read a key from a source such as an Amazon S3 bucket (even if the bucket is encrypted). Instead, define an IAM role that has appropriate permissions for your application and launch the Amazon EC2 instance with roles for EC2. This associates an IAM role with the Amazon EC2 instance and lets the application get temporary security credentials that it can in

turn use to make AWS calls. The AWS SDKs and the AWS CLI can get temporary credentials from the role automatically.

Q42. A, B
AWS Documentation Reference:
https://docs.aws.amazon.com/IAM/latest/UserGuide/introduction_access-management.html
Federated users don't have permanent identities in your AWS account the way that IAM users do. To assign permissions to federated users, you can create an entity referred to as a role and define permissions for the role. When a federated user signs in to AWS, the user is associated with the role and is granted the permissions that are defined in the role.

Q43. C, D
AWS Documentation Reference:
https://docs.aws.amazon.com/IAM/latest/UserGuide/id_roles_terms-and-concepts.html
A principal can be an AWS account root user, an IAM user, or a role. You can grant permissions to access a resource in one of two ways:

- You can attach a permissions policy to a user (directly, or indirectly through a group) or to a role.
- For those services that support resource-based policies, you can identify the principal in the Principal element of a policy attached to the resource.

Q44. E
AWS Documentation Reference:
https://docs.aws.amazon.com/IAM/latest/UserGuide/id_roles_providers_oidc_manual.html

- To enable the mobile app to access AWS resources, you first need to register for a developer ID with chosen IdPs.
- Configures the application with each of these providers. In AWS account that contains the Amazon S3 bucket and DynamoDB table for the game, use Amazon Cognito to create IAM roles that precisely define permissions that the game needs. If using an OIDC IdP, also create an IAM OIDC identity provider entity to establish trust between AWS account and the IdP.
- In the app's code, call the sign-in interface for the IdP that was configured previously.
- The IdP handles all the details of letting the user sign in, and the app gets an OAuth access token or OIDC ID token from the provider.
- App can trade this authentication information for a set of temporary security credentials that consist of an AWS access key ID, a secret access key, and a session token. The app can then use these credentials to access web services offered by AWS. The app is limited to the permissions that are defined in the role that it assumes.

Q45. C

AWS Documentation Reference:

https://docs.aws.amazon.com/IAM/latest/UserGuide/id_roles_providers_oidc_cognito.html

The right sequence is:

- A customer starts your app on a mobile device. The app asks the user to sign in.
- The app uses Login with Amazon resources to accept the user's credentials.
- The app uses Cognito API operations to exchange the Login with Amazon ID token for a Cognito token.
- The app requests temporary security credentials from AWS STS, passing the Cognito token.
- The temporary security credentials can be used by the app to access any AWS resources required by the app to operate. The role associated with the temporary security credentials and its assigned policies determines what can be accessed.

Q46. B, C, D, E

AWS Documentation Reference:

https://docs.aws.amazon.com/IAM/latest/UserGuide/id_roles_terms-and-concepts.html

Some AWS services allow you to attach a policy directly to a resource (instead of using a role as a proxy). These are called resource-based policies, and you can use them to grant principals in another AWS account access to the resource. Some of these resources include Amazon Simple Storage Service (S3) buckets, Glacier vaults, Amazon Simple Notification Service (SNS) topics, and Amazon Simple Queue Service (SQS) queues.

Q47.D

AWS Documentation Reference:

https://docs.aws.amazon.com/IAM/latest/UserGuide/id_roles_providers_create.html

When you want to configure federation with an external identity provider (IdP) service, you create an IAM identity provider to inform AWS about the IdP and its configuration. This establishes "trust" between your AWS account and the IdP.

Q48. A, B, C, D

AWS Documentation Reference:

https://docs.aws.amazon.com/IAM/latest/UserGuide/access_policies_managed-vs-inline.html

An AWS managed policy is a standalone policy that is created and administered by AWS. Standalone policy means that the policy has its own Amazon Resource Name (ARN) that includes the policy name. For example, arn:aws:iam::aws:policy/IAMReadOnlyAccess is an AWS managed policy.

AWS managed policies are designed to provide permissions for many common use cases. Full access AWS managed policies such as AmazonDynamoDBFullAccess and IAMFullAccess define permissions for service administrators by granting full access to a service.

One particularly useful category of AWS managed policies are those designed for job functions. For example, the AdministratorAccess job function provides full access and permissions delegation to every service and resource in AWS.

You cannot change the permissions defined in AWS managed policies.

## Q49.B

AWS Documentation Reference:

https://docs.aws.amazon.com/IAM/latest/UserGuide/access_policies_boundaries.html

AWS supports permissions boundaries for IAM entities (users or roles). A permissions boundary is an advanced feature for using a managed policy to set the maximum permissions that an identity-based policy can grant to an IAM entity. An entity's permissions boundary allows it to perform only the actions that are allowed by both its identity-based policies and its permissions boundaries.

User creation fails because the permissions boundary does not allow the iam:CreateUser operation. You could update the permissions boundary to allow him to create a user in IAM.

## Q50. .B

AWS Documentation Reference:

https://docs.aws.amazon.com/cognito/latest/developerguide/what-is-amazon-cognito.html

Amazon Cognito provides authentication, authorization, and user management for your web and mobile apps. Your users can sign in directly with a user name and password, or through a third party such as Facebook, Amazon, or Google.

## Q51. B, C, D

AWS Documentation Reference:

https://docs.aws.amazon.com/cognito/latest/developerguide/what-is-amazon-cognito.html

Social and enterprise identity federation: With Amazon Cognito, your users can sign-in through social identity providers such as Google, Facebook, and Amazon, and through enterprise identity providers such as Microsoft Active Directory using SAML.

Access control for AWS resources: Amazon Cognito provides solutions to control access to AWS resources from your app. You can define roles and map users to different roles so your app can access only the resources that are authorized for each user.

Standards-based authentication

Amazon Cognito uses common identity management standards including OpenID Connect, OAuth 2.0, and SAML 2.0.

Adaptive authentication: Using advanced security features for Amazon Cognito to add adaptive authentication to your applications helps protect your applications' user accounts and user experience. When Amazon Cognito detects unusual sign-in activity, such as sign-in attempts from new locations and devices, it assigns a risk score to the activity and lets you choose to either prompt users for additional verification or block the sign-in request. Users can verify their identities using SMS or a Time-based One-time Password (TOTP) generator, such as Google Authenticator.

Protection from compromised credentials: Advanced security features for Amazon Cognito helps protect your application users from unauthorized access to their accounts using compromised credentials. When Amazon Cognito detects users have entered credentials that have been compromised elsewhere, it prompts them to change their password.

## Q52. C

AWS Documentation Reference: Policies and the Root User

https://docs.aws.amazon.com/IAM/latest/UserGuide/access_policies.html

The AWS account root user is affected by some policy types but not others. You cannot attach identity-based policies to the root user, and you cannot set the permissions boundary for the root user. However, you can specify the root user as the principal in a resource-based policy or an ACL. As a member of an account, the root user is affected by any SCPs for the account.

## Q53. C, D

AWS Documentation Reference:

https://docs.aws.amazon.com/cognito/latest/developerguide/what-is-amazon-cognito.html

The two main components of Amazon Cognito are user pools and identity pools. User pools are user directories that provide sign-up and sign-in options for your app users. Identity pools enable you to grant your users access to other AWS services. You can use identity pools and user pools separately or together.

## Q54. A, B, D

C is wrong as that is the feature of Identity pools.

AWS Documentation Reference:

https://docs.aws.amazon.com/cognito/latest/developerguide/cognito-user-identity-pools.html

## Q55. B, D

AWS Documentation Reference:

https://docs.aws.amazon.com/cognito/latest/developerguide/cognito-identity.html

Amazon Cognito identity pools (federated identities) enable you to create unique identities for your users and federate them with identity providers. With an identity pool, you can obtain temporary, limited-privilege AWS credentials to access other AWS services.

## Q56. D

AWS Documentation Reference:

https://docs.aws.amazon.com/cognito/latest/developerguide/cognito-identity.html

Amazon Cognito identity pools support the following identity providers:

- Public providers: Login with Amazon (Identity Pools), Facebook (Identity Pools), Google (Identity Pools).
- Amazon Cognito User Pools

- Open ID Connect Providers (Identity Pools)
- SAML Identity Providers (Identity Pools)
- Developer Authenticated Identities (Identity Pools)

Q57. B
AWS Documentation Reference:
https://aws.amazon.com/blogs/compute/secure-api-access-with-amazon-cognito-federated-identities-amazon-cognito-user-pools-and-amazon-api-gateway/
As it is mentioned that you need RDBMS therefore Aurora serverless service , for Serverless design you will be using Lambda , Cognito is the service you will need for federated user authentication from Facebook/Google/Amazon and API gateway as custom API to your code running in AWS Lambda and also for calling the Lambda code from your API. API Gateway can invoke AWS Lambda code in your account.
You don't need DynamoDB as the design doesn't require NoSQL database nor Elastic Beanstalk which is appropriate for a web application deployment.

Q58. C, G
C is the feature of AWS Certificate Manager.
G is the feature of AWS Key Management Service (KMS).
AWS Documentation Reference:
https://docs.aws.amazon.com/directoryservice/latest/admin-guide/ms_ad_use_cases.html

Use Case A: Sign In to AWS Applications and Services with AD Credentials
You can enable multiple AWS applications and services such as the AWS Management Console, Amazon WorkSpaces, and Amazon RDS for SQL Server to use your AWS Managed Microsoft AD directory. When you enable an AWS application or service in your directory, your users can access the application or service with their AD credentials.
For example, you can enable your users to sign in to the AWS Management Console with their AD credentials.

Use Case B: Manage Amazon EC2 Instances
Using familiar AD administration tools, you can apply AD group policy objects (GPOs) to centrally manage your Amazon EC2 for Windows or Linux instances by joining your instances to your AWS Managed Microsoft AD domain. In addition, your users can sign in to your instances with their AD credentials. This eliminates the need to use individual instance credentials or distribute private key (PEM) files. This makes it easier for you to instantly grant or revoke access to users by using AD user administration tools you already use.
Use Case D: Provide Directory Services to Your AD-Aware Workloads
AWS Managed Microsoft AD is an actual Microsoft AD that enables you to run traditional AD-aware workloads such as Remote Desktop Licensing Manager and Microsoft SharePoint and Microsoft SQL Server Always On in the AWS Cloud.

Use Case E: SSO to Office 365 and Other Cloud Applications
You can use AWS Managed Microsoft AD to provide SSO for cloud applications. You can use Azure AD Connect to synchronize your users into Azure AD, and then use Active Directory Federation Services (AD FS) so that your users can access Microsoft Office 365 and other SAML 2.0 cloud applications by using their AD credentials.

Use Case F: Extend Your On-Premises AD to the AWS Cloud
If you already have an AD infrastructure and want to use it when migrating AD-aware workloads to the AWS Cloud, AWS Managed Microsoft AD can help. You can use AD trusts to connect AWS Managed Microsoft AD to your existing AD. This means your users can access AD-aware and AWS applications with their on-premises AD credentials, without needing you to synchronize users, groups, or passwords.

For example, your users can sign in to the AWS Management Console and Amazon WorkSpaces by using their existing AD user names and passwords. Also, when you use AD-aware applications such as SharePoint with AWS Managed Microsoft AD, your logged-in Windows users can access these applications without needing to enter credentials again.

Q59.E
AWS Documentation Reference:
https://docs.aws.amazon.com/directoryservice/latest/admin-guide/directory_ad_connector.html
Once set up, AD Connector offers the following benefits:

- Your end users and IT administrators can use their existing corporate credentials to log on to AWS applications such as Amazon WorkSpaces, Amazon WorkDocs, or Amazon WorkMail.

- You can manage AWS resources like Amazon EC2 instances or Amazon S3 buckets through IAM role-based access to the AWS Management Console.

- You can consistently enforce existing security policies (such as password expiration, password history, and account lockouts) whether users or IT administrators are accessing resources in your on-premises infrastructure or in the AWS Cloud.

- You can use AD Connector to enable multi-factor authentication by integrating with your existing RADIUS-based MFA infrastructure to provide an additional layer of security when users access AWS applications.

Q60. C
AWS Documentation Reference:
https://aws.amazon.com/compliance/shared-responsibility-model/
Customer/AWS shared responsibility model also extends to IT controls. Just as the responsibility to operate the IT environment is shared between AWS and its customers, so is the management, operation and verification of IT controls shared. AWS can help relieve

customer burden of operating controls by managing those controls associated with the physical infrastructure deployed in the AWS environment that may previously have been managed by the customer. As every customer is deployed differently in AWS, customers can take advantage of shifting management of certain IT controls to AWS which results in a (new) distributed control environment. Customers can then use the AWS control and compliance documentation available to them to perform their control evaluation and verification procedures as required. Below are examples of controls that are managed by AWS, AWS Customers and/or both.

Q61. A, B, C
AWS Documentation Reference:
https://aws.amazon.com/premiumsupport/technology/trusted-advisor/
Checks buckets in Amazon Simple Storage Service (Amazon S3) that have open access permissions.
Checks security groups for rules that allow unrestricted access (0.0.0.0/0) to specific ports.
Checks for your use of AWS Identity and Access Management (IAM).
Checks the password policy for your account and warns when a password policy is not enabled, or if password content requirements have not been enabled.
Checks the permission settings for your Amazon Elastic Block Store (Amazon EBS) volume snapshots and alerts you if any snapshots are marked as public.
Checks the permission settings for your Amazon Relational Database Service (Amazon RDS) DB snapshots and alerts you if any snapshots are marked as public.
Checks for service usage that is more than 80% of the service limit.

Q62. A, C, D
AWS Documentation Reference:
https://aws.amazon.com/premiumsupport/technology/trusted-advisor/

Q63. C

Q64. B, C, D
AWS Documentation Reference:
https://aws.amazon.com/premiumsupport/technology/trusted-advisor/best-practice-checklist/
Amazon EC2 Reserved Instances Optimization: Checks your Amazon Elastic Compute Cloud (Amazon EC2) computing consumption history and calculates an optimal number of Partial Upfront Reserved Instances.

Low utilization Amazon EC2 Instances: Checks the Amazon Elastic Compute Cloud (Amazon EC2) instances that were running at any time during the last 14 days and alerts you if the daily CPU utilization was 10% or less and network I/O was 5 MB or less on 4 or more days.

Checks Amazon Elastic Block Store (Amazon EBS) volume configurations and warns when volumes appear to be underused. Checks your Amazon Redshift configuration for clusters that appear to be underutilized.

Q65. B

AWS Documentation Reference:

https://docs.aws.amazon.com/IAM/latest/UserGuide/access_policies_managed-vs-inline.html#inline-policies

An inline policy is a policy that's embedded in a principal entity (a user, group, or role)—that is, the policy is an inherent part of the principal entity.

Q66. C

AWS Documentation Reference: Access Control Lists (ACLs)

https://docs.aws.amazon.com/IAM/latest/UserGuide/access_policies.html#policies_acl

Access control lists (ACLs) are service policies that allow you to control which principals in another account can access a resource. ACLs cannot be used to control access for a principal within the same account. ACLs are similar to resource-based policies, although they are the only policy type that does not use the JSON policy document format. Amazon S3, AWS WAF, and Amazon VPC are examples of services that support ACLs.

Q67. C

AWS Documentation Reference:

She should create a group called AllUsers and attach every user to that group so that she can easily apply any account-wide permissions to all users in the AWS account.

Q68. B, C, E, F

AWS Documentation Reference: Determining Whether a Request Is Allowed or Denied Within an Account

https://docs.aws.amazon.com/IAM/latest/UserGuide/reference_policies_evaluation-logic.html#policy-eval-denyallow

The following is a high-level summary of the AWS evaluation logic on those policies within a single account.

- By default, all requests are implicitly denied. (Alternatively, by default, the AWS account root user has full access.)
- An explicit allow in an identity-based or resource-based policy overrides this default.
- If a permissions boundary, Organizations SCP, or session policy is present, it might override the allow with an implicit deny.
- An explicit deny in any policy overrides any allows.

Q69. A, C

AWS Documentation Reference: Evaluating Identity-Based Policies with Resource-Based Policies https://docs.aws.amazon.com/IAM/latest/UserGuide/reference_policies_evaluation-logic.html#policy-eval-basics

Identity-based policies and resource-based policies grant permissions to the identities or resources to which they are attached. When an IAM entity (user or role) requests access to a resource within the same account, AWS evaluates all the permissions granted by the identity-based and resource-based policies. The resulting permissions are the total permissions of the two types. If an action is allowed by an identity-based policy, a resource-based policy, or both, then AWS allows the action. An explicit deny in either of these policies overrides the allow.
https://docs.aws.amazon.com/IAM/latest/UserGuide/access_policies_identity-vs-resource.html
John can perform list and read actions on Resource X. He is granted this permission by the identity-based policy on his user and the resource-based policy on Resource X.

Mary can perform list, read, and write operations on Resource X, Resource Y, and Resource Z. Her identity-based policy allows her more actions on more resources than the resource-based policies, but none of them deny access.

Q70. C, D
AWS Documentation Reference: Evaluating Identity-Based Policies with Resource-Based Policies
https://docs.aws.amazon.com/IAM/latest/UserGuide/reference_policies_evaluation-logic.html#policy-eval-basics

Identity-based policies and resource-based policies grant permissions to the identities or resources to which they are attached. When an IAM entity (user or role) requests access to a resource within the same account, AWS evaluates all the permissions granted by the identity-based and resource-based policies. The resulting permissions are the total permissions of the two types. If an action is allowed by an identity-based policy, a resource-based policy, or both, then AWS allows the action. An explicit deny in either of these policies overrides the allow.

https://docs.aws.amazon.com/IAM/latest/UserGuide/access_policies_identity-vs-resource.html

Zhang has full access to Resource Z. Zhang has no identity-based policies, but the Resource Z resource-based policy allows him full access to the resource. Zhang can also perform list and read actions on Resource Y.

Carlos can perform list, read, and write actions on Resource Y, but is denied access to Resource Z. The identity-based policy on Carlos allows him to perform list and read actions on Resource Y. The Resource Y resource-based policy also allows him write permissions. However, although his identity-based policy allows him access to Resource Z, the Resource Z resource-based policy denies that access. An explicit Deny overrides an Allow and his access to Resource Z is denied.

## Q71. C
AWS Documentation Reference:
https://docs.aws.amazon.com/IAM/latest/UserGuide/reference_policies_elements.html

## Q72.B
AWS Documentation Reference:
https://aws.amazon.com/iam/faqs/#Permissions
By default, IAM users, groups, and roles have no permissions; users with sufficient permissions must use a policy to grant the desired permissions. To set permissions, you can create and attach policies using the AWS Management Console, the IAM API, or the AWS CLI. Users who have been granted the necessary permissions can create policies and assign them to IAM users, groups, and roles.

## Q73. B, C
A and D are incorrect because AWS Simple AD doesn't have the feature to form a trust relationship with on-premise AD or identity federation.
AWS Documentation Reference:
https://aws.amazon.com/blogs/security/how-to-connect-your-on-premises-active-directory-to-aws-using-ad-connector/
How to Connect Your On-Premises Active Directory to AWS Using AD Connector
AD Connector is designed to give you an easy way to establish a trusted relationship between your Active Directory and AWS. Provide federated sign-in to the AWS Management Console by mapping Active Directory identities to AWS Identity and Access Management (IAM) roles.

https://aws.amazon.com/blogs/security/how-to-access-the-aws-management-console-using-aws-microsoft-ad-and-your-on-premises-credentials/
How to Access the AWS Management Console Using AWS Microsoft AD and Your On-Premises Credentials
With AWS Microsoft AD, you can grant your on-premises users permissions to resources such as the AWS Management Console instead of adding AWS Identity and Access Management (IAM) user accounts or configuring AD Federation Services (AD FS) with Security Assertion Markup Language (SAML).
By using an AD trust between AWS Microsoft AD and your on-premises AD, you can assign your on-premises AD users and groups to IAM roles. This gives the assigned users and groups the IAM roles' permissions to manage AWS resources. By assigning on-premises AD groups to IAM roles, you can now manage AWS access through standard AD administrative tools such as AD Users and Computers (ADUC).
After you assign your on-premises users or groups to IAM roles, your users can sign in to the AWS Management Console with their on-premises AD credentials. From there, they can select

from a list of their assigned IAM roles. After they select a role, they can perform the management functions that you assigned to the IAM role.

Q74.A

Q75. C, E
AWS Documentation Reference: JSON Policy Document Structure
https://docs.aws.amazon.com/IAM/latest/UserGuide/access_policies.html

The different elements are:
- Version – Specify the version of the policy language that you want to use. As a best practice, use the latest 2012-10-17 version.
- Statement – Use this main policy element as a container for the following elements. You can include more than one statement in a policy.
- Sid (Optional) – Include an optional statement ID to differentiate between your statements.
- Effect – Use Allow or Deny to indicate whether the policy allows or denies access.
- Principal (Required in only some circumstances) – If you create a resource-based policy, you must indicate the account, user, role, or federated user to which you would like to allow or deny access. If you are creating an IAM permissions policy to attach to a user or role, you cannot include this element. The principal is implied as that user or role.
- Action – Include a list of actions that the policy allows or denies.
- Resource (Required in only some circumstances) – If you create an IAM permissions policy, you must specify a list of resources to which the actions apply. If you create a resource-based policy, this element is optional. If you do not include this element, then the resource to which the action applies is the resource to which the policy is attached.
- Condition (Optional) – Specify the circumstances under which the policy grants permission.
https://docs.aws.amazon.com/IAM/latest/UserGuide/reference_policies_elements.html

Q76. A, B, C
AWS Documentation Reference:
https://docs.aws.amazon.com/IAM/latest/UserGuide/what-is-access-analyzer.html

IAM Access Analyzer informs you which resources in your account that you are sharing with external principals. It does this by using logic-based reasoning to analyze resource-based policies in your AWS environment. Once enabled, Access Analyzer analyzes the policies applied to all of the supported resources in your account. When analyzing the policies, if Access Analyzer identifies one that grants access to an external principal that isn't within your zone of trust, it generates a finding. Each finding includes details about the resource, the external entity that has access to it, and the permissions granted so that you can take appropriate action.

### Q77. A, C, D, E
AWS Documentation Reference:
https://aws.amazon.com/iam/faqs/
*What are the features of IAM roles for EC2 instances?*
*What problem does IAM roles for EC2 instances solve?*
IAM roles for EC2 instances simplifies management and deployment of AWS access keys to EC2 instances. Using this feature, you associate an IAM role with an instance. Then your EC2 instance provides the temporary security credentials to applications running on the instance, and the applications can use these credentials to make requests securely to the AWS service resources defined in the role.

IAM roles for EC2 instances provides the following features:
- AWS temporary security credentials to use when making requests from running EC2 instances to AWS services.
- Automatic rotation of the AWS temporary security credentials.
- Granular AWS service permissions for applications running on EC2 instances.

### Q78. B, C, D
AWS Documentation Reference:
https://aws.amazon.com/iam/faqs/
*What are the benefits of temporary security credentials?*
Temporary security credentials consist of the AWS access key ID, secret access key, and security token. Temporary security credentials are valid for a specified duration and for a specific set of permissions. Temporary security credentials are sometimes simply referred to as tokens. Tokens can be requested for IAM users or for federated users you manage in your own corporate directory. Temporary security credentials allow you to:
- Extend your internal user directories to enable federation to AWS, enabling your employees and applications to securely access AWS service APIs without needing to create an AWS identity for them.
- Request temporary security credentials for an unlimited number of federated users.
- Configure the time period after which temporary security credentials expire, offering improved security when accessing AWS service APIs through mobile devices where there is a risk of losing the device.

### Q79. A
B is incorrect, you cannot have trust relationship between AD and IAM. You can have trust relationship between on-premise AD and AWS Managed Microsoft AD or Active Directory Connector.

C is incorrect because web identity federation, you don't need to create custom sign-in code or manage your own user identities. Instead, users of your app can sign in using a well-known external identity provider (IdP), such as Login with Amazon, Facebook, Google, or any other OpenID Connect (OIDC)-compatible IdP. Here we want to login using AD user accounts.

AWS Documentation Reference:
https://docs.aws.amazon.com/IAM/latest/UserGuide/id_roles_providers_enable-console-saml.html
You can use a role to configure your SAML 2.0-compliant identity provider (IdP) and AWS to permit your federated users to access the AWS Management Console.
Users can sign in to a portal in your organization hosted by a SAML 2.0 compatible IdP, select an option to go to AWS, and be redirected to the console without having to provide additional sign-in information. Before you can use SAML 2.0-based federation as described in the preceding scenario and diagram, you must configure your organization's IdP and your AWS account to trust each other. The general process for configuring this trust is described in the following steps. Inside your organization, you must have an IdP that supports SAML 2.0, like Microsoft Active Directory Federation Service (AD FS, part of Windows Server), Shibboleth, or another compatible SAML 2.0 provider.
https://aws.amazon.com/blogs/security/aws-federated-authentication-with-active-directory-federation-services-ad-fs/
AWS Federated Authentication with Active Directory Federation Services (AD FS)
The following describes the process a user will follow to authenticate to AWS using Active Directory and ADFS as the identity provider and identity brokers:
1. Corporate user accesses the corporate Active Directory Federation Services portal sign-in page and provides Active Directory authentication credentials.
2. AD FS authenticates the user against Active Directory.
3. Active Directory returns the user's information, including AD group membership information.
4. AD FS dynamically builds ARNs by using Active Directory group memberships for the IAM roles and user attributes for the AWS account IDs, and sends a signed assertion to the user's browser with a redirect to post the assertion to AWS STS.
5. Temporary credentials are returned using STS AssumeRoleWithSAML.
6. The user is authenticated and provided access to the AWS management console.

Q80. A, B, C
D is incorrect as AWS Certificate Manager is a service that lets you easily provision, manage, and deploy public and private Secure Sockets Layer/Transport Layer Security (SSL/TLS) certificates for use with AWS services and your internal connected resources.

AWS Documentation Reference:
https://aws.amazon.com/kms/

The benefits are:

Centralized key management: AWS KMS presents a single control point to manage keys and define policies consistently across integrated AWS services and your own applications. You can easily create, import, rotate, delete, and manage permissions on keys from the AWS Management Console or by using the AWS SDK or CLI.

Manage encryption for AWS services: AWS KMS is integrated with AWS services to simplify using your keys to encrypt data across your AWS workloads.

Encrypt data in your applications: AWS KMS is integrated with the AWS Encryption SDK to enable you to used KMS-protected data encryption keys to encrypt locally within your applications. Using simple APIs you can also build encryption and key management into your own applications wherever they run.

Digitally sign data: AWS KMS enables you to perform digital signing operations using asymmetric key pairs to ensure the integrity of your data. Recipients of digitally signed data can verify the signatures whether they have an AWS account or not.

Built-in auditing: AWS KMS is integrated with AWS CloudTrail to record all API requests, including key management actions and usage of your keys.

Secure: AWS KMS uses hardware security modules (HSMs) that have been validated under FIPS 140-2, or are in the process of being validated, to generate and protect keys. Your keys are only used inside these devices and can never leave them unencrypted.

## Q81. B, C
AWS Documentation Reference:
https://docs.aws.amazon.com/kms/latest/developerguide/concepts.html#master_keys
Symmetric CMKs and the private keys of asymmetric CMKs never leave AWS KMS unencrypted.

## Q82. D
AWS Documentation Reference:
https://docs.aws.amazon.com/kms/latest/developerguide/concepts.html#enveloping
When you encrypt your data, your data is protected, but you have to protect your encryption key. One strategy is to encrypt it. Envelope encryption is the practice of encrypting plaintext data with a data key, and then encrypting the data key under another key.

## Q83. B, C, E
A, D and F are incorrect because AWS KMS uses Envelope encryption of encrypting plaintext data with a data key, and then encrypting the data key under another key.

AWS Documentation Reference:

https://docs.aws.amazon.com/kms/latest/developerguide/concepts.html#data-keys

Create a Data Key: To create a data key, call the GenerateDataKey operation. AWS KMS uses the CMK that you specify to generate a data key. The operation returns a plaintext copy of the data key and a copy of the data key encrypted under the CMK.

Encrypt Data with a Data Key: AWS KMS cannot use a data key to encrypt data. But you can use the data key outside of KMS, such as by using OpenSSL or a cryptographic library like the AWS Encryption SDK. After using the plaintext data key to encrypt data, remove it from memory as soon as possible. You can safely store the encrypted data key with the encrypted data so it is available to decrypt the data.

Decrypt Data with a Data Key: To decrypt your data, pass the encrypted data key to the Decrypt operation. AWS KMS uses your CMK to decrypt the data key and then it returns the plaintext data key. Use the plaintext data key to decrypt your data and then remove the plaintext data key from memory as soon as possible.

## Q84. C, F
AWS Documentation Reference:

https://docs.aws.amazon.com/kms/latest/developerguide/concepts.html#encrypt_context

All AWS KMS cryptographic operations (Encrypt, Decrypt, ReEncrypt, GenerateDataKey, and GenerateDataKeyWithoutPlaintext) that use symmetric CMKs accept an encryption context, an optional set of key–value pairs that can contain additional contextual information about the data.

You cannot specify an encryption context in a cryptographic operation with an asymmetric CMK.

When you include an encryption context in an encryption request, it is cryptographically bound to the ciphertext such that the same encryption context is required to decrypt (or decrypt and re-encrypt) the data. If the encryption context provided in the decryption request is not an exact, case-sensitive match, the decrypt request fails. Only the order of the key-value pairs in the encryption context can vary.

An encryption context can consist of any keys and values. The key and value in an encryption context pair must be simple literal strings. They cannot be integers or objects, or any type that is not fully resolved. If you use a different type, such as an integer or float, AWS KMS interprets it as a string.

## Q85. B
AWS Documentation Reference:

https://docs.aws.amazon.com/IAM/latest/UserGuide/id_roles.html

An IAM role is an IAM identity that you can create in your account that has specific permissions. An IAM role is similar to an IAM user, in that it is an AWS identity with permission policies that determine what the identity can and cannot do in AWS. However, instead of being uniquely associated with one person, a role is intended to be assumable by anyone who needs it. Also, a role does not have standard long-term credentials such as a password or access keys associated with it. Instead, when you assume a role, it provides you with temporary security credentials for your role session.

You can use roles to delegate access to users, applications, or services that don't normally have access to your AWS resources.

Q86. A, C

AWS Documentation Reference:

https://aws.amazon.com/compliance/shared-responsibility-model/

AWS responsibility "Security of the Cloud" - AWS is responsible for protecting the infrastructure that runs all of the services offered in the AWS Cloud. This infrastructure is composed of the hardware, software, networking, and facilities that run AWS Cloud services.

Customer responsibility "Security in the Cloud" – Customer responsibility will be determined by the AWS Cloud services that a customer selects. This determines the amount of configuration work the customer must perform as part of their security responsibilities. For example, a service such as Amazon Elastic Compute Cloud (Amazon EC2) is categorized as Infrastructure as a Service (IaaS) and, as such, requires the customer to perform all of the necessary security configuration and management tasks. Customers that deploy an Amazon EC2 instance are responsible for management of the guest operating system (including updates and security patches), any application software or utilities installed by the customer on the instances, and the configuration of the AWS-provided firewall (called a security group) on each instance. For abstracted services, such as Amazon S3 and Amazon DynamoDB, AWS operates the infrastructure layer, the operating system, and platforms, and customers access the endpoints to store and retrieve data. Customers are responsible for managing their data (including encryption options), classifying their assets, and using IAM tools to apply the appropriate permissions.

This customer/AWS shared responsibility model also extends to IT controls. Just as the responsibility to operate the IT environment is shared between AWS and its customers, so is the management, operation and verification of IT controls shared.

Q87. B, C

AWS Documentation Reference:

https://aws.amazon.com/premiumsupport/knowledge-center/import-ssl-certificate-to-iam/

It's a best practice that you upload SSL certificates to AWS Certificate Manager (ACM). If you're using certificate algorithms and key sizes that aren't currently supported by ACM or the associated AWS resources, then you can also upload an SSL certificate to IAM using AWS Command Line Interface (AWS CLI).

Q88. A

AWS Documentation Reference:

https://docs.aws.amazon.com/cognito/latest/developerguide/cognito-user-identity-pools.html

A user pool is a user directory in Amazon Cognito. With a user pool, your users can sign in to your web or mobile app through Amazon Cognito. Your users can also sign in through social identity providers like Google, Facebook, Amazon, or Apple, and through SAML identity providers. User pools provides:

- Sign-up and sign-in services.
- A built-in, customizable web UI to sign in users.
- Social sign-in with Facebook, Google, Login with Amazon, and Sign in with Apple, as well as sign-in with SAML identity providers from your user pool.
- User directory management and user profiles.
- Security features such as multi-factor authentication (MFA), checks for compromised credentials, account takeover protection, and phone and email verification.
- Customized workflows and user migration through AWS Lambda triggers.

https://docs.aws.amazon.com/cognito/latest/developerguide/user-pool-settings-mfa.html

Multi-factor authentication (MFA) increases security for your app by adding another authentication method, and not relying solely on user name and password. You can choose to use SMS text messages, or time-based one-time (TOTP) passwords as second factors in signing in your users. With adaptive authentication, you can configure your user pool to require second factor authentication in response to an increased risk level.

Q89. D

AWS Documentation Reference:

https://aws.amazon.com/cloudhsm/features/

AWS CloudHSM is a cloud-based hardware security module (HSM) that allows you to easily add secure key storage and high-performance crypto operations to your AWS applications. CloudHSM complements existing data protection solutions and allows you to protect your encryption keys within HSMs that are designed and validated to government standards for secure key management. CloudHSM allows you to securely generate, store, and manage cryptographic keys used for data encryption in a way that keys are accessible only by you.

Q90. C

C is the reason for using KMS. AWS Key Management Service (KMS) is a multi-tenant, managed service that allows you to use and manage encryption keys.

AWS Documentation Reference:

https://aws.amazon.com/cloudhsm/faqs/

When should I use AWS CloudHSM instead of AWS KMS?
You should consider using AWS CloudHSM if you require:

- Keys stored in dedicated, third-party validated hardware security modules under your exclusive control.
- FIPS 140-2 compliance.
- Integration with applications using PKCS#11, Java JCE, or Microsoft CNG interfaces.
- High-performance in-VPC cryptographic acceleration (bulk crypto).

Q91. B, E

AWS Documentation Reference:

https://aws.amazon.com/certificate-manager/

AWS Certificate Manager is a service that lets you easily provision, manage, and deploy public and private Secure Sockets Layer/Transport Layer Security (SSL/TLS) certificates for use with AWS services and your internal connected resources.

https://aws.amazon.com/kms/

AWS Key Management Service (KMS) is a managed service that makes it easy for you to create and manage cryptographic keys and control their use across a wide range of AWS services and in your applications.

Q92. A, D

AWS Documentation Reference:

https://docs.aws.amazon.com/cloudhsm/latest/userguide/clusters.html

AWS CloudHSM provides hardware security modules (HSMs) in a cluster. A cluster is a collection of individual HSMs that AWS CloudHSM keeps in sync. You can think of a cluster as one logical HSM. You can create a cluster that has from 1 to 28 HSMs (the default limit is 6 HSMs per AWS account per AWS Region).

When you create a cluster, you specify an Amazon Virtual Private Cloud (VPC) in your AWS account and one or more subnets in that VPC. Each time you create an HSM, you specify the cluster and Availability Zone for the HSM.

When you create an AWS CloudHSM cluster with more than one HSM, you automatically get load balancing. Load balancing means that the AWS CloudHSM client distributes cryptographic operations across all HSMs in the cluster based on each HSM's capacity for additional processing.

When you create the HSMs in different AWS Availability Zones, you automatically get high availability. High availability means that you get higher reliability because no individual HSM is a single point of failure. AWS recommends that you have a minimum of two HSMs in each cluster, with each HSM in different Availability Zones within an AWS Region.

Q93. D

AWS Documentation Reference:

https://aws.amazon.com/macie/

Amazon Macie is a security service that uses machine learning to automatically discover, classify, and protect sensitive data in AWS. Amazon Macie recognizes sensitive data such as personally identifiable information (PII) or intellectual property, and provides you with dashboards and alerts that give visibility into how this data is being accessed or moved. The fully managed service continuously monitors data access activity for anomalies, and generates detailed alerts when it detects risk of unauthorized access or inadvertent data leaks. The Amazon Macie service supports Amazon S3 and AWS CloudTrail management API and S3 object-level events for the buckets and prefixes enrolled with Amazon Macie.

Q94.A, B

AWS Documentation Reference:

https://docs.aws.amazon.com/macie/latest/userguide/macie-concepts.html

To classify and protect your data, Macie analyzes and processes information from the following data sources:

- AWS CloudTrail event logs, including Amazon S3 object-level API activity
- S3

Q95.D

AWS Documentation Reference:

https://aws.amazon.com/macie/faq/

What are some examples of suspicious activity that Amazon Macie can detect?

Amazon Macie analyzes activity of user, application, and service accounts associated with sensitive data that suggests risk to the business, such as inadvertent exposure of data, insider threats, or targeted attacks. Amazon Macie can alert on suspicious activity such as compromised user accounts enumerating and downloading large amounts of sensitive content from unusual IP addresses, or the download of large quantities of source code by a user account that typically does not access this type of sensitive content. A compliance-focused example of Amazon Macie includes detection of large quantities of high-risk documents shared publicly or to the entire company, such as files containing personally identifiable information (PII), protected health information (PHI), intellectual properties (IP), legal or financial data. Additionally, customers also have the ability to use Amazon Macie's dashboard to define their own alerts and policy definitions based on their security needs.

# Answer Chapter 9 Developer Tools, Management & Governance

Q1. D

AWS Documentation Reference:

https://docs.aws.amazon.com/awscloudtrail/latest/userguide/cloudtrail-user-guide.html

AWS CloudTrail is an AWS service that helps you enable governance, compliance, and operational and risk auditing of your AWS account. Actions taken by a user, role, or an AWS service are recorded as events in CloudTrail.

Q2.D

AWS Documentation Reference:

https://docs.aws.amazon.com/awscloudtrail/latest/userguide/how-cloudtrail-works.html

AWS CloudTrail is a web service that records activity made on your account and delivers log files to your Amazon S3 bucket. CloudTrail event log files are delivered to a S3 bucket that you specify on trail creation.

Q3. A

AWS Documentation Reference:

https://aws.amazon.com/devops/

AWS CodePipeline is a continuous integration and continuous delivery service for fast and reliable application and infrastructure updates. CodePipeline builds, tests, and deploys your code every time there is a code change, based on the release process models you define. This enables you to rapidly and reliably deliver features and updates.

Q4. B

AWS Documentation Reference:

https://aws.amazon.com/devops/

AWS CodeBuild is a fully managed build service that compiles source code, runs tests, and produces software packages that are ready to deploy. With CodeBuild, you don't need to provision, manage, and scale your own build servers. CodeBuild scales continuously and processes multiple builds concurrently, so your builds are not left waiting in a queue.

Q5. C

AWS Documentation Reference:

https://aws.amazon.com/devops/

AWS CodeDeploy automates code deployments to any instance, including Amazon EC2 instances and on-premises servers. AWS CodeDeploy makes it easier for you to rapidly release new features, helps you avoid downtime during application deployment, and handles the complexity of updating your applications.

Q6. E

AWS Documentation Reference:

https://aws.amazon.com/devops/

AWS CloudFormation allows you to model your entire infrastructure in a text file.in JSON or YAML to describe what AWS resources you want to create and configure. If you want to design visually, you can use AWS CloudFormation Designer to help you get started with AWS CloudFormation templates.

Q7. D
AWS OpsWorks is a configuration management service that uses Chef, an automation platform that treats server configurations as code. OpsWorks uses Chef to automate how servers are configured, deployed, and managed across your Amazon Elastic Compute Cloud (Amazon EC2) instances or on-premises compute environments. OpsWorks has two offerings, AWS OpsWorks for Chef Automate, and AWS OpsWorks Stacks.

Q8. B
AWS Documentation Reference:
https://aws.amazon.com/devops/
With AWS Config, you are able to continuously monitor and record configuration changes of your AWS resources. Config also enables you to inventory your AWS resources, the configurations of your AWS resources, as well as software configurations within EC2 instances at any point in time.

Q9. D
AWS Documentation Reference:
https://aws.amazon.com/devops/
Amazon CloudWatch is a monitoring service for AWS cloud resources and the applications you run on AWS. You can use Amazon CloudWatch to collect and track metrics, collect and monitor log files, set alarms, and automatically react to changes in your AWS resources.

Q10. E
AWS Documentation Reference:
https://aws.amazon.com/devops/
AWS X-Ray helps developers analyze and debug production, distributed applications, such as those built using a microservices architecture. With X-Ray, you can understand how your application and its underlying services are performing to identify and troubleshoot the root cause of performance issues and errors. X-Ray provides an end-to-end view of requests as they travel through your application, and shows a map of your application's underlying components. You can use X-Ray to analyze both applications in development and in production, from simple three-tier applications to complex microservices applications consisting of thousands of services.

Q11. C
You can code your infrastructure with CloudFormation template language in either YAML or JSON format, or start from sample templates.

Q12. B

AWS Systems Manager allows you to centralize operational data from multiple AWS services and automate tasks across your AWS resources.

AWS Documentation Reference:

https://aws.amazon.com/systems-manager/features/

Q13. B

B is the use case for AWS CloudFormation. AWS CloudFormation provides a common language for you to model and provision AWS and third party application resources in your cloud environment.

AWS Documentation Reference:

https://aws.amazon.com/cloudtrail/faqs/

*Q: What are the benefits of CloudTrail?*

CloudTrail provides visibility into user activity by recording actions taken on your account. CloudTrail records important information about each action, including who made the request, the services used, the actions performed, parameters for the actions, and the response elements returned by the AWS service. This information helps you to track changes made to your AWS resources and to troubleshoot operational issues. CloudTrail makes it easier to ensure compliance with internal policies and regulatory standards. For more details, refer to the AWS compliance white paper "Security at scale: Logging in AWS".

Customers who need to track changes to resources, answer simple questions about user activity, demonstrate compliance, troubleshoot, or perform security analysis should use CloudTrail.

Q14. A, C, D, E

B is the feature of AWS Systems Manager which gives you visibility and control of your infrastructure on AWS.

AWS Documentation Reference: Ways to Use AWS Config

https://docs.aws.amazon.com/config/latest/developerguide/WhatIsConfig.html

AWS Config is designed to help you oversee your application resources in the following scenarios:

Resource Administration

To exercise better governance over your resource configurations and to detect resource misconfigurations, you need fine-grained visibility into what resources exist and how these resources are configured at any time. You can use AWS Config to notify you whenever resources are created, modified, or deleted without having to monitor these changes by polling the calls made to each resource.

You can use AWS Config rules to evaluate the configuration settings of your AWS resources. When AWS Config detects that a resource violates the conditions in one of your rules, AWS

Config flags the resource as noncompliant and sends a notification. AWS Config continuously evaluates your resources as they are created, changed, or deleted.

Auditing and Compliance
You might be working with data that requires frequent audits to ensure compliance with internal policies and best practices. To demonstrate compliance, you need access to the historical configurations of your resources. This information is provided by AWS Config.

Managing and Troubleshooting Configuration Changes
When you use multiple AWS resources that depend on one another, a change in the configuration of one resource might have unintended consequences on related resources. With AWS Config, you can view how the resource you intend to modify is related to other resources and assess the impact of your change.
You can also use the historical configurations of your resources provided by AWS Config to troubleshoot issues and to access the last known good configuration of a problem resource.

Security Analysis
To analyze potential security weaknesses, you need detailed historical information about your AWS resource configurations, such as the AWS Identity and Access Management (IAM) permissions that are granted to your users, or the Amazon EC2 security group rules that control access to your resources.
You can use AWS Config to view the IAM policy that was assigned to an IAM user, group, or role at any time in which AWS Config was recording. This information can help you determine the permissions that belonged to a user at a specific time: for example, you can view whether the user John Doe had permission to modify Amazon VPC settings on Jan 1, 2015. You can also use AWS Config to view the configuration of your EC2 security groups, including the port rules that were open at a specific time. This information can help you determine whether a security group blocked incoming TCP traffic to a specific port.

Q15. C
By default, Amazon EC2 sends metric data to CloudWatch in 5-minute periods.

Q16. B
To send metric data for your instance to CloudWatch in 1-minute periods, you can enable detailed monitoring on the instance.

Q17.D
AWS Documentation Reference:
https://docs.aws.amazon.com/config/latest/developerguide/how-does-config-work.html
If you are using AWS Config rules, AWS Config continuously evaluates your AWS resource configurations for desired settings. Depending on the rule, AWS Config will evaluate your resources either in response to configuration changes or periodically. Each rule is associated

with an AWS Lambda function, which contains the evaluation logic for the rule. When AWS Config evaluates your resources, it invokes the rule's AWS Lambda function. The function returns the compliance status of the evaluated resources. If a resource violates the conditions of a rule, AWS Config flags the resource and the rule as noncompliant. When the compliance status of a resource changes, AWS Config sends a notification to your Amazon SNS topic.

Q18. A, B

AWS Documentation Reference:

https://aws.amazon.com/config/faq/

*How does AWS Config work with AWS CloudTrail?*

AWS CloudTrail records user API activity on your account and allows you to access information about this activity. You get full details about API actions, such as identity of the caller, the time of the API call, the request parameters, and the response elements returned by the AWS service. AWS Config records point-in-time configuration details for your AWS resources as Configuration Items (CIs). You can use a CI to answer "What did my AWS resource look like?" at a point in time. You can use AWS CloudTrail to answer "Who made an API call to modify this resource?" For example, you can use the AWS Management Console for AWS Config to detect security group "Production-DB" was incorrectly configured in the past. Using the integrated AWS CloudTrail information, you can pinpoint which user misconfigured "Production-DB" security group.

Q19. C

AWS Documentation Reference:

https://aws.amazon.com/cloudwatch/features/

Amazon CloudWatch is a monitoring and management service that provides data and actionable insights for AWS, hybrid, and on-premises applications and infrastructure resources. With CloudWatch, you can collect and access all your performance and operational data in form of logs and metrics from a single platform. This allows you to overcome the challenge of monitoring individual systems and applications in silos (server, network, database, etc.). CloudWatch enables you to monitor your complete stack (applications, infrastructure, and services) and leverage alarms, logs, and events data to take automated actions and reduce Mean Time to Resolution (MTTR). This frees up important resources and allows you to focus on building applications and business value.

CloudWatch gives you actionable insights that help you optimize application performance, manage resource utilization, and understand system-wide operational health. CloudWatch provides up to 1-second visibility of metrics and logs data, 15 months of data retention (metrics), and the ability to perform calculations on metrics. This allows you to perform historical analysis for cost optimization and derive real-time insights into optimizing applications and infrastructure resources.

Q20. B

A is wrong because VPC Flow Logs is a feature that enables you to capture information about the IP traffic going to and from network interfaces in your VPC. It doesn't capture information about the modifications of security group or NACL.

C and D are wrong because Cloudtrail or Cloudwatch alone cannot meet the requirements of given scenario.

AWS Documentation Reference:
https://docs.aws.amazon.com/awscloudtrail/latest/userguide/monitor-cloudtrail-log-files-with-cloudwatch-logs.html
You can configure CloudTrail with CloudWatch Logs to monitor your trail logs and be notified when specific activity occurs.

1. Configure your trail to send log events to CloudWatch Logs.

2. Define CloudWatch Logs metric filters to evaluate log events for matches in terms, phrases, or values. For example, you can monitor for ConsoleLogin events.
   F. https://docs.aws.amazon.com/AmazonCloudWatch/latest/events/Create-CloudWatch-Events-Rule.html

3. Assign CloudWatch metrics to the metric filters. In the given scenario it will look like below for 'security group' events
{ ($.eventName = AuthorizeSecurityGroupIngress) || ($.eventName = AuthorizeSecurityGroupEgress) || ($.eventName = RevokeSecurityGroupIngress) || ($.eventName = RevokeSecurityGroupEgress) || ($.eventName = CreateSecurityGroup) || ($.eventName = DeleteSecurityGroup) }

https://docs.aws.amazon.com/awscloudtrail/latest/userguide/cloudwatch-alarms-for-cloudtrail.html#cloudwatch-alarms-for-cloudtrail-security-group

4. Create CloudWatch alarms that are triggered according to thresholds and time periods that you specify. You can configure alarms to send notifications when alarms are triggered, so that you can take action.

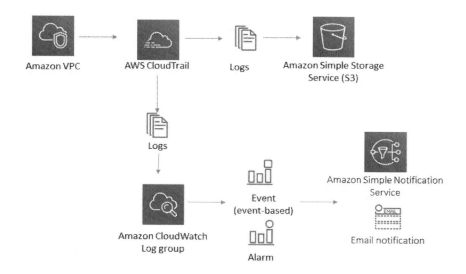

Q21. A, B, C
D is the feature of Elastic Beanstalk.

AWS Documentation Reference:
https://docs.aws.amazon.com/AWSCloudFormation/latest/UserGuide/Welcome.html
AWS CloudFormation is a service that helps you model and set up your Amazon Web Services resources so that you can spend less time managing those resources and more time focusing on your applications that run in AWS. You create a template that describes all the AWS resources that you want (like Amazon EC2 instances or Amazon RDS DB instances), and AWS CloudFormation takes care of provisioning and configuring those resources for you. You don't need to individually create and configure AWS resources and figure out what's dependent on what; AWS CloudFormation handles all of that.

Q22. B
AWS Documentation Reference: Verify Quotas for All Resource Types
https://docs.aws.amazon.com/AWSCloudFormation/latest/UserGuide/best-practices.html#limits
Before launching a stack, ensure that you can create all the resources that you want without hitting your AWS account limits. If you hit a limit, AWS CloudFormation won't create your stack successfully until you increase your quota or delete extra resources.

https://docs.aws.amazon.com/AWSCloudFormation/latest/UserGuide/stacks.html
AWS CloudFormation ensures all stack resources are created or deleted as appropriate. Because AWS CloudFormation treats the stack resources as a single unit, they must all be created or deleted successfully for the stack to be created or deleted. If a resource cannot be

created, AWS CloudFormation rolls the stack back and automatically deletes any resources that were created. If a resource cannot be deleted, any remaining resources are retained until the stack can be successfully deleted.

Q23. B, C, D, E
A is the feature of Cloudtrail.
AWS Documentation Reference:
https://aws.amazon.com/xray/

AWS X-Ray works with Amazon EC2, Amazon EC2 Container Service (Amazon ECS), AWS Lambda, and AWS Elastic Beanstalk. You can use X-Ray with applications written in Java, Node.js, and .NET that are deployed on these services.

Review request behavior: AWS X-Ray traces user requests as they travel through your entire application. It aggregates the data generated by the individual services and resources that make up your application, providing you an end-to-end view of how your application is performing.

Designed for a variety of applications: AWS X-Ray works for both simple and complex applications, either in development or in production. You can analyze simple asynchronous event calls, three-tier web applications, or complex microservices applications consisting of thousands of services. With X-Ray, you can trace requests made to applications that span multiple AWS accounts, AWS Regions, and Availability Zones.

Discover application issues: With AWS X-Ray, you can glean insights into how your application is performing and discover root causes. With X-Ray's tracing features, you can follow request paths to pinpoint where in your application and what is causing performance issues. X-Ray provides annotations so you can append metadata to traces, making it possible to tag and filter trace data so you can discover patterns and diagnose issues.

Improve application performance: AWS X-Ray helps you identify performance bottlenecks. X-Ray's service maps let you see relationships between services and resources in your application in real time. You can easily detect where high latencies are occurring, visualize node and edge latency distribution for services, and then drill down into the specific services and paths impacting application performance.

Q24. A
AWS Documentation Reference:
https://docs.aws.amazon.com/whitepapers/latest/microservices-on-aws/auditing.html
The solution is depicted in the diagram below to detect, inform and automatically react to non-compliant configuration changes within your microservices architecture. If a member of the development team has made a change to the API Gateway for a microservice to allow the endpoint to accept inbound HTTP traffic, rather than only allowing HTTPS requests. Because

this situation has been previously identified as a security compliance concern by the organization, an AWS Config rule can be created to monitor for this condition.

The rule identifies the change as a security violation, and performs two actions: it creates a log of the detected change in an S3 bucket for auditing, and it creates an SNS notification. Amazon SNS is used for two purposes in this scenario: to send an email to a specified group to inform about the security violation, and to add a message to an SQS queue. Next, the message is picked up, and the compliant state is restored by changing the API Gateway configuration.

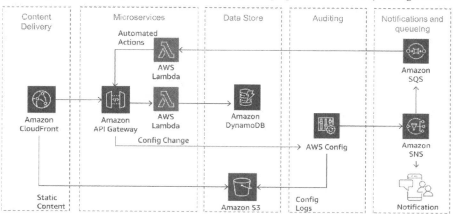

Q25. A, B
AWS Documentation Reference:
https://docs.aws.amazon.com/AmazonCloudWatch/latest/monitoring/publishingMetrics.html#high-resolution-metrics
Standard resolution, with data having a one-minute granularity
High resolution, with data at a granularity of one second

Q26.A, B
AWS Documentation Reference:
https://aws.amazon.com/premiumsupport/technology/trusted-advisor/
https://aws.amazon.com/blogs/mt/monitoring-service-limits-with-trusted-advisor-and-amazon-cloudwatch/
Use the AWS Trusted Advisor Service Limits check to monitor service limits.
You can configure alarm in Cloudwatch using TrustedAdvisor servicelimitusuage metrics.

Q27.A, C
AWS Documentation Reference:
https://docs.aws.amazon.com/awscloudtrail/latest/userguide/cloudtrail-user-guide.html

AWS CloudTrail is an AWS service that helps you enable governance, compliance, and operational and risk auditing of your AWS account. Actions taken by a user, role, or an AWS service are recorded as events in CloudTrail. Events include actions taken in the AWS Management Console, AWS Command Line Interface, and AWS SDKs and APIs.
https://aws.amazon.com/config/
AWS Config is a service that enables you to assess, audit, and evaluate the configurations of your AWS resources. Config continuously monitors and records your AWS resource configurations and allows you to automate the evaluation of recorded configurations against desired configurations. With Config, you can review changes in configurations and relationships between AWS resources, dive into detailed resource configuration histories, and determine your overall compliance against the configurations specified in your internal guidelines. This enables you to simplify compliance auditing, security analysis, change management, and operational troubleshooting.

Q28.D
AWS Documentation Reference:
https://docs.aws.amazon.com/config/latest/developerguide/remediation.html
The AWS Config Auto Remediation feature automatically remediates non-compliant resources evaluated by AWS Config rules. You can associate remediation actions with AWS Config rules and choose to execute them automatically to address non-compliant resources without manual intervention. AWS Config allows you to remediate noncompliant resources that are evaluated by AWS Config Rules. AWS Config applies remediation using AWS Systems Manager Automation documents. These documents define the actions to be performed on noncompliant AWS resources evaluated by AWS Config Rules. You can associate SSM documents with using the AWS Management Console or by using APIs.

https://aws.amazon.com/blogs/mt/aws-config-auto-remediation-s3-compliance/
Refer to above blog link to follow the steps.

A is a custom option to achieve the remediation as described in blog link below
https://aws.amazon.com/blogs/security/how-to-use-aws-config-to-monitor-for-and-respond-to-amazon-s3-buckets-allowing-public-access/

C is wrong as there is no S3 documents feature to work with AWS Config.

Q29. B
AWS Documentation Reference:
https://aws.amazon.com/blogs/aws/aws-cloudtrail-update-turn-on-in-all-regions-use-multiple-trails/
https://docs.aws.amazon.com/awscloudtrail/latest/userguide/receive-cloudtrail-log-files-from-multiple-regions.html

You can simply specify that a trail will apply to all regions and CloudTrail will automatically create the same trail in each region, record and process log files in each region, and deliver log files from all regions to the S3 bucket or (optionally) the CloudWatch Logs log group you specified.

In addition to turning on CloudTrail for all existing regions, when AWS launches a new region CloudTrail will create the trail in the new region and turn it on. As a result, you will receive log files containing API activity for your AWS account in the new region without taking any action.

## Q30.C

AWS Documentation Reference:

https://docs.aws.amazon.com/AmazonCloudWatch/latest/logs/AgentReference.html

The CloudWatch Logs agent provides an automated way to send log data to CloudWatch Logs from Amazon EC2 instances. The agent is comprised of the following components:

* A plug-in to the AWS CLI that pushes log data to CloudWatch Logs.

* A script (daemon) that initiates the process to push data to CloudWatch Logs.

* A cron job that ensures that the daemon is always running.

## Q31. D

AWS Documentation Reference:

https://docs.aws.amazon.com/AmazonCloudWatch/latest/events/WhatIsCloudWatchEvents.html

Amazon CloudWatch Events delivers a near real-time stream of system events that describe changes in Amazon Web Services (AWS) resources. Using simple rules that you can quickly set up, you can match events and route them to one or more target functions or streams.

Events – An event indicates a change in your AWS environment. AWS resources can generate events when their state changes. For example, Amazon EC2 generates an event when the state of an EC2 instance changes from pending to running, and Amazon EC2 Auto Scaling generates events when it launches or terminates instances. AWS CloudTrail publishes events when you make API calls. You can generate custom application-level events and publish them to CloudWatch Events. You can also set up scheduled events that are generated on a periodic basis.

Rules – A rule matches incoming events and routes them to targets for processing. A single rule can route to multiple targets, all of which are processed in parallel. Rules are not processed in a particular order. This enables different parts of an organization to look for and process the events that are of interest to them. A rule can customize the JSON sent to the target, by passing only certain parts or by overwriting it with a constant.

Targets – A target processes events. Targets can include Amazon EC2 instances, AWS Lambda functions, Kinesis streams, Amazon ECS tasks, Step Functions state machines, Amazon SNS topics, Amazon SQS queues, and built-in targets. A target receives events in JSON format. A rule's targets must be in the same Region as the rule.

## Q32. D
AWS Documentation Reference:
https://docs.aws.amazon.com/AmazonCloudWatch/latest/events/WhatIsCloudWatchEvents.html
You can configure the following AWS services as targets for CloudWatch Events:

- Amazon EC2 instances
- AWS Lambda functions
- Streams in Amazon Kinesis Data Streams
- Delivery streams in Amazon Kinesis Data Firehose
- Log groups in Amazon CloudWatch Logs
- Amazon ECS tasks
- Systems Manager Run Command
- Systems Manager Automation
- AWS Batch jobs
- Step Functions state machines
- Pipelines in CodePipeline
- CodeBuild projects
- Amazon Inspector assessment templates
- Amazon SNS topics
- Amazon SQS queues
- Built-in targets: EC2 CreateSnapshot API call, EC2 RebootInstances API call, EC2 StopInstances API call, and EC2 TerminateInstances API call.
- The default event bus of another AWS account

## Q33. C
AWS Documentation Reference:
https://docs.aws.amazon.com/AWSCloudFormation/latest/UserGuide/stacks.html
A stack is a collection of AWS resources that you can manage as a single unit. In other words, you can create, update, or delete a collection of resources by creating, updating, or deleting stacks. All the resources in a stack are defined by the stack's AWS CloudFormation template. A stack, for instance, can include all the resources required to run a web application, such as a web server, a database, and networking rules. If you no longer require that web application, you can simply delete the stack, and all of its related resources are deleted.
AWS CloudFormation ensures all stack resources are created or deleted as appropriate. Because AWS CloudFormation treats the stack resources as a single unit, they must all be created or deleted successfully for the stack to be created or deleted. If a resource cannot be created, AWS CloudFormation rolls the stack back and automatically deletes any resources that

were created. If a resource cannot be deleted, any remaining resources are retained until the stack can be successfully deleted.

## Q34. A, B

AWS Documentation Reference:
https://docs.aws.amazon.com/AWSCloudFormation/latest/UserGuide/using-cfn-updating-stacks.html

When you need to make changes to a stack's settings or change its resources, you update the stack instead of deleting it and creating a new stack. When you update a stack, you submit changes, such as new input parameter values or an updated template. AWS CloudFormation compares the changes you submit with the current state of your stack and updates only the changed resources.

AWS CloudFormation provides two methods for updating stacks: direct update or creating and executing change sets. When you directly update a stack, you submit changes and AWS CloudFormation immediately deploys them. Use direct updates when you want to quickly deploy your updates.

With change sets, you can preview the changes AWS CloudFormation will make to your stack, and then decide whether to apply those changes.

## Q35.D

AWS Documentation Reference:
https://docs.aws.amazon.com/AWSCloudFormation/latest/UserGuide/using-cfn-updating-stacks-update-behaviors.html

For updated resources, AWS CloudFormation uses one of the following update behaviors:

Update with No Interruption: AWS CloudFormation updates the resource without disrupting operation of that resource and without changing the resource's physical ID. For example, if you update any property on an AWS:: CloudTrail::Trail resource, AWS CloudFormation updates the trail without disruption.

Updates with Some Interruption: AWS CloudFormation updates the resource with some interruption and retains the physical ID. For example, if you update certain properties on an AWS: EC2::Instance resource, the instance might have some interruption while AWS CloudFormation and Amazon EC2 reconfigure the instance.

Replacement: AWS CloudFormation recreates the resource during an update, which also generates a new physical ID. AWS CloudFormation creates the replacement resource first, changes references from other dependent resources to point to the replacement resource, and then deletes the old resource. For example, if you update the Engine property of an AWS:: RDS::DBInstance resource type, AWS CloudFormation creates a new resource and replaces the current DB instance resource with the new one.

Q36. A, C

AWS Documentation Reference:

https://docs.aws.amazon.com/awsaccountbilling/latest/aboutv2/ri-recommendations.html

If you enable Cost Explorer, you automatically get Amazon EC2, Amazon RDS, ElastiCache, Amazon ES, and Amazon Redshift Reserved Instance (RI) purchase recommendations that could help you reduce your costs. The RI recommendation page shows you your estimated potential savings, your RI purchase recommendations, and the parameters that Cost Explorer used to create your recommendations. You can change the parameters to get recommendations that might match your use case more closely. The top of the RI recommendations page show you three numbers:

- Estimated Annual Savings – Your Estimated Annual Savings is how much Cost Explorer calculates that you could save by purchasing all the recommended RIs.
- Savings vs. On-Demand – Your Savings vs. On-Demand is your estimated savings as a percentage of your current costs.
- Purchase Recommendations – Your Purchase Recommendations is how many different RI purchase options that Cost Explorer found for you.

https://docs.aws.amazon.com/awsaccountbilling/latest/aboutv2/ce-rightsizing.html

Rightsizing recommendations helps you identify cost saving opportunities in Cost Explorer, downsizing or terminating instances in your Amazon Elastic Compute Cloud (Amazon EC2). Rightsizing recommendations analyzes your Amazon EC2 resources and usage to show opportunities on how you can lower your spending. You can see all of your underutilized Amazon EC2 instances in every Region and linked account in a single view to immediately identify how much you can save. You can see the following top-level key performance indicators (KPIs) in your rightsizing recommendations:

- Optimization opportunities – The number of recommendations available based on your resources and usage
- Estimated monthly savings – The sum of the projected monthly savings associated with each of the recommendations provided
- Estimated savings (%) – The available savings relative to the direct instance costs (On-Demand) associated with the instances in the recommendation list

Q37. A

AWS Documentation Reference:

https://docs.aws.amazon.com/AWSCloudFormation/latest/UserGuide/what-is-cfnstacksets.html

AWS CloudFormation StackSets extends the functionality of stacks by enabling you to create, update, or delete stacks across multiple accounts and regions with a single operation. Using an administrator account, you define and manage an AWS CloudFormation template, and use the template as the basis for provisioning stacks into selected target accounts across specified regions.

https://aws.amazon.com/blogs/aws/use-cloudformation-stacksets-to-provision-resources-across-multiple-aws-accounts-and-regions/

## Q38. C
AWS Documentation Reference:
https://aws.amazon.com/devops/
AWS CloudTrail is a web service that records AWS API calls for your account and delivers log files to you. The recorded information includes the identity of the API caller, the time of the API call, the source IP address of the API caller, the request parameters, and the response elements returned by the AWS service.

## Q39.B
AWS Documentation Reference:
https://docs.aws.amazon.com/AWSCloudFormation/latest/UserGuide/using-cfn-updating-stacks-changesets.html
When you need to update a stack, understanding how your changes will affect running resources before you implement them can help you update stacks with confidence. Change sets allow you to preview how proposed changes to a stack might impact your running resources, for example, whether your changes will delete or replace any critical resources, AWS CloudFormation makes the changes to your stack only when you decide to execute the change set, allowing you to decide whether to proceed with your proposed changes or explore other changes by creating another change set.

## Q40. D
AWS Documentation Reference:
https://docs.aws.amazon.com/AWSCloudFormation/latest/UserGuide/using-cfn-nested-stacks.html
As your infrastructure grows, common patterns can emerge in which you declare the same components in multiple templates. You can separate out these common components and create dedicated templates for them. Then use the resource in your template to reference other templates, creating nested stacks.
For example, assume that you have a load balancer configuration that you use for most of your stacks. Instead of copying and pasting the same configurations into your templates, you can create a dedicated template for the load balancer. Then, you just use the resource to reference that template from within other templates.
https://aws.amazon.com/blogs/devops/use-nested-stacks-to-create-reusable-templates-and-support-role-specialization/

## Q41. A

AWS Documentation Reference:

https://aws.amazon.com/organizations/

AWS Organizations helps you centrally govern your environment as you grow and scale your workloads on AWS. Whether you are a growing startup or a large enterprise, Organizations helps you to centrally manage billing; control access, compliance, and security; and share resources across your AWS accounts.

https://aws.amazon.com/organizations/faqs/

What is the difference between AWS Control Tower and AWS Organizations?

AWS Control Tower abstracts multiple AWS services (including AWS Organizations) to provide automated set-up of a secure, well-architected environment. AWS Control Tower is best suited if you want an automated deployment of a multi-account environment with AWS best practices. If you want to define your own custom multi-account environment with advanced governance and management capabilities, AWS recommends to use AWS Organizations.

Q42. D, F

These are features of AWS Control Tower and not of AWS Organizations.

AWS Documentation Reference:

https://docs.aws.amazon.com/controltower/latest/userguide/what-is-control-tower.html

AWS Control Tower has the following features:

Landing zone – A landing zone is a well-architected, multi-account AWS environment that's based on security and compliance best practices. This is the enterprise-wide container that holds all of your organizational units (OUs), accounts, users, and other resources that you want to be subject to compliance regulation.

Guardrails – A guardrail is a high-level rule that provides ongoing governance for your overall AWS environment.

Account Factory – An Account Factory is a configurable account template that helps to standardize the provisioning of new accounts with pre-approved account configurations. AWS Control Tower offers a built-in Account Factory that helps automate the account provisioning workflow in your organization.

Dashboard – The dashboard offers continuous oversight of your landing zone to your team of central cloud administrators.

https://docs.aws.amazon.com/organizations/latest/userguide/orgs_introduction.html#featur es

AWS Organizations offers the following features:

Centralized management of all of your AWS accounts: You can combine your existing accounts into an organization that enables you to manage the accounts centrally. You can create accounts that automatically are a part of your organization, and you can invite other accounts to join your organization. You also can attach policies that affect some or all of your accounts.

Consolidated billing for all member accounts: Consolidated billing is a feature of AWS Organizations. You can use the master account of your organization to consolidate and pay for all member accounts.

Hierarchical grouping of your accounts to meet your budgetary, security, or compliance needs: You can group your accounts into organizational units (OUs) and attach different access policies to each OU. For example, if you have accounts that must access only the AWS services that meet certain regulatory requirements, you can put those accounts into one OU. You then can attach a policy to that OU that blocks access to services that do not meet those regulatory requirements. You can nest OUs within other OUs to a depth of five levels, providing flexibility in how you structure your account groups.

Control over the AWS services and API actions that each account can access: As an administrator of the master account of an organization, you can use service control policies (SCPs) to specify the maximum permissions for member accounts in the organization. In SCPs, you can restrict which AWS services, resources, and individual API actions the users and roles in each member account can access. You can also define conditions for when to restrict access to AWS services, resources, and API actions. These restrictions even override the administrators of member accounts in the organization. When AWS Organizations blocks access to a service, resource, or API action for a member account, a user or role in that account can't access it. This block remains in effect even if an administrator of a member account explicitly grants such permissions in an IAM policy.

Q43. A, B, D, E
AWS Documentation Reference:
https://docs.aws.amazon.com/organizations/latest/userguide/orgs_getting-started_concepts.html
Root: The parent container for all the accounts for your organization. If you apply a policy to the root, it applies to all organizational units (OUs) and accounts in the organization.

Organization unit (OU): A container for accounts within a root. An OU also can contain other OUs, enabling you to create a hierarchy that resembles an upside-down tree, with a root at the top and branches of OUs that reach down, ending in accounts that are the leaves of the tree. When you attach a policy to one of the nodes in the hierarchy, it flows down and affects all the branches (OUs) and leaves (accounts) beneath it. An OU can have exactly one parent, and currently each account can be a member of exactly one OU.

Account: A standard AWS account that contains your AWS resources. You can attach a policy to an account to apply controls to only that one account. There are two types of accounts in an organization: a single account that is designated as the master account, and member accounts.

Service control policies (SCPs) are one type of policy that you can use to manage your organization. SCPs offer central control over the maximum available permissions for all accounts in your organization, allowing you to ensure your accounts stay within your organization's access control guidelines.

Q44. A, B, C, E, F
AWS Documentation Reference:
https://aws.amazon.com/premiumsupport/technology/trusted-advisor/

Q45. B, C, D
A is incorrect because AWS CodeCommit is a fully-managed source control service.

AWS CodePipeline is a fully managed continuous delivery service that helps you automate your release pipelines for fast and reliable application and infrastructure updates. CodePipeline automates the build, test, and deploy phases of your release process every time there is a code change, based on the release model you define. This enables you to rapidly and reliably deliver features and updates.

AWS Elastic Beanstalk is an easy-to-use service for deploying and scaling web applications and services developed with Java, .NET, PHP, Node.js, Python, Ruby, Go, and Docker on familiar servers such as Apache, Nginx, Passenger, and IIS.You can simply upload your code and Elastic Beanstalk automatically handles the deployment, from capacity provisioning, load balancing, auto-scaling to application health monitoring. At the same time, you retain full control over the AWS resources powering your application and can access the underlying resources at any time.

AWS CloudFormation provides a common language for you to describe and provision all the infrastructure resources in your cloud environment. CloudFormation allows you to use programming languages or a simple text file to model and provision, in an automated and secure manner, all the resources needed for your applications across all regions and accounts.

You can create a CI/CD on AWS with CodePipeline, CloudFormation and AWS Elastic Beanstalk. You can fully automate the provisioning of all of the AWS resources in CloudFormation to achieve Continuous Delivery for a web application in Elastic Beanstalk.

Q46. C
AWS Documentation Reference:
https://aws.amazon.com/organizations/

Following are the use cases for using AWS Organizations:

Implement and enforce corporate security, audit, and compliance policies: Use AWS Organizations to implement Service Control Policy (SCP) permission guardrails to ensure that users in your accounts can only perform actions that meet your corporate security and compliance policy requirements. Additionally, you can configure central logging of all actions performed across your organization using AWS CloudTrail and centrally aggregate data for rules that you've defined using AWS Config, enabling you to audit your environment for compliance and react quickly to changes.

Share resources across accounts: AWS Organizations makes it easy for you to share critical central resources across your accounts. For example, you can share your central AWS Directory Service Managed Active Directory with all accounts in your organization for applications to access your central identity store. Additionally, you can ensure application resources across your accounts are created on your AWS Virtual Private Cloud (VPC) subnets by centrally defining them once and sharing them across your organization using AWS Resource Access Manager.

Automate the creation of AWS accounts and categorize workloads: AWS Organizations helps you simplify IT operations by automating AWS account creation and management. The Organizations APIs enable you to create new accounts programmatically, and to add the new accounts to a group. The policies attached to the group are automatically applied to the new account. For example, you can automate the creation of new accounts for workload or application isolation and grant entities in those accounts access only to the necessary AWS services.

Q47. A, D, E, G
AWS Documentation Reference:
https://docs.aws.amazon.com/organizations/latest/userguide/orgs_manage_policies_scp.html

Service control policies (SCPs) are one type of policy that you can use to manage your organization. SCPs offer central control over the maximum available permissions for all accounts in your organization, allowing you to ensure your accounts stay within your organization's access control guidelines. SCPs are available only in an Organization that has all features enabled. SCPs aren't available if your Organization has enabled only the consolidated billing features.

SCPs are necessary but not sufficient for granting access in the accounts in your organization. Attaching an SCP to the organization root or an organizational unit (OU) defines a guardrail for what actions accounts within the organization root or OU can do. You still need to attach IAM policies to users and roles in your organization's accounts to actually grant permissions to them. With an SCP attached to those accounts, identity-based and resource-based policies grant permissions to entities only if those policies and the SCP allow the action. If both a permissions boundary (an advanced IAM feature) and an SCP are present, then the boundary, the SCP, and the identity-based policy must all allow the action.

SCPs are similar to IAM permission policies and use almost the same syntax. However, an SCP never grants permissions. Instead, SCPs are JSON policies that specify the maximum permissions for an organization or organizational unit (OU).

Q48. A, D
AWS Documentation Reference:
https://aws.amazon.com/premiumsupport/knowledge-center/iam-policy-service-control-policy/

The IAM user Bob is part of the Dev OU, and the IAM policy associated with Bob allows full access to the Amazon S3 and Amazon EC2 services. Because the SCP associated with the Dev OU allows the use of the S3 service, and Bob has an IAM policy that grants him full access to S3, Bob can use S3. However, even though the IAM policy also grants Bob admin access to EC2, since the SCP only allows the use of S3, Bob cannot use EC2.

For the IAM user David, even though the S3 service is whitelisted for the users, groups, and roles in the Sales OU (by the SCP), David's IAM policy doesn't allow access to any AWS services. David will not be able to access any AWS services until he has an IAM policy that grants permissions to services.

Q49. B
AWS Documentation Reference:
https://docs.aws.amazon.com/codestar/latest/userguide/welcome.html
AWS CodeStar is a cloud-based service for creating, managing, and working with software development projects on AWS. You can quickly develop, build, and deploy applications on AWS with an AWS CodeStar project. An AWS CodeStar project creates and integrates AWS services for your project development toolchain. Depending on your choice of AWS CodeStar project template, that toolchain might include source control, build, deployment, virtual servers or serverless resources, and more. AWS CodeStar also manages the permissions required for project users (called team members). By adding users as team members to an AWS CodeStar project, project owners can quickly and simply grant each team member role-appropriate access to a project and its resources.

Q50. A
AWS Documentation Reference:
https://aws.amazon.com/devops/continuous-delivery/
https://aws.amazon.com/devops/continuous-integration/
You can set up a continuous integration workflow with AWS CodePipeline, which lets you build a workflow that builds code in AWS CodeBuild every time you commit a change.

You can set up continuous delivery by using AWS CodePipeline, which lets you build a workflow that builds code in AWS CodeBuild, runs automated tests, and deploys code.

Q51. D
AWS Documentation Reference:
https://aws.amazon.com/xray/
AWS X-Ray helps developers analyze and debug production, distributed applications, such as those built using a microservices architecture. With X-Ray, you can understand how your application and its underlying services are performing to identify and troubleshoot the root cause of performance issues and errors. X-Ray provides an end-to-end view of requests as they travel through your application, and shows a map of your application's underlying components.
https://aws.amazon.com/blogs/developer/new-analyze-and-debug-distributed-applications-interactively-using-aws-x-ray-analytics/
AWS X-Ray Analytics helps you quickly and easily understand:
• Any latency degradation or increase in error or fault rates.
• The latency experienced by customers in the 50th, 90th, and 95th percentiles.
• The root cause of the issue at hand.
• End users who are impacted, and by how much.
• Comparisons of trends, based on different criteria. For example, you can understand if new deployments caused a regression.

Q52. C
AWS CloudFormation automates and simplifies the task of repeatedly and predictably creating groups of related resources that power your applications.

Q53. A, B, C, E
AWS Documentation Reference:
https://docs.aws.amazon.com/AWSCloudFormation/latest/UserGuide/gettingstarted.templatebasics.html
A template is a declaration of the AWS resources that make up a stack. The template is stored as a text file whose format complies with the JavaScript Object Notation (JSON) or YAML standard. In the template, you declare the AWS resources you want to create and configure. A stack is a collection of resources that result from instantiating a template. You create a stack by supplying a template and any required parameters to AWS CloudFormation. Based on the template and any dependencies specified in it, AWS CloudFormation determines what AWS resources need to be created and in what order.
Q54. B
AWS Documentation Reference:
https://docs.aws.amazon.com/AWSCloudFormation/latest/UserGuide/parameters-section-structure.html

You can launch stacks from the same template but with variations such as different AMI, RDS size, security group etc. You can use parameters to customize template at runtime when the stack is built for a specific environment. Parameters enable you to input custom values to your template each time you create or update a stack. By leveraging parameters you can use a single template for creating different infrastructure with different configuration values.

Q55. C
AWS Documentation Reference: Updating a Stack with Change Sets
https://docs.aws.amazon.com/AWSCloudFormation/latest/UserGuide/cfn-whatis-howdoesitwork.html
When you need to update your stack's resources, you can modify the stack's template. You don't need to create a new stack and delete the old one. To update a stack, create a change set by submitting a modified version of the original stack template, different input parameter values, or both. AWS CloudFormation compares the modified template with the original template and generates a change set. The change set lists the proposed changes. After reviewing the changes, you can execute the change set to update your stack or you can create a new change set.

Q56. A, B, D
AWS Documentation Reference: Deleting a Stack
https://docs.aws.amazon.com/AWSCloudFormation/latest/UserGuide/cfn-whatis-howdoesitwork.html
When you delete a stack, you specify the stack to delete, and AWS CloudFormation deletes the stack and all the resources in that stack. If you want to delete a stack but want to retain some resources in that stack, you can use a deletion policy to retain those resources.
After all the resources have been deleted, AWS CloudFormation signals that your stack has been successfully deleted. If AWS CloudFormation cannot delete a resource, the stack will not be deleted. Any resources that haven't been deleted will remain until you can successfully delete the stack.

Q57. A, B, D
C is incorrect as there is no 'Echo' property.
AWS Documentation Reference:
https://docs.aws.amazon.com/AWSCloudFormation/latest/UserGuide/best-practices.html
Q58.B
AWS Documentation Reference:
https://docs.aws.amazon.com/systems-manager/latest/userguide/what-is-systems-manager.html
AWS Systems Manager is an AWS service that you can use to view and control your infrastructure on AWS. Using the Systems Manager console, you can view operational data from multiple AWS services and automate operational tasks across your AWS resources.

Systems Manager helps you maintain security and compliance by scanning your managed instances and reporting on (or taking corrective action on) any policy violations it detects. For example:

- Group AWS resources together by any purpose or activity you choose, such as application, environment, region, project, campaign, business unit, or software lifecycle.
- Centrally define the configuration options and policies for your managed instances.
- Centrally view, investigate, and resolve operational work items related to AWS resources.
- Automate or schedule a variety of maintenance and deployment tasks.
- Use and create runbook-style SSM documents that define the actions to perform on your managed instances.
- Run a command, with rate and error controls, that targets an entire fleet of managed instances.
- Securely connect to a managed instance with a single click, without having to open an inbound port or manage SSH keys.
- Separate your secrets and configuration data from your code by using parameters, with or without encryption, and then reference those parameters from a number of other AWS services.
- Perform automated inventory by collecting metadata about your Amazon EC2 and on-premises managed instances. Metadata can include information about applications, network configurations, and more.
- View consolidated inventory data from multiple AWS Regions and accounts that you manage.
- Quickly see which resources in your account are out of compliance and take corrective action from a centralized dashboard.
- View active summaries of metrics and alarms for your AWS resources.

Q59.B, C, D
AWS Documentation Reference:

https://docs.aws.amazon.com/systems-manager/latest/userguide/prereqs-operating-systems.html
Your Amazon EC2 instances, on-premises servers, and virtual machines (VMs) must be running one of the following operating systems in order to be used with AWS Systems Manager.

Windows Server, Linux, Raspbian

Q60. D
D defines CloudFormation Templates.
AWS Documentation Reference:

https://docs.aws.amazon.com/systems-manager/latest/userguide/sysman-ssm-docs.html
An AWS Systems Manager document (SSM document) defines the actions that Systems Manager performs on your managed instances. Systems Manager includes more than a dozen pre-configured documents that you can use by specifying parameters at runtime. Documents use JavaScript Object Notation (JSON) or YAML, and they include steps and parameters that you specify.

Q61. B, C
AWS Documentation Reference:
https://docs.aws.amazon.com/systems-manager/latest/userguide/session-manager.html
Session Manager is a fully managed AWS Systems Manager capability that lets you manage your Amazon EC2 instances, on-premises instances, and virtual machines (VMs) through an interactive one-click browser-based shell or through the AWS CLI. Session Manager provides secure and auditable instance management without the need to open inbound ports, maintain bastion hosts, or manage SSH keys. Session Manager also makes it easy to comply with corporate policies that require controlled access to instances, strict security practices, and fully auditable logs with instance access details, while still providing end users with simple one-click cross-platform access to your managed instances.
https://docs.aws.amazon.com/systems-manager/latest/userguide/execute-remote-commands.html
AWS Systems Manager Run Command lets you remotely and securely manage the configuration of your managed instances. A managed instance is any Amazon EC2 instance or on-premises machine in your hybrid environment that has been configured for Systems Manager. Run Command enables you to automate common administrative tasks and perform ad hoc configuration changes at scale. You can use Run Command from the AWS console, the AWS Command Line Interface, AWS Tools for Windows PowerShell, or the AWS SDKs. Run Command is offered at no additional cost.
Administrators use Run Command to perform the following types of tasks on their managed instances: install or bootstrap applications, build a deployment pipeline, capture log files when an instance is terminated from an Auto Scaling group, and join instances to a Windows domain, to name a few.

Q62. A, B, C, E
D is not a feature of AWS System Manager, AWS Config is a separate AWS service.
AWS Documentation Reference:
https://aws.amazon.com/systems-manager/features/
AWS AppConfig helps you deploy application configuration in a managed and a monitored way just like code deployments, but without the need to deploy the code if a configuration value changes. AWS AppConfig scales with your infrastructure so you can deploy configurations to any number of Amazon EC2 instances, containers, AWS Lambda functions, mobile apps, IoT devices or on-premises instances.

Inventory: AWS Systems Manager collects information about your instances and the software installed on them, helping you to understand your system configurations and installed applications. You can collect data about applications, files, network configurations, Windows services, registries, server roles, updates, and any other system properties.

Automation: AWS Systems Manager allows you to safely automate common and repetitive IT operations and management tasks. With Systems Manager Automation, you can use predefined playbooks, or you can build, run, and share wiki-style automated playbooks to enable AWS resource management across multiple accounts and AWS Regions.

Patch Manager: AWS Systems Manager helps you select and deploy operating system and software patches automatically across large groups of Amazon EC2 or on-premises instances. Through patch baselines, you can set rules to auto-approve select categories of patches to be installed, such as operating system or high severity patches, and you can specify a list of patches that override these rules and are automatically approved or rejected. You can also schedule maintenance windows for your patches so that they are only applied during preset times. Systems Manager helps ensure that your software is up-to-date and meets your compliance policies.

## Q63. A, B

AWS Documentation Reference:
https://docs.aws.amazon.com/organizations/latest/userguide/orgs_manage_policies_about-scps.html
Because the SCP attached to the organization root doesn't allow D or E, no OUs or accounts in the organization can use them. Even though the SCP attached to the OU explicitly allows D and E, they end up blocked because they're blocked by the organization root. Also, because the OU's SCP doesn't allow A or B, those permissions are blocked for the OU and any of its child OUs or accounts. However, other OUs under the organization root that are peers to the parent OU could allow A and B.

## Q64. A, B, D

AWS Documentation Reference:
https://aws.amazon.com/aws-cost-management/
AWS Budgets gives you the ability to set custom budgets that alert you when your costs or usage exceed (or are forecasted to exceed) your budgeted amount. You can also use AWS Budgets to set reservation utilization or coverage targets and receive alerts when your utilization drops below the threshold you define. Reservation alerts are supported for Amazon EC2, Amazon RDS, Amazon Redshift, Amazon ElastiCache, and Amazon Elasticsearch reservations.

AWS Cost Explorer has an easy-to-use interface that lets you visualize, understand, and manage your AWS costs and usage over time. AWS Cost Explorer lets you explore your AWS costs and usage at both a high level and at a detailed level of analysis, and empowering you to dive deeper using a number of filtering dimensions (e.g., AWS Service, Region, Linked Account, etc.) AWS Cost Explorer also gives you access to a set of default reports to help you get started, while also allowing you to create custom reports from scratch.

The AWS Cost & Usage Report contains the most comprehensive set of AWS cost and usage data available, including additional metadata about AWS services, pricing, and reservations (e.g., Amazon EC2 Reserved Instances (RIs)).The AWS Cost & Usage Report lists AWS usage for each service category used by an account and its IAM users in hourly or daily line items, as well as any tags that you have activated for cost allocation purposes. You can also customize the AWS Cost & Usage Report to aggregate your usage data to the daily or hourly level.

Q65. D

Q66. A
AWS Documentation Reference:
https://aws.amazon.com/blogs/aws/aws-compute-optimizer-your-customized-resource-optimization-service/
https://aws.amazon.com/compute-optimizer/faqs/
*When should I use AWS Compute Optimizer and when should I use AWS Cost Explorer?*
You should use AWS Compute Optimizer if you want to look at instance type recommendations beyond downsizing within an instance family. You can use AWS Compute Optimizer to get downsizing recommendations within or across instance families, upsizing recommendations to remove performance bottlenecks, and recommendations for EC2 instances that are parts of an Auto Scaling group. AWS Compute Optimizer provides you additional capabilities to enhance recommendation quality and the user experience, such as using machine learning to identify workload types and automatically choose workload-specific recommendation methodology for them. You should also use AWS Compute Optimizer if you want to understand the performance risks and how your workload would perform on various EC2 instance options to evaluate the price-performance trade-off for your workloads.
You should use AWS Cost Explorer if you want to identify under-utilized EC2 instances that may be downsized on an instance by instance basis within the same instance family, and you want to understand the potential impact on your AWS bill by taking into account your RIs and Savings Plans. Cost Explorer offers recommendations for all commercial regions (outside of China) and supports the A, T, M, C, R, X, Z, I, D, H instance families.

Q67. A, B, C, D, E
AWS Documentation Reference:
https://aws.amazon.com/architecture/well-architected/

Q68. A, C, D, E, F

Q69. B, C
AWS Documentation Reference:
https://docs.aws.amazon.com/awsaccountbilling/latest/aboutv2/ce-default-reports.html
Cost and Usage Reports has following reports:

- The AWS Marketplace report shows how much you have spent through AWS Marketplace.
- The Monthly costs by linked account report shows your costs for the last six months, grouped by linked account.
- The Monthly costs by service report shows your costs for the last six months, grouped by service.
- The Monthly EC2 running hours costs and usage report shows how much you have spent on active Reserved Instances (RIs).

Reserved Instance Reports:

RI Utilization Reports: The RI Utilization reports show how much of your Amazon EC2, Amazon Redshift, Amazon RDS, Amazon Elasticsearch Service, and Amazon ElastiCache Reserved Instance (RIs) that you use, how much you saved by using RIs, how much you overspent on RIs, and your net savings from purchasing RIs during the selected time range. This helps you to see if you have purchased too many RIs. It also shows how much you saved over On-Demand Instance costs by purchasing a reservation, the amortized costs of your unused reservations, and your total net savings from purchasing reservations.

RI Coverage Reports: The RI Coverage reports show how many of your Amazon EC2, Amazon Redshift, Amazon RDS, Amazon Elasticsearch Service, and Amazon ElastiCache instance hours are covered by RIs, how much you spent on On-Demand Instances, and how much you might have saved had you purchased more reservations. This enables you to see if you have under-purchased RIs.

Q70. A, B, D
Capacity reservation is not a feature of Consolidated Billing.
AWS Documentation Reference:
https://docs.aws.amazon.com/awsaccountbilling/latest/aboutv2/consolidated-billing.html
https://docs.aws.amazon.com/awsaccountbilling/latest/aboutv2/useconsolidatedbilling-procedure.html
AWS Organizations provides consolidated billing so that you can track the combined costs of all the linked accounts in your organization. The payer account is billed for all charges of the linked accounts. However, unless the organization is changed to support all features in the organization (not consolidated billing features only) and linked accounts are explicitly restricted by policies, each linked account is otherwise independent from the other linked accounts. For example, the owner of a linked account can sign up for AWS services, access resources, and use AWS Premium Support unless the payer account restricts those actions. Each account

owner continues to use their own IAM user name and password, with account permissions assigned independently of other accounts in the organization.

# Answer PRACTICE EXAM 1

Q1. A

AWS Documentation Reference: General Purpose SSD (gp2) Volumes: I/O Credits and Burst Performance

https://docs.aws.amazon.com/en_pv/AWSEC2/latest/UserGuide/EBSVolumeTypes.html

General Purpose SSD (gp2) volumes offer between a minimum of 100 IOPS (at 33.33 GiB and below) and a maximum of 16,000 IOPS (at 5,334 GiB and above), baseline performance scales linearly at 3 IOPS per GiB of volume size.

When your volume requires more than the baseline performance I/O level, it draws on I/O credits in the credit balance to burst to the required performance level, up to a maximum of 3,000 IOPS. When your volume uses fewer I/O credits than it earns in a second, unused I/O credits are added to the I/O credit balance. Each volume receives an initial I/O credit balance of 5.4 million I/O credits, which is enough to sustain the maximum burst performance of 3,000 IOPS for 30 minutes.

The 500 GB gp2 storage will have baseline performance of 500*3 = 1500 IOPS. As the volume uses fewer I/O credits of 1000 IPS than it earns 1500 IOPS in a second, unused I/O credits are added to the I/O credit balance.

When your volume requires 3000 IOPS which is more than the baseline performance I/O level of 1500 IOPS, it draws on I/O credits in the credit balance to burst to the required performance level

Q2. B, D, E

AWS Documentation Reference:

https://docs.aws.amazon.com/AmazonS3/latest/dev/UsingBucket.html#access-bucket-intro

Amazon S3 supports both virtual-hosted–style and path-style URLs to access a bucket.

In a virtual-hosted–style URL, the bucket name is part of the domain name in the URL. For example:

http://*bucket*.s3.*aws-region*.amazonaws.com.
http://*bucket*.s3.amazonaws.com

In a virtual-hosted–style URL, you can use either of these endpoints. If you make a request to the http://bucket.s3.amazonaws.com endpoint, the DNS has sufficient information to route your request directly to the Region where your bucket resides.

Virtual style url that will work are

https://mywestwebsite.s3.amazonaws.com
https://mywestwebsite.s3.us-west-1.amazonaws.com
https://mywestwebsite.s3-us-west-1.amazonaws.com

For

https://s3.amazonaws.com/mywestwebsite

it will throw an error with suggested endpoint "mywestwebsite.s3.amazonaws.com"

In a path-style URL, the bucket name is not part of the domain. For example:

Region-specific endpoint, http://s3.*aws-region*.amazonaws.com/*bucket*

Valid endpoint names for this west region:
s3.us-west-1.amazonaws.com

For a bucket in the region us-west-1
Path url that will work are:
https://s3.us-west-1.amazonaws.com/mywestwebsite
https://s3-us-west-1.amazonaws.com/mywestwebsite

Q3. D
The key criteria is to deploy minimum servers to meet the fault tolerance requirement of availability of at least six servers (66% of total 9) when on AZ goes down and also meeting requirement of at least nine servers for normal scenario.
Though A and C will ensure availability of at least six servers when one of the AZ goes down but total number of servers is more than that of option D

Q4. C
AWS Documentation Reference: Web serving & content management
https://aws.amazon.com/efs/
Amazon EFS provides a durable, high throughput file system for content management systems and web serving applications that store and serve information for a range of applications like websites, online publications, and archives.
Amazon EFS provides secure access for thousands of connections for Amazon EC2 instances and on-premises servers simultaneously using a traditional file permissions model, file locking capabilities, and hierarchical directory structure via the NFSv4 protocol.

Q5. A, D
AWS Documentation Reference:
https://docs.aws.amazon.com/autoscaling/ec2/userguide/as-scaling-target-tracking.html
https://docs.aws.amazon.com/autoscaling/ec2/userguide/Cooldown.html
A recommended best practice is to scale out quickly when needed but scale in slowly to avoid having to relaunch if there is workload fluctuation up and down more frequently.
It will also be better to analyze what should be the value of the metric which would reduce the fluctuation of scaling up and down.

Q6. D
None of the other options provide static ip address.
AWS Documentation Reference:
https://aws.amazon.com/global-accelerator/features/
https://aws.amazon.com/blogs/aws/new-aws-global-accelerator-for-availability-and-performance/

AWS Global Accelerator uses AWS's vast, highly available and congestion-free global network to direct internet traffic from your users to your applications running in AWS regions. With AWS Global Accelerator, your users are directed to your workload based on their geographic location, application health, and weights that you can configure. AWS Global Accelerator also allocates static Anycast IP addresses that are globally unique for your application and do not change, thus removing the need to update clients as your application scales.

## Q7. C, D, E
A is wrong because you cannot modify the operating system.
B is wrong because instance size footprint of a1.large and a1.xlarge is not same as shown in table below.

| Instance size | Normalization factor |
|---|---|
| medium | 2 |
| large | 4 |
| xlarge | 8 |

AWS Documentation Reference:
https://docs.aws.amazon.com/AWSEC2/latest/UserGuide/ri-modifying.html#ri-modification-limits
You can modify these attributes as follows:

| Modifiable attribute | Supported platforms | Limitations |
|---|---|---|
| Change Availability Zones within the same Region | Linux and Windows | - |
| Change the scope from Availability Zone to Region and vice versa | Linux and Windows | If you change the scope from Availability Zone to Region, you lose the capacity reservation benefit. If you change the scope from Region to Availability Zone, you lose Availability Zone flexibility and instance size flexibility (if applicable). |
| Change the instance size within the same instance family | Linux only | The reservation must use default tenancy. Some instance families are not supported, because there are no other sizes available. |
| Change the network from EC2-Classic to Amazon VPC and vice versa | Linux and Windows | The network platform must be available in your AWS account. If you created your AWS account after 2013-12-04, it does not support EC2-Classic. |

## Q8. B

## Q9. D, E
EC2 instance with windows based AMI along with Amazon FSx for Windows File Server to provide the environment similar to on-premise
AWS Documentation Reference:
https://aws.amazon.com/fsx/windows/
Amazon FSx is built on Windows Server and provides you with the native Windows file system features and performance that your applications need from a file store. By providing fully managed native Windows file shares with features like Microsoft AD integration and automatic backups, you can easily migrate Windows-based applications to AWS. Amazon FSx

supports Windows-native file system features such as Access Control Lists (ACLs), shadow copies, and user quotas to help you move your applications to AWS with minimal disruption. Amazon FSx provides NTFS file systems that can be accessed from up to thousands of compute instances using the SMB protocol. Amazon FSx works with Microsoft Active Directory (AD) to easily integrate your file system with your Windows environments.

## Q10. A, D
B is incorrect as there no option called 'validating' the file.
C replacing the old file with new file having same name will not have effect of newer file getting served to user request. The new file will be served only after the expiration time setting.
AWS Documentation Reference:
https://docs.aws.amazon.com/en_pv/AmazonCloudFront/latest/DeveloperGuide/Removin gObjects.html
If you want to remove a file right away before it expires, you must do one of the following:

* Invalidate the file from edge caches. The next time a viewer requests the file, CloudFront returns to the origin to fetch the latest version of the file.

* Use file versioning. When you use versioning, different versions of a file have different names that you can use in your CloudFront distribution, to change which file is returned to viewers.

## Q11. D
Since 'cost' is the most important criteria, spot instances pricing provides least pricing compared to other purchasing options.
AWS Documentation Reference:
https://docs.aws.amazon.com/AWSEC2/latest/UserGuide/using-spot-instances.html
A Spot Instance is an unused EC2 instance that is available for less than the On-Demand price. Because Spot Instances enable you to request unused EC2 instances at steep discounts, you can lower your Amazon EC2 costs significantly. Spot Instances are a cost-effective choice if you can be flexible about when your applications run and if your applications can be interrupted.

## Q12. C.
AWS Documentation Reference:
https://docs.aws.amazon.com/en_pv/AWSEC2/latest/UserGuide/EBSVolumeTypes.html

## Q13. C
AWS Documentation Reference:
https://docs.aws.amazon.com/AWSSimpleQueueService/latest/SQSDeveloperGuide/sqs-delay-queues.html
When the wait time for the ReceiveMessage API action is greater than 0, long polling is in effect. Long polling helps reduce the cost of using Amazon SQS by eliminating the number of

empty responses (when there are no messages available for a ReceiveMessage request) and false empty responses (when messages are available but aren't included in a response).

Long polling offers the following benefits:

- Eliminate empty responses by allowing Amazon SQS to wait until a message is available in a queue before sending a response. Unless the connection times out, the response to the ReceiveMessage request contains at least one of the available messages, up to the maximum number of messages specified in the ReceiveMessage action.

- Eliminate false empty responses by querying all—rather than a subset of—Amazon SQS servers

## Q14. B

AWS Documentation Reference:

https://aws.amazon.com/blogs/compute/secure-api-access-with-amazon-cognito-federated-identities-amazon-cognito-user-pools-and-amazon-api-gateway/

As it is mentioned that you need RDBMS therefore Aurora Serverless service , for Serverless backend design you will be using Lambda , Cognito is the service you will need for federated user authentication from Facebook/Google/Amazon and API gateway  as custom API to your code running in AWS Lambda and also for calling the Lambda code from your API. API Gateway can invoke AWS Lambda code in your account.

You don't need DynamoDB as the design doesn't require NoSQL database nor Elastic Beanstalk which is appropriate for a web application deployment.

https://aws.amazon.com/rds/aurora/serverless/

Amazon Aurora Serverless is an on-demand, auto-scaling configuration for Amazon Aurora (MySQL-compatible and PostgreSQL-compatible editions), where the database will automatically start up, shut down, and scale capacity up or down based on your application's needs.

## Q15. B

AWS Documentation Reference:

https://docs.aws.amazon.com/AmazonS3/latest/dev/how-to-set-lifecycle-configuration-intro.html

Based on the requirement S3 is the most cost effective storage giving different storage options based on the accessibility and life duration time based requirements. Hence C and D is not correct. You didn't need Redshift data warehouse to store for this requirement. EBS provides block storage and is specifically meant for EC2 (Elastic Computing Cloud) instances and is not accessible unless mounted to one

S3 lifecycle rules are applied based on object creation date. Hence A is not correct.

Option B provides the appropriate transition of data based on the life time from creation date to right S3 storage tier.

## Q16. D

AWS Documentation Reference:

https://aws.amazon.com/waf/

AWS WAF is a web application firewall that lets you monitor the HTTP and HTTPS requests that are forwarded to an Amazon API Gateway, Amazon CloudFront or an Application Load Balancer. AWS WAF gives you control over which traffic to allow or block to your web applications by defining customizable web security rules.

## Q17. A, C
There is no option of performance networking for instances.
AWS Documentation Reference:
https://docs.aws.amazon.com/AWSEC2/latest/UserGuide/placement-groups.html#placement-groups-cluster
A cluster placement group is a logical grouping of instances within a single Availability Zone. Cluster placement groups are recommended for applications that benefit from low network latency, high network throughput, or both. They are also recommended when the majority of the network traffic is between the instances in the group. To provide the lowest latency and the highest packet-per-second network performance for your placement group, choose an instance type that supports enhanced networking.

## Q18. D
Multi-AZ deployment doesn't improve performance.

## Q19. C
AWS Documentation Reference links:
https://docs.aws.amazon.com/AmazonS3/latest/dev/WebsiteHosting.html
https://docs.aws.amazon.com/AmazonS3/latest/dev/WebsiteEndpoints.html
https://docs.aws.amazon.com/general/latest/gr/rande.html#s3_website_region_endpoints

After configuring a S3 bucket for website hosting, website content are uploaded to the bucket. The bucket must have public read access. The website is then available at the AWS Region-specific website endpoint of the bucket, which is in one of the following formats:

<bucket-name>.s3-website-<AWS-region>.amazonaws.com
<bucket-name>.s3-website. <AWS-region>.amazonaws.com

Which format is used for the endpoint depends on what Region the bucket is in.
In the given scenario the website endpoint for us-west-2 regions is
's3-website-us-west-2.amazonaws.com' therefore the url for the website will be

http://west-bucket.s3-website-us-west-2.amazonaws.com/

## Q20. B
AWS Documentation Reference:
https://docs.aws.amazon.com/elasticbeanstalk/latest/dg/Welcome.html

With Elastic Beanstalk, you can quickly deploy and manage applications in the AWS Cloud without having to learn about the infrastructure that runs those applications. Elastic Beanstalk reduces management complexity without restricting choice or control. You simply upload your application, and Elastic Beanstalk automatically handles the details of capacity provisioning, load balancing, scaling, and application health monitoring.

## Q21. A, B, D

AWS Documentation Reference: Examples of Applying Reserved Instances
https://docs.aws.amazon.com/AWSEC2/latest/UserGuide/apply_ri.html
The Reserved Instance benefits are applied in the following way:

- The discount and capacity reservation of the four m3.large zonal Reserved Instances is used by the four m3.large instances because the attributes (instance size, Region, platform, tenancy) between them match.
- The m4.large regional Reserved Instances provide Availability Zone and instance size flexibility, because they are regional Amazon Linux Reserved Instances with default tenancy.
- An m4.large is equivalent to 4 normalized units/hour.
- You've purchased four m4.large regional Reserved Instances, and in total, they are equal to 16 normalized units/hour (4x4). Account A has two m4.xlarge instances running, which is equivalent to 16 normalized units/hour (2x8). In this case, the four m4.large regional Reserved Instances provide the billing benefit to an entire hour of usage of the two m4.xlarge instances.
- The c4.large regional Reserved Instance in us-east-1 provides Availability Zone and instance size flexibility, because it is a regional Amazon Linux Reserved Instance with default tenancy, and applies to the c4.xlarge instance. A c4.large instance is equivalent to 4 normalized units/hour and a c4.xlarge is equivalent to 8 normalized units/hour.
- In this case, the c4.large regional Reserved Instance provides partial benefit to c4.xlarge usage. This is because the c4.large Reserved Instance is equivalent to 4 normalized units/hour of usage, but the c4.xlarge instance requires 8 normalized units/hour. Therefore, the c4.large Reserved Instance billing discount applies to 50% of c4.xlarge usage. The remaining c4.xlarge usage is charged at the On-Demand rate.

## Q22. B

The key point to consider here is file size in the range of 10-20 MB and upload resiliency in low speed network.
C is not suitable because Amazon S3 transfer acceleration is used mainly when:

- You have to upload to a centralized bucket from all over the world.
- You have to transfer gigabytes to terabytes of data on a regular basis across continents.

A is feasible as you can upload up to 5 GB object size in one PUT operation to S3 bucket. But using single put operation may not be suitable in low bandwidth scenario.

Correct answer is B, to use multipart upload api to upload the files to S3. If you're uploading over a spotty network, multipart uploading increases resiliency to network errors by avoiding upload restarts. Multipart upload can be used for file sizes greater than 5 MB.

### Q23. C, D
AWS Documentation Reference:
https://docs.aws.amazon.com/AmazonRDS/latest/UserGuide/Overview.Encryption.html
You can only enable encryption for an Amazon RDS DB instance when you create it, not after the DB instance is created. However, because you can encrypt a copy of an unencrypted DB snapshot, you can effectively add encryption to an unencrypted DB instance. That is, you can create a snapshot of your DB instance, and then create an encrypted copy of that snapshot. You can then restore a DB instance from the encrypted snapshot, and thus you have an encrypted copy of your original DB instance.

### Q24. C, D, E
AWS Documentation Reference:
https://docs.aws.amazon.com/efs/latest/ug/whatisefs.html
Amazon Elastic File System (Amazon EFS) provides a simple, scalable, fully managed elastic NFS file system for use with AWS Cloud services and on-premises resources. Using Amazon EFS with Microsoft Windows–based Amazon EC2 instances is not supported.
Multiple Amazon EC2 instances can access an Amazon EFS file system at the same time, providing a common data source for workloads and applications running on more than one instance or server.
https://docs.aws.amazon.com/fsx/latest/WindowsGuide/what-is.html
Amazon FSx for Windows File Server provides fully managed Microsoft Windows file servers, backed by a fully native Windows file system. Amazon FSx has native support for Windows file system features and for the industry-standard Server Message Block (SMB) protocol to access file storage over a network.
https://docs.aws.amazon.com/fsx/latest/LustreGuide/what-is.html
Amazon FSx for Lustre makes it easy and cost-effective to launch and run the popular, high-performance Lustre file system. You use Lustre for workloads where speed matters, such as machine learning, high performance computing (HPC), video processing, and financial modeling. Amazon FSx for Lustre is POSIX-compliant, so you can use your current Linux-based applications without having to make any changes. Amazon FSx for Lustre provides a native file system interface and works as any file system does with your Linux operating system.

### Q25. A
AWS Documentation Reference:
https://docs.aws.amazon.com/AmazonECS/latest/developerguide/service-load-balancing.html

Your Amazon ECS service can optionally be configured to use Elastic Load Balancing to distribute traffic evenly across the tasks in your service.

Amazon ECS services support the Application Load Balancer, Network Load Balancer, and Classic Load Balancer load balancer types. Application Load Balancers are used to route HTTP/HTTPS (or Layer 7) traffic. Network Load Balancers and Classic Load Balancers are used to route TCP (or Layer 4) traffic.

Application Load Balancers offer several features that make them attractive for use with Amazon ECS services:
- Each service can serve traffic from multiple load balancers and expose multiple load balanced ports by specifying multiple target groups.
- They are supported by tasks using both the Fargate and EC2 launch types.
- Application Load Balancers allow containers to use dynamic host port mapping (so that multiple tasks from the same service are allowed per container instance).
- Application Load Balancers support path-based routing and priority rules (so that multiple services can use the same listener port on a single Application Load Balancer).

## Q26. B
AWS Documentation Reference:
https://docs.aws.amazon.com/sns/latest/dg/sns-common-scenarios.html
The "fanout" scenario is when an Amazon SNS message is sent to a topic and then replicated and pushed to multiple Amazon SQS queues, HTTP endpoints, or email addresses. This allows for parallel asynchronous processing.

## Q27. B, C, D
AWS Documentation Reference:
https://docs.aws.amazon.com/AmazonS3/latest/dev/NotificationHowTo.html#notification-how-to-event-types-and-destinations
Amazon S3 supports the following destinations where it can publish events:
- Amazon Simple Notification Service (Amazon SNS) topic
- Amazon Simple Queue Service (Amazon SQS) queue
- AWS Lambda

## Q28. B
A, C are wrong because transitive peering connection is not supported.
AWS Documentation Reference: Three VPCs Peered Together
https://docs.aws.amazon.com/vpc/latest/peering/peering-configurations-full-access.html

## Q29. A
Lambda function can be configured as S3 event notification target.

AWS Documentation Reference:

https://aws.amazon.com/lambda/

AWS Lambda lets you run code without provisioning or managing servers. You pay only for the compute time you consume - there is no charge when your code is not running. Just upload your code and Lambda takes care of everything required to run and scale your code with high availability.

Q30. A, B, C

AWS Documentation Reference:

https://docs.aws.amazon.com/vpc/latest/userguide/VPC_Scenario2.html

The configuration for this scenario includes a virtual private cloud (VPC) with a public subnet and a private subnet as shown below.

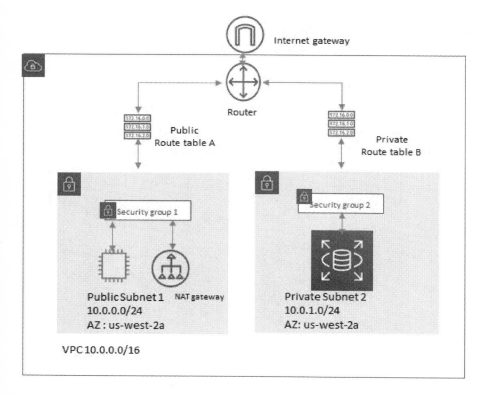

The web servers is in a public subnet and the database servers in a private subnet. You can set up security and routing so that the web servers can communicate with the database servers. The instances in the public subnet can send outbound traffic directly to the Internet, whereas the instances in the private subnet can't. Instead, the instances in the private subnet can access the Internet by using a network address translation (NAT) gateway that resides in the public subnet. The database servers can connect to the Internet for software updates using the NAT gateway, but the Internet cannot establish connections to the database servers.

Q31. A
AWS Documentation Reference:
https://docs.aws.amazon.com/Route53/latest/DeveloperGuide/routing-policy.html
Since the requirement here is routing based on 'location' of the user, the appropriate routing policy will be Geolocation Routing. Geoproximity routing policy is used when you want to route traffic based on the location of your resources and, optionally, shift traffic from resources in one location to resources in another.
There is no routing policy for C and D.

Q32. C
AWS Documentation Reference:
https://aws.amazon.com/directconnect/features/?nc=sn&loc=2
Transferring large data sets over the Internet can be time consuming and expensive. When you use the cloud, you can find that transferring large data sets can be slow because your business critical network traffic is contending for bandwidth with your other Internet usage. To decrease the amount of time required to transfer your data, you could increase the bandwidth to your Internet service provider, which frequently requires a costly contract renewal and a minimum commitment. With AWS Direct Connect, you can transfer your business critical data directly from your datacenter, office, or colocation environment into and from AWS bypassing your Internet service provider and removing network congestion. Further, AWS Direct Connect's simple pay as-you-go pricing, and no minimum commitment means you pay only for the network ports you use and the data you transfer over the connection, which can greatly reduce your networking costs.

Q33. A
AWS Documentation Reference:
https://aws.amazon.com/organizations/
AWS Organizations helps you centrally govern your environment as you grow and scale your workloads on AWS. Whether you are a growing startup or a large enterprise, Organizations helps you to centrally manage billing; control access, compliance, and security; and share resources across your AWS accounts.

Q34. A
AWS Documentation Reference:
https://docs.aws.amazon.com/amazondynamodb/latest/developerguide/Streams.Lambda.html
Amazon DynamoDB is integrated with AWS Lambda so that you can create triggers—pieces of code that automatically respond to events in DynamoDB Streams. With triggers, you can build applications that react to data modifications in DynamoDB tables.

If you enable DynamoDB Streams on a table, you can associate the stream Amazon Resource Name (ARN) with an AWS Lambda function that you write. Immediately after an item in the table is modified, a new record appears in the table's stream. AWS Lambda polls the stream and invokes your Lambda function synchronously when it detects new stream records. The Lambda function can perform any actions you specify, such as sending a notification or initiating a workflow.

## Q35. .B
AWS Documentation Reference:
https://docs.aws.amazon.com/vpc/latest/userguide/vpc-nat-comparison.html
Most appropriate solution is to use NAT gateway instead of NAT instance. Its bandwidth can scale up to 45 Gbps and software is optimized for handling NAT traffic.

## Q36. D
AWS Documentation Reference:
https://docs.aws.amazon.com/kms/latest/developerguide/concepts.html#enveloping
When you encrypt your data, your data is protected, but you have to protect your encryption key. One strategy is to encrypt it. Envelope encryption is the practice of encrypting plaintext data with a data key, and then encrypting the data key under another key.

## Q37. A, C, D
Cross region replication doesn't protect against object deletion, it enables automatic, asynchronous copying of objects across Amazon S3 buckets.
AWS Documentation Reference:
https://docs.aws.amazon.com/AmazonS3/latest/dev/object-lock.html
With Amazon S3 object lock, you can store objects using a write-once-read-many (WORM) model. You can use it to prevent an object from being deleted or overwritten for a fixed amount of time or indefinitely. Amazon S3 object lock helps you meet regulatory requirements that require WORM storage, or simply add another layer of protection against object changes and deletion.

https://aws.amazon.com/blogs/security/securing-access-to-aws-using-mfa-part-3/
https://docs.aws.amazon.com/AmazonS3/latest/dev/DeletingObjectVersions.html
Versioning keeps multiple versions of an object in the same bucket. When you enable it on a bucket, Amazon S3 automatically adds a unique version ID to every object stored in the bucket. At that point, a simple DELETE action does not permanently delete an object version; it merely associates a delete marker with the object. If you want to permanently delete an object version, you must specify its version ID in your DELETE request.

https://docs.aws.amazon.com/AmazonS3/latest/dev/UsingMFADelete.html
You can add another layer of protection by enabling MFA Delete on a versioned bucket. Once you do so, you must provide your AWS account's access keys and a valid code from the

account's MFA device in order to permanently delete an object version or suspend or reactivate versioning on the bucket.

## Q38. D
AWS Documentation Reference:
https://docs.aws.amazon.com/AWSSimpleQueueService/latest/SQSDeveloperGuide/sqs-visibility-timeout.html

When a consumer receives and processes a message from a queue, the message remains in the queue. To prevent other consumers from processing the message again, Amazon SQS sets a visibility timeout, a period of time during which Amazon SQS prevents other consumers from receiving and processing the message. Amazon SQS doesn't automatically delete the message. Thus, the consumer must delete the message from the queue after receiving and processing it.

In the given scenario as the processing is terminated before completion, the consumer program didn't deleted the message from the queue. Hence it will be visible again in the queue for other spot instance to receive it after the visibility time is over.

## Q39. B, C
AWS Documentation Reference:
https://docs.aws.amazon.com/amazondynamodb/latest/developerguide/GlobalTables.html

Amazon DynamoDB global tables provide a fully managed solution for deploying a multiregion, multi-master database, without having to build and maintain your own replication solution. DynamoDB global tables are ideal for massively scaled applications with globally dispersed users.

https://aws.amazon.com/dynamodb/dax/

Amazon DynamoDB Accelerator (DAX) is a fully managed, highly available, in-memory cache for DynamoDB that delivers up to a 10x performance improvement – from milliseconds to microseconds – even at millions of requests per second.

https://docs.aws.amazon.com/amazondynamodb/latest/developerguide/AutoScaling.html

Amazon DynamoDB auto scaling uses the AWS Application Auto Scaling service to dynamically adjust provisioned throughput capacity on your behalf, in response to actual traffic patterns. This enables a table or a global secondary index to increase its provisioned read and write capacity to handle sudden increases in traffic, without throttling. When the workload decreases, Application Auto Scaling decreases the throughput so that you don't pay for unused provisioned capacity.

https://docs.aws.amazon.com/amazondynamodb/latest/developerguide/bp-partition-key-design.html#bp-partition-key-partitions-adaptive

Adaptive capacity is enabled automatically for every DynamoDB table, at no additional cost. You don't need to explicitly enable or disable it. Adaptive capacity is a feature that enables DynamoDB to run imbalanced workloads indefinitely.

## Q40. D

AWS Documentation Reference:

https://docs.aws.amazon.com/vpc/latest/userguide/VPC_Subnets.html#vpc-sizing-ipv4

The first four IP addresses and the last IP address in each subnet CIDR block are not available for you to use, and cannot be assigned to an instance.

Q41. B

AWS Documentation Reference:

As it is mentioned that VPC and ALB routes only IPv4 traffic and not IPv6, option A and D is not applicable as AAAA record type is for IPv6 addresses.

Option C is incorrect because a Non Alias A record type should map to an ip address. In this case the ip address of ALB can change over time.

The correct option is B.

https://docs.aws.amazon.com/Route53/latest/DeveloperGuide/routing-to-elb-load-balancer.html

https://docs.aws.amazon.com/Route53/latest/DeveloperGuide/resource-record-sets-choosing-alias-non-alias.html

https://docs.aws.amazon.com/Route53/latest/DeveloperGuide/ResourceRecordTypes.html#CNAMEFormat

Amazon Route 53 alias records provide a Route 53–specific extension to DNS functionality. Alias records lets you route traffic to selected AWS resources, such as ALB, CloudFront distributions and Amazon S3 buckets.

To route domain traffic to an ELB load balancer, use Amazon Route 53 to create an alias record that points to your load balancer. An alias record is a Route 53 extension to DNS.

When you use an alias record to route traffic to an AWS resource, Route 53 automatically recognizes changes in the resource. For example, suppose an alias record for 'www.mycloudblogs.com' points to an ELB load balancer at lb1-1234.us-east-2.elb.amazonaws.com. If the IP address of the load balancer changes, Route 53 automatically starts to respond to DNS queries using the new IP address.

It's similar to a CNAME record, but you can create an alias record both for the root domain, mycloudblogs.com, and for subdomains, such as www. mycloudblogs.com.

E is not correct because the DNS protocol does not allow you to create a CNAME record for the top node of a DNS namespace, also known as the zone apex. For example, if you register the DNS name mycloudblogs.com, the zone apex is mycloudblogs.com. You cannot create a CNAME record for mycloudblogs.com, but you can create CNAME records for www. mycloudblogs.com and so on.

Q42. B

Key considerations are:

• VPC is mapped to one region but can span AZs

- A subnet is mapped to on AZ in VPC's region
- Both the application will be inside the same VPC but in different subnet of their own.
- To achieve fault tolerance in case one AZ goes down, each application should have one instances in two subnets which are mapped to two different AZs.

For example if you are deploying INTERNETApp and INTRANETApp by creating a VPC in us-east-1 region. Your network topology can be

- Subnet1, us-east-1a AZ having INTERNETApp instance.
- Subnet2, us-east-1b AZ having INTERNETApp instance.
- Subnet3 us-east-1c AZ having INTRANETApp instance.
- Subnet4, us-east-1d AZ having INTRANETApp instance.

This ensures that in case one AZ goes down, user request can be served by instance in subnet mapped to other active AZ.

Q43. B, C
AWS Documentation Reference:
https://docs.aws.amazon.com/vpc/latest/userguide/VPC_SecurityGroups.html
https://docs.aws.amazon.com/vpc/latest/userguide/vpc-network-acls.html
SG evaluate all rules before deciding whether to allow traffic
Network ACL process rules in number order when deciding whether to allow traffic.

Q44. A
AWS Documentation Reference: Whitepaper: Web Application Hosting in the AWS Cloud
https://d1.awsstatic.com/whitepapers/aws-web-hosting-best-practices.pdf

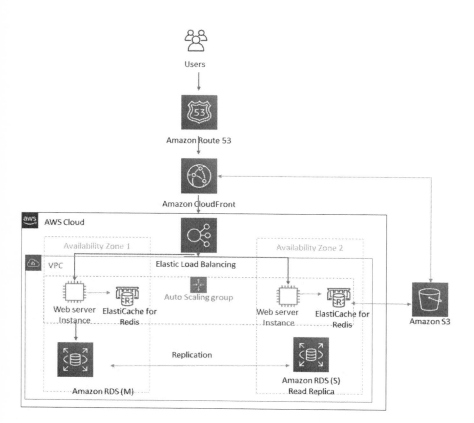

The above architecture achieves resiliency through failover based on multi-AZ architecture. The web EC2 instances are deployed across AZ, RDS is mutli-AZ enabled and Application Load Balancing with Elastic Load Balancing (ELB)/Application Load Balancer (ALB) – Allows you to spread load across multiple Availability Zones and Amazon EC2 Auto Scaling groups for redundancy and decoupling of services.

Caching with Amazon ElastiCache – Provides caching services with Redis or Memcached to remove load from the app and database, and lower latency for frequent requests. Also for storing session information.

Managed Database with Amazon RDS – Creates a highly available, Multi-AZ database architecture with six possible DB engines. Read Replica will improve read intensive transaction performance.

Edge Caching with Amazon CloudFront – Edge caches high-volume content to decrease the latency to customers.

Static Storage and Backups with Amazon S3 – Enables simple HTTP-based object storage for backups and static assets like images and video.

Q45. A, B

AWS Documentation Reference:

https://aws.amazon.com/blogs/aws/new-application-load-balancer-sni/

https://aws.amazon.com/premiumsupport/knowledge-center/acm-add-domain-certificates-elb/

To add multiple certificates for different domains to a load balancer, do one of the following:

- Use a Subject Alternative Name (SAN) certificate to validate multiple domains behind the load balancer, including wildcard domains, with AWS Certificate Manager (ACM).
- Use an Application Load Balancer (ALB), which supports multiple SSL certificates and smart certificate selection using Server Name Indication (SNI).

The Subject Alternative Name (SAN) is an extension to the X.509 specification that allows users to specify additional host names for a single SSL certificate.

SNI stands for Server Name Indication. It is an extension of the TLS protocol. It denotes which domain name the browser is trying to connect at the beginning of the handshake process. This technology allows a server to present multiple SSL Certificates to one IP address and port. Hence allows multiple secure (HTTPS) websites (or any other service over TLS) to be served by the same IP address without requiring all those sites to use the same certificate.

SNI is automatically enabled when you associate more than one TLS certificate with the same secure listener on an application load balancer. Similarly, SNI mode for a secure listener is automatically disabled when you have only one certificate associated to a secure listener.

Q46. B, C

AWS Documentation Reference:

https://docs.aws.amazon.com/AmazonRDS/latest/UserGuide/Concepts.MultiAZ.html

Amazon RDS provides high availability and failover support for DB instances using Multi-AZ deployments. In a Multi-AZ deployment, Amazon RDS automatically provisions and maintains a synchronous standby replica in a different Availability Zone. The primary DB instance is synchronously replicated across Availability Zones to a standby replica to provide data redundancy, eliminate I/O freezes, and minimize latency spikes during system backups. Running a DB instance with high availability can enhance availability during planned system maintenance, and help protect your databases against DB instance failure and Availability Zone disruption.

The high-availability feature is not a scaling solution for read-only scenarios; you cannot use a standby replica to serve read traffic.

https://aws.amazon.com/rds/details/read-replicas/

To service read-only traffic, you should use a Read Replica. Amazon RDS Read Replicas provide enhanced performance and durability for database (DB) instances. This feature makes it easy to elastically scale out beyond the capacity constraints of a single DB instance for read-heavy database workloads. You can create one or more replicas of a given source DB Instance and serve high-volume application read traffic from multiple copies of your data, thereby increasing aggregate read throughput.

Q47.C

Q48. A, B, D
AWS Documentation Reference:
https://docs.aws.amazon.com/AmazonS3/latest/dev/restoring-objects.html
The following table summarizes the archival retrieval options.

| Storage Class | Expedited | Standard | Bulk |
|---|---|---|---|
| GLACIER | 1–5 minutes | 3–5 hours | 5–12 hours |
| DEEP_ARCHIVE | Not available | Within 12 hours | Within 48 hours |

Q49. A, B, D
AWS Documentation Reference:
https://aws.amazon.com/caching/web-caching/
Caching web content helps improve upon the responsiveness of your websites by reducing the load on backend resources and network congestion. Web caching is performed by retaining HTTP responses and web resources in the cache for the purpose of fulfilling future requests from cache rather than from the origin servers.
One form of server side web caching includes utilizing key/value stores such as Memcached and Redis. A key/value object store can be used to cache any web content desired by the application developer. The web content is retrieved typically by means of application code or use of an application framework that can leverage the In-Memory data store. Another benefit to using key/value stores for web caching is they are also commonly used for storing web sessions and other cached content. This provides a single solution to serve various use cases. Amazon ElastiCache offers fully managed Redis and Memcached.

https://aws.amazon.com/autoscaling/
AWS Auto Scaling monitors your applications and automatically adjusts capacity to maintain steady, predictable performance at the lowest possible cost. Using AWS Auto Scaling, it's easy to setup application scaling for multiple resources across multiple services in minutes. The service provides a simple, powerful user interface that lets you build scaling plans for resources including Amazon EC2 instances and Spot Fleets, Amazon ECS tasks, Amazon DynamoDB tables and indexes, and Amazon Aurora Replicas. AWS Auto Scaling makes scaling simple with recommendations that allow you to optimize performance, costs, or balance between them. If you're already using Amazon EC2 Auto Scaling to dynamically scale your Amazon EC2 instances, you can now combine it with AWS Auto Scaling to scale additional resources for other AWS services. With AWS Auto Scaling, your applications always have the right resources at the right time.

https://aws.amazon.com/blogs/networking-and-content-delivery/dynamic-whole-site-delivery-with-amazon-cloudfront/
https://aws.amazon.com/cloudfront/

Amazon CloudFront is a fast content delivery network (CDN) service that securely delivers data, videos, applications, and APIs to customers globally with low latency, high transfer speeds, all within a developer-friendly environment.

Amazon Elastic Compute Cloud (Amazon EC2) origins serving dynamic and/or static content using CloudFront because it offers a number of additional benefits including performance, security, and cost benefits.

## Q50. C

AWS Documentation Reference:

https://aws.amazon.com/about-aws/whats-new/2014/03/20/elastic-load-balancing-supports-connection-draining/

https://aws.amazon.com/blogs/aws/elb-connection-draining-remove-instances-from-service-with-care/

When you enable Connection Draining on a load balancer, any back-end instances that you deregister will complete requests that are in progress before deregistration. Likewise, if a back-end instance fails health checks, the load balancer will not send any new requests to the unhealthy instance but will allow existing requests to complete.

This means that you can perform maintenance such as deploying software upgrades or replacing back-end instances without impacting your customers' experience.

Connection Draining is also integrated with Auto Scaling, making it even easier to manage the capacity behind your load balancer. When Connection Draining is enabled, Auto Scaling will wait for outstanding requests to complete before terminating instances.

## Q51. D

AWS Documentation Reference:

https://aws.amazon.com/macie/

Amazon Macie is a security service that uses machine learning to automatically discover, classify, and protect sensitive data in AWS. Amazon Macie recognizes sensitive data such as personally identifiable information (PII) or intellectual property, and provides you with dashboards and alerts that give visibility into how this data is being accessed or moved. The fully managed service continuously monitors data access activity for anomalies, and generates detailed alerts when it detects risk of unauthorized access or inadvertent data leaks. The Amazon Macie service supports Amazon S3 and AWS CloudTrail management API and S3 object-level events for the buckets and prefixes enrolled with Amazon Macie.

## Q52. A, B

By using Server-Side Encryption, you request Amazon S3 to encrypt your object before saving it on disks in its data centers and decrypt it when you download the objects.

By using Client-Side Encryption, you can encrypt data client-side and upload the encrypted data to Amazon S3. In this case, you manage the encryption process, the encryption keys, and related tools.
SSL connection given data in transit encryption.

Q53.B

Q54. C
She should create a group called AllUsers and attach every user to that group so that she can easily apply any account-wide permissions to all users in the AWS account.

Q55. B, C
A and D are incorrect because AWS Simple AD doesn't have the feature to form a trust relationship with on-premise AD or identity federation.
AWS Documentation Reference:
https://aws.amazon.com/blogs/security/how-to-connect-your-on-premises-active-directory-to-aws-using-ad-connector/
How to Connect Your On-Premises Active Directory to AWS Using AD Connector
AD Connector is designed to give you an easy way to establish a trusted relationship between your Active Directory and AWS. Provide federated sign-in to the AWS Management Console by mapping Active Directory identities to AWS Identity and Access Management (IAM) roles.

https://aws.amazon.com/blogs/security/how-to-access-the-aws-management-console-using-aws-microsoft-ad-and-your-on-premises-credentials/
How to Access the AWS Management Console Using AWS Microsoft AD and Your On-Premises Credentials
With AWS Microsoft AD, you can grant your on-premises users permissions to resources such as the AWS Management Console instead of adding AWS Identity and Access Management (IAM) user accounts or configuring AD Federation Services (AD FS) with Security Assertion Markup Language (SAML).
By using an AD trust between AWS Microsoft AD and your on-premises AD, you can assign your on-premises AD users and groups to IAM roles. This gives the assigned users and groups the IAM roles' permissions to manage AWS resources. By assigning on-premises AD groups to IAM roles, you can now manage AWS access through standard AD administrative tools such as AD Users and Computers (ADUC).
After you assign your on-premises users or groups to IAM roles, your users can sign in to the AWS Management Console with their on-premises AD credentials. From there, they can select from a list of their assigned IAM roles. After they select a role, they can perform the management functions that you assigned to the IAM role.

Q56. C, D
AWS Documentation Reference:

https://docs.aws.amazon.com/en_pv/AmazonCloudFront/latest/DeveloperGuide/private-content-restricting-access-to-s3.html

CloudFront doesn't expose Amazon S3 URLs, but your users might have those URLs if your application serves any files directly from Amazon S3 or if anyone gives out direct links to specific files in Amazon S3. If users access your files directly in Amazon S3, they bypass the controls provided by CloudFront signed URLs or signed cookies, for example, control over the date and time that a user can no longer access your content and control over which IP addresses can be used to access content.

To ensure that your users access your files using only CloudFront URLs, regardless of whether the URLs are signed or signed cookies, do the following:

- Create an origin access identity, which is a special CloudFront user, and associate the origin access identity with your distribution. You associate the origin access identity with origins, so that you can secure all or just some of your Amazon S3 content. You can also create an origin access identity and add it to your distribution when you create the distribution.

- Change the permissions either on your Amazon S3 bucket or on the files in your bucket so that only the origin access identity has read permission (or read and download permission). When your users access your Amazon S3 files through CloudFront, the CloudFront origin access identity gets the files on behalf of your users. If your users request files directly by using Amazon S3 URLs, they're denied access. The origin access identity has permission to access files in your Amazon S3 bucket, but users don't.

## Q57. B
AWS Documentation Reference:
https://aws.amazon.com/big-data/datalakes-and-analytics/
For real-time analytics, Amazon Kinesis makes it easy to collect, process and analyze streaming data such as IoT telemetry data, application logs, and website clickstreams. This enable you to process, and analyze data as it arrives in your data lake, and respond in real-time instead of having to wait until all your data is collected before the processing can begin.

## Q58. A

## Q59. . D
AWS Documentation Reference:
https://aws.amazon.com/appsync/faqs/
AWS AppSync is a service that enables developers to manage and synchronize mobile app data in real time across devices and users, but still allows the data to be accessed and altered when the mobile device is in an offline state.

The service further allows developers to optimize the user experience by selecting which data is automatically synchronized to each user's device when changes are made, minimizing storage and bandwidth requirements, with a query language called GraphQL.

Using these capabilities, developers can, in minutes, build real time collaborative experiences spanning browsers, mobile apps, Alexa skills, and IoT devices that remain usable when network connectivity is lost.

Q60. A, B
AWS Documentation Reference:
https://docs.aws.amazon.com/vpc/latest/userguide/VPC_Security.html

Q61. B, C
AWS Documentation Reference: Comparison of Security Groups and Network ACLs
https://docs.aws.amazon.com/vpc/latest/userguide/VPC_Security.html

Q62. A, C, D

AWS Documentation Reference:
https://aws.amazon.com/single-sign-on/features/
If the users in your organization already have a way to be authenticated, such as by signing in to your corporate network, you don't have to create separate IAM users for them. Instead, you can federate those user identities into AWS.
https://docs.aws.amazon.com/IAM/latest/UserGuide/id_roles_providers_saml.html
AWS supports identity federation with SAML 2.0 (Security Assertion Markup Language 2.0), an open standard that many identity providers (IdPs) use. This feature enables federated single sign-on (SSO), so users can log into the AWS Management Console or call the AWS API operations without you having to create an IAM user for everyone in your organization. By using SAML, you can simplify the process of configuring federation with AWS, because you can use the IdP's service instead of writing custom identity proxy code.

You must configure your organization's IdP and your AWS account to trust each other. Inside your organization, you must have an IdP that supports SAML 2.0, like Microsoft Active Directory Federation Service (ADFS, part of Windows Server), Shibboleth, or another compatible SAML 2.0 provider.

https://docs.aws.amazon.com/IAM/latest/UserGuide/id_roles_providers_enable-console-saml.html
You can use a role to configure your SAML 2.0-compliant identity provider (IdP) and AWS to permit your federated users to access the AWS Management Console.

Q63.A, B

Q64. D

Q65. B, D
File Gateway and Volume Cached Gateway maintain local copy of frequently accessed data.

# Answer PRACTICE EXAM 2

## Q1. A
AWS Documentation Reference: RAID Configuration Options
https://docs.aws.amazon.com/en_pv/AWSEC2/latest/UserGuide/raid-config.html

## Q2. D
AWS Documentation Reference:
https://docs.aws.amazon.com/AmazonS3/latest/dev/replication.html
Although Amazon S3 stores your data across multiple geographically distant Availability Zones by default, compliance requirements might dictate that you store data at even greater distances. Cross-region replication allows you to replicate data between distant AWS Regions to satisfy these requirements.

This also minimizes latency in accessing objects by maintaining object copies in AWS Regions that are geographically closer to your users.

If you have compute clusters in two different AWS Regions that analyze the same set of objects, you might choose to maintain object copies in those Regions. This will help to increase operational efficiency.

## Q3. C
AWS Documentation Reference:
https://docs.aws.amazon.com/AWSEC2/latest/UserGuide/apply_ri.html
Regional Reserved Instances provide instance size flexibility where the Reserved Instance discount applies to instance usage within the instance family, regardless of size. Instance size flexibility is determined by the normalization factor of the instance size. The discount applies either fully or partially to running instances of the same instance family, depending on the instance size of the reservation, in any Availability Zone in the Region. The only attributes that must be matched are the instance family, tenancy, and platform. Instance size flexibility is applied from the smallest to the largest instance size within the instance family based on the normalization factor.

A t2.medium instance has a normalization factor of 2 and t2.small has a normalization factor of 1. Therefore you will get benefit applicable to both running t2.small instances. 2/ (2x1) =100%

## Q4. A
AWS Documentation Reference:
https://aws.amazon.com/efs/
Amazon Elastic File System (Amazon EFS) provides a simple, scalable, fully managed elastic NFS file system for use with AWS Cloud services and on-premises resources. It is built to scale on demand to petabytes without disrupting applications, growing and shrinking automatically as you add and remove files, eliminating the need to provision and manage capacity to accommodate growth.

Media workflows like video editing, studio production, broadcast processing, sound design, and rendering often depend on shared storage to manipulate large files. Amazon EFS provides a strong data consistency model with high throughput and shared file access which can cut the time it takes to perform these jobs and consolidate multiple local file repositories into a single location for all users.

## Q5. A
Schedule based auto scaling policy allows you to scale out or in at a specific time.

## Q6. A, D
AWS Documentation Reference:
https://docs.aws.amazon.com/global-accelerator/latest/dg/introduction-how-it-works.html
There are two ways that you can customize how AWS Global Accelerator sends traffic to your endpoints:

- Change the traffic dial to limit the traffic for one or more endpoint groups
- Specify weights to change the proportion of traffic to the endpoints in a group

You configure traffic dials for endpoint groups. The traffic dial lets you cut off a percentage of traffic—or all traffic—to the group, by "dialing down" traffic that the accelerator has already directed to it based on other factors, such as proximity.

You use weights, on the other hand, to set values for individual endpoints within an endpoint group. Weights provide a way to divide up traffic within the endpoint group. For example, you can use weights to do performance testing for specific endpoints in a Region.

## Q7. D
Having 6 reserved instances will give the best cost benefit and adding 12 on-demand instances only for those three days gives the flexibility.
A is not cost optimized, having all 18 instances on-demand will be most costly.
B having 8 spot instances, there is risk that not all of them may be provisioned or there may be early termination of instances.
C having 18 reserved instances is not an optimized strategy as it will be applicable only for three days and you will be paying for 18 instances for rest of the days of month when you are using only 6 instances.

## Q8. A, B, C
AWS Documentation Reference: Elastic Fabric Adapter (EFA)
https://docs.aws.amazon.com/AWSEC2/latest/UserGuide/efa.html
An Elastic Fabric Adapter (EFA) is a network device that you can attach to your Amazon EC2 instance to accelerate High Performance Computing (HPC) and machine learning applications. EFA enables you to achieve the application performance of an on-premises HPC cluster, with the scalability, flexibility, and elasticity provided by the AWS Cloud.

EFA provides lower and more consistent latency and higher throughput than the TCP transport traditionally used in cloud-based HPC systems. It enhances the performance of inter-instance communication that is critical for scaling HPC and machine learning applications. It is optimized to work on the existing AWS network infrastructure and it can scale depending on application requirements.

https://aws.amazon.com/ec2/faqs/
High Performance Computing (HPC) applications distribute computational workloads across a cluster of instances for parallel processing. Examples of HPC applications include computational fluid dynamics (CFD), crash simulations, and weather simulations. HPC applications are generally written using the Message Passing Interface (MPI) and impose stringent requirements for inter-instance communication in terms of both latency and bandwidth. Applications using MPI and other HPC middleware which supports the libfabric communication stack can benefit from EFA.

EFA brings the scalability, flexibility, and elasticity of cloud to tightly-coupled HPC applications. With EFA, tightly-coupled HPC applications have access to lower and more consistent latency and higher throughput than traditional TCP channels, enabling them to scale better.

An ENA ENI provides traditional IP networking features necessary to support VPC networking. An EFA ENI provides all the functionality of an ENA ENI, plus hardware support for applications to communicate directly with the EFA ENI without involving the instance kernel (OS-bypass communication) using an extended programming interface.

Q9. A, B, C
AWS Documentation Reference:
https://aws.amazon.com/fsx/windows/faqs/?nc=sn&loc=7
When should I use Amazon FSx Windows File Servers vs. Amazon EFS vs. Amazon FSx for Lustre?
For Windows-based applications, Amazon FSx provides fully managed Windows file servers with features and performance optimized for "lift-and-shift" business-critical application workloads including home directories (user shares), media workflows, and ERP applications. It is accessible from Windows and Linux instances via the SMB protocol.

If you have Linux-based applications, Amazon EFS is a cloud-native fully managed file system that provides simple, scalable, elastic file storage accessible from Linux instances via the NFS protocol.

For compute-intensive and fast processing workloads, like high performance computing (HPC), machine learning, EDA, and media processing, Amazon FSx for Lustre, provides a file system that's optimized for performance, with input and output stored on Amazon S3.

Q10. B
AWS Documentation Reference:
https://docs.aws.amazon.com/en_pv/AmazonCloudFront/latest/DeveloperGuide/georestrictions.html

When a user requests your content, CloudFront typically serves the requested content regardless of where the user is located. If you need to prevent users in specific countries from accessing your content, you can use the CloudFront geo restriction feature to do one of the following:

- Allow your users to access your content only if they're in one of the countries on a whitelist of approved countries.

- Prevent your users from accessing your content if they're in one of the countries on a blacklist of banned countries.

## Q11. B

AWS Documentation Reference:

https://docs.aws.amazon.com/AWSEC2/latest/UserGuide/user-data.html

When you launch an instance in Amazon EC2, you have the option of passing user data to the instance that can be used to perform common automated configuration tasks and even run scripts after the instance starts. You can pass two types of user data to Amazon EC2: shell scripts and cloud-init directives. You can also pass this data into the launch wizard as plain text, as a file (this is useful for launching instances using the command line tools), or as base64-encoded text (for API calls).

## Q12. A, B

AWS Documentation Reference:

https://docs.aws.amazon.com/AWSEC2/latest/UserGuide/EBSVolumeTypes.html

## Q13. B, D, E

AWS Documentation Reference:

https://docs.aws.amazon.com/AWSSimpleQueueService/latest/SQSDeveloperGuide/FIFO-queues.html#FIFO-queues-exactly-once-processing

https://aws.amazon.com/es/blogs/aws/new-for-amazon-simple-queue-service-fifo-queues-with-exactly-once-delivery-deduplication/

SQS FIFO queue provides FIFO (First-In-First-Out) delivery and exactly-once processing:

- The order in which messages are sent and received is strictly preserved and a message is delivered once and remains available until a consumer processes and deletes it.

- Duplicates aren't introduced into the queue.

Unlike standard queues, FIFO queues don't introduce duplicate messages. FIFO queues help you avoid sending duplicates to a queue. If you retry the SendMessage action within the 5-minute deduplication interval, Amazon SQS doesn't introduce any duplicates into the queue.

To configure deduplication, you must do one of the following:

- Enable content-based deduplication. This instructs Amazon SQS to use a SHA-256 hash to generate the message deduplication ID using the body of the message—but not the attributes of the message.
- Explicitly provide the message deduplication ID (or view the sequence number) for the message.

Q14.A, B
AWS Documentation Reference:
https://docs.aws.amazon.com/AmazonRDS/latest/AuroraUserGuide/aurora-serverless.html
Amazon Aurora Serverless is an on-demand, autoscaling configuration for Amazon Aurora

Q15. B, D
AWS Documentation Reference:
https://docs.aws.amazon.com/AmazonS3/latest/user-guide/using-folders.html
For the sake of organizational simplicity, the Amazon S3 console supports the folder concept as a means of grouping objects. Amazon S3 does this by using a shared name prefix for objects (that is, objects that have names that begin with a common string). Object names are also referred to as key names.

Amazon S3 console supports displaying objects stored in the buckets in form of folders. The console treats all objects that have a forward slash "/" character as the last (trailing) character in the key name as a folder.
In the given scenario all the files have 'alaskaphotos/*.jpg' in their key name, hence there is a folder 'alaskaphotos' inside the bucket in the S3 console.

You can have folders within folders, but not buckets within buckets. You can upload and copy objects directly into a folder. Folders can be created, deleted, and made public, but they cannot be renamed. Objects can be copied from one folder to another.

Q16. B
AWS Documentation Reference:
https://aws.amazon.com/shield/

AWS Shield is a managed Distributed Denial of Service (DDoS) protection service that safeguards applications running on AWS. AWS Shield provides always-on detection and automatic inline mitigations that minimize application downtime and latency, so there is no need to engage AWS Support to benefit from DDoS protection. There are two tiers of AWS Shield - Standard and Advanced.

All AWS customers benefit from the automatic protections of AWS Shield Standard, at no additional charge. AWS Shield Standard defends against most common, frequently occurring network and transport layer DDoS attacks that target your web site or applications. When you use AWS Shield Standard with Amazon CloudFront and Amazon Route 53, you receive comprehensive availability protection against all known infrastructure (Layer 3 and 4) attacks.

For higher levels of protection against attacks targeting your applications running on Amazon Elastic Compute Cloud (EC2), Elastic Load Balancing (ELB), Amazon CloudFront, AWS Global Accelerator and Amazon Route 53 resources, you can subscribe to AWS Shield Advanced. In addition to the network and transport layer protections that come with Standard, AWS Shield Advanced provides additional detection and mitigation against large and sophisticated DDoS attacks, near real-time visibility into attacks, and integration with AWS WAF, a web application firewall. AWS Shield Advanced also gives you 24x7 access to the AWS DDoS Response Team (DRT) and protection against DDoS related spikes in your Amazon Elastic Compute Cloud (EC2), Elastic Load Balancing (ELB), Amazon CloudFront, AWS Global Accelerator and Amazon Route 53 charges.

Q17. C
AWS Documentation Reference:
https://docs.aws.amazon.com/AWSEC2/latest/UserGuide/instancedata-data-retrieval.html
To view all categories of instance metadata from within a running instance, use the following URI.
http://169.254.169.254/latest/meta-data/
The IP address 169.254.169.254 is a link-local address and is valid only from the instance.

Q18. C, D
AWS Documentation Reference:
https://docs.aws.amazon.com/AmazonRDS/latest/UserGuide/Overview.Encryption.html#Overview.Encryption.Enabling
To enable encryption for a new DB instance, choose Enable encryption on the Amazon RDS console. If you use the create-db-instance AWS CLI command to create an encrypted DB instance, set the --storage-encrypted parameter to true. If you use the CreateDBInstance API operation, set the StorageEncrypted parameter to true.

When you create an encrypted DB instance, you can also supply the AWS KMS key identifier for your encryption key. If you don't specify an AWS KMS key identifier, then Amazon RDS uses your default encryption key for your new DB instance. AWS KMS creates your default encryption key for Amazon RDS for your AWS account. Your AWS account has a different default encryption key for each AWS Region.

On a database instance running with Amazon RDS encryption, data stored at rest in the underlying storage is encrypted, as are its automated backups, read replicas, and snapshots. Encryption and decryption are handled transparently.

Q19. C

AWS Documentation Reference links:
https://docs.aws.amazon.com/AmazonS3/latest/dev/WebsiteHosting.html
https://docs.aws.amazon.com/AmazonS3/latest/dev/WebsiteEndpoints.html
https://docs.aws.amazon.com/general/latest/gr/rande.html#s3_website_region_endpoints

After configuring a S3 bucket for website hosting, website content are uploaded to the bucket. The bucket must have public read access. The website is then available at the AWS Region-specific website endpoint of the bucket, which is in one of the following formats:

<bucket-name>.s3-website-<AWS-region>.amazonaws.com
<bucket-name>.s3-website. <AWS-region>.amazonaws.com

Which format is used for the endpoint depends on what Region the bucket is in.

In the given scenario the website endpoint for us-west-2 regions is
's3-website-us-west-2.amazonaws.com' therefore the url for the website will be

http://west-bucket.s3-website-us-west-2.amazonaws.com/

Q20. B
AWS Documentation Reference:
https://docs.aws.amazon.com/autoscaling/ec2/userguide/as-scaling-target-tracking.html
With target tracking scaling policies, you select a scaling metric and set a target value. Amazon EC2 Auto Scaling creates and manages the CloudWatch alarms that trigger the scaling policy and calculates the scaling adjustment based on the metric and the target value. The scaling policy adds or removes capacity as required to keep the metric at, or close to, the specified target value. In addition to keeping the metric close to the target value, a target tracking scaling policy also adjusts to the changes in the metric due to a changing load pattern.

Q21. B, C
AWS Documentation Reference:
https://docs.aws.amazon.com/AWSEC2/latest/UserGuide/enhanced-networking.html
Enhanced networking uses single root I/O virtualization (SR-IOV) to provide high-performance networking capabilities on supported instance types. SR-IOV is a method of

device virtualization that provides higher I/O performance and lower CPU utilization when compared to traditional virtualized network interfaces. Enhanced networking provides higher bandwidth, higher packet per second (PPS) performance, and consistently lower inter-instance latencies.

https://docs.aws.amazon.com/AWSEC2/latest/UserGuide/enhanced-networking.html#supported_instances

Depending on your instance type, enhanced networking can be enabled using one of the following mechanisms:

Elastic Network Adapter (ENA)

The Elastic Network Adapter (ENA) supports network speeds of up to 100 Gbps for supported instance types.

Intel 82599 Virtual Function (VF) interface

The Intel 82599 Virtual Function interface supports network speeds of up to 10 Gbps for supported instance types.

## Q22. C

AWS Documentation Reference:

https://docs.aws.amazon.com/AmazonS3/latest/dev/transfer-acceleration.html

Amazon S3 Transfer Acceleration enables fast, easy, and secure transfers of files over long distances between your client and an S3 bucket. Transfer Acceleration takes advantage of Amazon CloudFront's globally distributed edge locations. As the data arrives at an edge location, data is routed to Amazon S3 over an optimized network path.

You might want to use Transfer Acceleration on a bucket for various reasons, including the following:

- You have customers that upload to a centralized bucket from all over the world.
- You transfer gigabytes to terabytes of data on a regular basis across continents.
- You are unable to utilize all of your available bandwidth over the Internet when uploading to Amazon S3.

## Q23. B

AWS Documentation Reference:

https://docs.aws.amazon.com/AmazonRDS/latest/UserGuide/USER_ReadRepl.html

You can reduce the load on your source DB instance by routing read queries from your applications to the Read Replica. Using Read Replicas, you can elastically scale out beyond the capacity constraints of a single DB instance for read-heavy database workloads.

## Q24. D

AWS Documentation Reference:

https://aws.amazon.com/blogs/storage/transferring-files-from-on-premises-to-aws-and-back-without-leaving-your-vpc-using-aws-datasync/

AWS DataSync is a service to simplify, automate, and accelerate data transfer between on-premises storage and AWS, such as Amazon Elastic File System (EFS) and Amazon S3. DataSync can be leveraged to migrate on-premises storage to AWS, in order to shut down entire data centers, or move cold data to more cost-effective storage. DataSync adheres to high standards of information security: all data transferred between the source and destination is encrypted via TLS, data is never persisted by DataSync, and access to AWS storage locations is entirely in your control. DataSync is also managed by standard AWS tools such as IAM (for S3) and security groups (for EFS). In addition to these security measures, data can be moved from on-premises storage to AWS via Direct Connect or VPN, without traversing the public internet, to further increase the security of the copied data.

https://aws.amazon.com/blogs/storage/migrating-storage-with-aws-datasync/

Q25. A, B, D, E
AWS Documentation Reference:
https://docs.aws.amazon.com/AmazonECS/latest/developerguide/task_execution_IAM_role.html
The Amazon ECS container agent makes calls to the Amazon ECS API on your behalf, so it requires an IAM policy and role for the service to know that the agent belongs to you. This IAM role is referred to as a task execution IAM role. You can have multiple task execution roles for different purposes associated with your account.
The following are common use cases for a task execution IAM role:
Your task uses the Fargate launch type and

- is pulling a container image from Amazon ECR.
- uses the awslogs log driver.

Your tasks uses either the Fargate or EC2 launch type and

- is using private registry authentication.
- the task definition is referencing sensitive data using Secrets Manager secrets or AWS Systems Manager Parameter Store parameters.

https://docs.aws.amazon.com/AmazonECS/latest/developerguide/instance_IAM_role.html
The Amazon ECS container agent makes calls to the Amazon ECS API on your behalf. Container instances that run the agent require an IAM policy and role for the service to know that the agent belongs to you. Before you can launch container instances and register them into a cluster, you must create an IAM role for those container instances to use when they are launched.
https://docs.aws.amazon.com/AmazonECS/latest/developerguide/codedeploy_IAM_role.html
Before you can use the CodeDeploy blue/green deployment type with Amazon ECS, the CodeDeploy service needs permissions to update your Amazon ECS service on your behalf. These permissions are provided by the CodeDeploy IAM role (ecsCodeDeployRole).
https://docs.aws.amazon.com/AmazonECS/latest/developerguide/CWE_IAM_role.html

Before you can use Amazon ECS scheduled tasks with CloudWatch Events rules and targets, the CloudWatch Events service needs permissions to run Amazon ECS tasks on your behalf. These permissions are provided by the CloudWatch Events IAM role (ecsEventsRole).

## Q26. D
AWS Documentation Reference:
https://docs.aws.amazon.com/amazon-mq/latest/developer-guide/welcome.html#difference-from-sqs-sns
Amazon MQ is a managed message broker service that provides compatibility with many popular message brokers. AWS recommend Amazon MQ for migrating applications from existing message brokers that rely on compatibility with APIs such as JMS or protocols such as AMQP, MQTT, OpenWire, and STOMP.

## Q27. A, B, D, F
C, E are ways to encrypt data in transit and data at rest in S3.
AWS Identity and Access Management (IAM) user policies can be defined in way so as to specify the users that can access specific buckets and objects.
You can use a bucket policy to grant access across AWS accounts, grant public or anonymous permissions, and allow or block access based on certain conditions.

## Q28. B, C, D
AWS Documentation Reference: VPC Peering Limitations
https://docs.aws.amazon.com/vpc/latest/peering/vpc-peering-basics.html

## Q29. A
AWS Documentation Reference:  Image recognition & processing
https://aws.amazon.com/serverless/resources/?serverless.sort-by=item.additionalFields.createdDate&serverless.sort-order=desc#Reference_architectures
https://github.com/aws-samples/lambda-refarch-imagerecognition
The architecture is depicted in the diagram below.
1. An image is uploaded to the S3 bucket
2. The S3 upload event triggers the Lambda function, which kicks off an execution of the state machine in AWS Step Functions, passing in the S3 bucket and object key as input parameters.
3. The state machine has the following sub-steps:
    a. Read the file from S3 and extract image metadata
    b. Based on output from previous step, validate if the file uploaded is a supported file format (png or jpg). If not, throw NotSupportedImageType error and end execution.
    c. Store the extracted metadata in the DynamoDB table
    d. In parallel, kick off two processes simultaneously:

    i.   Call Amazon Rekognition to detect objects in the image file. If detected, store the tags in the DynamoDB table

    ii.   Generate a thumbnail and store it under the S3 bucket

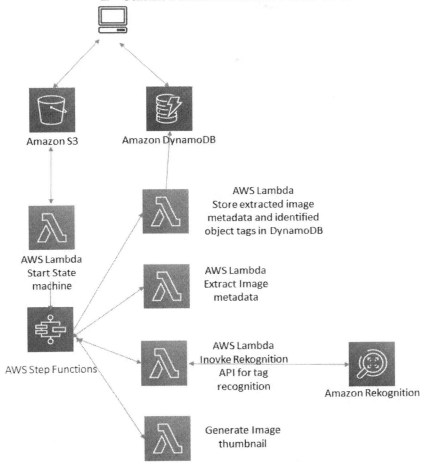

Q30. A, B, C

AWS Documentation Reference:

https://docs.aws.amazon.com/vpc/latest/userguide/VPC_Security.html

Amazon Virtual Private Cloud provides features that you can use to increase and monitor the security for your virtual private cloud (VPC):

Security groups — Act as a firewall for associated Amazon EC2 instances, controlling both inbound and outbound traffic at the instance level

Network access control lists (ACLs) — Act as a firewall for associated subnets, controlling both inbound and outbound traffic at the subnet level

Flow logs — Capture information about the IP traffic going to and from network interfaces in your VPC

The following diagram illustrates the layers of security provided by security groups and network ACLs. For example, traffic from an Internet gateway is routed to the appropriate subnet using the routes in the routing table. The rules of the network ACL associated with the subnet control which traffic is allowed to the subnet. The rules of the security group associated with an instance control which traffic is allowed to the instance.

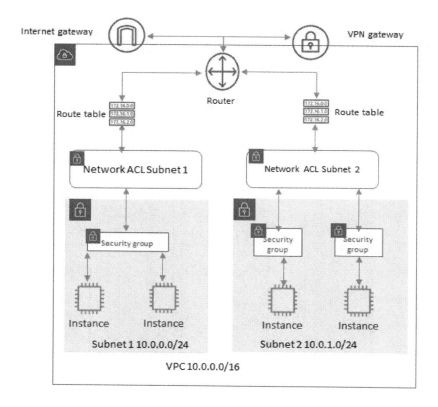

Q31. A, B, C, E

AWS Documentation Reference:

https://docs.aws.amazon.com/en_pv/AmazonCloudFront/latest/DeveloperGuide/CNAMEs.html#alternate-domain-names-requirements

Q32. B

AWS Documentation Reference:

https://docs.aws.amazon.com/vpn/latest/s2svpn/how_it_works.html

A virtual private gateway is the VPN concentrator on the Amazon side of the Site-to-Site VPN connection. You create a virtual private gateway and attach it to the VPC from which you want to create the Site-to-Site VPN connection.

## Q33. A, D
AWS Documentation Reference:

https://aws.amazon.com/premiumsupport/knowledge-center/iam-policy-service-control-policy/

The IAM user Bob is part of the Dev OU, and the IAM policy associated with Bob allows full access to the Amazon S3 and Amazon EC2 services. Because the SCP associated with the Dev OU allows the use of the S3 service, and Bob has an IAM policy that grants him full access to S3, Bob can use S3. However, even though the IAM policy also grants Bob admin access to EC2, since the SCP only allows the use of S3, Bob cannot use EC2.

For the IAM user David, even though the S3 service is whitelisted for the users, groups, and roles in the Sales OU (by the SCP), David's IAM policy doesn't allow access to any AWS services. David will not be able to access any AWS services until he has an IAM policy that grants permissions to services.

## Q34. A, B
AWS Documentation Reference:

https://docs.aws.amazon.com/amazondynamodb/latest/developerguide/HowItWorks.CoreComponents.html

## Q35. A, C, D, E
AWS Documentation Reference:

https://docs.aws.amazon.com/vpc/latest/userguide/VPC_Internet_Gateway.html

To enable access to or from the internet for instances in a VPC subnet, you must do the following:

- Attach an internet gateway to your VPC.
- Ensure that your subnet's route table points to the internet gateway.
- Ensure that instances in your subnet have a globally unique IP address (public IPv4 address, Elastic IP address, or IPv6 address).
- Ensure that your network access control and security group rules allow the relevant traffic to flow to and from your instance.

## Q36. A, B, C, E, F

AWS Documentation Reference:
https://aws.amazon.com/premiumsupport/technology/trusted-advisor/

Q37. A, D
AWS Documentation Reference:
https://docs.aws.amazon.com/AmazonS3/latest/dev/storage-class-intro.html#sc-glacier
GLACIER—Use for archives where portions of the data might need to be retrieved in minutes.
DEEP_ARCHIVE—Use for archiving data that rarely needs to be accessed.

Q38. B
B is correct. If you use only one queue there will be scenario where premium messages are far behind the free messages. Create two queues, one for premium members and one for free members editing task. EC2 processing program should poll premium member's queue first and only if message request is empty then it should poll the free member's queue.

A is incorrect. Message timers let you specify an initial invisibility period for a message added to a queue. For example, if you send a message with a 45-second timer, the message isn't visible to consumers for its first 45 seconds in the queue. But this will not have an effect on priority for processing.

C is incorrect as SQS doesn't provide a feature to set priority in individual messages.

D is incorrect as you cannot create a delay queue only for a subset of messages. Moreover delay queue will not have an effect on priority of message processing.

Q39. A, D
AWS Documentation Reference:
https://docs.aws.amazon.com/amazondynamodb/latest/developerguide/bp-partition-key-uniform-load.html
The partition key portion of a table's primary key determines the logical partitions in which a table's data is stored. This in turn affects the underlying physical partitions. Provisioned I/O capacity for the table is divided evenly among these physical partitions. Therefore a partition key design that doesn't distribute I/O requests evenly can create "hot" partitions that result in throttling and use your provisioned I/O capacity inefficiently.
It does mean that the more distinct partition key values that your workload accesses, the more those requests will be spread across the partitioned space.
Option A and D will result in more distinct values.

Q40. B
A is wrong as security group doesn't have option to create DENY rules.

C is wrong as this is an internet application you cannot move it private subnet.

D is wrong as internet gateway doesn't have option to create DENY rules.

AWS Documentation Reference:

https://docs.aws.amazon.com/vpc/latest/userguide/vpc-network-acls.html

A network access control list (ACL) is an optional layer of security for your VPC that acts as a firewall for controlling traffic in and out of one or more subnets. You might set up network ACLs with rules similar to your security groups in order to add an additional layer of security to your VPC. A network ACL has separate inbound and outbound rules, and each rule can either allow or deny traffic

https://docs.aws.amazon.com/vpc/latest/userguide/VPC_SecurityGroups.html

In a security group you can specify allow rules, but not deny rules.

Q41. D

AWS Documentation Reference:

https://docs.aws.amazon.com/Route53/latest/DeveloperGuide/routing-policy.html#routing-policy-weighted

Weighted routing lets you associate multiple resources with a single domain name (example.com) or subdomain name (acme.example.com) and choose how much traffic is routed to each resource. This can be useful for a variety of purposes, including load balancing and testing new versions of software.

To configure weighted routing, you create records that have the same name and type for each of your resources. You assign each record a relative weight that corresponds with how much traffic you want to send to each resource. Amazon Route 53 sends traffic to a resource based on the weight that you assign to the record as a proportion of the total weight for all records in the group:

Formula for how much traffic is routed to a given resource:

weight for a specified record / sum of the weights for all records.

For example, if you want to send a tiny portion of your traffic to one resource and the rest to another resource, you might specify weights of 1 and 255. The resource with a weight of 1 gets 1/256th of the traffic (1/1+255), and the other resource gets 255/256ths (255/1+255). You can gradually change the balance by changing the weights. If you want to stop sending traffic to a resource, you can change the weight for that record to 0.

In the given scenario record with weight 3 will receive (3/4) i.e 75% of traffic and record with weight 1 will receive (1/4) i.e 25% of traffic.

Q42. B

Using VPC Endpoints for S3 calls is the solution. There is no additional charge for using endpoints.

AWS Documentation Reference:

https://docs.aws.amazon.com/vpc/latest/userguide/vpce-gateway.html

A VPC endpoint enables you to privately connect your VPC to supported AWS services and VPC endpoint services powered by PrivateLink without requiring an internet gateway, NAT device, VPN connection, or AWS Direct Connect connection. Instances in your VPC do not require public IP addresses to communicate with resources in the service. Traffic between your VPC and the other service does not leave the Amazon network.

Q43. B, C, D

AWS Documentation Reference:

https://docs.aws.amazon.com/vpn/latest/s2svpn/how_it_works.html

Q44. B

AWS Documentation Reference: Auto Discovery

https://aws.amazon.com/elasticache/faqs/

Auto Discovery enables automatic discovery of cache nodes by clients when they are added to or removed from an Amazon ElastiCache cluster. To take advantage of Auto Discovery, an Auto Discovery capable client must be used to connect to an Amazon ElastiCache Cluster.

To use the Auto Discovery feature a client must be able to use a Configuration Endpoint and determine the cluster node endpoints. You may either use the Amazon ElastiCache Cluster Client or extend your existing Memcached client to include the Auto Discovery command set.

Upon initialization, the client will automatically determine the current members of the Amazon ElastiCache cluster using the Configuration Endpoint. When you make changes to your cache cluster by adding or removing nodes or if a node is replaced upon failure, the Auto Discovery client automatically determines the changes and you do not need to initialize your clients manually.

Q45. B

Application tier and Database tier need to be in separate private subnet. For fault tolerance and availability they should be redundantly deployed in two separate AZs. Therefor you will need two private subnet in two separate AZs.

To use elastic load balancer you must create public subnets in the same Availability Zones as the private subnets that are used by your private instances. Hence you will need to create one public subnet in each of the two AZ.

AZ-1: public subnet-a -> Load balancer, private subnet-a -> application tier, private subnet-b -> database tier

AZ-2: public subnet-b -> Load balancer, private subnet-c -> application tier, private subnet-d -> database tier

Q46. B, C

AWS Documentation Reference: Read Replicas and Multi-AZ Deployments

https://aws.amazon.com/rds/details/read-replicas/

https://aws.amazon.com/rds/features/multi-az/

Q47. C

AWS Documentation Reference: Failover Process for Amazon RDS

https://docs.aws.amazon.com/AmazonRDS/latest/UserGuide/Concepts.MultiAZ.html

In the event of a planned or unplanned outage of your DB instance, Amazon RDS automatically switches to a standby replica in another Availability Zone if you have enabled Multi-AZ. The failover mechanism automatically changes the DNS record of the DB instance to point to the standby DB instance.

Q48. C

AWS Documentation Reference:

https://docs.aws.amazon.com/AmazonS3/latest/dev/cors.html

https://docs.aws.amazon.com/sdk-for-javascript/v2/developer-guide/cors.html

Cross-origin resource sharing (CORS) defines a way for client web applications that are loaded in one domain to interact with resources in a different domain.

Cross-origin resource sharing, or CORS, is a security feature of modern web browsers. It enables web browsers to negotiate which domains can make requests of external websites or services. CORS is an important consideration when developing browser applications with the AWS SDK for JavaScript because most requests to resources are sent to an external domain, such as the endpoint for a web service. In this case S3 web service.

In the simplest case, your browser script makes a GET request for a resource from a server in another domain. Depending on the CORS configuration of that server, if the request is from a domain that's authorized to submit GET requests, the cross-origin server responds by returning the requested resource.

If either the requesting domain or the type of HTTP request is not authorized, the request is denied.

Amazon S3 buckets require CORS configuration before you can perform operations on them.

To configure your bucket to allow cross-origin requests, you create a CORS configuration, which is an XML document with rules that identify the origins that you will allow to access your bucket, the operations (HTTP methods) that will support for each origin, and other operation-specific information. When Amazon S3 receives a preflight request from a browser, it evaluates the CORS configuration for the bucket and uses the first CORSRule rule that matches the incoming browser request to enable a cross-origin request.

Q49. A, C

AWS Documentation Reference:

https://docs.aws.amazon.com/en_pv/AmazonCloudFront/latest/DeveloperGuide/PrivateContent.html

Many companies that distribute content over the internet want to restrict access to documents, business data, media streams, or content that is intended for selected users, for example, users who have paid a fee. To securely serve this private content by using CloudFront, you can do the following:

- Require that your users access your private content by using special CloudFront signed URLs or signed cookies.
- Require that your users access your content by using CloudFront URLs, not URLs that access content directly on the origin server (for example, Amazon S3 or a private HTTP server). Requiring CloudFront URLs isn't necessary, but it is recommended to prevent users from bypassing the restrictions that you specify in signed URLs or signed cookies.

Q50. C
AWS Documentation Reference:
https://docs.aws.amazon.com/elasticloadbalancing/latest/application/load-balancer-listeners.html#path-conditions
https://aws.amazon.com/blogs/aws/new-host-based-routing-support-for-aws-application-load-balancers/
You can use path conditions to define rules that route requests based on the URL in the request (also known as path-based routing).

The path pattern is applied only to the path of the URL, not to its query parameters.

A path pattern is case-sensitive, can be up to 128 characters in length, and can contain any of the following characters.

A–Z, a–z, 0–9

_ - . $ / ~ " ' @ : +

& (using &amp;)

* (matches 0 or more characters)

? (matches exactly 1 character)

In the given scenario you can create path pattern as
www.statefair.com/web/*
www.statefair.com/mobileweb/*
www.statefair.com/mobileapp/*

Network load balancer doesn't support path based routing.

Q51. C
AWS Documentation Reference:
https://aws.amazon.com/guardduty/
Amazon GuardDuty is a threat detection service that continuously monitors for malicious activity and unauthorized behavior to protect your AWS accounts and workloads. The service uses machine learning, anomaly detection, and integrated threat intelligence to identify and prioritize potential threats. GuardDuty analyzes tens of billions of events across multiple AWS data sources, such as AWS CloudTrail, Amazon VPC Flow Logs, and DNS logs.

Q52. D
For first 30 days as there are lot of users frequently accessing the data, therefore STANDARD class will be most appropriate.
After 30 days as there is infrequent access so STANDARD_IA will be more appropriate.
After 30 days as it is rarely accessed and retrieval time is not a criteria, so most cost effective storage will be DEEP_ARCHIVE.

DEEP_ARCHIVE is used for archiving data that rarely needs to be accessed. Storage costs for DEEP_ARCHIVE are less expensive than using the GLACIER storage class.

Q53. A, B
AWS Documentation Reference:
https://aws.amazon.com/glue/
AWS Glue is a fully managed extract, transform, and load (ETL) service that makes it easy for customers to prepare and load their data for analytics.

C is incorrect because AWS Data Pipeline is a web service that helps you reliably process and move data between different AWS compute and storage services, as well as on-premises data sources, at specified intervals.

D is incorrect because EMR is not a data warehouse service but it Runs and Scales Apache Spark, Hadoop, HBase, Presto, Hive, and other Big Data Frameworks

Q54. A, C, D, E
AWS Documentation Reference:
https://aws.amazon.com/iam/faqs/
*What are the features of IAM roles for EC2 instances?*
*What problem does IAM roles for EC2 instances solve?*
IAM roles for EC2 instances simplifies management and deployment of AWS access keys to EC2 instances. Using this feature, you associate an IAM role with an instance. Then your EC2 instance provides the temporary security credentials to applications running on the instance,

and the applications can use these credentials to make requests securely to the AWS service resources defined in the role.

IAM roles for EC2 instances provides the following features:

- AWS temporary security credentials to use when making requests from running EC2 instances to AWS services.
- Automatic rotation of the AWS temporary security credentials.
- Granular AWS service permissions for applications running on EC2 instances.

## Q55. A, C, D

AWS Documentation Reference:

https://docs.aws.amazon.com/IAM/latest/UserGuide/id_roles_providers_oidc.html

With web identity federation, you don't need to create custom sign-in code or manage your own user identities. Instead, users of your app can sign in using a well-known external identity provider (IdP), such as Login with Amazon, Facebook, Google, or any other OpenID Connect (OIDC)-compatible IdP. They can receive an authentication token, and then exchange that token for temporary security credentials in AWS that map to an IAM role with permissions to use the resources in your AWS account.

https://docs.aws.amazon.com/IAM/latest/UserGuide/id_roles_providers_oidc_cognito.html

For most scenarios, AWS recommends that you use Amazon Cognito because it acts as an identity broker and does much of the federation work for you.

https://docs.aws.amazon.com/IAM/latest/UserGuide/id_roles_providers_oidc_manual.html

If you don't use Amazon Cognito, then you must write code that interacts with a web IdP, such as Facebook, and then calls the AssumeRoleWithWebIdentity API to trade the authentication token you get from those IdPs for AWS temporary security credentials. If you have already used this approach for existing apps, you can continue to use it.

## Q56. A, C

AWS Documentation Reference:

https://docs.aws.amazon.com/AmazonS3/latest/dev/ObjectVersioning.html

When you PUT an object in a versioning-enabled bucket, the noncurrent version is not overwritten. The following figure shows that when a new version of photo.gif is PUT into a bucket that already contains an object with the same name, the original object (ID = 111111) remains in the bucket, Amazon S3 generates a new version ID (222222), and adds the newer version to the bucket.

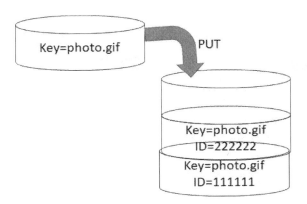

When you DELETE an object, all versions remain in the bucket and Amazon S3 inserts a delete marker, as shown in the following figure. The delete marker becomes the current version of the object.

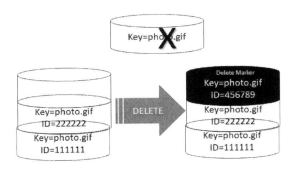

Q57. B
AWS Documentation Reference:
https://aws.amazon.com/quickstart/architecture/clickstream-analytics/

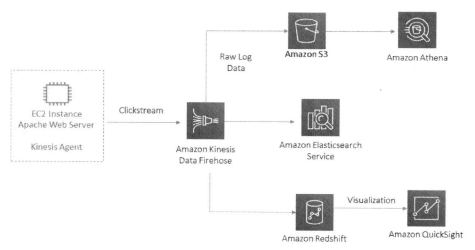

The clickstream data as users navigate through a website captured in the web server logs is sent to the Kinesis Data Firehose delivery stream using Kinesis Agent installed on the web servers.

Once the data is processed, the Kinesis Data Firehose delivery stream sends the data in near real-time to Amazon Redshift. You can build a recommendation engine with Amazon Redshift application programming interfaces (APIs).

Kinesis Data Firehose with an Amazon S3 destination persists managed feeds to a curated datasets bucket in Amazon S3.

Kinesis Data Firehose with an Amazon ES destination stores and indexes the dataset in Amazon ES.

Amazon CloudWatch metrics monitor the health of the services.

You can run ad-hoc queries on the data in Amazon S3 with Amazon Athena, create and share visualization dashboards on the Amazon Redshift data using Amazon QuickSight, and use Kibana to visualize the data in Amazon ES.

Q58. A, B, C, D
AWS Documentation Reference:
https://docs.aws.amazon.com/general/latest/gr/aws-access-keys-best-practices.html

Remove (or Don't Generate) Account Access Key: Anyone who has the access key for your AWS account root user has unrestricted access to all the resources in your account, including billing information. You cannot restrict the permissions for your AWS account root user. One of the best ways to protect your account is to not have an access key for your AWS account root user. Unless you must have a root user access key (which is very rare), it is best not to generate one. Instead, the recommended best practice is to create one or more AWS Identity and Access Management (IAM) users, give them the necessary permissions, and use IAM users for everyday interaction with AWS.

Use Temporary Security Credentials (IAM Roles) Instead of Long-Term Access Keys
In many scenarios, you don't need a long-term access key that never expires (as you have with an IAM user). Instead, you can create IAM roles and generate temporary security credentials. Temporary security credentials consist of an access key ID and a secret access key, but they also include a security token that indicates when the credentials expire.

Don't embed access keys directly into code. The AWS SDKs and the AWS Command Line Tools allow you to put access keys in known locations so that you do not have to keep them in code. Put access keys in one of the following locations:

- The AWS credentials file. The AWS SDKs and AWS CLI automatically use the credentials that you store in the AWS credentials file.
- Environment variables. On a multitenant system, choose user environment variables, not system environment variables.

Rotate access keys periodically. Change access keys on a regular basis.

Q59. A
AWS Documentation Reference:
https://aws.amazon.com/blogs/aws/aws-compute-optimizer-your-customized-resource-optimization-service/
https://aws.amazon.com/compute-optimizer/faqs/
*When should I use AWS Compute Optimizer and when should I use AWS Cost Explorer?*
You should use AWS Compute Optimizer if you want to look at instance type recommendations beyond downsizing within an instance family. You can use AWS Compute Optimizer to get downsizing recommendations within or across instance families, upsizing recommendations to remove performance bottlenecks, and recommendations for EC2 instances that are parts of an Auto Scaling group. AWS Compute Optimizer provides you additional capabilities to enhance recommendation quality and the user experience, such as using machine learning to identify workload types and automatically choose workload-specific recommendation methodology for them. You should also use AWS Compute Optimizer if you want to understand the performance risks and how your workload would perform on various EC2 instance options to evaluate the price-performance trade-off for your workloads.
You should use AWS Cost Explorer if you want to identify under-utilized EC2 instances that may be downsized on an instance by instance basis within the same instance family, and you want to understand the potential impact on your AWS bill by taking into account your RIs and Savings Plans. Cost Explorer offers recommendations for all commercial regions (outside of China) and supports the A, T, M, C, R, X, Z, I, D, H instance families.

## Q60. D

AWS Documentation Reference:

https://aws.amazon.com/transit-gateway/

AWS Transit Gateway is a service that enables customers to connect their Amazon Virtual Private Clouds (VPCs) and their on-premises networks to a single gateway. As you grow the number of workloads running on AWS, you need to be able to scale your networks across multiple accounts and Amazon VPCs to keep up with the growth.

With AWS Transit Gateway, you only have to create and manage a single connection from the central gateway in to each Amazon VPC, on-premises data center, or remote office across your network. Transit Gateway acts as a hub that controls how traffic is routed among all the connected networks which act like spokes. This hub and spoke model significantly simplifies management and reduces operational costs because each network only has to connect to the Transit Gateway and not to every other network. Any new VPC is simply connected to the Transit Gateway and is then automatically available to every other network that is connected to the Transit Gateway. This ease of connectivity makes it easy to scale your network as you grow.

## Q61. B

AWS Documentation Reference:

https://docs.aws.amazon.com/vpc/latest/userguide/vpc-network-acls.html

As a packet comes to the subnet, network ACL evaluate it against the ingress rules of the ACL the subnet is associated with (starting at the top of the list of rules, and moving to the bottom). Here's how the evaluation goes if the packet is destined for the SSL port (443). The packet doesn't match the first rule evaluated (rule 100). It does match the second rule (110), which allows the packet into the subnet.

## Q62. D

AWS Documentation Reference:

https://docs.aws.amazon.com/directoryservice/latest/admin-guide/what_is.html#choosing_an_option

Simple AD is a Microsoft Active Directory–compatible directory from AWS Directory Service that is powered by Samba 4. Simple AD supports basic Active Directory features such as user accounts, group memberships, joining a Linux domain or Windows based EC2 instances. Simple AD is a standalone directory in the cloud, where you create and manage user identities and manage access to applications. You can use many familiar Active Directory–aware applications and tools that require basic Active Directory features. Simple AD is compatible with the following AWS applications: Amazon WorkSpaces, Amazon WorkDocs, Amazon QuickSight, and Amazon WorkMail. You can also sign in to the AWS Management Console with Simple AD user accounts and to manage AWS resources.

Simple AD does not support multi-factor authentication (MFA), trust relationships, DNS dynamic update, schema extensions, communication over LDAPS, PowerShell AD cmdlets, or FSMO role transfer.

You can use Simple AD as a standalone directory in the cloud to support Windows workloads that need basic AD features, compatible AWS applications, or to support Linux workloads that need LDAP service.

Q63. B
AWS Documentation Reference:
https://aws.amazon.com/blogs/compute/implementing-serverless-video-subtitles/
Using Serverless managed services such as AWS Lambda and AWS Step Functions will be most appropriate for this PoC. A custom code base on Amazon EC2 would take too long to code and will be excessive computation for what is needed; a container with the code base on Amazon Elastic Container Service would be better, but still will be overkill from a compute perspective. Step Functions would take care of coordinating the workflow of the application and the different Lambda functions. Set up an Amazon DynamoDB table to store the state of each file for further processing on the front end.

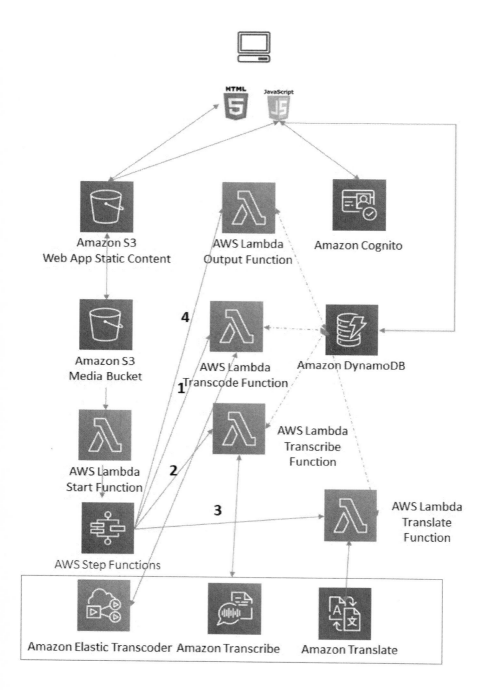

Q64. B

AWS Documentation Reference:

https://docs.aws.amazon.com/elasticloadbalancing/latest/application/application-load-balancers.html#connection-idle-timeout

For each request that a client makes through a load balancer, the load balancer maintains two connections. A front-end connection is between a client and the load balancer, and a back-end connection is between the load balancer and a target. The load balancer manages an idle timeout that is triggered when no data is sent over a front-end connection for a specified time period. If no data has been sent or received by the time that the idle timeout period elapses, the load balancer closes the connection.

Q65. D

Volume Gateway works with your existing applications through the industry-standard iSCSI protocol. The Cache Volume Gateway maintains on-premises of recently accessed data

Made in the USA
Columbia, SC
28 February 2021